Imagine Paul

Imagine Paul

Apostle of God

G. Roger Greene

PICKWICK Publications • Eugene, Oregon

IMAGINE PAUL
Apostle of God

Copyright © 2024 G. Roger Greene. All rights reserved. Except for brief quotations in critical publications or reviews, no part of this book may be reproduced in any manner without prior written permission from the publisher. Write: Permissions, Wipf and Stock Publishers, 199 W. 8th Ave., Suite 3, Eugene, OR 97401.

Pickwick Publications
An Imprint of Wipf and Stock Publishers
199 W. 8th Ave., Suite 3
Eugene, OR 97401

www.wipfandstock.com

PAPERBACK ISBN: 979-8-3852-0389-5
HARDCOVER ISBN: 979-8-3852-0390-1
EBOOK ISBN: 979-8-3852-0391-8

Cataloguing-in-Publication data:

Names: Greene, G. Roger, author.

Title: Imagine Paul : Apostle of God / by G. Roger Greene.

Description: Eugene, OR: Pickwick Publications, 2024 | Includes bibliographical references and index.

Identifiers: ISBN 979-8-3852-0389-5 (paperback) | ISBN 979-8-3852-0390-1 (hardcover) | ISBN 979-8-3852-0391-8 (ebook)

Subjects: LCSH: Paul, the Apostle, Saint. | Bible.—Epistles of Paul—Theology. | Paul, the Apostle, Saint—Journeys—Mediterranean Region. | Paul, the Apostle, Saint—Travel—Mediterranean Region.

Classification: BS2506.3 G74 2024 (paperback) | BS2506.3 (ebook)

VERSION NUMBER 10/15/24

Permission to use copyrighted material is gratefully acknowledged. Travel data is from ORBIS, The Stanford Geospatial Network Model of the Roman World (http://orbis.stanford.edu). Artwork as indicated is licensed from *Archaeology Illlustrated* © Balage Balogh (http://archaeologyillustrated.com). Lexington Books/Fortress Academic graciously permitted reuse of previously published material from *The Ministry of Paul the Apostle: History and Redaction* by G. Roger Greene, all rights reserved (http://rowman.com). Images of Roman coins is afforded by Classical Numismatic Group, LLC (http://cngcoins.com). Public domain material may be accessed through Wikimedia (http://en.wikipedia.com). Maps and cover art are provided by Jason Greene (http://greenelbow.com).

This work is dedicated to my grandfather,
Andrew Jackson Hargis,
Who taught a grandson how to live love

Contents

List of Illustrations | x
Preface | xiii
Acknowledgments | xxiii
Abbreviations | xxv
Orientation | xxvii
    Map of Paul's World | xxvii
    Travel Times and Distances | xxviii

1. The Gift of Imagination | 1
   Imagination   1
   Contextual Illumination   4
   Imagine Interpretation   15
   Imagine Paul's Letters   20
   Conclusion   34

2. Imagine Christian Beginnings | 37
   Four Gospels and Acts   38
   Jesus and His Ministry   40
   The Prologue of Christian Beginnings   53
   Conclusion   65

3. Imagine the Person and Worlds of Paul | 70
   The Worlds of Paul   75
   The Personal World of Paul   94
   A Customary Picture of Paul   101
   A Summary Evaluation   110

4. Imagine Paul's Foundation Campaign | 114
   Imagine the Ministry of Paul   115
   The Foundation Campaign   125
   Conclusion   164

5. Imagine Paul's Collection Campaign and Its Aftermath | 167
    The Collection Campaign   168
    The Post-Collection Period   194
    Conclusion   212

6. Imagine the Gospel of Paul | 215
    Second Thessalonians (49 CE)   216
    First Thessalonians (51 CE)   218
    Galatians (53–54 CE)   220
    Philippians (54 CE)   223
    First Corinthians (54 CE)   225
    Second Corinthians (56 CE)   234
    Romans 1–15 (56 CE)   237
    Colossians (60 CE)   256
    Ephesians (60 CE)   257
    Romans 16 (60 CE)   260
    Second Timothy (60 CE)   261
    Conclusion   261

7. Now, Re-Imagine the Theology of Paul | 269
    Introductory Considerations   270
    One Story   276
    One God of Israel   286
    One Gospel   289
    One Lord   293
    One Spirit   298
    One Faith   299
    One Hope   304
    One New Creation   306
    Conclusion   310

8. Re-Imagine the Legacy of Paul | 315
    Paul's Person   315
    Paul's Gospel   321
    Theology   328
    God   337
    Christ   340
    Salvation   344

Church   347
Eschatology   352
The Cross and Resurrection   357
A Gospel Imperative   361

9. Imagine Incarnation | 363
    Images   363
    The Essence of What Paul Believed   370
    A Concluding Postscript   379

Appendix A: A Chronology of the Ministry of Paul | 383
Appendix B: God's Table Spread | 387
Glossary | 389
Bibliography | 395
About the Author | 407
Scripture Index | 409

Illustrations

Figure 1   Map of Paul's World | xxvii
Figure 2   Heel Bone of Yehonanan ben Hagkol | 9
Figure 3   Papyrus 46 Page, 2 Corinthians 11:33—12:9 | 12
Figure 4   Map of the Galilee of Jesus | 44
Figure 5   Augustus of Prima Porto | 64
Figure 6   Reconstruction of the City of Corinth | 71
Figure 7   Augustus Divi F. Denarius | 82
Figure 8   Tiberius-Augustus Aureus | 82
Figure 9   Vespasian Judea Capta Sestertius | 89
Figure 10   First-Century Jerusalem Model | 90
Figure 11   Map of Paul's Asia Minor | 103
Figure 12   Paul and Barnabas | 104
Figure 13   Map of Paul's World of Ministry | 108
Figure 14   Map of Paul's Foundation Campaign | 122
Figure 15   Sailing for Macedonia | 134
Figure 16   First-Century Athens | 141
Figure 17   Map of Area of Corinth | 145
Figure 18   Stone Mason and Corinthian Capital | 146
Figure 19   The Bema at Corinth | 152
Figure 20   A Roman Grain Ship | 154
Figure 21   Harbor Gate at Ephesus | 155
Figure 22   Gateway Harbor City of Caesarea Maritima | 157
Figure 23   Famine Relief from Antioch | 161
Figure 24   Map of Paul's Collection Campaign | 174
Figure 25   The Temple of Artemis at Ephesus | 177
Figure 26   The Taurus Mountains | 190
Figure 27   Herod's Temple in Jerusalem | 194

Figure 28   A Final Journey Begins | 197
Figure 29   Shipwreck! | 199
Figure 30   A Roman Merchant Ship | 200
Figure 31   A Roman Soldier | 205
Figure 32   Tombs in the Necropolis of Pompeii | 219
Figure 33   Jewish Concept of the Two Ages | 284
Figure 34   Paul's Concept of the Three Ages | 284
Figure 35   Augustus of Prima Porto, cropped | 291
Figure 36   The Christ Event | 302
Figure 37   The Christian Life | 302
Figure 38   Icon of Saint Paul | 320

Preface

IN THE LOST VALLEY of dry bones, the prophet Ezekiel was asked the question by God, "Can these bones live?" In valleys as dry as that of Ezekiel's vision (Ezek 37), a question posed by this book is "Can the real Paul live again?"

The question is perhaps surprising, in that one may hear a great deal *about* Paul in many circles. Still, Paul himself has been lost in theological valleys filled with doctrinal and technical "dry bones." Paul has been lost in countless sermons populated with big, mysterious words ending in "-tion" or "-logy," words like "justification," "propitiation," or "expiation," words like "soteriology," "hamartiology," or "pneumatology." Paul has been lost in stacks of scholarly tomes that have pursued the most minute details of Paul's life or theology. Paul has been lost in artists' images that come from a much later date and offer only a caricaturish anachronism of a first-century Paul. Although it is certainly permissible to paint an artist's portrait of anything or anyone, one should realize that the product is a portrait or a particular artist's rendition. Paul has been lost in a modern, contemporary world that in many respects has passed him by and left his remains in an antiquated theological and religious valley of "dry bones."

Yet there are still those who, like the author, study Paul. Critical books on the life and thought of Paul have not abated. They offer arguments and conclusions that "establish" facts pertaining to his life, ministry, and thought. The number of books about Paul, his theology, and commentary founded upon Paul's letters appear to be unending and as overwhelming as a tsunami. Laypersons and students fear to approach Paul because he is perceived as too difficult and hard to understand, or, on the other hand, irrelevant. Both issues may be successfully addressed by actual study and appropriation. The reason for such study of Paul is the belief held by many who feel Paul still has something significant to say, even in a postmodern, technological age.

The author has spent almost fifty years studying and contemplating Paul and his ministry and introducing Paul and his theology to university students. The present task is to write an informed treatment of Paul for the person who, unencumbered by scholarly documentation, might wish to consider the story of Paul the apostle—the man and his thought, and his ministry in the worlds in which he lived. This book about Paul is written thereby for students, non-specialists, laypersons, and even interested non-Christians. The work is based upon critical scholarship as may be seen in the bibliography. It is deliberately presented without footnotes and reference to the immense and often technical body of secondary literature pertaining to Paul, even though the work of many scholars may underwrite this work.

The largely neglected factor in Pauline studies has surprisingly been the ministry of Paul himself, which from a surface point of view should be seen as foundational to Paul's thought. Such neglect is in part a testimony to the quality of Luke's narrative in Acts. We assume we know the story with its "Damascus road" experience and its "three missionary journey" interpretation, such that Paul's story requires no further attention than Luke's presentation.

Contemplation of Paul's theology is often made complicated and difficult by the debates of scholars and theologians. His theology has been the playground of biblical scholars and clergy alike even as it has withheld its mysteries from the casual gaze of laypersons. The issue is not one of "digging deeper" with "in-depth" Bible study. Frequently, the issue is one of a willingness to hear before one speaks and to live out what one has heard as one creatively seeks to address living with all of the issues presented by a postmodern world.

For readers who wish to pursue the study of Paul at a more advanced or specialized level, one may pursue works of interest given in the selective bibliography. What is written herein is drawn from the author's understanding as garnered and developed from extensive research and experience. It is representative of conclusions reached, whether those be traditional or not. It is focused upon the fruit of scholarly labor, yet it is expressed in a more reader-friendly format based on the light of scriptural evidence that we have for Paul, namely, Paul's letters and the book of Acts, all of which should be taken seriously.

Usually, Paul's *story* is drawn from Acts and his *thought* is drawn from his letters. However, this book will emphasize a different approach. One should always consider Paul's letters first, for his identity, his story, and his thought. Paul's own letters must always be primary, according to the usual canons of historical study. Luke's treatment in Acts should always be considered secondary. The letters are attributed to Paul himself; Luke's work is a later account about the gospel and the early church that features Paul. Admittedly, any secondary presentation of Paul will only be a *portrait* of his life, ministry, and thought. That is true of Luke's work in Acts. That is also the best that historical research can produce. All portraits are not equal, however.

There are many gaps in the sources as it would pertain to the story of Paul—a story of a ministry that extended for more than a quarter of a century. Paul himself is known only through his occasional letters and through Luke's account of his ministry given in Acts or Luke's underlying source material. Luke in crafting the book of Acts had access to a significant source, designated as the "STA" or "Source Tradition of Acts" and found in the author's earlier work on *The Ministry of Paul the Apostle: History and Redaction*.

To set forth a narrative story of Paul is the only way to allow Paul to live again, although by nature of the case and the available sources, such an account must involve the imagination. Understanding should involve the imagination, but not the imaginary. While such an account of Paul's story and ministry must be hypothetical and speculative at many points as a result of gaps in our sources, one may allow one's imagination to be informed and guided by critical facts and interpretation. This book offers just that, based upon careful scholarship. One's own aptitudes and experience will likewise stimulate and inform one's imagination. One's own ability to imagine can be developed through exposure to Paul's world and comprehension of what he writes in his letters.

The author may present alternative viewpoints of understanding as appropriate, but he does not intend to encumber the text with scholarly quotes or notes unless deemed absolutely necessary. An occasional note of explanation or reference to further sources may be given as an aid for understanding. A glossary is given to help in definition of concepts, whether common or technical. One person's familiar summary may be another person's first-time discovery. There is some purposeful repetition in the work that is deliberate, in view of the intended audience of readers. Unless otherwise indicated, translation of New Testament scripture references are representative of the author's own personal translation from the Greek.

As desired, the reader may pursue numerous scripture references that are offered in support of perspectives or theological positions presented by the author. In fact, the reader is encouraged to read this book with a Bible at hand. Instead of immersing oneself in the finer points of scholarly debate, it is recommended that the reader spend time in reflection upon the scriptural texts cited, in the light of one's religious experience and perceptions. One is encouraged to "imagine" the New Testament, to engage in the *activity* of "imagining," but to do so with an open Bible.

If one truly engages the New Testament, one should be prepared for surprises that encourage spiritual growth and a new mind-set ("repentance") that goes beyond mere religious indoctrination. As 2 Tim 3:16 suggests, every writing inspired by God is also beneficial not only for teaching or instruction, but also for refutation of error, for correction of faults, for discipline inherent in righteousness. We too often prefer to emphasize scripture and the matter of divine inspiration as a dogma, rather than to emphasize our own need for discipline and instruction, the refutation of our errors, and the correction of our faults.

This work is meant to be primarily a book about the Gospel of God as understood by a man, the apostle Paul, who is responsible for the earliest Christian literature that we possess, including the reference in 2 Timothy cited above. His own letters were written even earlier than the four Gospels, which, of course, tell the story of Jesus. While necessarily the account of the Gospel of God must begin with the story of Jesus, and while other early Christian interpreters in the New Testament followed after Paul, the primary focus and emphasis of this book will be upon the apostle Paul and his gospel.

Jesus was the "Christ," he was not a "Christian," a term which by definition points to one who is a follower of the "Christ." The term "Christ" is actually a Greek equivalent of the Hebrew word "Messiah," both of which suggest "anointed one." According to Acts, it was at Antioch that the disciples were first called "Christian" (Acts 11:26). In actual fact, as any concordance will demonstrate, the word "Christian" occurs only three times in the New Testament—in Acts 11:26 and 26:28, as well as in 1 Pet 4:16. Whether it was a name given by others—"they're only 'Christians'"—or whether it was self-chosen—"we're Christians"—is lost to history. Paul never identifies himself as a "Christian," but he repeatedly suggests he was a man "in Christ."

In order to provide an appropriate initial context for understanding Paul, some attention will be given to the ministry of Jesus and the birth of the earliest church that existed before Paul. Attention given to Christian beginnings is an important stage for imagining Paul in his historical context. Without Jesus, there is no Gospel of God, no church, no Christianity, and no Paul the apostle. While he apparently never met the pre-resurrection Jesus in the flesh, Paul includes himself as a distinctive witness of the resurrection (1 Cor 15:8–10). He experienced an encounter with the risen Christ, according to his own testimony and the secondary witness of the book of Acts (Gal 1:15–16; 1 Cor 15:8–10; Acts 9:1–9). Paul believed that God had revealed his risen Son to him, and that he was called to be an *apostle* who proclaimed the Gospel of God to the gentiles.

Paul, in actuality, is the most brightly illuminated figure or person in the New Testament. Jesus is known only through the presentation of the four later Gospels (65–95 CE), all of which are written after the time of Paul. They incorporate early Christian tradition and remembrance. Jesus himself left nothing in writing, such that all of his teachings and remembrance of his mighty works were handed down through the developing Christian tradition of the early church. Paul is known through *his own* letters (ca. 50–60+ CE), which are to be dated to within twenty to thirty years of the death of Jesus (30 CE). While the Gospel material was being handed down orally in the period 30–65 CE, the Gospels themselves were not likely written down before 65–95 CE.

Paul himself received his apostolic call within five years of Jesus's death and resurrection, or, around 34 CE. He was martyred around 61 CE, according to the present writer. Paul, for example, never read any one of the Four Gospels, for they only appeared after his death. In addition to Paul's letters, fully half or more of the book of Acts is devoted to the story of the spread of the gospel through his apostolic ministry. Paul never read Acts either, nor did he have the opportunity to augment or correct Luke's work.

In this present work, one is invited to imagine Paul in the most positive sense of the word. Instead of entertaining a fictitious Paul of later Christian orthodoxy, one is invited to imagine being with Paul, going about his ministry in a first-century Greco-Roman world. One is invited to see Paul as a real person, who was encountered by the risen Christ in the context of a first-century Greco-Roman world. He became a "man in Christ," an evangelist of the Gospel of God, and a pastoral shepherd of some of the very earliest Christian churches. He was called to be an apostle within five years of the death and resurrection of Jesus. One is invited to let Paul, "the man in Christ," breathe again. Through the window of the New Testament record, one is invited to go with him and to "look over his shoulder," as it were, as he lives out his ministry.

This book related to Paul will begin with a thematic appreciation for imagination and the work that scholars do. It will move to a brief description of the beginnings of the Gospel story in terms of the remembrance of Jesus's ministry and passion, as well as the foundations of the early church as best known from the book of Acts. The world of earliest Christianity is one of the determinative contexts of the ministry and thought of Paul. The book's title, *Imagine Paul: Apostle of God*, calls upon the reader to see Paul historically in his own first-century context and to understand his ministry and message in the light of a Jewish gospel carried to a Greco-Roman world.

The sectional and chapter headings fairly represent the inherent presentation of Paul, from an understanding of his person in the context of the worlds in which he lived, to his legacy and expressed hope. There is a certain logic that guides the work from beginning to end. An outline of the entire work is provided. However, there is another theme for Christians to consider that is introduced here, that plays in the background, and that will be more fully developed at a later point in the book. That is the theme of actively *imagining* Paul in terms of his world, his person, his ministry, and his gospel. *One is called upon to engage Paul as an active participant and not as a passive, uninvolved observer.* Only as we seek to participate with Paul and allow the renewing action of imagination shall we come to a more full appreciation of a man called Paul, a man "in Christ." Only then will "dry bones" live again.

While it may be difficult to truly imagine the historical Paul—it requires the work of commitment and engagement—one may begin with an easier task. *Imagine the New Testament without Paul*. No Pauline letters. No Pauline churches. Most of the book of Acts disappears from view, aside from the Jerusalem traditions and the material associated with Peter. Acts would only be a shadow of its former self. Actually, Acts would be very minimal if the Lukan speeches and redaction should be removed. One does not fully realize how much of the book of Acts is taken up with the story of Paul. Who knows? Without Paul, there may have been no Jerusalem Conference (Acts 15)—certainly not one of the nature that Luke reports.

While not often studied in church circles today, the Jerusalem Conference (Acts 15) was a crucial event in the early history of Christianity. It addressed the question of what was necessary for a gentile to become a Christian. Must gentiles within the Christian church observe Jewish boundary markers, such as food laws (see Lev 11)? Must male gentiles be circumcised? In other words, must one embrace the requirements of Jewish torah (Mosaic instruction) in order to become a Christian? As the gospel moved out into the larger Hellenistic world to reach a gentile audience, the question of obedience to Jewish torah became an intense one. And, lest one forget, the Gospel of God (Rom 1:1) began with the ministry of Jesus on Jewish soil and represented the fulfilment of God's promises to Israel (Rom 9:4–5). All of the earliest Christians were Jews, including Jesus's earliest disciples and those who responded to the Gospel on the day of Pentecost (Acts 2:5). Those present on the day of Pentecost may have also included proselytes of the Jewish religion (Acts 2:10).

Without Paul, there would be no Philippians or Galatians with their vignettes of Paul's personal testimony. There would be no 1–2 Corinthians with insightful windows into the social and religious life of a first-century church. There would be no book of Romans, so instrumental in the conversion of church fathers like Augustine and Luther. It is hard to imagine a Christianity without the book of Romans, which has been such a keystone in the development and debate of Christian theology throughout the entire history of the Christian church. The sublime expression of Ephesians would be nowhere found in the New Testament, regardless of whether that book was written by Paul or a "Paulinist." In fact, there would be no "Paulinists," or, admirers of Paul who even produced works under his name.

Libraries would be devoid of books and articles on Paul. The entire scholarly guild would lose a primary focus of inquiry, theological studies would lose their vibrancy, preachers would lose a wealth of sermon texts, church liturgies would become far more restricted. The basic nature of the gospel itself would be re-defined. *Imagine a world without Paul.* If the Christian faith even existed, it would certainly assume a different cast. Christianity may never have become a separate, world-wide religion. It may have succumbed at a very early period to the sectarianism of a fractured Judaism that did not survive the aftermath of the destruction of Jerusalem by the Romans in 70 CE or the reformative threat of a movement called "Gnosticism" in the second and third centuries CE.

Imagine a Christian religion without Paul. Imagine a New Testament without Paul. Rightly or wrongly, some have identified Paul as the "founder" or "second founder" of *Christianity*. Indeed, even though he did not employ the term, Paul *was* a "Christian," whereas Jesus was not. Jesus was a Jew, or, as some like to add, "at least on his mother's side." Paul himself was a Jew until the day he died, although a messianic Jew of a movement that came to be known as "Christian." Imagine a world of a New Testament or Christian religion without Paul. Such a world changes from a brightly lit and colorful world to a backdrop and palette of dim, dark, and dull gray.

The current work calls upon the reader to "imagine." It calls for activity, for one to employ all the faculties of the mind. It calls for a reader to read the scripture text. It calls upon the reader to imagine Paul in *his* context, whether that be his world, his ministry, his churches, or the gospel he proclaimed. It calls upon the reader to "walk with Paul." As one "walks," either literally or metaphorically, one takes only a step at a time. As this presentation proceeds, one is invited to briefly imagine the person and ministry of Jesus and the foundational context of the early church before one turns to the person of Paul himself. One is invited to view the person of Paul as one imagines his worlds. As one begins to "walk with Paul," one is invited to re-imagine the contours of Paul's years of ministry. It is Paul's actual ministry that calls forth his theological expression.

"Walking with Paul" is perhaps easier than following Paul's expressed thought, most certainly if one has no appreciation for Paul's contextual ministry. Paul does not write theology; rather, he applies gospel in the first-century crucible of the Greco-Roman world. As one imagines Paul's world, one becomes equipped to imagine the depth of the thought of Paul. And, as one comes to appreciate the depth of Paul's thought, one begins to imagine with Paul the depth of God's incredible and inscrutable Gospel. The logic of the presentation thus moves from the more simple to the more complex, from description of Paul and his worlds to the analysis of his thought. Hopefully, however, the presentation will focus upon simplicity that represents the imaginative and manageable side of complexity. The reader is invited to "walk with a real Paul" as he may be imagined and to think Paul's real thoughts with him through his letters, as one comes to more fully experience the Gospel Paul knew and proclaimed.

As the reader imagines, he or she will come to a renewed and deeper comprehension of this man "in Christ," not only in terms of *what* Paul did but also in terms of *why* Paul did and said what he did. Imagine if there were no Paul. But, now, actively begin to imagine Paul.

To begin with, we may need to repent (to think differently, to adopt a different mind-set) of some usual time-worn models for understanding Paul that have actually led to misunderstandings. *Our* maps, for example, are generally oriented north-south, with the most important point of the compass seen to be "north," the direction located at the top of the map. Even Google Earth appears for those in North America with the north pole of the globe at the top of the screen.[1] As the familiar map of the United States appears, north is at the top. But Google Earth can be rotated. Does the very land mass that is the United States look different if the globe is rotated ninety degrees, such that "east" is now at the top and the equator vertical? In similar fashion, how does the appearance of the Mediterranean change, when "east" is rotated to the top? One might try the exercise with Google Earth. Now, begin to imagine a different world that comes with a different orientation.

Contemporary maps of the ancient biblical world are likewise usually oriented on a north-south axis, with north at the top. It is suggested that people who lived in the world of Paul and Jesus at the eastern end of the Mediterranean (the *Mare Nostrum* or Roman Sea) lived in a world they understood to be oriented east-west, rather than north-south. The sun rose in the east and set in the west. The Romans came from the west to establish their presence in the world of the middle-east. Metaphorically, at least, church buildings later than Paul were oriented with the apse toward the east, resurrection itself associated with the rising of the sun. As one rotates our usual maps ninety degrees counter-clockwise, one begins to imagine Paul and others living in that

1. See https://www.google.com/earth/resources/ for current Google Earth resources.

first-century world that may already begin to look different. A new orientation may bring with it a new mind-set. One begins to re-imagine.

While one might be quite familiar with the concept of "Paul's three missionary journeys," Paul would not have understood himself to be on a "journey" as we understand that word, nor would Paul have understood himself as a "missionary," nor would the character of Paul's work be classified in terms of "three." In fact, the concept of "three missionary journeys" has only been in vogue since the rise of Western missionary societies (ca. 1700 CE). The earliest reference to "three missionary journeys" apparently occurs only in 1742 CE as a biblical model in support of eighteenth-century English missionary causes. The concept is foundationally misleading and anachronistic as applied to Paul. As we shall see, Paul's ministry is better understood in terms of two major campaigns—one in which Paul carried out foundational ministry as a directly called apostle of Christ and a second one in which he gathered a collection of funds from his gentile churches for the impoverished Jewish Christians in the church in Jerusalem. Again, a new mind-set is called for, as one re-imagines the ministry of Paul. He did not hold short-term revivals, but engaged in a long-term evangelistic and pastoral ministry.

The average layperson may feel that the first-century Greco-Roman world of Paul is too far removed from the postmodern world of today to be of any relevance. If we are honest, such a perspective connotes many things for both Christians and non-Christians, including the relevance of Paul's thought, "scripture" itself, and even the very nature of Christianity. There is a difference in meaning and reality between the words "Christian" and "Christendom." The latter is a religio-social entity in which the word "Christian" is increasingly used as a convenient adjective. The word "Christian" as a noun, on the other hand, historically describes a "Christ-follower," or as Paul would say, one "in Christ." An adjective describes; a noun denotes.

Today, there is a distinct difference in the broad use of the descriptive term and the claim of personal identity. One need not read nor understand Paul (or any scripture, for that matter) in order to be a member of a contemporary "Christendom." However, if one claims the personal identity of "Christian," i.e., one who is a follower of Christ, then one must read Paul. It is Paul himself, and not the historical theologians of "Christendom," who define what it means to be one "in Christ" at the very headwaters of Christian experience.

The present writer would acknowledge the relevance of these three realities—Paul, scripture, and Christianity—as one begins to understand and appreciate these through the divine gift of imagination. One cannot get away from interpretation. All interpretations are not equal. Some offer a new freedom, while others simply enforce an old or a new slavery to codified dogma.

Appropriate interpretation leads to a very colorful world laced with the legacy of Paul that offers something comparatively rare in contemporary society, namely, hope. That hope in the Gospel of God that Paul expressed has unfortunately often been occluded or obscured by multitudinous debates and varying theological interpretations that have often been at loggerheads with one another. As previously suggested, this has left the average layperson with the impression or the conclusion that Paul is too difficult to understand, much less comprehend. Paul has too often been overlaid with what the present writer terms "theological barnacles," which have tightly attached themselves to the Pauline "wood" and in themselves have become "theological barriers." When these are scraped away, the message of the good news of God shines brightly through the apostle Paul into a world that desperately stands in need of a hope that is real and transformative. Indeed, one may encounter a Pauline gospel that is quite different than the one customarily offered.

The first passage of scripture that the author took seriously and personally as a sixteen-year-old boy was Phil 4:4–8. In the light of Paul's own words, with acknowledgment and encouragement to all who may read that work, Paul's words present the Gospel of God with a clarion call to joy and peace. As one embraces what is true, honorable, just, pure, lovely, and gracious, one indeed may be filled with the joy and peace of God in Christ Jesus.

So, welcome to a pilgrimage into the colorful, illuminating world of imagining Paul, a "man in Christ," who expressed the victory of the Gospel of God. Three points need to be stated here. First, the word "gospel" already existed in the Greco-Roman world of Caesar before it ever appeared in Christian usage. In the present work, it will be spelled with a capital if the reference is to the Gospel of God in its reality. Any proclamation of that Gospel, by Paul or anyone else, will be spelled as "gospel." No proclamation by humans captures the totality of the Gospel of God. Secondly, the word "Christian" will be employed even if anachronistic for Paul and those who came to accept the Gospel. No suitable alternative has yet emerged that would convey clarity to contemporary readers. And, thirdly, the reminder is given that unless otherwise noted, the translation into English of New Testament texts belongs to the work of the present author. As a first step, however, one needs to gain a new orientation and come to understand and appreciate the gift of imagination.

Acknowledgments

MORE YEARS AGO, NOW, than this writer would like to count, the author set out to write a single book on Paul and his theology as that is expressed in his letters. Having studied Paul and his letters in seminary through fine seminary professors who offered the freedom to think rather than indoctrination, and having taught university courses on Paul, "the man and his writings," the time came to express positions and conclusions that had been reached through long years of exposure to Paul. It became a case of "now or never."

The work seemingly took on a life of its own. First there was one book that grew into two then into three and now into four. The author's pilgrimage has been akin to the little house that grew by add-ons as each of the children came along the way. The original house has been remodeled several times over, such that it is hardly recognizable. Still, there has been a certain foundational logic and spiritual awareness that has guided a soon-to-be twenty-year directed pilgrimage with Paul the apostle.

The mists of time shroud the memory and contributions of many persons who have significantly influenced the author's life and perspectives, from family members to teachers, pastors, professors, authors of books that the author has read, and friends. Collective appreciation is expressed for all of these mentors.

A work like this does not just happen. Appreciation is expressed to the entire production staff at Wipf and Stock for their customary and consistent able assistance at every level. A word of appreciation is certainly accorded to Matt Wimer, managing editor at Wipf and Stock, for his effective efficiency and flexibility in overseeing a process supported by so many extremely capable eyes and hands.

The author once again expresses his deepest gratitude to his two colleagues at Mississippi College for their support and encouragement, and, yes, correction in protracted discussions of Paul and his letters through working lunches in busy semesters of teaching. Their time was generously given even during summer breaks. One could not ask for greater encouraging support and abiding friendship. To Michael Johnson and Eddie Mahaffey, the writer extends a joyful expression of gratitude that goes far beyond the confines of these present pages.

The author's wife Mary Ann has been supportive in every way through an extended time frame that has now included four books. She has read each manuscript, including this one, almost as many times as the author has, as she offered her constructive commentary. Stacks of books and papers have seemingly become a way of life. She has served as the author's chief critic, editor, and publicist. For her support and love, I am most grateful.

To my son Jason, an artist by profession, the author expresses a deep word of thanks for the artwork of the included maps and for the exclusive art provided for the cover. His art has decorated all of the covers of the author's works on Paul, as he has very ably carried out a thematic portrayal of Paul at Corinth suitable for calling forth one's imagination.

To my son Ramsey, the engineer, appreciation is expressed for many thoughtful dialogues. This book actually had its birth at a time that called for my presence with him at a critical juncture of life.

Finally, this work is dedicated to the memory of my grandfather, Andrew Jackson Hargis, who perhaps more than any other person influenced a young grandson during his growing up years. As the dedication indicates, it was my grandfather who taught a grandson how to actually live love. He conveyed this through his actions of love and ever-present servant mentality. Physically, he was a rather small man who always exhibited a large heart. He was not a man of many words and came from humble beginnings. He was known, respected, and appreciated throughout the larger community as "Mr. Andy." For many years, he served in a significant elective office through many terms without any elective opposition.

As the oldest grandchild in the family, I had the privilege of being able to give him a new "grandparent name." While others called him "Mr. Andy" throughout the community and beyond, I was proud to call him "Po." He always introduced me in whatever public encounter or forum as "my grandson" and he always called me "Man." He would do anything for anyone at any time, living out a service mentality, living out love. And so, from the heart of a grandson now much older who became a man, "Thank you. Po, this one is for you, with love."

Abbreviations

adj.	adjective
a.k.a.	also known as
Ant.	Josephus, *Jewish Antiquities*
aor.	aorist verb tense in Greek
aor. pass.	aorist passive in Greek verbs
BCE	Before the common era
CE	Common era
cf.	compare
Cor	Corinthians (1 and 2)
Dan	Daniel
Deut	Deuteronomy
Eph	Ephesians
Exod	Exodus
Ezek	Ezekiel
fig.	figure
Gal	Galatians
Gen	Genesis
Hab	Habakkuk
Heb	Hebrews
Hist. eccl.	Eusebius, *Ecclesiastical History*
Isa	Isaiah
J.W.	Josephus, *Jewish War*
L	special material found only in Luke among the Synoptic Gospels
Lev	Leviticus
lit.	literal or literally
LXX	Septuagint, Greek translation of the Old Testament
M	special material found only in Matthew among the Synoptic Gospels

ABBREVIATIONS

Macc	Maccabees (1 and 2)
Matt	Matthew
NAB	*New American Bible*
NJB	*New Jerusalem Bible*
NRSV	*New Revised Standard Version*
par.	parallel
pf.	perfect verb tense in Greek
pres.	present, as in a present tense verb
Q	Material found in Matthew and Luke that is not found in Mark
Pet	Peter (1 and 2)
Phil	Philippians
Phlm	Philemon
Ps	Psalms
Rev	Revelation
Rom	Romans
RSV	*Revised Standard Version*
sing.	singular
STA	Greene, "Source Tradition of Acts"
sub.	subjunctive mode in Greek or English
subj.	subject of a verb
subj. gen.	subjective genitive
Thess	Thessalonians (1 and 2)
Tim	Timothy (1 and 2)
YHWH	Yahweh, the Old Testament covenant name for God
Zech	Zechariah

Orientation

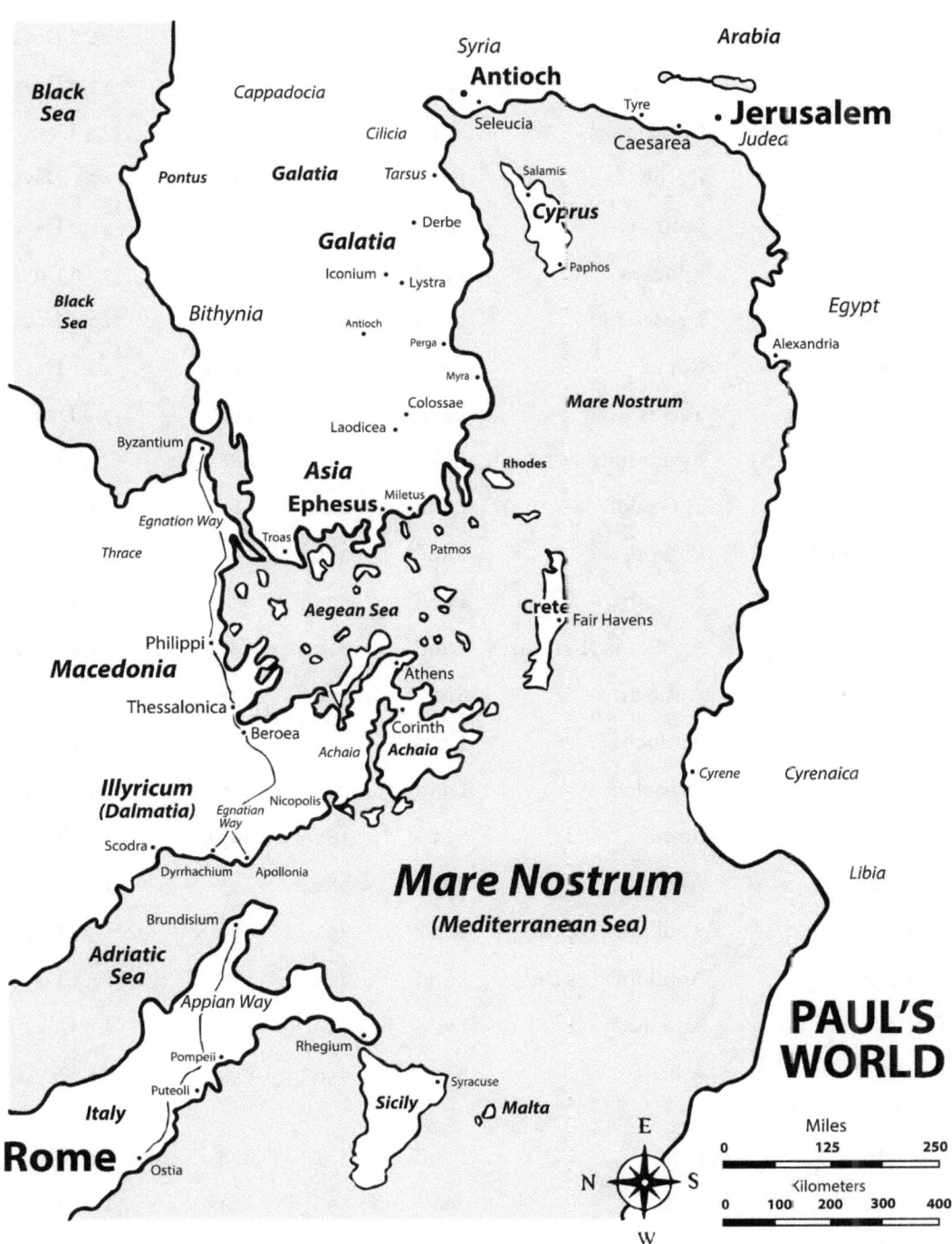

Fig. 1. Map of Paul's World. © Jason Greene. Used with permission.

ORIENTATION

Travel Times and Distances

From	To	Mode	Miles	Kilometers	Time
Alexandria	Rome	Sea	1607	2588	21.2 Days
Antioch	Athens	Sea	907	1460	13.0 Days
Antioch	Caesarea	Sea	356	574	4.3 Days
Antioch	Derbe	Land	381	614	17.1 Days
Antioch	Ephesus	Sea	748	1192	11.0 Days
Antioch	Ephesus	Land	666	1073	37.0 Days
Antioch	Jerusalem	Land	371	598	20.0 Days
Antioch	Rome	Sea	1878	3024	26.1 Days
Antioch	Tarsus	Land	124	200	7.0 Days
Apollonia (Epirus)	Byzantium	Land	614	988	32.9 Days
Apollonia (Epirus)	Thessalonica	Land	241	388	12.9 Days
Apollonia (Epirus)	Philippi	Land	319	514	18.1 Days
Athens	Corinth	Land	53	85	2.8 Days
Byzantium	Apollonia (Epirus)	Land	614	988	32.9 Days
Caesarea	Antioch	Sea	356	574	4.3 Days
Caesarea	Antioch	Land	306	492	16.4 Days
Caesarea	Jerusalem	Land	78	126	2.6 Days
Caesarea	Rome	Sea	1820	2931	17.2 Days
Corinth	Antioch	Sea	984	1585	14.0 Days
Corinth	Apollonia (Epirus)	Sea	391	629	5.7 Days
Corinth	Apollonia (Epirus)	Land	445	716	24.5 Days
Corinth	Athens	Land	53	85	2.8 Days
(Around Peloponnesus)	Athens	Sea	530	854	6.1 Days
Corinth	Philippi	Land	421	678	22.6 Days
Corinth	Rome	Sea/Land	896	1443	12.3 Days
Corinth	Scodra	Sea/Land	504	812	6.0 Days

From	To	Mode	Miles	Kilometers	Time
Corinth	Thessalonica	Land	325	524	17.5 Days
Dyrrhachium	Philippi	Land	385	539	18.0 Days
Dyrrhachium	Philippi	Sea	1146	1845	12.7 Days
Ephesus	Athens	Sea	228	367	2.3 Days
Ephesus	Antioch	Land	666	1073	37.0 Days
Ephesus	Corinth	Sea	289	466	4.0 Days
Ephesus	Laodicea	Land	106	171	5.7 Days
Ephesus	Philippi	Sea	401	646	5.0 Days
Ephesus	Tarsus	Land	542	872	30.3 Days
Ephesus	Thessalonica	Sea	415	668	5.9 Days
Jerusalem	Antioch	Land	371	598	19.9 Days
Jerusalem	Antioch	Land/Sea	419	675	6.8 Days
Jerusalem	Caesarea Maritima	Land	78	126	2.6 Days
Jerusalem	Corinth	Sea	959	1545	10.3 Days
Jerusalem	Ephesus	Sea	751	1209	7.8 Days
Jerusalem	Ephesus	Land	1038	1671	56.9 Days
Jerusalem	Rome	Sea	1899	3058	19.6 Days
Jerusalem	Rome (Shortest)	Land/Sea	1817	2926	43.4 Days
Jerusalem	Philippi	Sea	1113	1793	12.0 Days
Jerusalem	Tarsus	Land	554	892	10.3 Days
Jerusalem	Thessalonica	Sea	1076	1733	10.2 Days
Rome	Byzantium	Sea	1692	2724	21.3 Days
Rome	Corinth	Sea/Land	897	1444	9.4 Days
Rome	Jerusalem	Sea	1899	3058	19.6 Days
Rome (Shortest by Land)	Jerusalem	Land	2405	3872	130.7 Days
Rome	Pompeii	Land	151	244	8.2 Days
Rome	Puteoli	Land	128	206	6.9 Days

ORIENTATION

From	To	Mode	Miles	Kilometers	Time
Rome	Scodra	Sea	860	1384	11.3 Days
Philippi	Jerusalem	Sea	1113	1793	12.0 Days
Philippi	Thessalonica	Land	96	154	5.1 Days
Scodra	Corinth	Land/Sea	504	812	6.0 Days
Scodra	Corinth	Land	568	915	30.3 Days
Tarsus	Caesarea	Land	430	692	23.1 Days
Tarsus	Jerusalem	Land	554	892	10.3 Days
Thessalonica	Athens	Land	298	479	16.0 Days
Thessalonica	Athens	Sea	335	540	4.6 Days
Thessalonica	Corinth	Land	325	524	17.5 Days
Thessalonica	Ephesus	Sea	415	668	5.9 Days
Thessalonica	Philippi	Land	96	154	5.1 Days

Source of data: ORBIS: The Stanford Geospatial Network Model of the Roman World. http://orbis.stanford.edu. Used by permission. *Note*: The data above generally indicates the fastest route for travel occurring in July. In terms of Paul's travels, one must allow for geography, topography, weather (winds, seasons as winter), availability of ship passage, and personal needs or intentions. Seldom can one travel in an absolute straight line and without interruption. One kilometer = 0.621 miles.

1

The Gift of Imagination

THE WORD "IMAGINATION" BELONGS to a very interesting word group, all based upon the root word "image." According to *Webster's New Collegiate Dictionary*, "image" is derived from the Latin *imagin-*, *imago*, and is perhaps to be related to the Latin *imitari*, "to imitate."[1] An "image" may thus be a reproduction of a person or a thing, such as a sculpted statue or photograph, which brings the real person or thing to mind and enables one to visualize or recall the person or thing captured in the "image." An image is thus a likeness or a semblance. It need *not* be an exact likeness. The Genesis account of creation affirms that God created humankind "in his own image," creating humankind simultaneously as both male and female (Gen 1:26–27). Humankind was commanded to be fruitful and to multiply, to have dominion over the remainder of creation as responsible stewards of God. While the Genesis text speaks anthropomorphically from the understanding of the biblical writer, it should be obvious that the use of the word "image" refers to more significant realities than mere physical statue or form.

Imagination

An "image" may be a tangible representation or a mental picture of something or someone not actually present. It may be a graphic representation or a vivid mental picture held only in the mind, as one conceptualizes reality. It can be a mental picture held and shared with others. In its verbal idea, "to image" is to form or call up a mental picture. It suggests the action of calling up and portraying an image in representative form. It is what artists do all the time—in the words of poetry, or a painting, or in sculpture. In the hands of an artist and from the mind of an artist, an image is brought to life.

It is what engineers and architects do, as one envisions a problem or a possibility and works to solve the problem or bring the possibility to reality, whether that be a bridge or a computer or a smart phone or an engine or beautiful architecture. It is what doctors do, as they seek to restore patients to a "picture of health." "Imagery" of various kinds is thus the product of image makers who engage in the art of bringing mental images to tangible or figurative expression. While an "artist" may excel

---

1. Mish, *Merriam-Webster's Collegiate Dictionary*, "Imagination."

in a given field of endeavor with his or her resultant "imagery," we are all engaged in the making of "images." Images are the "stuff" of life. One who has a developed sense of imagination is truly blessed. And, thankfully, imagination is an entity that *can be* skillfully developed.

There are other words belonging to the word group of imagination, some of which have a positive connotation and some of which possess a negative connotation. Words really do not have "meaning" in themselves, but they mean what we use them to mean. The word "imaginary" suggests something that exists *only* in the imagination—something that really doesn't exist and perhaps has never existed, something that lacks factual reality, even something truly impossible. It may suggest the unreal, the unbelievable, that which is purely fictitious, that which is only mental and existing in the imagination. To merely think something does not mean that it is real outside of one's thought context. Contemporary entertainment can create a "virtual world" that does not exist and has never existed, through a movie screen or video games. In our day, the "virtual world" can even become an addictive substitute for the real world. However, one cannot be personally healthy and live in a world that is only "fictive." Real life means more than being merely a "media" cyborg. A truly *human* being needs at least some *real* "friends," not just those of the fictive variety that live only in cyberspace or in a "secret garden" somewhere.

On the other hand, imagination can very positively suggest that which is visionary and capable of realization at some point in the future. While one may have had an imaginary playmate as a child that did not really exist ("Puff, the Magic Dragon"), without a vision of what one could become and be, few human beings would develop their abilities to their maximum potential of full personhood. We can imagine a career, where we want to live, a soul mate, and things we would actually like to experience. The more we develop our imagination, the richer our actual experience will become.

"Imagination" is thus an important, creative word. Drawn from the Latin (*imaginatus, imaginatio*), imagination is the creative power or action of an active, developing or developed mind. Imagination is the power of action that human beings have to form mental images of what is not readily present to our sensory perception. If one is present with a loved one, one's sensory perception is active. One may "sense" by sight or hearing or touch the loved one's presence. One may directly communicate—"I love you." If one is apart from a loved one, one may *imagine* how or what that person may be doing or how that person may look. One strongly "imagines" the loving relationship one shares with that person, as one draws upon delightful memories. One can strongly imagine the celebration of reunification with the loved one at some point in future time.

Imagination is thus not only an important, creative word, but it is a highly significant human activity that at least in part defines our humanity. The greater the power of our imagination (which can be richly developed), the greater fullness and overall satisfaction of our lives. This is true of our physical being, but it is also in a very positive sense true of our spiritual being and our religious experience. While one cannot live in a totally imaginary world and be considered mentally healthy, one cannot live in a world without the exercise of imagination. The ability to imagine contributes to being a healthy person who is able to grow and reach one's full ability and humanity. This is true physically and mentally. It is also true spiritually.

This brings us to the word "imagine" (Latin, *imaginari, imago*) which is used in the title of this book, *Imagine Paul: Apostle of God*. The word "imagine" suggests the formation of a mental image or understanding of a person or thing not present. In the sense the word is being used in this book, the word deals with the real and the actual, or what for a given person may become real and actual, not the virtual and unreal. At the same time, the word "imagine" has to do with interpretation. To think is to imagine. To evaluate is to imagine. To weigh and come to understand alternatives is to imagine.

The word "imagine" is an active verb and not a passive word. It involves activity on the part of the person who is willing to engage in the activity of imagining. One may image the actual past as well as the potential future. One may actively imagine and engage in working to achieve a better present. The act of imagining is a powerful ability and activity that can recreate the past, remake the present, and work toward a better future. One cannot get away from interpretation. To interpret the past, the present, or the future is to imagine. In the act of imagining, to feel and to show compassion and empathy for others is to imagine. Sometimes on the basis of our own personal experience we are enabled to imagine the experience of others and join with them in their sufferings and personal challenges, as well as their successes. Thank God for empathy and compassion wrought by imagination.

As an example, to truly understand Jesus's parables, such as the Good Samaritan and Prodigal Son so-called, *one must place oneself into the parable* and imagine the setting and the experience of the characters within the parables. Likewise, one cannot remain a disinterested and distant observer "sitting above" Jesus's stories if one is to comprehend. One needs to be "on the ground," immersed and participating in the story. One cannot appreciate Paul's letter to the Philippians and its resounding theme of joy without standing beside Paul and imagining his life-threatening experience in a Roman municipal prison (likely in Ephesus). To come to a more full appreciation of the ministry and person of Jesus, the development of early Christianity, and the ministry of Paul and the gospel he preached, one has to *imagine*. Otherwise, one only entertains a detached dogmatism laced with theological opinions found along the highway of history and nourished by another, alternative world far removed from the original world of Paul. In such instance, one participates in "Christendom," but not as an active *Christian*.

There *was* a real first-century world, now characterized as Greco-Roman, that was quite different from the world in which we now live. There *was* a real Jesus of Nazareth. There *was* a real Peter. There *was* a real Paul, a person who lived in a first-century Mediterranean culture and in a world ruled by the Roman Empire. Just as the future in our day has not yet become a present reality and may be imagined in terms of "a galaxy far, far away," so also the past must be "imagined" by those living in the present. If a time-travel machine should ever be invented (and people have "imagined" such), then one will be enabled to travel back in time and actually experience the first-century world of Paul for oneself. With a time machine, one could step out into the ancient streets of Corinth or "go up" to old Jerusalem for the Feast of Passover or Pentecost with the throng of pilgrims, maybe even the throng that welcomed Jesus, the prophet from Galilee. Of course, if one wished to communicate verbally with anyone living in that world, one would need to learn to speak Greek or Aramaic or Latin as it was pronounced in the first-century world! One would also need to change one's clothes and hair style, as well, lest one look completely strange.

Until a time-travel machine should be invented, however, one can only enter Paul's world or Jesus's world through the historical reconstruction of that world. One must learn better to imagine that world. The work of scholars may help one to better imagine. There are countless resources available today that can help one do just that—computer resources, video media, books, travel opportunities—both general and specific. Helps are available, but one must will to imagine. One must actively engage opportunities that are available.[2]

Contextual Illumination

If one is not a biblical scholar or a theologian, one must imagine what scholars do and how they go about their work. One may at times wonder whether scholars and theologians have any contribution to make at all. However, before one imagines a world without biblical scholars and theologians, one should imagine a world that includes them and come to appreciate what they do.

If one is a person whose native language is English, as is true for the present writer for example, every time one picks up an English Bible to read even a small portion in one's favorite translation, one is indebted to biblical scholars. It is they who have done the work of translating the original Hebrew and Greek into a language that one can actually read, provided one is literate. Otherwise, the Bible itself would remain inaccessible in its entirety to the average person. It would be filled with strange symbolic characters printed on a page, that in their own right would be as mysterious as Egyptian hieroglyphics or Mesopotamian cuneiform. English reading people only have ready access to the Bible because of biblical scholars who have labored to provide the biblical word in one's own language. This is true as well

---

2. While there are some illustrations included in the present work meant to stimulate one's imagination, one could supplement them with illustrative images found on the internet for virtually every physical topic that is addressed in this work. One should pursue them according to one's interest. These may range from still images to extended reconstructive videos.

for persons of native languages other than English. Without a ready and understandable translation of the biblical text, one would likely not even know about the apostle Paul, much less be able to imagine him and his ministry in any significant way other than hearsay in contemporary dress.

Some readers may not be familiar with an historical approach to "Scripture," having been taught that "Scripture" is simply the "word of God" meant for moral edification. A more serious and comprehensive approach to Scripture would perceive both that Scripture is that and more. If one actually reads Scripture and takes it seriously, rather than merely reciting summary doctrines, then one is compelled to acknowledge that the most common literary genre or form in the Bible is narrative or "story."

The Bible relates the story of God's relationship with human beings through Abraham, Moses, David, the prophets, and Jesus of Nazareth, through Israel, Judaism, and early Christianity, as examples of biblical content. The Bible covers a broad swath of human history, cultural experience, and religious development. One may even sometimes ask oneself, "Why is this in the Bible?," or "How is this the 'word of God'?"

The Bible is, in effect, the story of God as revealed to and by human beings inspired to re-present the divine revelation that has come to them. And as divine revelation, one should acknowledge that from the perspective of the biblical writers themselves, moral and edifying truths of God's creation and intended redemption of humankind (and the remainder of God's creation) is couched in and presented in narrative stories of historical events. The distinctive nature of God, in biblical thought, is the fact that Israel's God worked in history and historical events to accomplish his purposes.

A blind ignorance of historical context will inevitably lead to mis-appropriation, mis-interpretation, and mis-application of biblical truth, even that which may directly express moral or salvific/redemptive concerns. One actually betrays the Bible and biblical revelation if one neglects or denies the historical context which the Bible provides and upon which it focuses.

Second Timothy 3:15–17 is an apt description of the function of Scripture. The reference is more than a dogmatic definition, as it sets forth the function of Scripture, lest we forget while lost in imposed dogmatism. As a germane and relevant illustration to current discussion, the book of Acts may have its moments of edifying moral teaching, but the basic framework expresses the significance of historical development and story of the early church.

The historical development of Paul's churches call for Paul's pastoral address of differing issues of ethics and theology which arose in the context of living out the Gospel of God in various places within a first-century Greco-Roman world. The Bible is more than "post-it-note" theology meant for daily edifying consumption through a-contextual "daily Bible readings" chosen for personal devotions and gratification. The "word of God" is expressed through narrative story of human experience. This is true for the biblical writers, as much as it is for ourselves.

The Bible is more than a collection of "moral lessons" for cultural accommodation. The Bible itself recounts many events and stories and mentions many places and peoples. It sets forth conceptions which describe the relationship of God with humankind. All of these cry out for contextual interpretation and comprehension. The investigations of scholars and theologians provide a context for understanding. As an example, without an awareness of the geography of Galilee, one will not adequately comprehend the ministry of Jesus. Some have even termed the land itself the "fifth Gospel." Without some appreciation of the geographical nature of the Greco-Roman world and the distances Paul traveled over the course of his ministry, as well as the physical location of his mission centers, one will comprehend neither what Paul did nor what he wrote.

Without understanding the sociology and culture of the worlds of Jesus and Paul, one embraces biblical words that without a context become only pretexts for alternative gospels of misapplied meaning. *One practices a fallacy when one rushes to make application of a biblical text without an adequate appreciation of the biblical context.* The Bible can be approached with a sophisticated esotericism by laypersons, clergy, and scholarship alike that is uninformed by contextual realities. The biblical "why" is as important as the biblical "what" and often far more significant than a contemporary significance only anthropologically defined according to contemporary designs and desires. Scholars labor to provide avenues of contextual appreciation for the biblical world itself in terms of its geography, sociology, religions, and culture that enable a clarity of vision.

Scholars must work with the available evidence, whether that be written literary materials or whether that be archaeological artifacts and structures uncovered in the excavation of ancient sites. All available data calls for analysis by means of various methodologies. One may employ literary methodologies that reveal the underlying use of source materials in biblical writings and that reveal purpose and intent of the final author's theological understanding. One may seek to discern the "who, what, when, where, and why" questions in analyzing a literary work. One may set forth plot and character development of protagonists and antagonists in a given work. As an illustration on another level, it is interesting to become aware of the characters with whom Jesus populates his parables and to come to understand his deliberate intent in doing so. It is likewise significant to come to understand the rhetorical techniques that Paul may employ in structuring and setting forth what he writes in his letters. Such elements become vehicles for both understanding and appropriate development of understanding and meaning.

One may identify differences in genre and consequently the purpose and effect of given literary works. A Pauline letter is quite different from a Gospel or the book of Revelation. It is of a different literary genre and carries with it a different purpose. It exhibits a different means of accomplishing its purpose. On the basis of rhetorical analysis and contextual explication, one may even discern significant differences of Pauline purpose and expression in his various letters.

Among the Gospels, one may see how each Gospel writer approaches the story of Jesus and relates that story in his own manner. Scholars, for example, by employing methodologies like "source analysis" (what sources did a writer use?) and "redaction analysis" (how did the writer employ his sources?), seek to set forth the distinctive alteration of underlying source materials. The Gospel writers express their own distinctive purposes and theological understandings through their adaptation and alteration of the sources they utilized. For example, it is the suggestion of most scholars that when Luke wrote his Gospel, he made use of Mark as an underlying source. He felt free to modify Mark in the light of his own purposes. Mark 6:1–6 recounts the story of Jesus's rejection in his own home town of Nazareth at a middle point in Mark's presentation of the Galilean ministry of Jesus. Matthew, who (according to most) also used Mark as a source, likewise presents this episode according to the narrative ordering of Mark (see Matt 13:53–58), i.e., somewhere in the middle of Jesus's Galilean ministry.

On the other hand, Luke omits the account at that later point in the gospel story and instead moves it back to the very beginning of Jesus's public ministry (see Luke 4:16–30). He has theological purpose in doing so, in spite of what or when the actual historical occurrence may have been. With the inclusion of the Isaiah passage (Isa 61:1–2), Luke deliberately characterizes and emphasizes the kind of Messiah Jesus will be. He also stresses the fulfillment of the Isaiah passage in the person of Jesus, as the Lukan Jesus tells the crowd in Nazareth, "Today this scripture has been fulfilled [pf.] before your ears" (Luke 4:21). The verb employed is a perfect tense in Greek that suggests an action that has itself been completed but that continues to express the result or implication of that action in some manner. The episode of Jesus's rejection at Nazareth becomes the "programmatic introduction" to the entire ministry of Jesus that will be presented in the Lukan Gospel. In this single episode, Luke sets forth how Jesus's person and ministry should be understood through the remainder of his Gospel. Through the utilization of methodologies such as source, redaction, and rhetorical analysis, then, the scripture text is set forth with greater clarity of purpose and meaning.

One may engage in historical reconstruction, as one examines the biblical evidence that presents the ministry of Jesus, or the beginnings of earliest Christianity, or the overall ministry of Paul. We are so constituted as human beings that we have an appreciation for organized, rational thought. Historical context informs the literary content of Paul's letters or the teachings of Jesus. The evidence is not always clear, complete, or universal, such that evaluation may lead to more than a single *plausible* interpretation and reconstruction as offered by scholars. Archaeological findings may greatly augment and clarify socio-religious realities and the cultural context of a bygone age. They help us to imagine with factual clarity the "worlds" of Paul, for example, or the nature of a first-century Galilee in which Jesus carried out his ministry.

Historical reconstruction with a view toward understanding and appreciation is what scholars do. Biblical scholars seek to reconstruct and rediscover an actual world gone by. Imagination is involved in a very positive and practical sense. The biblical world was a very real world, even as was, let's say, the nineteenth-century Common Era world, as evidenced by both the archaeological remains and literary legacy of that world. One may find it difficult to imagine the reality of people traveling narrow dirt roads or streets on horseback or by horse-drawn wagons, when one lives today in a world of paved highways and fast-moving vehicles, some of which are now "self-driven." And should we mention air travel and even electricity?

The biblical world was not an imaginary world that never existed, but rather a world that had real existence—a world that on the basis of its remaining legacy may now be imagined. One may stand before Roman ruins and image an entire building or temple and the hustle and bustle of life that occurred there. This is comparatively easy at a location of the two cities of ancient Pompeii or Herculaneum located in southern Italy, which were frozen in time by the volcanic ash from the explosion of Vesuvius in 79 CE. Archaeological scholars have labored to recover, expose, and reconstruct the life of first-century Pompeiians whose skeletal remains have been found where they lived—and where they died. There are scholarly works that even seek to establish the presence of early Christianity in Pompeii.

Pliny the Younger, for example, produced a written account of the destruction of Pompeii and Herculaneum by the explosion of Vesuvius, an event in which his uncle, Pliny the Elder, died. Josephus, a colorful Jewish historian, produced accounts of the history of the Jews and the war between the Jews and Romans that is invaluable for understanding the context of the Judaism of Jesus's and Paul's day. The discovery of the "Dead Sea Scrolls" and the excavation of Qumran on the northwestern shore of the Dead Sea in southern Palestine have offered firsthand insight into a sectarian Jewish group in the time frame of Jesus's ministry and the development of earliest Christianity, including the ministry of Paul. The discovery of a first-century fishing boat in the mud of the Lake of Galilee illustrates full well the type of vessel in which Jesus and his disciples sailed across that lake. From the remains of all these things left behind, full illustrations have been drawn and models have been constructed. Imagination in the most positive sense comes into play through the work of archaeological scholars, as an ancient world is brought back to life.

Artifacts, things easily removed from an archaeological site (scrolls, coins, jewelry, pottery, a limestone sarcophagus) are objects used by real people of the past that defined in part their everyday living. Structures, on the other hand, are those things not easily removed from an archaeological site without destroying them. Structures would include entities such as houses, temples, arches, aqueducts, bathhouses, tombs, and even streets and roadways. Study of the actual skeletal remains of persons who lived in the first-century world enable insight into the diet and health of ancient people and offer a stark reminder that, indeed, it was a real world. Pottery cooking pots still containing food residue offer factual insights into the diets and appetites of ancient peoples. Artifacts are more than just objects to be seen in an archaeological "museum." They reveal the life of the ancient world and stimulate the imagination, such that it comes "to life" again, such that we may come to understand at least a portion of that world better.

Literary evidence beyond the Gospels, for example, testifies to the reality of Roman crucifixion in the time of Jesus. Literally, there is literary witness to thousands of persons crucified by the Romans and others. Jesus himself was crucified by the Romans on the orders of Pilate, likely in April of 30 CE at Passover season. However, physical evidence of crucifixion is meager indeed.

In 1968 a heel bone with a Roman nail driven through it was recovered from a tomb in Jerusalem, providing the first physical example of the Roman practice of crucifixion. It belonged to a young man in his twenties by the name of Yehonanan ben Hagkol.

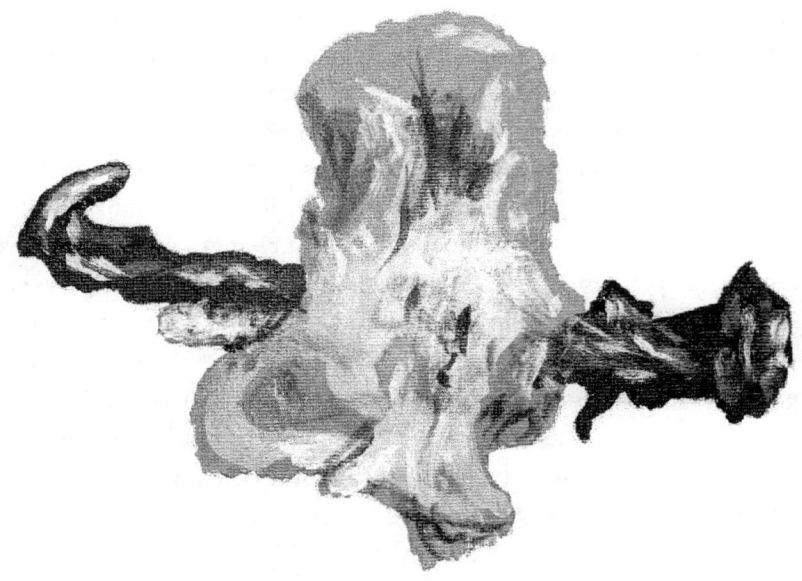

Fig. 2. Heel Bone of Yehonanan ben Hagkol. Painting by G. Roger Greene.

Coupled with structures and artifacts, and other physical evidence brought forth by archaeology, the literary remains from the ancient world help to "flesh out" and define the lives of ancient people and events. It was a real world that we can imagine from all of its evidence left behind. It was a real world that can come to life again by allowing its evidence to inform our imagination. Along with literary evidence and that revealed by archaeology, even a heel bone with a Roman nail can be a stark reminder to the *reality* of the Roman world. The internet affords immediate access to literally thousands of pictures and illustrations of Roman cities and culture of the Greco-Roman world.

In the case of Paul, one may "visit" the world of Paul in various ways. One may travel to ancient sites such as Corinth, Athens, Thessalonica, Philippi, Ephesus, or Jerusalem, or Caesarea Maritima. One may travel the lands themselves—Palestine-Syria, Asia Minor, Greece, or Italy—and gain a feel for Paul's travels. The internet affords ample resources for "virtual visits" to various places that are significant to the ministry of Paul. Scholarly works are available with ample illustrations that depict various sites and the nature of life in that ancient world.

Why did Paul primarily work in cities or urban areas? What was a Greco-Roman city like? What would life be like to live in such a city on a daily basis? How did life as a gentile differ from life as a Jew? What *would* it have been like to have lived in ancient Corinth at the time Paul preached and worked there? How would you, the reader, have responded to the gospel message preached by Paul if you had been a member of the Jewish synagogue in Corinth or a gentile shop-keeper with a shop near that of Aquila and Priscilla—and Paul (see Acts 18:3)? How would you have responded to the gospel message if you had been a gentile pagan who came to buy an awning at the shop of Aquila and Priscilla in the marketplace of old Corinth?

And, whether Jew or gentile, sociologically and religiously speaking, what changes would have been demanded in your lifestyle if you had embraced the gospel of a Lord called Jesus as proclaimed by Paul? What changes would you have made in your lifestyle, beyond moral issues generally heard in church today? What about all the gods one needed to worship in that ancient world, gods that would still be worshiped by pagan friends and neighbors? One might still pass by their temples daily—temples that one used to visit before becoming a Christian. Pagan temples abounded, although there was no standing "Temple of Christ." Why was meat sacrificed to idols such a big thing in the Corinthian context? How did the environment of Corinth contribute to the problems faced by the fledgling church in Corinth? Did "speaking in tongues" at Corinth have anything to do with the Pythia at the Oracle of Delphi, located just across the Bay of Corinth in the shadow of Mount Parnassus that was so visible from Corinth?

Would you have been willing to give up all the gods worshiped in Corinth—gods believed to protect the city and one's own life as well—in order to embrace a crucified Jew supposedly exalted by the singular Jewish God? Would you have been willing to exchange your entire circle of friends and totally revamp your social life? How would the gospel have affected your life lived in Corinth in real terms—or, for that matter, in Philippi or Ephesus or the region of Galatia?

Paul did not write the same words to every church, such that his letters are generally context specific. It is the context that indeed determines the message. Without appreciation of context, the message is either lost or misunderstood. To come to understand the letters that Paul wrote to Corinth and other church centers, one must seek to enter into the contextual world of Paul and his first-century audience that lived in those centers.

We can read what Paul wrote, but how often do we imagine and appreciate the audiences to whom Paul wrote? What were their social and cultural practices? What did they believe, religiously speaking? How did social roles between men and women vary? How did they dress? What did they eat? How did they spend their time? What were their hopes and dreams? What did the "gospel" offer and whose "gospel" was it—Caesar's or God's? One must be willing to "visit" Paul's world in order to hear Paul's gospel—and to more fully appreciate the Gospel of God.

While we have no originals of any of the New Testament documents as they left the hands of their human writers, we are quite fortunate to have some three thousand or more hand-written copies of various New Testament books. These date from the second through the seventeenth centuries. The printing press was not invented until the late fifteenth century. These manuscripts vary in terms of precise content and completions. For example, we have an early collection of Paul's letters written on papyrus that has been called Papyrus 46 (or p46). Pictures of pages from this manuscript may be easily found on the internet, as illustrated by the accompanying illustration.[3]

---

3. One may note even from the small sample of p46 how different a "page of the Bible" actually looked, compared to modern-day Bibles. It is written in Greek capital letters, without chapter or verse divisions, without separation between words, and without punctuation marks. Be thankful for the work of scholarly translators.

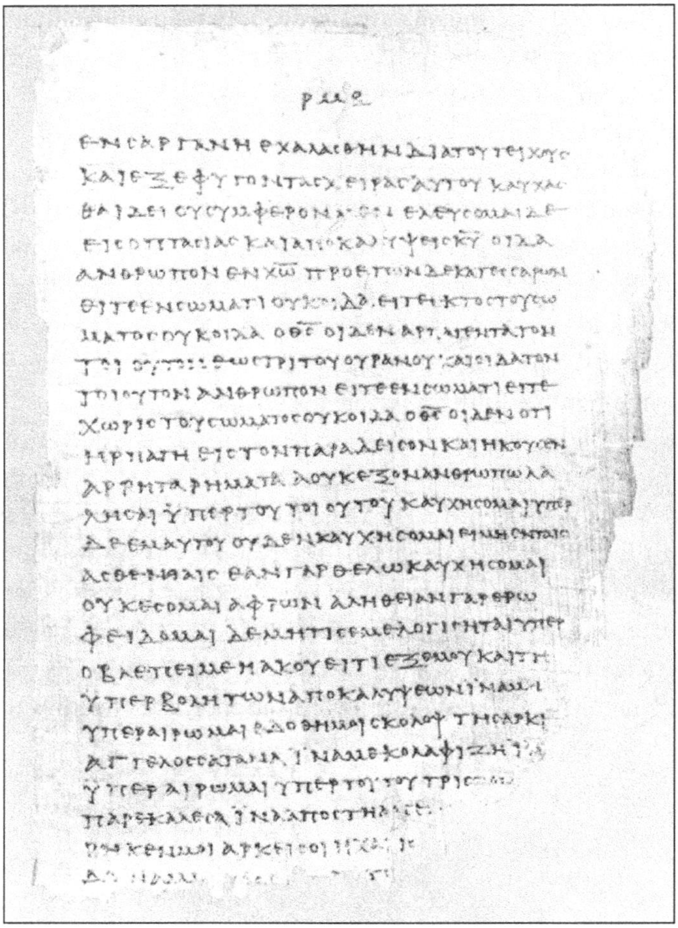

Fig. 3. Papyrus 46 Page, 2 Corinthians 11:33—12:9. Chester Beatty II; Ann Arbor, University of Michigan, Inv. 62382. Public domain.

Papyrus 46 is missing seven leaves at the beginning (which likely contained the beginning of the letter to the Romans) and seven leaves at the end. It presently lacks 2 Thessalonians, Philemon, and the so-called Pastorals of 1 Timothy, 2 Timothy, and Titus. It includes the book of Hebrews, which was thought by some in the ancient world to have been written by Paul. Strictly speaking, Hebrews is anonymous. All titles to New Testament books have been added along the way—none are original, and the book of Hebrews nowhere identifies its author within the pages of the text itself. Papyrus 46 is now dated to the late second century and becomes the earliest collection of Paul's letters that we possess.

However, there are other relatively early manuscripts that contain copies of Paul's letters. Because every manuscript represents something copied by the hand of a particular scribe, no two manuscripts are exactly alike. There are variations—some deliberate and some accidental—that characterize every hand-produced manuscript. Scholars are called upon to evaluate every available manuscript in order to seek to discern what appears to be the most original reading of any given passage or verse. The process is known as "textual analysis," and it must necessarily be completed before any English translation may be published. One encounters marginal notes in many English editions that give some of the alternative readings found in various manuscripts. Once again, one is the recipient of careful work supplied by biblical scholars.

Scholars engage in contextual illumination and historical reconstruction. Scholars engage in commentary on biblical texts, including Paul. One cannot avoid interpretation, if one actually reads a biblical text and takes it seriously. However, one should be aware of the basis of one's interpretation. Often, our interpretation of Scripture is simply based upon "what we have always heard" or mere personal opinion. This may be true for one who is a professing Christian, for one who embraces another religion, for one who is an agnostic or even an atheist. It is truly difficult to climb out of canyons carved by long-flowing cultural waters. Many times in many areas of life, our "beliefs" are simply the result of our long ingrained social enculturation. The mind-set we have is a result of our past experience. Sometimes that calls for affirmation; sometimes that calls for repentance.

There is a real sense that *we are what we have been*. Life, however, is about growth and not about stagnation. We grow through the flowering of imagination, as we dare to experience new things and think new thoughts. Biblical scholars help us move beyond or further develop previous frames of reference. They offer insight into difficult biblical texts by illuminating the meaning of words and concepts. They develop historical reconstructions which shine light upon the context of biblical thought. If one does not understand the context, then at best one is likely to comprehend a biblical text only partially and at worst misunderstand the text altogether. There is a sense that we become what we are, i.e., what we *will* to become.

Sometimes the results of biblical scholarship have appeared rather "barren" to those who look to canonical Scripture to find only spiritual encouragement for the day ahead or contemporary moral application to their lives. It should be stated that not all Scripture has direct application to one's individual life, nor does every scripture convey a moral lesson. In fact, the dominant literary genre in the Bible is narrative story that intends far more than a mere "moral lesson." It should go without saying that none of the biblical writers wrote for us; we were not their audience. The twenty-first century would have been for them a "galaxy far, far away," in a day and age when people believed the Earth was at the center of the universe or cosmos and they did not even know that such things as "galaxies" even existed. Biblical scholars apply historical and literary analysis in order to discover what the biblical writers intended to convey to the audiences to whom they wrote, who were people of their own day. No single methodology offers an exclusive hermeneutical certainty or comprehension of author and audience. However, hermeneutical truth should be based upon more than just opinion or dogmatic interpretation. "Hermeneutics" is the science and process of interpretation.

One cannot get away from interpretation. The only uninterpreted biblical text, Paul included, is an unread biblical text. If one reads, one interprets. Scholars use big words translated into English from the Greek, words such as hermeneutics, exegesis, and eisegesis. Hermeneutics simply means "interpretation," a process of translating the language conceptuality and original meaning of the writer's contextual experience into that of a later or more modern applicational context. Appropriate interpretation (hermeneutics) involves both the task of seeking to discover the original meaning and the task of applying that meaning to a contemporary setting of modern categories. It thus involves historical exegesis, as well as hermeneutical application that carries with it contextual validity.

Everyone holds opinions. This fact is actually unavoidable, for it belongs to what it means to be human. However, all opinions are not the same. Nor should biblical interpretation reside at the level of mere opinion, which may be informed, uninformed, or even misinformed. Biblical interpretation may be based upon many things ranging from contextual appreciation of the available evidence to ignorance to mere dogma. To be somewhat technical for a moment, biblical scholars engage in what is called "exegesis," i.e., the illumination of meaning inherent to the author's intended meaning of a given text. They seek to avoid what is called "eisegesis," or reading into a text a meaning that was never intended or suggested by a given writer. The two words are derived from Greek—"exegesis" a "leading out of" and "eisegesis" a "reading into." The term "exegesis" marks the attempted recovery of ancient meaning in the context of its own original setting. "Eisegesis" marks a "leading into" or reading into an ancient text what was not found in the text originally. It is meaning improperly imposed upon a text that does not fairly represent the meaning implied by the text.

To be honest, we all engage in both activities. Our vision is always limited by the point in which we live in history and even by our own sinfulness or perversity or dogmatism, as well as by our total wealth of experience. One's vision may be limited by ignorance or by apathy. One's vision may be limited by a lack of maturity, by a lack of opportunity, or by an unwillingness to experience new thought and understanding. Paul, for example, charged the Corinthians with being "babies in Christ" long after they should have been maturing in Christ (1 Cor 3:1–4). "Infantile paralysis" sometimes affects our entire realm of living and not just physical bodies.

One's vision may be limited by a paucity or lack of developed imagination. As an ancient Jewish proverb suggests, we see the world as we are and not as it is. To be human is to experience limitations—we cannot do all things, we cannot know everything, nor do we see all things without personal bias, prejudice, or preference. The best one can do is to offer an informed interpretation based upon the evaluation of all of the evidence that is available.

Imagine Interpretation

The practice of private, silent "Bible reading" was virtually absent in the ancient world. The "Bible" as we know it did not exist. The so-called Old Testament works would be read aloud from separate scrolls in synagogue worship services (see Luke 4:16–21). New Testament writings were read aloud in worship in the context of a small community of believers gathered in a house church. Most people were not literate, they could not read nor write. Writing services and materials were expensive. The culture was an oral and aural one, such that reading aloud in collective worship became a part of the selection process for which writings would become canonical New Testament scripture. The "Bible" of the earliest church was what we call the "Old Testament," especially in the Septuagint (LXX) or Greek translation of the Hebrew, until specifically Christian writings were included alongside the "Old Testament scripture." Second Peter 3:15–17, for example, includes Paul's letters alongside the "other scriptures."

As an ex post facto judgment, the early church affirmed inspiration by the Spirit for those works which had come to be considered authoritative by the church. The letters of Paul and other early Christian writings (such as the Gospels) continued to be read and used in worship. Questions of perceived apostolic authorship were settled on the basis of perceived apostolic theology and the earlier date of a work. The nature of the mediation or representation of the original revelatory events came into play. The early church made judgments as to what represented the apostolic faith and what did not. Over time, countless gospels, letters, acts, and apocalyptic writings were produced by early Christians. Not all were deemed to be early, apostolic, or orthodox in their content. Most of these writings, thereby, were not included in the New Testament.

The church of the early centuries ultimately assembled a body of twenty-seven works deemed to be suitable for worship and instruction. Although development of the New Testament canon occurred over time, the exact listing of the twenty-seven works that constitute the New Testament appeared for the first time in the Easter letter of Athanasius, bishop of Alexandria, in 367 CE. That date is 337 years after the execution and resurrection of Jesus—almost seventeen Christian generations later, if a generation is considered to be twenty years. Even at that point, some seven works remained disputed in some other quarters of the church—2 John, 3 John, 2 Peter, Jude, James, Hebrews, and Revelation. These works had difficulty gaining universal acceptance as "scripture."

Although our present New Testament comes to us as a printed text replete with book titles, chapter divisions, verse divisions, paragraphs, punctuation marks, and separation between words, none of these things are to be found in the earliest manuscripts of the New Testament documents. One may look again at the illustration of p46 given earlier. In fact, as indicated, one did not have access to a full New Testament collection of works prior to the fourth century, when the New Testament "canon" was acknowledged by Athanasius (367 CE). Instead, one would encounter individual works or perhaps only partial collections represented by various "manuscripts." Written documents could only be produced by hand, such that copies of New Testament works would be very expensive and time-consuming to produce.

Imagine, however, the absence of the aforementioned things to which we have grown so accustomed in written texts, along with arbitrary word division governed by available spaces on a given line.

MARYHADALITTLELAMBLITTLELAMBLITTLELA

MBWHOSEFLEECEWASWHITEASSNOW

Imagine all capital letters without punctuation marks and separation between words—and written in Greek or Latin, with some words abbreviated. To give a biblical example in Greek, one might confront the following text.

ΟΥΤΩΣΓΑΡΗΓΑΠΗΣΕΝΟΘΕΟΣΤΟΝΚΟΣΜΟΝ

ΩΣΤΕΤΟΝΥΙΟΝΤΟΝΜΟΝΟΓΕΝΗΕΔΩΚΕΝΙΝ

ΑΠΑΣΟΠΙΣΤΕΥΩΝΕΙΣΑΥΤΟΝΜΗΑΠΟΛΗΤΑ

ΙΑΛΛΕΧΗΖΩΗΝΑΙΩΝΙΟΝ

What text is it? Why John 3:16, of course, presented in capital letters with thirty characters per line.

Or, to give another biblical example, again given in thirty characters per line, imagine Paul's words in Rom 12:1—in English, instead of Greek!

IBESEECHYOUALLTHEREFOREBRETHRE

NTHROUGHTHETENDERMERCIESOFGODT

OPRESENTYOURBODIESASASACRIFICELI

VINGHOLYACCEPTABLETOGODYOURLOG

ICALSERVICE

The number of characters that could be printed by a scribal hand on a given line would have to be considered, such that the above example employs an arbitrary thirty characters per line. The number of characters per line would be determined by the size of the papyrus sheet and the penmanship of the scribe, and might vary between twenty-eight to thirty-six characters, for example. Sometimes, the lack of word separation or abbreviation could lead to alternative interpretations or even misinterpretation, such as in the sentence "GODISNOWHERE" or perhaps "ḠISNOWHERE," where the word "GOD" would even be abbreviated. One cannot get away from interpretation.

The story of how the English Bible came to be is a fascinating one. Chapter divisions are attributed to Stephen Langdon, archbishop of Canterbury, in the thirteenth century, while the present verse divisions were introduced in the 1551 edition of a printed Greek text by Robert Stephanus. The first English Bible to contain both chapter and verse divisions was the Geneva Bible first published in 1560. This was but a scant fifty-one years before the publication of the first edition of the King James Version of the Bible published in 1611.

Paul's letters were actually the first New Testament documents written and the first to be gathered into a collection. Collection implies some type of ordering. While originally written individually to particular churches (as "Philippians," to the church at Philippi), once they were all collected together they became transformed into Pauline tradition addressed to all churches universally. The question of ordering also arises at that point, such that Paul's letters are not presented in the New Testament in the order in which he wrote them.

Paul's letters are not presented chronologically—Romans was not the first written. Rather, the present order is on the basis of relative length (Romans is the longest), with letters written to churches given first and those addressed to individuals given after. Philemon, for example, is the shortest of Paul's attributed letters and is assumed to be addressed to an individual, while Romans is the most lengthy and addressed to one or more churches in Rome.

It should not be missed that all of this is to say we do not have Paul's letters or any other New Testament document in the form in which the original left the author's hand. All of our New Testament documents have been edited by the early church and by the course of transmission since the earliest days of the development of Christianity. This fact has implications for many doctrines of inspiration.

So, imagine a letter of Paul as it left his hand or that of the recording secretary he had employed. Imagine sheets of papyrus written upon with a quill pen in the common Greek of the day. Imagine a fragile document without a heading or date, without paragraphs, word separation, punctuation or accents, and without chapters and verses. Imagine also the delivery time that would be needed, as one had to dispatch or wait for a courier to deliver the letter in a process that could take weeks or even months. One may aid one's imagination by looking up various pictures of papyrus leaves of p46 on the internet. It is as Paul said, by way of analogy, "Now we have this treasure in ceramic vessels, in order that the surpassing power might be of God and not of us" (2 Cor 4:7).

It is as Paul wrote, "*You all* are our epistle, having been written in our hearts, being made known and being read by all men; because you all are openly manifest that you are an epistle of Christ having been ministered to by us, having been written not with ink but with the Spirit of the living God, not on stone tablets but on tablets of human hearts" (2 Cor 3:2–3). The truth of the Gospel of God, according to Paul, is not to be found on a printed page valuable as that may be, but rather it is to be found in human hearts and changed lives.

When one comes to Paul's letters, one already confronts a history of interpretation. With reference to Paul, this is mostly perceived in terms of theology or ethics. It is largely crystallized in what we term "doctrines," whether they be "doctrines" of belief or of behavior. A "doctrine" is an establishing principle that is taught. A doctrine formally stated and authoritatively proclaimed and held as established opinion is known as "dogma," whether it has adequate support (warrants) or not. All doctrines are stated interpretations that have been formulated at particular points in time to address specific issues that have arisen. What may be customarily referred to as "Pauline theology" may also be referred to as "Pauline doctrine."

Not all "Pauline" theology is the same, however. What Paul actually wrote represents his theological understanding expressed in writing to foundational situations that arose in his churches in the context of a first-century Greco-Roman world. As we read Paul's letters, we are exposed to his expressed "epistolic" (found in the letters) theology. Paul's total theological understanding would be more personal and more extensive, as it would be for anyone who might write an essay on "My Understanding of God and His Actions."

One would not express everything one believed or understood. Not every interpretation of Paul is exegetically or contextually based. Not every interpretation of Paul offers adequate awareness of Paul's first-century historical context, so as to more completely understand *why* Paul wrote *what* he wrote. Not every interpretation of Paul is the same. Paul is imagined differently. So is his thought. Also, one should not forget that when Paul's letters are read aloud in oral presentation, interpretation is present through tone of voice, emphasis, and a selection process in a community context. Even the liturgical year of the church today may set forth a limited passage of a few verses without respect to the larger context of Paul's entire letter. The application of Pauline texts may be imagined differently depending upon the context, whether that be private devotions, a classroom, or a church community at worship.

The Pauline texts become a living voice again only in the context of a living people. Otherwise, Paul's words that were representative of at least some of his thought when he wrote or dictated them remain for us only as black carbon deposits on a dormant, printed page of paper or virtual characters on a computer screen. Whether one reads the Greek or the English, and whether one reads silently or aloud, interpretation becomes evident in emphases, intonation, and thought. Interpretation becomes the vehicle that facilitates both hearing and comprehension. We may "hammer" Paul's words to fit our pre-conceived theology and ideology, or we may seek to first understand them in Paul's own context and that of his audience as we struggle with meaning in terms of a contemporary application. In either case, imagination is at work, whether we have realized it or not.

One approach only requires the dogma of what one "already knows," while the other brings contextual discovery enabled by the active gift of imagination or re-imagination. To become a more competent and responsible interpreter is to enrich one's repertoire of comprehension and experience. That desired result is achieved only in the context of one or more communities—no one is a self-made individual.

Various aspects of human living interpenetrate, whether gender, social, political, religious, racial, or ethnic issues.

A cathedral may be studied or analyzed architecturally, but it can only be fully experienced as a whole in worship. Paul's letters can be imagined in terms of dogmatic theology, but they will only be experienced as they result in the worship of the God responsible for the Gospel contained therein. They will only be experienced when we "hear" what Paul is saying and why. When Paul's letters were first written, they were not considered "scripture." Paul did not take out a sheet of papyrus and begin addressing the Corinthian church by stating, "Dear Corinthians, let me write some scripture for you today." Such a view would represent the height of ignorance and naiveté.

Still, what Paul may have written to the Corinthians (or any other church) would have been perceived by the recipients as written to them and for them. By nature of the case, Paul addresses specific churches in the light of specific, contingent needs and issues. This should serve as a reminder that Paul did not write to us, even though his letters may be applied to us and by us. Paul's churches varied in character and needs, much as the seven churches mentioned in Rev 2–3 differed.

People living in a pre-sixteenth-century world prior to the Reformation may have perceived themselves to be living in much the same world as Paul and the recipients of his letters, in spite of some very real differences that had come to exist. Paul would have been an historical, canonical, and theological icon, to be sure, but the worldview would have been much the same in many respects. The authority of tradition perpetuated a long-standing continuum through the Middle Ages, even despite political changes. However, with the Copernican revolution and the rise of critical and analytical scientific thought, major gaps were introduced. What could be read in the Bible, Paul included, stood in marked contrast to scientific fields like astronomy, geology, geography, and biology.

With the invention of the microscope, a hitherto unseen and unknown micro world became visible for the very first time. With the invention of the telescope, Copernican astronomy now realized that the sun and not the Earth was at the center of the solar system. Geographically, and because some dared to imagine, a whole "new" world was discovered on the other side of the Atlantic Ocean. That "new" world actually dwarfed the Roman Empire world of Paul, situated as Paul's world was around the Mediterranean Sea (the *Mare Nostrum*, "Our Sea").

Almost simultaneously, the *world* became a larger place, the *earth* a smaller and much older place. A larger and older extended universe had to be imagined. And, with the rise of analytical study of the Bible itself, Paul included, the ancient world of the Bible became more strange and distant in a post-sixteenth-century world. The realization had dawned that the Bible was not written to us nor was it written in our "language." The Bible comes to us as the history of events of an earlier time And, as someone has observed, they did things and saw things differently "back then."

The bifurcated response to the rise of modern scientific understanding was somewhat schizophrenic. On the one hand, there was apologetic defense of the Bible coupled with the fear of the onslaught of radically different worldviews. On the other hand, there was liberation from outmoded dogma that offered new opportunity to explore freedom of thought. Religion itself was divided in response. In the wake of the Renaissance, the Reformation, and the Enlightenment, dogmatic naiveté was no longer a realistic option. The rise of analytical methodologies meant for some that they were free *from* the Bible and for others that they were free *for* more informed study of the Bible. While the Reformation offered the opportunity for individual interpretation of the Bible, all interpretations take place within a community of some kind, such that no interpretation is truly individualistic. That is true for the interpretation of Paul.

One may envision the early church in a later, post-70 CE world, reflecting upon what Paul wrote in a pre-70 CE world, as the early Christians came to grips with the destruction and fall of Jerusalem—and the delay of the return of Christ. One may imagine the task of second-century Christians, as they sought to rescue Paul from the heresies of Gnosticism. The word "Gnosticism" characterizes a group of movements of the late first-century and second-century worlds that generally placed emphasis on salvation by secret "knowledge." One may imagine the interpretation of Paul in the world of Constantine and the significance of the Pauline gospel and writings by the Nicene fathers who drafted the Nicene Creed following the council of 325 CE.

One may imagine an Augustine or a Luther reading Paul until the truth of Romans or Galatians flooded their minds, hearts, and souls. One may imagine Calvin crafting rational doctrines of the Christian religion from the pages of Paul's letters. One may imagine the utilizations of Paul's letters in polemical battles against the steady onslaught of the development of modern scientific thought and advances. One may imagine the place of Paul and his letters in the entire sweep of Christian history. However, one can scarcely imagine the New Testament or Christian history itself without Paul.

Imagine Paul's Letters

Paul's letters are historically real. They are not imaginary or fictional. Interpreting them, and interpreting them appropriately, however, is another issue. Interpretation requires the employment of imagination, for there is a large and distinct cultural and historical time gap between Paul and our own day. To illustrate the point further, imagine a blindfolded and ear-muffed Paul led into a large church or cathedral service and then "unbound." Assuming *we* might understand him in communication and he us, what would Paul's response be to the modern expression of Christianity? How would Paul react? How would his reaction vary if he were exposed to a cathedral, to a traditional worship service in a church, or to a contemporary youth service in "fellowship hall" in a gymnasium? How would he respond to a formal service permeated with liturgy? How would he react to a rock band versus a pipe organ? Informal dress versus formal robes? Which do you imagine Paul might prefer? Or, would he find a "different" (heterodox) gospel being performed in them? Would it be Galatians all over again?

What would be his understanding of what was occurring in the church service, even if (and perhaps especially!) the preacher or priest should be offering a sermon or homily drawn from one of Paul's own letters? How would he react to formal clerical dress? How would he respond? What would he seek to communicate? And in reverse, how would we receive the historical Paul? For starters, he certainly would have a different look about him, as we would to him, regardless of what might be said or sung. He might well look like a left-over from a "Christmas manger scene," according to our stereotype. Or, perhaps he would appear totally and unexpectedly different.

Paul was a real, historical person who lived in a time and culture quite different from our own age. Neither he nor his letters were imaginary, but they do require our imagination to understand both his person and his thought. The ball is in our court. It is not Paul's task to understand us, but it is our task to comprehend Paul, if we value Christian Scripture and Christian experience at all. Approximately 25 percent of the New Testament makes a claim to have been written by Paul. His letters represent the earliest New Testament literature that we possess. Through the gift of imagination, we can avail ourselves of scholarly understanding and historical research, allowing such avenues to introduce us more fully to the real man Paul and his very real letters in his own time.

The theologians of the Christian church have for virtually all the centuries of Christian history looked to Paul in order to formulate a *system* of Christian theology. That is not to say that the remainder of Christian Scriptures (both the Old Testament and the New Testament) do not contribute greatly to theological understanding. It is to affirm, however, that Paul's thought expressed in his letters is central, that, historically speaking, his understanding of God and the gospel stands at the very heart of Christian belief.

That is very remarkable for a first-century Jewish Pharisee called by God to proclaim the Gospel of God to the gentile world, who left behind but a handful of occasional letters addressed to the house churches he founded or established or encouraged. Paul did not leave behind an extended and systematic treatise of carefully developed theological topics according to some logical ordering. In short, not even the letter to the Romans offers a systematic theology of Paul.

Paul's letters were written at specific points in time to address particular situations or particular problems or issues being faced in particular church settings. They are thereby "occasional" and "situation specific." They are letters and not theological treatises. When we read them, we are reading someone else's mail. We are privy to Paul's expressed thought and beliefs found in those letters, from which we may draw principles and guidelines for theological understanding. We may even further develop Paul's themes in the light of our own day. We may debate with Paul's expressed thought, even disagree with him, but we should not succumb to the conclusion that all Paul thought or believed is to be found in his very occasional letters or that he wrote Christian doctrine for us.

While scholars differ in their conclusions as to which letters are "authentic" and written by Paul and which letters may have been written by someone else under his name (a practice known as *pseudonymity*), the present writer assumes a very broad Pauline canon of scripture. Some scholars may assume as few as four letters that bear his name may actually be ascribed to Paul with certainty, while others assume that all letters ascribed to Paul plus Hebrews (which nowhere contains Paul's name) should be accepted as Pauline. The present writer, for reasons argued elsewhere and without further apology, assumes a Pauline canon of eleven letters as authentic to Paul, excluding only 1 Timothy and Titus (both pseudonymous), and of course, Hebrews (anonymous).

There are other letters acknowledged by Paul that we may not have—the so-called Previous Letter (see 1 Cor 5:9) and the Painful Letter (see 2 Cor 2:3–4), both written to Corinth. Again, the reader should understand that the titles contained in contemporary Bibles have been added in the course of history and are not original to the text. Paul himself did not take a sheet of papyrus as he began to compose Romans and neatly letter at the top "The Epistle of Paul to the Romans."

With the considerations of material presented in this chapter in mind, it is appropriate at this point to briefly consider the letters of Paul in terms of their basic address. The task here is description of church and correspondence. The later thrust (chapters 6 and 7) is upon the analysis of letter content in terms of gospel and theology. Further pursuit of appreciation of the historical nature and context of Paul's various churches and their issues, as well as the central elements of his theology, will be developed in the later chapters of this book. The letters will be treated in the order in which the current author believes them to have been written.

Paul's own ministry, which provides his own personal context of the letters, will also be treated in subsequent chapters in terms of Paul's two central campaigns. This perspective of two major campaigns instead of the "three missionary journeys" offers a new paradigm for understanding and imagining Paul's ministry, mission, and theology. It also offers new avenues for imagining the application of time-worn Pauline thought in a postmodern world.

The present writer will present the facts of Paul's two campaigns within the illustrative framework of what could be termed "historical fiction." However, within the current work, the emphasis is upon "imagine the two campaigns of Paul," which are deemed to be historical in terms of the actual course of Paul's ministry. It is helpful for understanding to consult the map and other information included in the orientation material given at the beginning of this book. One needs a clear awareness of Paul's movements and the relative location of his churches in order to understand his ministry.

The Thessalonian Letters

Second Thessalonians is understood by the author as the earliest of the Pauline letters that we possess. It was likely written in 49 CE from either Athens or Corinth, both of which were located in the Roman province of Achaia. Thessalonica itself was in the province of Macedonia, as were Philippi and Beroea. Paul encourages the Thessalonians to keep their faith intact in the face of ongoing persecution. He seeks to clarify the understanding of these gentile Christians regarding the return of Christ and the sequence of events that must precede his return (2 Thess 2:1–12), apparently in response to either a misunderstanding or to questions that had been raised in the interim time since Paul had been in the church. His basic answer that he offers them is that of a Jewish apocalyptic schema of the time of fulfillment rather literally interpreted.

That which is "apocalyptic" suggests a perspective of a radical and sudden inbreak of God to make things right. While there are various explanations offered in interpretation of 2 Thess 2:1–12, at a minimum the earlier "sign" of Caligula's order to have a statue of himself set up and worshiped in the Jerusalem Temple appears to have relevance. This was an event that would have had apocalyptic ramifications akin to those of the time of Antiochus IV Epiphanes, the Seleucid ruler who sparked the now much earlier Maccabean Revolt (168–165 BCE). The Thessalonians had been led to believe that the parousia (Christ's "return") would occur very soon, such that some had even ceased working at their jobs in order to wait for heavenly fulfillment.

By the time Paul writes the letter known as 1 Thessalonians, one or more of the believers in Thessalonica have apparently died. There is the expressed concern that those who had died had missed out on the parousia. The believers appear to have weathered the storm of persecution and to have maintained their faith. Still, Paul seeks to admonish the three problem groups that had arisen in Thessalonica—the morally weak, the fainthearted who have lost loved ones, and those who have become idle by quitting work as they awaited the parousia that had not yet materialized (see 1 Thess 4:9—5:22).

Although many accept the canonical ordering of 1 Thessalonians–2 Thessalonians, the reminder is offered that Paul's letters are not given in the New Testament in the chronological order in which they were actually written. The basic principle of order is that of length with those ostensibly addressed to individuals given after those addressed to churches. At the point when titles were appended, the titles given reflect the canonical order already adopted (e.g., 1 Corinthians–2 Corinthians, 1 Thessalonians–2 Thessalonians). "First" Thessalonians has five chapters, "Second"

Thessalonians only has three. In the present writer's judgment, it is the content that suggests the chronological ordering of 2 Thessalonians–1 Thessalonians.

The author also believes the so-called Previous Letter to Corinth (see 1 Cor 5:9) to have been written between the writing of 2 Thessalonians and 1 Thessalonians, such that the three letters may be placed in the time period of 49–51 CE. We no longer possess Paul's "Previous Letter to Corinth," unless a fragment of it is preserved in 2 Cor 6:14—7:1. As will be seen, these three letters may be dated to the time of Paul's "Foundation Campaign" (ca. 38–51 CE). All of Paul's other letters are written later, either during the time of Paul's "Collection Campaign" (52–56 CE) or Post-Collection imprisonment (56–60 CE).

The Galatian Letter

Paul, along with Barnabas, had apparently established several churches in the region of southern Galatia during the first phase of his Foundation Campaign, during the time frame of 38–43 CE. The Galatian epistle itself, written about 53 or 54 CE, differs from Paul's other letters, in that Paul writes with rather obvious anger. There is no opening "thanksgiving," such as characterizes Paul's other letters. Paul is disappointed with the Galatian Christians in the multiple churches located there—they have proven themselves to be very gullible in the acceptance of alternative gospels proclaimed by interlopers who have invaded the church fields of Galatia.

Scholars disagree concerning Galatians, as to whether it is relatively early or later in the Pauline sequence, whether it was written to the northern part of ethnic Galatia or the southern part of the combined Roman province of Galatia. The "Nomistic Evangelists" (those who preached a "law gospel"), who were Paul's opponents, proclaimed a more Jewish version of the gospel that called for obedience to the Law or Torah for those gentile believers who wished to be incorporated into the new people of Israel. Specific issues involved food laws and circumcision.

The gentile Christians needed encouragement and correction as to the nature of the gospel and the expected morality that gospel called forth. For Paul, it was not a case of the gospel that required a sealing by a literal circumcision mandated by Torah. In fact, Paul asserts that if one chooses the route of a Torah gospel, then one has departed from the Gospel of God's grace in Christ. God's Gospel calls for a life characterized by the "fruit of the Spirit," not "works of the flesh." Generally speaking, Christians were called upon to live life at a higher level of moral behavior than that acceptable to gentiles.

The Philippian Letter

Philippians and 1 Corinthians were both written from Ephesus in 54 CE. Philippians is identified as a "prison epistle" of Paul (see Phil 1:12–14). Some scholars view

Philippians as a composite of three letter fragments, although the present writer accepts it as a single, unified letter.

While Philippians has traditionally been placed in the period of Paul's Roman imprisonment (hence, 59–61 CE), there are good reasons to place it into the early part of the period of Paul's Collection Campaign (52–56 CE). The Philippians had sent aid to Paul on more than one occasion while he was headquartered in Ephesus during his Collection Campaign. They even sent one of their own, Epaphroditus, to minister to Paul and care for his needs (Phil 2:25–30). It is not expressly stated anywhere in Paul's letters or Acts that Paul was imprisoned *in Ephesus*, although Paul himself acknowledges multiple imprisonments prior to those in Caesarea and Rome (see 2 Cor 11:23–25; Acts 24–26; 28:16–31).

The immediate occasion for the letter to the Philippians appears to be at least five-fold. First, Epaphroditus had become quite ill at some point, prompting concern among the Philippians for his well-being. Now better, Epaphroditus needed to return to Philippi. Secondly, Paul wishes to allay the concerns the Philippians had for Paul's own welfare during his imprisonment, now that it appeared that his release was imminent (Phil 1:19–26). Thirdly, Paul wished to warn the Philippians about the conservative Jewish Christians most often referred to as "Judaizers," but whom the present writer terms "Nomistic Evangelists." They were conservative Jewish Christians who were insisting upon the necessity of circumcision for gentile males as a rite of incorporation into the new eschatological Israel marked by observance of the Torah. They had already created havoc among Paul's Galatian churches, and Paul saw them as potentially threatening all of his mission fields and the very gospel apart from the ritual Law of Judaism that he proclaimed.

Whereas in the Galatian letter Paul consigned them to "hell," not once but twice (Gal 1:6–9), he simply gives a strong warning to the Philippian Christians to "watch out for the dogs, watch out for the evil workers," and with polite English translation, "watch out for the mutilation folk" (Phil 3:2). A fourth concern emerges with regard to two women in the church, Euodia and Syntyche, who are threatening the church with disunity because they are not getting along with each another (Phil 4:2–3). This is a serious problem for a small developing church, but also a particularly significant problem at a time when Paul is engaged in his Collection Campaign, the purpose of which was to unify a potentially divided church (see Rom 15:25–27). Paul needed church unity and unified support. Any causes of inner division would threaten Paul's collection effort. A fifth purpose for Paul was the matter of celebration and encouragement in the light of the gospel, such that Paul calls for rejoicing on the part of all (Phil 4:4–6). Nonetheless, in spite of everything, the twin themes of joy and unity permeate the Philippian letter.

The Corinthian Correspondence

Paul wrote at least three letters (and perhaps as many as nine) and made at least three visits to the church at Corinth in the course of his stormy relationship with that church. He received at least one letter from the church at Corinth (see 1 Cor 7:1), to which he responded in reply to their questions (1 Cor 7–16). Paul wrote a letter prior to our canonical 1 Corinthians that is dubbed the "Previous Letter" by scholars (see 1 Cor 5:9). It is a lost letter, unless 2 Cor 6:14—7:1 preserves a fragment of that letter as some scholars think (including the present author). The Previous Letter apparently addressed the issue of immorality in the Corinthian church.

First Corinthians addresses personal issues of self-centeredness and petty envy, gross immorality characteristic of gentile standards, and questions of theological inquiry posed by the church to Paul, ranging from marriage to the matter of resurrection (1 Cor 7–15). The central problem appears to have been an "I" problem of self-centeredness that was creating a "cliqueish" kind of loyalty given to separate leaders (see 1 Cor 1:10–13). This self-centeredness also manifested problems in relation to other issues, such as spiritual gifts and even the celebration of the Eucharist or Lord's Supper (see 1 Cor 12–14; 11:17–22).

There obviously was a time when Paul made an earlier foundational visit to Corinth. Paul's second visit, however, was a painful visit in which tempers flared and Paul was at best treated rudely. Paul acknowledges that he determined not to make another painful visit during his Collection Campaign, for there was nothing to gain and much to lose if the Corinthians rejected his authority again. Paul is again focused upon church unity during his collection period.

While many assume that the "Painful Letter" Paul wrote as a substitute to avoid another painful visit has been lost, a minority of scholars including the present writer assume its identity with our current 1 Corinthians. The question of Paul's authority resounds throughout the letter. It is not likely that Paul made an impromptu visit to Corinth from Ephesus ahead of his later third and final visit to that church at the point of his reception of Collection gifts from the Corinthians. Both the Painful Letter and the Painful Visit are acknowledged by Paul in 2 Cor 2:1–4.

Many scholars suggest that 2 Corinthians is a composite of as many as six different letter fragments rather than a unity. The present author accepts 2 Corinthians as a unity, although the dominant partition theory would attribute 2 Cor 1–9 and 10–13 to two separate letters in Paul's original correspondence. This minimal division theory acknowledges the change in tone between 2 Cor 1–9 and 10–13. Second Corinthians 8–9 certainly reflect a time when Paul is in Macedonia preparing to come to Corinth in order to receive Corinth's contribution to the Collection. In the present writer's judgment, Paul's Corinthian relationship was as follows: Founding Visit; Previous Letter to Corinth (from Illyricum); Painful Visit (time of Gallio); Painful Letter (1 Corinthians); 2 Cor 1–13; Collection Visit.

A number of issues were brought to Paul's attention prior to his writing of 1 Corinthians, both by oral reports from Corinthian envoys (1 Cor 1:11; 5:1; 11:18) and by letter sent by the Corinthian church to Paul (1 Cor 7:1). Divisions within the community represent Paul's major concern (1 Cor 1:10–13), as might well be expected during his Collection Campaign, for that campaign was predicated upon Christian unity (see Rom 15:25–27). Other issues included sexual immorality, court lawsuits, marriage and divorce, food offered to idols, Paul's apostolic authority, conduct and appearance of men and women at worship, improper celebration of the Lord's Supper, pride and use of spiritual gifts in worship, a questioning of the resurrection, clarification of Paul's Collection for the Jerusalem church, and information concerning future visits by Timothy and Apollos.

The Roman Letter

It is likely Paul wrote Romans as he spent the winter of 55–56 CE in Corinth during his Collection Campaign and time of his final visit with the church there. It is apparent he has decided he must accompany his Collection to Jerusalem (Rom 15:25–29), such that the Roman letter becomes a substitute for a long-anticipated and immediate visit to Rome (see Rom 1:8–15; 15:22–24, 32). He will be delayed once more. As Paul writes, he had never been to Rome. It is not likely that he knew many people in the Roman church or churches, such that Rom 16 is understood by the present writer to actually be a later letter of Paul written from Rome to Ephesus during the time of Paul's Roman imprisonment. Romans 16 likely accompanied Paul's letter that we know as "Ephesians." It likely became attached to the Roman letter (Rom 1–15) after Paul's death by those in Rome who had access to copies of Paul's correspondence.

Romans 1–15 is certainly Paul's longest letter and one of his most systematic in the light of his intention and lack of relationship with Rome. Paul's purpose, however, is not to write a "systematic theology" treatise. It does not represent a complete statement of Paul's theology, for many of his "theological doctrines," known from his other letters, are either omitted entirely or only given brief treatment in Romans. Careful reading of the letter suggests that Paul wrote what was "on his mind" in the light of both his recent and anticipated experiences with the Judaizing opponents or the Nomistic Evangelists, coupled with his troubles with Corinth. The content of the letter is framed by his problems with the Nomistic Evangelists, his troubles with Corinth, his anticipated difficulties with opponents in Jerusalem, and his future hope of an anticipated visit to Rome and ministry to Spain (see Rom 15:28–29).

Paul had neither founded, nor had he ever previously visited, the Roman church/es. The letter reflects the particular circumstances of Paul's own life as well as that of the Roman churches as known to Paul. Paul sought to set forth his gospel in a manner that would commend him to the Roman Christians in a way that would allay rumors about himself and his gospel brought about by tensions that existed between Jewish and gentile Christians.

Paul emphasizes that the Gospel of God in Christ has leveled the playing field between Jew and gentile, that all humankind has sinned and is subject to the powers of Sin and Death and other enslaving elements, personified. God's salvation is available to all on the basis of faithfulness, which indeed marked the response of Abraham to God and by which "rightness" was accorded to him. Both Jew and gentile are made right with God on the basis of faithful response, are released from all enslaving powers by "dying" with Christ and by beginning a new life lived by the power of the Spirit of God.

It is in the context of such a Gospel, based upon God's victory over the power of Sin and Death, a Gospel marked by the resurrection and universal equality, that problems related to the place of the Law and Israel emerge. Questions are raised, particularly in view of the fact that many of the Jews had not responded positively to the Gospel. Paul thus seeks to address the issue of the place of the Law and what is to become of ethnic Israel and God's covenant promises made to Israel (Rom 4; 9–11).

Paul seeks to make sense of God's saving purposes past and present, seeking to demonstrate that God has been faithful throughout in his dealings with lost and enslaved humanity. He provides a lengthy theological argument in Rom 1–11, before he turns to more practical instruction and ethical implications of the Gospel of God in Christ (Rom 12–15). The letter closes with announcement of his travel plans, his hope for reconciliation in Jerusalem in the context of his Collection. See the treatment of Rom 16 given below.

Colossians

There are five letters of Paul that the present writer understands to have been written to Asia Minor from a Roman imprisonment, most of which that are often seen to be pseudonymous—Colossians, Philemon, Ephesians, what is now Rom 16, and 2 Timothy. Two remaining letters attributed to Paul are deemed by the present writer to be pseudonymous, i.e., to have been written under Paul's name—1 Timothy and Titus.

Even though Colossians contains a number of vocabulary words not evidenced in the undisputed Pauline letters, Colossians appears to be clearly Pauline in character. The distinctiveness of style, coupled with perceived development of some aspects of theology and ethics, prompt many scholars to deny Pauline authorship. The author of Colossians appears to have a more realized eschatology that presents the resurrection hope of Christians, seen to be a future happening in Romans, as already having occurred in Colossians (see Col 3:1). Elsewhere, Paul views the decisive battle as already won with a final triumph yet to occur (see Phil 2:5–11; 1 Cor 15:23–28).

While it is a subjective call on the part of scholars, perceived differences of change of thought and theological development appear to be very natural in the light of Paul's imprisonment in Rome toward the end of his life. Paul has begun to realize he may not live until the Telos (End) and that the present age may be extended beyond his own lifetime. Household behavioral codes governing inter-household relationships (Col 3:18—4:1) would appear to be more appropriate in that setting—codes that are repeated in Ephesians with some apparent development (see Eph 5:21—6:9). Paul addresses various parties within a typical Greco-Roman household, stressing mutual responsibilities of wives and husbands, children and parents, slaves and masters. Those who in that society enjoyed greater freedom are charged with greater responsibility. The perceived "weaker" party, socially speaking, is addressed first in each of the paired relationships.

Colossians also appears to address the threat of some type of rival or alternative "philosophy," to which some Christians were being attracted (see Col 2:8–23). While the nature of this philosophy (or "theosophy") is disputed as a result of lack of detail, it appears to have involved the worship of angels, coupled with visions and submission to rules concerning foods, festivals, Sabbaths, etc. (Col 2:16-23).

Overall, the style and vocabulary is similar enough to that of Paul, such that differences may be explained in terms of the time and nature of the problem addressed. The false teachings appear to be an amalgam of Jewish (see Col 2:11, 16) and Greek (see Col 1:15-16; 2:8-9; 2:20-21) elements that are wrongly impacting undiscerning Christians. The basic issue appears to be the superiority of Christ in the face of a *pleroma* (πλήρωμα, "fullness") structure of the worship of multiple entities. Paul counters such by his use of an early hymn that celebrates the superiority of God's fullness in Christ (Col 1:15-20), as he emphasizes the central essence of Christian life. He characterizes other alternatives as subsidiary, unnecessary, or external.

Philemon

The letter to Philemon is a brief, basically personal letter meant to appeal to Philemon, both a householder and slave-owner, on behalf of Onesimus. Careful reading of the letter will note that the church as a whole is also included in the address and the final blessing (Phlm 2, 25). Onesimus had apparently run away or wronged his master, such that he had become "useless," belying his name, which means "useful." Paul apparently encountered Onesimus in an imprisonment setting. He had proven to be very useful to Paul, who now seeks to prevail upon Philemon to take Onesimus back as more than a slave, as a beloved brother in Christ. Paul "pulls out all the stops," such that the brief letter becomes a model of Christian diplomacy. It is a brief but valuable document, even though it lacks attention given to any explicit theological issues or concerns. Its personal nature makes it both delightful and serious at the same time, offering potent pleading for the life of a Christian brother. The letter was likely sent from Rome to the Roman province of Asia at the same time as Colossians (see Col 4:7-17; Phlm 23-24).

Ephesians

Ephesians appears to be closely related to Colossians in its form and content, as may be noted in its Christology (Eph 1:20–23), its vision of life in Christ (Eph 4:14—5:20), and its household code (Eph 5:21—6:9). It also betrays a realized eschatological view (Eph 2:6). Ephesians does not appear to address any threatening heresy or danger, unlike Colossians. While phrases and words may be related to Colossians, there is a rather wide vocabulary difference between Ephesians and the other letters of Paul deemed to be "authentic."

Perhaps the most telling argument against Pauline authorship (whose usual style is rather choppy, employing short sentences) is the difference in style of Ephesians that employs long, smooth, flowing sentences. Ephesians 1:3–14 is one long, extended sentence in Greek, although English translations tend to break it into multiple sentences and even paragraphs. The style of Ephesians reaches great heights of expressive emotion.

Ephesians is a magnificent work that stresses God's action of reconciling work in Christ, as it offers inspiring praise to God (Eph 1:3–14). Paul prays for the Ephesians in memorable prayers (Eph 1:17–23; 3:14–21), as he celebrates the victory of God in the resurrection and exaltation of Christ (Eph 1:17–23). He exults in the unity of Jews and gentiles in Christ, such that two peoples formerly at enmity have now become one. What Paul writes in Ephesians echoes and develops the content of the concluding doxology of Rom 16:25–27. Dividing walls (such as that of gentile exclusion placed around the Jerusalem Temple), established on the basis of ritual laws and ordinances, have been broken down and abolished (Eph 2:11–22).

Reconciliation has been wrought, hostility has been ended, and peace through the Spirit of God has been effected. A unified and reconciled church represents God's new Temple in form of the living body of Christ. Paul affirms unity in manifold ways and encourages growth toward the maturity of Christian calling in Christ (Eph 4:1—5:20). Christian unity remains a central theme for Paul, even as it had been during his Collection Campaign.

Romans 16

The present writer believes Rom 16 to be a brief and highly personal letter sent to Ephesus at the same time as the letter to "the Ephesians." It became attached to the Roman letter at some early point after Paul's death when Paul's letters were being collected together for wider circulation among early Christian churches. Paul's letters were not significant beyond the immediate church to which they were sent until Paul himself began to be venerated.

The textual issue of the omission of the words "in Ephesus" (see Eph 1:1) in the greeting of many early existing manuscripts has prompted some to identify Ephesians as a circular letter meant to circulate among various churches in Asia Minor. The absence of personal names in the letter is seen to strengthen the case. However, the present writer believes Rom 16 to have been an accompanying letter of Paul sent at the same time to the church at Ephesus, personally remembering and thanking all God's "little saints" in the Ephesian church for their support in the gospel during the lengthy time Paul was headquartered there at the time of the Collection Campaign.

Paul would have known many Christians in Ephesus, to whom he could recommend Phoebe, whereas he had never visited Rome. He did not have to repeat personal greetings in the Ephesian letter proper thereby, in the light of the accompanying letter we know as Rom 16. In fact, an argument could be made that had Rom 16 originally been a part of the Roman letter, it is likely Paul would have also included other personal references early in Romans as he did in 1 Cor 1:11–16. It is Romans that is not "personal," save for the later appended copy of an Ephesian letter that we know as Rom 16.

While it must remain a hypothesis, Tertius, the secretary who copied or recorded Rom 16 at Paul's dictation, may well have been the amanuensis (recording secretary) for Ephesians, and perhaps Colossians and Philemon. Written one by one, they would have been gathered to await a suitable courier who could transport them to Ephesus and Colossae. The present writer sees all four of these letters to have been sent by Paul to Asia Minor at the same time.

Tertius was the recording secretary in Rome (not Corinth, from which Romans was written!) selected by Paul to draft this letter and perhaps other letters of Paul sent to Asia. Generally, when an amanuensis was employed in the ancient world, two copies of a letter would be made—one to be sent, and the other to be retained by the sender. If so, Paul himself would have had the original first collection of all his letters and correspondence, which he apparently asked Timothy to retrieve and bring to Rome when he came (see 2 Tim 4:13). If Timothy so complied, Paul's effects would have been preserved by someone in Rome after Paul's death. The source for Rom 16 specifically could have been Tertius, Paul's amanuensis, who had retained copies of Paul's later letters.

Because of a lack of evidence one way or another, we can never know for sure. Such a scenario as suggested, however, solves a number of issues. First of all, Rom 16 is the most personal of all of Paul's letters. Nowhere else does Paul mention such a large number of people or groups. This is very strange if Paul were writing to Rome, to churches he did not found and had never visited. On the other hand, Ephesus had been his headquarters for his Collection campaign. According to Luke, Paul spent several years there (see Acts 19:8–10). Prisca and Aquila had apparently worked with Paul in Ephesus after they left Corinth together (see Acts 18:18–21). They apparently remained in Ephesus (see Rom 16:3–4). It is not necessary to predicate their movement back to Rome (see Acts 18:2). Others greeted by Paul are also to be associated with Ephesus or "Asia." It simply makes most sense that Paul would greet intimately these friends and associates whom he had come to love dearly. Those named at the end of the listing that are given in Rom 16:22–23 are actually Roman Christians and friends of Tertius.

While Ephesians has been seen as most impersonal and is often rejected as being by Paul on that basis, the objection may be set aside if the letter to "the Ephesians" was accompanied by Rom 16. A number of manuscripts of Ephesians omit the words "in Ephesus" (among them p46, Sinaiticus, Vaticanus), prompting development of the hypothesis that what we know as "Ephesians" was actually a circular letter sent to several churches (the so-called Goodspeed theory). However, this hypothesis carries with it some serious questions and is unnecessary if Paul had already addressed personal issues separately. Having already separately acknowledged their faithfulness, Paul simply greets "those who are indeed faithful in Christ Jesus," if the words "in Ephesus" should be excluded (see Eph 1:1).

Romans 16 is not a "letter fragment." It is a complete letter, less necessary redaction that occurred when it was joined to Romans. It is what it purports to be—a letter of support and recommendation for Phoebe (Rom 16:1–2) and greetings and thanksgiving for those in Ephesus. When it became joined to the Roman letter, some redaction had to occur—omission of a grace wish at the end of Rom 15 and omission of any greeting, for example, at the beginning of Rom 16. Many technical issues are involved here and these are thoroughly developed in the author's earlier work, *The Ministry of Paul the Apostle: History and Redaction*.

Other than a virtual roll call of these "little saints of God," many of whom are otherwise unknown, Rom 16 ends with a significant doxology that may have been known in the Ephesian church. As previously indicated, its content echoes themes found in Ephesians. It certainly expresses with significant definition the basic nature and content of Paul's gospel to which he was called and for which he labored. It highlights the revelation of the mystery of the Gospel of God as a Gospel of inclusion based upon faith. It should be noted that Paul praises the only wise God, *through* Jesus Christ—to whom be glory unto the ages (Rom 16:27). What makes the doxology and Rom 16 all the more remarkable is that Paul was incarcerated and facing potential martyrdom when he dictated it to Tertius. He had learned the abiding nature of joy in the Gospel during the earlier time of threat from his imprisonment in Ephesus (see Philippians).

Second Timothy

Since the eighteenth century (seventeen hundred years after Paul), 2 Timothy has been most often grouped with 1 Timothy and Titus and characterized as a group of three "Pastoral Epistles" in the light of pastoral advice given in the three letters. All three letters are most often seen as pseudonymous by scholars, written later under Paul's name by a loyal admirer in order to claim Pauline authority. The debate regarding authorship revolves around vocabulary and style, development of official offices in the church (bishops and deacons), the rise and nature of false teachings, and the historical place of the letters within Paul's overall ministry.

Perhaps a brief note on the issue of pseudonymity is in order at this juncture, before further treatment of 2 Timothy. Pseudonymity, or writing under the name of a notable and generally earlier figure, was a common occurrence in the ancient world, at least within Judaism and early Christianity. There are Jewish works later written under the names of Enoch, Ezra, Solomon, Baruch, and early patriarchs such as Abraham and Moses. The book of Jude in the New Testament even quotes from 1 Enoch 1:9 (see Jude 14–15). Some of the Psalms may have been written under the name of David in honor of David.

In like manner, a number of early Christian writings including various gospels were written under the name of Peter or one of the other apostles, even under the name of Mary. These works were judged to be later (second–third centuries) by the early church and consequently were not included in the New Testament canon. There is even a letter designated "Third Corinthians" attributed to Paul, as well as a series of supposed Pauline correspondence with Seneca, none of which was ultimately deemed to be authentic by the early church.

The intent of pseudonymity was not to "lie" or to be deliberately deceptive. In an early time before there were written commentaries on scriptural texts and before there was even a body of works that could be termed "New Testament scripture," the intent was to re-present for a new age the teaching and authority of an earlier significant figure. It was seen to be a worthy and not deceptive undertaking that venerated and extended the influence of an earlier personage, such as a Peter or a Paul.

With regard to 2 Timothy and the Pastorals, criteria such as vocabulary and style do matter as standards of judgment regarding authorship, but conclusions drawn may be somewhat subjective. For the English reader who reads an English translation, the New Testament may all "sound the same." That is usually because the final overall translation work has been smoothed over by an English translation committee or the single translator. Paul may sound like Peter or John. For one who reads the New Testament in Greek, the differences are often stark and plain. Even those in the early church, for example, recognized the distinct differences in the Greek of 2 Peter compared to that of 1 Peter. Theology and official church organization develops over time, suggesting perhaps an early second-century origin for the "Pastorals" (1 Timothy and Titus) at a time after Paul. Still, judgment may be subjective when it comes to development, such that scholars may divide on the issue of authorship.

It appears to the current writer that the historical setting is perhaps the most important and least subjective consideration in the present instance. If one accepts all three of the "Pastorals" as Pauline, then one generally must accept early church tradition beyond the New Testament that Paul was released from his first Roman imprisonment, that he had a subsequent ministry to the east and west, that he was martyred in

Rome following a second period of arrest, ca. 64 CE or as late as 68 CE. This scenario may account for the historical situation reflected in the "Pastorals" as a group, but it moves well beyond Luke's accounting of Paul's story in the book of Acts.

It is the writer's judgment that 2 Timothy may be properly fitted into the end of Paul's ministry as we know it from the New Testament, that, indeed, it forms Paul's "last will and testament," as it were (see 2 Tim 4:6–18). This is not true for 1 Timothy and Titus. There are also some stylistic and theological distinctives that suggest to the present writer that 1 Timothy and Titus are pseudonymous, compared to 2 Timothy, which is authentic to Paul. In fact, 2 Timothy may be identified as a final "prison" epistle of Paul, rather than a "pastoral" epistle to be grouped with the other two Pastorals. In 2 Timothy Paul is imprisoned; in 1 Timothy and Titus, Paul is a free man without a firm historical context.

Second Timothy, like the letter to Philemon, is a personal letter intended for a corporate church setting. Paul's first word in his letters to each of his churches is "grace to all of you and peace from God the Father and the Lord Jesus Christ," as seen in all his salutations. Paul's last words to Timothy are "The Lord be with your [sing.] spirit," followed by a grace wish for the church—"Grace be with all of you" (see 2 Tim 4:22).

Conclusion

There are no perfect interpreters of biblical texts, even should one affirm the "infallibility" and "inerrancy" of the texts themselves. To assume perfect interpretation is to assert human arrogance and idolatry, both of which lie at the root of human sinfulness. However, one cannot get away from interpretation. To interpret is to think, to investigate, to weigh, *and* to imagine. Not all interpretation is the same, however. One should strive in one's interpretation to do "exegesis" and not "eisegesis."

Not all scholarly works are the same either. In this writer's judgment, one should avail oneself of those scholarly resources that enable one to better contextualize the biblical word and world, Paul included, rather than those that simply dogmatize or seek to indoctrinate. One should avail oneself of scholarly works that help one to imagine and to develop one's imagination in the most positive contextual sense of those words. Interpretation enlarges one's horizons. One should not seek out works that "tell" one what one should or must believe, but rather one should seek those works that encourage thought and interaction and personal development. Maturity comes through participative actualization of truth into one's living, not through non-participative recitation of impersonal and imposed dogma.

If one wishes to understand the biblical text, and especially Paul, then one must develop one's imagination and engage in the activity of imagining the contexts that called forth a given biblical text. One must positively imagine the ministry of Jesus in order to understand his person and his message. One must imagine the beginnings of early Christianity in order to appreciate the successful spread of the gospel. One must imagine the historical factuality of the world and person of Paul. One must imagine the ministry and theology of Paul—how and why he preached the gospel that he proclaimed. And whether one be a friend of Paul or a foe of Paul, or simply see him to be irrelevant in a postmodern world, one needs to imagine his legacy—pro or con.

Paul stands at the headwaters of the Christian movement. He stands as close as we can get to the beginnings of the Gospel and the early Christian church. One needs to imagine the hope of that Gospel which Paul expressed. One may embrace Paul. One may debate with Paul. One may reject Paul by calling attention to all of the problematic issues faced in the modern or postmodern world, a number of which are supposedly even wrought by Paul's writings. One may call attention to many other issues that are neglected by Paul, even though they were not issues in the time of Paul.

The apostle Paul provides opportunity for theological affirmation of one's own closely held beliefs, but Paul also provokes us by providing a "theology of irritation" as his thought prods our own, even when we are forced to deal with issues of which Paul never thought. One may choose an alternative to affirmation or irritation—one may simply choose to ignore Paul. And in our day, many do. To ignore Paul may be deemed appropriate for one who is not a Christian, but it is hardly acceptable for one who claims to be Christian.

However, if one fails to imagine Paul (whether in agreement or disagreement), the contemporary Christian only entertains an impoverished Christian New Testament Bible and impoverished Christian theology set forth in shades of grey. If one is a Christian who cares about the New Testament at all, then one must actually imagine Paul and his theology, his understanding of the Gospel of God. Whether we like Paul's answers or not, the gospel of Paul calls forth issues that dare not be ignored, provided one identifies oneself as Christian. What Paul has to say may also prod us toward other, alternative answers to issues faced in common. Or, again, what Paul has to say as he brings the Gospel to his world may provide insight to a way forward as we seek to deal with the new issues of our age.

However, the present writer would affirm that one first needs to "imagine Paul" and imagine Paul in his own context. It is not enough to merely "quote" Paul with a misappropriated "post-it note" theological statement. Paul understood himself to be an "apostle of God." Who was this Paul? What was his world like? What did he believe? What was the nature of his gospel? And, why did he believe it so strongly that it changed and reoriented his entire life, causing him to travel more than ten thousand miles (much of it on foot) as an evangelist of the Gospel of God in Christ?

As the present work develops and moves forward, Paul's ministry and his theology will be imagined on the basis of his letters. It has been seen that the present writer imagines a Pauline canon of scripture consisting of eleven of the thirteen New Testament letters that bear his name and that were attributed to him. Only 1 Timothy and Titus are seen to be pseudonymous, written by someone else under Paul's name at a time well after Paul. While many scholars have detected fragments of multiple letters of Paul pieced together (e.g., Philippians a combination of three letter fragments; 2 Corinthians a combination of as many as six letter fragments), the present writer, on the basis of a lengthy pilgrimage of the study of Paul, imagines the unity of the letters with two possible exceptions.

Second Corinthians 6:14—7:1 appears to interrupt the text (see 2 Cor 6:13 and 7:2), such that it may be a fragmentary insertion of Paul's "Previous" letter to Corinth into the body of 2 Corinthians. This could have resulted from a single misplaced papyrus leaf. Also, Rom 16 is seen to be a letter originally sent to Ephesus, a copy of which was later joined to the letter to the Romans (Rom 1–15). The book of Hebrews nowhere claims to have been written by Paul and is so different in stylistic and theological content that it is deemed to have been written by someone other than Paul. When it comes to authorship of Hebrews, the early church father Origen perhaps gave the best answer—"God knows."

It is only through imagining that one comes to *understand* oneself and the world in which one lives. It is only through imagining that one comes to *define* oneself and the world in which one lives. It is only through imagining that one comes to understand Paul and his world. It is only through active imagining that Paul may be brought into a postmodern world. One may choose not to embrace Paul's hope, but then what hope is to be imagined in its place? Life without hope is a dismal life, indeed. Imagination is a gift of God. It provides the avenue by which to seize the day or to envision tomorrow. It also provides the opportunity to reach across the centuries to comprehend different cultures and the scripture text more fully.

To imagine beyond one's current experience level, even in some small way, is the gift of scholars to everyday Christians. To enable and to nourish the imagination is the gift of God, for which one should be thankful. Imagining is an activity that enables one to grow in the grace and knowledge of God, as one experiences in larger measure the good news of the Gospel of God through a man called Paul. It is that experience of the Gospel of God that in itself makes life worth living.

2

Imagine Christian Beginnings

ONE CANNOT APPRECIATE EITHER Paul or his ministry without an understanding of Jesus and antecedent Christian beginnings prior to Paul's call to mission by God. Lost to history is whether Paul ever saw or met Jesus in the flesh prior to Jesus's death and resurrection. We do know from both the book of Acts and Paul's own letters that he was a persecutor of the early church (Acts 8:1–3; 9:1–2; 22:4–5; 26:9–11; Gal 1:13, 23). The earliest followers of Jesus were known, according to Luke in Acts, as followers of "the Way" (Acts 9:2). According to Acts, the disciples were first called "Christians" in the church at Antioch (Acts 11:26). For followers of the Way, Jesus himself was the Christ. While Jesus was not a "Christian," there would have been no Christians apart from Jesus, the Christ.

Paul himself became part of what we know as the Christian movement within five years of Jesus's death and resurrection. The literature we know as the four "Gospels" and the "Book of Acts" are *later* historical documents that narrate the *earlier* history. All five of these works actually would date to the time after Paul's own death, even though they narrate events earlier than the ministry of Paul. The canonical ordering of the New Testament suggests a logical ordering in framing the Christian narrative, but it creates a chronological misimpression. Paul's letters are the earliest Christian documents that we have. The focal point of Paul makes best sense only in the light of a contextual awareness of the earlier historical antecedents of the person and ministry of Jesus, as well as the beginnings of Christianity.

Paul came after Jesus, although the two were roughly contemporaries. Jesus was likely born 7–4 BCE and Paul at some point between 5 BCE and 10 CE. Jesus was executed in 30 CE, according to most, while Paul was likely martyred in 61 CE (some say as late as 68 CE). By every reckoning, Paul's life had ended prior to that crucial date of 70 CE when Jerusalem fell to the Romans.

Those whom the Pharisee Paul had initially persecuted were in Christ and followers of the Way (see Acts 9:2; 24:22) before Paul received his own call from God through the risen Christ. The Gospels and Acts are important for the contextual awareness of the ministry of Jesus and the beginnings of the early church. The historical ministry of Jesus and the pre-Pauline church provide the antecedent beginnings for the story of Paul, apostle of God.

Four Gospels and Acts

Scholars date the four Gospels to ca. 65–95 CE, with Mark being the earliest and John being the latest. If Paul died in 61 CE, as suggested by the current work, then all of the Gospels were written after the time of Paul. If Paul died as late as 68 CE according to some scholars, then Mark's Gospel was extant during Paul's lifetime. If written in Rome, Mark's Gospel would have emerged just after Paul's death or would have existed in Rome at the time of Paul's supposed second arrest and subsequent martyrdom. The present author does not deem this to be likely. The book of Acts has been variously attributed to a date range from 62–150 CE, although perhaps the majority of scholars (including the present writer) would date the book to 80–95 CE.

Three "Synoptic" Gospels

Mark, Matthew, and Luke are known as "Synoptic" Gospels, in that they may be "seen together." They offer a similar but not identical presentation of Jesus's ministry, which lasted essentially little more than one year. Jesus begins his ministry in Galilee, makes a single journey to Jerusalem for a Passover feast, has a one week ministry in Jerusalem, at which time he is arrested, condemned, and crucified on the eve of the Passover. John's Gospel by contrast is approximately 90 percent different from the Synoptics. Jesus makes many journeys back and forth from Galilee to Jerusalem. The Gospel of John mentions three different Passovers, which suggests a three-year ministry. In John's Gospel, Jesus "cleanses" the temple in John 2:13–22, whereas Jesus performs that prophetic action near the end of the Synoptic presentation during that final week in Jerusalem (see Mark 11:15–19; Matt 21:12–17; Luke 19:45–48). The Gospel of Mark contains sixteen chapters. While not often realized, fully three-eighths of Mark's Gospel is devoted to Jesus's final week in Jerusalem. It is the passion of Jesus in Jerusalem that is the focal point emphasized by Mark, our earliest "gospel."

John and the Synoptics

The two traditions, John and the Synoptics, cannot easily be harmonized, although some have tried. Among many laymen, John has been the favorite Gospel and Mark the least favorite. Of the three Synoptics, Matthew has probably been the favorite of the three. It contains a birth narrative (Matt 1:18—2:12) and the Sermon on the Mount (Matt 5:1—7:29) and stands first in the New Testament order. Hermeneutically speaking and informally among laymen, however, the Synoptics have often been interpreted on the basis of John, with *Matthew as interpreted in the light of John* having influenced the interpretation of Mark and Luke.

The common belief that Jesus was thirty-three when he died makes an assumption that combines Luke's assertion that Jesus was "about thirty" when he began his ministry (see Luke 3:23) with the mention of three Passovers in the Gospel of John (see John 2:13; 6:4; 11:55). One needs to recall that the duration of Jesus's ministry according to the Synoptics (Luke also!) included only a single Passover, thus, a one to one and one-half year ministry. To repeat, the content of the Gospel of John is roughly 90 percent different from that of the Synoptics, such that again the accounts cannot readily be harmonized.

The Synoptic Problem

It is evident on the basis of comparison of content that some type of relationship exists among the three Synoptic Gospels. This has given rise to what is called the "Synoptic Problem," which simply asks the question, "How does one best explain the similarities and differences that exist among Matthew, Mark, and Luke?" The majority of scholars would posit that both Matthew and Luke made use of Mark in the production of their Gospels. Out of Mark's over 650 verses, fewer than forty verses do not appear to be repeated in Matthew and/or Luke. In addition, scholars propose the hypothesis of a Q source (*Quelle* or "source") that Matthew and Luke had in common. Q is basically a sayings tradition (handed down orally?) that represents a large body of Jesus's teachings presented without attendant narrative. In addition to the use of Mark and Q, there is material unique to Matthew that is identified as "M" material and material unique to Luke that is identified by the symbol "L." Jesus's most famous parables, the Good Samaritan and the Prodigal Son so-called, are to be found only in Luke (see Luke 10:30–35; 15:11–32) and may thus be identified as "L" material.

The Book of Acts

The book of Acts represents the second volume of the Lukan work (see Luke 1:1–4; Acts 1:1). Luke, in his prologue, acknowledges that he is not a "first generation" Christian. He belonged to one of the subsequent generations following the eye-witnesses. The Gospel of Luke features the story of Jesus and his ministry. It begins in the temple in Jerusalem with the service of Zechariah and the announcement of the birth of John the Baptizer (Luke 1:5–25). It features a long, single journey from Galilee to Jerusalem consisting of almost ten chapters of material (Luke 9:51—19:28). Luke ends where he began, with the disciples worshiping in the temple and praising God (Luke 24:52–53). All of Jesus's resurrection appearances occur in and around Jerusalem.

With the book of Acts, Luke tells the story of the early church beginning in Jerusalem and then moving out from Jerusalem in a universal mission, of which Paul is the primary figure inherent in that mission. Although the book is often referred to as the "Acts of the Apostles," most of Jesus's original disciples are never heard from again after the first chapter. The original Twelve (including Matthias as Judas's replacement) disappear entirely from the book after the Jerusalem Conference narrated in Acts 15 (see Acts 15:22). The focus of the remaining part of the book is upon the gentile mission of Paul. Luke's story of the development and movement of the early church away from Jerusalem ends *as it must* with Paul in Rome still proclaiming the gospel of the kingdom of God and the Lord Jesus Christ "quite openly and unhinderedly" (Acts 28:31). Luke had a story to tell and he tells it well, while making use of source materials.

It is altogether appropriate to set the stage for understanding the person of Paul, his ministry, and his gospel by first briefly considering the ministry of Jesus and the beginnings of the Christian church. The two together provide a consecutive contextual matrix for understanding and imagining Paul.

Jesus and His Ministry

It comes as a shock to some to learn that Jesus was not a "Christian." He was born into a Jewish family in the town of Bethlehem according to the New Testament Gospels of Matthew and Luke (Matt 2:1; Luke 2:4–7). He grew up in Nazareth village and hence became known as "Jesus of Nazareth, son of Joseph" (John 1:45). Nazareth is estimated to have had a population of approximately four hundred persons in Jesus's day. It was so insignificant, that Nathaniel asked the question, "Can anything good come out of Nazareth?" (John 1:46). Philip's reply to Nathaniel was "Come and see."

Beginnings

The two Gospels that offer miraculous birth stories regarding Jesus (Matthew and Luke) also offer genealogies that trace Jesus's lineage through the line of Joseph (Matt 1:16; Luke 3:23). While the two genealogies vary, both Gospels present virgin birth stories that are different in content and in emphasis (see Matt 1:18–25; Luke 1:26–35). Although a "Christmas story" is fashioned from the combination of the two accounts, each Gospel writer has a different stress and each has his own particular theological emphases. It would be helpful to read Matt 1–2 and Luke 1–2 separately and to imagine the different scenes in their respective narrative stories, in order to discern their individual and particular emphases through a following comparison.

The promise of Jesus's birth is given to Joseph in a dream in Matthew, while Luke presents announcement given to Mary in a waking state. Each Gospel offers a different perspective. Matthew presents Jesus as a royal king of the line of David at his birth, such that the wise men or magi (not *three kings*!) bring royal gifts to present to the child who is "born a king" (Matt 2:2, 11). In Luke's Gospel, an announcement of universal import is given to shepherds by angels, who bring good news of a savior whose glory will extend to all the world (Luke 2:8–14). A reminder is given by Luke that it was a Roman world governed by Augustus Caesar, who himself was proclaimed "lord" and "savior" by the Roman gospel prevalent in that world (Luke 2:1–2). Mark and John, of course, have no birth narratives. John instead speaks of the eternal "Logos" or "Word" who was in the beginning with God (John 1:1). Jesus, of course, still had to be actually born. Mark simply announces the beginning of the "good news" (gospel) of "Jesus Christ, Son of God" (Mark 1:1). It is God's Gospel, of which the person of Jesus and his proclamation is the content.

Joseph and Mary had other children, according to the Gospel record (Mark 6:3). Joseph worked as a craftsman or tradesman, although in common thought this has been popularized as a "carpenter" (Matt 13:55), an identification which Jesus himself acquired (Mark 6:3). Wood was scarce in Palestine. The underlying Greek simply suggests a builder, perhaps one who worked with wood or stone. During the time Jesus was growing up in Nazareth, Herod Antipas was building his capital at Sepphoris, on a hillside a scant four miles from Nazareth.

Although there is no way to prove one way or the other, it is really inconceivable to think that Joseph was not involved in the work that was taking place in Sepphoris. If so, it is likely that Jesus would have accompanied and aided Joseph in the work. At the very least, Jesus's boyhood curiosity would have taken him and his boyhood friends to see this Greco-Roman style city developing on a neighboring hillside before their very eyes, a scant hour's walk away. While Nazareth was but a small village of perhaps four hundred persons, Sepphoris was the capital and "ornament" of all Galilee (see Josephus, *Ant.* 18.27), then ruled by Herod Antipas. At some point Jesus and his family moved from Nazareth to Capernaum, a fishing village located on the north shore of the Lake of Galilee, slightly more than twenty miles away. Capernaum, or the "Village of Nahum," was a small "townlet," the inhabitants of which were largely engaged in the fishing industry. It was located on the frontier between the ruling domains of Herod Antipas and Herod Philip. The occasion for the move may have been the death of Joseph (who is not further mentioned in the gospel record), or perhaps the reason was to find renewal of work. While a traditional interpretation, it is not likely that the move from Nazareth to Capernaum was occasioned by the event of Jesus's rejection at Nazareth that historically occurred at a later point (see Mark 6:1–6; Luke 4:16–30). Herod Antipas decided to move his capital from Sepphoris to the Lake of Galilee, some sixteen miles distant from Nazareth. This new city of Tiberius was named after Antipas's new Roman benefactor, Tiberius Caesar.

Jesus's life is lost from view until he begins his public ministry following the arrest of his cousin, John the Baptizer. While Jesus was baptized by John according to the Gospel record (see Mark 1:9–11; Matt 3:13–17; Luke 3:21–22), Mark tells us that Jesus began his public ministry after John was arrested (Mark 1:14; see Matt 4:12–17). Jesus came preaching the kingdom of God saying, "The rule of God has already drawn near, repent and come to faith in the good news" (Mark 1:15). Jesus's stark but exciting announcement was coupled with an invitation of participation. Something long-expected and new was happening. It called for a new mind-set.

The glad tidings announced to shepherds years earlier were now coming to fruition. God's salvation perceived by Spirit-filled people like Simeon and Anna in the Temple in Jerusalem at the time of Jesus's birth was now coming to pass (see Luke 2:25–38). And according to Luke, Jesus was about the age of thirty when he began his public ministry (Luke 3:23).

Jesus's Good News

One should be clear about the nature of Jesus's message. It was different from the message of judgment proclaimed by John the Baptizer. John proclaimed a message of repentance leading to the forgiveness of sins—national, corporate, and individual (Mark 1:4; Luke 3:3). Jesus proclaimed a message of good news of the now-present dawning of the rule of God in his person, coupled with an imperative of invitation to become a part of what God was doing. Come to faith in the gospel was Jesus's message (Mark 1:15). That which had been long-expected was now coming to pass, as referenced by Old Testament scripture.

Because of our long-ingrained religious enculturation, we have at best only partially understood and at worst greatly misunderstood the nature of Jesus's message and invitation of participation in God's kingdom. The idea of the Hebrew word for "repentance" is that of a "turning," followed by a journey or pilgrimage with God. A proper relationship with God is envisioned as an ongoing journey characterized by covenant, vigilance of living, and clarity of purpose. The Greek word for repentance in the New Testament (μετανοέω, μετάνοια) is perhaps even more provocative and evocative. It suggests a "change of mind-set"—to go beyond the current understanding, customary view, intention, or mind-set one now has, so as to incorporate a new way of thinking and, hence, a new way of living.

Repentance in the New Testament is anchored in a change of thinking, that issues forth in action of greater faithfulness or alternative commitment. The emphasis upon what one is "turning toward" is at least equal if not greater than the emphasis upon that which one is "turning from." One is called upon to *imagine* a new reality that calls for a new lifestyle. Repentance is thus a change in direction for living brought about by a permanent change of mind-set or life orientation. Repentance involves imagining what alternative life may be like. It is far more than a "moment of decision." Having imagined a new reality, one is to take steps to actualize the new reality by the way one lives.

We have perhaps taken our usual understanding of Jesus's message from the earlier message of John the Baptizer or the later message of the Latin Church rather than from Jesus. We have made "repentance" to be almost exclusively about individual sin, guilt, and forgiveness. We have sinned; we need to "turn" from our sins, such that we can be forgiven. The noun for "repentance" (μετάνοια) occurs but once in Mark's Gospel as a descriptor of the message of John the Baptizer (Mark 1:4). The verbal form occurs but twice in Mark's Gospel, in Jesus's original public announcement as an imperative of invitation (Mark 1:15) and as a description of the preaching of the

Twelve whom Jesus sent out (Mark 6:12). The English word "repentance" has been strongly colored by concepts such as "penance" and "penitence" drawn from a Latin background, thus conveying the nuance of "regret" and "remorse."

This is not Jesus's meaning in his announcement of good news. The usage of Jesus is totally different. There is no "regret" or "remorse" in his announcement and his imperative of invitation. None. Jesus only offered a new vision of God to be imagined—the kingdom of God had come near. Imagine what that would mean! He invited people of all social classes to participate in God's rule. To "repent," according to Jesus, is to move beyond the mind-set one currently had in order to embrace a dawning new reality. Things would be different when God's rule was realized. And, Jesus offered a new vision of God. Imagine what Jesus's invitation might mean for Galilean peasants living in Galilee under heavy taxation or for the nation as a whole living under a Roman occupation.

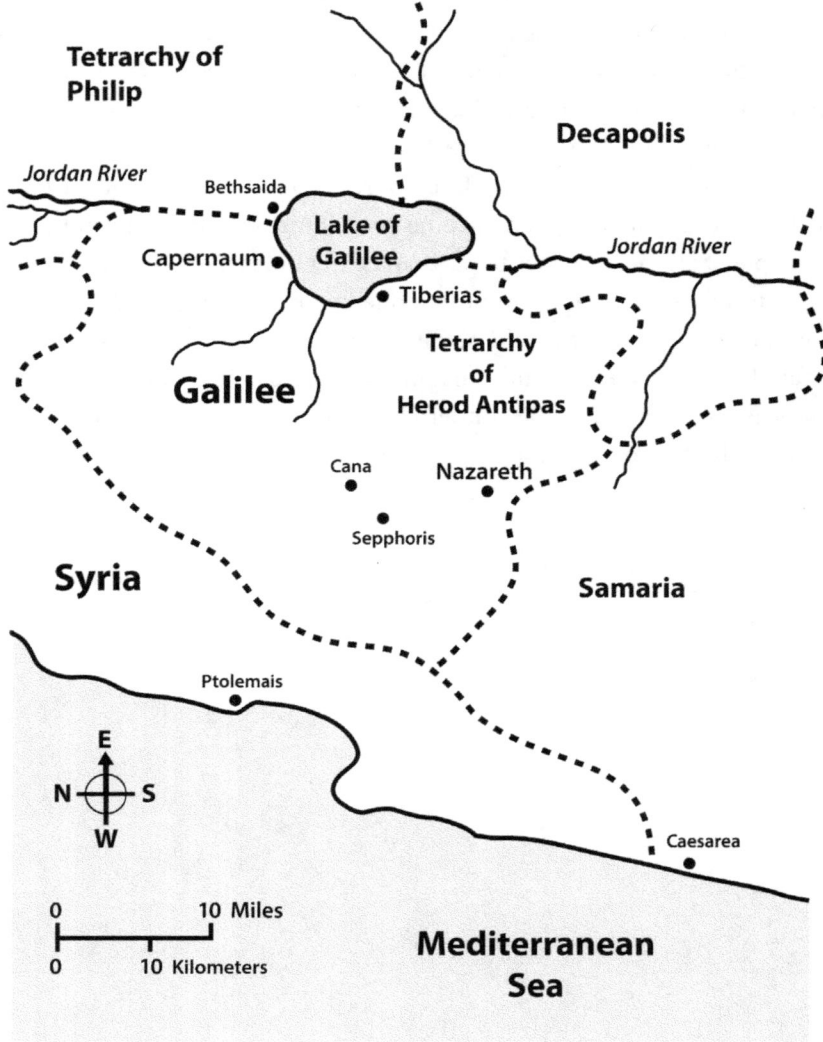

Fig. 4. Map of the Galilee of Jesus. Map © Jason Greene. Used with permission.

Luke actually describes the inauguration of Jesus's public ministry as the fulfillment of the promises of God given in Isa 61:1–2, a poetic passage that echoes the Servant Songs of Isa 42–53. It is the day of deliverance. The longed-for restoration of the Spirit now rests upon Jesus, the Prophet like Moses (Acts 3:22–23), who has been anointed to "preach good news to the impoverished, to proclaim release to the captives, to enable the blind to see again, to send those who have been oppressed unto freedom," all of which heralds "the acceptable year of the Lord" (see Luke 4:17–19). With radical affirmation, Jesus proclaimed, "Today this scripture has been fulfilled [perfect tense] in your hearing" (Luke 4:21). The perfect tense in Greek suggests action that has been completed, with a focus upon existing results. Jesus's proclamation offered a vision of fulfillment of God's promises that called for an immediate change in the way one viewed the world in terms of its politics, social order, and even staid customary religion. Even so, the people in Jesus's hometown synagogue in Nazareth did not "repent," for they did not have eyes to see or ears to hear.

We have interpreted the content of Luke 4:18 as a rather literal *religious* statement by Jesus, when it may actually have been far more metaphorical and political. Economically, those in Galilee were heavily taxed, which made it difficult to eke out a living. They were captive to a mind-set that marked the maintenance of Roman oppression. Eyes blinded to the power of God by Roman military standards erected in place needed to once again be able to see what God was now doing to bring about revolution (the kingdom of God). Personal freedom and national freedom awaited the proclamation of the acceptable year of YHWH that had now dawned in the beginning of the ministry of Jesus in a small village called Nazareth.

In a nearby small village called Nain, Jesus resuscitated a young man who had died. All were filled with religious awe and reverence, such that the people cried out and glorified God, saying that "a great prophet has been raised among us," that indeed, "God has visited his people." Luke affirms that "this report concerning him spread throughout the whole of Judea and all the surrounding countryside" (a clue to Luke's identity or place of writing; see Luke 7:11–17). In the sequel that followed, John the Baptizer sent disciples to question Jesus as to whether or not he was the expected "Coming One," apparently meaning "the Messiah" or perhaps the "Prophet like Moses" (see Luke 7:18–23; Matt 11:2–6).

According to Luke, in that very hour Jesus healed many and cast out demons, as directly witnessed by the messengers from John. Jesus instructed them to go and tell John what they had just experienced—"the blind see again, lame people are walking again, lepers are now clean again and those deaf now hear, dead people are being raised, the gospel is being preached to the poor"—all in active fulfillment of God's promise found in the passage of Isa 61 that Jesus read in the synagogue in Nazareth. Jesus then pronounced a beatitude—"Indeed, whoever is not scandalized by me is blessed" (Luke 7:23), after which he continued to speak about John, his own ministry, and the kingdom of God in the face of criticism and rejection (Luke 7:24–35).

In John's Gospel, Jesus called Philip of Bethsaida to follow him. Philip confessed to Nathaniel, "We have found the one concerning whom Moses in the Law and the Prophets wrote, Jesus son of Joseph, the one from Nazareth" (John 1:45). Nathaniel replied immediately, "Is anything good able to come out of Nazareth?" (John 1:46). It is interesting that Nathaniel's question in John 1:46 comes after the confession by Andrew that Jesus had been identified as the Messiah (John 1:41). After Nathaniel himself encounters Jesus, he offers confession—"*you* are the Son of God, *you* are the King of Israel" (John 1:49). We have simply ignored the political dimension of Jesus's person and ministry, even in the Gospel of John. We need to re-imagine the Gospel narrative.

Jesus announced the revolutionary rule of God. In a day in which religion and politics were bound together, Jesus's message was far more political than we have imagined it to be. Jesus was not just a religious moralist proclaiming an eternal religious salvation for another world after death. He came proclaiming *a redemption of this present world* from an oppressive Roman rule.

Jesus proclaimed the revolutionary rule of God to a people who knew that God would one day judge "sinners" and vindicate the "righteous." Jesus proclaimed that he had not come to call the "righteous," but sinners. He coupled that proclamation with a proverb that it is not "the well" who need a doctor, but rather those who are "sick" (Mark 2:17). The message of Jesus was redemptive and not judgmental, as he redefined the community of Israel. The religious leaders objected to the nature of the community that Jesus gathered around him. They were embarrassed by his authoritative words and mighty works and sought to destroy him from a very early point in his ministry (Mark 3:6).

Jesus also spoke metaphorically of the need for new, flexible wineskins and not those which were old, stiff, and brittle (Mark 2:22). His message was about the kingdom of God, a theme that occurs approximately 120 times in the Synoptic Gospels. Jesus offered a good news announcement, coupled with an imperative of invitation (Mark 1:15). The dawning of the rule of God *was* Jesus's message, which he proclaimed with authority in both his mighty words and deeds. It was *exclusive* in terms of its content. It was *inclusive* in terms of its outreach. It was new. It was powerful. And its reception required "repentance," going beyond the current religious and political mind-set and customary expectations of the day. Jesus called upon people to imagine what life would be like now that God's long-promised and expected rule was breaking in. It would overcome both the celestial rule of the demonic and the earthly rule of Rome exercised through Caesar and puppet kings.

Imagine God's promised rule as compared with that of Tiberius and Herod Antipas! Imagine the freedom of God's rule compared to the destructive personal slavery of Satan and the demonic. Those whom Jesus healed and upon whom he performed exorcisms certainly came to know the difference, as they experienced new life (see Mark 5:1–20). Jesus demonstrated what the rule of God would be like for those with whom he came in contact through his mighty words and works that changed individual lives. Jesus re-introduced people to the active power of God that was able to change the potential of living. Jesus lifted burdens, even as he created new opportunities of living on the other side of "repentance."

In the course of his ministry, Jesus performed mighty works. The word "miracle" is our word. The Gospels prefer words such as "wonders," "signs," or "mighty works." Jesus healed people—the sick, the blind, the lame, those with other infirmities. Jesus performed exorcisms of demons, at least according to the Synoptic Gospels of Matthew, Mark, and Luke. The Gospel of John contains no exorcisms, just as it contains no parables. The only mighty work that occurs in all four Gospels is the feeding of the five thousand (see Mark 6:30–44 par.; John 6:1–15), although other "nature works" occur in the Gospels. The first of the "signs" that Jesus performed according to the Gospel of John was the changing of the water into wine, for example (see John 2:1–12). John also presents the account of the resuscitation of Lazarus (John 11:1–44), while the Synoptics recall the raising of Jairus's daughter (Mark 5:21–24, 35–43 par.) and the widow's son at Nain (Luke 7:11–17). Jesus thus performed healings, exorcisms, resuscitations, and nature works of various kinds. In fact, one of the most certain things we know about Jesus from the available evidence is that he did wondrous works. That which had been imagined by the prophet Isaiah was now coming to pass and, indeed, was now reality (see Isa 61:1–2; Luke 4:18–21; 7:21–23).

Jesus taught with mighty *words*, in addition to his mighty *works*. Jesus taught in short sayings (aphorisms) employing many figures of speech. He did not always speak literally. He could use metaphors, puns, overstatement, and hyperbole. Very few people have understood Jesus to be speaking literally when he suggested plucking out the right eye or cutting off the right hand as a solution to lust (Matt 5:29–30). On the other hand, few have perceived Jesus's humor in hyperbole of a person "with a log in one's eye" (see Matt 7:4–5). Jesus could employ humor in his teachings, although we today generally entertain a rather serious and somber Jesus. We have made Jesus to be too "religious."

Parables of Jesus

More than 30 percent (35 percent) of Jesus's recorded teachings in the Synoptic Gospels are in the form of parables. Parables draw a comparison between earthly examples and spiritual realities, but they need not be fully developed stories. They convey spiritual reality for earthly living. They are not "earthly stories with a heavenly meaning." They are earthly stories and metaphors charged with earthly meaning associated with the rule of God. While they may draw an illustrative analogy, they are not allegories which require an interpretive key to unlock the hidden meaning of every separate element within the parable.

If one understands Jesus's story or illustration, then one can make application concerning Jesus's proclamation of the kingdom of God. Jesus, for example, can convey the nature of grace or discipleship through a parable. The nature of the kingdom—its apparent small beginnings with its final great result—is expressed through parables, as is the crisis that the coming and presence of the kingdom creates. While Jesus may have pointed briefly to a direction or application, he did not apparently intend his parables as thorough-going allegories.

The extended allegorical interpretations of the parable of the Sower (Mark 4:15–20 par.) and the Weeds (Matt 13:36–43) likely go back to the early church rather than to Jesus. This is likely for several reasons. First of all, Jesus placed the responsibility upon the hearer to hear and to apply and to understand his message, his person, and God's kingdom, as well as one's own relationship to that kingdom. He called upon people to imagine. He did not tell people what they must "believe," such that they were relieved of personal responsibility. He challenged people to "repent," to move beyond the mind-set they currently had.

Jesus's parables were not intended to teach mere "moral lessons" to guide individual behavior. Rather, they were potent directions that pointed to the in-break of the kingdom of God for the collective life of the people of Israel. Secondly, Jesus's overall intention was to reveal and relate the kingdom of God to everyday life, i.e., what life in the kingdom would be like in comparison to life they currently lived. The parables were open windows for those who had eyes to see. They were pictorial realities for those who had ears to hear. They drew one in and expressed significant meaning with an economy of words. They appealed to the imagination and called for imaginative response. They were meant to be life changers, not vehicles of entertainment.

Certain parables of Jesus are found in all three Synoptic Gospels, while others are found in only one or two Gospels. Some of Jesus's best-known parables, like the parable of the "Good Samaritan" and "Prodigal Son" are found only in Luke's Gospel, while that of the "Sower" is found in Mark as well as Matthew and Luke (Mark 4:1–9; Matt 13:1–9; Luke 8:4–8). In Luke 10:29–37, Jesus tells a story about a man who fell among robbers who was helped by a Samaritan (Jesus nowhere calls the Samaritan "good"). Jesus told the parable in order to clarify a Torah lawyer's question about the definition of neighbor. Jesus did not tell the lawyer what to think or believe. Jesus did not offer a definition of neighbor in theory, but rather he offered a storied demonstration of neighbor in fact. With his story, he led the lawyer to draw his own, appropriate conclusion. The parable resides in the context of a theological discussion that began with the lawyer's question, "What must I do to inherit eternal life?" (Luke 10:25–29). In essence, Jesus's answer is to live out of love and compassion *now*, in this world.

The parable of the "Prodigal Son" (found only in Luke's Gospel) is a parable of grace. It is the third of a series of three parables in Luke 15. Because we have imagined them as moral lessons for use in evangelism, we have failed to understand. In reality, the three parables are really mis-named. Jesus tells a parable about a *shepherd* who lost a sheep (not the "Lost Sheep"), one about a *woman* who lost a coin (not the "Lost Coin"), and another about a *father* who had *two* sons (not the "Prodigal Son"). The parables address the matter of joy in finding that which was lost as characteristic of the redemptive grace of God. The Lukan context is one of religious leaders murmuring concerning the nature of the messianic community that Jesus was gathering around himself—a community of "tax collectors and sinners" who heard Jesus gladly and with whom Jesus dared to eat a meal (Luke 15:1). The messianic community being formed by Jesus was inclusive and not exclusive.

Jesus spoke the parable of the "Sower" along with other agricultural parables in a Galilean context where farming pursuits upon very rocky ground were common. Exposed limestone and basalt rock is found everywhere in the area around the Lake of Galilee. The parable itself is a parable of contrast and assurance regarding the kingdom of God (see Mark 4:11, 26, 30). Just as a sower sows seed with the expectation of a harvest, so it is with Jesus and the kingdom of God.

The allegorical interpretation of the parable (Mark 4:15-20 par.) redirects attention to the hearers in terms of types of "soils" and away from the assurance of harvest. As it stands, and for a number of reasons, the interpretation appears to be the product of the early church that at a quite early point in time began to wrestle with the allegorical interpretation of Jesus's parables. When (according to Mark) the disciples asked Jesus about the meaning of the parables, Jesus did not tell them what to believe. Instead, Jesus gave them a clear hint of application. He drew a parallel. He identified himself as the Sower who sows the word concerning the kingdom of God (Mark 4:14) and offered several other parables which clarified the meaning of the parable of the Sower and the nature of the kingdom of God (see Mark 4:21-34). Wake up! Repent! Open your eyes! Come to a different mind-set! God himself is now doing something new in one's very midst. Planting time is here now, but there will soon come a great harvest. Jesus's message was other than the "be good soil" (a passive metaphor) of a moralistic imperative.

The Authority of Jesus

Jesus also clarified Mosaic Torah by stressing the intent of the Torah (Matt 5:17-48). He claimed personal authority even over Moses with his emphatic "but *I* say to you" (Matt 5:22, 28, 32, 34, 39, 44), an emphasis generally ignored in English translation. Jesus claimed authority as "Son of Man" over the sacred Sabbath (Mark 2:28).

Jesus spoke with authoritative words and performed mighty works which heralded the dawning of the rule of God in ways long-expected as well as in ways inherently new. His message was strongly political, even as it addressed even deeper religious needs and yearnings. God's day of redemption and reconciliation had come. Jesus announced that the kingdom of God's rule had already drawn near and he offered a participatory imperative of invitation for all to participate in God's kingdom rule. In particular, those persons who had been classed as "sinners," often as a foil to define those who were "righteous," were invited to come under God's rule. And, many did. They now had a place at God's table.

Time in Jerusalem

While John's Gospel presents Jesus as traveling back and forth many times between Galilee and Jerusalem, the Synoptic Gospels present only the single journey to Jerusalem at Passover season. As already indicated, while John mentions three Passovers, the Synoptics present only a single Passover. According to the Synoptics, Jesus will enter Jerusalem on a Sunday and will be crucified on the coming Friday of

Passover eve. The tomb will be found empty on the following Sunday morning. Everything that happens in the course of the Judean ministry will take place within the span of a single week—i.e., eight days. Jesus will render a prophetic action of judgment against what the Temple had become because of its current practices orchestrated by the wealthy priestly families in collaboration with Rome. Jesus will again teach the people, while he will be challenged repeatedly by the various factions of the Jewish religious leadership. According to Mark, the religious leadership has been trying to get rid of Jesus since an early time in his Galilean ministry (Mark 3:6).

There is now a unified opposition from the highest levels of Jewish authorities. As the writer of John suggests, the high priest's position is that it is expedient that one man die and not the whole nation perish (John 11:46–50). Such a statement heralds the danger of a more widespread political revolution. In the Synoptics, Jesus is challenged by chief priests, scribes, and elders (Mark 11:27–33 par.). Among other things, Jesus responds with the parable of the Wicked Tenant Farmers—a parable found in all three Synoptics (Mark 12:1–12; Matt 21:33–46; Luke 20:9–19). While the parable may tend toward allegory, especially in Matthew, the Markan presentation suggests an autobiographical identification with Jesus. If so, one gains understanding in terms of divine intention. God is not the "murderer" of Jesus, nor is he a co-conspirator in Jesus's death, as some contemporary "theology" suggests. The owner of the vineyard in Jesus's parable did not send either his servants or his son to be mistreated or killed. Rather, he sent both the servants and the son to claim what was rightfully his. The evident reasoning was that of respect for his authority through the son. And this in Jesus's own words.

Death and Resurrection

The execution of Jesus is a significant part of the gospel story with which the early church had to wrestle in its interpretation of the Christ event as a whole. And for the most part, the earliest Christians sought to interpret the death of Jesus in the light of the resurrection. How could God's promised Messiah, long expected and hoped for in Jewish thought, be killed by Israel's enemies, the Romans? And especially, how could he be killed by a cross execution which seemed to evoke the curse of Torah itself (see Deut 21:23)? If Jesus died under God's curse *for any reason whatsoever*, how could he be God's true representative deliverer? These were very real issues with which the earliest Christians had to wrestle, as they came to comprehend a gospel truly worth proclaiming.

Fully three-eighths of Mark's Gospel (Mark 11–16, 37.5 percent) focuses upon the *final week* of Jesus's life, i.e., his ministry in Jerusalem at Passover season. It is the end of the story that gives supportive sense to the whole story of Jesus. Paul, in every one of his letters, proclaims Jesus as "Lord" and "Christ," even as does Luke's presentation of Peter's sermon on the day of Pentecost (Acts 2:36). Apart from the resurrection, at best Jesus would have been remembered as a dead founder of a movement or as another failed Messiah (see Acts 5:33–39). With the resurrection, however, one finds divine vindication of both Jesus's person and ministry.

God's "justice" is demonstrated in the resurrection, although much theology restricts it to the cross as associated with divine wrath. Once this is realized, one readily begins to imagine a rather different view of God. God righted a grievous wrong, overcoming all powers of evil in the process. Rather than a divine need for a perfect sacrifice, God met the human need for a perfect, i.e., complete, salvation by his Gospel. Much is at stake in how one imagines the nature of God.

Aside from Paul's earlier accounts of his encounter with the resurrected Christ based upon his physical experience of the commanding presence of a risen Lord, the Gospels (written after the time of Paul) offer two kinds of resurrection narratives. There is the testimony of the "empty tomb" narratives (Mark 16:1–8; Matt 28:1–8; Luke 24:1–11; John 20:1–10). The body of Jesus is no longer found in the place of burial. The tomb is portrayed not only as empty, but as *open*. The stone has been rolled away. While John has no mention of an angelic messenger, the Synoptic tradition speaks of a figure (Luke has two!) who testifies to the resurrection. The testimony of the figure or figures echoes the testimony of Jesus himself given prior to his passion (see Mark 8:31; 9:31; 10:33–34 and par.). There is the echo of Jesus's prior promise to go before the disciples to Galilee (Mark 14:28; Matt 26:32).

The Gospels also present "appearance" narratives that identify the risen one with the Jesus who died (see Matt 28:9–10, 16–20; Luke 24:13–49; John 20:11—21:23). Jesus intrudes into the lives of the disciples with a powerful, life-changing, commanding presence. The appearances provoke doubt, fear, fascination, and assurance. They elicit confession of lordship. The appearance narratives, especially in Luke, offer the opportunity for the interpretation of the church's scripture as represented by what Christians today refer to as the "Old Testament" (Luke 24:27, 44–47; cf. 1 Cor 15:3–4).

Written after the time of Paul, the Gospels later narrate stories illustrative of the Easter faith that earlier had called the church into being. While Mark 16:9–20 represents a later addition to what was perceived to be an incomplete text (see Mark 16:8), Mark depicts three women who go to the tomb only to find it empty. The figure who appears within the tomb speaks of Jesus's earlier promise that they will see him when they return to Galilee (see Mark 14:28; 16:7). There are no appearances in Jerusalem. In Matthew's Gospel, only two women go to the tomb and Jesus appears to both, appearing later to all the apostles in Galilee, where a commission to universal mission is given (Matt 28:19–20). In Luke's Gospel, three named women plus other women discover the tomb empty and are addressed within the tomb by *two* figures dressed in white.

The risen Jesus appears incognito to two disciples on the road to Emmaus (Luke 24:13–27), two disciples not numbered among the apostles. Following an offstage appearance to Simon Peter, Jesus appeared to all the apostles *in Jerusalem*. While there are no Galilean appearances in Luke, all of the Jerusalem area encounters occurred on Easter Sunday within seventy-two hours of Jesus's death. It is interesting that Luke alone narrates the ascension of Jesus into heaven—twice, in different ways. In the Gospel, the risen Jesus leads the disciples out as far as Bethany before he departs from them (Luke 24:51). The disciples, for their part, return to Jerusalem and are portrayed as continually blessing God in the Temple (Luke 24:52–53), indicative of the fulfillment of Old Testament promises.

In Acts, Luke speaks of the risen Jesus being with his disciples for a period of forty days before he is taken up into heaven out of their sight (Acts 1:3–9). The two Lukan accounts are different and really cannot be harmonized (Luke 24:52–53; Acts 1:3–9). Luke makes use of the event in Acts to set the stage for the day of Pentecost and development of early Christianity or the Christian movement.

Luke presents a drama in two parts—the story of Jesus and the story of the development of the early church. His drama begins in Jerusalem. After a ministry in Galilee, a central feature of Jesus's ministry in Luke is Jesus's lengthy journey to Jerusalem (see Luke 9:51—18:14). Luke's Gospel ends with resurrection appearances in Jerusalem. The story in Acts is a movement away from Jerusalem. It ends with the Gospel having reached Rome. It has become an unhindered movement (Acts 28:31). Luke likely writes sometime after the Jewish-Roman War (66–70 CE) and the destruction of Jerusalem and its Temple in 70 CE. He depicts a story of divine fulfillment that begins in Jerusalem but that claims the entire Roman world. Luke is a literary artist in his presentation of the gospel story.

The Gospel of John presents resurrection appearances in Jerusalem—first to Mary Magdalene on Easter Sunday morning, then to ten disciples on Easter evening, and a week later to the eleven disciples (including Thomas, who was earlier absent; see John 20:19–29). Jesus also reveals himself to eleven disciples beside the Sea of Tiberius (Lake of Galilee) at a subsequent time (John 21). The writer of John indicates that this was the "third time" that Jesus was revealed to the disciples after his resurrection from the dead (John 21:14).

The Gospels thus employ two means of stressing the reality of the resurrection of Jesus—the empty tomb and actual appearances of the risen Jesus. While there is the materialization of Jesus's raised body in the later Gospel accounts, the resurrection faith is based upon the fact of remembered appearances and not upon a particular conception of a post-Easter resurrection body of Jesus. The appearance narratives are woven into the conception of the empty tomb, such that the faith in the resurrection is not based simply upon the fact of the empty tomb. There could indeed be other explanations for an "empty tomb," including a mistaken tomb or the theft of the body (Matt 27:62–66; John 20:13). Paul's own expressed faith in the resurrection is based upon an appearance of the risen Christ (Gal 1:15–16; 1 Cor 15:8). Paul makes no mention of the "empty tomb."

The Gospel accounts, Acts, and Paul's letters offer differing traditions and perspectives that need not be and should not be harmonized. All represent early Christian testimony. The narrative accounts become a vehicle for expressing the resurrection faith, although that faith is not identical to the affirmation of the historical factuality of any or even all of the narrated stories. Each one bears witness to an extraordinary divine event in its own unique way. Each of the Gospel writers "envisioned" the story of Jesus and the early church with their own unique presentation of the fulfillment of divine promise in the person of Jesus of Nazareth.

As noted above, the four Gospels handle post-resurrection appearances of the risen Christ differently. In the last authentic verses of Mark's Gospel, the women flee from the now empty tomb (Mark 16:8). On the basis of our earliest extant manuscripts, Mark 16:9–20 appears to have been added at a later time. Those verses appear to contain echoes of the other, later Gospels, as well. Unless the original ending has been lost, Mark's original witness is that of an open-ended gospel story. Mark offers three predictions of Jesus's suffering and death (Mark 8:31; 9:30–32; 10:32–34 par.). Prior to his death, after the Supper and on the Mount of Olives, Jesus told his disciples that he would go before them to Galilee (Mark 14:28). With the completion of events in Jerusalem, there is now open-ended attention directed to the place of beginnings.

Matthew's Gospel largely follows the Markan account but offers a distinctive presentation of Jesus's Passion which includes resurrection appearances in both Jerusalem and Galilee (Matt 28:9–10, 16–20). It is Matthew's Gospel that includes the so-named "Great Commission" to make disciples of all nations (Matt 28:19–20). The commission and appearance take place on a mountain in Galilee, to which Jesus had directed his disciples. Luke's Gospel presents post-resurrection appearances only in the area of Jerusalem or Judea, coupled with a brief account of Jesus's ascension (Luke 24:13–53; cf. Acts 1:1–11). Both Luke and Acts present an ascension into heaven from the area of Jerusalem. The Gospel of John presents resurrection appearances in both Jerusalem (John 20) and in the Galilean epilogue (John 21).

Again, the accounts of each Gospel are unique and should not be harmonized. It is instructive for the reader to read and compare the similarities and differences that exist among the four Gospels, as well as the beginning of Acts. Paul personally attests to the traditional witness to the resurrection and includes himself among those to whom Jesus appeared (1 Cor 15:3–8). It is the resurrection and exaltation that provide a basis for the development of the gospel and the beginnings of Christianity, both of which are predicated upon the "good news" of Jesus's resurrection.

The Prologue of Christian Beginnings

Jesus had proclaimed the kingdom of God. The early church proclaimed Jesus through the effective power of the resurrection and consciousness of the presence of the Spirit of God as the fulfillment of Old Testament promise (Acts 2; Joel 2:28–32). It was not until the church had spread to Hellenistic Antioch of Syria that the followers of Christ were first called "Christians" (see Acts 11:26). To repeat a point of note, the word "Christian" occurs but three times in the entire New Testament (see Acts 11:26; 26:28; 1 Pet 4:16). Prior to that time they had been referred to as "Galileans" (Acts 1:11; 2:7; 13:31), "disciples" (Gospels; Acts 2:44), "Nazarenes" (Acts 24:5; cf. Matt 2:23), or followers of "the Way" (see Acts 9:2).

The term *Messiah* or *Christ* (Greek, χριστός) or "Anointed One" became the word of designation as the church spread into the gentile world. While the Jewish term "Messiah" would have little meaning in the larger gentile world, it could be used as a term of derision, as in "the Messiah people." The Greek equivalent, "Christ" (χριστός) became virtually a second name that clearly identified the risen Jesus. No longer "Jesus of Nazareth," suitable as a localized identifier of the historical Jesus, as also "Jesus of Galilee," the risen Jesus as the "Christ" becomes unbound from localized geographical designation.

A Generative Event

The development of Christianity centers around the person of Jesus of Nazareth, who died upon a Roman cross, but who through post-resurrection appearances became known as the risen Lord. Apart from the resurrection event, there would have been only the veneration of a martyr or a dead founder of what would likely have been a rather temporary and local movement. In fact several messianic movements of the time are brought to remembrance in the book of Acts. When Gamaliel addresses the council that had already charged Peter and the other apostles to speak no more in the name of Jesus (Acts 4:17–18; 5:26–28), he reminds them of the movements associated with Theudas and also Judas the Galilean (Acts 5:35–37).

As Gamaliel spoke of the present case involving Jesus of Nazareth, he advised the council that if the movement was but another zealotic uprising or pretended messianic deliverer wrought by humans, it would fail on its own. If, on the other hand, the movement of Jesus followers was of God, no one would be able to stop it (see Acts 5:38–39). There were many in that first-century world of Judaism who came proclaiming themselves to be the messiah (see Josephus, *Ant.* 20.97–8). Apparently there was an "Egyptian" who stirred up revolt by leading a significant force of some four thousand out into the wilderness (see Acts 21:38).

It was Jesus's resurrection that distinguished him in the eyes of his followers from all others. God had raised Jesus from the dead and exalted him, thus executing his justice and validating his identity. The resurrection was the keystone of the early Christian message proclaimed by the earliest Christian preaching or kerygma (see Acts 2:22–24; 2:32; 3:14–15; 4:10; 5:30–32).

It was the generative event of the resurrection that created the need to remember Jesus in any long term fashion and to interpret those memories in a particular manner. Those who had followed Jesus, who had heard him teach and who had seen his mighty works performed, now had a transformative "religious experience" unlike anything that had ever happened before. While those followers of Jesus may have had a "commemorative experience" that remembered Jesus's teachings or his mighty works or even his crucifixion and death upon a Roman cross, none of these commemorative experiences was sufficient to generate the claims and sustain the support of the Christian gospel represented by the earliest Christian communities. It was experience that called forth memory—and interpretation. What did it mean for God to raise a crucified prophet from the dead?

The resurrection was *the* event that gave rise to the development of the early church. All of the earliest Christians were Jews, who affirmed that the God of the Jewish covenant had raised Jesus from the dead. Something happened beyond a mere "empty tomb" that turned a frightened band of followers with frustrated hopes into a fearless and committed group willing to suffer personal martyrdom for their convictions. Something happened beyond visionary hallucinations that caused Paul, a Jewish Pharisee, to become a life-long proclaimer of the Christian gospel rather than a persecutor of a fringe Jewish movement.

Christian history thus began with the highly paradoxical event of the resurrection as experienced among a small group of Jesus followers in the environs of Jerusalem in 30 CE. All were Jews. The next forty years would be tumultuous, as Christianity would leave its sectarian identity within Judaism behind. The date of 70 CE marks a watershed date, for the Romans destroyed Jerusalem and its great Herodian Temple in that year. The prior decade of the sixties CE was marked by the death of Christian leaders like Paul and James and Peter. In the present writer's judgment, Paul was martyred in 61 CE, although other traditions may date his death as late as 68 CE, following a subsequent ministry to Spain or the eastern Mediterranean—a ministry not reflected in the New Testament. Some traditions suggest both Peter and Paul died in the Neronian persecutions in Rome in 64–65 CE. We do know that James, the brother of Jesus, was martyred in Jerusalem in 62 CE by the high priest Ananus, during a transition period of the absence of a Roman governor (Josephus, *Ant.* 20.200).

In the present writer's judgment, Paul's active ministry basically occupied the period of time from his call (34 CE) to his final journey to Jerusalem (56 CE), with Paul's final years (56–61 CE) being spent under incarceration in either Jerusalem, Caesarea Maritima, or Rome, as suggested by the Acts account and its underlying source. This "Source Tradition of Acts" (STA) is proposed and developed elsewhere by the present author (see *The Ministry of Paul the Apostle: History and Redaction*). One should not assume that Paul and company were the only Christian evangelists at work during the formative period—indeed, the New Testament bears witness to the independent mission of Barnabas, as well as the Nomistic Evangelists (Judaizers) who proclaimed the necessity of embracing the Torah of Moses in order to become a part of the "new Israel" now composed of gentiles as well as Jews.

While Paul's mission is the one about which we know the most, there were undoubtedly other formal (Peter?) and informal missions responsible for the spread of Christianity into the larger Greco-Roman world. The informal spread of Christianity would have likely begun as early as the time of Jesus's death and resurrection (30 CE), following the climactic Pentecost of 30 or 31 CE (Acts 2).

Foundational Beliefs

The book of Acts is the basic source for information about earliest Christianity in terms of the history of the early church. It has been variously dated from ca. 62–150 CE. One gains insight into the period of time following the resurrection from the ending of the Gospels, all likely written in the period 65–95 CE. One may piece together insight into individual church communities through careful reading of Paul's own letters, which constitute our earliest Christian literature, likely written in about a twelve year period from 49–60 CE. From Paul's letters, one may also glean an awareness of the struggles and issues faced by the larger church that were then so current. Paul's letters do not come with a date and are not arranged in chronological order in the New Testament. They appear in canonical order from longest to shortest, with those addressed to churches preceding those ostensibly written to individuals. The dating and arrangement of Paul's letters must be worked out. Our sources are thus limited in number, but they are significant.

Some of the basic beliefs of the early Christians emerge in the proclamation or kerygma of the early church. One may think of the basic kerygma developing through the first twenty years or so, following the death and resurrection of Jesus (30 CE). A half dozen themes constitute the basic proclamation. First, in keeping with the Jewish concept of the Two Ages, the new age of the Age to Come had dawned. It had been promised in Scripture and long hoped for (Luke 2; 24; cf. Joel 2:28–32). Secondly, fulfillment had come in a most unexpected way—through the life, death, and resurrection of Jesus of Nazareth. He was (a) descended from David, (b) did many mighty works, (c) was unjustly condemned by collusion of Jewish and Roman authorities, (d) was crucified on a Roman cross, and (e) was affirmed to have been raised from the dead by the power of God. Thirdly, one of the earliest confessions was that of "Jesus is Lord!," which heralded exaltation to the right hand of God as viceroy of the new Israel (see 1 Cor 15:20–28).

Fourthly, the sign that Jesus was alive and presently active with those who expressed faith in him was to be found in the Spirit active in the church. A fifth belief was that Jesus would return *soon* to consummate the kingdom and return full rule to God, after subduing all enemies (1 Cor 15:20–28). The technical term for the return of Jesus is *parousia*, which was an apocalyptic concept literally interpreted by the early church. While other sub-points could be introduced, a final point could be given as the appeal to repent and accept the fulfillment of new life offered by the Gospel of God. While repentance is often restricted in contemporary Christian thought to "turning from sin," its broader usage and implication is that of embracing a new mind-set and lifestyle that frees one from a narrow, wrong, or outmoded theological vision. There was but one God, who now fulfilled his elective purpose through Christ to create a new Israel consisting of both Jews and gentiles. This purpose, however, was inherent in the promise originally made to Abraham.

The earliest church was not a separate entity from Judaism. The early followers of Christ worshiped in both the temple and the synagogue, as well as in private houses. For them, the time of the fulfillment of Judaism had come. And, quite unexpectedly, the kingdom rule of God had come in the person, ministry, and passion of Jesus of Nazareth, in whom the rule of God had dawned.

There are a paucity of references to early Christianity found in the vast array of Roman literature during the first hundred years after the death of Jesus. One reason for this may be that the Romans did not much distinguish between Christians and Jews until the clear separation of Christianity and Judaism in the aftermath of the pivotal events of 70 CE. Judaism had long been recognized as a "legal religion" (*religio licita*) by Rome, such that earliest Christianity was simply accepted as sectarian Judaism. While Josephus barely mentions Jesus himself (*Ant.* 18.63–64), he does mention the execution of James and others in 62 CE without indicating their specifically Christian identity. The testimony of Tacitus (ca. 56–120 CE, *Annals* 15.44.2–5) and Suetonius is later (ca. 69–122 CE, *Divus Claudius* 25.4). Tacitus mentions the blame Nero placed upon Christians for the fire of 64 CE in Rome, which resulted in the martyrdom of many followers of Christ. Suetonius mentions the earlier banishment of Jews from Rome as a result of unrest and disturbance over a certain "Chrestus," a Romanized Greek name that would have been pronounced virtually the same as "Christos" (=Christ).

The event of expulsion under Claudius would be the earliest event involving Christians found in secular sources. It most likely occurred ca. 46–47 CE. Outside of the church's writings, there is no trace to be found of the first twenty years of Christianity. We are virtually dependent upon Luke's account in the book of Acts and upon Paul's letters for the time between the execution of Jesus in 30 CE and the appearance of Paul before Gallio in Corinth in the summer of 51 CE. The earliest of Paul's letters, 2 Thessalonians and 1 Thessalonians, date from 49–51 CE. Traditional source materials underlying Acts and Paul's letters offer information for reconstructing the developing history and theological understanding of the early church and earliest Christians. While the speeches attributed to Peter and Paul and others are Lukan characterization, the Lukan presentation of early church development is likely sound tradition in terms of the underlying STA (Source Tradition of Acts, see *The Ministry of Paul the Apostle*), once Lukan redaction is taken into account.

Paul himself offers creedal material in 1 Cor 15:3–5 and Rom 1:3–5. He bears witness to hymnic material representative of earliest Christianity, whether borrowed or self-created, in Phil 2:6–11 and Rom 8:28–30. Such references offer indications of the development of Christian thought and practice in the earliest period. There are flourishing churches in existence—many of which were not established by Paul, such as those at Jerusalem, Damascus, Caesarea Maritima, Antioch, Ephesus, and Rome. There were yet others that Paul established in his great foundational movement around the Mediterranean—in Galatia, Philippi, Thessalonica, and Corinth. Characterization of Pauline churches has been given in the first chapter of the present work.

Acts and the Gospels were written in the decades following the period of 30–52 CE, the time of Jesus's own death and resurrection (30 CE) to the time of the crucial Jerusalem Conference of 52 CE. Paul's ministry and that of other early Christian evangelists fit into this gap. The early sixties CE mark the time of the death of early Christian leaders (Paul, James, Peter). The time of the Jewish-Roman War (66–73 CE) marks the time of the likely appearance of Mark's Gospel, the destruction of the temple, and the fall of Jerusalem (70 CE). Masada held out until 73 CE. These years marked a period of clear separation of Christians from Jews, as well as a period of Christian consolidation in the diaspora of the Greco-Roman world.

Literarily, Paul's letters represent the decade of the fifties (49–60 CE), the Gospels the three decades following (65–95 CE), followed by Acts (85–100? CE), and later New Testament writings are to be placed in the final three decades (90–125 CE). Second Peter is likely the latest New Testament book and was in existence by 125 CE. Second Peter testifies to some type of collection of Paul's letters plural (see 2 Pet 3:15–16) that is already having interpretive impact within Christian churches. By that time, other non-canonical works such as the Apostolic Fathers (1 Clement, Didache, Letters of Ignatius, etc.) were likewise in existence and in use in some quarters of the early Christian church. All of the New Testament documents themselves were likely produced within a hundred years of Jesus's death and resurrection, over a span of approximately seventy-five years.

Jesus proclaimed the kingdom of God (Mark 1:15) and the early church proclaimed the risen Jesus. It was faith in Jesus's resurrection that effected the change and marked the development of the Gospel. It is the resurrection that is the central building block of the Christian faith and the development of the New Testament. Whether implicit or explicit, the resurrection becomes the presupposition of all the New Testament writings, Paul's letters included. Christian faith is not based upon a set of religious ideas and ideals, old or new. It is not based upon a theology. Rather, it is based upon an event believed to have been effected by God.

Christian faith was not based upon the distillation of wise advice, but rather upon the announcement of good news of God's action in raising Jesus from the dead. The resurrection was about God and his action; it was not an additional accomplishment of Jesus. With the exaltation of Jesus as Lord over all powers and authorities and the proclamation of the Gospel of God to the gentiles, one sees the culmination of and fulfillment of God's promises to Abraham.

No one witnessed the moment of resurrection. As a unique, transcendent event, it is not in itself subject to the study of historians. Historians may study the perceived effect of God's action in the lives of those who embraced the reality of faith in the resurrection. From the very beginning one is confronted with the remembrance and interpretation of an event that obviously produced a life-changing effect. Jesus died a truly human death in which it appeared that conspiratorial forces of evil consisting of Jewish priestly authorities and official representatives of Rome won out. Beginning on the third day following his death, Jesus's followers were proclaiming that he was alive. Their proclamation was not that of a theory of the "immortality of the soul," but was rather a way of affirming the action of God in terms of a theological conception already present within the Jewish party of the Pharisees (see Mark 12:18–27). It was God who "raised Jesus from the dead" (see 1 Thess 1:9–10; Gal 1:1; 2 Cor 4:14; Rom 4:24; 6:4; 8:11; 10:9; Eph 1:20; Col 2:12).

There are some things that the resurrection was not, in terms of expressed New Testament faith. It was not a belief in immortality, whereby the "immortal soul" of Jesus survived death. It was not a matter of mere resuscitation, whereby Jesus was restored to this-worldly life. It had nothing to do with para-psychological phenomena. It was not just a powerful subjective and collective memory experience, whereby Jesus "lived on" in the hearts and memory of his disciples. It was not a new call to commitment in Jesus's name to Jesus's cause. It was first of all something that happened to the dead Jesus, not something that happened first of all to his disciples and would-be disciples. The resurrection was not an adaptation of the myth of dying-and-rising of fertility gods of antiquity. The resurrection faith was not merely the belief that a corpse had come back to life, nor was it the basic belief that the tomb was empty on Easter morning. It was more than that.

The focal point was not upon debate as to whether there is "life after death," but rather the focus was upon divine vindication, justice, and affirmation. The resurrection marked the faithful recognition by God of the life Jesus had lived as he embodied the will of God throughout his entire life.

The earliest Christians could affirm the resurrection in creeds, hymns, or kerygma, all of which were based upon the experience of the risen Christ within the community. It came to be interpreted in the thought categories of apocalyptic which provided a ready-made vehicle for expressing the eschatological action of God. Elements of Old Testament and Jewish thought portrayed the resurrection of the dead at the end of history in terms of God's promise and divine victory over all enemies, cosmic and domestic.

Jesus's resurrection came to be interpreted as the vanguard of God's new age, in keeping with the Jewish concept of the Two Ages. Just as the Present Evil Age was personified by Sin, Law, Flesh, and Death, so now the hoped-for Age to Come had broken into history, personified as it was by Righteousness/Justice, Grace, Spirit, and Life. The resurrection of Jesus was but the "first fruit" of everything else God was doing and would soon do. Just as one may see the leading edge of a weather front in the sky, so in the interpretation of the earliest Christians the resurrection and exaltation of Jesus was but the leading edge of the fulfillment of God's total victory over all cosmic powers and their embodiment upon earth.

Jesus did not found a church, nor did he establish an institutionalized religion. He did not institute a "movement" in the modern sense of the word. Rather, he proclaimed the advent of the kingdom (rule) of God and called upon his followers to embrace his message proclaimed in words and mighty works. In the first weeks following Jesus's death, his followers formed a distinct gathered group within Judaism in Jerusalem. It is perhaps too strong to assume they formed a distinct religious community. The arrest and execution of Jesus marked a shattering of the hopes of his followers (see Luke 24:21). There may well have been a scattering of the disciples and even a return to Galilee, while it is Luke-Acts that suggests or creates the impression that the disciples remained in Jerusalem. That scenario, however, is in keeping with Luke's theological purpose.

While there is much we do not know about the earliest community, the *ekklesia* (church) began as a distinct group within Judaism. All of the original disciples were Palestinian, Aramaic-speaking Jews, like Jesus himself. They would have formed a group within Judaism, much like the Pharisees, Sadducees, Essenes, or followers of John the Baptizer. Their closest kinship may have been with the followers of John as a grass-roots movement. If they followed the emphases of Jesus, the disciples would not have entertained the idea of an individualistic personal relationship with God in terms of a modern Western "personal savior" image apart from membership in a community of faith. The concept of the kingdom of God includes the prediction of a *community* of faith established by God's saving action and attuned to God's eschatological mission of world transformation.

For all the emphasis upon the cross in a contemporary church context, the New Testament and the earliest Christian faith emphasize the resurrection. Life, not death, is the focus of the New Testament gospel. The cross is important, but in ways that are ignored or overlooked in contemporary Christianity. Jesus spoke about taking up one's own cross (Mark 8:35 par). The early church, Paul included, came to symbolize the entire Christ event with the symbol of the cross. Indeed, how could one symbol the resurrection? The cross—a symbol of death and shame in the ancient Roman world— became a symbol of how to live, through what may be termed a "rebirth of images" for those "in Christ." It became a symbol of victorious life.

The eschatological gift of the Spirit and the restoration of prophecy characterized the community. It was God who had exercised the initiative to raise Jesus from the dead and to send the Spirit. Very early, Jesus became confessed as "Son of Man," as "Lord" and "Christ." The exalted Christ now continued to speak through inspired Christian prophets, thus fulfilling a role that in the Old Testament had belonged to God alone. The historical Jesus now spoke from heaven as the risen Christ through the prophets, in keeping with the eschatological expectation of the prophet Joel (Joel 2:28–32 [3:1–5 LXX]).

The Lukan Accounting

The terms "disciples" and "Christian" are absent in Paul. The term "disciple" is found only in the Gospels and Acts in the New Testament, such that the term does not appear to be a self-designation of the earliest church. The term "Christian," according to Luke, was first used in Antioch in the forties CE (Acts 11:26). It is used sparingly in the New Testament—only three occurrences (Acts 11:26; 26:28; 1 Pet 4:16). It is not clear whether it was a self-chosen term or whether a term applied by opponents. An early term used in Acts was that of "the Way" (Acts 9:2; 18:25–26; 19:9, 23; 24:22). This term seems to be in accord with the term "saints" or "holy ones," as the early church saw itself to be a holy community of the "last days" or time of fulfillment.

According to the Lukan presentation, at least some of Jesus's Galilean followers resettled in Jerusalem. This is apparently historically true, although the centrality of Jerusalem is theologically significant to the Lukan presentation. In Luke's story, Jerusalem is the point of origination of eschatological fulfillment (Luke 1–2), the ultimate goal of Jesus's ministry (Luke 9:51—19:28), the point of origination of the Christian church and mission (Acts 1–2), and ultimately the place of sacred memories, as the gospel moves out to the larger world and to Rome (Acts 28:23–31). The earliest Galilean followers remain observant Jews who worship in the temple and synagogue, participating fully in Jewish rituals and festivals. This is hardly surprising for those earliest believers in the risen Jesus. Judaism is what they knew, and their belief was that God was now fulfilling his promise of eschatological fulfillment through the risen Jesus. Jerusalem was "ground zero" for all eschatological events. For Luke, it was the originating center of sacred memories of promise and fulfillment.

Luke is a gifted writer and he tells the Christian story with distinct purpose, such that his own interests are very evident. As the story of the church begins in Acts, one assumes a swift continuation of Luke's Gospel (Luke 24:50–53) in the unfolding events of Acts. One tends to overlook the difference in the Lukan narration between the end of the Gospel and the beginning of Acts (Acts 1:1–11). Jesus was executed at Passover season as all the Gospels affirm. As the book of Acts implies, the sequence of events rapidly leads to the Day of Pentecost in Acts 2, followed by subsequent events pertaining to the fledgling church, including localized harassment by the official Jewish religious leadership and "growing pains" (Acts 3–6). This is an issue that might be raised with the Lukan presentation, however.

The tradition of appearances suggested by the other three Gospels includes appearances in Galilee. Luke's current presentation in Acts precludes and even contradicts that traditional evidence. It may well be that there is a much overlooked "time gap" suggested by the Lukan "in those days" of Acts 1:15. Luke certainly has many time gaps in his later presentation of Paul's ministry, and he only gives vignettes of initial Christian developments and mission (Acts 1–12). While it can only be speculative, if the Day of Pentecost reflected in Acts 2, historically speaking, was a year later than the time of Jesus's death and resurrection, all the evidence available could be more easily accommodated.

A plausible suggestion would be that those Galilean disciples returned to Galilee, the place of Jesus's ministry and announcement of the kingdom of God (Mark 1:15; cf. 14:28). Through encounters with the risen Jesus, they experienced and remembered and reflected. A year later, they returned to Jerusalem, at which point the events reflected in the early chapters of Acts began to unfold. In essence, historically speaking, Jesus was executed in 30 CE and the Day of Pentecost reflected in Acts 2 may have occurred in 31 CE, after the disciples had returned to Jerusalem for Passover, 31 CE, in commemoration of Jesus's death and resurrection. This would also mark the deliberate beginning of the Christian mission of proclamation of eschatological fulfillment. Lukan redaction is certainly much in evidence in Acts 1:1–11, as is the materializing of the risen Jesus's continuing presence.

Jesus in the Memory of the Church

While the *recording* of the early Christian kerygma set forth in Acts would date to a time long after the death of Paul, Paul himself acknowledges the basic kerygma prevalent in his day in 1 Cor 15:1–8 and Rom 1:1–4. First Corinthians is likely to be dated to 54 CE (Romans to 56 CE), such that within a quarter of a century after Jesus's execution (30 CE), what Paul and others have been preaching is termed "gospel" and involves a developed understanding of Jesus's death and resurrection. The fact of resurrection is being supported by the acknowledgment of resurrection appearances to Cephas (Peter?), the Twelve (apparently including Matthias, Acts 1:15–26), and to an undifferentiated group of five hundred, and last of all to Paul himself. Paul's gospel was based squarely upon the reality of the resurrection. That gospel had already been interpreted in the light of Old Testament scripture.

The resurrection is the singular event apart from which there would have been no lasting Christian movement. It is significant that the Corinthians asked Paul about clarification of the resurrection (1 Cor 15), although they apparently did not have a similar question about the cross-death of Jesus. As supported by Paul, the Gospel tradition, and the book of Acts, it is the resurrection faith that marks the birth of Christianity. In one of Paul's earliest letters written to the Thessalonians in 51 CE, Paul affirms faith in the resurrection of Jesus (1 Thess 1:10; 4:14). Paul's testimony represents more than a conviction, for it rests ultimately upon his own experience of the "risen Christ" (see Gal 1:15–17; 1 Cor 15:8–10). In what this writer feels is the earliest letter of Paul that we have, the focus of Paul upon the parousia implicitly affirms the resurrection, for the exalted Jesus will be revealed from heaven (2 Thess 1:7–10; 2:1).

Although Paul's gospel was misunderstood by gentiles, such that Paul had to clarify the nature of the resurrection (1 Cor 15) and the projected timing of the parousia (2 Thess 2:1–12), Paul never wavered in his faith in the reality of the resurrection. It was the foundation stone of Christian kerygma (1 Cor 15:3–8), the basis of Christian faith (1 Cor 15:12–28), the paradigm and goal of Christian living (Phil 1:21; 3:8–16), and eternal hope (2 Tim 4:18). The birth of resurrection faith is indeed the birth of Christianity and the "birth" of Paul the apostle. The maintenance of that resurrection faith is, indeed, the heart of Christianity.

Paul's encounter with the risen Jesus was personal, commanding, and empowering. According to his own testimony, as well as that of Luke in Acts (Acts 9:1–8; 22:6–11; 26:12–18), Paul had an experiential encounter that was more than visionary. It was a full spiritual and physical experience of the risen Jesus alive and present in a powerful, life-changing manner revealed to the messianic community.

The resurrection was experienced as a tremendous mystery (a *mysterium tremendum*) that was coupled with the action of proclamation of the outpouring of the Spirit of God. Revelation in the highest sense led to an encounter with the Holy Spirit that was marked by unfolding action. It was not the illusion of vain hope or psychological adjustment. The transcendent, transforming power that emerged from the reality of the resurrection was more than a resuscitation or a vague vision restricted to a local group. It issued forth in a commission of proclamation and witness to the Good News of God (Matt 28:18–20; Luke 24:47–49; Acts 1:8; 2:16–36). The present possession of the Holy Spirit becomes the correlative power associated with the confession that God has made the risen Jesus both Lord and Christ (Acts 2:36; Rom 1:4–7).

It was the presence of the resurrected Jesus through the power of the Holy Spirit of God that called the church into being and shaped its life, proclamation, mission, and beliefs. The resurrection was the generative experience of Christianity that defined its conviction and confession, its spiritual empowerment and actions. It was that which meant the very re-ordering of life, of which Paul himself might be the prime example (Phil 3:4–11).

A Clarity of Vision

The word "gospel," in Greek εὐαγγέλιον, literally suggests an "exceedingly good announcement." Transposed into English characters, the word appears as *evangelion*, from which the English words "evangelism" and "evangelist" are derived. An "evangelist" is one who is actively engaged in the activity of proclamation of "exceedingly good announcement." The word "angel" (Greek ἄγγελος, "messenger") belongs to the same word grouping.

The word "evangelical" likewise belongs to the English word grouping, although the usage today as an adjective (as, "evangelical Christian") for the outside world carries with it the baggage of a particular religious or political persuasion of conservative identity. It may be a word used positively by those who embrace the politics and theology of the right, or it may be used pejoratively by those in opposition who represent the religious or political left. While the Sunday school definition of "gospel" is "good news," it is not altogether inaccurate, although it is rather trite and static. It too often refers to a body of statements to be "believed." Contemporary usage tends to lack the dynamism of the use of the word in Paul's day.

Although most think that "gospel" is a Christian word, in fact it is not. The very word was used to describe the accomplishments of Caesar Augustus, as he brought order and restored civility to a fractured Roman world following the assassination of his adoptive father, Julius Caesar. Neither was "salvation" a Christian word, for among other usage it was Augustus who brought "salvation" to that world. So significant were the accomplishments of Augustus that he was hailed as "Lord" and "Savior." Thus, words like "gospel," "salvation," "Lord," and "Savior" were Roman words before they were ever appropriated as Christian words to proclaim the Gospel of God in Christ.

Fig. 5. Augustus of Prima Porto. By FollowTheMedia, CC BY-SA 3.0.
https://commons.wikimedia.org/w/index.php?curid=5561975.

Thus, when Paul and others went forth to engage in the activity of proclaiming the "gospel" (an activity with a particular content), they were proclaiming a message that was sometimes deemed treasonous in a world that already was governed by the alternative gospel of Caesar. That world proclaimed Caesar as Lord, *Kurios Caesar*. The early Christians proclaimed the risen Jesus as Lord, *Kurios Christos*. In terms of Christian proclamation, if Christ was Lord, then Caesar was not.

It was a high stakes enterprise, although we have totally missed the political nature of the gospel in first-century terms. Even the Christmas story that we so idealize is a strong political statement in terms of the actual Gospel presentation. Luke 2 certainly fits the definition of "gospel" as an "exceedingly good announcement" delivered yet to "shepherds," a lower and sometimes despised class of people. One should not, however, miss Luke's underlying message. It was the time of Caesar Augustus (Luke 2:1), a statement that implies much more than temporal characterization.

An angel (divine messenger) brings a message of great joy ("gospel") to those who belong to *Israel* (even shepherds) that a "Savior" has been born "in the city of David" (Bethlehem, not Rome), who is "Christ" (the Messiah, the expected anointed one of God) and "Lord" (one who will rule). Luke 2:1–11 could hardly be more explicit and more political, although we have missed Luke's message by idealizing (idolizing?) a babe in a manger (Luke 2:16). The message of a heavenly host of messengers in Luke 2:14 is "Glory to the Most High God!" (not Caesar, who was proclaimed divine) and "peace among men on earth" (a "peace" far greater than Caesar's *Pax Romana*).

Luke, of course, writes after the time of Paul, but he accurately and subtly describes a Roman world in which Roman power prevailed. We should perhaps set aside our idealism with regard to the "Christmas story" and spend some time meditating upon the deeper meaning of the words found in the "Magnificat" of Mary (Luke 1:46–55) and the "Benedictus" of Zechariah, John's father (Luke 1:67–79). Both are highly crafted political statements regarding the Gospel of God in Christ. Simeon's statements in the temple when the baby Jesus is presented for dedication is likewise insightful, in that God's provision of salvation for *all peoples* has come in the person of a newborn babe, "a light unto revelation for gentiles and glory for your people Israel" (Luke 2:30–32). It is interesting that the two primary Christological terms used by Luke in Luke 2:11, "Lord" and "Christ," are the same two terms that identify the risen Jesus at the conclusion of Peter's Pentecost sermon in Acts 2:36.

Conclusion

Perhaps with a degree of surprise to the reader, this chapter has focused upon the person of Jesus and the beginnings of the Christian movement. There are several reasons for this. First of all, it is hoped that the reader has begun to engage one's imagination. Initially, one may find it easier to imagine concrete narratives (as both the stories of Jesus and the early church development represent) than to imagine abstract thought (as much of Paul's letters represent). The stage upon which the events of the New Testament unfold is much clearer in a narrative genre as compared with a letter genre. Secondly, the story of Jesus and the development of the early church provide the overall context for the person and thought of Paul. Imagine the subtraction or absence of all four Gospels and the book of Acts from the New Testament. Imagine only the letters of Paul themselves.

Who was this man Paul? What exactly is he talking about? Who was this Jesus of whom he speaks? As previously suggested, at best the New Testament and Christianity would only be a shadow of itself without Paul's letters. By contrast, one can scarcely imagine a New Testament at all—even a Paul, apart from the Gospels and Acts. The context is the message. Apparently, in the early decades of the church there were oral sources (Q?) and written gospels that preserved or interpreted only the teachings of Jesus (the Gospel of Thomas, for example). In the story of gospel development and canon formation, the early church rightly preferred Gospels with a historical context and not just a collection of preserved sayings. Even Marcion, to whom is attributed the honor of a first New Testament canon, combined an abbreviated Gospel of Luke with ten letters of Paul. Where there is not an adequate context, an adequate message is not conveyed.

One cannot understand Paul in isolation from the person and ministry of Jesus, as well as the prologue of Christian beginnings. The church understood itself to have an eschatological mission of the proclamation of the gospel from the very beginning. According to the Synoptic tradition, the pre-Easter Jesus had sent his disciples out on mission. The resurrected Jesus commissions his disciples to a universal mission (Matt 28; Acts 1). The church expanded numerically, but it also expanded across boundaries that were ethnic, cultural, religious, and ideological. The Pauline mission included Syria, Asia Minor, Macedonia, Achaia, and Illyricum. Acts mentions churches or Christians along the Palestinian coast, as well as Samaria, Galilee, Cyprus, Cilicia, Cyrene, Alexandria, and Rome itself. Attention to the person and message of Jesus and the early church frames the person and thought of Paul. One can hardly imagine otherwise.

The *Pax Romana* or "Roman peace" effected by Augustus made transportation and communication throughout the empire possible. Earlier, Alexander the Great had made Greek to be the universal language or *lingua franca* of that world. The even earlier spread or diaspora of the Jews at the point of the Babylonian exile had likewise prepared the way for the incursion of an essentially Jewish gospel to move out into the gentile world. The Christian faith did not remain a localized, sectarian group within Judaism, as for example had the community at Qumran located at the north end of the Dead Sea (the Jewish community of "Dead Sea Scrolls" fame). The Christian faith became a universal movement with appeal to gentile pagans. While Jewish eschatology was not necessarily understood or fully appreciated, the Gospel's appeal to inclusion was significant.

The church experienced growing pains with regard to organization and structure. Initially, there was little organizational structure. Following the execution and resurrection of Jesus, the disciples simply met together to regroup. Several resurrection appearances occur in such a Jerusalem context, others occur in Galilee as the disciples have returned to an earlier occupational context. It is suggested that the Pentecost reflected in Acts may have historically occurred a year later, on the basis of a temporal gap reflected in Acts 1:15. A year's interlude would have given Galilean Christ-followers the opportunity to get their affairs in order and to relocate in Jerusalem by the time of the first anniversary of Jesus's death. It would also have offered time for reflection and developing interpretation of the meaning of the Christ event and their own commitment to the beginning of the Christian mission in the light of eschatological fulfillment. Where better to live and work than Jerusalem, "ground zero" of God's eschatological fulfillment.

Be that as it may, by the time of Pentecost 30 or 31 CE, the "Twelve" are reflected as having a place of authority. While Jesus is presented to be in charge in the Gospels, Peter appears to be prominent among the disciples (see Matt 16:13–20). He certainly is predominant in the early chapters of Acts, as in John. An early attempt at economic communal living in the area of Jerusalem that may reflect a relocation of Galilean disciples appears to have been an ultimate failure (see Acts 4:32–37). There appears to be no long term vision for an ongoing future of the church, in view of the near expectation of the parousia. "Daily distribution" called for better organization as seven men were chosen to fulfill these everyday duties. Among them were numbered Stephen, the first Christian martyr (Acts 7:54–60), and Philip, the first to preach to Samaritans (Acts 8:4–13).

The Gospel will be carried to gentile God-fearers by Philip and Peter (Acts 8:26–40; 10:1–48). For Luke, Peter's episode with Cornelius and his household marks the proclamation of the gospel to the gentiles (Acts 11:1–11). Paul has been called to a mission to the gentiles (Acts 9:1–22; cf. Gal 1:11–17) and will later begin that mission, sent out as he was by the church at Antioch, *after* Peter (an Apostle) and the Jerusalem church have affirmed the mission to the gentiles (Acts 11:1–18). It took the testimony of two witnesses who affirmed the same story to establish truth in a Jewish court. Luke is fond of this "rule of two" and thus affirms divine sponsorship of the gentile mission in the Spirit through the original witness of the Apostle Peter and through the apostle Paul, both of which came about through the Spirit.[1]

Growing pains continue with the controversy of the Jerusalem Conference (Acts 15), that occurred more than twenty years after the resurrection of Jesus. The basis for admittance of gentiles in the Christian church remained an issue. Specifically, the twin

---

1. While Paul may be Luke's hero, Luke does not see Paul as an Apostle with a "capital A." Paul in Acts is identified as an apostle of the church at Antioch. He did not qualify as an "Apostle" like Peter, according to the qualifications set forth in Acts 1:21–26. As Paul's own letters indicate, there were those who questioned the legitimacy of his apostolate. See Gal 1–2; 1 Cor 9:1–2.

issues involved were, what is necessary for salvation (circumcision or not?) and what is necessary for table fellowship (Jewish food laws or not?). These may seem like insignificant issues today, but they were apparently major issues in the early church's struggle to integrate gentiles into the new Israel in the age of fulfillment. There have been significant church controversies in the centuries since Paul's day over lesser issues.

Christianity faced a tremendous problem in the beginning—it was cradled in Judaism. Jews were generally not well thought of in the ancient world. In part, this was because they were strict monotheists who rejected all of the other gods in the larger Greco-Roman world. From a gentile perspective, the very safety of the city and even life itself depended upon the proper worship of these gods. Opposition, in part, was because Jewish customs were different. Who but the Jew practiced bodily mutilation in a rite of circumcision? Who but the Jew observed strict food laws that prohibited pork, among other things? Who but the Jew observed the Sabbath day in worship, while the rest of the world went about its business? And, then, these Jews came to town who proclaimed that a man named Jesus had been crucified on a Roman cross, yet the Jewish God had raised him from the dead and made him to be "Lord of the world" in the place of Caesar. What sense did that make? Christians faced a tremendous problem of credibility in that ancient world where the Gospel of God first began in competition with the gospel of Caesar.

If there were ever a Jew steeped in Judaism, it was Paul. Unalterably, he proudly and stubbornly remained a Jew to the end of his life. Called upon to defend his Christian apostleship, he affirmed he was an Israelite of the tribe of Benjamin, a "Hebrew born of Hebrews," one of the seed of Abraham (2 Cor 11:22). Paul was one who had been circumcised on the eighth day, in accordance with Torah (Phil 3:4–6). Paul was wedded to ancestral covenant and religion. Paul knew Judaism at its best and highest level as an insider. He was a Pharisee, a devout Jew who brought the Torah to every aspect of daily living. He could even claim to being "blameless" under the Torah.

Regardless of what "Christianity" has become in the contemporary world, the original movement called "Christian" was born into a world now long past. It was a world generally described as "Greco-Roman," in that it was still marked by things Greek and ruled by Rome. The age of classical Greece had been transformed by the conquests of Alexander the Great, such that Hellenistic culture and a common Greek language (Koine) had come to permeate the world of the Mediterranean basin long before the political ascendancy of Rome. Even with Roman rule, Rome assimilated "things Greek" as it made that world its own. The phrase "Greco-Roman" thus describes the historical and symbolic world of the first century into which the Christian movement was born. If one deems these things to be unimportant, then one is simply dismissing the foundations of the "Jesus Way" at the headwaters of Christianity in favor of some later version of "Christendom" or gospel not at all.

The person of Jesus, early Christians (such as Peter and Paul), as well as the writings that we know as the "New Testament," all have their origin within the matrix of that first-century Greco-Roman world, specifically within the matrix of first-century Judaism. It is a world long past. The three realities of Jesus himself, the earliest Christians, and specifically Christian writings all had their being and birth in the midst of social structures quite different from our own. As Dorothy suggested in the movie the *Wizard of Oz*, it is a case of "Toto, we are not in Kansas anymore."

If we are to understand Jesus—who he was and what he was about—we have to understand him in his context. If we are to understand the earliest Christian movement, we must reconstruct the world in which it developed, to the best of our knowledge and imagination. It is one thing to imagine religious fiction. That is done all too often today in the halls of "Christendom," even in the form of common theological doctrines. It is quite another to imagine the development of historical and religious reality from an earlier time now gone by. If we are to comprehend the New Testament writings in terms of the original intentions of their authors, we have to take seriously *why* they wrote *what* they actually did write to the real audiences they addressed. Otherwise, we live only with a truncated, caricaturish, and irrelevant characterization of Jesus, early Christians (Paul included), earliest Christianity, and the writings known as the New Testament. It is time, now, to imagine constructively and more accurately the person and worlds of Paul.

3

Imagine the Person and Worlds of Paul

AND, SO, WE COME explicitly to Paul the apostle. When we consider Paul, we do not deal with a fictional character. Paul himself, like Jesus, was a real historical person who lived in a first-century Greco-Roman world. He had historical roots and lived out his life in the light of the Gospel of God. When we first encounter him, he is a persecutor of the fledgling Christian church, called into being by the Gospel of God and focused on the resurrected Jesus of Nazareth. When we gain a last glimpse of Paul, he is about to be martyred because of his faithful ministry in proclaiming the Gospel of God in Christ across a vast world that was under the political rule of Rome. Paul himself was the product of several cultural worlds that influenced who he was and who he became.

Imagining the person of Paul does not suggest the production of an historical novel. There is a difference between creating an historical novel populated by fictional characters (or historical characters fictionalized), governed by fictional situations. One may speculate (as many scholars do) and remain within the domain or realm of plausible history. The employment of historical imagination may utilize the control of what is historically *typical* and known, in order to "colorize" or generalize individual historical experiences. One may remain in the domain of historical reality and plausibility, even though one may and must imagine.

There is a sense in which all history is fictionalized or "colored" to some degree. A phrase popular in our day is "revisionist history," in itself a neutral phrase that may suggest a positive correction or an inappropriate distortion. All recorded history, by nature of the case, is but partial and provisional. The book of Acts, for example, is a theological history that portrays Lukan purpose in its selection, arrangement, and presentation of historical events. It is a deliberate theological history. It is not an historical novel, but neither is it a filmed and unedited documentary.

While the lines may sometimes blur, especially when confronting secondary historical sources such as the book of Acts, there was a real person known as Paul the apostle and there was a real Greco-Roman city named "Corinth" in which he established a real church. And, we actually know quite a lot about each entity.[1]

---

1. One may view several excellent videos of reconstructions of ancient Corinth on the internet. One may simply look up "ancient Corinth videos" or "ancient Corinth images."

IMAGINE THE PERSON AND WORLDS OF PAUL

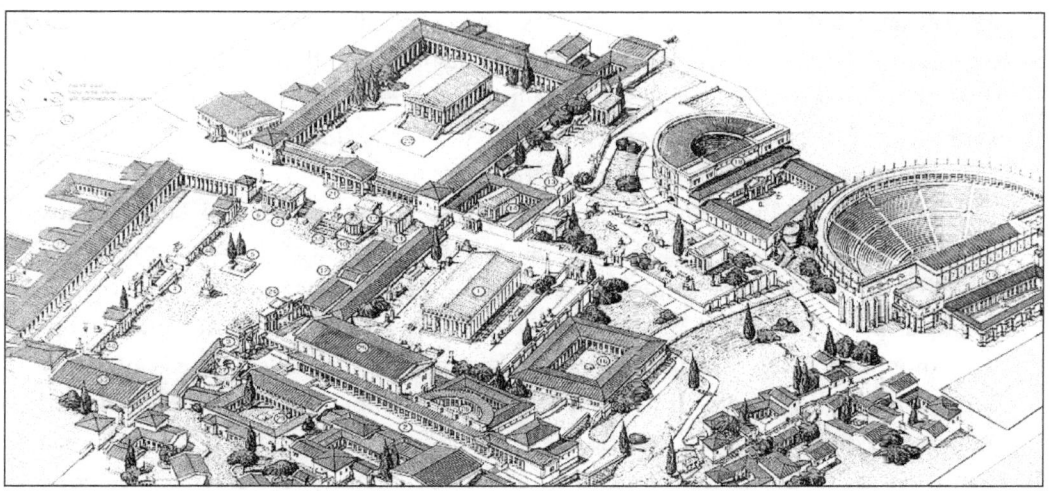

Fig. 6. Reconstruction of the City of Corinth. © Davide Mauro, CC BY-SA 4. Picture has been cropped. https://commons.wikimedia.org/wiki/File:Reconstruction_of_ancient_Corinthos.jpg.

One may note the central agora surrounded by shops at the left, with its row of small temples at the western end. The large temple of Augustus is at the upper center. The older temple of Apollo is shown in the center. The "bema" where Paul appeared before the Roman governor Gallio stands in the center portion of the agora at the left. The overall drawing depicts what we know from more than one hundred years of archaeological excavations of the central area of ancient Corinth, a metropolitan area of perhaps two hundred thousand people or more. Figure 19 in chapter 4 depicts a larger representation of the "bema," as well as the Acrocorinth that towered over the city.

We have letters of Paul to the church at Corinth that reveal the troublesome nature of a church loved by Paul. More than a century of archaeological work has revealed much about the Roman city of Corinth. Once one exhausts examination of the specific evidence available, one must interpret that evidence in the light of the general context. One employs both deductive and inductive reasoning.

On the other hand, one could suggest that the line between a novel and imagination is somewhat artificial and anachronistic as applied to the ancient world. Which is it for Luke's writing in Acts, for example? Did he write a redactional "history"? Or did he seek to create a fictional novel in the light of history? The speeches in Acts are widely acknowledged as a Lukan creation that are used to characterize and express Luke's own theological perspectives. They are not verbatim recordings. For example, there is not a lot of difference between the speeches attributed to Peter and those attributed to Paul in either content or style. One ought to compare them (see, for example, Acts 10:34–43 and 13:26–41).

Luke offers his own summary or synopsis, even if the speeches of his characters were historical events. For example, Peter's "Pentecost Sermon" in Acts (Acts 2:14–36) may be read aloud in less than three minutes. (So why are there so many long sermons today?) And, many scholars see the so-called first missionary journey to be the creation of Luke, a point with which the present author would not agree. As demonstrated elsewhere, it represents the first phase of Paul's Foundation Campaign according to Luke's underlying source (see STA, in *The Ministry of Paul the Apostle : History and Redaction* by the present writer).

Did Luke write an "historical novel" of inspired fiction, or did Luke employ historical imagination in redaction of source materials to describe "the way it must have been"? Did he write in the light of the knowledge and source material that he had available to him and in the light of his own purpose? Historical imagination appears more probable. Luke is not interested in just facts for "facts sake," but rather he interprets and presents his account according to deliberate purpose. He writes as one who lived in a post-70 CE world. He employs historical imagination in the most positive sense, as he relates the story of earliest Christianity, of which he was not a participant (see Luke 1:1–4). The present writer would affirm that Luke writes history in the first-century definition of that term, even though that history may include some imaginative and even fictive elements.

All history is interpretive. Both ancient and modern history involve events that happen, facts that are remembered, and interpretations that are given. One cannot escape interpretation, accurate or not. Luke writes history, but he does not write history according to a twenty-first-century definition of the word fixated on "facticity." Even facts and events must be interpreted in order to have meaning. Cause and effect are related. Luke writes history, but history with a purpose: he offers a theological history both *of* and *for* the early church in the light of his own interests and his understanding of the way it was (see Luke 1:1–4; Acts 1:1–3).

As an illustration, one might examine one's own identity of personhood and purpose. One may well recall where one grew up—whether it be the country, a community, town, or city, and whatever region or even nation. "Who one comes to be" is influenced by the values and perspectives of a larger community that extends well beyond one's own immediate household or town. Different social, political, economic, and religious forces exert their formative influences upon a person in ways that are largely subconscious. For example, as the present writer imagines with his recollection, he grew up in a town of approximately fourteen thousand people in the Southern United States in the post-war period of the mid-twentieth century. The writer's family heritage was that of a median middle class, characterized by maintenance personnel, postal workers, teachers, and office workers. The town was a college town surrounded by agriculture, which translated into an environment of higher literacy and generally stable employment. There was a fluid, multi-racial environment of at least three or more ethnic identities. The town had a significant historical heritage, such that long-standing cultural values both defined and sustained the community and its inter-relationships.

The present writer chose to attend college in another town within his home state, in the light of a projected and chosen field of study in engineering. Personal experiences led to a change of personal focus and to graduate studies in the field of theology in a *large city* in yet another state, hundreds of miles distant. A first employment opportunity arose in a small, private, newly established college in yet another large city in another culturally diverse Southeastern state. A subsequent employment opportunity arose at another private institution, this one long-established, that was closer to the writer's home town and extended family. Each station in the author's pilgrimage offered unique and diverse cultural values and opportunities within a very broad and general continuum. The current author's point is made, although the author's personal story could be developed at some length. The reader may likewise recount his or her own unique life pilgrimage, and one may recall with colorful imagination "the way it was," even relating memorable anecdotes.

There is a sense in which we are who we have been, i.e., our past experiences define our present identity. We are the product of our heritage, our environment, and our cumulative experience. One can recount basic facts of one's own life story, as the writer has done autobiographically. The reader may even now write a limited "biography" of the author, as one imagines a single specific life generally speaking, as it may have been lived in a "college town" in the "South" in the mid-twentieth century. One can imagine a shift from "engineering" to "theological" studies. One can imagine personal, family, cultural, and educational values that were definitive for a given time, place, and overall context in history. The result will likely be factual, as well as fictional. The author has not divulged his precise home town, although to do so would be to "factionalize" the author's pilgrimage and assist the reader in factionalizing a limited biography. The reader may further "factionalize" the author's pilgrimage by drawing upon additional source materials, such as the very brief "About the Author" given at the end of this volume. Our interpretations are not always accurate, nor necessarily complete. Our recollections at times represent "revisionist history," intentional or not.

The more detail that is provided, the more "colorful" an account of one's own personal experience will be. The point at issue here, however, is that one can imagine without forsaking historical reality in its basic contours. One can imagine beyond historical reality. One can even imagine a different scenario of one's own life as lived. The writer, for example, can imagine however accurately or inaccurately, by way of contrast, a life begun in a *large* city in another region of the United States or even Europe. One may imagine the result of different choices made, even in the realm of career decisions and personal relationships. One can imagine a different marital choice. One can imagine the result of a different career choice—perhaps as an engineer, accountant, or lawyer, instead of a college professor in the area of Christian studies. And, regardless of how satisfied we may be with our identity or with the choices we have made, we can always imagine alternatives. Imagination is an important, everyday aspect of being human. It is a gift of God.

Secondly, we are reminded of the importance of elements of our cultural contexts in the formation of who we are and who we may become. We can imagine alternatives, whether those alternatives be significant or insignificant. Should I take a new job in another place? What impact would that have upon my life? Should I choose this dress or that suit, rather than another? Which one would be more flattering on me? One can imagine before one ever looks in a mirror. Imagination involves weighing different scenarios and enters into many of the choices—significant or not—that we make, even on a daily basis.

The real, historical Paul likewise had a context of origin and of living that determined who he was and who he was to become. It makes a difference whether Paul grew up in Tarsus or Jerusalem, whether he was a Jew or a gentile. It makes a difference whether Paul accepted his dramatic call to proclaim the gospel to gentiles or not. It made a difference to carry out a counter-clockwise ministry in provincial capitals of the Roman Empire, rather than a clockwise movement that remained in Arabia and Egypt. Paul made conscious choices based upon personal experience, but he was also influenced by the various cultural, social, political, economic, and religious contexts that impinged upon him. Of all these things, so important for the creation of a biography of Paul, we have only partial information.

When one considers the "person of Paul," one cannot assume that (like the present author) he shared the values of a boy growing up in the "Southern" United States in the mid-twentieth century. The reader may re-imagine one's own contextual background. What about one's current age and educational level? Did one grow up in a city, town, or countryside? Did one live in the same place during one's formative years, or did one move from one community to another? How would the reader describe his or her family heritage? What were one's formative religious experiences? As one reflects and re-imagines, it becomes readily apparent that the reader did not grow up in a first-century Roman world. One's orientation and belief system is conditioned by one's personal experience based upon and drawn from a contemporary world.

In similar vein, Paul's person must be understood in the light of his own context, not ours. One must consider the "worlds of Paul" that shaped who he was or who he became. Examination of the worlds of influence—Greco-Roman, Jewish, and Christian worlds—is not an irrelevant exercise in pursuit of historical curiosity. It has distinct relevance for how one understands the person, mission, and theology of Paul. The better one comes to understand Paul's person, the better one shall come to understand Paul's theology. Paul cannot be properly understood apart from what we may discern as his historical context, or shall we say, "contexts." While one should not assume Paul was a contemporary personality with Western values and a Western conscience, a profile of ancient personality emerges as one comes to appreciate first-century worlds, contexts, and values. Background study is not irrelevant. In fact, the context is largely the message.

The exercise of imagination in the light of available evidence offers opportunity to employ methods and to develop models that address the dynamic of the universal human search for meaning. It is the human search for meaning that creates symbolic worlds for the living of everyday life. One may begin at the basic level of communication, where the very language we use is symbolic. Human beings organize themselves and relations with others on the basis of symbolic conceptualization of the world in which we live. While the phrase "symbolic world" may first of all appear to be rather abstract, it is really not. We live by symbols—they pervade every level of life.

A symbolic world simply defines that which brings shared meaning to our lives. Needs, perceptions, ideology, rituals, relationships, self-understandings, expression of divine realities—and the list could go on—all share in and create a symbolic world of meaning shared with others. What happens when a specific group confronts other, alternative symbolic worlds in a wider, pluralistic context? Tension that may even threaten group identity is engendered. Tragically, sometimes even violence ensues. Response may involve closing ranks to outsiders, communication with outsiders, or even conversion to the alternative symbolic world of outsiders.

The Worlds of Paul

The New Testament was not written for us, although we may appropriate its truths. When one approaches the study of the New Testament, one may speak in terms of the symbolic worlds that are complex and pluralistic. Paul's "world" was a combination of Mediterranean culture, Hellenistic civilization, Roman rule, and Judaism. The better one understands the symbolic "world of Paul," the better one will understand Paul's writings and his theology.

The more we seek to create a "modern Paul," the more likely it is that we deal with only a "false Paul" or a "fictive" Paul of our own making. We gravitate from "imagining Paul" to an "imaginary Paul" who expresses our thoughts and not his own. Paul was not one who embraced *our* contemporary social and cultural values, nor did he espouse *our* contemporary theological perspectives. Paul was not a "child of the Reformation" (sixteenth century) nor a child of the Enlightenment (seventeenth-eighteenth centuries). He certainly was not a postmodernist of the twentieth or twenty-first century. We do not perceive Paul's own true relevance by making him over in our own image in the light of our world. This is a temptation of which we must ever be aware and which we should seek to avoid.

Each of us is conditioned by our experience and our accumulated presuppositions. This is true for the average layperson, student, and accomplished scholar. One may be governed by what one has "always heard," by "we've always done it that way," by associative dogma, by essential ignorance, rigidity of rejection, or by the flexibility of extensive study and learning. By nature of the case, these things can create tension between those who approach a subject (Paul, in this case) on different levels from beginner to accomplished scholar. The antidote for such tension is to first of all openly acknowledge the issues involved, followed by both *self* and *subject* examination based upon available facts or warrants. One needs to acknowledge and be aware of one's level of knowledge, experience, limitations, and skills and abilities.

No one has a total corner on the truth, such that one must always allow for alternative interpretation, be it better or worse. The very word "disciple" actually means to be a learner. One, at whatever level, must be willing to become a student rather than a dogmatician. As one grows, re-imagining becomes a necessary yet humble enterprise. Otherwise, one only lives with an ossified doctrine of limiting understanding.

We need to learn to let Paul be Paul in his world, even as we seek to admit him to our world. As we learn about the first-century world and employ historical imagination, by nature of the case, it is best to begin with the more general context of Paul's day by which we come to understand and into which we may place the specific person of Paul.

Paul was a product of background matrices and influences that melded together in the first-century world. The larger context is that of the Greco-Roman world and the Roman Empire. Within that world, Paul was born and lived as a Jew. He was not a gentile or a pagan. He became a Christian Jew or Jewish Christian, firmly convinced that God was bringing to fulfillment all of the promises that God had made to Abraham and the covenant people of Israel. Whether "Christian Jew" or "Jewish Christian," he never lost his Jewish heritage and identity. He became a "man in Christ" as a Jew who believed Jesus was the promised Messiah (Christ) according to the Gospel of God.

The Greco-Roman World

The first-century Greco-Roman world was a world different from our own in many respects, but it is not a "lost world." Ancient literature and archaeological remains offer opportunity of access and reconstruction. Our sources are fragmentary and partial, however, such that any reconstruction may involve impressionistic sketches rather than full delineation.

Geographically, the Greco-Roman world was the world of the Mediterranean. The Romans described the Mediterranean Sea as the *Mare Nostrum*, "our sea." This world was Paul's world, geographically speaking, and is illustrated by the map at the beginning of this book. Even more than geographically, however, this world was considered to be the "civilized world." Temporally speaking, it had begun with the conquests of Alexander the Great (356–323 BCE). The influence of Hellenistic civilization ushered in by Alexander continued well into the new political reality of the Roman Empire that began with the accession of Augustus in 31 BCE. While Rome had begun territorial conquests during the time of the late Roman Republic, Augustus ratified a Roman rule that brought political stability diffused with the ideals of Hellenization.

Alexander utilized the model of the *polis* or city-state as the symbol that brought Greek culture to its best expression and full dissemination, including organization of religious activity. The city and civilization were considered to be coterminous, such that the Hellenistic world was conceived as an *urban* world. Greek became the universal language, serving as a powerful tool to convey all of the symbols of Hellenistic culture. It was so pervasive that even the Hebrew scriptures were translated into Greek (the Septuagint or LXX) by the mid-second century BCE.

Even new Jewish writings now began to be written in Greek and not Hebrew. For Hellenistic Jews living in the diaspora, as well as for the later early Christians, their "Bible" was the Septuagint. One should know, however, that literacy rates were low in the ancient world (estimated at 5–10 percent). Individual Jews or Christians would not possess individual and complete copies of the "Bible," a term that only loosely applied to differing collections of writings. The Christian "Bible" as known today only comes into being subsequent to 367 CE, some three hundred years and more after the time of Paul—and Jesus, for that matter.

A universal language fostered trade and commerce, as well as the rapid diffusion of ideas both old and new. It fostered a cosmopolitan identity that oftentimes transcended local identity and culture—one that in the process created local confusion. Greek became the language of trade, government, philosophy, and religion. It remained so under Rome, with Latin becoming the official imperial language at a later point in time.

Cultural patterns of the symbolic Greco-Roman world included an economy based upon land, characterized by village agriculture. It was a world of slaves and owners, of large households run by patriarchs. It was a world of status-seeking based upon patronage, in which severe disparities in status were negotiated on a continuing basis. It was a world of trade and warfare. Paul, for example, lived in a world in which all goods tangible and intangible were considered to be in limited supply. The Greco-Roman world was one in which the value of honor-shame predominated. One sought to accumulate honor and sought to avoid shame. Wealth itself became a means of accumulating public honor, a more highly valued commodity, as one provided funds for public projects. In a world of honor-shame, honor was to be sought and preserved and shame was to be avoided. It was a world in which family values of the time were protected and maintained. Once again, background study is not irrelevant. In fact, the context is largely the message.

While the ideals of classical Greece had been based upon the vibrancy of local traditions and identities, the Hellenistic world was one of universal empire and cosmopolitan syncretism. This syncretism affected religion and religious feeling. Local gods were identified with Greek counterparts. Yet the world became more ominous. As official and traditional religion suffered a loss of prestige, influence, and credibility, the encroaching sense of alienation fostered by impersonal empire led to perception of a world ruled by fate or chance. Official religious expression provided ritual but few answers, such that a new religious search for meaning originated that often found the answers for which it sought in the philosophies of the day. The growth of empire fostered bureaucracies, military enforcement, oppressive taxation, and a sense of personal alienation and lost identity.

The Roman Rule

The Roman version of empire was preoccupied with power, legitimized by its legions. Peace was maintained on a long-term basis through a complex system of governance that involved military colonies and explicit military governance through prefects and procurators. The empire grew through conquest, which resulted in a stratified society populated by a large number of displaced persons and slaves. Slave labor supported the economy of empire. Taxation of subject peoples could be severe. Under Julius Caesar, as much as 25 percent of a year's harvest could be required in taxes for Rome. In addition, client kings like Herod the Great and client tax agents (publicans) would gouge even more from the local populace.

Such an empire characterized by the *Pax Romana* or "Roman peace" required efficient transportation and communication. The Mediterranean provided ready passage between May and October, although it could be extremely perilous from October to April. Built for the ready movement of Roman legions, an extensive Roman road system of approximately fifty thousand miles by the year 100 CE provided for rapid transportation and communication by land. Imagine a Roman legion traveling an ancient Roman road, legionnaires walking in step and talking, as provincials are forced to carry the packs of Roman soldiers. Picture local provincials cursing as they see the dust stirred up by the measured gait of an approaching legion. Imagine small children peering from behind mothers' robes at Roman soldiers as they passed by arrayed in their uniforms and armor. It was a Roman world. The twin realities of availability of travel and Roman security encouraged both mobility and communication, two things very evident in the ministry of Paul. A universal language inherent in Koine Greek enabled preaching on the one hand and the acceptance of the Christian message on the other.

While on balance the Roman world proved to be a significant and positive force for the development and spread of Christianity, that fact did not mean that life was easy. Life was hard in the ancient world. Many children died by the age of five. Unwanted newborn baby girls, in particular, could be left on trash heaps to die or to be gathered by slave traders for future profit. Wars, famine, disease, and natural disasters could leave many adults dead by the age of thirty. It could be a world with few medicines, unreliable harvests, poor diet, poor shelter, and few economic opportunities.

Life, in fact, could be very harsh for provincials who were not Roman. Jewish Palestine is a case in point. Given the high context taxation and social marginalization, it is no accident that the Jewish revolt against Rome began in Galilee. Life in the great urban centers and even Rome itself could be difficult. Rome was fed at the expense of the provinces. Grain ships ploughed the Mediterranean constantly between Rome and Egypt, Rome's breadbasket. The threat of shortages always loomed large. Famines were a particular problem during the reign of Claudius (41–54 CE), the primary time of Paul's ministry. Streets in a city like Rome could be narrow, crowded, and dirty. Population density in urban tenements was high. Food was simple and sometimes scarce. Meat was a luxury item. Enjoyment of aristocratic privileges (upper 2–5 percent) claimed wide public spaces and sometimes country villas. The tenements, on the other hand could be sparse, smelly, and dark. Chamber pots of raw sewage could be emptied from tenement windows upon the streets below.

One commonly entertains a picture of total depravity of the "pagan" society of the Roman Empire. From the perspective of Judaism, the gentile world was considered to be morally degenerate and spiritually lost. Even pagan satirists and moralists, who sought to embody the highest standards within "pagan" society, could delight in exaggerating gentile vices in dramatic fashion. So, it is not surprising to find Jewish or New Testament writings that condemn life lived "according to the flesh" (see Gal 5:16–21; 1 Cor 6:9–11; Rom 1:18–32). It is not likely, however, that the life of the average person was one of "total depravity" that consisted of intoxicated sexual orgies, indifference to suffering, and infliction of occasional torture upon one's slaves.

Rootlessness, loss of a personal sense of self-worth, longing for real community, and a sense of hopelessness before powerful impersonal forces can all give rise to the awakening of religious responses in a search for meaning. In Paul's day, a sense of the need for identity in a chaotic world seemingly ruled by cosmic powers opened the door for religious solutions to one's plight. Traditional Greek and Roman religion with its temples and official forms of public liturgy and sacrificial offerings could be found everywhere. Magic, astrology, and superstition became very popular substitutes even among the sophisticated as means of overcoming the power of fate and controlling cosmic forces. Such religiosity was quick to be exploited by spiritual frauds and religious charlatans of all kinds who promised ready solutions to one's plight—usually for a fee.

In first-century man's search for meaning in everyday life, as well as one's search for solutions to life's problems, the religious spirit of Hellenism provided revelation for transformation that would bring a sense of identity and well-being. Prophecy was held in honor, as it marked either revelation or even a literal possession of the human by the divine. It could involve the inspection of animal entrails to discern the future, or it could involve ecstatic speaking in tongues as found at oracle sites such as ancient Delphi. Wandering charismatic figures, like Apollonius of Tyana, performed wonders and healings, being regarded as "divine men." Healings could be sought at shrines dedicated to Asklepios, where a "visitation" of the god would effect cures. Devotion to gods like Asklepios or Serapis could be deep, personal, and stimulative of a sense of community and belonging carried out through cultic ritual meals.

The so-called mystery cults gained wide appeal during the Roman period, as new deities from the eastern end of the Mediterranean found broad acceptance. Cults dedicated to Isis and her consort Osiris emanated from Egypt, while the mother goddess Cybele from Phrygia in Asia Minor was likewise worshiped. These cults were attractive, for they were both ancient and exotic in their expression, offering divine revelation, personal transformation, and a sense of belonging and community. People today yet seek for a "sound and a feeling" that will bring personal meaning and a sense of belonging in what may increasingly appear to be a callous, uncaring world.

The Greek spirit fed a pervasive religious response known as Gnosticism, which became a full-blown threat to Christianity as an organized second-century heresy. In Paul's day, *gnosis* or knowledge was more a mood related to a particular perception of the world. It tended to offer a pessimistic and dualistic worldview, characterized by flesh-spirit and good-evil. Matter or flesh was evil, spirit was good. Human life was seen to be imprisoned in materiality and thus alienated from its true source. Material existence was captive to cosmic forces, such that "salvation" marked escape from the power of materiality and the forces of fate, often personified.

The need of the "soul" was marked by escape from the "flesh," in order to effect a return to a heavenly, spiritual home. Such an escape heralded "eternal life." The Corinthian church was fixated upon a form of *gnosis* in Paul's day, such that knowledge resulted in self-exaltation of personal spiritual gifts. Many elements that are representative of the misunderstandings of Gnosticism that plagued the early church have become entrenched in some expressions of contemporary Christianity.

While "philosophy" (or the love of wisdom) in our day tends to be equated with the art of living in terms of metaphysics and politics, philosophy was a way of life in the first-century world represented by great philosophical schools of thought. In a sense, it was a first-century "religion" in which people sought meaning. According to Luke in Acts, Paul preached a sermon to the Epicurean and Stoic philosophers in Athens at the Areopagus (Acts 17:16–34). In Paul's day, greatest influence may have been exerted by Stoicism. Tarsus itself, recognized by Luke as Paul's city of origin (Acts 22:3), was a great center of Stoic learning. Recognizing that Fate, Chance, and political realities may be beyond one's control, Stoicism offered a positive response to reality with a focus upon the mind and personal desires.

One could focus upon personal virtues and duties, irrespective of external circumstance. The cosmos was deemed to be a rational place, governed by a kind of divine providence. Thus, if one lived a reasonable or rational life according to nature itself, one could become a fully realized human being. Stoicism featured the idealism of a virtuous, happy, self-controlled life of contentment. Death itself was a natural phenomenon and was not to be feared. Even social status (slavery, for example) could not threaten self-realization. Focus on personal virtue and independence of outward circumstance represented by Stoicism held great appeal for many in Paul's world.

While Stoicism was rather idealistic in its emphasis upon a perfection difficult to attain, Cynicism on the other hand was more practical and less theoretical. It focused upon freedom and free speech, associated with individualism. To live as one pleased, regardless of societal standards, meant freedom. The willingness to revile the "establishment" represented free speech. Uninhibited individualism was championed in the face of alienating social structures. As ancient satirists suggested, the cynics could be described as traveling would-be philosophers who did not want to work too hard at being a philosopher. Other schools of philosophy included the Pythagoreans and Epicureans.

The point in present context is that philosophies in Paul's world could be described as quasi-religious, in terms of modern understanding. They offered a sense of identity and experience of community. They offered association or group belonging. They offered deliverance from powers of alienation. They offered freedom. In their own way, they offered "salvation." Both the many forms of religion and philosophy marked responses to changing times brought about by the collapse of more traditional norms and symbols that came with the advent of empire. The values of ancient Greece were over-written by an alienating social structure of a Roman age couched in Hellenistic dress. As the old gods lost their force, the lines between religion and philosophy became blurred in an age that searched for and embraced meaning wherever it might be found.

Paul lived his life in one Roman province after another, under the control of a Roman governor, whether or not he was a "Roman citizen" who grew up in Tarsus. Jerusalem, likewise, was located in a Roman province, that of Judea. Paul's life and ministry existed during the reign of five Roman emperors who belonged to the Julio-Claudian dynasty—Augustus (31 BCE–14 CE), Tiberius (14–37 CE), Caligula (37–41 CE), Claudius (41–54 CE), and Nero (54–68 CE). One may inform one's imagination by pursuing articles on the worldwide web or internet pertaining to any of these emperors.

Picture Paul paying for lodging and a meal or a ship's fare with a silver denarius (about the size of a dime, enlarged below) that along with Caesar's image would proclaim Caesar as divine.

IMAGINE PAUL

Fig. 7. Augustus Divi F. Denarius. Photograph © Classical Numismatic Group, LLC. Used with permission.

On this coin Caesar is proclaimed with the strength of a bull, while on the reverse side of other such coins Caesar might be proclaimed as Pontifex Maximus, high priest of Rome. The Illustration is that of a silver denarius of Augustus Caesar that proclaims Augustus as "son of a god." A denarius essentially represented a day's wage for the working class. The gold aureus of Tiberius (worth twenty-five denarii) is also shown below and depicts the heads of both Augustus and Tiberius. Tiberius was the adopted son and successor of Augustus. If one looks carefully at the inscription, one sees that the aureus features Tiberius as "divine" on the obverse (DIVI) and the glorification of Augustus as divine on the reverse (DIVOS, DIVIF). One learns a lot through the study of Roman coinage. It provided a strong, everyday propaganda of Roman rule.

Fig. 8. Tiberius-Augustus Aureus. Photograph © Classical Numismatic Group, LLC. Used with permission.

Coins of all five Caesars who belonged to the Julio-Claudian dynasty likely passed through Paul's hands on a regular basis. They would be as common as coins featuring American presidents or the British queen or king. They would be the basis of commercial trade and payment throughout the empire, including small awning tent or leather shops where Paul may have worked. Within Judea itself from the time of Paul's boyhood until the time of his death, a full dozen Roman governors ruled and maintained order, from Coponius (6–8 CE) to Festus (58–62 CE).

Paul was at home in the Hellenistic-Roman world. He walked Roman roads and traveled a Roman sea (*Mare Nostrum*). Roman justice both aided Paul and condemned him. Fluent in Greek, he projected a Hellenistic heritage alongside his Jewish heritage.

Paul was evidently a diaspora Jew (a Jew of non-Palestinian origin), who felt very much at home in a Hellenistic environment. He was at home in the Greek language as well as the world of Greek thought, although he shows no interest in harmonizing his Jewish heritage with Greek wisdom, as seen in Philo. His writing style betrays a good Greek education, although he does not exhibit formal training in Greek philosophy and culture in any manner akin to a Philo (died ca. 50 CE). Paul could employ terminology borrowed from Stoicism or the mystery religions and use that to reach his gentile audiences where they lived. Paul proclaimed a Jewish gospel in a manner relevant to gentile audiences and culture. He exhibits the use of literary devices and rhetoric employed in popular contemporary teaching, such as that of the *diatribe* style of debate with an imaginary opponent (see 1 Cor 9; Rom 2:1–20).

Paul used imagery derived from Hellenistic-city culture, including legal and commercial and political terminology (see Gal 3:15; 4:1–2; Rom 7:1; Phlm 18; Phil 1:17; 3:20). Paul could reference Greek games (Phil 2:16; 1 Cor 9:24–27) or Hellenistic slave trade (1 Cor 7:22; Rom 7:14) or celebrations that a city might accord a visiting emperor (1 Thess 2:19; 4:16). One point to note here is the stark contrast between Jesus's rural orientation toward agrarian life in Galilee compared to Paul's urban orientation toward a larger Greco-Roman world. The Hellenistic Greco-Roman world was where Paul lived and worked alongside his audiences and various publics.

Paul lived and worked in the midst of a world characterized by things Greek and ruled by Rome and its deified Caesars. The "gospel of Augustus" existed long before there was ever a "gospel of Christ." As previously indicated, Paul preached an alternative gospel that proclaimed "Lord Christ" and not "Lord Caesar." The message of Paul and other early Christians thus challenged the accustomed political gospel of the day with a new gospel of what God had done in Christ. Paul's message and that of other early Christians was in the end antithetical to that of Rome. Paul owed nothing to the Greco-Roman world in terms of the *content* of his message, even though he could borrow some of its *expression* from that world. His mission was God-given, although the *contours* of that mission were in part dependent upon a Greco-Roman world that facilitated the spread of the Gospel of God.

The World of Judaism

In the first-century world of Paul, many more Jews lived outside the area of Palestine than within Galilee and Judea. Of an estimated seven million Jews in the first-century world, five million were to be found in the diaspora. One should not, however, confuse the phrase "diaspora Judaism" with "Hellenistic Judaism," for Hellenism was a significant characteristic of Judaism in Palestine and not every expression of Judaism in the diaspora was Hellenistic. A perennial problem that faced Judaism in general, as well as early Christianity, was cultural and religious assimilation versus separation. Assimilation to contemporary culture is a continuing problem for a contemporary Christendom that struggles to maintain a biblical identity as it searches for a gospel to proclaim to a postmodern world.

Separation from the prevailing culture in Paul's day marked the attempt to maintain the distinctive cultural and religious values of Judaism, as one resisted and insulated oneself from assimilation to the larger world. Judaism outside Palestine by necessity was forced to deal with the pluralism of Greco-Roman culture to a greater degree than Jews living in more localized Galilee or Judea. This is demonstrated by the fact that the Jewish-Roman war of 66–70 CE did not impact an already distinct, yet assimilated diaspora Judaism as it did the devastation of Judaism within Palestine. Still, Judaism in Palestine was not isolated from long-standing Hellenistic influences, which in themselves dated back to the conquests of Alexander the Great.

A thriving Jewish culture had been located outside Palestine for centuries that even antedated Alexander, following the much earlier deportations to Assyria (722 BCE) and Babylon (586 BCE). By Paul's day, the diaspora provided a natural centuries-old context and an accepted identity within the pluralism of the Greco-Roman world. Synagogues were established wherever Jews had migrated, such that they provided a center for the maintenance of Jewish identity and conservation of Jewish values in the larger first-century world. Indeed, as Christianity moved into the larger gentile world through evangelists like Paul, it was the Jewish synagogue that provided the model for preaching, teaching, and worship in the midst of Hellenistic culture.

Jewish monotheism, the high moral code of Torah, and covenant identity as the people of God had strong appeal for many gentiles who were attracted to synagogue worship. Initial success in the proclamation of the gospel was marked by the conversion of these gentile "God-fearers" found in the synagogues. Examples of such "God-fearers" (as contrasted with full "converts" to Judaism) may be seen in the book of Acts in the figures of the Ethiopian eunuch and Cornelius, a Roman centurion (see Acts 8:26–40; 10:1–48).

Paul could preach in an urban center synagogue and reach Jews attracted to fulfillment of ancestral religion, as well as gentile "God-fearers" who found the Christian gospel of grace and faith more appealing than the ritual requirements of circumcision and food laws. Through "God-fearers" already associated with Judaism and familiar with its Greek Bible (Septuagint or LXX), their pure pagan-gentile friends could more easily be reached by the gospel. Paul made use of this most natural approach to evangelism among his own people, even though he did not always meet with success.

Jews were significantly privileged within the Roman Empire, where in the light of Roman tolerance, they experienced freedom. They had autonomy in their place of residence. They were exempt from the obligation to worship other gods or Caesar in syncretistic worship, even civic gods upon whom the protection of the city depended. Failure to worship such gods might engender suspicions. They were allowed to meet freely in synagogues and observe Sabbath day worship. They were exempt from required military service. They were allowed to pay the annual temple tax in support of the Jerusalem religious center. Jewish exclusivism and privilege at times engendered resentment among pagan neighbors.

A Jew like Philo who grew up and flourished in Alexandria, Egypt, ca. 20 BCE to 50 CE, was able to effect a synthesis between Jewish values and Greek thought through use of allegorical method learned through his Hellenistic education. Teachings of Torah were expressed in terms of Greek wisdom without any sense of incompatibility. Through allegory, synthesis of Jewish and Greek thought proceeded naturally—inevitably and unconsciously. Even Jewish apologetic strengthened community identity, as Judaism was presented as a superior form of Greek philosophy and wisdom expressed in Torah. In a Philo, one encounters a diaspora Jew who was totally at home within Greek culture, who interpreted the deeper meaning of Torah according to Greek allegory and mystical connotations. One finds attention given to the immortality of the soul, but no attention given to apocalyptic preoccupation or expectation of a messiah or conception of resurrection.

Judaism in Palestine prior to 70 CE was anything but uniform. Ideological differences created multiform, competing Judaisms within a larger, consistent framework. Palestine was a small area, but a strategically located land bridge at the eastern end of the Mediterranean. The Jews who lived there had been influenced by empire builders who passed through the region time and again. The security of Palestine affected rule in the East. This was true for Rome as well. In the period prior to the New Testament era, as well as the New Testament era itself, Palestine was a land marked by strife. Following the time of Alexander the Great, the land was caught up in the struggle between his successors, the Ptolemies and the Seleucids. Antiochus IV Epiphanes sought to unify his empire by imposing syncretistic worship upon the Jews, insisting that a statue of Zeus Olympus be erected in the temple and that Jews no longer follow Torah (1 Macc 1:41–57; 2 Macc 6:1–6).

The ensuing rebellion on the part of Mattathias and his family, those "zealous for the law" (1 Macc 2:27), was aided by Roman support (1 Macc 8). The restoration under the Maccabean or Hasmonean dynasty marked a kingdom that was ultimately dependent upon Roman rule. The period of quasi-freedom under the Maccabees or

Hasmoneans (167–63 BCE) marked the only time the Jews in Palestine lived as a free people prior to the formation of the modern state of Israel in 1948.

Tensions and strife were thus especially true from the time of the Maccabean revolt (167 BCE) through the time of the Bar Kochba rebellion (132–135 CE). From the time of Seleucid rule (198–167 BCE) to the time of Roman rule (63 BCE on), the fervor of freedom from foreign domination and messianic hope reigned. Following defeat by the Romans in 135 CE after the second Jewish-Roman war, the hope of messianism collapsed. No longer was there any hope of a temporal rule over Palestine by a king of the line of David who would be guided by Torah. In fact, following the destruction of Jerusalem and the temple in 70 CE, Judaism was restructured around the study of the Torah. This came as a result of the survival of Pharisaism, after the demise of other Jewish groups such as the Sadducees, Essenes, and Zealots.

Tensions were already present and building during the time of the years of Jesus's ministry, such that when he came proclaiming "the kingdom of God is at hand," to have faith and come to a new mind-set in the light of the good news (Mark 1:15), that was a radical proclamation. His message was both religious and political, as previously indicated. To proclaim the advent of another kingdom, a messianic kingdom of God, was inflammatory, ambiguous, and even treasonous (see Luke 23:2). In the light of Christian emphasis upon Jesus as a divine religious figure, the political nature of Jesus's ministry and proclamation has been overlooked or even sublimated within Christendom, even though it is present on the surface of the Gospel records. According to all four Gospels, the placard above Jesus on the cross identified him as the "King of the Jews" (see Mark 15:9, 26; Matt 27:22, 37–43; Luke 23:38; John 19:19–22).

Response to the external influences of Hellenism and foreign rule were different among the various groups that developed within the area of Palestine. The use of Greek was pervasive, especially in Galilee. Warning inscriptions surrounding the temple in Jerusalem were carved in Greek, warning gentiles to go no farther beyond the dividing wall. Hellenistic architecture became evident with the building of Sepphoris in Galilee and structures in Jerusalem that included a gymnasium. The books of Maccabees that chronicled Hasmonean times, as well as other works, were either written in or quickly translated into Greek.

Even the rise of differentiated and antagonistic parties, groups, and sects owed their origin to the political turmoil of the times, from the zealotic, nationalistic rebels on the political left and religious right to the cooperative, collaborationist Sadducees on the political and religious right. While the Sadducees tended to be representatives of the wealthier, more aristocratic, high priestly families, the Pharisees tended to be more middle-class, urban, and Judean. They tended to become more a-political over time, focusing upon the extension of Torah to every aspect of life. They were not focused on either cooperation with or active opposition against Rome. The Sadducees may thus be characterized as politically liberal and religiously conservative, living cooperatively under Roman rule, while the Pharisees were politically conservative or neutral and religiously liberal. Their interpretation of Torah was "innovative," as they developed interpretations known as the "oral law."

The Essenes are the only group identified by Josephus that are not mentioned in the New Testament, though they are described as being thoroughly separatist in ideology, hence, politically conservative and religiously fundamental. One should not think, however, that every Jew in Palestine was either a Zealot, Sadducee, Pharisee, or an Essene. Collectively, the various parties were a fraction of the overall population. The bulk of the population, who have left no records as did the Essenes of Qumran, would fall into the category of the *am-ha-aretz* or "people of the land."

Ideological political and religious differences separated the groups, even if only by degrees. Pharisees could despise the *am-ha-aretz* for their failure to observe ritual regulations of Torah, such as tithes and purity rules. They could despise Sadducees for their power and ignorance of the Torah (the five books of Moses) and rejection of a larger canon of "scripture," including the Pharisees' own oral torah. Essenes could despise both Pharisees and Sadducees for not being holy enough in their social contacts or ritual functions. What would appear to be surface distinctions were actually definitional descriptions of what it meant to live as the "people of God," as interpreted by the various parties or groups.

The Pharisees were an urban phenomena generally limited to the area around Jerusalem, with some possible urban influence in Galilee, such as at Tiberias. If Paul became a Pharisee, he did so by personal decision in Jerusalem. Paul may have had limited choice of groups in which to lodge his youthful idealism. Josephus mentions the four different Jewish groups in addition to the hereditary priesthood—Pharisees, Sadducees, Essenes, and Zealots (*Ant.* 18.11–25). The Zealots became an organized political group of revolutionary tendencies at a time later than Paul, were more localized to Palestine, and would not likely have great appeal for a diaspora Jew, unless one was a "freedom fighter." The Essenes were highly exclusive and sectarian, having marginalized themselves in separate communities or isolated settlements such as Qumran. A diaspora Jew familiar with a much larger world would not likely find solace at an isolated location in the Judean wilderness beside the Dead Sea.

While mainstream, the Sadducees were the aristocratic wealthy class bent on power and political control. The great high priestly families, who ruled the country in cooperation with the Romans after the deposition of Archelaus, Herod's son, in 6 CE, belonged to the party of the Sadducees. Their autocratic style embraced a narrow canon of scripture (only the five books of Moses), which they interpreted literally and strictly. It was easier that way—strict religious conservatism supportive of a liberal cooperation with the Romans, who enabled their power. Wealth, power, and position mattered. High priests were appointed and deposed by Rome.

The power of the Pharisees in the day of Jesus and Paul rested in their influence of the clarification of the Torah as applied to all matters of everyday, domestic life. They commanded respect because they lived in accordance with the written Torah of Moses, extended and clarified by their development of the oral interpretation of the Torah in every manner imaginable. Celebration of meals was especially to be a time of absolute purity. More than half of their surviving teachings pertain to dietary laws, ritual purity for means, and tithing of agricultural produce. While Jesus judged them to be hypocritical (see Matt 23), they enjoyed the respect of the common people as an ideal religious figure. The Pharisees survived in measure the destruction of Jerusalem in 70 CE, such that post-70 CE Judaism in Palestine was largely Pharisaic. The writing down of the oral interpretation of Torah by the third century is known today as the *Mishnah*. It is the Mishnah, along with additional oral interpretation, that forms the basis of the Jewish *Talmud*.

Pharisees spent time in study and common discussion and had a tendency to concentrate in group activity with those of like persuasion. This facilitated the practice of separatism and holiness, especially at the high point of table fellowship. One is mindful of the social and religious setting of the dinner party in Simon the Pharisee's house, where Jesus told the parable of the Two Debtors after a "sinner woman" of the city had rendered the whole dinner unclean (see Luke 7:36–50).

All of this is to suggest that Judaism even in Palestine was pluriform as it perceived different gradations of religious purity and political expediency. Appreciation of religious symbols and realities was in flux, as different groups valued components of Judaism differently. Those who kept Torah most "religiously" or rigidly were seen to be descriptive of the "people of God" most perfectly. Consequently, different views existed with regard to temple, Torah, messianism, and the like. Different ideologies and perceptions of the times issued forth in different types of Jewish literature. Apocalyptic literature that expressed hope for rather immediate political and religious renewal in the midst of perceived persecution from without and transformational erosion from within also became prevalent. Strictly sectarian literature (as at Qumran) with its separatist guidelines and hope for living, to the development of what became known as rabbinic tradition following the catastrophe of the Jewish-Roman War of 66–70 CE flourished. Judaism in Palestine was centered upon the many aspects of what it meant to be the people of God. The catastrophe of the Jewish-Roman War was a tragedy for Judaism, as illustrated by the "Judea Capta" coin of Vespasian that depicts Judea as a "weeping woman." Rome is the "victor" and Judea the "weak" and the "vanquished."

Fig. 9. Vespasian Judea Capta Sestertius. Photograph © Classical Numismatic Group, LLC. Used with permission.

One should not, however, think that Judaism in Palestine existed in isolated, watertight compartments. Categories of what may be termed "apocalyptic," "rabbinic," "ritualistic," or "liturgical" were somewhat fluid, such that a given group could be described in multiple terms. For example, all Jewish groups were monotheistic and worshiped the single God of Israel. Jews observed the Sabbath day and circumcised their male children. Most worshiped and sacrificed at the temple at one time or other (the feast days), although regular meetings would occur in the synagogue (of which there were many). While there were particular group distinctives, there were common elements that constituted all Jews as Jews and distinguished Jews from gentiles. In similar fashion, one could identify differing groups within Christendom today (even within the same "denomination"), although the terminology might be different. Common factors might serve to identify one as "Christian," although differing doctrines or practices would tend to establish separate communities.

Jewish worship in the time of the New Testament was to be found in the home, in the synagogue, and in the temple in Jerusalem. While the pilgrimage festivals such as Passover beckoned Jews from throughout the diaspora, the locus of everyday worship and piety was to be found in the synagogue and in the home. Worship in the synagogue was not centered upon sacrifice, for there was none offered there. The temple was the place of sacrifice and where ritual activities were carried out by the priests.

The synagogue was centered upon the study of Torah, such that ritual actions were kept to a minimum. The synagogue was a place of meeting, prayer, and learning. Readings from the Torah and Prophets were given and interpreted, followed by a sermon that interpreted the text and its implications. Meals were considered to be sacred; they symbolized fellowship and spiritual unity. While it could be celebrated anywhere, the most sacred meal of all was to celebrate the Passover supper *in Jerusalem* as a celebration of community renewal and remembrance of the exodus as the paradigmatic event of redemption. It also expressed a contemporary hope for deliverance from foreign domination. Jesus's mission in Mark is a straight line from public announcement

(Mark 1:15) to Passover. The kingdom of God expressed hope in redemption. The Passover marked remembrance, but also hope of new deliverance. Passover was the "radiant" in reverse of Jesus's message and ministry.

In Paul's day, as one drew near Jerusalem one would see the great Herodian Temple on the eastern side of the city, with the smoke rising from the sacrifices offered there. One would also be reminded of the presence of Rome, especially at the time of the major feasts.

Fig. 10. First-Century Jerusalem Model. Public domain.

The tower fortress of Antonia north of the Temple Mount (upper right) housed a garrison of Roman soldiers who maintained order. The impressive palace of Herod the Great with its three massive towers on the western side of the city (top upper left) housed the Roman governor or prefect when he came to Jerusalem from his normal domicile of Herod's seaside palace at Caesarea Maritima. Between the Temple Mount and Herod's palace one would find the sumptuous quarter in which the high-priestly families lived in spacious houses with tiled mosaic floors (upper left). Business was good, even and especially under the Romans, in spite of the inconvenience of Roman rule. As for Herod's palace (top upper left), the towers stood as high as 150 feet and were named for his murdered wife, Mariamne, his friend Hippicus, and his brother Phasael. A portion of Herod's palace still stands in Jerusalem today.

To the south of Jerusalem, Herod built a theater, as well as a hippodrome or amphitheater, although the exact location is unknown. Offensive to pious Jews, the sites hosted pagan games and festivals and provided stark reminder of the incursion of Greco-Roman paganism even into the holy city of Jerusalem. While buildings and structures in Greco-Roman style were in evidence in Caesarea, Antioch, or Tarsus, as were Roman garrisons of soldiers, these things represented an alien presence for

Jews in Jerusalem. They provided a constant reminder of Roman subjection; the Jews were not a free people.

Still, it was the commanding presence of the temple that defined the nature and culture of the city. In order to placate the Jews over whom he ruled as a client king of Rome, Herod had greatly enlarged and remodeled the temple. The result was the construction of the largest religious complex of the Greco-Roman world, covering an area of thirty-six acres. It was built over three slopes, and supported by huge retaining walls. Covered galleries or stoa surrounded the Courtyard of the Gentiles on three sides—again echoing Greco-Roman style.

The original building was surrounded by a low wall with warning inscriptions that forbade the entry of non-Jews into the courtyards of increasing holiness. The Court of Women was superseded by the Court of Israel, the Court of the Priests, and ultimately the Holy of Holies within the temple structure itself. The outer façade of the sanctuary was layered with gold, which would have caused it to shine with a radiance that even superseded that of the golden Jerusalem limestone that gave the walled city a brilliance in the bright sunlight.

Paul, as a Jewish Pharisee living in Jerusalem, would have attended the temple many times. Paul's God was the God of Judaism. Paul himself was an uncompromising Jewish monotheist (Gal 2:20; Rom 3:30), such that he rejected pagan religion, worship, and pagan standards of morality (1 Cor 10:14, 21; Rom 1:26–32; Col 2:8). He did not propose a new conception of God. God was the living God whose dynamic actions could be seen in the promise to Abraham or the exodus from Egypt as well as in the Christ event. It was this God who had acted to demonstrate his power and justice, as he acted in Christ to usher in the long hoped-for Age to Come for the rectification of all humankind (see chapter 7).

Paul did not seek to create a new "religion," but simply adjusted his understanding of Judaism in the light of the coming, death, and resurrection of Jesus Christ, the one exalted by the singular God of Judaism. When one begins to think about Paul's perspectives, the implications for much customary and conventional characterization of Paul and Christian theology are highly significant as one begins to re-imagine dogmatic viewpoints long held. Many of these developed long after Paul, even though as "scripture" Paul's letters were used in support and crafting of doctrines that addressed much later issues that had nothing to do with Paul and that Paul himself never addressed.

The Christian Experience

Jewish theology within the broad spectrum of what it meant to be a Jew in the first-century Greco-Roman world was focused upon monotheism, election, and eschatology. Paul the Jew affirmed all three, but Paul the Christian was also forced to re-imagine his understanding of each of these three elements. There was only one true God, but the power and grace of Israel's God was now at work in the fulfillment of Israel and the blessing of the gentiles. The Gospel of God now at work meant the redemption of all humankind and the entire cosmos. Election was not ethnically exclusive, but rather was radically inclusive as a fulfillment of the promise made to Abraham.

And it was the time of fulfillment. The Age to Come had dawned in the present, such that the resurrection of Christ and the gift of the Spirit were the harbingers of its advent. Paul did not seek to formulate a speculative system of theology, but he rather sought to proclaim the reality of and the need for the Gospel of God in a new age. As a Pharisee, Paul had a broad canon of torah that extended beyond the written law, prophets, and writings. The oral torah was also deemed authoritative. While he came to question the supremacy of some of the ritual requirements of Jewish scripture—especially for gentiles, that same scripture remained the norm for Paul's thought and action. His Jewish scripture was now interpreted in the light of the Christ event.

Paul's ethnic and religious background predisposed him to look for a promised messiah who would establish God's reign. That reign would come through actions and deeds, not through new ideas. Paul moved beyond older, traditional, and nationalistic conceptions of the messiah as a divinely anointed king. Paul's gospel was an eschatological gospel, in that he believed the Age to Come had dawned with the resurrection of Christ. The apocalyptic thought of Palestinian Judaism became significant for him. Within Hellenistic Judaism, the temple was superseded by the synagogue, sacrifice by Torah, and priests by scribes and lawyers who were Torah scholars. Paul shared the expectation of the prophets, who emphasized gentile participation in the fulfillment of Israel (see Mic 4:1–4; Isa 2:2–4). The fulfillment of the promises of Israel's restoration were needed by the whole world, both Jew and gentile.

Paul and the earliest Christians did not create a new "religion," but rather came to see the Christ event as the fulfillment of their Jewish faith. To understand that Jesus was the expected Jewish Messiah, especially after crucifixion by the Romans, called for revolutionary re-evaluation. Jesus, risen and glorified, represented the fulfillment of God's promises. This, in turn, had to transform and redefine God's dealings with his own people. The focal point shifted from the Torah of Moses to the divine promise given directly to Abraham. Though it retained much value in many ways in terms of promises, the foundational story of Israel, and expectations, the Gospel of God in Christ suggested the Torah of Moses had been superseded. While not obsolete in many respects, it had served its temporary function (see Gal 3:23–29). Paul's experience was conditioned and redirected by the appearance of the risen Christ and his commission to go to the gentiles.

Paul inherited some of his understanding concerning Christ from those who were in Christ before him (1 Cor 15:3–7). Paul's zeal as a Pharisee had caused him to persecute Christians. Now, that same enthusiasm was directed to the proclamation of the gospel, as Paul became a man "in Christ." In fact, he became an "apostle" of God "in Christ," one sent with the authority of the Sender (see Gal 1:13–16). A dependence upon the early kerygma, liturgy, hymns, theological terminology, confessional formulas, and general exhortation are all evidence of early Christian influences upon Paul. The prophecies had indeed been fulfilled, the new age had been inaugurated. Jesus, born of the seed of David, had died in accordance with the scriptures (the Old Testament) to deliver humankind from the Present Evil Age. He had been buried, but he was raised on the third day by God, again in accordance with scripture, and had been exalted as Son of God and Lord of all. He would soon return as judge and savior.

Paul came to understand the gospel as the true expression of Jewish fulfillment. The resurrection convinced Paul that the Christian proclamation was, indeed, correct. Paul was not awakened from a dead orthodoxy of legalism, as a long-standing Christian caricature of Judaism might suggest. Nor did Paul rise from his visionary experience on the "Damascus Road" to embrace a new theology called "Christian" based upon a collection of objective doctrines to be affirmed. Rather, a Paul zealous for Judaism came to a vibrant, new, personal awareness of his Jewish faith as now fulfilled in Messiah Jesus. Paul now joined with other witnesses as a witness of what God had done in Christ.

Paul had cultural roots in Hellenism and training in Pharisaism. He lived in and was influenced by the Greco-Roman world and the world of Judaism. However, it was ultimately his Christian experience that determined his life and theological development. The compulsion of divine calling pressed Paul into the service of the Gospel of God as a distinct witness to that Gospel. Paul's vision and call did not bring with it a new God, but rather a new understanding of the God Paul had always worshiped and served. Paul's commitment was still to the one God of Israel. He remained committed to Torah, so foundational to his Pharisaic identity, but now its significance was transformed as Paul developed a new appreciation of eschatology, Christology, soteriology, and even ecclesiology, of what it meant to belong to the people of God through Abraham.

The "game-changer" for Paul, as for the other earliest Christians, was not the death of Jesus but the assurance of the resurrection. Even though "Christ crucified" (1 Cor 1:23) may have been an initial "stumbling block," the answer to a long-standing conundrum came in the form of "Christ raised." The resurrection and the parousia were like "bookends," circumscribing God's new age. Paul wanted to be a part of that, as he stretched forward, "forgetting" what lay behind (Phil 3:12–16).

The "Christian" Paul did not think of separate compartments of "Judaism," "Hellenism," and "Christianity." There was now a single Israel fulfilled in Christ. There was now no difference between Jew and Greek, slave and free, male and female (see Gal 3:25–29). The Gospel had transformed Paul, and through it Paul sought to transform the world until Christ should return.

The Personal World of Paul

When it comes specifically to the matter of sources for the life and ministry of Paul, most people know "Paul" best through Luke's narrative presentation of the development of the early church. Paul is introduced under the name "Saul" at the point of the stoning of Stephen. He is portrayed as a consenting bystander (Acts 7:58) and then as a persecutor of the church in both Jerusalem and Damascus (Acts 8:3; 9:1–2). From Acts 13:9 onward, he is known by the name Paul (Παῦλος in Greek). Roman citizens might have a tripartite name consisting of a formal first name or *praenomen* (as Gaius), a second name or *nomen* (as *Julius*) of the Roman tribe (or gens) that linked one to one's ancestry or patron of citizenship. The third element or *cognomen* was the name which identified the individual (the name most commonly used to identify, as *Caesar*). All three elements would be present in one's full name, as in "Gaius Julius Caesar" or "Tiberias Julius Caesar." Jews and Greeks normally used a single name. The name Paul (*Paulus*) is a Latin cognomen and is the name Paul always used to refer to himself in all of his letters.

Prior to Acts 13:9 and in the accounts of Paul's call (Acts 9:4, 17; 22:7, 13; 26:14), Luke makes use of the name "Saul" (Σαῦλος). The Greek form is Σαῦλος in the nominative case or Σαούλ in the vocative case of direct address. Paul never refers to himself as "Saul," an honored name within Judaism ("asked of God/Yahweh") but perhaps suggestive of the provocative walking of a courtesan in the Greek world. The Lukan usage is interesting or perhaps curious. On the other hand, *Paulus* in Latin could refer to "small" or "little." We know nothing, however, about Paul's stature or physical appearance. The apocryphal description of Paul given in the *Acts of Paul and Thecla* 3:3 (ca. 190 CE) as a man of small stature, with bald head and crooked legs is not deemed to be an accurate historical description. The New Testament does not tell us what Paul actually looked like. Paul's opponents at Corinth charged him with being weak in his bodily presence (2 Cor 10:10), although Paul's experiences through an extended, lengthy ministry would suggest personal strength and endurance (see 2 Cor 6:4–10; 11:21b–29). Generally speaking, we mostly imagine what Paul looked like on the basis of medieval or renaissance portraits and iconography that has come to surround us in the contemporary world. One finds these manifold anachronistic portraits of Paul on the many book covers of scholarly and popular works on Paul.

We have no idea of the actual date of Paul's birth, although Paul referred to himself as an "old man" or πρεσβύτης in Phlm 9. Paul uses a Greek term that can be translated either "ambassador" (*RSV*, *NAB*) or "old man" (*NRSV*, *NJB*). In the ancient world this term might describe someone over fifty years of age (fifty to fifty-six). It would seem that it could also refer to one who felt like an "old man," one who was "spent" after long years of hardship in ministry (see 2 Cor 11:23–29). While different ancient writers may address the "ages of man," there is an element of artificiality introduced by dividing the proverbial "three score and ten" into periodic limits or stages.

And while a given schema might suggest that the term Paul utilizes would refer to a man in his early fifties, one could conclude that an "old man" might describe one near or over sixty years of age as well. In the present writer's understanding, Paul's ministry after his call extended for at least twenty-seven years.

The prime of life for a "man" (a different term, ἀνήρ) might be defined by a range of years from twenty-nine to forty-nine years of age. Without further evidence, it is precarious to date the individual life of Paul on such a slender thread of a single reference that in Paul's letters is not rigidly defined. It could be a metaphor, rather than a literal designation. Most scholars feel Paul was born around the "turn of the century," although suggested dates range from 10 BC to 10 CE. That is a twenty year date span, such that one may only guess. We do not know definitively, although one may certainly speculate.

According to the chronology of the present author, Paul was martyred in 61 CE. He would have been between fifty-one and seventy-one years of age when he died. If he were martyred in 68 CE (as suggested by some chronologies), Paul could have been as old as seventy-eight when he died. We simply don't know. However, the present writer envisions Paul as a man in his early sixties at the time of his martyrdom. The younger Paul was a Jewish contemporary of Jesus.

According to Luke (Acts 22:3; 21:39), Paul was a "Jew," born in Tarsus, a Roman citizen from birth (Acts 22:25–29; 16:37; 23:27), who had a sister and nephew in Jerusalem (Acts 23:16). Luke presents Paul as a Pharisee who was brought up in Jerusalem, having studied at the feet of Gamaliel (Acts 22:3). The reference would be to Gamaliel I, who flourished in Jerusalem circa 20–50 CE. Luke's statement provides the only evidence for such rabbinical training. Paul himself is also silent with regard to the matter of Roman citizenship, perhaps because he centered his identity on being an "apostle of Christ" rather than a "citizen of Rome."

Paul does not tell us where he was born, although he boasted of a proud Jewish heritage. He was an "Israelite" of the tribe of Benjamin (Phil 3:5; 2 Cor 11:22; Rom 11:1), a "Hebrew born of Hebrews" who understood the Torah from a Pharisaic perspective (Phil 3:6). He exhibits a zeal for "the traditions of my fathers," as one who had excelled his peers in Judaism.

Paul was proud of his Jewish heritage (Phil 3:4–5; 2 Cor 11:21–22). Paul claimed the pride of an Aramaic-speaking Jew, suggesting his family was of Palestinian origin. According to Jerome, in his commentary on Phlm 23–24 written in 387 or 388 CE, Paul's parents were from Gischala in "Judea" and were moved to Tarsus by the hand of the Romans. Essentially, the same information is conveyed in his biographical dictionary of famous men (*Famous Men*, 5).

Disturbances followed the death of Herod in 4 BCE, one of which was led by Judas, son of Ezekias, in Galilee (*Ant.* 17.271). He broke into the arsenal at Sepphoris and armed his followers, which prompted the Roman general Varus to burn the city of Sepphoris and make slaves of its inhabitants (*J.W.* 2.68). These were then sold off to cover military campaign expenses, according to standard Roman practice. Gischala may have suffered a similar fate. Paul may have thus migrated with his parents to Tarsus in Cilicia, after Gischala was captured by the Romans. Josephus speaks of the fate of Gischala in his *Jewish War* (*J.W.* 4.84–120). Human slaves were a commodity, as much as other living animals (see Rev 18:11–13).

The village of Gischala was located perhaps twelve miles northwest of the Lake of Galilee in Upper Galilee. It was the last Jewish stronghold to fall in Galilee after the capture of Gamla during the Jewish-Roman War of 66–70 CE. Gischala in Palestine is today known in Arabic as *el-Jish* and as *Gush Halav* in modern Hebrew. It is located several miles north of Mount Meiron. It was famous for its olive oil. Jerome inherited the post-70 CE designation of the entire area of Palestine under the control of the Romans. Post-70 CE, the entire area was simply "Judea," as readily seen on Judea Capta coinage issued in commemoration of Roman victory in 70 CE as earlier illustrated.

Some feel that Paul's parents may have become slaves in Tarsus, ultimately freed and granted Roman citizenship. One could assume, for example, on the basis of Jerome, that Paul was a Galilean by birth whose parents lived in Gischala. Paul's parents are assumed to have been taken into slavery, following Varus's destruction of Sepphoris, capital of Galilee. They were settled in Tarsus, Roman capital of the province of Cilicia Pedias, as their new home. Whether Jerome's information is accurate is questioned by many. Such a scenario, however, could well explain Paul's Roman citizenship as set forth by Luke in Acts.

Tarsus had a long history of four thousand years as a result of its strategic location, ten miles inland on the River Cydnus on the trade route that linked Syria with Asia Minor and the Aegean. Paul's parents could well have been bought by a Roman citizen in Tarsus, who at some point set them free, at which time they would have acquired Roman citizenship. The Romans exhibited a consistent interest in Tarsus, such that Octavian confirmed that it was a free city and not a Roman colony, following his defeat of Mark Antony at the battle of Actium in 31 BCE. We simply do not know about Paul's date of birth nor about his childhood and teen years. The early years are simply lost from view. Nonetheless, we still know a lot about Paul.

Paul's use of imagery involving freedom and slavery may well reflect the earlier period of his childhood as a child of slaves in Tarsus early in the first century CE. Paradoxically, what some thought of as liberty, Paul thought of as slavery (Gal 4:9; Rom 6:17). What others thought of as a slave market transaction, Paul could think of as freedom (1 Cor 6:19–20). While for freedom Christ has set one free (Gal 5:1)—such that one is set free from the slavery of Torah—one is at the same time free of Sin, only to belong to another master (Rom 6:15–23). Paradoxically, the gracious gift of God comes to those who are "slaves of God," as one is freed from Sin and Death and becomes enslaved to a process of sanctification leading to Righteousness and Life—all, in Christ Jesus our *Lord*. In any event, one may discern that the world in which Paul lived conditioned the expression of his theology.

It is evident from his letters that Paul had considerable education. It is possible, according to Luke (Acts 22:3), that Paul was born in Tarsus and sent to Jerusalem for his education at the feet of Gamaliel. If Paul should have begun his schooling in Tarsus, the city was large enough to support at least one Jewish school (elementary) where basic values and skills would be taught from the age of five or six. In part he would have studied the Torah for inculcation of Jewish religious values. Any Jewish school in the diaspora would need to train Jewish students for life in a Hellenistic world. Paul would have learned many things informally in the midst of a busy commercial Greco-Roman city. Secondary studies would have begun about the age of eleven or twelve and would have continued for approximately three years and would prepare a boy for the beginning of the study of rhetoric at about the age of fourteen or fifteen years. One would learn to write and to write well, before one would begin to learn the art of eloquence under the tutelage of a learned orator.

Paul's letters exhibit a strong mastery of rhetorical style and structure, as were recognized by those of his churches (2 Cor 10:10–12). His letters indicate an underlying Greek education, in that he could write Greek and quote the Old Testament from the Greek Septuagint. He also made use of stylistic devices of rhetoric, such as the rhetorical diatribe common to Stoicism. He had such a grasp of basic principles of the art of persuasion that he could adapt them to his own purposes, either by way of parody or inversion or transformation of expected content. This is evident in the "fool's speech" of 2 Cor 11:1—12:13, as well as in his carefully crafted arguments in Galatians and Romans.

Paul's letters thus suggest he had an excellent education, both secular and religious, such that his parents had moderate means. Paul knew the LXX and quotes it almost ninety times. Paul had a command of Greek, with a mastery of rhetorical structure and figures of style. He exhibits a grasp of principles associated with persuasive presentation, whether he is enumerating his achievements, pressing an argument, or listing his failures.

It is also evident that he had some exposure to philosophical thought and training. The study of rhetoric would also by nature of the case expose one to philosophical thought. Tarsus was a center of Stoic thought, as illustrated by Athenodorus of Tarsus, friend of Cicero and court philosopher of Augustus. What effectively could be called "the University of Tarsus" was thus in particular associated with Stoicism, which was "in the air" in Tarsus. By the time Paul would have finished his formal schooling he would have been about nineteen or twenty. Because the influence of Stoicism was "in the air" in the first-century world, Paul could have caught its influence informally whether he studied it or not, whether or not he was influenced by Tarsus itself.

Paul lived within the tension between both the Jewish and gentile worlds. Paul made the choice to immerse himself in Judaism, which meant he had to immerse himself in the Torah of Moses. One can imagine Paul as a young man about the age of twenty in the early years of Tiberius Caesar's reign, joining a group of Cilician pilgrims traveling to Jerusalem for Passover, embarking on a five hundred-mile journey that could take six weeks. Such a journey would be an expensive proposition for a Jewish pilgrim attending such a feast. While the distance may be irrelevant in the light of speedy travel in the modern world, the time frame (six weeks in Paul's day) would still be expensive. Antioch, the Roman capital of Syria, would be a stop along the way. They could follow the narrow coastal highway south all the way to Caesarea Maritima, before they turned eastward for the two or three day walk toward Jerusalem. Once in Jerusalem, the first task would have been to find lodging, which would not be easy at the crowded season of Passover. One can imagine Paul electing to remain in Jerusalem after Passover and Pentecost to become a Pharisee engaged in the most serious study of Torah.

Paul identifies himself as a Pharisee (Phil 3:5), a connection that really can only be identified with Jerusalem. It would have been virtually impossible to practice Pharisaism in the larger Greco-Roman world of the diaspora, given the Pharisaic emphasis upon separatism and holiness in all things in the everyday world. While Jesus experienced Pharisaic opposition in Galilee, the opposition likely originated from Jerusalem or perhaps Tiberias, such that there was no widespread indigenous presence in Galilee. Defined "holiness" decreased, the farther one moved from Jerusalem.

While Palestine had long been Hellenized to a degree, it is not likely that the degree of Hellenization evidenced in Paul could have been gained in Jerusalem nor that his identity as a Pharisee could have been acquired outside of Jerusalem. In terms of formative forces, Paul appears to be a product of both the diaspora and Jerusalem, a combination that served him well in Christian ministry to a larger world.

Thus, one might conclude that Paul did not likely grow up in a Pharisaic household, but rather came to Pharisaism as a young assimilated diaspora Jew. Paul could have been moved to embrace Pharisaism as a result of a pilgrimage experience in Jerusalem that moved him to relocate to Jerusalem. We simply have no way of knowing precisely the details of Paul's earlier life beyond what he himself says and Luke's introduction of Paul at the point of the stoning of Stephen.

So, where did that leave a youthful Paul, a diaspora Jew with a bent toward religious but not political zeal (Gal 1:13–14)? Paul had a pride of origin, a strong grounding in Torah, a desire to excel, and a commitment to achieve (Phil 3:5–6). Theological debates stimulated group activity and belonging. This would have been appealing to Paul. As a result of debates between the "*zugoth*" of Hillel and Shammai before the time of Paul, Pharisaism could be sub-divided into a Hillel faction (more liberal) and a Shammaite faction (more conservative, more zealous). The *zugoth* were paired scholars of the Torah who represented alternative theological positions and interpretations. Some scholars have suggested the pre-Christian Paul was more aligned with the conservative Shammaite faction, given his zeal in persecuting the early Christian movement.

Thus, Paul would have likely been a young man in Jerusalem at the time Gamaliel I flourished (ca. 20–50 CE). He may well have belonged to Shammaite Pharisaism, a more zealotic faction than that of Gamaliel (see Acts 5:34–39; 8:1). We do not know how long Paul was in Jerusalem prior to his persecution of Christians and his call experience. If his call occurred within four years of Jesus's execution (April 7, 30 CE), he could have been between twenty-four to thirty-four years of age in the present writer's viewpoint. In contrast to the viewpoint of others, the present author views Paul as a *younger* contemporary of Jesus, who was likely in his early twenties at the time of Jesus's death. When Paul later writes 1 Corinthians (see 1 Cor 7:8), he was not married. Most Jewish men were married not later than the age of twenty. One can only speculate as to whether Paul was ever married, and if he were, what happened to his wife. If he were married, it is likely he would have married into a Pharisaic family.

There is no suggestion in either Paul's letters or in Acts that Paul ever met the historical Jesus of Nazareth. The beginning of Galatians where Paul gives autobiographical material would be the perfect place to affirm such, although he makes no mention. In fact, to affirm he had met the historical Jesus would have enhanced his argument pertaining to his apostolic authority given by God in his encounter with the risen Christ (Gal 1:12–17).

Paul was born a Jew and remained a Jew to the day he died, albeit a Jewish believer of the fulfillment of Judaism in Christ. Paul himself referred to his Jewish heritage in several of his letters—Gal 1:13–17; Phil 3:4–6; 1 Cor 15:8–10; 2 Cor 11:22; and Rom 11:1.

Once Paul came to be "in Christ," the strictly Jewish boundary markers such as pride of origin and ritual prescriptions of Torah became relativized (see Phil 3:7–9; Gal 6:15; Rom 2:17–29). Neither Paul nor anyone else can change one's ethnic origin—Paul *was* a Jew. However, on the basis of Torah itself, Paul came to understand that the righteousness which he sought through Torah rested on faith through the covenant with Abraham and was to extend to all, gentiles included. Paul came to realize that boundary identities were relativized by faith in Christ and supported by the example of Abraham's faith long before the giving of the Torah through Moses (Rom 4:1–25; Gal 3:23–29).

Paul had pursued Torah with zeal as the path to righteousness, but now he realized that in Christ the righteousness he sought was found in the Gospel of God. This left him with an ambivalent attitude toward the Torah, which is so evident in his letters. Paul did not and could not give up his Jewish identity of origin, but instead he found that identity realized in Christ. He did have to reform his Pharisaic views. Given his personality with his desire to excel and his commitment to achieve, Paul's zeal was re-channeled in Christ. Just as he had been totally committed to Judaism defined by Torah, for which the party of the Pharisees offered him greatest opportunity, now he became totally committed to Judaism defined by Christ. The turning point was his life-changing visionary experience of the *risen* Christ directly afforded him by God in his prophetic call.

We do not know how political Paul actually was, but it is possible that a pattern of false messiahs in a time of political tension with Rome led to his strong objection to the assumption that one who had been crucified by Rome (of all things!) could actually be the anointed one of God, the one who fulfilled God's long-standing promises to Israel. Tensions were building in the aftermath of Herod the Great's rule as a client king of Rome, followed as it was by the appointment of Roman governors to rule specifically in Judea after the deposition of Herod's son Archelaus in 6 CE. Luke certainly portrays Gamaliel as a much more moderate Pharisee than the more brash Paul/Saul (Acts 5:33–39; 8:1–3; 9:1–2).

The world was swiftly changing in Palestine and the Pharisees were equipped to change with it. Their agenda and vision of social and religious identity was much more flexible than that of the Sadducees. Respected for their learning and admired for their strict observance of the Torah, albeit as interpreted through the developing oral law, the Pharisees enjoyed popularity among the people. They were far more "down to earth" than the priestly and aristocratic Sadducees, in that they dealt with matters of domestic life, such as dietary laws and ritual purity. They were not tied to "Temple."

In the view of Gamaliel I, Jesus was not the first misguided "Messianist" (*Ant.* 18.64). One could ignore the followers of Jesus, for now that Jesus was dead and if his movement were merely of men, it would fade away. On the other hand, if it were of God it could not be stopped. Jews like the Pharisees thought in terms of sequential ages. The Present Age, characterized by Torah, would be superseded by the Age to Come, inaugurated by the Messiah. The Age to Come would be an age of blessings, joy, and gladness in which holiness reigned, such that in a perfect world the Torah would have little relevance. However, it was still God's Torah, such that speculative efforts sought to mention a role for Torah in the Messianic Age.

The Pharisaic Paul rejected the view that the Torah had no place in the Messianic Age as proclaimed by the Jesus movement, because he saw Jesus as a false messiah such that the Messianic Age was still to come. In the present, the Torah remained distinctly relevant. Once Paul was convinced that, indeed, the Messianic Age had dawned with the resurrection of Christ (which confirmed Jesus was the Messiah), Paul was left with an ambivalent understanding of the place of the Torah. It was still "holy and just and good" (Rom 7:12) and Paul could not condemn it, but if gentiles were to be admitted to Israel in the new Messianic Age on the basis of faith, what place did the Torah have (see Rom 7:1–25)? Once Paul changed his appreciation for Christ (2 Cor 5:16), he necessarily had to change his perspective with regard to Torah. Still, he found the faith of Abraham narrated within the Torah of Moses.

As a Pharisee, Paul's general impression of Christ may find a later echo in Josephus's statement that Jesus was a novelistic teacher who attracted followers (*Ant.* 18.63–64). He was perceived as a wise man and worker of miraculous deeds, who was crucified under Pontius Pilate. Paul apparently even went further, seeing the claims of Jesus's followers to be preposterous and Jesus himself to be a religious charlatan. However, Paul had a personal experience in which "he saw the Lord" (see Gal 1:15–16; 1 Cor 9:1; 15:8–9). Paul emerged from his experience with the absolute conviction that he had seen the risen Jesus, which meant Jesus was alive, just as his followers had been proclaiming him to be. It was a moment of illumination, a moment of change, and a moment of re-evaluation. It was a moment of revelation; it was a moment of encounter.

Paul had been a zealous persecutor of the church prior to his direct call by God (Gal 1:13–16). This was a turning point in his life that is best likened to a prophetic call. He was given a commission to preach Christ among the gentiles; he was not "converted" from one religion to another. It was his vision of the risen Christ that constituted his original identity as an apostle, as he became a "servant of Christ" (Gal 1:10) through his experience of a "revelation of Jesus Christ" (Gal 1:12). The divine revelation and encounter with Christ did result in a theological conversion of sorts (shall we say, "repentance"), for he had to revise his understanding of Jesus from one cursed by God (Gal 3:13) to one blessed by God as the long-expected Messiah of Israel (Gal 1:3–5).

Paul admits he was a persecutor of the church (Gal 1:13, 23) who had carried out violent actions against it. Luke likewise suggests Paul (Saul) "ravaged" the church in Jerusalem following the martyrdom of Stephen (Acts 8:1–3) and sought to extend opposition and threats as far as synagogues in Damascus (Acts 9:1–2), some 160 miles from Jerusalem.[2] It is in the latter setting that Paul experienced his call (Acts 9:3–19), which Luke recounts three times in Acts—once in historical narrative and twice more in defense speeches following his arrest in Jerusalem (Acts 22:6–16; 26:12–18). While the details vary, the fact that Luke presents the event of Paul's call in threefold manner is indicative of its significance for Luke. The event is connected with Paul's persecution of the church and is stressed by Luke in terms of its unexpected and overwhelming character. Paul's call did not mark the rejection of Judaism, but it did mark a reorientation of Paul's life with regard to sectarian Judaism, both Pharisaic and Christian.

A Customary Picture of Paul

The customary picture of Paul is generally drawn from the secondary book of Acts rather than Paul's own letters. The career of Paul's ministry as an evangelistic apostle sent to the gentiles is organized into three segments or phases, according to Acts. These are commonly referred to as Paul's "three missionary journeys" and are documented on countless maps with colored and dotted lines. Luke, the author of Acts,

---

2. The verb that Luke uses is λυμαίνομαι in Greek, which means something like "to destroy savagely, as with a mania." It conveys a strong verbal idea.

does not label or distinguish them as we have generally tended to do in contemporary presentation.

Luke is not telling the "story of Paul," but rather his purpose is to present a story that treats the spread of the gospel and the development of the early church through vignettes. It should also be noted at this point that our label of "three missionary journeys" only dates back to about 1742 CE, after missionary societies began to multiply and flourish in England. Paul did not see himself as a "missionary," but rather as an apostle (one sent with authority) and as an evangelist (one who proclaims the Gospel of God). It is we who have characterized Paul as a "missionary" who made "three missionary journeys." To think of Paul as a "missionary" on "three missionary journeys" is totally anachronistic and wrongly conceived on several counts. Paul did not journey forth to save "the heathen." He was commissioned to proclaim inclusion of the gentiles according to the fulfillment of the promise given to Abraham.

According to the Acts presentation as it now stands, Paul's "pre-Council" (see Acts 15) activity is set forth solely in Acts 13:3—14:28. Paul himself gives no details pertaining to his activity for the period of fourteen years immediately prior to his second visit to Jerusalem in Gal 2:1 (the Famine visit). However, the *underlying source* used by Luke to craft his account preserved in Acts does not contradict the rather sparse details found in Paul's letters. For a time, Paul worked in the areas of Syria and Cilicia (Gal 1:21, 23), working "among the gentiles" as he summarizes (Gal 2:2). He likely worked in the churches of south Galatia (Acts 13:13—14:25), following which time after a return visit to Antioch he moved on to Asia Minor and to Macedonia.

IMAGINE THE PERSON AND WORLDS OF PAUL

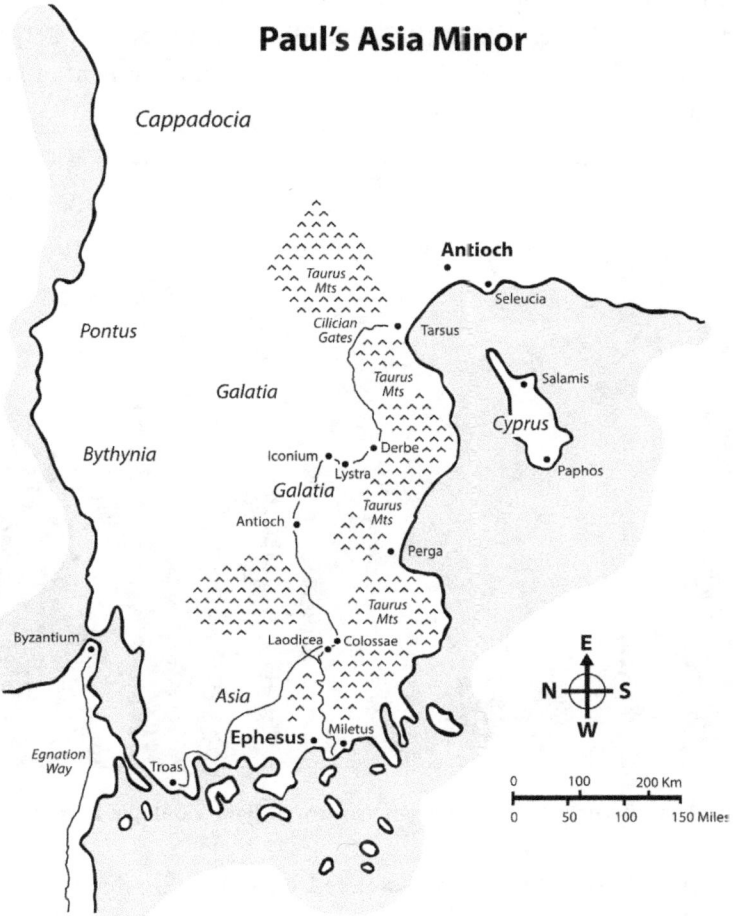

Fig. 11. Map of Paul's Asia Minor. Map © Jason Greene. Used with permission.

Acts presents Barnabas and Saul (Paul) being sent out by the church at Antioch. John Mark, the cousin of Barnabas, accompanied them. They depart from Seleucia (port of Syrian Antioch) for Cyprus. They travel through the island from Salamis to Paphos, converting the Roman proconsul Sergius Paulus, among others. They sail to Perga in Pamphylia. John Mark leaves them to return to Jerusalem, while they make their way to towns in South Galatia—Pisidian Antioch, Iconium, Lystra, Derbe. According to Luke, Paul first preached in synagogues if he had such opportunity. He could thus proclaim fulfillment of scriptural promises to Jews, as well as gain entrée to gentiles through "God-fearers" present in synagogue attendance.

While Paul first preaches to Jews in their synagogue, he announces he is turning to the gentiles after he meets Jewish resistance (Acts 13:46). This is the first of three occurrences in Acts where Paul states he is turning to the gentiles (see Acts 13:46; 18:6; 28:24–29). He never, however, forsakes his own people in Luke's presentation, in spite of continuing opposition. Paul and Barnabas retrace their steps, as they leave Derbe and go back through Lystra, Iconium, Psidian Antioch, to Perga. They sail from Attalia for Antioch of Syria. This completes the first segment of Paul's overall mission as narrated by Luke in Acts.

Fig. 12. Paul and Barnabas. *Archaeology Illustrated*, © Balage Balogh. Used under license.

In the Lukan presentation, the so-called Jerusalem Conference or Council is utilized by Luke to separate the first two segments of Paul's evangelistic activity. Compared to his source, Luke has shifted the location of this event, even as he did the event of the rejection of Jesus at Nazareth in his Gospel (see Luke 4:16–30; cf. Mark 6:1–6; Matt 13:53–58). Questions arose in Antioch with regard to gentile converts. Must gentile converts be circumcised and observe Jewish food laws according to the Torah of Moses (Acts 15:1–3)? A dispute arose that led the church at Antioch to send Paul, Barnabas, and others to Jerusalem for consultation with the leaders of the Jerusalem church regarding the requirements and status that should pertain to gentile converts. It is an issue pressed by Pharisaic members of the church.

After thorough debate and discussion of the issues, Peter's testimony pertaining to his experience with Cornelius, along with the testimony of Barnabas and Paul, seemingly prevailed (Acts 15:1–12). James (literally, "Jacob") appears as the leader and spokesman of the Jerusalem church and renders a minimal list of regulations, with which the apostles and elders of the Jerusalem church will agree (Acts 15:13–29).

The times were changing and so was the leadership of the Jerusalem church. The last mention of the "apostles and elders" is to be found in Acts 16:4. Given Luke's own emphases, Acts 15 is often viewed as a problematic and composite chapter in his storied presentation of the development of the early church. On the other hand, it is out of place, historically speaking.

In the Lukan presentation, the second segmented phase of Paul's mission begins following the Jerusalem Conference. It marks a continuation of foundational work, albeit now with clarification of the gospel, as Paul returns to South Galatia, travels through the upper regions of Asia Minor, and moves to southern Europe via the Roman province of Macedonia. Paul and Barnabas begin two separate missions with new partners. Paul chooses Silas and sets out from Antioch of Syria. They go through Syria and Cilicia, before Paul returns to Derbe and Lystra in South Galatia (Acts 15:40—16:1). A young Christian disciple by the name of Timothy, who was well thought of in both Lystra and Iconium, joins with Paul and Silas (Acts 16:1–3). Paul and company travel through portions of the area or region of Phrygia and Galatia.

Some see Paul as founding churches in North Galatia at places like Pessinus, Ancyra, and Tavium. Neither Paul nor Luke clearly delineate this, although Luke suggests they were forbidden by the Spirit to carry out work in either Asia or Bithynia (Acts 16:6–7, note the "Spirit of Jesus" in v. 7). They passed through Mysia on the way to Troas, where Paul had a vision that invited him to come to Macedonia (Acts 16:7–9). It is here that the so-called we source appears for the first time in Acts (Acts 16:10).

While some scholars will assume the *presence* of the writer of Luke-Acts in conjunction with the "we source," there are alternative explanations, including Luke's use of a source, or on the other hand, use of mere literary convention. The "we source" does not appear uninterrupted throughout the remainder of Acts, but rather breaks off and resumes. To assume the author is a "sometimes companion" of Paul is only a modern accommodation to a theological assumption of a particular view of authorship of the book of Acts.

Paul traveled from Troas to Neapolis, port city of Philippi of Macedonia, by sea and from there travels inland to Philippi. There was apparently no synagogue in Philippi, such that those converted by Paul were gentiles. Philippi was a Roman colony, which had figured prominently in Roman history. The church that was founded there by Paul was a church loved by Paul and one that loved him. They continued to offer support to him even after he left Philippi, as evidenced by the Philippian letter.

Early in Paul's ministry, the Philippian Christians partnered with Paul and later sent Epaphroditus to minister to his needs while he was imprisoned, likely in Ephesus (Phil 4:14–20). Paul's heart had been warmed and his spirit encouraged by this church. Luke recounts the story of Paul's arrest in Philippi at the time of the founding visit on the basis of economic disturbance and advocation of unlawful customs (Acts 16:19–21). Paul and company were beaten with rods and thrown into prison, only to experience a miraculous, natural intervention. Paul was freed from prison as a result of an earthquake (Acts 16:22–30).

The nucleus of the church at Philippi, at least according to Acts, was Lydia and her household along with the Philippian jailer and his household (Acts 16:14–15,

33; see 16:40). Paul is portrayed as invoking Roman citizenship only at the point of their release by the city magistrates. This struck fear because it marked a violation of Roman law to so ill-treat un-condemned Roman citizens (Acts 16:35–39). Upon their release they proceeded to travel on the Via Egnatia to Thessalonica, traveling through both Amphipolis and Apollonia. Paul's ill-treatment in Philippi is acknowledged in 1 Thess 2:1.

Paul likely spent more time in Thessalonica than Luke's acknowledged "three weeks" (Acts 17:2). Paul's message to the Jews in Thessalonica involved identification of the resurrected Jesus as the expected Messiah of Judaism (Acts 17:3). The proclamation of the gospel was deemed to be treasonous, involving another king than Caesar (Acts 17:7).

A controversy erupted that left the city in turmoil and Paul in danger, such that members of the church ferreted Paul away to Beroea (Acts 17:10). From there, he made his way to Athens by sea, leaving Silas and Timothy in Beroea (Acts 17:15).

Paul sought to proclaim the gospel of the risen Christ to the Athenians on the basis of general revelation (Acts 17:22–30). The Athenians misunderstood Paul to be preaching about a pair of gods—Jesus (masculine noun in Greek) and his female companion *Anastasis* (ἀνάστασις, a feminine noun for "resurrection" in Greek). According to Luke, they raised the question "what's this 'seed-picker' saying?" (Acts 17:18), perhaps in Southern English, "What's this 'woodpecker' trying to say?" The Athenian philosophers were not impressed.

Paul was apparently not very successful in Athens and moved on to Corinth, where he teamed up with Aquila and Priscilla, who had recently moved there from Italy (Acts 18:2). Silas and Timothy came from Macedonia and caught up with Paul in Corinth (Acts 18:5).

Corinth would be the western-most mission center of Paul according to the Lukan presentation in Acts (see Acts 18:1–17). Luke does not mention Illyricum at all (see Rom 15:19). According to the manner in which the text of Acts is usually read, Paul stayed in Corinth for eighteen contiguous months, during which time the Jews brought him before the tribunal of Gallio, the Roman governor (Acts 18:11–16). Gallio dismissed his case. Paul stayed many days longer, before he sailed for Syria, taking Priscilla and Aquila with him (Acts 18:18). He left them in Ephesus and went on to Caesarea Maritima.

Acts 18:22 is commonly assumed among scholars to reflect a visit to the church at Jerusalem, based upon the rubric that one always goes "up to Jerusalem" and "down from Jerusalem" in biblical thought. It should be noted, however, that the verse is rather vague and nondescript and does not mention Jerusalem at all. The return to Antioch marks the end of the second segment of Paul's initial ministry that retraced steps in South Galatia and moved as far west as Corinth.[3] As significant as Jerusalem

---

3. A reminder is offered that a summary portrayal of the customary ministry of Paul as presented by Luke in Acts is being offered. In contrast to Paul's own letters, Luke does not mention a mission to

is for Luke, in both Luke and Acts, had Paul traveled to Jerusalem Luke would have surely and clearly mentioned Jerusalem by name. Such a visit to Jerusalem at this point appears to be an unwarranted assumption. Overall, Paul in the course of this segment worked in Galatia, Asia (Ephesus), Macedonia, and Achaia. This was the provincial basin of Paul's evangelistic work. It is likely that Paul had his sights set on Rome and had traveled as far as Illyricum by this point in time.

In the third segment given in Acts, Paul travels overland once again from Antioch through the region of South Galatia and Phrygia to Ephesus, where he had earlier left Priscilla and Aquila. Ephesus would become his headquarters for this final segment of his active ministry. According to the Lukan presentation, this period lasted for two or three years (Acts 19:10; 20:31). While Acts says nothing of a Pauline imprisonment in Ephesus, a severe imprisonment may have occurred at this time (see 1 Cor 15:32; Phil 1:20–26; 2 Cor 1:8–9; 11:24–27). There was an uproar in Ephesus involving Demetrius and the silversmiths of Artemis (see Acts 19:23—20:1), after which Paul left Ephesus and traveled to Macedonia (the location of Philippi and Thessalonica), after which he spent three months in "Greece" (likely Achaia, location of Corinth).

Paul returned to Philippi and sailed for Troas after the days of Unleavened Bread (Passover, Acts 20:3–5). Although Paul celebrated Passover in Philippi, his intention was to be in Jerusalem for the day of Pentecost (Acts 20:16). The time associated with travel by sea to Troas and time in Troas occupied twelve days (Acts 20:6), which left but thirty-eight days to reach Jerusalem by the day of Pentecost. He would have skirted the coast of Asia Minor—Assos, Mitylene, Chios, Samos, Miletus, sailing on to Cos, Rhodes, Patara in Lycia, Tyre in Phoenicia, Ptolemais, and finally Caesarea Maritima. Nineteen more days would have been taken up in travel from Troas to Caesarea Maritima, where Paul spent "some days" (Acts 21:10, 15). The temporal references become generalized in Acts, although Paul apparently made it to Jerusalem in time for the Feast of Pentecost. Paul and company traveled with other disciples from Caesarea, all joining with other pilgrims traveling to Jerusalem for Pentecost.

Illyricum (see Rom 15:19). Should Acts 18:22 be a vague reference to a Jerusalem visit, the absence of any *direct* reference to Jerusalem would be very strange for Luke, given the overall emphasis to Jerusalem in the combined work of Luke-Acts.

IMAGINE PAUL

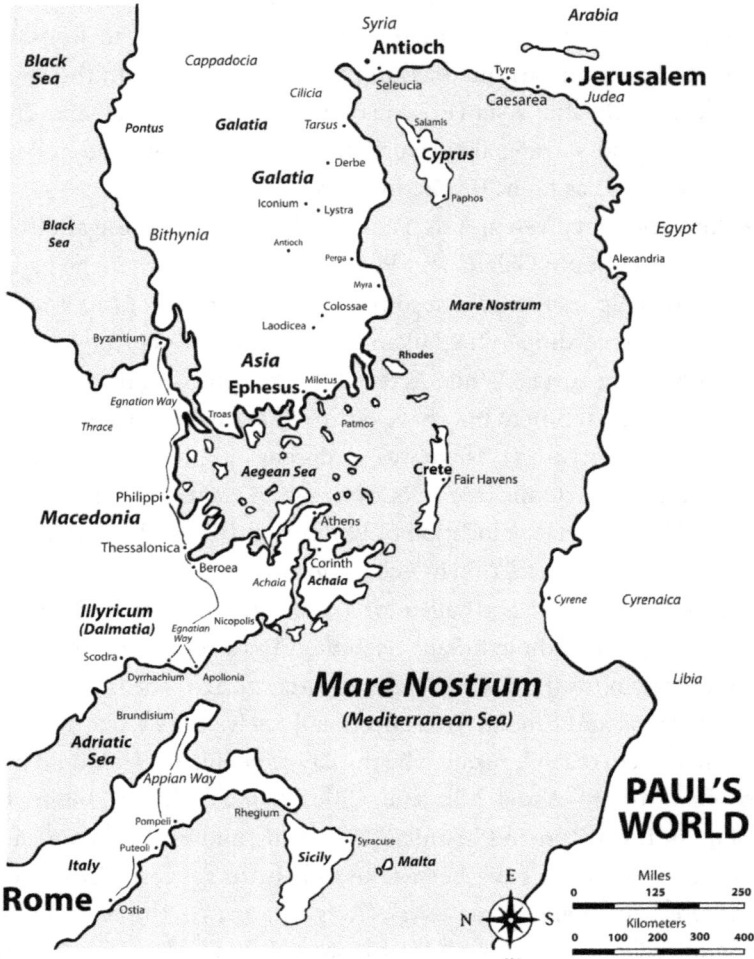

Fig. 13. Map of Paul's World of Ministry. Map © by Jason Greene. Used with permission.

Luke gives no reason for the third segment of Paul's ministry, although it is known from Paul's own letters that he was busy taking up a collection among his gentile churches for the poor saints in Jerusalem (see 1 Cor 16:1–9; 2 Cor 8–9; Rom 15:25–29; see Gal 6:7–10). Acts 19:21–22 does appear to echo Pauline travel intentions, without any statement of definite purpose. Acts 20:1–6 may be an oblique reference to the Collection in the underlying tradition, although it is not so acknowledged by Luke.

Paul likely arrived in Jerusalem with his collection in time for Pentecost, 56 CE. For the remainder of Paul's career as an apostle and evangelist, one is solely dependent upon Lukan information in Acts (Acts 21–28), which is essentially a period of multiple incarcerations. Paul is arrested in Jerusalem for his own protection during a feast period, a time of high alert for Roman overseers. Paul is brought before the Sanhedrin by a Roman tribune, who decides that he should be sent to

Caesarea Maritima to appear before Antonius Felix, the procurator of Judea (Acts 23). Paul remained under arrest in Caesarea for two years until the arrival of Porcius Festus, the new procurator, at which time Paul appealed to Caesar on the basis of his Roman citizenship (Acts 25:11). Festus granted his request. Paul's final journey took him, finally, to Rome, but under vastly different circumstances than Paul himself had planned (see Rom 15:22–29).

On the voyage from Caesarea Maritima to Rome, Paul was shipwrecked and forced to spend the winter on the island of Malta. At the beginning of the new sailing season, Paul is escorted by ship to Syracuse in Sicily, then to Rhegium, then to Puteoli (near Naples, modern Pozzuoli). He traveled the Via Appia to Rome, where he was kept under house arrest for two years. Paul was able to evangelize those who visited him in his quarters (Acts 28:17–28). According to traditional and usual view of the dating of letters that bear Paul's name, he wrote Philemon, Colossians, and Ephesians at that time.

Luke's reference to Paul's stay in Rome for "two whole years" (Acts 28:30) need not mark the end of Paul's life, despite the somewhat enigmatic ending of Acts. It should be stated again that Luke has a story to tell in which Paul is a principal character, but it is not Luke's purpose to write a "life of Paul." Luke may "characterize" Paul, but his overall focus is upon the spread of the gospel.

Did Paul survive the first Roman incarceration? Luke likely knew the end of Paul's story yet simply chose not to narrate it. It was not in keeping with Luke's purpose. Luke's characters, when he is through with them, are simply left aside. No one dies or is martyred, other than Stephen (Acts 7:60) and James, the brother of John (Acts 12:2). Peter and the other Apostles do not die or suffer martyrdom, neither does Barnabas. In like manner, Paul is simply left aside at the end of Luke's intended story. It was not in keeping with Luke's purpose that he narrate Paul's further life or the end of his life.

Those who regard the three Pastoral Epistles as a group assume they were written by Paul after his release from Roman house arrest. They would be testimony to a subsequent ministry to the eastern end of the Mediterranean. Titus was set up by Paul as head of the church in Crete. First Timothy would bear witness to Timothy as head of the church at Ephesus. Second Timothy would appear to be Paul's "last will and testament," following a subsequent arrest at Troas (2 Tim 4:13) and return travel to Rome (2 Tim 1:17).

Most scholars today regard the three "Pastoral Epistles" (1 Timothy, 2 Timothy, and Titus) as written by someone other than Paul but under Paul's name. Hence, they are termed "pseudepigraphical," likely written by a disciple of Paul. Later church traditions, perhaps heavily laced with legends, suggest Paul went to Spain after his first two years of house arrest in Rome, thus testifying to the fulfillment of his announced plans seen in Rom 15:24, 28.

Clement of Rome testifies that Paul reached the limits of the West, which would have been Spain (Clement, 1 Cor 5.7). Clement's testimony (ca. 95 CE) suggests thereby a further ministry to the *west* and another trial, followed by martyrdom. Eusebius (*Hist. eccl.* 2.22.3) is the first to mention a second imprisonment in Rome, with a following martyrdom under Nero. Second Timothy would have been written at this time, according to this view. The testimony of Eusebius (d. 339 CE), which is widely accepted, would place Paul's death at some point during the Neronian persecution of Christians in Rome, that began in the summer of 64 CE and lasted until the time of Nero's death on June 9, 68 CE. Eusebius's testimony comes more than 250 years—some two and one-half centuries—after the death of Paul.

A Summary Evaluation

The above sketch is primarily based upon the account found in Acts. The present author will propose an alternative paradigm for understanding Paul's ministry in the following two chapters. While it may commonly be assumed that "Luke the physician, the companion of Paul" is responsible for the writing of Acts, that presuppositional conclusion is not likely correct. The assumption is made on the basis of the appearance of the "we source" travel diary, among other things. On the basis of reference to a Luke in the Colossian letter (Col 4:11, 14), it is also assumed that Luke is the "only gentile writer" of a New Testament work. Both assumptions or presuppositions are likely wrong.

First of all, Luke (the author of Luke-Acts) was a gifted writer. It was common in the ancient world to employ a "recording secretary" or *amanuensis*. One may see this reflected in Rom 16:22 or 1 Pet 5:12. There is never an acknowledgment in any of Paul's extant letters that Luke served as an amanuensis. And, if Paul had such ready access to such an accomplished writer, then why not use him? Secondly, many of Paul's letters have co-senders, such as "Paul, Silvanus, and Timothy." Luke is never listed as a co-sender of any of Paul's letters. Thirdly, Paul wrote letters to his churches as a substitute for a visit. However, if we only had the book of Acts, we would never know Paul ever wrote a single letter. Fourthly, significant theological themes that are basic to Paul's own letters are absent in the speeches of Acts attributed to Paul. Finally, as will be shown, the latter part of Paul's active ministry involved taking up a collection of money from his gentile churches for the poor saints in Jerusalem. As will be shown, this was the dominant intent and force of Paul's latter ministry after the Jerusalem Conference. Luke never mentions the Collection, such that again, we would never know about it if we only had the book of Acts and did not have Paul's own letters.

Altogether, it appears that Acts was written at a time significantly later than the life of Paul by one who was not a companion of Paul. Estimates for the time of writing of Acts as earlier stated vary from about 80 CE to 120 CE. We call the author "Luke" (his name never appears in the *text* of the Gospel or Acts) and he was a very skilled writer. The collective evidence, however, would suggest that he was not the companion of Paul. In fact, he identifies himself as a second or perhaps a third generation Christian (see Luke 1:1–4). He makes use of earlier source material available to him, such as the Gospel of Mark in the writing of his gospel and a connected source tradition for the production of Acts.

This source tradition as it would pertain to Paul has been developed in the present writer's earlier book, *The Ministry of Paul the Apostle: History and Redaction*, as the "Source Tradition of Acts" or STA. It may be found there in its entirety. In the current work, occasional reference will be made to Luke's Source, STA, with a chapter and verse designation. Such designation will recognize Luke's use of underlying source material. For simplicity's sake, such reference will employ the chapter and verse designation found in the present Acts account, although the ordered location or wording of content may not accord exactly with what one might read in the Lukan account in Acts.

If one is to observe the usual canons of historical investigation, then one should consult the primary sources as central for the study of Paul's life and ministry (in this case, Paul's own letters), against which the secondary presentation of Luke in Acts should then be understood. Two additional points may be made, however. First, given the incomplete and periodic nature of both source materials (the letters and Acts), an adequate sketch of Paul's ministry requires the use of both the letters and Acts. Secondly, while the letters are primary, the underlying source tradition used by Luke in Acts appears to be quite valuable.

A ready comparison of the ministry of Paul reflected in his letters comports quite well as compared with the presentation of Paul's ministry *in the underlying source material of Acts* that is not characterized by Lukan redaction (i.e., the STA). Perceived discrepancies and problems that arise in comparison of the *present* book of Acts and the letters of Paul must be charged to Lukan adaptation or redaction, i.e., the deliberate changes that Luke made in the available source material in order to tell the story of the development of the early church he wished to relate. This is thoroughly treated in the author's earlier aforementioned work.

When the underlying source material (the STA) used by Luke in Acts is taken into account along with Paul's letters, it is necessary to re-imagine the overall ministry of Paul. Paul did not engage in "three missionary journeys," but rather in two major campaigns. He moved counter-clockwise through major Roman provinces surrounding the Mediterranean Sea, working to proclaim the gospel in great urban centers or provincial capitals of that Greco-Roman world. His intent was always to work his way to Rome and to claim the whole world (as far as Spain!) for Christ. From his call to his death, Paul engaged in a ministry/mission that extended beyond a quarter of a century—a period of approximately twenty-seven years.

When one realizes this fact, it becomes self-evident that all of our sources for the life of Paul are limited and can only offer vignettes of understanding. We do not have a full and entire documentary by any stretch of the imagination. We have nothing like the "memoirs of Paul" that would offer a connected and orderly twenty-seven year long account. We only have a collection of snapshots given in no particular order by the canonical collection of Paul's letters and a single, connected and comparatively brief summary in Acts offered by Lukan redaction of underlying source material. There are many temporal gaps in the sixteen chapters of Acts that feature Paul as part of Luke's story of the development and spread of the early church. Luke "imagined Paul" in the most positive sense of that phrase, and we are called upon to do the same.

Paul was a man of three worlds—Jewish, Hellenistic (or Greco-Roman), and Christian. Paul's experience both blends and transcends these three worlds. Still, he is informed by all three. Born a Jew, Paul was reared within a strict, Jewish heritage of which he was very proud (Phil 3:5–6; Rom 9:3; 11:1). He lived the early part of his adulthood as a zealous Pharisee in faultless obedience to Torah (see Gal 1:14; Phil 3:6; 2 Cor 11:22). He may have belonged to the Shammaite branch of Pharisaism, a more right-wing movement within Pharisaism that zealously worked for the fulfillment of scriptural prophecies.

Neither Judaism nor Pharisaism, however, existed in a water-tight compartment, for Hellenism in the form of Greek language, thought, and culture had invaded Palestine some three hundred years earlier with the conquest of Alexander the Great. From the time of the exile, Jews had spread throughout the Mediterranean world in a movement known as the diaspora. Paul himself may have been a diaspora Jew, if, indeed, he was from Tarsus (see Acts 22:3), a claim Paul himself never makes. His ministry was carried out within the larger Greco-Roman world, such that his audiences comprised Hellenistic Jews, "God-fearers," and pagan gentiles. Paul was embraced by God through a vision of the risen Christ and commissioned to preach the gospel to the larger gentile world. That larger gentile world was the Roman Empire. He became a man "in Christ," a "Christian" (although he doesn't use the term), or one who found the fulfillment of Israel to rest in what God had done through Christ. While Hellenistic influences may have determined his interactions with his gentile congregations, Judaism was the basic matrix of Paul's thought.

Paul did not turn his back on Torah, but rather his shared Christian experience and personal call drove him back to the foundational story of Abraham *found in Torah*. It is Torah itself that informs much of Paul's theology, as the matter of faith became universally paramount over legalistic elements within Torah. It is a false caricature drawn from earlier Christian history that assumes Paul was "converted" from a load of guilt and psychological baggage. Paul was not "converted" from disbelief to faith, from irreligion to religion, from sinfulness to righteousness, or even from one religion to another. Paul came to understand the gospel as the true expression of Jewish fulfillment.

While the word "conversion" might apply to the change that occurred in Paul as he moved from persecutor to proclaimer as a result of his call, perhaps surprisingly the word "repentance" (a change of mind-set or understanding) or "rededication" might better describe his embrace of Christianity in terms of theological understanding. Paul experienced a "call" and underwent a necessary revision of his thought as a result of that call.

The resurrection convinced Paul that the Christian proclamation was, indeed, correct. Paul was not awakened from a dead orthodoxy of legalism, as a Christian caricature of Judaism might suggest. Nor did Paul rise from his visionary experience on the "Damascus Road" to embrace a new theology called "Christian" based upon a new collection of objective doctrines to be affirmed. Rather, a Paul zealous for Judaism came to a vibrant, new, personal awareness of his Jewish faith as now fulfilled in Messiah Jesus. Paul now joined with other witnesses as a witness of what God had done in Christ. Paul witnessed to the Gospel of God.

If one consults Paul's letters first, before consulting Acts, a new paradigm for understanding Paul's ministry emerges. As will be seen, the new paradigm involves a *Foundation Campaign* by Paul carried out in two phases, followed by a singular *Collection Campaign*. The purpose of the Foundation Campaign is self-evident, namely, the proclamation of the Gospel of God in Christ in the larger gentile Greco-Roman world. The purpose of the Collection Campaign was to unify a divided church at the eastern end of the Mediterranean prior to any new work to be undertaken by Paul in areas as far west as Rome and Spain (Rom 15:22–29). In the present writer's judgment, the suggested new paradigm of two campaigns offers greater historical clarity for appreciating Paul's service of the Gospel of God "in Christ."

4

Imagine Paul's Foundation Campaign

MOST PEOPLE APPEAR TO enjoy a good mystery. In this instance, the mystery is how to define the contours of Paul's mission and ministry. One might think—given the traditional or customary contours of "missionary journeys" set forth in the prior chapter—there is no issue. Others might think that Paul's ministry itself is really irrelevant to his "theology" and various theological doctrines based upon what Paul says. The truth of the matter is different. The "context is the message."

Paul's theological and ethical instruction is largely tied to the *who, where*, and *what* Paul was facing as he wrote his very occasional letters. The abiding relevance of Paul is couched in his ministry. The mystery of his mission that governed his theology awaits discovery in the correlation of our sources that set it forth. One may develop and set forth a brief outline as is done in many scholarly works, but it should be remembered that Paul was more than an outline and more than a religious icon. According to his own testimony, he was a "man in Christ," given a mission by the direct call of God (Gal 1:11–17).

Paul's visits to Jerusalem provide an organizational key for developing the overall ministry of Paul. Why, for example, does he emphatically state that he did not go up to Jerusalem following his call (see Gal 1:17)? Why does he organize his own autobiographical account around visits to Jerusalem (see Gal 1:18; 2:1)? Given the different accounts in Paul's letters and the book of Acts, the correlation regarding Paul's visits to Jerusalem following his call is the most difficult matter regarding any reconstruction of Paul's ministry. Even though at points perhaps technical, the reader is invited to participate in the equivalent of the investigation of a mystery, maybe even a long-standing "cold case."

The problem is the correlation of what Luke says in Acts and what Paul says in his letters. Paul recounts two visits to Jerusalem after his call (Gal 1:18; 2:1) and announces a third planned visit to take his collection to Jerusalem (Rom 15:25). Luke, on the other hand, according to many scholars, suggests five or even six visits to Jerusalem (see Acts 9:26–29; 11:29–30; 12:25; 15:1–2; 18:22; 21:15–17). For convenience, these may be labeled P1–3 for Paul's references and A1–6, according to the order given, for the supposed references in Acts.

As a solution to this problem, many scholars have suggested that Luke has created separate visits on the basis of references to a single visit found in multiple sources. Some find the best solution to be the equating of Acts 11:29–30 (A2) with Acts 12:25 (A3) with Acts 15:1–2 (A4), i.e., A2 = A3 = A4, all referring to the same visit. Announcement of visits in Paul's letters may also be enumerated as follows: P1 (Gal 1:18); P2 (Gal 2:1); P3 (Rom 15:25). Thus, many scholars would suggest a solution along the lines of P2 = A2 = A3 = A4. Other "doublet" solutions have been proposed, as has the denial of the historicity of the so-called "first missionary journey" as set forth by Luke in Acts 13–14. Some simply see Acts 13–14 as the creation of Luke. All proposed solutions mark an attempt to correlate the evidence found in the sources that we have available, to correlate Paul's letters with the Acts accounting.

The reader should not overlook the significance of this problem or issue, for it determines how the overall mission of Paul will be understood. It would seem that some reorientation and re-examination of the evidence is in order, such that one is enabled to come to a more appropriate understanding of Paul's ministry. A thorough critical study of all of the issues involved may be found in the author's work *The Ministry of Paul the Apostle: History and Redaction*. The evidence and argumentation is thoroughly developed and presented there, whereas in the present work the results will be assumed as a working hypothesis.

The customary or traditional understanding of the ministry of Paul in terms of "three missionary journeys" based upon the reading of the Acts account has been presented in the prior chapter. The customary "three missionary journeys" model is highly problematic on multiple fronts. The reader is now called upon to imagine a new paradigm of *two major campaigns* instead of "three missionary journeys" to describe Paul's ministry, drawn primarily and first of all from his letters. It is a paradigm, as we shall see, that correlates quite well with what appears to be the underlying source used by Luke in Acts. The development of this source, the "Source Tradition of Acts" (STA) has been fully developed in the author's book *The Ministry of Paul the Apostle*.

Imagine the Ministry of Paul

Galatians 1–2 and Phil 3:5–11 provide the primary and foundational references for understanding the personal ministry of Paul based upon his own words. The two texts are not "neutral" texts, in that both texts were called forth during Paul's confrontation with "Nomistic Evangelists" or Judaizers who called his person and his gospel into question. A controversy was sparked in early Christianity, once gentiles began to respond to the gospel. The essential question was whether a gentile must become a Jew first in order to become a Christian, i.e., must a gentile essentially become a Jew in order to belong to God's "new Israel." As seen in the narration of the Jerusalem Conference in Acts 15, the essential issue was crystallized in terms of the issues of (1) circumcision and (2) Jewish food laws. These resulted in the general questions of (1) "What was necessary for salvation?" and (2) "What was necessary for table fellowship?" with regard to gentile Christians. Had it not been for the theological controversy that arose, we would not likely have Paul's own testimony regarding his person and ministry.

Galatians 1–2 is charged with a rhetorical defense of the integrity of both the gospel that Paul preached and his own person. The two go hand in hand. If either lacks integrity, the other is undermined and called into question. Paul himself was an extremely zealous Jew. As he states in Philippians, he was "circumcised on the eighth day, of the tribe of Benjamin, a Hebrew born of Hebrews, according to the Law a Pharisee, according to zeal a persecutor of the church, according to righteousness defined by law one who had become blameless" (Phil 3:5–6). He was zealous for the traditions of the fathers, such that by his own admission he had advanced beyond many of his contemporaries in his own generation (Gal 1:14).

It is interesting that Paul never identifies his birthplace. If Tarsus, that may not have served his present argument well, for it was far removed from the aura of Jerusalem. Paul, however, writes to gentile Christians. If Jerusalem, he may have appeared to be something of a renegade, out of step with Jerusalem authorities. It was simply best not to stress his birthplace. No one, however, could question Paul's Jewish credentials with regard to faith and practice. In both Philippians (Phil 3:6) and in Galatians (Gal 1:13), Paul identifies himself as a persecutor of the church.

In contemplating Paul's life on the basis of his letters, one can certainly speak of his *Pre-Christian Period*—"Pre-Christian" rather than "Jewish," even should the term "Christian" be somewhat anachronistic. Paul was born a Jew and remained a Jew to the day he died. Yet this Pharisaic Jew, who is known as Paul, was directly called by God to become a proclaimer of the Gospel of Jesus Christ among the gentiles (Gal 1:12, 15–16; Rom 1:1–5). Paul's Jewish identity and practice prior to his call appear to be unimpeachable. By all appearances, Paul was an orthodox Jew, although one marked by Hellenistic thought of the diaspora and by Pharisaic achievement.

The pre-Christian Paul may have been a Shammaite Pharisee, one who was revolutionary in spirit, a strict and zealous hardliner. Alternatively, some scholars have even suggested that the pre-Christian Paul was a missionary of the Jewish faith to the gentiles. At any rate, Paul was a staunch defender of the Jewish faith. While Palestinian Judaism was focused on temple, sacrifice, and priesthood, practically speaking, diaspora Judaism recognized synagogue over temple, study of Torah over sacrifice, and scribes and lawyers over priests.

When one seeks to understand the career of Paul as a Jewish Christian and proclaimer to the gentiles, Paul's life and work may be further characterized. In addition to Paul's *Pre-Christian Period*, one may consider four more periods of Paul's ministry that belong to Paul's Christian period, once he embraced Christ. These will be set forth in chart form following the discussion given below. The time frames given remain to be developed.

The first period is the *Initial* or *Post-Call Period*, as narrated by Paul in Gal 1:16–24. Apparently, this time was spent in Arabia or in Damascus. Paul provides no allocation of time spent, although the suggestion seems to be that most of the three-year time period was spent in Damascus (Gal 1:17–18; Acts 9:20–23). Paul traveled to Jerusalem for the first time as a Christian after this initial three-year time period. Paul narrates what he says in Galatians for rhetorical effect as he addresses the matter of the Nomistic Evangelists who are questioning his gospel and the very integrity of his apostleship. One should not expect him to give a complete, detailed account of all his movements and activities. He only gives attention to that which advances his current argument. He indicates that after he spent a fortnight (fifteen days) in Jerusalem, he "went away into the regions of Syria and Cilicia" (Gal 1:21), likely Antioch and Tarsus. It is not known how long Paul remained there.

In his next temporal reference, Paul indicates that it was another fourteen years before he returned to Jerusalem for the second time (Gal 2:1). This "fourteen year" period of time may be termed Paul's *Foundational Period* of ministry. Paul himself gives few details for this "silent period," but he does offer some clues. Paul describes himself as a very zealous Pharisee, who had surpassed many of his peers, as he pursued the traditions of the fathers. A re-evaluation of the Messiah and divine action with regard to Jesus of Nazareth would certainly have been in order. However, there is no reason to suppose that Paul needed any lengthy period of time for reflection or study or learning once he embraced the Christian gospel. Paul received a revolutionary divine calling by a direct revelation from God. He would have interpreted the revelation as the fulfillment and eschatological realization of his Jewish faith. Zealous as a Jew, he became a zealous proclaimer of Christ (Gal 1:23–24). He would not have succumbed to the inertia of remaining in place for "ten plus silent years."

Paul was already a man of faith and zealous for God. His zeal prompted him to go to Jerusalem for the first time "after three years" (Gal 1:18). It is not likely that Paul spent the next fourteen years ministering in the comparatively small area of Syria and Cilicia, during what many term the "silent years." The "silent years" were not as silent as many assume.

Fourteen years after his first visit to Jerusalem as a Christ-follower, Paul made a second visit to Jerusalem (Gal 2:1). He went up *with* Barnabas (suggesting equality), although he *took* Titus along with him. Titus, who is not mentioned in Acts at all, is identified as a Greek by Paul.[1] When one considers Paul's overall ministry, Titus may well have been from either the area of Corinth or Illyricum (see 2 Cor 8:6, 16, 23; 2 Tim 4:10). Paul himself affirms that he reached Illyricum (Rom 15:19). It is suggested that by the time Paul came to Jerusalem for the second time, his foundational missionary work had already been completed. Thus, the fourteen-year period from the time of his abbreviated first visit may be termed the *Foundation Campaign*

---

1. It is possible that "Titus" is an alternative name for Titius Justus, a "God fearer" whose home was next to the synagogue in Corinth, as witnessed by a few ancient texts. See Acts 18:7.

Period of Paul's ministry. While most will identify this second visit to Jerusalem in some way with the so-called Conference visit (Gal 2 = A4 = Acts 15), this is *not* the position suggested by a careful comparison of Paul's letters with Acts, nor the position taken in the present work.

The Corinthian correspondence and the letter to the Romans make plain the fact that Paul's next campaign was concerned with taking up a collection for the poor saints in Jerusalem (1 Cor 16:1; 2 Cor 8–9; Rom 15). As Paul writes Romans, he has made the decision that he must accompany this collection back to Jerusalem. These letters belong to Paul's *Collection Period* in his ministry, which marked his second great campaign. The *Collection Campaign* followed upon Paul's *Foundation Campaign*, separated by essentially two visits to Jerusalem that were comparatively close together.

Potentially, at least, letters such as Philippians and Philemon and the so-called Deutero-Paulines such as Colossians, Ephesians, and the Pastorals (notably 2 Timothy) offer testimony to the ministry of Paul following the delivery of the Collection to Jerusalem. Thus, a fifth period of Paul's ministry may be posited—the *Post-Collection Period*. On the basis of the evidence of Paul's letters alone, as contained within the New Testament and as will be set forth in this work, five periods of Paul's life and ministry may be discerned:

1. *Pre-Christian Period* (pre-34 CE)

2. *Initial or Post-Call Period* (three-year period, 34–37 CE)

3. *Foundation Campaign Period* (fourteen-year period, 38–51 CE)

4. *Collection Campaign Period* (a five-year period, 52–56 CE)

5. *Post-Collection Period* (56–61 CE)

As may be readily seen, Paul engaged in two major campaigns, the second of which was squarely focused upon his collection. It is this outline of Paul's life and ministry that offers clarity based upon the primary sources of Paul's letters alone.

Little is actually known about the first two periods beyond what Paul tells us. Paul's story as presented in Acts begins with the persecution of Stephen. Acts 22:3 is evaluated differently by scholars, but it offers the suggestion that Paul was born in Tarsus (in Cilicia), that he was reared in Jerusalem, and that he studied at the feet of Gamaliel. The reference occurs in Paul's first defense speech given in Jerusalem in a speech supplied by Luke to "colorize" his primary character of Paul. The concluding context also suggests that Paul was a Roman citizen (Acts 22:25). With lack of hard evidence, one may offer only general speculation about the time of Paul's birth and early years as seen in the prior chapter. Paul himself gives limited details that are neither complete nor chronological. Luke places Paul's first appearance at the persecution of Stephen. Aside from his divine call by God, Paul would apparently have lived and died as an unknown Jewish Pharisee.

In contrast to the traditional way in which Acts has been understood in terms of the "three missionary journeys of Paul" (see prior chapter), it is more accurate in the present writer's judgment to understand Paul's ministry in terms of two campaigns. This is true both from the perspective of Paul's letters *and* perhaps surprisingly from the book of Acts itself. The "three missionary journeys" nomenclature was apparently only first used in 1742 (Bengel) at a time when the concept was created to support developing European missionary societies.

The customary designation of "three missionary journeys" is actually a misnomer at every point. Paul's mission should not be construed as "journeys," for he settled down and worked in a given locale for an extended period of time. It was not "missionary" in a contemporary sense. It was not "three" in number. Paul was called by God to proclaim the fulfillment of Judaism in Christ marked by the inclusion of gentiles on the basis of faithful response to the Gospel of God. If Paul's ministry should be misunderstood, it is likely Paul's theology will likewise be misconstrued. A more adequate comprehension of Paul's ministry itself at least opens the possibility for a more adequate appreciation and clarification of his thought and theology found in his letters.

Paul's letters are contextual. Without an adequate comprehension of Paul's personal context, one will misunderstand and misapply what Paul writes. As a simple illustration, it is already apparent, given the length and time frames of Paul's campaigns, that he was not a man "in a hurry" who sought to move through the Greco-Roman world with apocalyptic haste before a soon-to-come judgment and the "end of the world." Paul's overall demeanor will color his gospel and theology. Whatever understanding we have of Paul's ministry will determine *our* interpretation of Paul's theology.

The latter three periods as outlined above are those of primary concern for the student of Paul. These are the periods for which we have New Testament evidence, both chronologically and theologically speaking. When Paul's own written testimony is considered, it becomes evident that Paul engaged in two great mission campaigns—a *Foundation Campaign* and a *Collection Campaign*. The *reality* of the Foundational Campaign is self-evident. There had to be initial, foundational work in all of the places to which Paul wrote letters. The work was carried out consecutively. The Collection Campaign is likewise evident as a "red thread" in Paul's major epistles—1 Cor 16:1–4; 2 Cor 8–9; Rom 15:25–33; and likely Galatians (see 1 Cor 16:1; Gal 6:7–10).

Acts lends support to the *reality* of the two campaigns. The first campaign was foundational and carried out in two phases by Paul working with two different partners. Phase I involved work with Barnabas in Galatia, while phase II involved work with Silas in Galatia, Asia, Macedonia, and Achaia. Acts does bear witness to a second major campaign, although it is virtually silent with regard to the nature of the second campaign. It does not identify Paul's work as the Collection Campaign (see Acts 20:1–6).

In its *present* form, Acts has been traditionally misunderstood in terms of "three missionary journeys," although Acts properly understood does support the idea of two major campaigns and hence two primary time periods of Paul's ministry. One might ask why the issue is important. One should consider the point that if we have misunderstood the nature of Paul's evangelistic work we may well have also misunderstood the nature and contemporary relevance of his theology—even at the point of its foundational emphasis. Our goal should be the best understanding of Paul in both areas, given his overall relevance to contemporary Christianity.

For the Post-Collection Period, one is virtually entirely dependent upon Acts. Other than travel to Rome by sea, Paul is mostly stationary in imprisonment in Caesarea Maritima and Rome. Whether or not one admits details from particular letters of Paul depends upon one's position taken with regard to the time of writing and the authenticity of individual letters. In the light of many variables, the *reality* of Paul's ministry is one thing, while the *ordering* of Paul's ministry becomes quite another.

Comparison of the "authentic" letters of Paul, Acts, the so-called Deutero-Paulines (letters written by others in Paul's name), and Lukan redaction will affect how Paul's total ministry is ultimately *ordered*. The present writer assumes that all letters in the New Testament bearing Paul's name were written by Paul, except for the two Pastoral letters of 1 Timothy and Titus. None of Paul's letters come with "dates," and the current New Testament order is based essentially upon length. Paul's letters do not appear in the New Testament in chronological order of when they were written.

On the basis of content in relation to Paul's ministry reflected in largely incidental details given within the letters, Paul's letters may easily be arranged and fitted into the periods of Paul's ministry as follows:

Foundational Campaign:	2 Thessalonians; Previous Letter to Corinth; 1 Thessalonians
Collection Campaign:	Galatians; Philippians; 1 Corinthians ("The Painful Letter"); 2 Cor 1–13; Rom 1–15
Post-Collection Imprisonment:	Colossians; Philemon; Ephesians; Rom 16; 2 Timothy

The letters are listed in a chronological ordering within each period as held by the author. Full supporting arguments and documentation are given in the author's earlier volume on Paul's ministry. Space and the nature of the current work does not permit development here, although a fully developed presentation may be found in *The Ministry of Paul the Apostle: History and Redaction*. First Timothy and Titus are deemed to be pseudonymous. The letters of Paul that we have were written in a time span of approximately twelve years, from 49 CE (2 Thessalonians) to 61 CE (Colossians; Philemon; Ephesians; Rom 16; 2 Timothy).

Paul's ministry began with his prophetic call and commission by God himself, who, according to Paul, was pleased to reveal his son to him (Gal 1:15–16). Paul was not "converted" from one religion to another, but he was called to proclaim a Jewish gospel to a gentile world. Paul acknowledges his early persecution of the Christian church, but he became its foremost proclaimer in the first-century Greco-Roman world. The story of Paul is recounted in the book of Acts according to Luke's purposes (see Acts 7–28), even as it may be pieced together through careful examination of Paul's own letters. Virtually all scholars would acknowledge source materials utilized by Luke in Acts, although they may disagree as to the exact nature of the Lukan source material.

As previously indicated, the present writer has developed an underlying source tradition for Acts as related to Paul (STA or "Source Tradition of Acts") in his earlier redactional and chronological study of Paul's letters and Acts. One may consult *The Ministry of Paul the Apostle: History and Redaction*. That work is thorough and somewhat technical. For convenience, an abbreviated rendition of the resultant chronology of the developed ministry of Paul may be found in appendix A of the present work. It also contains a listing of Paul's letters according to their projected dating. The only sources that we have for developing the historical contours of the ministry of Paul are his letters and the book of Acts.

Fig. 14. Map of Paul's Foundation Campaign. Map © Jason Greene. Used with permission.

Paul's Foundation Campaign occurred in two phases (see Acts 13–18). Phase I of this campaign was centered in Asia Minor in provinces like Galatia, while phase II moves from Anatolia through Macedonia and Achaia to Illyricum. Essentially, phase I involves what may be currently identified as Asia Minor and phase II encompasses a portion of southern Europe. The Foundation Campaign would have occurred in the time period of 38–51 CE, following Paul's call in 34 CE. Paul's earlier intervening years were spent in Damascus, Arabia, and Antioch. Following a Famine Visit to Jerusalem (Fall, 51 CE) and the Conference Visit (Spring, 52 CE), Paul engaged in his Collection Campaign (52–56 CE), gathering funds for the Jewish Christians in Jerusalem. His reasoning (aside from their physical needs) was that just as the gentiles had received spiritual blessings from the Jews, there was now the opportunity to offer physical blessings to the poor Jewish saints in Jerusalem (Rom 15:25–27). It was a time of opportunity for the nations to bring gifts to Jerusalem in fulfillment of scriptural promise (see Mic 4:1–2; Isa 2:1–3).

It was an attempt by Paul to *achieve unity* among the Christian churches in the East, before he sought new ministry in Rome and to Spain. While Paul's collection was intended to have practical consequences for the impoverished church in Jerusalem that had experienced the after-effects of severe famine, the eschatological intention of the collection was far greater. Paul sought to establish theological unity on the basic nature of the gospel before he sought any further new work to the West (i.e., Spain). Paul had a calm, methodical approach to evangelism that was eschatological but not overwhelmed by apocalyptic fervor.

A careful examination of Paul's letters, the book of Acts, and Lukan redaction reveals that Paul's ministry may be understood not only in terms of two major campaigns, but also in terms of four visits to Jerusalem. These four visits may be labeled respectively, the "Acquaintance" Visit (Gal 1:18; see Acts 9:26–27), "Famine" Visit (Gal 2:1–10; see Acts 11:27–30), "Conference" Visit (see Gal 2:11–21; cf. Acts 15), and the "Collection" Visit (Rom 15:25–29; cf. Acts 21:15–17). These may be correlated with what Paul says in his letters, as summarized in the following chart.

Historical Visits of Paul to Jerusalem

Actual Historical	*Characterization*	*Reference*
J1	Acquaintance	Gal 1:18; Acts 9:26–30
J2	Famine	Gal 2:1–10; Acts 11:27–30
J3	Conference	Acts 12:25; 15:1–35 (Paul chooses not to narrate)
J4	Final (Collection)	Rom 15:25–32; Acts 21:17

According to Acts and its underlying source material, Paul spent his Post-Collection years imprisoned in either Caesarea or Rome. Paul likely experienced martyrdom in Rome in the spring or summer of 61 CE. To posit release from a first Roman imprisonment and a subsequent ministry prior to a second Roman imprisonment and martyrdom (ca. 68 CE) is to move to later church tradition beyond the New Testament.

As has been seen, it has been customary to look to Acts for an understanding of Paul's life and ministry (supplemented by Paul's letters) and to look to the "authentic" letters of Paul for his theology. His theology has sometimes been inappropriately supplemented by Paul's speeches in Acts and Pauline thought in the "Deutero-Paulines." Methodologically speaking, since the time of John Knox (1950), it has been deemed more appropriate to look first to Paul's letters for his life as well as his thought. Since the time of Dibelius (1956) and others, the speeches of Acts have been recognized as the work of Luke, who uses them to "colorize" his narrative characters and to advance his gospel purposes.

The story of Paul in Acts is marked by Lukan purpose and redaction, as the work of this writer and others have underscored. Paul's theological perspectives will be found in his own authentic letters, although scholars since F. C. Baur (1792–1860) have differed as to which letters are Paul's. Everyone agrees that 1 Thessalonians, 1 Corinthians, Galatians, Philippians, 2 Corinthians, Romans, and Philemon are Pauline, although scholars may differ on the order or the unity of individual letters. Composite theories of multiple letters are posited for Philippians and 2 Corinthians in particular, with fragments of as many as six different letters being perceived in 2 Corinthians. The other letters—2 Thessalonians, Colossians, Ephesians, and the "Pastorals"—are subject to widely differing claims of authenticity.

While Paul certainly wrote other letters during the course of his quarter of a century of ministry (e.g., the "Previous Letter" to Corinth, 1 Cor 5:9), the letters of Paul we possess that are deemed authentic are our only sources for discerning Paul's theological perspectives. However, even Deutero-Pauline or pseudonymous letters attributed to Paul may offer radiant trajectories of insight into Pauline thought. Again, a reminder is given that we can only recover Paul's *literary* theology, his "epistolic" theology. Yet, that theology comes from the formative period of the early church.

Thus, in the light of a rereading of Paul's own letters and a more careful appraisal of Luke's presentation in the book of Acts, the present writer contends that the contours of Paul's ministry should be re-imagined with a new model of his ministry. Every current map of Paul's ministry that documents his "three missionary journeys" is based solely on a misconception of the book of Acts as it stands. Such understanding offers a mischaracterization that is relatively modern that does not take into account either the evidence of Paul's own letters or Luke's alteration of his underlying source material. Paul himself clearly indicates that he has fully preached the gospel of Christ from "Jerusalem to Illyricum" (Rom 15:19). One may find the locations of both Jerusalem and Illyricum depicted on the map of "Paul's World" given at the beginning of this book. One may find the so-called three missionary journeys of Paul in the map section of many Bibles or other resource materials. Which of the "three journeys" takes Paul to Illyricum? And the answer is—not a single one. Check it out.

Not a single map based upon the traditional "three missionary journeys" of Paul documents his ministry in Illyricum, which means according to Paul's own statement that none of those maps are accurate. And, in the light of the fact that the earliest mention of "three missionary journeys" first appears only in 1742 CE—almost seventeen hundred years after Paul—a re-evaluation calls for a new model. The person of Paul and the background matrices which formed and influenced him have already been treated, including a brief historical sketch of his ministry according to the understanding of the present writer. It remains to develop this further, with a renewed invitation to "imagine Paul."

The Foundation Campaign

The remainder of this chapter will treat the period of Paul's Foundation Campaign. It will be crafted with alternating blocks of what could be called "historical fiction" followed by historical presentation. The fictional portions are presented in italics for clarity's sake. Also, it should be stated that many of the references drawn from Acts are representative of content and perhaps a different order reflected in Luke's underlying source material. Elsewhere, the author identifies these as "STA" references ("Source Tradition of Acts") in order to make plain Lukan redaction.

In the interest of simplicity, references given in this work will either be identified with the usual "Acts" nomenclature if the customary book of Acts as it stands is referenced. If Luke's underlying source tradition is referenced, it will be identified as "Luke's Source, STA" accompanied by chapter and verse numbering. Thus, the present Acts chapter and verse nomenclature will be retained, although the order and precise content and order of Luke's Source and his redacted presentation may vary. Luke felt free to alter his source in various ways, in order to recount the story he wished to tell. The author does not wish to make things complicated in this present work, but he deems the differences to be significant. The reader may wish to ignore the differences in the present context and may always consult the author's other work for full development of the STA.

While the author is not attempting to be novelistic, the acknowledged fictional portions are included to make several points with regard to our available evidence. First of all, good fiction may sound like history and may even be firmly based upon history. James Michener's *The Source* comes to mind as an example. In appearance, fiction may closely approximate "history" in the ancient world, as well as in the modern world. Secondly, an attempt is made to "personalize" Paul by an historical appeal to the imagination. It is altogether too easy to forget that Paul and other persons mentioned in the "scripture" of Acts and the Pauline letters were real people, and to remember that there is more to their own human story than what is given in a comparatively narrow scriptural address.

It is sometimes difficult to get outside the box of "Scripture" and "theology." If this chapter (and this overall work) creates a greater appreciation, understanding, and awareness of the *person* of Paul who lived as an apostle of the Gospel of God in the first-century Roman world, then it will have been worth the journey. The intent is not to write an "historical novel," populated by non-biblical fictional characters, but rather to personalize Paul through the employment of a degree of historical imagination in the light of our available source material and contextual understanding employed as historical evidence.

If one is not familiar with the first-century Roman world, it is strongly suggested that one follow Paul's movements on a suitable map that delineates clearly the general topography and outline of the provincial Roman Empire. A basic map of "Paul's World" is included in the orientation materials of this volume, but more detailed maps are available on the internet in color—many with topographical relief indicated. One may even develop a topographical awareness and discern locations of ancient biblical sites through the use of Google Earth. Regardless of which map one consults, the present author suggests that one needs to think in terms of an east-west orientation, rather than the customary north-south orientation. Try rotating Google Earth ninety degrees, for example. Do things look different? A listing of distances between various cities important to Paul, based upon ORBIS (The Stanford Geospatial Network Model of the Roman World), is also offered in the beginning of this volume. One needs a sense of scale and relative time, even though actual historical time itself is a distinct variable.

In a modern world in which one may quickly and rather effortlessly cover great distances in rapid time, one needs to allow for much slower movement in the ancient world on the part of Paul. The reader not only needs to *slow* one's thinking down, but one must *shrink* one's thinking. The entire Mediterranean basin was much smaller than the United States, for example. The Mediterranean basin is perhaps but a quarter of the size of the United States.

And so, let the story of Paul, the "man in Christ," begin . . . .

> *Stephen's words still hung in the air, as an enraged crowd rushed upon him. Some went before him, picking up stones as they moved hurriedly to the city gate. Others dragged Stephen along the paved street that ran along in full sight of the great Herodian Temple of Jerusalem—that temple with its huge, glistening stones that stood immortalized as the most holy place at the heart of Jewish religious practice. Just beyond the threshold of the city gate, they threw Stephen to the ground. Before he could rise up on his hands and knees, the first stone hit him. And then as he knelt, another. And another. As Stephen prayed and cried out, those who joined in the stoning piled their garments beside a young Pharisee by the name of Saul. And Saul looked on approvingly, as this messianic Jew (Stephen by name) took his last breath.*
>
> *Saul had heard enough already about this "Jesus of Nazareth" and Stephen's challenge to the heritage of the fathers. It wasn't that Saul didn't believe in the resurrection—after all, he was a Pharisee. Most certainly, God would act to declare his Messiah one day, but when he did, it would become clear to all. No more of these impostors—Theudas, Judas the Galilean, and now this "Jesus of Nazareth." Who could possibly believe in a Messiah who was crucified on a Roman cross beside the main road from Caesarea? And why must this impostor's followers keep criticizing the temple and the Law and the traditions of the fathers?*

> *Although he did not cast the first stone—or any others for that matter, this young Jewish Pharisee by the name of Saul, whose Roman name was Paul, looked approvingly upon what had taken place. All such "messiahs"—and their followers, as well—deserved what they got. Saul resolved to expose as many of these false messianists as he could, as he turned to walk away from the now lifeless body lying on the ground outside the city gate. Saul was zealous to preserve the traditions of the Fathers in these times of Roman rule. The very heritage of Israel was at stake. . . .*

So begins the story of Paul, the apostle of God in Christ Jesus, that one also known as "Jesus of Nazareth." It was the year 34 CE. Tiberius (14–37 CE) was still emperor of Rome in name, although he had been living in isolated safety in the refuge of his Villa of Jupiter on the island of Capreae since 26 CE, the same year in which Pontius Pilate had been appointed governor in Judea. Tiberius continued to administer the empire from his fortress of solitude. Pilate had an exceptionally long tenure in Judea, especially given his lack of popularity among the Jewish people (Josephus, *Ant.* 18.55–62). Subject to the governor of the province of Syria, he had ruled over the "special territory" of Judea as *praefectus Iudaeae*. A Pilate inscription was found in Caesarea Maritima in 1961. Bronze coins minted during the tenure of Pilate abound. Pilate was removed from office by Lucius Vitellius, governor of Syria, sometime after the Passover of 36 CE.

Several years earlier, at the instigation of the Jewish high-priestly authorities, Pilate had handed over the Jewish prophet Jesus of Nazareth to be crucified (most probable date, April 7, 30 CE). The question might be asked as to when Jesus began his ministry. There may well be a connection with the Jewish Sabbatical Year of 27/28 CE, an anticipated Year of Release according to Isa 61:1–2. Luke's inaugural sermon of Jesus at Nazareth (Luke 4:16–30) may well reflect this thematic background. Tiberias died in March, 37 CE, at his villa on Capreae. Gaius Caligula, who had been living on Capreae with Tiberius since 32 CE, became emperor. When Caligula came to the Roman throne in 37 CE, he appointed Marullus as governor of Judea (Josephus, *Ant.* 18.237).

While it is possible that the martyrdom of Stephen could have occurred during the procuratorial interim of 36/37 CE, this cannot be proven nor is it compelling. Stephen's death appears to be the action of a lynch mob. The Roman governor for the most part remained at his domicile in Caesarea on the coast, making such consideration largely irrelevant. A Roman garrison quartered in the tower of Antonia maintained order in Jerusalem. While the garrison might quell any general crowd disturbance, it could not necessarily prevent a spontaneous lynch mob from forming. It is at the point of Stephen's martyrdom, however, that Luke introduces Paul (see Acts 8:1). While Paul himself acknowledges that he persecuted the churches of Judea (Gal 1:22–23), Luke may well have enhanced Paul's identity as a persecutor of the church.

According to the Lukan portrayal in Acts, the early church in Jerusalem endured both internal struggle (Acts 4:32—5:11; 6:1–6) and external Jewish persecution (Acts 4:1–31; 5:17–40). Luke offers snapshot vignettes without a time frame, as he portrays struggle, persecution, and phenomenal church growth that overcomes all challenging obstacles (see Acts 2:41–47; 4:32–37; 5:12–16; 5:41–42; 6:7).

There is no question that Paul was a persecutor of the earliest church (see Gal 1:13, 23). Paul himself is silent on the cause and specific accounting of his persecution, but he suggests that he practiced a destructive violence against the church. Somewhere in the vicinity of Damascus, Paul experienced a compelling divine vision that changed his life. God revealed Jesus the Christ to him (Gal 1:12–16). God gave him a commission to preach the Gospel among the gentiles. Paul simply describes his experience in terms of a "revelation," a "setting apart," a "call," and a "commission." His life would never be the same, for this experience sent him in a diametrically opposite direction. Paul the persecutor became Paul the proclaimer. He apparently maintained a repentant attitude toward his former persecutorial zeal, now trumped by his evangelistic zeal for the Gospel (see Gal 1:23–24).

As a Pharisee, Paul was zealous for the Law and the traditions of the fathers. This called for *practice* of everyday purity in isolation from gentiles and even *persecution* of aberrant theologies of misplaced messianic identities that threatened the Jewish way of life—certainly given the hotbed of Jewish nationalistic fervor that had steadily risen in the face of Roman occupation and oppression. After his call, however, this Jewish Pharisee had to come to a new way of thinking and a new way of living. Paul's encounter with the risen Christ confirmed that Jesus was alive and was, indeed, the expected and longed-for Messiah. Paul's call confirmed eschatological fulfillment in the inclusion of gentiles into the people of God. God's final plan of inclusion was now taking place. Those who embraced Jesus as the Christ were not following one more false messianic claimant, but rather they were those who stood in the vanguard of God's announced Gospel for Israel and the entire world. Paul went away for a time into the broad expanse known as Arabia—where and for how long, we do not know. Paul implies it was not too long, however. Paul perhaps came to realize the ministry of Jesus had been a non-violent movement of proclaimed fulfillment, rather than another zealotic uprising.

While he was there, he apparently deeply offended the Nabateans, who controlled Arabia at that time. Petra (what a magnificent place!) was the royal seat of Arabia, or the kingdom of the Nabateans, which lay on the desert side of the easternmost cities of the Decapolis, south of the Roman province of Syria and the contiguous Herodian territory east of the Lake of Galilee, beginning roughly south of the Yarmuk River. One should take time to look at a detailed map. Paul suggests that he returned to Damascus and spent several years there (Gal 1:17). Once the Nabateans gained control of Damascus in 37 CE, Paul's days in Damascus were apparently numbered (see 2 Cor 11:32–33). Incidentally, Herod Phillip had ruled until

34 CE, the year of Paul's call/commission, and Herod Agrippa I now ruled over Phillip's territories in the year Paul went to Jerusalem, 37 CE.

In biblical thought, because of its theological significance, one always "goes up" to Jerusalem or "down from" Jerusalem. Paul did not "go up" to Jerusalem until three years after his call/commission experience (Gal 1:18). Paul thus left Damascus in the year 37 CE, and for the first time since his call/commission to become an apostle of the Gospel to the gentiles, he determined to go to Jerusalem to meet with some of the leaders of the church. The source underlying Acts suggests Paul was preaching the gospel in Jewish synagogues in Damascus.

According to Acts 9:21, the content of Paul's preaching was focused upon Christology. It was apparently in the synagogues of Damascus and around Damascene Christians that Paul hammered out or sharpened his specifically Christian identity and message. As a Pharisee, Paul did not begin from "scratch," but rather developed a revisionist understanding of the scripture and scriptural expectations in the light of his call experience and association with Christians in Damascus. In a sense, Paul rediscovered the faith of Abraham in relation to divine promise. While there may have been periods of solitude, Paul appears to have been a social person, such that he was no monastic during this time. As a result of rising *Jewish* opposition, which had hitherto characterized the experience of all Christian disciples in the book of Acts, Paul left Damascus on his way to Jerusalem.

> *Paul welcomed the sight of Jerusalem as he came over the hill on the road from Damascus. He had to pause, as he first saw once again the Great Temple, where he had so often presented his offerings and discussed matters of the Torah with his fellow Pharisees and others. A wry smile came to his lips, as he remembered a particularly lengthy debate with a Sadducee—oh, they were so unskilled in the finer matters of the Law. It was such a welcome sight, after three—or had it been four?—years' absence from the Holy City. In the next moment, he uttered a prayer for his safe arrival, as he began his walk down the hill toward the city. Paul had been glad to have escaped the clutches of King Aretas IV in Damascus, as he reached the territory now controlled by King Agrippa. He had earlier skirted around the Lake of Galilee, as he set his sights on the road to Jerusalem.*

> *Ah! What a welcome sight! Jerusalem glistening in the sun! And the Great Temple with its golden colored stone! It would be a good thing to make an offering and to celebrate once again in the Great Temple, especially now that he understood in such personal terms the mighty work that God was now doing in Jesus Christ. He walked carefully down the hill, staff in hand, looking up every few steps. He could not help but reflect upon how much his life had changed since he was last here. He could not wait to have discussions with members of his old synagogue. He was prepared to demonstrate from the scripture to all who would listen that Jesus of Nazareth, who had been crucified just a few years earlier, was, indeed, the messianic Son of God. Wait until he told them about the revelation that had*

come to him! Yet he was deeply reflective, keenly aware that when he had last lived here he had strongly persecuted those who held the faith that he was now so ready to proclaim.

A wave of deep remorse swept over him, as he remembered his own earlier activity of persecuting the followers of the executed Jesus. Yet now, he himself was a follower of "the Way." He cast a glance at the very city gate by which Stephen had been martyred. After slight hesitation, he quickly looked back down at the rocky roadway he was following and decided to enter the city by another gate . . . .

Having reached the Holy City, he hurried down the narrow, stone-paved street moving past the small shops, to find a place to stay in the city. He was lucky that it was not a time of the Feast. There were many people here whom he knew— even his sister's family; surely he could readily find lodging, share a good meal with friends, and get some rest. Then he would get about the business at hand. Some followers of "the Way" who had come to Damascus had told him about the fledgling church and, in particular, about the work of Cephas. Tomorrow, he thought he would inquire about how the new sect of believers who expressed faith in Jesus of Nazareth was doing and discover where Cephas lived . . . .

Paul acknowledges that he went up to Jerusalem for the very first time as a Christian only after living three years as a messianic Jew in the area of Damascus (Gal 1:17–18). He stayed in Jerusalem for but a brief time—fifteen days, a fortnight. One may imagine Paul's meeting with Cephas. Was Cephas deeply suspicious of Paul? What topics marked their discussion? Surely one topic must have been the reality and experience of the resurrection of Jesus and all that meant.

Writing later in the context of the Galatian threat by the Judaizers or Nomistic Evangelists during his Collection Campaign, Paul indicates that he met only with Cephas and James the Lord's brother among the Christian leadership in Jerusalem. He may well have met with other members of the church there, but he wishes to refute any idea that the Galatian Christians may have been falsely taught, namely, that he and his Gospel were unduly influenced or defined by the leaders of the church in Jerusalem. Luke's Source account is a brief synopsis that records the initial fear of Paul by the Jerusalem disciples (Luke's Source, STA 9:26), his own testimony about his vision (Luke's Source, STA 9:27), and the action of the Jerusalem Christians in assisting him to get to Caesarea and ultimately to Tarsus (Luke's Source, STA/Acts 9:30).

Phase One: Cyprus and Galatia

Paul's own testimony simply says that after he left Jerusalem, he went into the regions of Syria and Cilicia (Gal 1:21). Tarsus was the capital of Cilicia and Antioch was the capital of Syria. Paul engaged in a ministry here of undetermined length, but one still long enough for word to travel back the more than five hundred miles to Jerusalem

(Gal 1:23). Paul could have been headquartered in Antioch—he does not say. The next time he is introduced in the Acts, he is portrayed as one of the "prophets and teachers in Antioch" who was commissioned and sent out by the Antiochene church as an evangelistic missionary along with Barnabas (Luke's Source, STA/Acts 13:1, 3). What discussions must have entered into developing relationship between Barnabas and Paul? What differences were to be perceived between the outlook of the church in Jerusalem and that in Antioch regarding the nature of the Gospel?

Paul himself does not give any information about a mission to Cyprus, although such a mission should be neither surprising nor suspect, geographically and personally speaking. Cyprus was geographically close to Antioch, without the barrier created by the Anatolian mountains. According to Acts 4:36, Barnabas was a native of Cyprus. Also, in Luke's listing of diaspora Jews and proselytes present on the day of Pentecost (Acts 2:9–11), Cyprus is not listed. So, where better to begin a mission sponsored by Antioch? Study of any map of the Mediterranean world will illustrate the wisdom of the choice. However, the details of this entire mission must be filled in by material given only in Luke's Source/Acts.

As has been demonstrated, this ministry represents phase I of the Foundation Mission Campaign of Paul, which likely occurred 38–42/43 CE. After the first portion of the campaign was completed on Cyprus, Paul and his company sailed across to Perga in Galatic Pamphylia (Luke's Source, STA 13:13), a southern region associated with Galatia. Pamphylia is best thought of as a region in Paul's day, rather than a separate province. It was joined with Galatia from 25 BCE until 43 CE, when Claudius established the province of Lycia-Pamphylia. It was simply a geographical area which marked the coastal region of "south Galatia," such that Galatia should be understood as extending all the way to the sea. Galba (68–69 CE) reunited Pamphylia with the region of Galatia, while Vespasian (69–79 CE) reunited Pamphylia with Lycia as a separate province. Pamphylia was essentially a regional district about eighty miles long and thirty miles wide. Paul would have first passed through the area at a time earlier than 43 CE

Again, the choice seems very logical. One may assume that cities along the eastern Mediterranean coast from Caesarea to Antioch itself could readily have been reached by disciples emanating from Judea. The mission field of Antioch itself would have been to the east, north, and west. While travel from Antioch to the central Anatolian highland could have been effected through Tarsus and the Cilician Gates of the Taurus Mountains (a route later followed by Paul), the sea route from Cyprus took them directly to the port city near Perga. From Perga they moved through the river valley over the Taurus Mountains into the central Anatolian plateau of Pisidian Galatia, finally arriving in Antioch of Pisidia in Asia Minor (Luke's Source, STA 13:14). To be clear, this "Antioch" is other than the Antioch of Syria that sent out Paul and Barnabas.

Modern people who travel by mechanized machines do not generally appreciate what a barrier a mountain range like the Taurus Mountains presented to ancient people walking on foot or moving by wagon. On an altogether different matter, phase II of the Foundation Mission Campaign was *not* occasioned by a falling out of Barnabas and Paul over John Mark's earlier "desertion" (see Acts 13:13; cf. Acts 15:36; Acts 15:37–40). That story belongs to Lukan redaction. The historical explanation may be as simple as the fact that John Mark saw the opportunity to return home to Jerusalem and took it. This may even have been agreed upon at the beginning of the mission, or mission plans may have changed. Whatever the reason, John Mark chose *not* to participate in the additional mission in Anatolia.

During Paul's day, the *regions* of Pamphylia, Pisidia, and Lycaonia were all part of the larger province of Galatia. Paul, in writing to the Galatians at a later time, reminds them of his first visit in the Galatian province (42/43 CE), when he preached to them "because of a bodily ailment" (Gal 4:13). The provincial term "Galatians" was the common denominator for the various peoples who lived within the border of the province created by Augustus in 25 BCE. Prior to 43 CE, "Galatia" would have included at least parts of the regions designated Pamphylia, Pisidia, and Lyconia at a later point in time.

Luke's Source (see Acts 13:14—14:21) presents Paul and Barnabas as carrying out a foundational ministry in Antioch, Iconium, Lystra, and Derbe. Paul himself confirms this in 2 Tim 3:11. It is also tempting to connect the stoning mentioned by Paul in 2 Cor 11:25 with that of the stoning in Lystra, where he was left for dead (Luke's Source, STA 14:19). After working in the area of the Galatian plateau, Paul and Barnabas returned through Pisidia of Galatia to Pamphylia, where they preached in Perga (Luke's Source, STA 14:25). Subsequently, they returned to Antioch of Syria, where they were commended for their work by the church that had sent them out (Luke's Source, STA 14:26). Phase I of the Foundation Mission Campaign was then complete—a campaign that had begun in 38 CE had lasted until 42/43 CE.

Phase Two: Galatia to Illyricum

Phase II of the Foundation Mission Campaign actually begins with two missions—Barnabas and John Mark return to Cyprus (Luke's Source, STA 15:36), while Paul and Silas/Silvanus return to Galatia, passing through Syria and Cilicia on the way. Although stated nowhere in the texts, Paul and Silas/Silvanus would have traveled to Tarsus and from there would have traveled through the Cilician Gates to gain access to the Galatian plateau of Anatolia. The first-century world was one of high contextual knowledge and awareness, such that much background detail could be assumed and need not be written down. Paul shared the same world as that of his various constituencies. A map of Paul's Asia Minor illustrates the barrier of the Taurus Mountains, as well as a Roman road that extended from Tarsus through the Galatian plateau all the way to Troas. One might consider the use of Google Earth to begin to gain a feel of the formidable topographical and geographical barriers Paul faced.

IMAGINE PAUL'S FOUNDATION CAMPAIGN

Paul and company would have followed ancient Roman roads that had been built by Roman engineers to facilitate speed of travel for the legions and for official communication. The by-product of this "government work" was that the populace of the various provinces could use the roads as well. Roman roads fostered travel, trade, commerce, and communication.

> *As Paul walked the last few miles from Derbe to Lystra with Silvanus, he was tired and reflective. The visit to the provincial Galatian churches was different without Barnabas. They had left Derbe behind four days ago and would be in Lystra by nightfall. Things had gone well at Derbe, even though Paul had had to answer a lot of questions about Barnabas. He and Silvanus had walked the just over one hundred miles from Tarsus to Derbe on the Roman road, passing through the Cilician Gates and through the Taurus Mountains in a week's time. They had stayed with Gaius in Derbe and Paul had renewed acquaintance with other disciples in the fledgling church he had founded with Barnabas on his prior visit a year earlier. Everyone in the church wanted to know all about Barnabas. He told them about Barnabas's renewed work on his home island of Cyprus to which Barnabas had felt called. Paul had introduced them to his new mission partner, Silvanus. He thanked the church once again for caring for him during his founding visit with them, as he recuperated from the earlier stoning he had received at Lystra.*
>
> *Ah, Lystra! It was a place he could never forget, given the stoning he received there. He still did not have full use of his left arm that he had used to shield the blows. It had been very difficult to return there with Barnabas after the completion of their ministry in Derbe last year. At that time, he had really wanted to travel the road that he and Silvanus had just traversed. They could go to Tarsus and then on to Antioch, but instead Barnabas had wanted to check on the churches and retrace their route by land before sailing for Syria. Barnabas had won that one. And given the absence of outside Jewish agitation, the return with Barnabas had been without incident. But now Paul would again be passing the "place of the stoning." He had been encouraged, though, by the recent response he received at Derbe and hoped that the reunion in Lystra would be equally as productive. It was going to be good to take off his sandals. His thoughts began to center upon where they would spend the night . . . .*

Paul's visit to Lystra proved to be one of his most significant moves. It was there that he met a disciple by the name of Timothy, son of a Jewish mother and a Greek father. The value that Timothy added to Paul's mission enterprises is not to be minimized. Phase II of the Foundation Mission Campaign would take Paul and his associates all the way from central Anatolia (Galatia) to Illyricum. Most of the major mission centers that are normally associated with the letters of Paul are found here: Galatia; Philippi; Thessalonica; Corinth. Romans belongs to the Collection Period, while Colossians and Ephesians belong to the Post-Collection Period.

Overall, phase II required about eight years to be brought to completion, from 43–51 CE. Together, phase I and phase II of the *Foundation Campaign* occupy fourteen years or slightly over half of Paul's ministry, as Paul himself indicates in Gal 2:1. The time required for each individual phase can only be estimated. Altogether, it is clear that Paul's ministry and mission consisted of much more than a series of compressed "summer revival" meetings.

After visiting Iconium and Antioch of Pisidia, Paul contemplated a ministry in the direction of Bithynia along the Black Sea, and perhaps a current move in the direction of Ephesus. A revelatory vision, however, directed him to cross the Aegean Sea and begin a new work in the province of Macedonia at Philippi. That vision helped to define Paul's ultimate hope to get to Rome. Macedonia would be a step in the right direction. This move proved to be decisive as well. Any movement toward Bithynia would have taken Paul away from the heart of what truly was the Roman Empire. There was a reason the Mediterranean was called the *Mare Nostrum*, "Our Sea." The eastern Mediterranean basin, with all its provincial centers and colonies, provided the foundational focus of Paul's ministry.

Fig. 15. Sailing for Macedonia. Original painting by G. Roger Greene.

Paul and his company made the crossing from Troas to Neapolis [modern day Kavalla] without incident. The Aegean Sea had been fair, and the winds had been favorable. The white caps that appeared as frosting on the tops of the deep blue waves seemed to push the ship along, as its bow split the water, creating its own cascading trail. Perhaps the smooth sailing was a good omen for what lay ahead. Paul had a seat near the bow of the ship, from which he could see the port town of Neapolis drawing ever nearer, as the island of Thasos receded behind. He would soon set foot in Macedonia! Paul, Silvanus, and Timothy gathered their meager belongings as the ship docked by the wharves to begin unloading its cargo of amphora storage jars filled with wine, nuts, and grain. After a night's rest, they spoke with some Greeks at a taverna overlooking the harbor. They made ready to travel to the Roman colony known as Philippi, a day's journey away. Philippi was the leading city of the easternmost district of Macedonia, located little more than ten miles inland. Paul was on new evangelistic ground. What would Philippi bring? Paul was positively anxious. He was excited about settling down for a time. It was the year 44 CE and Claudius remained as emperor in Rome. . . .

Travel from Troas to Neapolis went well for Paul. The island of Samothrace was a halfway point that provided a visible landmark for navigation from both Troas and Neapolis. Favorable winds and weather offered a two day passage, with overnight on the island. Philippians 4:10–16 offers insights into the circumstances and success of Paul's mission in Macedonia. Although Philippians is a letter written from a later Ephesian imprisonment, it chronicles something of the warmth of the Philippian Christians and the success of Paul at Philippi. The church at Philippi was the first church established on European soil and became Paul's initial gateway to the West, the land of the Greeks, which led to Rome.

In Paul's day, Philippi was the leading city of the easternmost district of Macedonia, an area covering some seven hundred square miles, from the mineral rich Pangion mountain range in the north to the port of Neapolis in the south. The last great battle of the Roman republican war had been fought on the "Plains of Philippi" southwest of the city, with the forces that sought to avenge the assassination of Caesar emerging victorious in 42 BCE. The city was given the status of a colony. After Octavian's victory at the Battle of Actium in 31 BCE, Octavian renamed the city *Colonia Julia philippensis* in honor of his daughter.

Philippians 4:15 refers to the time "in the beginning of the gospel, when I left Macedonia . . . ." The most natural way to understand Paul's reference in Phil 4:15 is to see the verse as referring to Paul's initial work in Philippi and his reminiscence of how the Philippian church supported him even after he moved on to Thessalonica and Corinth (Achaia). It is not at all clear how long Paul stayed in Philippi on his first visit there. It is evident from Paul's letter that he remained long enough to establish a strong and vibrant church that provided financial support for him in his continued mission to Thessalonica and Corinth (Phil 4:16). Paul acknowledges the partnership of the Philippians in the gospel "from the first day" until the present (Phil 1:5). He reiterates their partnership in the gospel in Phil 4:15. The theme of joy pervades the epistle (see Phil 1:4, 18, 25; 2:2, 17–18; 3:1; 4:1, 10). Paul's affection for this church is without peer among the letters of Paul. And, it was a church that was predominately gentile in membership.

When one considers the evidence in Luke's Source, the plural "we" shows up for the first time in conjunction with travel from Troas to Macedonia (Luke's Source, STA/Acts 16:10). The two day sea voyage is briefly, yet aptly described with a clear geographical awareness—i.e., by someone who knew the route and area well. No indication is given with regard to any length of stay in Neapolis, nor are any details given about traveling the ten miles to Philippi. Luke's Source (STA 16:12) simply states that when Paul and his company arrived in Philippi, they remained in the city "for some days." This summary statement allows for what must have historically been a significant length of time. Compare the reference to Paul's stay in Thessalonica, which characterizes according to Acts an inordinately brief time (three weeks, Acts 17:2). The Thessalonian letters themselves suggest Paul's stay there was much longer than a mere three weeks. Luke's Source that underlies Acts supports this more extended perspective.

Luke's Source offers three vignettes associated with Philippi not mentioned in Paul's letters. The three vignettes belong more to historical presentation of the ministry of Paul and the spread of the gospel, rather than to the theological requirements of salvation (e.g., "believe and be baptized"). The first is the encounter with a business woman by the name of Lydia, who was a God-fearer (Luke's Source, STA 16:13–15). When Paul reached Philippi, he found no Jewish synagogue in the city. When the Sabbath day came, he and Silvanus and Timothy went to a place outside the city which they had heard was frequented by those who worshiped the God of Judaism. It was there they encountered Lydia. At some point following her conversion, Lydia apparently sponsored the church in her house (Luke's Source, STA 16:15, 40). Although it is nowhere stated, it is entirely possible that she became a significant patron of Paul and his work. Literarily, the story involving Lydia provides the foundational story for work in Philippi.

The second Philippi vignette offered in the Luke's Source involves the encounter with the slave girl who was a *mantis* ("one who divined the future," Luke's Source, STA 16:16–24). After Paul performs an exorcism of the spirit which inspired her, her owners brought public charges against Paul for their economic loss. It is this event that resulted in Paul and Silas being beaten with rods (see 2 Cor 11:25) and being cast into prison. It is interesting that Timothy is not jailed along with Paul and Silas. The account involving the slave girl provides an accounting as to why Paul and Silas were imprisoned.

The third vignette portrays the episode of the conversion of the Philippian jailer and his family (Luke's Source, STA 16:25–34). It is a significant episode in Luke's Source, for it marks the conversion of the first gentile pagan in Europe. The so-called we source is intertwined in the first two vignettes, although it is not in evidence in the account of the trial and imprisonment of Paul and the conversion of the jailer. For Luke, this third vignette becomes climatic in its narration of the unhindered spread of the gospel even to pure gentile pagans. In its own right, it is as significant as the earlier accounting of the gospel going to gentile God-fearers in the Cornelius story (see Acts 10:1—11:18). Taken together, the two stories support Luke's "rule of two" in his historical narration.

Historically speaking, none of the three vignettes are implausible once the Lukan redaction is removed. In fact, with the removal of the dialogue involving Paul's Roman citizenship and improper treatment, Paul and his companions are not even asked to leave the city (Luke's Source, STA 16:35). The magistrates only gave orders regarding Paul's release. It becomes apparent that Luke created an exit strategy regarding Paul's departure from Philippi through his redaction. The rapid movement from scene to scene in both Acts and Luke's Source creates a misimpression that the vignetted events took place in a more rapid order than was historically the case. Paul's stay in Philippi was longer than the three vignettes supplied by Acts and Luke's Source would imply.

Traveling the ninety-six miles from Philippi to Thessalonica could have been made in six days. Paul would have traveled the Egnatian Way, the major Roman highway which ran across Macedonia. Just as Phil 4:15-16 points to the warmth and partnership of the Philippian church with regard to Paul's ministry, so also it connects the ministry in Thessalonica with that initial work in Philippi. The Philippians sent financial support to Paul more than once while he was working in Thessalonica. Philippians 4:15-16 itself refutes the misconception apparent in Acts 17:2 that Paul only spent "three weeks" in Thessalonica. The whole tenor of the Thessalonian correspondence confirms this. Luke's Source suggests a potential "time gap" between Luke's Source, STA 17:9 and STA 17:10, which if so, could obscure a much longer period than that suggested by Lukan redaction. Paul's own letters suggest warmth toward the Thessalonians, as well as criticism of those who persecuted these early gentile Christians (see 2 Thess 1:4-12; 1 Thess 2:14-16).

We know nothing more about the situation that prompted Paul to leave Thessalonica than the account given in Acts and Paul's letters (Acts 17:5-15; 1 Thess 2:1-20). Second Thessalonians is likely the earlier of the two letters and the very earliest of Paul's letters that we have. While the present writer accepts 2 Thessalonians as the earliest Pauline letter that we have, it will only be treated below after attention is given to 1 Thessalonians.

Virtually half of 1 Thessalonians deals with Paul's relationship with the church, as he looks back in retrospect and reminds them of his initial work with them. First Thessalonians provides much information associated with the route Paul took during his founding mission in Greece. Paul goes from Philippi to Thessalonica to Beroea to Athens and sends Timothy from Athens back to Thessalonica. Timothy then linked up with Paul at Corinth, the likely place of the composition of 1 Thessalonians. The Corinthian congregation had just been founded about the time 1 Thessalonians was composed.

The founding visit to Corinth occurred at this point in time and *not* at the time the current Acts account would suggest during the time the Collection was being organized in the course of Paul's second campaign. Paul had good success in Thessalonica, as evidenced by the witness the church became (see 1 Thess 1:7–8; 2:1). He was welcomed among the gentiles there, who responded to his preaching of the gospel by turning from the worship of idol gods (1 Thess 1:9). Paul worked day and night such that he might support himself while he preached the gospel. He made converts, but he also made dear friends, as he grew this fledgling congregation (1 Thess 2:1–12). The family metaphors that Paul uses to describe his work among the Thessalonians—that of a nurse and that of a father—should not be lost. As he reflects, Paul cannot but help to contrast his reception in Thessalonica with his shameful treatment in Philippi by the city magistrates (1 Thess 2:2). Lifestyle conversion from paganism to the gospel Paul proclaimed did not occur over a fortnight nor were lasting relationships established in such a brief time.

Paul has nothing but praise for this church and felt bereft of them when he had to leave Thessalonica (1 Thess 2:17). The kind of affection that is evident in 1 Thessalonians is the kind of affection that can only develop in shared experiences over time. Paul had modeled selfless ministry and exhibited genuine pastoral care without impure motives or pleasing flattery or personal greed. Paul loved this church and saw it to be his "hope and joy and crown of boasting" before the Lord at the time of the parousia (1 Thess 2:19). Again, the opposition that he experienced in Thessalonica was external and not internal. Even after Paul moved on to Athens (1 Thess 3:1), he sent Timothy back to Thessalonica to check on the church. He was simply elated when Timothy brought back a good report of how the church was maintaining its faith even in the face of opposition and affliction (1 Thess 3:1–10).

Paul expresses thanksgiving for their growing faith and increasing love for one another (2 Thess 1:3). In the present writer's judgment, 2 Thessalonians is authentic and written at a time earlier than 1 Thessalonians. A reminder is offered that the present canonical arrangement of the Pauline letters is based upon length and not upon chronology nor the order in time when the letters were written.

Paul boasts about the steadfastness of the Thessalonians "in the churches of God" (2 Thess 1:4), even in the face of the afflictions which they are being called upon to endure. The "churches of God" (plural) mentioned here could include churches like Philippi, Beroea, Athens (?), Corinth—i.e., especially those churches in the European theater seem to be implied.

Aside from the difficult eschatological passage found in 2 Thess 2:1–12, Paul basically offers a word of comfort, encouragement, and exhortation (2 Thess 2:13—3:5). Some few problems had begun to arise in the church itself since his departure, such that the problem groups of "the weak, the fainthearted, and the idle" had to be addressed (2 Thess 3:6–13; see 1 Thess 5:14). His exhortations are very much characterized by comfort and encouragement in *both* Thessalonian letters, as he encouraged them to imitate his own example (2 Thess 2:16–17; 3:7–9; 3:15; 3:30–5; 1 Thess 4:1, 9–10, 18; 5:14–22).

Luke's underlying Source suggests that Paul's ministry in Thessalonica reached three categories of converts—Jews, God-fearing Greeks, and a number of leading women (Luke's Source, STA 17:4). At Philippi, Paul had already discovered how valuable "leading women" (such as Lydia) could be to the church in terms of both patronage and provision of houses in which to meet. The three categories of converts mentioned here describe the membership of Pauline churches, with the exception of inclusion of gentile pagans (such as the Philippian jailer).

While the proportionate membership might vary, Paul's churches reflect these four categories of members. The internal evidence of the Thessalonian correspondence depicts a growing gentile opposition, while Acts /Luke's Source reflects growing opposition to Paul on the part of the Jews of Thessalonica, who began to employ rabble rousers from the marketplace to stir up the crowds. According to Luke's Source, STA 17:6–9, charges of treason or sedition against Paul and Silas were brought before the authorities by the Jewish opposition. In view of Lukan redaction, this could have been more serious than is suggested by Acts/Luke's Source.

The situation apparently became grievous enough at some point, that the people of the church decided it was best for Paul and Silas to leave (Luke's Source, STA 17:10). Paul and company went to Beroea and found a more "noble" reception in the synagogue there than they had found in Thessalonica (Luke's Source, STA 17:11). Beroea itself was located near the base of Mount Bermius, some fifty miles from Thessalonica and several miles south of the main road or Egnatian Way. Note once again, that both Jews and "leading Greek women" came to believe in the gospel (Luke's Source, STA 17:12).

Although there is no surviving correspondence of Paul written to the "Church at Beroea," there was apparently a church established in Beroea. The fact that Silas and Timothy remain behind suggests a fledgling church in which there was more work to be done. The fact that only Timothy apparently caught up with Paul in Athens suggests a significant amount of time and work spent in Beroea, even after Paul left. When Paul returned to Judea upon the completion of his collection ministry during his Collection Campaign, Sopater of Beroea, son of Pyrrhus, accompanied him (Luke's Source, STA 20:4).

However, when Jews from Thessalonica came to Beroea and began to incite the crowds there, some of the brethren escorted Paul away, ultimately taking him to Athens by sea (Luke's Source, STA 17:14). The strength of Paul's opposition from the Jewish quarter in Thessalonica is illustrated by the fact they were willing to travel the fifty miles from Thessalonica to Beroea (at least a three-day journey) in order to incite the crowds against Paul. Silas and Timothy remained behind in Beroea. Paul sent back instructions for them to join him in Athens as soon as they could (Luke's Source, STA 17:15). Timothy apparently did join Paul in Athens for a time. However, there is no indication in Luke's Source that either Timothy or Silas connected with Paul in Athens, even though that was Paul's intention (Luke's Source, STA 17:15–16).

Luke's Source suggests Paul had already moved to Corinth, that Silas and Timothy met Paul in Corinth (Luke's Source, STA 18:1, 5). On the other hand, Paul mentions that he sent Timothy back from Athens to Thessalonica to check on the state of the Thessalonian church and to encourage them (1 Thess 3:1–5). The reference in Luke's Source (STA 18:5) portrays both Silas and Timothy joining Paul in Corinth after a trip from Macedonia. Both Silvanus and Timothy are listed as the co-senders of the two letters to Thessalonica (2 Thess 1:1; 1 Thess 1:1). A critical combination of the information gained from Paul's letter and Luke's Source may suggest that Silas remained in Beroea, while Timothy reported to Paul in Athens. Timothy apparently returned to Macedonia (Philippi, Thessalonica, and also Beroea), such that the two of them then rejoined Paul later in Corinth. Both 2 Thessalonians and 1 Thessalonians appear to have been written from Corinth.

> *Paul's passage to Athens had been anything but uneventful. A sudden storm between the Northern Sporades and Euboea had caused the small ship he was on to flounder and sink, with the loss of the cargo and some life. As luck would have it—or was it Providence?—Paul and several others were able to cling to planks of the ship and were finally rescued by some fishermen after a day and night of being adrift at sea. It had been a harrowing escape, with all having feared for their very lives. Although Paul could not have known it at the time, this was not the last time he would experience a shipwreck.[2] Paul and those with him discovered they were near the southern end of the island of Euboea and that they were not far from Geraestus and Carystus, which offered the best chance of obtaining passage to Piraeus/Athens. Smaller coastal packet ships came once a week—sometimes twice—and at most it should take only three days to arrive at Piraeus. The fishermen provided passage to Carystus, and when the packet ship came, Paul boarded the ship with some concern and trepidation. The voyage was without further incident. As they rounded Cape Sunium, the temple of Poseidon towered high above the sea from its natural prominence. The sheltered waters of the Saronic Gulf brought them safely to Piraeus.*
>
> *When he had first approached Athens, Paul had come up from the Port of Piraeus, walking steadily the four miles or so into the city. He remembered well the awe he had felt as the acropolis of Athens loomed ever larger in the distance. Although the city of Athena was past its heyday, the ancient splendor of Athens was still in evidence. As he had walked through the outer Ceramicus, where the road was lined with graves and cenotaphs, he could not help but notice the fine marble monuments to the dead. Athens was famous for its marble. Athens, however, was no different from other Greco-Roman cities, where the roads into the city passed through a necropolis before one reached the city of the living. It was in the city of the living that he would seek to proclaim Jesus as the living one,*

---

2. See 2 Cor 11:25. Paul was shipwrecked on three separate occasions and this would not include the shipwreck narrated in Acts/Luke's Source that occurred on the final voyage to Rome. Sailing the Mediterranean was a dangerous enterprise in the ancient world.

whom God had raised from the dead. Paul entered the city through the Dipylon Gate, where the main street took him into the agora of Athens. As he walked about the agora and the surrounding area looking for work and a place to stay, he could not fail to notice the temples dedicated to various gods.

During the time he was in Athens, Paul visited the Areopagus, from which he enjoyed an excellent view of the agora and surrounding city, as well as a view of the imposing acropolis which rose yet another 140 feet higher. Athens was far more imposing than any city he had ever visited. As he ascended to the Propylaea, the monumental gateway to the Acropolis, he marked the temples in evidence—a small temple to Athena Nike, the huge Parthenon dedicated to Athena Polias, along with its frieze of triglyphs and sculpted metopes and statuary depicting the gods of the Panathenaic procession. Both Athena and Poseidon were worshiped at the Erechtheum, its lower north porch overlooking the Roman agora. And to the southeast, the huge temple of Olympian Zeus remained unfinished but could not be missed. The hills outside the city walls were covered with grapevines and olives and fig trees that thrived in the thin soil of the rocky terrain surrounding the city. Paul could see in the distance both the port of Piraeus and the Sacred Way to Eleusis . . . .

Paul himself tells us nothing about a ministry in Athens, other than that he was willing to be left alone in Athens while Timothy returned to Thessalonica to further establish the church in its faith even in the face of continuing afflictions (1 Thess 3:1–5).

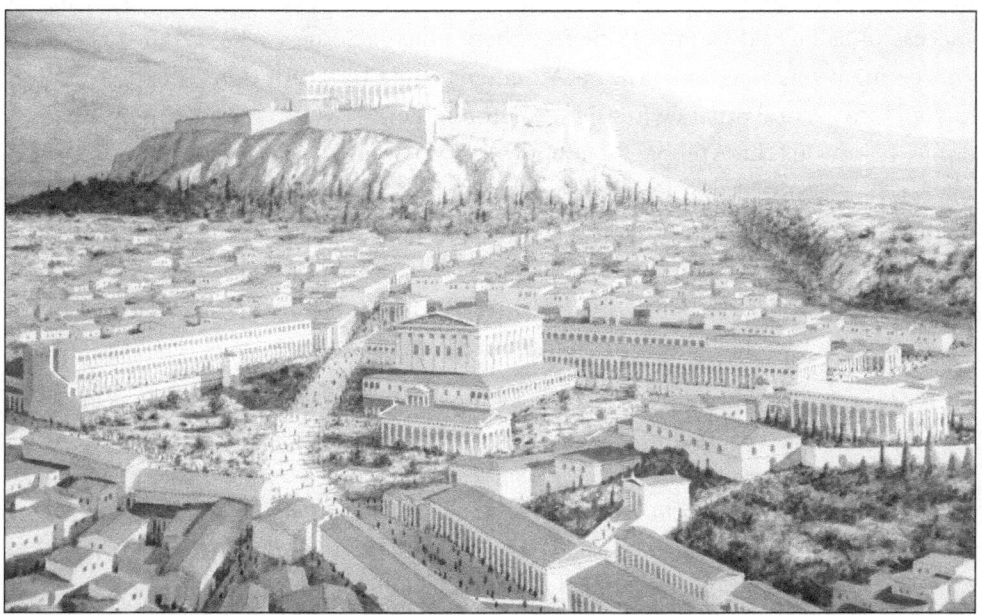

Fig. 16. First-Century Athens. *Archaeology Illustrated*, © Balage Balogh. Used under license.

Paul did not want the ministry in Thessalonica to have been in vain. No mention is made of the movements of Silas/Silvanus, which may suggest he remained in Beroea or elsewhere in Macedonia. Although speculative, Paul apparently sent Timothy back to Macedonia to rejoin Silvanus even after he brought a good report concerning the Thessalonican church, with the instructions that they should join him in Corinth as soon as they could see fit to come.

It is possible Timothy also carried a report back to Philippi about the progress of gospel, in view of the fact that Philippi was a patron church supporting Paul (Phil 4:15). When Timothy along with Silvanus returned to Paul, apparently at Corinth, he brought a good report about the strength of the Thessalonian church (1 Thess 3:6) and may well have brought funding from Philippi.

Luke's Source reflects a similar ministry of Paul seen elsewhere, as Paul repeats a pattern carried out both in Asia Minor and in Macedonia. Paul proclaimed the gospel in the synagogue, for there he could make appeal to both Jews and God-fearing gentiles (Luke's Source, STA 17:17). In addition, he had opportunity to proclaim the gospel to gentile pagans that he might encounter in the Roman agora, including Epicurean and Stoic philosophers. Stoicism was "in the air" of that first-century world, and Paul himself utilized some perspectives and vocabulary of Stoicism in the proclamation of the gospel. Tarsus, after all, had been a center of Stoic learning.

While many of the philosophers found Paul to be entertaining, others simply made fun of this Jewish ex-Pharisee who proclaimed a message that ran so counter to the tenets of Greek philosophies. Paul was less than successful, or at least not as successful as he had wanted to be in Athens (Luke's Source, STA 17:18–33). Luke's Source mentions that some of the Athenians came to faith ("some of the men following him . . . and others with them"), although only two persons are mentioned by name: Dionysius the Areopagite and a woman named Damaris (Luke's Source, STA 17:34). It is possible that Damaris was a wealthy woman, who became the patron of the small church and provided a place for their meeting, although there is no statement to that effect. These two persons are not mentioned further in the New Testament. There are no surviving letters of Paul to the "Athenians," such that nothing more is known about this fledgling Christian community.

> *Paul was glad to have left Athens. As it turned out, it had been a somewhat lonely time. Paul had worked in Athens for several more months and had become increasingly concerned when Silvanus and Timothy had not joined him there. He had hoped to hear good news about Philippi and Thessalonica and Beroea. Timothy finally came and brought news of Beroea, although he reported to Paul that Silvanus had returned to Thessalonica and intended to go back to Philippi. Paul waited another month, but when no word came from Silvanus, he dispatched Timothy back to Thessalonica. He had instructed him to find Silvanus and to rejoin him at Corinth whenever they could. Paul had discussed plans to move to Corinth, suggesting to Timothy that the remaining time in Athens would*

not be long. Paul felt that Corinth would be a better gateway to the West than Athens, situated as it was on the Gulf of Corinth and having two ports—one at Cenchreae and the other at Lechaeum. By moving to Corinth, Paul would be in the major city of Greece and much closer to Rome.

While in Athens, Paul had found plenty of work and supported himself at his trade of working leather and making awnings. Awnings provided shade from the hot and bright Mediterranean sun. He remained rather busy. The small shop in Athens in which he had worked and found lodging was only a street or two away from the agora. The location had afforded ample opportunity to come in contact with numerous gentiles from all stations in life. He had lived daily in sight of the acropolis, immersed in the business of the agora. With sacred temples constructed of Pentellic marble and dedicated to pagan deities seemingly everywhere, Paul could not help but think about that singular Temple of golden stone which stood in Jerusalem and the singular God worshiped there. It was that God who had called him and commissioned him to proclaim the singular gospel, irrespective of how that gospel might sound to the mind of Athenian philosophers. Paul uttered a brief prayer of thanksgiving to the One God of Heaven.

The time came to leave Athens, even though Timothy had not yet returned with Silas.

And Paul was glad when he finally left Athens, traveling as he did on the road to Eleusis. He was glad to be at Isthmia—it was only a few more miles to Corinth. As Paul contemplated his own move, the thought occurred to him that maybe Silvanus and Timothy had decided to bypass Athens entirely and travel the Via Egnatia farther west. Or, maybe they had gone by sea to Cenchreae and then to Corinth. Maybe they were already in Corinth; perhaps he was the laggard. He certainly hoped that they had suffered no further ill in Thessalonica.

Paul had contemplated the rather brief sail across the Saronic Gulf to Cenchreae, but he preferred to go by land when he could. It was cheaper to go on foot, without having to book passage on a ship. Besides, he had wanted to travel the "sacred way" that he had heard so much about from the Athenian philosophers. He had seen and heard enough in Athens, such that he decided to proceed according to the old sacred way to Eleusis some thirty miles distant, then through Megara and Isthmia and on to Corinth. His three days walking had been pleasant enough, with the sea on his left and the mountains on his right. He had found it more than interesting to visit the birthplace of the Eleusirian mysteries. As he crossed over the narrow isthmus at Isthmia that separated the Gulf of Corinth from the Saronic Gulf, he could not help but stop and watch a small ship being rolled across the land on the diolkos.[3]

---

3. The *diolkos* (δίολκος) was the overland rail system that transported ships across the three-and-one-half mile wide isthmus which separated the Gulf of Corinth from the Saronic Gulf, thus saving sailors a two hundred-mile journey around the Peloponnesus peninsula of Achaia. It is today the

Several of the people with whom Paul was traveling began to say that it would not be long now before they reached Corinth. Someone quoted the well-known adage, "Not for every man is a journey to Corinth!"[4] There was laughter among the Greek men with whom Paul traveled, as they turned their faces westward and began to walk the final few miles to Corinth, that city which had such a reputation for revelry and more . . . .

A part of Paul's task at Athens—here, as elsewhere—was to convince the Athenians that what could be seen and was so apparent was not real. What was real was what could not in fact readily be seen. However, it was not to Platonism that Paul appealed. It was not a Platonic gospel to which Paul appealed—i.e., that the real existed in heaven, while all around were mere copies of reality. The Athenians were familiar with that. No, it was an alternative Gospel of the One God who had raised a crucified Jesus from the dead, the One God who offered new life in a new age.

A Time in Corinth

When Paul first arrived in Corinth, it was the year 49 CE; he had now been involved in some type of Christian mission for some fifteen years. In the early years he had first worked with Barnabas, after he had become associated with the church at Antioch. They had completed that early mission to Cyprus, which had led to the suggestion that they go to Pamphilia and the southern region of Galatia. After a time spent in the church at Antioch in Syria, Barnabas had wanted to return to Cyprus. Paul, on the other hand, had decided to return to southern Galatia and then to develop additional churches in Asia Minor.

In this second phase of what would become his *Foundational Campaign*, a visionary experience had led him in the direction of Macedonia. And way had led on to way. Yet his overall mission had begun to crystallize, as Paul began to understand some things he had never even contemplated earlier in his career. He was in striking distance of Rome, the capital of the empire. He would work his way toward Rome, preaching the gospel as he went. Now after a time in Athens (Achaia), he found himself in the relatively new city of Corinth (Achaia), which had been rebuilt by Julius Caesar beginning in 44 BCE following its earlier destruction by the Romans a hundred years earlier. Although the old city had reached its "golden age" in Classical times, Caesar created a new colony with a settlement of freedmen and named the colony for

---

location of the Corinth Canal, contemplated by Nero, but completed only at the end of the nineteenth century.

4. As a major city with two seaports and much cosmopolitan traffic, Corinth had quite a reputation for lax morality. There was even a verb coined, "to play the Corinthian" or "to Corinthianize," known in many quarters of the Mediterranean world since classical times—such was the city's reputation for sexual immorality.

himself—*Colonia Laus Julia Corinthiensis*. This new city, expanded on the old site, was the city in which Paul lived and worked.

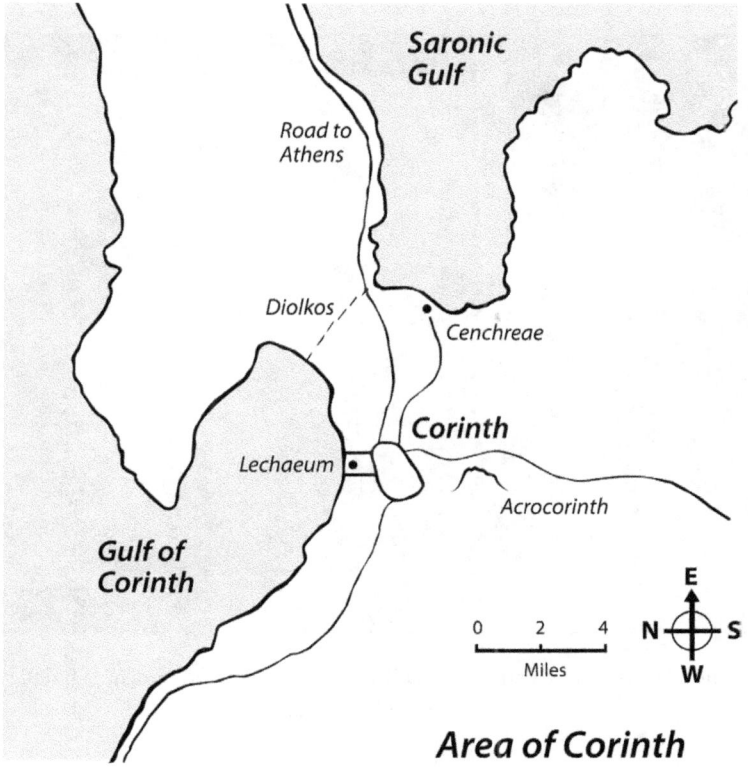

Fig. 17. Map of Area of Corinth. Map © by Jason Greene. Used with permission.

The city of Corinth was blessed by its strategic location. Located as it was near the narrow isthmus that separated the Peloponnese meant that it had two ports—a southeastern port at Cenchreae on the Saronic Gulf and a northern port at Lechaeum on the Gulf of Corinth. It was a thriving center of commerce, energetic vigor, and teeming life. Every two years, the city played host to the Isthmian Games celebrated to honor Poseidon, god of the sea. The city itself was inland and lay on a plateau (some two hundred feet above sea level), the backdrop of which was dominated by a single, steep mountain peak to the south known as the Acrocorinth, that towered some sixteen hundred feet over the city. There were natural springs in the area and the city itself was founded over the Peirene Spring, located in the center of the city. The Peirene Spring still flows today.

In the century after Paul, Corinth became the undisputed commercial and political center among Greek cities during the Roman period and, indeed, the finest city in all of Greece. It became known for its natural resources, such as fine wine and currant fruit, as well as for its manufactured goods of fine pottery and bronze sculpture. Corinth gave its name to a particular architectural feature of an ornate column top decorated with carved acanthus leaves. Paul was now in the heartland of Roman Greece.

Fig. 18. Stone Mason and Corinthian Capital. *Archaeology Illustrated*, © Balage Balogh. Used under license.

Literary references as well as archaeological remains testify to the multitudinous deities worshiped in the city of Corinth. In spite of Mummius's destruction in 146 BCE, Doric columns of the sixth-century BCE temple of Apollo remained standing. Older Greek cults persisted, including the worship of Dionysus, god of wine and revelry. A temple of Aphrodite may have once stood on the Acrocorinth. Temples have been found in Corinth that were erected to the Egyptian gods Isis and Osiris. There was a temple to Asclepius, the god of healing. A number of Roman temples were dedicated after 44 BCE—temples to Tyche (Fortune), Hermes, Poseidon, Jupiter, as well as an imperial cult shrine to Octavia, sister of Augustus. The emperor Augustus himself was the adopted son of Julius Caesar, the one who began the earlier rebuilding of Corinth. There were monuments celebrating other gods, such as Apollo and "Athena the Bridler," and in case any had been missed, there was a Pantheon shrine erected to all the gods.

While "paganism" tends to be tagged with the word "atheism" today, in Paul's world paganism was in a sense the dominant religion. The Christians, in fact, at a later point were persecuted as "atheists," because they did not believe in the gods. In addition to worship of the gods, Corinth was characterized by the common moral religion of the day as popularized by wandering philosophers like the Cynics. Diogenes of Sinope (on the Black Sea), a recognized founder of the Cynic movement, had lived and died in Corinth. Paul thus came to a very "cosmopolitan" and a very "religious" city. There was apparently at least one or more Jewish synagogues in the city as well.

Paul writes 1 Corinthians from Ephesus during his Collection Campaign, and we learn a great deal from this first surviving letter to Corinth concerning his initial work there. Issues dealing with the problems the church was facing at that time, as well as the matter of Paul's Collection, can be postponed until later. The point at issue here is Paul's initial work in Corinth and the founding of the church. When Paul first arrived in Corinth, he was at a low ebb. It had been more than five years since he had left Antioch with Silvanus. His work in Macedonia and Athens had not been easy, and he now found himself in the capital city of the Roman province of Achaia. "I came to you in weakness and fear, and with much trembling" (1 Cor 2:3), Paul would later write to the Corinthian church.

Indeed, Paul's work at Corinth would prove to be one of his most fruitful mission centers, but it would also prove to be one of his most troublesome and difficult churches. The hard flint of Corinth would help Paul to develop both pastoral sympathy and theological acumen—it would severely put him to the test, as he would be called upon to defend both his gospel and his person.

As Paul recalls his foundational work, he mentions having baptized Crispus and Gaius and the household of Stephanas, as well as possibly others (1 Cor 1:14–16). He identifies the household of Stephanas as the "first converts in Achaia" (1 Cor 16:15). Paul became the spiritual father of the Corinthian church, an indication that he was the founder of the church (1 Cor 4:15), along with his associates Silvanus and Timothy (2 Cor 1:19). Not many of the initial converts at Corinth were "wise according to worldly standards" or powerful or of noble birth (1 Cor 1:26).

There is a focus on words like "wise" and "wisdom" in 1 Corinthians, although one must remember that Paul has come to Corinth from Athens. He has been accustomed to debating the "wisdom of the age" (see 1 Cor 1:17—2:5; 3:18–20). In the proclamation of the gospel, Paul sought to proclaim the wisdom of God, a wisdom of "Christ crucified," which must have sounded rather audacious and strange to Greek ears, even as the proclamation of "Jesus and Resurrection" (ὁ Ἰησοῦς and ἡ ἀνάστασις) had sounded strange to the Greek philosophers of Athens who envisioned a coupled pair of deities (Luke's Source, STA 17:18). As previously indicated, in Greek "Jesus" is a masculine proper name and "resurrection" is a feminine noun. For the Greek philosophical viewpoint that prided itself regarding "wisdom" (ἡ σοφία), it sounded as though Paul was preaching about two gods—a male deity named "Jesus" and a female deity named "Resurrection."

As Paul had come to understand, there were many in Corinth who prided themselves in "wisdom" and "things spiritual." Whether they were mere sophists or sophic pneumatics made no difference to Paul, because Paul essentially had to treat them as "babes in Christ" and (ironically) not as "spiritual" persons (1 Cor 3:1). In his work,

Paul had sought to lay the basic foundation of the gospel, which as he states is "Jesus Christ" both crucified and resurrected (1 Cor 3:11). For Paul, the gospel involved both Jesus's crucifixion and his resurrection. While he may mention one or the other separately, the other is always nearby. Jesus died by crucifixion, a Roman means of execution. That was an historical fact. Yet, apart from resurrection there would be no gospel—and no "Paul, apostle of the *Lord* Jesus *Christ*." Compare Rom 1:1–4; see 1 Cor 15:1–4 for his basic traditional statement of the early Christian kerygma.

Paul reminds the Corinthians that "neither those who practice sexual immorality, nor idolaters, nor the immoral, nor adulterers, nor those who play the female role or male role in homosexuality, nor thieves, nor the greedy, nor drunkards, nor slanderers, nor those who seize by violence will inherit the kingdom of God," but then he adds the words, "some of you were these things" (1 Cor 6:9–11). It is evident that the church at Corinth consisted of folk from different social strata and varied religious experience. It is evident there was a problem with various forms of immorality, which was very much in keeping with the nature of Corinth itself. Corinth was a center of prostitution, both sacred and otherwise. Paul's awareness of Corinthian immorality judged according to Jewish standards is clear.

Paul's work in Corinth apparently reached a wide spectrum of the Corinthian populace. Some were Jews (see 1 Cor 7:18–19; 9:20); some were slaves (see 1 Cor 7:21–23); some were powerful and of noble birth, some were educated (see 1 Cor 1:26). Apparently, many were gentile pagans (see 1 Cor 8:1–6; 9:21; 10:14–21; 12:2). This broad spectrum of people in itself opened the door for the multitudinous problems that both the church and Paul would face. Pagan immorality apparently was a continuing and pressing problem in the church at Corinth (1 Cor 5:9; 2 Cor 12:21). When Paul first worked among the Corinthians, he was supported by other churches (as Philippi) and was not financially dependent upon the Corinthians (1 Cor 4:12; 2 Cor 11:8–9).

The Acts presentation or Luke's Source account suggests that Paul came to Corinth after his time in Athens and that he encountered a Jewish Christian couple, Aquila and Priscilla, who had recently come from Italy as a result of Claudius's edict. At some time earlier than their arrival in Corinth, Claudius had Jews banished from Rome for creating unrest and disturbance (see *Suetonius*, "The Deified Claudius," 5.25), including unrest involving a certain "Chrestus" (Christ?). Whether or not Aquila and Priscilla were Christian before their encounter with Paul is not known. If so, they were not the first converts at Corinth—an honor which belongs to the household of Stephanas (1 Cor 16:15). While the point at which they became Christian may be an issue, the fact that they became Christian is not. Paul himself mentions them in 1 Cor 16:19, 2 Tim 4:19, and Rom 16:3 in conjunction with Ephesus. The year of their arrival in Corinth was apparently 48/49 CE, although Claudius's edict is to be dated several years earlier. They may have relocated elsewhere in Italy for a time after being banished from Rome, prior to the time they moved to Corinth.

Paul had several things in common with Aquila and Priscilla, in that they were Jewish, apparently Christian, and all worked at the same trade as tent or awning makers. This could also include small leather goods (Luke's Source, STA 18:3). There is no reason to doubt Paul's usual manner of witness as reflected in Acts/Luke's Source, namely, that he would begin work in the synagogue preaching to Jews and God-fearers until he encountered resistance, at which time he would turn primarily to gentiles. There is a certain logic to that kind of approach, even though the threefold Pauline assertion in Acts (Acts 13:44–47; 18:6; 28:28) belongs to Lukan redaction. What Paul needed to establish a church in any location was a patron who could provide a place for meeting for worship and fellowship.

According to Luke's Source (STA 18:4), Paul sought to persuade both Jews and God-fearers (Greeks) every Sabbath in the synagogue. When Silas and Timothy came from "Macedonia" (Luke's Source, STA 18:5), Paul was involved in emphatic Christological proclamation to Jews. By the time synagogue opposition and insults had increased, Paul had already established the beachhead that he needed, such that he could pull away from the synagogue (Luke's Source, STA 18:6–7). The house of Titius Justus, a God-fearer, became the locus of Paul's proclamation (Luke's Source, STA 18:7).

The name Titius Justus appears to be much like the nomen and cognomen of a Roman citizen, such that his full name might have been Gaius Titius Justus—the person whom Paul personally baptized (1 Cor 1:14). An alternative textual reading gives the name "Titus" rather than "Titius," such that this could possibly reference Paul's associate Titus (see Gal 2:1; 2 Cor 8:16–17). Titus was an uncircumcised gentile God-fearer (Gal 2:3; cf. Acts 18:7). The ruler of the synagogue, Crispus, was apparently one and the same person that Paul lists among the converts he personally baptized (1 Cor 1:14). Crispus, Gaius, and Stephanas were apparently persons of means who may have been patrons of the synagogue and then of the newly formed church.

Paul was apparently quite successful at making converts in Corinth, in contrast with Athens. There is an air of dynamism in Luke's Source account of Paul's ministry in Corinth as compared with Luke's Source account of Athens (see Luke's Source, STA 17:34; 18:7–8, 11). There is also a potential time gap between Luke's Source, STA 18:11 and 18:12, which suggests Lukan redaction has telescoped two different accounts of Paul's work in Corinth. Luke's Source (STA 18:11) suggests Paul worked in Corinth for eighteen months. This extraordinary length of time would refer to the period of Paul's initial work in the city. If the current thesis is correct, Paul left Corinth and moved on to Illyricum after this eighteen month period, at least as far as Apollonia at the terminus of the Via Egnatia. However, it was not too long before Paul felt compelled to return to Corinth to seek to remediate some very serious issues that had arisen in the church since his departure. Paul generally appears to have left associates or, at any rate, an established church behind as he moved on to a new work. Such an approach echoes Paul's earlier procedure with regard to Thessalonica. It would not have taken long for word from Corinth to have reached him in Apollonia (Illyricum)—less than a week. The terminus of the Via Egnatia in Illyricum would have been a strategic location for the establishment of a church congregation—a final point of significance before Italy itself.

It is quite possible that Paul converted Titus while he was in Corinth or perhaps in Illyricum (see Gal 2:1–3). Titus is not mentioned at all in Acts (unless Titius in Acts 18:7), although he plays a prominent role in Paul's own letters. In Galatians, he is identified as an uncircumcised Greek who accompanied Paul to Jerusalem at the time of the Famine Visit (Gal 2:1–10). In 2 Corinthians, he is one whom Paul trusts to be his envoy in working out the difficult problems that existed between Paul and the Corinthians during the time of the Collection Campaign (2 Cor 2:13; 8–9).

When Paul is imprisoned in Rome, he indicates in 2 Timothy (likely his last extant letter) that Titus has returned to Dalmatia (Illyricum, 2 Tim 4:10). Titus was thus a very significant individual in the context of Paul's ministry and mission. The fact of his absence in the book of Acts may well suggest Lukan redaction at the point of Lukan omission of a ministry in Illyricum and the Lukan combination of two separate visits to Corinth (Luke's Source, STA 18:1–11 and STA 18:12–18).

We know by Paul's own testimony that he made three visits to Corinth (2 Cor 12:14; 13:1). The first visit would have been the "Founding" visit, while the last visit would have been the "Collection" visit. Paul himself alludes to a "Painful" visit that occurred between the "Founding" and "Collection" visits (2 Cor 2:1). The book of Acts as it stands presents only a single "Founding" visit to Corinth (Luke's Source, STA 18:1–18) and merely hints at the "Collection" visit (see Acts 20:3). It nowhere records a second, "Painful" visit, a point that would certainly not support Luke's apologetic in his telling of the gospel story. Luke does not appear to be aware of Paul's Collection mission, or perhaps he suppresses the underlying purpose.

In seeking to understand Paul's ministry, scholars are confronted with the dilemma of how to account for Paul's second and "Painful" visit to Corinth, as well as Paul's time spent in Illyricum (Rom 15:19). Many posit an abrupt visit to Corinth from Ephesus during the Collection period. Others posit the idea of Paul beginning a new work in Illyricum at the time he comes to Corinth to receive the Collection. Both of these options, however, appear to be rather artificial solutions to a real and often ignored problem of what to do with Illyricum, as well as Paul's second and "Painful" visit to Corinth. At least one scholar has termed Rom 15:19 a "throw-away" verse because he found no place for Paul's work in Illyricum. All options are speculative to some degree, because of the lack of developed evidence. Correlation must be made with the dating of the Gallio reference as well, for that is a cornerstone of any developed Pauline chronology (Luke's Source, STA 18:12/Acts 18:12).

It is the thesis of this writer that Paul's ministry to Illyricum best fits into the temporal gap between Luke's Source, STA 18:11 and 18:12. Other than Rom 15:19, Paul himself says nothing specific about work in Illyricum, although 2 Tim 4:10 may be suggestive of such, as well, for it mentions Titus having gone to Dalmatia (Illyricum).

The position taken here is that Paul left Corinth after a lengthy initial period of working to establish the church there. During the time he was in Corinth, he wrote both 2 and 1 Thessalonians. When he left Corinth, Paul likely walked the coastal road from Corinth to Aegium to Patrae, where he boarded a ship that took him to Nicopolis (see Titus 3:12) and perhaps on up the coast to Apollonia and even Dyrrhachium, the beginning points of the Via Egnatia. They were both a part of Illyria in Paul's day. Within another week, he could have been in Scodra in Illyricum. Although speculation, it is reasonable speculation based upon Paul's prior patterns. Although perhaps tempted by Rome, Paul's intention may well have been to travel back along the Via Egnatia to Thessalonica and to Philippi, before returning to Antioch.

Paul had been away from Antioch for almost eight years. Had it really been that long? However, as a result of his work in Macedonia, he now had support (such as Philippi) that was independent of Antioch. In other words, Paul will complete this second phase of his Foundational Campaign with Silvanus, but he now knows that he has the wherewithal to mount an evangelistic campaign independent of Antioch yet even farther to the west. Paul apparently always left word as to where he was going next, such that anyone who needed to do so could reach him in due time. We do not know the extent of his communication with Antioch during the course of this phase of the Foundational Campaign, but there must have been some. Within reason, surely Antioch knew approximately where Paul might be, or at least how to find him, in view of the fact they were at least a semi-sponsor of his mission.

It is presupposed that over time word reached Corinth concerning the famine in Judea and the developing need among the Christians in Judea. News of severe famine (or earthquake, for that matter) likely traveled far and fast in the interconnected world of the Roman Empire. Jewish synagogues and Jewish merchants would provide an additional means of communication, especially when Jerusalem was the center of concern. Paul wrote 1 Thessalonians from Corinth, and although there are other possible interpretations, famine was traditionally interpreted as a sign of God's wrath (1 Thess 2:16). Jewish envoys could have brought news to the Jews of Corinth, even making an appeal for funds. News could have easily spread from Jews to Jewish Christians, who could have easily informed Paul, who was now in Illyricum. Paul, of course, had associates whom he could send back to Corinth to find out how the church was faring.

Indeed, Paul was informed that there was immorality in the church at Corinth. He wrote a letter to Corinth, now known as the "Previous Letter" (see 1 Cor 5:9), that warned the Corinthian Christians not to tolerate immorality of various kinds within the church. It is suggested that 2 Cor 6:14—7:1 may represent a fragment of this letter, a single leaf of papyrus which was mixed at an early point with the papyrus leaves of 2 Corinthians.

The letter was apparently misunderstood and did not correct the situation, such that Paul's work in Illyricum was interrupted, as he determined to return to Corinth to deal with church problems. He would then return to Antioch to give a direct report on his extensive campaign and to address in some way the matter of the famine in Judea. He could even appeal to Antioch for a mission farther west—to Rome and to Spain. The earliest Christians were living in eschatological times. And so from Illyricum Paul returned to Corinth for a second time, which proved to be a very "painful" visit (see 2 Cor 2:1–4). Although speculative, this is a very plausible scenario and is equally as viable or even more viable than a hurried, surprise visit made by Paul to Corinth from Ephesus during the Collection Campaign. To have made a "painful" visit in the middle of the Collection Campaign would have quite possibly spelled the end to collection efforts in Corinth.

It is during Paul's second visit to Corinth on the return from Illyricum that Paul has his encounter with Gallio in the summer of 51 CE. The Jewish opposition, as had been the case in other places according to Luke's Source, made an attack upon Paul and hauled him before the judgment seat of the new proconsul, Gallio (Luke's Source, STA 18:12). Paul's appearance before Gallio has become the linchpin of Pauline chronology, the one link between general history and Paul's career accepted by virtually all scholars. Gallio drove the Jews from his judgment seat (the *bema*), refusing to hear the case.

Fig. 19. The Bema at Corinth. *Archaeology Illustrated*, © Balage Balogh.
Used under license.

What is depicted is a new Roman proconsul who refuses to become involved in Jewish internecine disagreements, so long as city order is not threatened. Luke's Source simply states that Paul "remained many days longer with the brethren" (Luke's

Source, STA 18:18). This is an indeterminate time, but it affirms that Paul did not feel endangered as at Thessalonica (Luke's Source, STA 17:10). He continued to address the problems that existed within the church, although as it turned out, he was rather unsuccessful. This is illustrated by Paul's recall of that visit several years later (2 Cor 2:1–2), at the point of his Collection campaign. Paul was determined not to make another "painful visit," and so he wrote a letter (1 Corinthians) in response to reports and questions from Corinth. Yet, perhaps surprisingly, 1 Corinthians turned out to be a "painful letter" that made a bad situation worse. The dispatch of Titus and others to Corinth, as well as the writing of 2 Corinthians, becomes a tenuous attempt by Paul at reconciliation in the light of the Collection.

> *As the morning sun rose over the harbor at Cenchreae, Paul, along with Priscilla, Aquila, and Titus, watched as the last of the cargo was loaded onto the ship bound for Ephesus. They felt quite fortunate to have booked passage on a ship sailing directly across the Aegean the almost three hundred miles to Ephesus. If they were able to sustain good winds, they would be at Ephesus before the week was out. As water and food stuffs were loaded on board the ship, Paul and his party said their good byes to the several folk from the Corinthian church who had brought them by wagon to Cenchreae. As they moved their remaining belongings on board, they settled in on the port side of the ship just ahead of the mast. Perhaps that would afford them some shade from the western sun.*

Fig. 20. A Roman Grain Ship. Original painting by G. Roger Greene.

This would be the second major move for Priscilla and Aquila in about as many years. Paul had grown close to them during his stays in Corinth and had spoken with them about the possibilities of work in Ephesus. Paul had heard Ephesus was a grand city with great resources and opportunities. It was much closer to Macedonia and Achaia than was Antioch of Syria. In fact, it was a centralized location—Galatia lay to the south, Macedonia and Achaia to the north.

Paul had convinced Priscilla and Aquila that he sincerely needed their service in the foundational work in Ephesus, just as he had come to depend so strongly upon them in Corinth. Paul was glad they had an adventuresome spirit. They had received their share of criticism in the church when they had taken up for Paul during this most recent "painful" visit, but they had stood their ground. Corinth was not home; they would give Ephesus a go. Titus, on the other hand, was quite at home in the Corinthian basin. Paul had grown to love this gentile Christian, who had accepted so many tasks at Paul's behest. He had proved to be a good mediator during the very difficult second visit. Paul had finally convinced him to go with him to bear testimony in Antioch, assuring him that he would send him back to Corinth once they settled in Ephesus.

A Return to Antioch

When Paul finally sailed for Antioch in Syria, Priscilla and Aquila sailed with him. Although not mentioned at all in Luke's Source/Acts, Titus apparently also sailed with Paul (Gal 2:1–3). No mention is made of the whereabouts of either Silvanus or Timothy in Luke's Source/Acts or in Paul's letters. If Silvanus is the same person as the Silas of the Jerusalem Conference (as is herein assumed), then it is likely he accompanied Paul back to Antioch and then to Jerusalem. This is a reasonable assumption, in the light of the fact that the church at Antioch had commissioned both Paul and Silas to the second and great phase of the Foundational Campaign (Luke's Source, STA 15:40). Timothy is not mentioned again until later in Luke's Source (STA 19:22), at a time that must have coincided with the Collection Campaign.

Fig. 21. Harbor Gate at Ephesus. *Archaeology Illustrated*, © Balage Balogh.
Used under license.

Paul had earlier wanted to begin a ministry in Ephesus, but he was prevented from doing so by the Macedonian vision. He now leaves ("plants") Priscilla and Aquila at Ephesus to begin a work there (Luke's Source, STA 18:19), while he and others traveled on to Antioch. In all likelihood, Paul had not yet formulated in any full measure his intentions of a collection campaign, even though the possibility may have occurred to him. Support of the Jerusalem Temple by diaspora Jews was a customary practice, which could have served as a model for financial support of the Jerusalem church. A full comprehension of need combined with theological purpose could have only been formulated after his visit to Jerusalem (Gal 2:1–10, "Famine"; Acts 15, "Conference"). However, it is clear that Paul intended to return to Ephesus after a time at Antioch.

> *From Ephesus, Paul booked passage for himself and Titus upon a ship sailing for Caesarea. He had hoped to find one sailing more directly to Seleucia, the harbor of Antioch, but he had been unsuccessful. The merchant ship sailed among the islands off the coast of Asia until it finally put in at the harbor on Rhodes. After exchanging part of the cargo for supplies, the crew made ready for the open sea voyage which would first take them toward Crete and then toward Caesarea. Paul never liked the open sea, but the strong north-east wind of summer determined the route. . . .*

> *With five hundred miles of open sea now behind him, the ship was at last in sight of the lighthouse of Herod's artificial harbor at Caesarea which he had built some sixty years earlier. Paul had sailed from Caesarea years earlier when the brethren at Caesarea had sent him off to Tarsus, but he had never approached the city by sea from the northwest. The harbor now lay in the distance, drawing ever closer. Paul began to pick out the colossal statues of the imperial family standing on elevated columns guiding vessels to the harbor entrance. The lighthouse tower, named after Drusus, Augustus's heir apparent at an earlier time, began to loom larger and larger. Herod had named his great port city "Caesarea," to honor his patron, Caesar Augustus. The harbor itself was named "Sebastos," Greek for "Augustus." Paul began to point out the various features to Titus and his other companions. The large temple dedicated to Augustus stood at the head of the harbor and could not be missed as it loomed ever larger.*

IMAGINE PAUL'S FOUNDATION CAMPAIGN

Fig. 22. Gateway Harbor City of Caesarea Maritima. *Archaeology Illustrated*, © Balage Balogh. Used under license.

As Paul's ship drew closer to the harbor's entrance, Paul was captivated by the magnificent promontory of Herod's palace, now the residence of the provincial Roman governor. Paul pointed it out to Titus. Rising in the distance behind the palace stood the Roman theater, with its opening toward the Mare Nostrum—*the sea which Rome claimed as its own. As the ship entered the quay of the harbor, Paul's attention was immediately drawn to the large and magnificent temple that Herod had erected near the inner harbor dedicated to the goddess Roma and the now deified Emperor Augustus. Upon disembarking, Paul and his company did not stop to marvel—they had seen Roman temples before,—at Athens, Corinth, Ephesus and elsewhere. Still, the thought crowded his mind that only the Jewish God could raise one from the dead [Jesus's resurrection], as he and Titus, along with his other companions, went up into the city from the harbor to visit with the Jewish believers who dwelled there. Little did he know that he would one day return to Caesarea under much different circumstances. Tomorrow, though, he would inquire at the harbor about any ships sailing along the coast toward Seleucia. . . . He was now getting anxious to be back in Antioch. . . .*

It was the latter part of the summer of 51 CE when Paul and his company arrived at Seleucia, the port city of Antioch. It had been eight years since Paul had been in Antioch. The time had slipped by. He hoped that while he was in Antioch, he might have opportunity to see Barnabas and hear firsthand about his mission to Cyprus and otherwise be brought up to date. Paul certainly had some stories to tell—Philippi, Thessalonica, Athens, Corinth, Illyricum. He had lived and worked in some of the largest cities of the empire. After his trying time in Corinth, having been recalled from Illyricum, Paul was ready for a rest in Antioch. He could not wait for Titus and the others with him to relate to the church at Antioch how those in Corinth had received the gospel. It would be good to get his feet back on the land. Even though the lengthy voyage from Corinth to Ephesus to Antioch had been uneventful, he had long ago decided he was no seaman—especially after his earlier shipwreck in the Aegean Sea. . . .

While Acts 18:22 is most often interpreted as a fourth visit to Jerusalem in the *Acts* presentation, this is likely a misunderstanding wrought by the Lukan redaction which combined the two visits of Paul to Corinth. Given the centrality of Jerusalem to the Lukan presentation (in both Luke and Acts), Luke would have directly stated such rather than merely leaving a Jerusalem visit undescribed and only possibly implied. Paul simply "went up" into the city of Caesarea from the area of the harbor.

Once Paul landed at Caesarea, he had to wait for and locate a ship traveling up the coast of Palestine and Phoenicia to Syria (see Luke's Source, STA 18:19–21c). Paul simply greets and spends some time with members of what had come to be a significant church in Caesarea, before he embarks on a ship going to Antioch. Such a meeting would also enable Paul to find out significant details about the scourge of the famine that had now been affecting Judea for several years. Luke's Source (STA 18:22) actually brings phase II of the Foundation Campaign to a close and sets the stage for Paul's upcoming two visits to Jerusalem in what was a Jerusalem visit complex in Luke's Source prior to Luke's redaction.

A Mission to Jerusalem

Paul's return to Antioch would be both a joyous one and a challenging one. The results of the ongoing famine in Judea would necessitate a visit of Paul and Barnabas to Jerusalem in the fall of 51 CE.

Having returned to Antioch, a welcome respite, Paul listened to Agabus with interest as he spoke of worsening famine in Judea and the grave economic challenges that were being endured by the church there. He had been told about some of the difficulties being faced when he had visited with the church in Caesarea earlier in the summer, but now the situation had apparently worsened. The fall harvest did not look good. Paul had now been several months in Antioch. To his delight, he had found Barnabas there when he arrived. He had not seen him in almost a decade and they reminisced about their work in Cyprus and Galatia. Paul had shared his story of the gospel he had been preaching, testifying to the work that he had carried out as far as the province of Illyricum. He had introduced Titus to the Christians at Antioch, with the result that Titus became something of a cause célèbre *in Antioch of the impact of the gospel in Achaia.*

As the church at Antioch listened to Agabus, they determined to take up a collection to send as economic aid to the saints in Jerusalem. Because of their connection with Jerusalem, it was decided that Paul and Barnabas could accompany those who were designated to carry the famine funds to the Holy City. This would afford them opportunity to share their experiences among the gentiles with the Jewish Christians in Jerusalem. It would mark an anniversary of sorts....

The journey overland with famine relief funds had taken the better part of a month. Now Jerusalem was in sight. Paul tried to remember how long it had been—twelve years? No, fourteen. Fourteen years.... Those fourteen years had been climactic. Memories of his entire Foundational Campaign coursed through his mind—Galatia, Philippi, Thessalonica, Athens, Corinth. Ah, Corinth! He thought about how close he had gotten to Italy—and to Rome—in Illyricum, before word of trouble in Corinth and the famine in Judea had demanded his return east. He had shared the gospel that he had preached with Antioch, which was supportive of his success. But now, what reception would he receive in Jerusalem? His own life had certainly turned since he had personally persecuted the earliest followers of the "Way" in Judea.

He walked, staff in hand and purse by his side, as he looked down at the roadway before him that had almost reached the top of the hill. Paul's mind was flooded with a host of memories, some good and some very difficult. He was distracted as he walked along, oblivious to the conversation going on around him, until his attention was redirected. "Look, Titus, there is the Great Temple!...

Titus was familiar with pagan temples, but the virtual glow of the golden Jerusalem limestone in the sunlight was an awesome sight indeed. Titus was anxious to meet those original disciples of Jesus who had known Jesus and who became the first witnesses to the resurrection—Peter, John, and others, whose testimony must indeed be impressive. Barnabas, for his part, tugged at his robe and patted the portion of the famine relief funds that he was carrying. While being most familiar with Jerusalem and the location of its significant house church, with staff in hand, Barnabas pointed to the way he thought they should go. They would descend the hill and walk through the Kidron Valley and enter the city from the south, following a time-worn pilgrim path. They would be able to refresh themselves at the Pool of Bethesda, before they walked up the street roadway that would take them into the Holy City.

They would surely be able to find lodging with members of the church who would welcome them in Christ and who would welcome the monetary relief that accompanied them.

Paul had not been in Jerusalem since he had visited with James (Jacob) and Cephas for that brief time three years after his call and commission (Gal 1:18–24). It was now fourteen years later (Gal 2:1) and Paul had completed his foundational work, having traveled through much of the Roman Empire. It was the late summer or early fall of 51 CE. He had had time to spend with the church at Antioch and share with them his experiences in Macedonia, Achaia, and Illyricum. He introduced them to Titus and told them about Priscilla and Aquila and his future/further plans in Ephesus. That was unfinished business for Paul, ever since the Spirit had directed him away from a ministry in the province of Asia and toward a mission in Macedonia (Luke's Source, STA 16:7–10). By the time prophets came down from Jerusalem, Paul had also had time to meet with Barnabas. According to Luke's Source (STA 11:28), a prophet by the name of Agabus "foretold" a great famine about to come upon all the inhabited world. Luke's Source (STA 11:28) further confirms that this "happened" in the days of Claudius.

Josephus refers to famines in the times of the governorships of Cuspius Fadus (44–46 CE) and Tiberius Alexander (46–48 CE) (see Josephus, *Ant.* 20.5.2). "Famine" was not just a matter of the production of foodstuffs, but also a matter of *distribution* and the ability of the poor to purchase grain at inflated prices. "Famine" was a "class calamity." The effects of a severe famine could last for years. It was not a day and age when food and other aid could be airlifted to address the problem in a month's time. We need to learn to better imagine and appreciate the difference between our day and Paul's.

The reference stated in Luke's Source (STA 11:28) is rather general and is exactly what might be expected in tradition that has been handed down and remembered or interpreted some years later. The reference to the time of Claudius could in fact be Lukan redactional commentary. Surely, if Agabus and his prediction are historical, he had much more to say in the historical context pertaining to what the famine actually meant or how it should be interpreted.

> *Barnabas, Paul, and others from Antioch opened their purses and piled the coinage sent for famine relief on the table. Christians at Antioch had been very generous and most of the offering was silver, represented by Roman denarii that included the portrait of multiple emperors. Denarii with the bust of Tiberius [14–37 CE] and Claudius [41–54 CE] were most common, with some well worn and others appearing almost new. Those with the bust of Claudius were most plentiful. There were even some shekels and half-shekels of Tyre mixed in. The shekels were the coinage provided by the money changers in Jerusalem for worship in the temple offerings. The priestly officials could trust the silver content of Tyrian shekels; they could not always trust Roman coinage. The shekels had apparently been contributed by Jewish Christians who had made earlier pilgrimages to Jerusalem. They had apparently been brought back to Antioch as keepsakes of remembrance by those who had made earlier pilgrimages to feasts in Jerusalem in years past. Now, they were given up as an offering to aid brothers and sisters in Christ who were in deep need. A fitting return!*

IMAGINE PAUL'S FOUNDATION CAMPAIGN

Fig. 23. Famine Relief from Antioch. Photograph by G. Roger Greene.

James and Cephas and others in the Jerusalem church were overcome as they stared at the pile of coins on the table. As Cephas stirred the coins with his fingers, a gold aureus or two were even to be seen, each worth twenty-five silver denarii. Paul and Barnabas and the other representatives from Antioch on their part were only too glad to relieve themselves of the burden and responsibility of the offering sent by Antioch church. Although the famine had been severe when it had first occurred several years earlier, the gravity of the crisis had been significantly increased by a locust plague in agricultural regions normally rich in production. Severe drought had occasioned the famine in the first place. The inflationary economy that had resulted made it difficult for those in a city like Jerusalem who had no access to their own land to either obtain or afford even basic foodstuffs over a time of continuing drought. Jerusalem imported everything it needed, given its rather isolated location. And, the entire situation had even been aggravated by the required observance of a sabbatical year as prescribed by Torah.

The church at Jerusalem had few wealthy patrons, such that it had been quickly affected by the ensuing famine. Distribution of even basic foodstuffs became more and more difficult over time. Old divisions that had arisen earlier between the Aramaic-speaking faction and the more liberal Greek-speaking faction [see Acts 6:1] flared up again in the face of food scarcity. The tax system required by Rome in Judea was not abated, but was even elevated by the expectations of the Herodian tetrarch Antipas in Galilee and other areas of the country subject to local taxation.

> *This particular Feast of Tabernacles [in 51 CE] had been awaited with great expectations. What would fall fruits of harvest bring? It was hoped that the full harvest brought from the surrounding countryside would be sufficient to end the bad years. The supply of animals available for sacrifice at the temple had even been impacted by the years of drought. Pasturage had been limited. The wadis [stream beds] were dry. Reservoirs around Jerusalem that had been built by Herod the Great remained at a very low level. It was hoped that this would be the year when pilgrims returned to a pre-famine number, resulting in an economic boon to the city, There had not yet been clear signs of pilgrimage improvement. While people waited for Tabernacles, they already looked beyond Tabernacles to the beginning of the hoped-for rainy season to begin.*
>
> *Paul and company verbally conveyed greetings and concern from the church at Antioch, although the coins piled on the table spoke for themselves. Indeed, each carried its own unspoken story from those saints of God at Antioch who had given so sacrificially. Members of the Jerusalem church felt like the windows of heaven had indeed been opened and God had poured out a blessing in the form of the funds sent from Antioch [see Mal 3:10]. . . . Could the longed-for rains be far behind? . . .*

The famine sparked a lingering economic crisis for the church in Jerusalem that continued for several years. One might think of lingering times of recession or even depression in the modern world, a period when "times are hard." Within the ancient world, famine and hard times could be construed as eschatological signs. The point at issue here is the ministry of Paul. There is no reason to doubt the historical veracity of Paul's famine relief visit to Jerusalem in the fall of 51 CE, supported as it is by both Gal 2:1–10 and Luke's Source (STA 11:27–30), once one recognizes the Lukan redaction. The church at Antioch took up a voluntary offering (διακονία) as a ministry of provision and sent it to the church in Jerusalem by the hands of Barnabas and Paul. The term διακονία is the same term later used by Paul to describe his Collection (see Rom 15:25, 31; 2 Cor 8:4; 9:1, 12, 13). Paul also took Titus along with him. It is tempting to maintain that there was no better time to do this than the time of the Feast of Tabernacles in the fall of 51 CE, in view of the inherent symbolism and meaning of the feast related to the fall harvest.

Paul's accounting of this "second" visit to Jerusalem (J2, "Famine Relief") in Gal 2:1–10 involved both a private meeting with the leaders of the church, as well as a more public meeting. Privately, Paul shared the experience of his Foundational Campaign and the basic gospel that he had been preaching. One must keep in mind that everything Paul writes in Gal 2:1–10 is being addressed to the churches *in Galatia*, albeit at a later point in time, such that the entire passage is colored by his rhetorical purpose vis-à-vis the then current situation in Galatia. The Galatian crisis occasioned by the Nomistic Evangelists would have arisen *after* Paul's Famine and Conference visits to Jerusalem.

While the Famine visit occurred in the fall of 51 CE (perhaps at the appealing, theologically significant Feast of Tabernacles), the follow-up Conference visit occurred in the spring of 52 CE. The troubling opposition that arose against Paul and his gospel of inclusion of gentiles into the new Israel during his Famine visit had reached Antioch in the form of Nomistic Evangelists who even challenged Peter's behavior in his table fellowship with Antiochene gentile Christians (Gal 2:11–13). Enduring legacies of lingering famine, as well as the unresolved and developing theological issues called forth the need for resolution of gospel growing pains in the mother church of Jerusalem. Time was set for the crucial Conference visit that would seek to resolve these continuing troublesome issues. It is highly tempting to connect the Conference visit in the spring of 52 CE with Pentecost or perhaps the fifty days earlier Passover.

Passover would symbolize covenant allegiance, while Pentecost would symbolize first fruits and would also communicate the outpouring of the Spirit and celebration of the Gospel as reflected in Acts 2. Each Jewish feast would mark a commemoration of sorts for these earliest Christians. The Jerusalem church was now more than twenty years old and every Passover or Pentecost marked not only a commemoration of Jesus's death and resurrection, but also the birth of the church and the hope of fulfillment. While Luke's source for Acts (the STA) narrated the Conference visit, Paul in his letter to the Galatians chose not to do so. It would not have served his need or his purpose very well in what he needed to say to the Galatians. While he very much supported Jerusalem, in no way did he want to appear to be subordinate to the Jewish authorities of Jerusalem before the Galatians.

The Foundation Campaign—A Summary

In the light of this chapter's presentation, Paul's Foundation Campaign may be summarized and set forth in the following chart. A full chart of Paul's entire ministry, replete with associated scriptural references, may be found in appendix A. For clarity's sake, only a simplified and summary sketch is offered here.

Foundational Ministry of Paul

Revelation and Initial Ministry—34–37 CE

    Revelation and Calling—34 CE

    Ministry in Damascus and Arabia—34–37 CE

    First Visit to Jerusalem (J1)—"Acquaintance" Visit, 37 CE (+3 years)

    Ministry in Syria and Cilicia—37 CE

Foundation Campaign around to Illyricum—38–51 CE

> Phase I of Foundation Campaign, Anatolia, with Barnabas (likely 3–5 years), 38–42/43 CE

> Return to Antioch

> Phase II of Foundation Campaign, Anatolia to Illyricum, with Silas and Timothy (likely 5–8 years), 43–51 CE
>> *2 Thessalonians*—Early 49 CE, from Achaia?
>>> *Previous Letter to Corinth* (see 2 Cor 6:14—7:1 Fragment)—Early 50 CE, from Illyricum

> Stay in Corinth—Summer, 51 CE, appearance before Gallio (July, 51?)
>> *1 Thessalonians*—Early 51 CE, from Corinth

> Return to Antioch, by way of Ephesus and Caesarea

> Antioch and Jerusalem (51–52 CE)

> Second Visit to Jerusalem (J2)—"Famine" Visit, Fall, 51 CE (calling + 17 years)

> Conflict with Nomistic Evangelists (Judaizers) in Antioch—Early Spring, 52 CE

> Third Visit to Jerusalem (J3)—"Conference" Visit, Spring, 52 CE

> Conflict with Nomistic Evangelists (Judaizers) in Antioch—Summer, 52 CE

Conclusion

It is clear that the leadership of the church had no problem with a gospel that did not insist upon gentile circumcision. It could perhaps be stated that they were more likely concerned with specific pressing physical and practical issues wrought by the lingering effects of famine than they were with more general theological matters (see Gal 2:10). They were grateful for the offering afforded by the church at Antioch. The gentile mission had been underway for at least twenty years. A lot had happened in that twenty year period, since the dispersion of the gospel following that first Pentecost (Acts 2). Titus, a "Greek," was not compelled to be circumcised (Gal 2:3). Paul underscores the fact that the Jerusalem leadership did not alter or add to his gospel (Gal 2:6–9).

The problem that resulted apparently came from a minority faction of a fundamentalist bent that infiltrated Paul's meeting with the church leadership. This "Judaizing" faction wanted to insist upon adherence to Mosaic Law and especially gentile circumcision, *in order for a gentile to be admitted into the people of Israel*. Paul stood his ground and would in no sense compromise the basic nature of the gospel by giving in to this faction (Gal 2:4–5). There were likely those in the Jerusalem church who still remembered that Paul had been a persecutor of the earliest church, such that they remained very suspicious of him. Even after such strong disagreement—likely personal, as well as theological, the leadership embraced Paul and Barnabas in their mission to the gentiles.

The mission field in the diaspora was large enough to support a dual mission both within and without the synagogue. Paul and Barnabas along with others had, of course, brought the Antioch famine offering to Jerusalem. It apparently was well received by those in the Jerusalem church, such that Paul and Barnabas were asked to continue to remember the poor. Paul indicates that he was eager to do that very thing (Gal 2:10). Paul's eagerness was likely as much theological as it was economic. In a time of eschatological fulfillment, it was expected that gentiles would stream to Jerusalem bearing gifts (see Isa 2:3; 60:2; Mic 4:1). Gentile Christians from Antioch had now sent their gifts to Jerusalem. The encouragement given to Paul and his intention led directly to his Collection Campaign designed to meet continuing physical needs but even more importantly to unify the divided family of the children of God in Christ in eschatological times.

While the present work is focused upon imagining Paul in his world at what might be termed the dawn of Christianity in the light of the scriptural resources that we have available, one might pause to imagine the implications and application of Paul's experience in the context of contemporary Christianity. First of all, Paul was a very religious individual (a Jewish Pharisee) who entertained a very exclusive theological perspective of who constituted the true people of God. Secondly, Paul did not *reason* a better theological doctrine that led him to change from persecutor to proclaimer of the Gospel. Paul experienced a direct *revelation* from God that called for a "theological repentance" on his part.

Thirdly, Paul's experience caused him (much as it did the early Christians) to re-search his scriptures to discern the will and ways of God. Paul went back to his foundations in Judaism and re-thought God's promise given to Abraham. It was through Abraham that all peoples would be blessed—an unconditional promise based solely upon faithfulness of trust in the promise of God. God's promise was not meant to establish favored ethnicity, but rather a universal inclusion of all peoples. The promise to Abraham was now eschatologically fulfilled in the resurrection and exaltation of Christ as Lord of all. The eschatological fulfillment was not based upon religious ritual (such as circumcision or food laws), but rather upon faithfulness, to divine revelation in Christ.

Paul re-imagined Judaism. He re-imagined doctrine. He re-imagined his theology in the light of Gospel fulfillment. He had to do so, if he were to be faithful to divine revelation. He re-imagined his ancestral religion. And it changed his life, behavior, and actions needed to enact a new mode of living in Christ. Life in Christ redefined the nature of the Christian community as an *inclusive* community that reached beyond limited and limiting borders of exclusion. When the Gospel is heard and embraced today, it may still have its redeeming effect upon our living out our lives "in Christ." While "Christendom" may seek to establish and preserve borders, "Christianity" moves beyond borders on the basis of the Gospel of God that stands openly revealed in Christ for all who may respond, even overcoming those borders erected and defined by *our* theologies.

5

Imagine Paul's Collection Campaign and Its Aftermath

ALTHOUGH THE COLLECTION FOR Jerusalem is the culmination point of Paul's ministry and runs like a "red thread" through Paul's major epistles, it is largely ignored in both ecclesiastical and scholarly circles in the interest of what is deemed to be more important themes. Scholars would rather debate and develop the finer points of Pauline theology, while topics of soteriology ("salvation") and ethical behavior dominate ecclesiastical or church interests within Christianity. And, within a self-serving Christendom, dogma and doctrine preserve the faithful and status quo.

Pragmatically, we take what appears useful from Paul to support our programs and agendas and do not wish to be bothered with other extraneous details or depth of comprehension. In this instance, the devil is in the dogma while the gospel is in the detail. Paul's ministry was all about God's eschatological Gospel.

It is not clear at what point Paul determined to take up a collection from among his gentile churches, but surely the collection that he and Barnabas took to Jerusalem from Antioch provided a model in kind. Paul would also have been familiar with the temple tax collected in the diaspora. The Antioch ministry certainly signified concern and cooperation between these two major Christian churches, as it addressed a real and continuing physical need. The theological intention behind Paul's later Collection ministry may have evolved over time. As Paul's Collection Campaign stretched out to encompass several years, its ultimate delivery may well have carried more symbolic than practical meaning. There is no way to know how much money was actually raised or the level of need that existed in the Jerusalem church at the time Paul delivered his Collection in the summer of 56 CE.

The present chapter, of which the title is not all-inclusive, will again alternate between "historical fiction" and supportive historical evidence. As indicated by the chapter heading, the focal point is the Collection Campaign of Paul, which was in the present writer's judgment his second and final campaign. Some would take the position that Paul had a subsequent ministry after his first Roman imprisonment, although such a perspective takes one beyond the evidence of the New Testament.

It is the Collection taken to Jerusalem that at least indirectly results in Paul's arrest and imprisonment, such that the final period of Paul's life may be termed the Post-Collection Period. This final period of Paul's life will also be treated in this chapter, in order to bring consideration of the ministry of Paul to a close.

The Collection Campaign

Some scholars assume that Paul did not participate in any kind of relief expedition to Jerusalem either during or prior to the Jerusalem Conference. The usual assumption is that Gal 2:1–10 is an account of the Jerusalem Conference of Acts 15 (G2 = A4). Other scholars have proposed the hypothesis that Luke placed an Antiochene report of a famine visit into Paul's earlier ministry where it did not belong, all in accordance with Lukan redactional purposes. The historical veracity of the famine visit narrated by Acts 11:27–30 is called into question by some scholars because of Paul's emphatic denial of any visit to Jerusalem between his acquaintance visit three years after his call/commission and the date of the Jerusalem Conference, on the assumption that what Paul narrates in Gal 2:1–10 is the Jerusalem Conference visit.

Some scholars who adopt the usual but wrong assumption regarding Gal 2:1–10 find the famine relief visit to be irrelevant to Pauline chronology and even historically suspect. Some do not even treat the matter of the famine visit. Others rule it out historically speaking, seeing it to be a Lukan duplicate of tradition associated with the Collection (in truth avoided by Luke in Acts 15–21) and the Jerusalem Conference. Historically reliable evidence of the tradition of a collection made by the community at Antioch for the Jerusalem community is generally ruled out, if one works with a wrong model of a visit to Jerusalem narrated in Gal 2. If one correctly understands the nature of (1) the Lukan redaction and (2) the Pauline rhetorical purpose, there simply is no historical problem.

Paul and Barnabas returned to Antioch after fulfilling the mission of the Famine Relief Visit. Paul spent the rest of 51 CE and the beginning of 52 CE in Antioch. It was winter time. He was mindful of the work that Priscilla and Aquila had begun in Ephesus, but with the sea lanes closed and snow in the mountains, he simply made plans to join them in the late spring/early summer of 52 CE. Titus would have likewise remained with Paul in Antioch through the winter of 51–52 CE.

Confrontations

As it turned out, the question of gentiles and the Mosaic Law was not settled. Cephas (Peter?) had come to Antioch and had fellowshipped with Paul, Barnabas, and the church at a time after the Famine Visit. Land travel in Palestine-Syria was not prohibited during winter in most places, given the milder climate. The church met together and shared meals without incident—both Jewish Christians and gentile

Christians, as was their regular custom (Gal 2:11–14). Things went smoothly, until some men who were insisting upon the necessity of Jewish circumcision came from Jerusalem (Gal 2:11; Acts 15:1), most likely in the early spring of 52 CE. The distance between Jerusalem and Antioch was less than 375 miles. It generally took between two and four weeks to travel between the two cities by land, less by sea from Caesarea during the season.

The harmony that had been shared in the church at Antioch was shattered with the arrival of the Judaizers or Nomistic Evangelists in Antioch. Earlier when Cephas had arrived in Antioch, he had not been bothered by strict Jewish food laws and by concern for ritual purity. The Cornelius episode, graphically narrated by Luke in Acts, may well have conditioned Peter's theological "repentance." If the climactic Acts account regarding the Cornelius episode be accepted, Peter had earlier come to realize that the gospel and outpouring of the Spirit were available to both Jew and gentile on the same basis (Acts 10:1—11:18). Peter had come to repentance in Christ.

Luke offers a reinforcing summary of Peter's earlier experience in his testimony at the Jerusalem Conference (Acts 15:7–11). Peter's initial behavior at Antioch, assuming Cephas is the same person, is consistent with his realized position portrayed in Acts. As an interesting aside, Luke alludes to the Cornelius episode three times in Acts (see Acts 10, 11, 15), even as he presents the story of Paul's call three times (see Acts 9, 22, 26). The significance of each story for Luke is highlighted in his accounting, again according to his "rule of two" narrated thrice.

The confrontation with the Judaizers or Nomistic Evangelists that had taken place in Jerusalem now had carried over to Antioch and Paul found himself once more in the thick of debate with them. The men who came from Jerusalem disapproved of Peter's eating with gentile Christians irrespective of Jewish food laws. As Paul acknowledges, both Peter and Barnabas drew back and changed their ways of relating to gentile Christians apart from the Law. They personally began to observe Jewish food laws once again. Paul has the harshest words for Peter (Gal 2:11–14), in view of Peter's shift to a policy of accommodation.

Paul understood the action as an inappropriate compromise of the gospel and accommodation to a fundamentalist faction. He even corrected Peter "before them all" in a face to face confrontation (Gal 2:14). Barnabas was temporarily carried away by the Judaizing faction, as well, until Paul offered correction. It is important to see what Paul says and does not say with regard to Barnabas. There is no permanent breach between Paul and Barnabas reflected in Galatians. While Paul corrects Peter, he simply states that Barnabas was "carried away." There is no direct suggestion that there was a great falling out between Paul and Barnabas as reflected in the rather artificial Acts account (Acts 15:39). Even in the Acts account, the disagreement is not over matters of Jewish Law, but over John Mark. Galatians 2 has generally been incorrectly read through the lens of Acts 15.

Luke apparently knew that Paul and Barnabas did not work together after the initial mission (phase I of the Foundation Campaign) as reflected in Acts 13–14, but he did not know why. Literarily, Luke supplied the Acts 15 reference to remove Barnabas from his account. Luke is through with Barnabas as a character in the story after the Conference visit of Acts 15, even as he is through with the Twelve Apostles (including Peter) after Acts 15. The last half of Luke's work in Acts focuses upon the spread of the gospel through the efforts of Paul and his associates until the Gospel has claimed even Rome (Acts 28). Beginning in Acts 15, the Jerusalem church exhibits new leadership under James (literally, "Jacob").

At Antioch, Paul insisted that the only badge of membership in God's people was faith in Christ and not Jewish food laws and circumcision. Paul sought to remind these Jewish Christian leaders about the basic nature of the gospel. It was decided by the parties involved that it would be good to air the issues once and for all in a conference to be held in Jerusalem later that spring, likely some time between Passover and Pentecost, 52 CE. If Paul's visit coincided with either Jewish feast, which makes sense, the time frame would have been twenty-one or twenty-two years after Jesus's death/resurrection and the first Christian Pentecost narrated in Acts 2.

Paul and Barnabas and others of the church at Antioch went up for the conference. It would have provided an opportunity to publicly air the issues and also to address the relief needs of the Jerusalem congregation. According to the chronology presented in the current work, the Conference Visit took place about fifteen years after Paul's initial visit to Jerusalem. The major point to be realized here is that the young Christian church, little more than twenty years old, is still undergoing significant growing pains in terms of the very definition of the Gospel. There have been severe disagreements in the first twenty years. The church is settling down to life in the Roman world, accompanied by a changing orthopraxy and developing orthodoxy shaped by the exigencies of everyday living. There have been ongoing Christian missions, including Paul's, throughout this entire period of time. And, the risen Christ has not yet returned.[1]

With the Galatian letter, Paul is writing to the churches in Galatia among whom Barnabas had originally worked as a partner. It would gain Paul nothing to criticize Barnabas to the Galatian churches, but it would rather tend to divide loyalties and create divisions in those churches. Rhetorically speaking, Paul could make his points regarding the nature of the gospel with reference to Peter and leave Barnabas out of the center of it. Paul and Barnabas had worked together for years in the first campaign (Luke's Source, STA 13–14). Paul's mention of Barnabas is simply provided as an illustration for the Galatians, using a person with whom they were very familiar.

---

1. Basic evangelism must have become more difficult with the continuing delay of the parousia. Imagine a gentile response: "You say that a Jew crucified twenty years ago is 'Lord of the world'? How credible is that? Where are his temples? Caesar rules—there's his temple over yonder and here in my hand are his coins. The gods be praised—'Jesus Christ,' you say."

Paul never mentions Barnabas in an otherwise negative manner. Luke's Source likewise presents Paul and Barnabas as cooperative representatives of the church at Antioch, both in terms of the Famine Visit and the Conference Visit. According to Luke's Source, STA 15:2, Paul and Barnabas are together as they dispute and debate with the Judaizing Christians or circumcision party that came to Antioch and who argued for ritual doctrine on the basis of Mosaic Torah.

Paul himself chose not to narrate the events of the Jerusalem Conference. Thus, Gal 2 is not equal to Acts 15. Instead, Paul has made the points he wished to make to the Galatians regarding circumcision through his narration of the earlier Famine Visit of Acts 11. And, for the Galatians, he was able to include Barnabas as a positive witness to his proclamation of the gospel. The powers that be in Jerusalem made no changes to the "gospel apart from the Law" that he had always preached. For that gospel, the same gospel Paul had originally preached among the Galatians, circumcision and observance of ritual purity and food laws was not a requirement (Gal 2:3, 6–10).

It should not be forgotten that Paul could make his appeal for a "law free" gospel to the gentiles *on the basis of Torah itself*, i.e., it was Abraham's faith and not his circumcision for which he was accorded "righteousness" (see Gen 15:6; 17:9–14). The Nomistic Evangelists could, of course, affirm that Abraham was also later circumcised, thus insisting that faith must be affirmed by observing the ritual Torah if one is to be incorporated into Israel. The Torah was foundational for Judaism. The debate would not be unlike insistence in a contemporary context that one is "saved" by confession of faith in Christ, but *now* one *must* be baptized to become a member of the church. And to go further, one must now be baptized according to a particular defined and acceptable mode as set forth by a particular church. Does a dogmatic legalism trump an authentic faith?

Paul does not want to appear in any way subservient to the authorities in Jerusalem. He chooses not to narrate the Jerusalem Conference or to mention the letter from James (intended for Antioch; see Acts 15:22–29) when he writes to the Galatian Christians. The entire gospel had earlier been on the line in Antioch, as it now was in Galatia. Justification and incorporation into the eschatological Israel, the "new Israel" (see Gal 6:11–16) did not come on the basis of works of the Law as the Nomistic Evangelists were wont to proclaim. Rather, it came by means of the grace of God in the Christ event. It came on the basis of faithfulness as it always had, even since the time of Abraham. If justification were on the basis of Law, then Christ died for no purpose (Gal 2:15–21) and Paul's whole eschatological gospel would be falsely based.

Luke's Source reflects a debate/disputation that occurred between Paul and Barnabas and the infiltrating Judaizers (Luke's Source, STA 15:1–2). The Antioch church appointed Paul, Barnabas, and others to convene in Jerusalem to discuss the issue with the apostles and elders. It is not known when Peter returned to Jerusalem. He was present and testified at the conference, representing a view quite close to Paul's own position (see Acts 15:7–11; Luke's Source, STA 15:7; Gal 2:14–21). It is entirely possible that James, the new leader of the Jerusalem church, modified his own earlier position as a result of the debate at the conference (Gal 2:9, 11; Luke's Source, STA 15:3; Acts 15:13–21).

Paul must have come away from the Conference with a sense of vindication and relief. The Jerusalem leadership, and indeed the whole church, essentially *once again* approved Paul's gospel to gentiles apart from the Law. The letter that was sent to Antioch by James would certainly clarify the issues for those in the Antioch church who had witnessed the earlier confrontations there. Basically, gentile converts to Christianity would be expected to abstain from idol worship and to maintain a basic level of morality and ritual purity that would enable purity of table fellowship with more conservative Jewish Christians. This would be entirely reasonable.

Evangelistic Plans

Paul himself had continued to formulate his future mission plans. He had learned much in this time of renewal of association with Barnabas and other members of the church at Antioch. He had become much more intimately acquainted with both Peter and James and other leaders at Jerusalem. He had seen firsthand the continuing physical needs of the poor saints in Jerusalem, in the light of the continuing economic pressures brought about by the famine that had been further aggravated by the observance of a sabbatical year. The original severity had lingered to a lesser degree, but it had nevertheless lingered.

However, Paul began to think beyond external crises and began to focus upon the possibilities of a ministry of reconciliation that could address both external needs and internal theological realities. A collection taken up among the gentile churches he had founded could certainly demonstrate a spirit of supportive unity. It could also mark fulfillment of eschatological prophecy (see Isa 2:3; 60:2; Mic 4:1). It could be an acknowledgment of interdependence on the part of both gentile and Jewish Christians, thus escaping the trap of bifurcation of the church fostered by either a spirit of dependence or independence. Now that the basic nature of the Gospel had been recognized and "settled," Paul could move on with his next campaign. Little did he know what lay ahead.

After his return to Antioch from the Jerusalem Conference in the late spring or early summer of 52 CE, Paul and Barnabas continued to teach and evangelize in Antioch (Luke's Source, STA 15:35). In all likelihood, Paul shared with Barnabas his mission plans as they related to a new mission headquartered in Ephesus, where he had left Priscilla and Aquila. He likely shared his hope to visit Rome and engage in an even more far-reaching ministry to the West. He likely shared his intention to take up a collection from among the various gentile churches as an offering for the Jewish saints in Jerusalem. It is possible that Paul had entertained thoughts of this collection since the time of the Famine Relief Visit the previous fall when he was accompanied by Barnabas

(Gal 2:10). For whatever reason, Barnabas elected not to accompany Paul to Ephesus. This will be the last time Paul would be associated with Barnabas, even though later references in the Pauline letters appear to reflect a positive relationship.

> *Paul and his companions left Antioch early in the morning for the almost seven hundred-mile journey to Ephesus. He had missed Titus, since he had dispatched him to Corinth by sea and by way of Ephesus two weeks earlier. Titus had instructions to inform Aquila and Priscilla in Ephesus of Paul's intentions to travel through Galatia before coming to Ephesus. In contrast to Paul, Titus, being a Greek, was quite the seaman. Paul himself had determined that he would visit Tarsus and then travel through the Cilician Gates and over the Taurus Mountains to Derbe. This would afford the opportunity to revisit churches founded during his first campaign. He could apprise the Galatian Christians of the events that had taken place in Jerusalem and Antioch and their impact upon the gospel. And, if he had already determined to take up his collection, Paul could explain the eschatological ramifications in person to his gentile churches in Galatia. He could follow the Roman road that led across the central Anatolian plateau and descended through the Lycus Valley to Ephesus.*
>
> *That had been his plan, and so far it had worked. His visit to Derbe and Lystra had gone well. Now it was on to Iconium and to Antioch and then to Ephesus. He would be in Ephesus within the month, and he wondered how Aquila and Priscilla were faring. He silently hoped that they had made good progress and were well, since he had left them there the previous summer to prepare a foundation in his new headquarters for Paul's ongoing mission. By now, they would know of his mission plans, having learned them from Titus. Paul could not have known at the time about his upcoming unexpected success in Colossae and Laodicea, even before he would reach Ephesus.*
>
> *As it turned out, his new ministry in Colossae—brief as it was—created unexpected delay in his travel plans. He barely left the Lycus Valley ahead of the winter snows. Once in Ephesus, he received a warm welcome from Aquila and Priscilla and the church which met in their house. . . .*

Paul left Antioch of Syria never to return again. Our sources do not tell us about Paul's parting. However, Paul owed much to Antioch if Luke's Source/Acts may be believed. Antioch had first sent Paul out and had undoubtedly extended support to him in both phases of the Foundational Campaign. It had provided a safe haven of emotional support through its more universal outlook supportive of the gentile mission. It is possible Paul maintained the support of patrons in the church, although when Paul left Antioch for this last time, he apparently left as an independent evangelist. In contrast to earlier times, there is no mention in Luke's Source of the church sending him out (see Luke's Source, STA 13:3; 15:40).

IMAGINE PAUL

Paul could have made the journey of 293 miles from Antioch to Tarsus to Derbe in about twenty days, not counting time in any stopovers. Another sixty miles to Lystra could be traveled in four or more days; the ninety to one hundred miles from Lystra to Antioch of Pisidia could take another week to ten days if he did not spend time in Iconium. The more than two hundred miles from Antioch of Pisidia to Ephesus could take two weeks or more. Luke's Source (STA 19:1) simply states that while Apollos was in Corinth, Paul passed through the higher country and came to Ephesus. Altogether, it would have taken Paul about forty-five days or a month and a half of travel time or more to go overland by foot from Antioch of Syria to Ephesus (a distance of more than 660 miles), not including stopovers.

Fig. 24. Map of Paul's Collection Campaign. Map © Jason Greene. Used with permission.

No one knows when Paul conceived his plan for the Collection ministry. If Paul indeed has the Collection in mind at this point (which the author deems likely), he would have had to have spent some time in each place, informing the Christians throughout southern Galatia about what had transpired since they had last seen him and about his intended Collection ministry for Jerusalem (see 1 Cor 16:1–4). After all, Paul understood his Collection ministry to have significant eschatological and Gospel ramifications (see Isa 2:3; 60:3; Mic 4:1; Rom 15:25–29). This time with various churches could have easily added another month to Paul's travel time, as could time in Colossae, such that he would have reached Ephesus in the early fall of 52 CE before the snows set in the "high country."

By the time he left Antioch of Syria (if not earlier) or most certainly from Tarsus, Paul would have likely dispatched Titus back to Corinth. Corinth would thereby learn of Paul's plans to relocate to Ephesus prior to his arrival in Ephesus in the fall of 52 CE. There was no reason for Titus to accompany Paul through the region of Galatia. Titus was more useful to Paul elsewhere and could have even stopped over at Ephesus to inform Aquila and Priscilla of Paul's experience in Antioch and Jerusalem, given the prevailing winds. Paul was bound to have been somewhat anxious about the state of the church in Corinth since the trouble he had experienced there on his second visit, especially since some of his staunchest supporters (Priscilla, Aquila, Titus) were now absent from the situation. Still, Titus would be able to inform the Corinthians about the Famine Visit to Jerusalem and the intended Collection, if Paul had already decided. He would also be able to bring Paul a report of the status of things in the Corinthian church since Paul's second and "painful" visit. Generally speaking, Titus was Paul's envoy of choice to deal with delicate issues in the church at Corinth (see 2 Cor 8; 1 Cor 16:1–3). Titus would be able to inform the Corinthian church about Paul's whereabouts and his mission intentions.

Paul undoubtedly reflected on his time in Antioch and his *two visits* to Jerusalem. He concluded that he could make his own contribution to the unity of the Christian church as a whole by taking up a collection from among the churches he had established and in which he had worked. The Famine Relief Visit provided a model for a collection from among his gentile churches. The Conference Visit provided an impetus toward theological unity. Once Paul completed his Collection ministry, he could set his sights on mission fields farther west and perhaps even realize his dream of visiting Rome.

The one thing that he felt he could not do was to begin a new campaign in the West to Rome and Spain and leave behind a *divided* church in the East. A Gospel of unity and peace could not be built or maintained upon a fractured foundation, nor would a gospel of division sustain appropriate eschatological realities introduced by the Gospel of God. Paul reasoned that the delay of Christ's return was dependent upon fulfillment of scriptural promise that would suggest continuing work to Rome and the western Roman Empire. God's Gospel in Christ was to be marked by full inclusion.

IMAGINE PAUL

Once Paul arrived in Ephesus, he connected with Priscilla and Aquila and began preaching in the Jewish synagogue there (Luke's Source, STA 19:8). This he did through the remaining months of 52 CE. According to Luke's Source, STA 19:10/Acts 19:10, Paul continued to preach there for another two years, i.e., 53–54 CE. Luke's Source, STA 19:11-12, 17/Acts 19:11-12, 17 suggests Paul enjoyed a great degree of success in Ephesus. It is *possible* that Paul conceived his Collection ministry only during this period. If so, he could have radiated a word about the Collection back to the Galatian churches and as far as Corinth.

However, it appears more likely that Paul personally would have conceived of such an endeavor at a point in time nearer the events in Jerusalem and Antioch, at a time when he could have informed the Galatian churches in person as he traveled through "the upper country," prior to settling in Ephesus. He could then make use of associates like Timothy to be a liaison with Galatia, even as Titus was such a liaison with Corinth. They would both be recognized and welcomed in their home territories and could address in persuasive terms whatever issues arose. Undoubtedly contact with his patron church of Philippi brought not only financial support but also the personal aid and service of Epaphroditus in behalf of the Philippians (see Phil 2:25-30).

Paul would spend some two and one-half to three years in Ephesus (see Luke's Source, STA 19:8, 10, 22; Acts 20:31), which had become the largest and most powerful city in the Roman province of Asia. It was the greatest trading center west of the Taurus Mountains. The main roads from the east converged in Ephesus, with Roman milestones calculating and marking the number of miles from Ephesus. It was the third largest city of the empire, with an estimated total population in excess of 250,000. The seating capacity of its great theater at the foot of Mount Pion was almost 25,000 (see Luke's Source, STA 19:29-34). After Antioch of Syria (300,000–500,000), Ephesus was the largest city on the Anatolian land mass. No doubt, the great Artemis temple brought large numbers of people to Ephesus.

Paul had moved from one provincial capital to the next and now felt ready to establish his ministry at this vital strategic and centralized capital that had flourished since the time of Augustus. Aquila and Priscilla had already made foundational inroads. They all agreed that Ephesus would provide a strategic center of unity for the Aegean churches located in Asia Minor and southern Europe during the time of the Collection Campaign. The time that Paul spent here was the longest time he spent anywhere during the time of his campaigns. It would prove to be a rather difficult and tumultuous period. A significant part of the time Paul spent in Ephesus was likely spent in an Ephesian imprisonment of indeterminate length (see 1 Cor 16:8-9; Philippians; Acts 19:8, 10, 23-41).

The great theater in Ephesus was open to the major street (later known as the Arcadian Way) which led to the harbor. The impressive way, some thirty-five feet wide, ran in a straight line eastward from the harbor for more than seventeen hundred feet. Paved in marble, it was flanked by fifteen-foot deep colonnades on both sides which provided stalls for small shops. Once in the city, one would also encounter a very large commercial Agora. About one and one-half miles north of the city was the temple of the goddess Artemis. The great Artemis temple, one of the "seven wonders" of the ancient world, was larger than the Parthenon in Athens.

Fig. 25. The Temple of Artemis at Ephesus. *Archaeology Illustrated*, © Balage Balogh. Used under license.

The economic wealth of the city was in part tied to the religious trade associated with the fertility goddess Artemis. The city of Ephesus was famous for its pagan worship and magical practices.[2]

For the casual visitor to Ephesus today, it is too easy to assume that everything one sees was there in Paul's day, when in fact many of the prominent structures (such as the Library of Celsus, the temple of Domitian, the temple of Hadrian, and even an expanded theater) date to a time after Paul. The ancient harbor, now silted up and some miles from the sea, with Mount Coressus in view on the left from the theater, must be imagined in the now wide plain which stretches out beyond the end of Harbor Street (later remodeled by Emperor Arcadius, 383–408 CE). It was still a very impressive city with quite a view in Paul's day!

---

2. One might imagine the contrast the religious industry associated with the goddess Artemis and her great temple—considered to be one of the "seven wonders" of the ancient world—and the simple, almost muted proclamation of Paul concerning a Galilean peasant named Jesus, who was crucified by the Romans, but who was now being proclaimed as "Lord of the world." While Paul preached daily for some two years in the hall of Tyrannus, according to Luke (Acts 19:10), the crowd of 25,000 that rushed into the theater cried out in a deafening voice for two hours, "Great is Artemis of the Ephesians" (μεγάλη ἡ Ἄρτεμις Ἐφεσίων, Acts 19:34).

The familiar pattern of preaching in the Jewish synagogue lasted for a three-month period of comparative welcome before opposition and rejection set in (Luke's Source, STA 19:8–9). Paul had preached there the prior year (Luke's Source, STA 18:19) toward the completion of phase II of the Foundational Campaign in the late summer of 51 CE at the time when he left Aquila and Priscilla in the city. After exclusion from the synagogue, Paul was able to make use of the "school" or "lecture hall" or "guild hall" (σχολή) of Tyrannus to preach during the hot portion of the day (Luke's Source, STA 19:9).

We tend to underestimate the time required to convince *Jews* that the heritage and story of Israel had now been fulfilled in the Galilean Jesus crucified by Rome, that his resurrection signaled the beginning of a new eschatological age. Not all diaspora Jews were attuned to eschatological speculation as suggested or called for by the gospel. The Torah of diaspora Judaism simply guided everyday life within the normalcy of a world ordered by Rome. The eschatological fervor of Palestinian Judaism that boiled over in the Jewish revolt of 66 CE in Palestine was apparently not present in the larger diaspora. There was no empire-wide uprising of Jews in 66–70 CE.

God had made provision for gentiles to become a part of Israel, completely apart from the Law and other customary identity markers, such as circumcision and food laws. The daily lives of diaspora Jews were maintained on the basis of such things, as well as Sabbath-day observance.

Furthermore, we tend to underestimate the time required to convince *gentile pagans* to give up the worship of multiple gods—personal, city, local, and state gods, as well as worship of a divine emperor—in order to embrace the singular God of Judaism. Why should a gentile become a Jew, a.k.a. a Christian? Paul's appeal was perhaps best received among gentile God-fearers associated with Jewish synagogues and already familiar with Jewish worship.

After all, it was Rome that ruled the world by the design and desire of the gods according to Roman propaganda, not Judea whose God could not be seen anywhere. God's statue was even absent from his own Temple—his only Temple—in Jerusalem. While statuary Platonic copies of pagan deities might populate pagan temples throughout the empire, Jews were to create no images. For a gentile to become Christian meant the disavowal not only of political and religious realities, but also many social and personal relationships as well. Why should one living in a polytheistic *Roman* world embrace a rather alien religious faith and practice, one tolerated but not necessarily respected by Rome, especially in an environment where little eschatological fervor existed? In effect, Paul and other early Christian evangelists exported the eschatological Gospel of God to a pagan gentile and Jewish world that did not know it truly needed such.

The major point here is that we subconsciously assume Paul simply moved through the Mediterranean world holding a series of weeklong revival meetings which met with immediate success. In part, this is because of Luke's skill evident in the writing of the Acts narrative, which moves along smoothly from place to place within seemingly short time frames. Such was not the case, by far. It took time—and much effort. The underlying reality of Paul's lengthy ministry is belied by the brief amount of time it may take us to read or hear the story summary presented by Luke or found in Luke's Source. In other words, our general misperception—conscious or not—is occasioned by the brevity of the very narratives themselves that stand completely aside from the actual historical, political, and social realities of Paul's time.

Climactic Time in Ephesus

The model for Paul's ministry is thus not a quick series of "missionary journeys," but rather the model set forth in this work of two extended campaigns carried out through the establishment of significant church centers. Ephesus, Paul's chosen headquarters for his Collection Campaign, proved to be a very strategic center from which the gospel could radiate. While Paul may have born witness to the gospel in new cities en route to Ephesus after his two Jerusalem visits (Famine and Conference), the real work at a place like Colossae was apparently done by Epaphras (Col: 1:7), who ministered in Paul's behalf.

The period of Paul's headquarters in Ephesus and establishment of a Pauline church there, as well as plans for the Jerusalem Collection and concerns for churches previously established, proved to be a busy and anxious time for Paul. Ironically, Luke's Source preserves comparatively little material related to this time. It offers a summary of the initial period (Luke's Source, STA 19:1, 8–12, 17) which testifies not only to Paul's daily proclamation but also to mighty works done through/by his hands. In addition, it elaborates upon an episode of a riot instigated by a certain Demetrius and a guild of silversmiths (Luke's Source, STA 19:23–25, 27–34) who felt their business was threatened by the growing influence of Paul and the "Way." There are potential time gaps in the account of Paul's stay in Ephesus, such that most of Paul's experience there goes un-narrated. The episodes narrated hardly account for the fullness of time spent there.

From Paul's own letters, it is evident this was a period of extensive letter writing. Paul tended to write letters to deal with specific problems and as a substitute for a visit. First Corinthians is written from Ephesus toward the end of Paul's time in Ephesus (1 Cor 16:8). Galatians was likely written during this time, as well, to address the serious problem of the Judaizing threat of the Nomistic Evangelists that had beset the Galatian churches in the time following Paul's visit with them as he had passed through the "upper country" on his way to Ephesus.

Although in all probability, Paul announced his intended Collection to the Galatians as he was on the way to Ephesus. Paul now received word that those churches were in danger of swerving from the truth of the gospel apart from the Law and instead were embracing a Nomistic Judaizing gospel of ritual prescriptions. Paul had felt that these sorts of issues had been settled at the Jerusalem Conference, but it becomes evident that Judaizing influences had begun to spread through Pauline mission fields in Galatia, Asia Minor, and perhaps even Macedonia.

The Galatian churches were plagued by what was in Paul's mind a perverted gospel that required the fulfillment of nomistic ritual prescriptions such as circumcision, i.e., the maintenance of distinctive Jewish identity markers (Gal 1:6–9; 3:1–5; 5:1–12). While these issues may seem irrelevant or insignificant to us, once again, it took time for the earlier church to work through these significant issues pertaining to gentile inclusion into the "new Israel" in terms of the outworking of the eschatological Gospel of God in Christ. These issues were still being faced more than two decades after the death and resurrection of Jesus. As an aside illustration, mentioned earlier, and by way of analogy, Christian groups today entertain differing positions on the mode and manner of baptism. Issues unsettled may become ingrained and remain as points of division. The issue of baptism is even linked to the celebration of the Eucharist in some contemporary churches. In the same vein, actual eschatological fervor related to Christ's return varies among contemporary Christian groups.

In addition to Galatia, the church in Philippi in Macedonia is likewise warned against the threat of a Judaizing faction (Phil 3:2–11). Paul does not acknowledge the presence of Judaizers in Philippi, but simply warns the church against such. This warning may be incidental evidence that Paul was being threatened by the Judaizers in Asia Minor and that Philippians was indeed written from an Ephesian imprisonment. (Philippians is a "prison epistle.") The Judaizing pressure against the Pauline gospel that arose following the Jerusalem Conference apparently became relentless on some of his mission fields, during the very time he was establishing his base of new work in Ephesus and the foundations of his Collection endeavor that was meant to unify the growing Christian church.

While Paul was engaged in a ministry predicated on reconciliation and unity, the Nomistic Evangelists made headway by criticizing Paul and his gospel, thus fostering alienation and division. If Paul's Collection Campaign took as much time as suggested in the present work, the Judaizers had time to work and seek to become established. If one only focuses upon the existent Pauline *literature* (or the book of Acts, for that matter), one easily loses the actual time perspective which the literature narrates, or the time over which it developed. Everything did not happen immediately nor all at once.

Paul also had to deal with the continuing deterioration of the situation in Corinth. The Corinthian letters that are extant reflect something of his extensive dealings with Corinth throughout the Ephesian period. The Corinthian church was crucial for the Collection ministry predicated upon unity. Paul had spent significant time in Corinth during his founding visit and had made a second and painful visit to the church on his return from Illyricum (2 Cor 2:1–2). The Previous letter was apparently written from Illyricum and addressed matters of immorality (see 1 Cor 5:9). The present author has independently identified 1 Corinthians as the "Painful Letter" mentioned in 2 Cor

2:3–4. This is also the position of some other scholars, although the letter is sometimes referred to as the "Letter of Tears."

It is evident Paul wrote 1 Corinthians from Ephesus (1 Cor 16:8). It was likely dispatched to Corinth through Chloe's people (Stephanus, Fortunatus, and Achaicus (see 1 Cor 1:11, 16:17). Corinth was across the Aegean Sea from Ephesus, a sailing distance of about three hundred miles. It was being reported to Paul that immorality of a grievous nature was still ongoing at Corinth (1 Cor 5:1–5). Chloe's people informed Paul of serious divisions in the church (1 Cor 1:11–17) involving allegiance given to leaders. Significant here is the fact that Apollos's and Cephas's names are mentioned. Also suggested and significant is the fact that the church was large enough to have multiple "divisions."

Apollos had been directed to Corinth by Aquila and Priscilla after their settlement in Ephesus prior to Paul's visits to Jerusalem (Luke's Source, STA 18:24–28). The surprise is the presence of Cephas in Corinth. How did he get there? When did he arrive there? Why did he go there? Is "Cephas" one and the same person with Simon Peter (see Gal 2:1–10; John 1:42)? No direct answers are given in the sources to these questions, although it appears "Cephas" traveled to Corinth at some time after the Jerusalem Conference, probably by 53 CE. Provided Cephas should be identified with Peter, he could claim firsthand pre-resurrection association with the historical Jesus as one of the "original apostles." And so, as narrated in Acts and Luke's Source, Peter was open to the gentile mission (see Acts 10:1—11:18; 15: 7–11; Luke's Source, STA 15:6–7). But he could also become a threat for Paul. It perhaps should be noted that later tradition associates Peter with Rome, such that he may well have been involved in evangelism outside the confines of Palestine.

Paul had his apostleship and his authority questioned at Corinth (1 Cor 9:1–7). There was apparently one individual who strongly opposed Paul (2 Cor 2:5–11), although Paul's potential opposition was more widespread (2 Cor 13:1–4). One is tempted to ask if the initial opposition originated from outside—from "Cephas" (see 1 Cor 1:12; Gal 2:11–16)—rather than from within the Corinthian church.[3] Not only did Chloe's people inform Paul of the developed factionalism, but Paul received a detailed letter from Corinth likely brought by Stephanas, Fortunatus, and Achaicus (1 Cor 7:1; 16:17). There is no reason to assume Paul left Ephesus to travel to Corinth personally, even though Corinth could be reached in a matter of days by sea. Rather, Paul had his hands full in Asia and Galatia and he had plenty of envoys he could send to Corinth, including Titus and Timothy and others. After his previous painful visit, Paul would not have risked a personal appearance until he was rather sure that he would be well received by the majority of Christians in the church. There was too much on the line for him to do otherwise. And 1 Corinthians did not necessarily

---

3. Peter's differences with Paul following his embarrassment in Antioch may well have continued and even bled over to Paul's own mission fields.

help the situation, probably much to Paul's surprise. Titus would become Paul's major liaison with Corinth during this time.

During the time Paul was in Ephesus, he experienced a time of severe imprisonment from which he was at one point not sure that he would be released (Phil 1:21–26). This likely occurred in 54 CE and brought about a change in earlier plans that he had previously announced to Corinth (1 Cor 16:5–9). While this could not be helped, it served to further undermine his credibility among his opponents in the church of Corinth. Paul's sour relationship with some in the Corinthian church had had time to fester since his previous "painful" visit. According to his opponents, Paul simply could not be trusted (2 Cor 1:8–23).

News of Paul's aborted departure from Ephesus reached both Philippi and Corinth, where it was met with differing responses. Corinth responded with suspicion. Philippi responded by sending Paul aid by the hand of Epaphroditus, who would further render aid to Paul in behalf of the Philippian church. During this time of imprisonment, Paul apparently despaired of life itself (Phil 1:19–24). The Philippians learned of Epaphroditus's own serious illness (Phil 2:25), such that the length of Paul's imprisonment was long enough to occasion Epaphroditus's ministry to Paul, his ensuing serious illness, and communication back and forth between Ephesus and Philippi. It was long enough to seriously disrupt his previously announced plans of a visit to Corinth.

The overall suggestion of the available evidence would be that Paul's imprisonment had some connection with the complaint voiced by the silversmiths and the ensuing riot in the city (Luke's Source, STA 19:23–34), although Paul himself does not say. In fact, the available evidence only supports the strong hypothesis of an imprisonment in Ephesus. Rhetorically speaking, however, it would not have served Paul's case at all to have directly stressed his imprisonment in Ephesus. That would have only been ammunition for the opposition in Corinth and the Judaizing faction to use against him. It would only further undermine his credibility. The available evidence points to a serious imprisonment in Ephesus, although it cannot be conclusively proven and must remain at the level of a strong hypothesis. Such an hypothesis best explains the available facts.

Paul's time in Ephesus was thus a time of "highs and lows." He acknowledges his great opposition (1 Cor 16:9). He speaks about "fighting wild beasts in Ephesus" (1 Cor 15:32). He has a near-death experience (2 Cor 1:8–9), which echoes sentiments expressed more personally in the Philippian letter (Phil 1:19–26). Paul indicates that Prisca and Aquila "risked their lives" for him (Rom 16:4). He mentions Andronicus and Junias (or Julius, p46) as persons of note *among the apostles* who were "his kinsmen and fellow prisoners" (Rom 16:7), who were actually "in Christ" before Paul. Contemporary interpreters seek to identify "Junias" as a female apostle in the interests of equality, although p46 has the reading "Julius" and Paul identifies the said person as a "fellow kinsman" and "fellow prisoner" in the remainder of the verse (see Rom 16:7).

Paul's experience in Ephesus may well be listed among his times of imprisonment and near-death experiences (2 Cor 11:23).

The riot in Ephesus was fed by both economic and religious concerns (Luke's Source, STA 19:23–24). Paul was accused of providing a direct threat to the metal craftsmen's trade and even to the Artemis cult itself. Some of the "Asiarchs" (local officials) were friends of Paul and sought to protect him from a mob lynching (Luke's Source, STA 19:30–31). Paul's imprisonment likely followed this riot, although Paul's time in prison and further time in Ephesus is indeterminate. Paul's imprisonment must have been of some months' duration, and it was most certainly severe. The overall experience provided a catalyst to encourage Paul to personally continue with his Collection ministry and his ultimate plans to visit Rome (see Luke's Source, STA 19:21–22). It served to underscore the urgency of Paul's own participation in the proclamation of the Gospel of God.

> Paul walked out of a Roman prison in Ephesus a free man and was met by Aquila and Apollos. They were a welcome sight. Paul clutched his few belongings ever more tightly, as he took his first steps of renewed freedom. And then, after taking a deep breath of fresh morning air, he dropped his small bundle to the ground and hugged his two friends warmly. Paul uttered a brief doxology to God as he looked heavenward, "Blessed be our God in Christ! Amen!" Paul bent down and gathered his belongings. He knelt there in silence for a while looking back at the prison in which he thought at one time he was surely going to die. Then, as his two friends lovingly lifted him up, the three of them walked together down the uneven Roman pavement toward the house of Aquila, where Prisca and others were anxiously waiting....

> Paul shared many tears of joy with his friends, his brothers and sisters in Christ, who had prayed for him and cared for him such as they could during his imprisonment. It was good to reunite with Andronicus and Junias, who had earlier actually been imprisoned with Paul. They had been released several months earlier. They had long been engaged in the work at Ephesus, even before Paul. The members of the church had not only maintained their support for Paul, but they had also provided care for Ephaphroditus during his protracted and serious illness. They had even paid for his passage back to Philippi. And Epaphroditus had carried with him Paul's earlier letter of thanksgiving and encouragement to those saints of Philippi....

> Free at last, Paul himself now had his sights on Macedonia, although he renewed worries about the Galatian situation and the threat posed by the Nomistic Evangelists from Jerusalem. Being but one person, and now needing rest and recuperation from his severe prison experience, he weighed his options: Would it be Galatia, or would it be Macedonia and Corinth? After much soul-searching and prayer, he would have to leave Galatia to his associates and hope that, backed by their efforts, his very pointed letter to the churches there would accomplish its

intended purpose. He had too much to lose otherwise. He simply had to complete his Collection. He simply had to try to mend his strained relationship with Corinth. He could not allow the Nomistic Evangelists to gain the upper hand in Macedonia or Achaia and Corinth, as they had apparently achieved in Galatia. Besides, he had to express personally a very heartfelt face-to-face thank-you to Philippi for their support, before he had to encounter troublesome Corinth. . . .

Yes, Paul thought, for the moment he had done all that he could with reference to Galatia, other than continue to pray for them. He had upheld the Gospel. Galatia would have to wait for another day. . . . It was a difficult, but strategic decision. . . . And, somewhere in the distance, there was always Rome. . . .

Paul went toward Macedonia (2 Cor 2:13; 7:5), while sending Titus to Corinth (2 Cor 7:6, 13, 14), who had now caught up with Paul in Macedonia. Paul had wanted to go from Ephesus to Corinth, then to Macedonia, then back to Corinth (2 Cor 1:16), and then perhaps Rome (Rom 15:22–29). He was keenly aware of the cruciality of Corinth in his belated Collection endeavor, now that his crushing experience in Asia had ended (see 2 Cor 1:8–11; 2 Cor 8–9). But he did not want to risk a visit there before he heard from Titus. Paul's second visit had been a strained and strident one which had caused pain (2 Cor 2:1), and even his letter (1 Cor) written in response to their subsequent inquiries had caused further pain (2 Cor 2:3)—much to his surprise. In the end, he had to reverse his original travel plans. He traveled to Macedonia, then to Corinth, then back to Macedonia, and then sailed for Judea and Jerusalem. Rome would have to wait a while longer (Rom 15:25–29).

Corinth had not been as sympathetic to his imprisonment in Ephesus as Philippi had been when they learned of it. So, having heard nothing from Titus, he moved instead in the direction of Macedonia. He still had heard nothing by the time he reached Troas (2 Cor 2:12–13), so although he had opportunity to preach the gospel, he moved on to Macedonia. Had he heard from Titus, he could have easily traveled from Troas to Corinth by sea. But Troas, as it were, was the last port-of-call before he decided to go to Macedonia instead of Corinth. After all, Paul owed Philippi a lot. Second Corinthians 7 also resounds with a renewed hope brought by the coming of Titus, who has assuaged Paul's fears in relation to Corinth (2 Cor 7:5–16). Paul could move ahead with his belated Collection (2 Cor 8–9).

Within the context of the Collection Campaign, Paul commends the Corinthians and beseeches them (2 Cor 9–10), but then he cannot refrain as he goes on to boast and to attack the false apostles (see 2 Cor 11:12–23). These opponents must belong to the group of Nomistic Evangelists who were threatening Paul's campaign, ministry, gospel, and person in the Galatian churches, Philippi, and Corinth. These were all areas of Paul's mission fields from his Foundational Campaign, about which he testified during his Famine visit to Jerusalem (Gal 2:1–10). Paul continues to express apprehension about his third visit to Corinth, as he boasts and exhorts, to the point that he may well have run the risk of offending the Corinthians again (2 Cor 11–13).

If indeed Romans was written in Corinth, then it appears he weathered the storm with regard to both the Corinthians themselves and the threat of the Nomistic Evangelists. Paul is likely to have rehearsed material in Romans within the Corinthian context before he sent the letter by courier to Rome. In the present instance, Romans may exhibit intertextuality issues with *both* the Galatian epistle as well as the Corinthian correspondence. It is far from certain that Paul deliberately carried on such an endeavor for the primary purpose of continuing an oblique address to Corinth. Paul has to continue to deal with whatever threat may have been posed by the Nomistic Evangelists and "mending fences" with Corinth. These separate issues may have well formed a constellation of challenge, but Paul really has his sight set upon his Collection, his upcoming delivery visit to Jerusalem (home of the Nomistic Evangelists), and upon his hoped for visit to Rome and ministry to Spain. Surely, he would be free of the Nomists as he moved to the West for new work following his Collection visit to Jerusalem.

Once released from an Ephesian imprisonment, Paul left for Macedonia at the beginning of the travel season in 55 CE. The three-year old Judaizing controversy involving the Nomistic Evangelists affecting Galatia and Asia had not been resolved, although Paul left associates behind in Ephesus to deal with this threat. Given the fact that Philippi was a predominantly gentile church and was so firmly supportive of Paul, if Judaizers in fact came to Philippi, they apparently were able to make no headway. Continuing negotiations were ongoing with Corinth, as illustrated by Paul's concerns expressed in 2 Cor 8–9.

During 55 CE Paul moved from Ephesus to Philippi and began to move through Macedonia and Achaia on his way to Corinth. Titus was apparently able to accomplish his mission for which Paul had dispatched him, such that Paul himself finally arrived in Corinth not later than the fall of 55 CE. Our sources are silent with regard to his time in Corinth, other than the reference in Luke's Source, STA 20:2–3 that the Jews stirred up trouble for Paul. This may occasion Paul's own expressed concern stated in Rom 15:30–31 as he prepared to take the Collection to Jerusalem. Thus, the letter to the Romans was apparently written in Corinth during the winter of 55–56 CE, as it became apparent to Paul that his long-delayed visit to the churches of Rome would be delayed yet once again.

The Collection Ministry

Too many events had transpired in the years following the Jerusalem Conference. The Collection had taken longer than Paul had anticipated. The strong personal opposition from the Nomistic Evangelists likewise needed to be addressed. It was not altogether clear anymore where the leadership of the Jerusalem church stood on the issue of the gospel. Much as he might want to go on to Rome, Paul simply had to make *this* journey to Jerusalem. It would prove to be an absolutely fateful decision, whereby his worst fears and more would be realized.

The Collection runs like a "red thread" through Paul's Pillar Epistles (1 Corinthians, 2 Corinthians, Romans, and Galatians?) and his own references take us to the eve of his departure from Corinth. There is no reason to doubt that Luke's Source (STA 20:1–4) references the Collection and some of the representatives of the contributing churches who accompanied Paul to Jerusalem—a delegation that included two representatives of the Galatian churches, Timothy from Lystra and Gaius from Derbe.

Luke's Source STA 20:1–6, coupled with Luke's Source STA 19:21–22, appears to be a certain allusion to Paul's Collection ministry. There is no reason not to regard those who are mentioned as members of the delegation of the churches who accompanied Paul. Sopater apparently represented Beroea, Aristarchus and Secundus represented Thessalonica, Gaius and Timothy served as representatives of the Galatian churches of Derbe and Lystra, Tychicus and Trophimus were Asian/Ephesian representatives. Conspicuously absent in this listing are representatives from Corinth and Philippi, although it is highly likely they participated in some measure (see 2 Cor 8:1–15; 9:1–5; Rom 15:26). Romans 15:26 indicates that both Macedonia and Achaia have made "some contribution." Romans was written before Paul left Corinth and before he returned through Macedonia (Luke's Source, STA 20:3). Their contributions may have increased further by the time of Paul's departure from Corinth and his return through Macedonia. Likewise, Asia (and perhaps Galatia) may have made further contributions as Paul traveled toward Jerusalem.

Some five years after he left Ephesus, when he was imprisoned in Rome, Paul remembered Onesiphorus for the many ways he had helped Paul in Ephesus and for his help during Paul's subsequent Roman imprisonment (2 Tim 1:16–18). He singled out his household for greetings, along with Prisca and Aquila, who had remained in Ephesus (2 Tim 4:19). On the other hand, Paul felt deserted by "all in Asia" (2 Tim 1:15), singling out in particular Phygelus and Hermogenes.

Paul surely makes an overstatement born of his despair, in the light of his greetings expressed in Rom 16, a separate accompanying letter sent to Ephesians but now attached to the Roman letter. Those mentioned in Rom 16 remained supportive of Paul, although he was most disappointed by others who deserted him. Alexander the metal worker apparently did Paul great harm with his testimony (2 Tim 4:14–15; cf. Luke's Source, STA 19:33–34) and no one spoke in Paul's first defense (2 Tim 4:16). Paul's time in Ephesus had been fruitful, but at the same time very, very difficult.

While Paul's final campaign cannot be understood apart from his Collection ministry, it is rather surprising that the book of Acts is virtually silent in this regard. Luke appears not to have known the significance of the Collection for Paul, or, on the other hand, he chose not to emphasize it at all. It is pointless to speculate, although the time of the Collection is long past when Luke writes, drawing upon his Source, the

STA. Luke's Source reflects a brief allusion to the Collection in a complex consisting of Luke's Source STA 19:21–22 and STA 20:1–6, which Luke breaks apart in his redaction. The reference in Acts 24:17 is usually cited as evidence of the Collection, but the verse is a part of Paul's defense speech and is representative of Lukan redaction. The vocabulary used does not suggest a reference to the Collection.

On the other hand, the Collection is a central theme in the letters of Paul written during this period of ministry. The letters make plain that Paul's final journey to Jerusalem was undertaken to deliver the Collection, which had been several years in the making (see 1 Cor 16:1–4; Rom 15:25–29). Paul was accustomed to multi-year ministry. Paul made two prayer requests of the Roman Christians as he wrote to them from Corinth (Rom 15:30–32). First, he asked that they pray he would be delivered from the non-Christian Jews in Judea; secondly, he wanted his Collection to be acceptable to the Christian community in Jerusalem. The two requests taken together are all-inclusive for the Jerusalem population—Jews and Christian Jews.

Perhaps neither one of these prayer requests met with a favorable outcome. While Paul's letters (Galatians; 1 Corinthians; 2 Corinthians; Romans) furnish us with a picture of Paul's Collection in terms of its practical and theological purposes, scope, and administration, there is no mention in Paul's post-Collection letters of its delivery and reception. Of course, one could argue that the so-called Deutero-Pauline letters are not by Paul and thus have no interest in the Collection. The silence of *Paul*, however, is at least as viable as the silence of non-Pauline authors and far more viable than seeing the entire Acts 21–28 account as total fiction.

The silence in Paul and in Luke's Source/Acts may suggest that the Collection was not the success that Paul had hoped it would be; i.e., its acceptability was marginal at best. Any number of reasons may be set forth as to why this was likely the case—e.g., limitation in the amount of funds raised, better economic times in a post-famine period, Judaistic reaction against Paul, etc.—one may only guess. The outcome of Paul's reception in Jerusalem (according to Luke's Source/Acts) was most certainly not what Paul had hoped it would be, for it marked the beginning of the end. Luke's Source/Acts provides the only framework that we have for understanding Paul's final visit to Jerusalem and its aftermath.

Galatians 2:10 with its present tense request (μνημονεύωμεν, pres. subj., "we should continue to remember the poor") and Paul's stated commitment ("the very thing I was eager to do") marks the establishment of the principle of Paul's Collection ministry. By the time he writes Romans, the theological purpose of unification has overtaken the principle of need in terms of its primary meaning. This may well have been aggravated by the actions of the Nomistic Evangelists who had plagued Paul's mission field during the Collection Campaign.

In his appeal to Corinth, Paul stressed ideas of Christian service or ministry (διακονία) on the basis of genuine love, Jesus himself having supplied the pattern (2 Cor 8:4, 19, 8–9). Two other principles underlying the Collection were those of equality (2 Cor 8:14–15) and unity (Rom 15:27). It was a ministry to demonstrate Christian solidarity. It was also a demonstration of eschatological realities for Paul (see Isa 2:3; 60:1–5; Mic 4:1). Ideological realities are often more difficult to address and establish than mere physical realities—i.e., the question of theological requirements for unity versus sheer physical need.

> Paul celebrated Passover in the spring of 56 CE in Philippi, which must have been a joyous occasion for him. Paul paused to think and reflect upon the years of his Collection Campaign since his departure from Antioch. Four years of difficult, yet fruitful labor were now past. He had successfully navigated his third visit to Corinth, where overall, thanks to Titus and others, he had been well received. Corinth was a troublesome church, which one had to treat like an unruly child in some ways. Yet in spite of everything, he loved that church. Now he was in Philippi, spending significant time with a church that had always loved him. His Collection had shaped up nicely and he felt that sufficient contributions had been made to render a significant statement regarding both his success among the gentiles and the badly needed theological unity of Jewish and gentile Christians.

> Before he had left from Corinth, Paul drafted the longest letter of his career and dispatched it to Rome. It represented an apology for the past as well as preparation for the future. Paul had long wanted to visit Rome, but he had been prevented. Still, after his upcoming collection visit to Jerusalem, his future intentions involved the West, beginning with Rome—until Christ should return in glory and with power.

> While the Collection had taken longer than he had originally anticipated, the aggregate result had been worth the years of hard reconciliation work. He did not regret his years of evangelical work in Ephesus, for a strong church had been established. Memory of his time of imprisonment in Ephesus and the despair he had felt suddenly flooded over him. He was fortunate to have survived such a trying time, when it appeared that everything including life itself would slip away from him with so many things yet undone. No, not just fortunate, he thought. Perhaps through that experience more than any other, he had come to a renewed sense of divine purpose and strength. He had come to a new understanding of God's peace, even in the midst of the greatest adversity. Joy flooded his soul as he commemorated this Passover in Philippi in such a personal way with Christian friends who had loved and supported him for so long.

> After Passover, Paul sailed for Troas to meet others of his party who had gone on ahead. As the ship neared Troas, Paul could not help looking backward in the direction of Samothrace, recalling a much earlier time when he was sailing in the opposite direction toward Macedonia in the time after he received his vision at Troas. By the time Paul's ship docked in the harbor at Troas, Paul realized that he had just over forty days to make it to Jerusalem if he were going to be there in time for Pentecost. How appropriate it would be to offer his

Collection as "first fruits" to the Jerusalem believers in Christ. Still, he would spend some time with the church that had formed in Troas.

How long ago had he had that Macedonian vision? Twelve years? Fourteen years? Longer? His friends met him at the harbor and took him to his place of lodging. He was glad to be back on solid ground. Paul spent a week with the church and worshiped with them on Sunday, intending to gather his party and leave the next day if they could book passage. He changed his mind after he preached too long and the episode involving Eutychus occurred. He decided to travel by land from Troas to Assos and meet the remainder of his party there.

Paul joined his party three days later at Assos, where they booked passage on another ship sailing for Syria. Assos to Mitylene, Mitylene to Chios, Chios to Samos, and Samos to Miletus. The sailing proved to be timely and uneventful. When the ship put in at Miletus, Paul sent an envoy by ship back to Ephesus to invite the Ephesian elders to meet him in Miletus. He felt it important to close out any unfinished business regarding the Collection and to find out firsthand how the church in Ephesus had fared over the past year. He knew that Prisca and Aquila and others would be more than glad to come and see him. Perhaps, they would even bring additional contributions for the Jerusalem Collection.

While it would take a number of days to accomplish the meeting, he could rest. The one thing he could not afford was to become bogged down in Ephesus for weeks or even longer, should opposition be stirred up were his presence to become known. So, he waited patiently at Miletus. When they finally came, he brought them up to date as they did him. And, they did bring with them some additional funding. Knowing that the time for the departure of his ship was drawing near, he outlined his plans to them. He was going to Jerusalem, but after he delivered the Collection, he planned to sail for Rome. It would likely be some years before he would have opportunity to pass that way again, especially if he made it to Rome and the churches there supported a ministry to Spain farther west. Goodbyes were never easy. Perhaps some would dare to join him in a new work, maybe even Aquila and Prisca would return to Rome. Perhaps the Ephesian church could become a patron or use its influence upon Christians in Rome.

Fig. 26. The Taurus Mountains. Original painting by G. Roger Greene.

Paul and his party sailed out of the harbor of Miletus, with its great theater finally disappearing behind them as they rounded the southern cape. They sailed a straight course for the island of Cos. The next day found them at Rhodus and the day following they docked at Patara on the southern tip of Anatolia. Three days were spent locating a ship that was sailing for Phoenicia. Paul had hoped to find a ship that might be sailing to Antioch, but none were immediately available. Mindful of the time until Pentecost, he decided to sail more directly to Tyre in Phoenicia, where a ship was scheduled to unload its cargo. And so from Patara, they sailed across open seas in sight of the Taurus Mountains on the port side, finally turning toward Cyprus and bringing it to port. From there they sailed across to Tyre.

Paul and his company remained in Tyre for the better part of a week waiting for a ship that could take them farther south. They could have perhaps saved some time by walking from Tyre all the way to Jerusalem, although they deemed it safer to travel the distance by sea, given the collection they carried with them. They found some disciples in Tyre, including several who had recently been to Jerusalem for Passover. Inspired by the Spirit, they warned Paul that it was not the best of times to go to Jerusalem. There seemed to be continuing strife between the Jews and the Jewish church in Jerusalem. Some of Paul's party thought Paul should heed the warning and perhaps go down to Antioch instead. Paul, however, was resolute.

When a ship was finally located that would take them to Ptolemais, Paul and company were on board. A day's sail took them to Ptolemais, where they spent the night with Christian brethren while the ship exchanged cargo. The next day's sail brought them to Caesarea. Although Paul had been here before, he could not help but marvel once again at the magnificent harbor that had been constructed by Herod the Great. As they sailed into the harbor between the two lighthouses, the Temple of Augustus dominated the landscape before them. Paul had preached the gospel of Christ in a world that had long believed in the gospel of Augustus. As Paul had preached, Christ had no temple but the church. But it was a living body, not a stone edifice.

As they disembarked and proceeded up into the city from the harbor, Paul sought out the house of Philip the evangelist, with whom he had stayed many years earlier when the brethren from the church in Jerusalem had first brought him to Caesarea and with whom he had stayed when he had returned from his Foundation Campaign. It was altogether fitting that he should stay with Philip once again at the end of his Collection Campaign.

Paul thus traveled with his companions from Miletus via Caesarea to Jerusalem. Hellenist Christians extended him hospitality—Philip in Caesarea and Mnason in Jerusalem. Mnason, like Barnabas, was from Cyprus (Luke's Source, STA 21:16). The Jewish Christian community in Jerusalem was presided over by James, and as might be expected, was faithful to the Law. When the prophet Agabus (see Acts 11:27–30) came to Caesarea, he foretold that the Jews in Jerusalem would bind Paul and hand him over to the gentile authorities (Luke's Source, STA 21:10–11). Members of the church in Caesarea begged Paul not to go up to Jerusalem, but he could not be persuaded to abandon his mission.

Paul had achieved his goal of arriving in Caesarea in plenty of time to spend some days there before going up to Jerusalem. Now, Paul and his company went up to Jerusalem to be there for Pentecost, which in 56 CE occurred on June 11. Some of the disciples from Caesarea guided Paul to the guest house of Mnason. It is interesting that Paul did not stay at his sister's house (see Luke's Source, STA 23:16). According to Luke's Source (STA 21:17), they were received warmly by the "brethren." Concerns were expressed by James, however, when Paul met with him and the Jerusalem elders the next day. The term διακονία is used to describe Paul's ministry among the gentiles in Luke's Source (STA 21:19), although the reference could be generic and not explicitly a reference to the Collection—it was a ministry "among the gentiles" and not one "for the saints."

The decision of the earlier Jerusalem Conference and the resultant letter that had been sent by James was directed toward gentile Christians and really said nothing about Jewish Christians. The issue of what was expected of *Jewish* converts to Christianity was thus largely unresolved. Although Paul could be a Jew to Jews and a "gentile to gentiles" (see 1 Cor 9:19–21), he apparently went beyond the focus of the Conference in his actions. Luke's Source is historically correct in suggesting that Paul was a controversial figure.

While Paul himself was not necessarily antinomian ("against the Law"), he was certainly no longer a Jewish legalist. The Nomistic Evangelists who had opposed both him and his gospel had proven that. The gospel which he proclaimed lent itself to antinomian (free from law) interpretation, as illustrated by the Corinthians' mantra of "all things are lawful" (see 1 Cor 10:23). Paul's own explosive response to the Judaizing problem of the Nomistic Evangelists in Galatia could certainly be misconstrued as it might apply to Jews, such that he could be understood as being "anti-circumcision." Paul was not so much "anti-circumcision" or "anti-law" as much as he was "pro-faith." Equality of Jew and gentile in Christ, of course, called for a new appraisal of the place of the Law by Paul. Equally significant, Paul had come to a new appraisal of Abraham's story of rectification—a story based upon faithfulness and not upon law.

Luke's Source specifically mentions Jews (and not Judaizers) who have been taught that Paul had been teaching the Jews among the gentiles to forsake the Law of Moses (Luke's Source, STA 21:21). The irony here is that this is apparently an aspect of the pre-Christian Paul's own persecution of Jewish Christians. This is in keeping with Jewish opposition elsewhere in Luke's Source/Acts, but it does not reflect the problem with the Judaizing Christians reflected in Paul's own letters. It is also "Jews from Asia" (Luke's Source, STA 21:27) who will incite the crowds against Paul and bring about his arrest. Paul's Jerusalem opposition in the source material does appear to be Jewish and not Christian in origin.

However, if Jews had been informed about Paul explicitly, the source is more likely to have been the Judaizers or the Nomists. Jewish opposition to Paul in the diaspora appears to have had more local and regional concerns related to "stealing" members from the synagogues than any real theological concerns. It would appear to be highly questionable as to how well Paul's ministry would be explicitly and generally known in Jerusalem among the "Jews." It is more likely that Luke's Source/Acts simply reflects the language of a later time post-70 CE world, when the Jewish mission is largely past and the church has gone its separate way. The later sources do not differentiate clearly between the Jews and Christian Nomists.

James called upon Paul to demonstrate his personal support of Jewish Law by undergoing his own purification rites in the temple and paying the expenses of four Nazirites who were fulfilling their vows. That there were "Nazirites" with Paul would be indicative of Jewish Christians among Paul's group, as well as Paul's personal continuing loyalty to Torah. From what Paul said in the Corinthian letter (see 1 Cor 9:19–21), he should have had no problem doing this—especially in Jerusalem. Such an action might indeed serve to dispel some of the rumors about Paul and serve to disperse some of the opposition to him among the more fundamentalist Jewish Christians.

Now that Paul was in Jerusalem, he was in the heartland of the fundamentalist Judaizing Christians, the Nomists. He had been in this position before. Accommodation to Jewish Law was the norm for *Jewish* Christians in Jerusalem. Paul should demonstrate that he could be a "Jerusalem Jewish Christian" out of respect for the Christians of the Jerusalem church. Although a lot of Lukan redaction is evident in the final chapters of Acts, the basic tradition appears to follow a source that is historically sound.

Jewish Christians *in Jerusalem* may well have seen Paul as an apostate from the Law who had gained the reputation of preaching apostasy among Jews and gentiles. There is nothing in Paul's letters which corresponds to the charge found in Luke's Source, STA 21:21. It is interesting that there is no remembrance of Paul's original persecutions of Christians or his strict nomistic orientation as a Pharisee in Jerusalem. These things are brought to remembrance only in the Lukan redaction of Paul's defense speeches in Acts (Acts 22:3–8; 26:4–11).

Paul's own letters testify to the aim of bringing the Collection of the Pauline communities to Jerusalem. Behind the issue of the Collection stands Paul's problematic relationship with the Jerusalem church. The question must thereby be why nothing concerning the Collection is mentioned in Luke's Source/Acts 21. Indeed, James would have found it difficult to acknowledge Paul's gentile mission by acceptance of the Collection and at the same time placate the concerns of the strict Jewish Christians concerning Paul. Ardent Jewish nationalists would be quick to criticize the Jewish Christian messianic movement if they suspected it of being "treacherously anti-Jewish." It may be the case that Luke omitted or deliberately avoided the issue of the Collection, perhaps because the underlying Lukan Source reported it as a failure or that it was rejected. In view of Luke's purpose, he certainly cannot report the grand finale of Paul's relation to Jerusalem as a failure.

Even more questions are raised about James's failure or the failure of the Jerusalem church to come to Paul's aid after his arrest—narration supposedly offered, according to some, by Luke the "eye-witness." If indeed Luke's Source (STA 21:18–26) exhibits an historical kernel, the entire episode of purification in the temple upon arrival in Jerusalem marks the conclusion of Paul's active missionary campaigns. Paul is portrayed as a good Jewish Christian who does what a good Jewish Christian would be expected to do *in Jerusalem*. There is nothing introduced prior to Luke's Source, STA 21:27, that would occasion Paul's arrest or confinement.

IMAGINE PAUL

Fig. 27. Herod's Temple in Jerusalem. *Archaeology Illustrated*, © Balage Balogh. Used under license.

The Lukan Source thus brings Paul's campaign to an end with Paul in the temple, where he had gone for his own purification. This is likely historical, but it also suits the Lukan purpose quite well and the overall attention Luke gives to Jerusalem in both his gospel and in Acts. But then, Luke's purpose at this point is focused upon Rome and not Jerusalem. Having begun with Jerusalem (Luke 1; Acts 1), Luke will soon bring closure to his story by leaving Jerusalem behind as the Gospel is proclaimed in Rome (Acts 28).

The Post-Collection Period

The occasion of Paul's arrest according to Acts thus had to do with the supposed charge of taking the gentile Trophimus into the inner precincts of the temple beyond the wall of exclusion (see Eph 2:14–15; Acts 21:29). Paul himself, in the light of his gospel, may have "pushed the envelope." However, Paul was not arrested on an intra-mural Judaizing charge. Jewish Christians neither testify for nor against Paul. Rather, he was arrested on the basis of having provoked a riot during the time of the Pentecost feast when both Jewish and Roman (and Christian!) sensitivities were at a peak. It was also at such times that Roman authorities would be at highest alert to quell any sort of disturbance that might fuel messianic uprising. The Jewish mob is upset about the possible profanation of the temple at a high holy time (Luke's Source, STA 21:27–31a), while the Roman tribune Claudias Lysias and the cohort of Roman soldiers is concerned about a potential uprising (Luke's Source, STA 21:31b–32a).

Although they represent Lukan redaction in their present form, the charges leveled by Tertullus in the hearing before Felix reflect rather clearly the charges that could be stated against Paul: he was a pestilent agitator among Jews throughout the world (hence, one who fomented disorder); he tried to profane the temple (hence, he was responsible for the riot); see Acts 24:5–6. The fact he belonged to the "sect of the Nazarenes" was immaterial from Rome's point of view. The label in all likelihood reflects an historical designation for the early Christian movement in Palestine, some quarter of a century after the execution of Jesus. The letter by Claudias Lysias finds Paul to have done nothing "worthy of death or imprisonment" (Luke's Source, STA 23:29), although Paul is sent by him to Felix for his own safety and for a disposition of his case.

> *Safely inside the Roman barracks of the Tower of Antonia, Claudias Lysias turned Paul over for interrogation by scourging in order to learn why Paul had been the cause of such an uproar. Paul already suffered from several bruises inflicted by the Jewish mob; he knew what Roman scourging was like. Paul decided he would make his identity known. "Is it according to Roman law that you scourge an uncondemned Roman citizen?" This was all it took for those soldiers who had been binding him with straps to loosen them and report immediately to Claudius Lysias. Paul rested overnight in the security of Antonia.*

> *The next day Claudius Lysias sent word to the chief priests and members of the Sanhedrin notifying them that he wanted all to meet face to face with Paul, in order that he could learn the facts of Paul's case. Paul turned the situation to his own advantage when he identified himself as a Pharisee who was being ill-treated because of his belief in the resurrection. A vigorous dispute ensued, which pitted Pharisees against the priestly Sadducees in a debate over resurrection. For the second time in two days, the Roman tribune had to rescue Paul. When a plot became known that the Jews planned to kill Paul, Claudias Lysias rescued Paul yet a third time by sending him under military protection along with a letter of explanation to Felix, the Roman governor, in Caesarea. Paul's final time in Jerusalem had been very brief. It had been less than a fortnight. His worst fears which he had expressed to the Roman Christians as he had penned his letter to the Romans just six months earlier in Corinth were now being realized.*

> *Paul found himself back in Caesarea before the beginning of July, 56 CE. Little did he know that he would be here under arrest for the next two years. Those who had accompanied Paul to Jerusalem likewise returned to Caesarea, carrying the news of Paul's reception and arrest in Jerusalem. One by one, they booked passage to return and report to their respective churches. There was nothing else for them to do. The church in Caesarea was in the older part of the city in the hills, while Paul was held in the newer administrative quarters*

of Herod's "Caesarea Maritima." Felix, as the Roman governor, enjoyed the luxury and view afforded by Herod's former palace, located as it was on the sharp promontory that extended into the Mediterranean between the main harbor and the theater. [See figure 22.]

Herod's city and harbor was a marvel of engineering, of which the Romans took full advantage. It was a secular city of maritime trade and Roman administration—a city vastly different from the Jewish religious center of Jerusalem. Yet both cities had their temple—Jerusalem had its great Herodian Temple in honor of the Jewish God, and Caesarea had its great temple in honor of the divine Augustus. It was that temple which overlooked the large harbor built by Herod the Great, Rome's client king. It overlooked that harbor, which was the gateway to Rome itself, far away to the west beyond the Mare Nostrum.

The Jewish high priest Ananias, Tertullus the lawyer, and others came down from Jerusalem to present their case against Paul before Marcus Antonius Felix, the Roman governor. Matters of Jewish theology—Torah and temple and the like—were of little concern to Felix. But if Paul were a member of the sicarii, *the growing Jewish liberation movement, that was another story that would have required swift judicial decision. Felix could have decided the case, but he decided to adjourn the proceedings until the tribune Claudius Lysias could come down from Jerusalem. The wait extended for two years, until Felix was recalled to Rome and was succeeded by Porcius Festus. When Festus went up to Jerusalem to curry favor with the Jewish leadership, they renewed their case against Paul. Jewish animosity toward Paul must have been strong to have endured a two-year interim period with such lasting fervor. Paul realized the precarious nature of his situation, as they pressed Festus to have him brought to Jerusalem to try his case.*

At a hearing held in Caesarea, Paul as a Roman citizen decided to appeal directly to Nero. It was the early summer of 58 CE—still within the early and good years of Nero's reign. If he could get a favorable verdict from the emperor himself, that would set the stage and open doors for an opportunity of fruitful ministry in Rome and Spain. Festus pronounced his decision: "You have appealed to Caesar; to Caesar you shall go."

Before Paul could sail for Rome, King Agrippa and his wife Bernice came down to visit Festus in Caesarea. Being himself inexperienced in Jewish matters, Festus placed Paul's case before the Jewish king. Paul himself was brought in and given permission to speak, at which point he made his defense as he had done many times previously. Agrippa confirmed that Paul had done nothing that was worthy of death and imprisonment and told Festus that he could have been set free if he had not already appealed to Caesar. Little did Paul know that Nero himself was becoming rather unpredictable. . . .

Finally, when the decision was made to transport Paul to Rome, Paul was handed over to Julius, a centurion of the cohort of Augustus. The voyage to Rome proved to be anything but uneventful. The cargo ship of Adramyttium sailed northward to Sidon and then into the sea lanes between Cyprus and Pamphylia, moving westward along the southern reaches of Anatolia with the formidable Taurus Mountains in sight.

Fig. 28. A Final Journey Begins. Original painting by G. Roger Greene.

Paul and the others changed ships at Myra, boarding a grain ship of Alexandria bound for Italy. Prevailing winds carried them to the southern coastline of Crete. The voyage had already been plagued by significant delays, such that the window for safe passage on the Mediterranean was fast drawing to a close. There was some discussion as to where they might best spend the winter, and before they could reach the agreed upon harbor at Phoenix at the western end of Crete, a dangerous northeasterner blew them out to the open seas of the Mediterranean. . . .

The Romans referred to the Mediterranean as the *Mare Nostrum*, "Our Sea." From the perspective of Palestine, the Mediterranean Sea was like a large "Roman lake." Things arrived from Rome and departed to Rome. The connection between Alexandria, Egypt, and Rome was the most vital trade link, for Egypt served as the granary of Rome. Because of its strategic importance, Egypt was always under direct *imperial* control and not the control of the Roman senate. Whoever controlled Egypt ruled Rome. It was a particularly important link in the time of Claudius, given several serious threats of famine during his reign.

The southbound journey from Rome to Alexandria could be made in fifteen days or less in a rather straight line with prevailing northwesterly winds. The return journey from Alexandria to Rome with a load of grain would often require a continuous "tacking" into the wind, thus carrying ships in a great counter-clockwise route along the eastern Mediterranean coast before heading westward toward Rome. The Roman Empire was not only connected by a vast fifty thousand plus miles of roads; it was connected by the *Mare Nostrum*. If one traveled very far, sooner or later travel would involve a journey of some kind on this great Roman sea.

A Fateful Journey

Sailing on the open sea was a dangerous enterprise in the ancient world, such that the seabed of the Mediterranean is today populated with literally thousands of ancient shipwrecks. The safest season for sailing was considered to fall between late May and mid-September, while the sea was closed to sailing between early November to early March. One might say that the sailing season extended from May 27 to September 14 and the closed season extended from November 11 to March 10. Mid-March to mid-May was risky, as was mid-September to early November. In the Jewish tradition, the Feast of Tabernacles marked the end of the safe sailing season.

Paul's entire voyage to Rome took place during the risky season, especially from the point of Myra onward (Luke's Source, STA 27:4). Even ships in harbor could be at risk. Fair Havens on Crete, despite its name, was not deemed to be a suitable harbor for the grain ship carrying Paul to spend the winter (Luke's Source, STA 27:12). The Roman historian Tacitus narrates that some two hundred corn ships were sunk by a bad storm in 62 CE, even as they were moored in Rome's home port of Ostia (Tacitus, *Annals* 15.18)!

The episode of Paul's journey to Rome is one of the finest examples of an ancient narrated sea voyage available to us today. Luke's Source, STA 27/Acts 27 offers considerable drama of an account filled with suspense and informed by the overarching providence of God (Luke's Source, STA 19:21). One is drawn into the account of a perilous sea voyage, but one knows Paul's story is not going to end or climax in a drowning at sea. Paul will reach Rome. Aristarchus of Thessalonica (Luke's Source, STA 20:4) travels with Paul (Luke's Source, STA 27:2) and the account is narrated with an interspersed "we" which rhetorically draws the reader/hearer into the account. Aristarchus is later described in Col 4:10 as Paul's "fellow prisoner," an incidental point of corroboration between the sources.

The storm that breaks upon them after they weigh anchor at Fair Havens prevents a safe passage to protected anchorage for the winter at Phoenix on the island of Crete. Instead, for a full two weeks they were at the mercy of the storm which blew them across an expanse of the Mediterranean Sea, obscuring even the sun and stars so as to prevent any kind of navigational orientation. After having been adrift at sea, with some damage of ship and loss of cargo, they finally encountered a mass of land, which turned out to be the island of Malta. While they planned to beach the ship, the ship was instead destroyed after it ran aground on a shoal. All were able to escape to land.

Fig. 29. Shipwreck! Original painting by G. Roger Greene.

The legendary drama surrounding Paul continues with the story of the snakebite (Luke's Source, STA 28:1–3, 5–6), in which he is acknowledged to be "a god." Paul performs healings on the island (Luke's Source, STA 28:7–10), even as he had done earlier at Ephesus (Luke's Source, STA 19:11–12) and Lystra (Luke's Source, STA 14:8–11). The islands of Melita ("refuge") or Malta provided a small and narrow window of rescue and safe haven for those on board Paul's ship. The three islands had a combined area of about 122 square miles, with Malta being the largest at around ninety-five square miles.

Once the sea lanes were open again at the close of the winter season, Paul and company were able to board a ship of Alexandria that had wintered on the island. It first took them to Syracuse in Sicily (some hundred miles to the northeast), then through the narrow straits of Messina to Rhegium on the mainland of Italy (another seventy-five miles). Two days later they were docking at Puteoli on the Bay of Naples (another 220 miles north).

Fig. 30. A Roman Merchant Ship. Original painting by G. Roger Greene.

They remained in Puteoli for a week with some "brethren," before traveling to Rome by land.[4] They joined the Appian Way, which brought them to Rome (Luke's Source, STA 28:14). Rome was roughly 128 miles from Puteoli by the *Via Appia*. Forty miles out of Rome was the Forum of Appius. Three Taverns was only ten miles from Rome. The final approach to Rome along the Appian Way, as in other major cities of the Roman Empire, passed through a necropolis of tombs. Paul passed through the city of the dead in order to reach the city of the living with the gospel of the Lord Jesus Christ. It was for that gospel that he gladly gave his life—he could do no less after his call that he had received so many years before on the road to Damascus.

The stay in Puteoli afforded the opportunity to notify the Roman Christians of Paul's coming. And they came out as far as the Forum of Appius and Three Taverns to meet this apostle from whom they had received a letter some three years earlier and about whom they had heard so much (Luke's Source, STA 28:15). Paul had finally realized his dream of many years to visit the Roman Christians (Rom 1:8–13; 15:22–24, 32), although he arrived under circumstances he could have never foreseen. It was the early spring of 59 CE.

---

4. That there were "brethren" at Puteoli is indicative of other Christian congregations not founded by Paul, and concerning which we have no information. Knowledge of the formation of Christian communities in Italy is limited at best. The reference is also interesting because Paul is still in custody.

Paul is portrayed by Luke's Source/Acts as enjoying a certain amount of personal freedom, being guarded only by a single soldier (Luke's Source, STA 28:16). He witnessed to leading Jews, whom he invited to visit him, "bearing witness to the kingdom of God, persuading them concerning Jesus from the Law of Moses and the prophets" (Luke's Source, STA 28:23). Paul's final preaching in Rome is an all too familiar spectacle of acceptance, rejection, and resultant division (Luke's Source, STA 28:23–25).

Paul's story of arrival in Rome for both Luke's Source and Acts is set within the larger context of the spread of the gospel and the development of the church—a story in which every obstacle has been overcome through the leading of the Spirit and through Divine Providence. Paul's story, like the Christian story itself, is left open-ended, rhetorically speaking. A host of questions may remain. What *did* happen to Paul? Did he ever come to trial before Nero Caesar? Why was his appeal not resolved after two years? The ending of Luke's Source/Acts has been building toward a dramatic climax, which now never comes and is never resolved. The ending of Acts is even more open-ended than the Gospel of Mark (see Mark 16:1–8), without the textual addition of Mark 16:9–20. This is why, just like Mark 16:9–20, developing church tradition sought to complete the story of Paul with a release, subsequent ministry, and finally a later martyrdom.

If one accepts several of the letters which bear Paul's name as having a Roman origin, then other details may be supplied. Luke's Source/Acts suggests Paul experienced not incarceration, but rather *libera custodia*, a form of imprisonment involving a rotational guard and a degree of personal freedom. Such custody would allow for Paul to continue a ministry of writing letters and receiving and dispatching associates. It was his appeal as a Roman citizen that had brought him to that point. Assuming the veracity of Luke's Source, things must have looked different to Paul once in Rome than they had looked earlier when he was in Caesarea. The full weight, might, awe, and splendor of Rome was self-evident and intimidating to the greatest degree. After all, it was *Rome*. Appeal to Rome had seemed like a good idea at the time. Then, too, the delicate relations between Jews and Christians in the capital city may have meant Paul quickly became something of a *persona non grata*, given his reputation and seeming penchant for conflict.

Paul's Final Letters

We have five extant letters, all written roughly during the year 60 CE, while Paul was awaiting an appearance before Nero, who had now reached the ripe old age of twenty-three. A notable event of the year 59 CE, the year of Paul's arrival, was that Nero had Agrippina, his mother, put to death (Tacitus, *Annals* 14.5–10). Such matricide was not easily overlooked. Tacitus recounts that a comet appeared in 60 CE, which was interpreted as "an apparition boding change to monarchies" (Tacitus, *Annals* 14.22). Inquiries began to be made as to who might succeed Nero, as though Nero had already been dethroned. Nero was perturbed, not only by his recent actions in the death of his mother, but also by rumors of succession.

According to Tacitus, the year 62 CE (likely after Paul's martyrdom) was marked by the poisoning of Burrus, the humbling of Seneca, the murder of Plautus, and the murder of Octavia, Nero's wife, so that he could marry Poppea. Paul happened to come to Rome at a very inopportune time. What would an appearance of a Roman provincial such as Paul before Nero be like? What difference would a Jewish provincial "Paul" make for an all-powerful Roman emperor? Can the *reader* imagine *oneself* appearing before the Roman Caesar? What defense would one make?

At some point, Timothy joined Paul in Rome, for he is listed as the co-sender of both Colossians and Philemon. Others are reflected as being with Paul in Rome—Epaphras, Tychicus, Onesimus, Mark, Jesus Justus, Luke, and Demas (Col 4:7–14). Aristarchus, who had traveled with Paul to Jerusalem with the Collection and to Rome as an apparent prisoner, remains a prisoner but sends greetings (Col 4:10; he is listed only as a "fellow worker" in Phlm 24). Tychicus will be the bearer of the letters to Ephesus, Colossae and to Philemon, accompanied by Onesimus (Col 4:7–9). Epaphras was instrumental in founding the church at Colossae (Col 1:7–8) and apparently had brought Paul word of the situation in Colossae (Col 4:12). In Phlm 23, he is listed as Paul's fellow prisoner. Paul's letters reflect ongoing communication with churches in Asia, as well as a changing stream of associates.

The so-called letter to the Ephesians (some manuscripts lack the words "in Ephesus"), also likely dispatched to Ephesus (and perhaps to the Lycus Valley), stands as a post-Collection bookend of Paul's thought after several years of reflection, just as Romans stands as a pre-Collection bookend of Paul's thought prior to his last journey to Jerusalem. Tychicus will likewise be the bearer of the Ephesian (some say, Laodicean) letter, as he was of the letter to the Colossians, and, along with Onesimus, the letter to Philemon. All three letters were likely dispatched at the same time from Rome and carried by Tychicus and Onesimus, having been written in the extended period of custody in the early spring of the year 60 CE (see 2 Tim 4:14). It is likely that a fourth letter accompanied them—namely, what we know as Rom 16.

Read in the light of his present setting as a prisoner in Rome, after some four years of deep reflection of his experience since he had left Corinth on his way to Jerusalem with the Collection, Ephesians becomes a powerful testimony to Paul's mature understanding of the Gospel in a period of quiet before his final trials. Imagine Paul writing the following words (real, not fiction) while in Roman custody in Rome, as he awaits an audience with Caesar:

> *Because I have heard of your faith in the Lord Jesus and your love unto all the saints,* I *do not cease to give thanks in behalf of all of you as I make mention of you in my prayers, in order that the God of our Lord Jesus Christ, the Father of Glory, might give to you all a spirit of wisdom in full knowledge of him, having the eyes of your heart enlightened that you all might know what is the hope*

> *of his calling, what is the wealth of the glory of his inheritance in the saints. Indeed what is the surpassing greatness of his power unto all of you who have faith according to the working of the power of his might, which he worked in Christ having raised him from the dead and having seated him at his right hand in the heavenly places, above every ruler and authority and power and lordship and every name which is named, not only in this age but in the coming [age]; indeed, he subjected all things under his feet and made him head over all things in the church, which is his body, the fullness of the one who fulfills all things in all.* (Eph 1:15–23; original translation)

These are amazing and bold words proclaimed by one who is not awed by Caesar and the trappings of Rome, especially given his circumstance. In the very lair and face of Roman power and Caesar, Paul was dependent upon the power of God and the lordship of Christ. A lifetime of experience in the Gospel and four years of reflection in the custody of Rome has filled Paul with pleonastic appreciation for what God had done in Christ. It has amazingly filled Paul with peace and affirmative joy and hope for all his "children" in the Gospel.

Imagine Paul writing the following words while in Roman custody awaiting appeal before Caesar, as he reflects upon the now four years ago event in the temple in Jerusalem involving the gentile Trophimus—that event that brought about his arrest in the first place:

> *Wherefore you all remember that at one time you [emphatic] gentiles in the flesh, the ones said to be the uncircumcision by what is called the hand-made circumcision in the flesh, because you all were at that time without Christ, being alienated from the commonwealth of Israel and strangers of the covenants of promise, because you had no hope and were without God in the world. But now in Christ Jesus you all [emphatic] who were once far off have been caused to come near in the blood of Christ. For he himself is our peace, the one who made both sides one and who destroyed the middle wall of division—the hostility—by his flesh, because he abolished the law of commandments in ordinances, that he might create in himself one new person in the place of two, thus making peace, indeed that he might reconcile both to God in one body through the cross, because he put to death the enmity in himself. Indeed, having come he proclaimed the good news of peace to you all who were far off and peace to the ones who were near; because through him we both have the right of entry in one Spirit to the Father, consequently therefore you are no longer strangers and sojourners but you all are fellow citizens of the saints and members of the household of God, having been built upon the foundation of the apostles and prophets, Christ Jesus himself being the cornerstone, in whom the entire structure having been joined together grows unto a holy temple [ναός] in the Lord, in whom you all also are built together into a dwelling place of God in the Spirit.* (Eph 2:11–22; original translation)

These are bold and revolutionary words that clearly set forth the gospel as Paul understood it—words which obliterate the artificial and useless distinctions that had brought about his arrest in Jerusalem. They may well reflect sentiment expressed by Paul before the church in Jerusalem, when he was called upon to defend his gospel at the time of representation of his Collection. "Appealing or appalling," Paul, in terms of the Gospel, proclaims a temple far greater than any found in either Jerusalem *or* Rome.

Imagine Paul writing the following words while in custody in Rome on a sunny morning, "bound" to a Roman guard standing by:

> *Finally, you all be strong in the Lord and in the strength of his might. You all put on the whole armor of God, that you may be able to stand before the wiles of the devil; because the struggle for us is not with blood and flesh but with ruling powers, with authoritative powers, with world dominions of this present darkness, with spiritual forces of evil in the heavenly places. Because of this, you all take up the whole armor of God, in order that you may be able to stand in the evil day, and being ones who have conquered all things, to stand. You all stand, therefore, having wrapped your waist with truth, having put on the breastplate of righteousness, having clothed (your) feet with the equipment of the gospel of peace, in everything taking up the shield of faith, by which you all are able to deflect all the flaming arrows of evil; and you all take the helmet of salvation and the sword of the Spirit, which is the word of God. Through every prayer and supplication being those who pray in every season in the Spirit, and in the same manner keeping alert with all perseverance and prayer concerning all the saints, and in my behalf, in order that utterance may be given to me in opening my mouth boldly to make known the mystery of the gospel, in behalf of which I am a representative in prison, such that I may boldly proclaim as it is necessary for me to speak.* (Eph 6:10–20; original translation)

Fig. 31. A Roman Soldier. Murrandazo Figurine. Photograph by G. Roger Greene.

Paul had the very model of that which he writes standing before him. His metaphors had been visualized daily in a literal sense. And yet as he awaited his trial before the ultimate tribunal power of Rome, he remained ever Christ's ambassador, even in his chains. Earthly metaphors, visibly close at hand, became avenues and implements for victory, even over cosmic powers of evil in the light of Paul's gospel. The thought of Ephesians has Rome as its backdrop, even as his letter to the Romans has Jerusalem as its foreground. We do not know the reception that Paul's letters to Asia received. We do know that the Lycus Valley was struck by a massive earthquake in 60–61 CE. Tacitus indicates "Laodicea, one of the famous Asiatic cities, was laid in ruins by an earthquake, but recovered by its own resources . . ." (Tacitus, *Annals* 14.27). Colossae apparently was not rebuilt.

Many of those who were with Paul when he wrote Colossians et al. were not with him when he wrote 2 Timothy. In fact, he affirms that Luke alone is with him (2 Tim 4:11). Tychicus was sent by Paul to Ephesus with the Asian letters (2 Tim 4:12; Col 4:7; Eph 6:21). Onesimus has returned to Philemon (Phlm; Col 4:9). Aristarchus, having been released from prison (see Col 4:10; Phlm 24), his whereabouts unknown, has perhaps returned to Thessalonica (see Luke's Source, STA 20:4). Jesus called Justus (Col 4:11) is apparently a Roman Christian. Epaphras has gone to Corinth (Col 4:12;

2 Tim 4:20). Demas had deserted Paul and returned to Thessalonica (Col 4:14; 2 Tim 4:10). Luke alone (not the compiler of Acts) remains with Paul at the time Paul pens the letter of 2 Timothy. Does the difference in style between say, Ephesians and 2 Timothy, written so close in time, offer question for Pauline authorship of Ephesians, stylistically speaking? Or, might that not be accounted for in other ways?

Perspectives

If Luke's Source (STA)/Acts is correct that Paul was arrested during his final visit to Jerusalem, imprisoned in Caesarea for two years, and transported to Rome upon appeal for at least a two-year imprisonment under house arrest—and we have no evidence in Paul or the early church to the contrary—it is the lack of evidence that creates a period of a "communication gap." Given the virtual silence of Acts in the matter of the Pauline Collection, how was it received? If there were representatives who accompanied Paul, how long did they remain in Jerusalem? What message did they carry back to their respective locales and church centers? While under arrest, how free was Paul to communicate with his associates and church centers?

In particular, the period of time associated with imprisonment in Caesarea appears as a "black out" period which is idealized by "Luke" (the author of Acts) in terms of Paul's localized appearances before Felix, Festus, and Agrippa. What is entirely absent, however, is any reporting or communication with anyone beyond the immediate environment of Caesarea or Jerusalem. Paul's central mission fields are never informed of Paul's fate in any way in the source materials available to us.

In the extant sources, "Luke," from a later vantage point, either had no information, or Paul's former mission fields had no continuing part in Luke's narrative purpose. Luke's sights are set on Rome and not Asia or Macedonia or Achaia. And Paul is explicably silent. Luke's silence in reporting any communication with former mission fields is an argument against "Luke the companion of Paul" being the author of the material in Acts. An intimate associate would have surely reported the results of the Collection and Paul's status back to those who would be most concerned. This would have been a crisis time for all who were associated with the Pauline mission.

In popular thought, it appears that there is an implicit assumption to make Luke, the author of Acts, to be a rather constant companion of Paul and thus a direct eye-witness to all of the events he narrates. The popular implicit assumption is that Luke's intent is to record an historical documentary for posterity's sake, upon which later Christian scripture may be firmly established. In popular thought, even the "speeches" of Acts are seen to be verbatim transcripts. That is altogether unlikely. The "Luke" of the Gospel and Acts was not likely the companion of Paul, even though he has a "story to tell" for a later generation after Paul.

The so-called Prison Epistles of Paul have been traditionally associated with Rome. The present writer attributes Philippians to Ephesus during the Collection

Period. Philemon, Colossians, and Ephesians are attributed to Rome toward the end of the Post-Collection Period by the present writer. Second Timothy may also be considered a Roman "Prison Epistle," rather than a "Pastoral." A minority of scholarly opinion would suggest at least some of the Prison Epistles were written from Caesarea rather than from Rome.

However, the point to be made here is that the Prison Epistles are silent with regard to the Collection. It is rather inconceivable that any letters written by Paul in close proximity or in the immediate aftermath of the delivery of his Collection and his subsequent arrest would not have mentioned the result of the delivery and Paul's status. Even so much as a brief "So and So will tell you about the reception we received in Jerusalem and my imprisonment when he comes" is not to be found anywhere. This is to suggest that the letters we have (Philemon, Colossians, Ephesians, and 2 Timothy) belong to a later period of time, i.e., they do not have a Caesarean provenance. In the light of Paul's transport to Rome and his imprisonment there, some years after the delivery of the Collection, his Jerusalem experience is no longer "news."

But there is a communication gap in the extant Pauline correspondence for the period from "Romans to Rome." Was Paul unable to communicate during a presumed Caesarean imprisonment (see Acts)? Was he able to maintain contact with his churches or not? Did his associates have access to him while he was imprisoned? Were any letters—especially immediate ones which may have been written during this time—simply discarded by the recipients? Might not at least one, perhaps written to a supportive church such as Philippi, have been preserved and have survived? Some would suggest Philippians was written from Caesarea, but there is no mention of Jerusalem or the Collection or other internal evidence that this is so.

Although an argument from silence (in this case a double *entendre*), the hypothesis is set forth that Paul did not have opportunity to engage in written communication while imprisoned at Caesarea because of the conditions of his imprisonment. At best his communication would have been limited to occasional oral communication through envoys. Even Acts 24:23 need not suggest, of itself, that Paul had the freedom to write letters. As a Roman citizen (Acts 23:27), one might argue that he may have had materials and opportunity, but then surely one or some of his communiqués would have survived. The easier assumption is that he was not able to write letters to the outside world while he was imprisoned at Caesarea. Even the Lukan presentation of the Roman imprisonment is presented in a different light (see Acts 28:16, 17–28, 30–31). On the other hand, and at an earlier time, there was communication with Corinth while Paul was either imprisoned or headquartered in Ephesus.

All of this is to suggest that most of the "Prison Epistles" that we have are far enough removed from the situation of Paul's last journey to Jerusalem so as not to reflect that several year period of Paul's Caesarean imprisonment. The Collection and Paul's arrest were no longer news, such that, unfortunately, we have no mention or record from Paul's own testimony. By the time Paul writes Philemon, Colossians,

Ephesians, Rom 16, and 2 Timothy, he is imprisoned in Rome and very near the end of this life. He has had several years to reflect upon his life's work, the basic nature of the Gospel of God which he still proclaimed, and the nature of the churches he had formerly established. His awareness of the current status and needs of those churches would be dictated by the availability of news from them and by the couriers and associates upon whom he could still depend. Surely, his available resources and contacts on all counts continued to diminish over time (see 2 Tim 4:9–17). And, one must surely allow travel time intervals for anyone who came to visit Paul or for those Paul dispatched. The world began to pass Paul by and Paul himself would soon pass from the world.

While one might assume that a pseudonymous author would seek to imitate personal details, such as those represented in Col 4:7–17; Eph 6:21–22; and 2 Tim 4:9–16, 19–21, the easiest explanation is that Paul himself is the author and that there is a distinct relation that connects Philemon with Colossians and Ephesians in view of the common persons mentioned in the respective letters (but see Titus 3:12–13).

In materials associated with Rome, the church at Philippi is conspicuously absent, unless the letter to the Philippians was written from Rome and not from an earlier Ephesian imprisonment. Paul likely sent Timothy from Rome to Ephesus, from which he would likely have traveled to Philippi via Troas before returning to Rome. Paul's hope that Timothy may come soon and will bring with him Mark, his cloak left at Troas, and the books and parchments seemingly best fits that locale. At any rate, Paul has already made a first defense (at which none testified in his behalf). He has been spared from the "lion's mouth" yet one more time, but he does not exhibit much hope for the future (2 Tim 4:6–8; 4:17). He realizes that he has "fought the good fight," that his ultimate reward is near.

His appeal to Timothy may reflect his hopeful concerns to prepare a more timely defense, while awaiting witnesses to appear in Rome for a second hearing before Nero. Paul is near the end of his life. Those who send greetings to Timothy mentioned in 2 Tim 4:21 are apparently members of the Roman church (Eubulus, Pudens, Linus, Claudia), none of whom incidentally are named in Rom 16. Those named in Philemon are not found in Rom 16, but then Philemon was not sent to Ephesus but to the Lycus Valley. Second Timothy was written at a time which would have made it possible for Timothy to reach Rome before winter, i.e., before the sea lanes shut down. Otherwise, Timothy would be delayed until the following spring, which might well be too late. In view of the fact that 2 Timothy is the last extant correspondence from Paul that we have, we do not know whether Timothy made it or not. One would like to believe that he did.

Whether in time or too late, if Timothy brought the "books and parchments" to Rome, it is likely they provided the foundation for a Pauline collection of letters. One may recall that it was Marcion in Rome (ca. 140 CE) who is credited with the first Christian canon of Scripture, consisting of an abbreviated Gospel of Luke *and* ten letters of Paul.

In the earlier letter of recommendation for Phoebe written to Ephesus (Rom 16) a matter of months before 2 Timothy, Timothy sends his greetings. While it is not likely that many folk from the Corinthian region would be visiting Paul in Rome, in view of the social nature of the church (see 1 Cor 1:26–29; 6:11), Phoebe could certainly be an exception and would likely have even known Prisca and Aquila. Paul apparently sent Timothy to Ephesus upon Tychicus's return, perhaps to explicitly gather materials for Paul's future defense.

There is a shadow of despondency in Rom 16, just as there is apprehension of what faced him in Jerusalem at the point of completion of his Collection (Rom 15:30–32). That shadow of despondency becomes even stronger in 2 Timothy. Paul had been through a lot in the final years of his Collection Campaign and his four years of imprisonment. He had longed for success in his Collection and for deliverance from Judaizers and Jews alike. Still, he had consoled himself with a long-cherished hope of even looking beyond Jerusalem to Rome and new opportunities in Spain. Yet what Paul had dared to dream would not come to pass.

If Rom 16 is a separate letter sent to Ephesus from Rome and later appended to Romans, with some redaction, Paul's copy of the letter retained by Tertius could have been included among his effects and later joined to his copy (retrieved by Timothy) or the Roman church's copy of Rom 1–15. A number of very plausible scenarios may be set forth. But if it were originally a separate letter, we can never be sure of its entire contents. Although a letter of recommendation for Phoebe, what else might it have contained? Might other material (if anything) have not been deemed redundant to Rom 1–15 by the editor who joined the two letters together, Rom 1–15 and Rom 16, at a time after the life of Paul?

In spite of all these textual and literary problems, there were many for whom Paul felt eternally grateful, as this writer would say, God's "little saints" in Ephesus. Paul sends greetings to everyone he can think of in Ephesus, the headquarters for his independent mission and Collection Campaign. He had not seen most of these friends for at least five years now, and yet they remained very dear to him. Should this indeed be a letter to the church at Ephesus, it may offer a clear indicator of the size of the church located there in terms of estimated number of members—at least those who remained friendly to Paul.

Finally, although textual problems abound with regard to the closing doxology of Rom 16, and it is generally acknowledged as non-Pauline, it provides a fitting closure near the end of the lengthy ministry of Paul.

> *To the One Who Is Able to Strengthen all of you according to my gospel and the proclamation of Jesus Christ, according to the revelation of mystery having been kept secret through eternal ages but now having been made known through prophetic writings through the authority of the eternal God unto an*

> *obedience of faithfulness unto all the gentiles—to the only wise God through Jesus Christ, through whom be glory unto the ages. Amen.* (Rom 16:25–27; original translation)

Even should the doxology not be original to Paul, it would be a doxology with which Paul would be in total sympathy. It certainly expresses sentiment with which Paul would agree. The author suspects it was a well-known doxology in use at Ephesus. Paul's final words in 2 Timothy are likewise a doxology, coupled with a grace wish, that the Lord be with Timothy's spirit and that "grace be with all of you" (2 Tim 4:22). It should also be noted that the grace wish of 2 Timothy employs a plural and not singular pronoun (2 Tim 4:22), although it appears formulaic. It is a grace wish extended to the church as a whole and not just to a single individual.

A Final Perspective

A reminder is given that all history is based upon the plausibility of the available evidence and its interpretation. In crafting this and the previous chapter as it has been written, with alternating blocks of historical summary and what some would call "historical fiction," the writer found it much easier to craft material for the places where he has personally traveled. Some would respond by saying, "All the more reason to call it subjective fiction!" That, however, is not the point addressed here. The writer might give a concrete example. The writer has never traveled to Antioch (of Syria, now modern-day Turkey). When he thought about writing a sketch with the backdrop setting of Antioch, there was nothing which came to mind—not even any kind of visualization, real or not, of the church located there. Nothing. When he thought about Paul in Jerusalem, or Ephesus, or Galatia, or Macedonia, or Achaia, or even sailing on the Mediterranean—the images of the those *places* readily flowed and informed the text, whether the text have been Paul's own letters or the Acts reconstruction (the STA source).

If one has an interest in the biblical texts, there is no substitute for travel in the lands where the events occurred. There is no substitute for drinking in the geographical, topographical, and archaeological realities that are reflected there. Indeed, as some have observed with reference to the four Gospels of the New Testament, the land itself is the "fifth" Gospel that documents and reveals the ministry of Jesus, even in spite of modern dress. This same reality holds true for understanding the ministry of Paul. Without the benefit of the lands, even Paul's own theology may become nothing other than a self-projected image on a blank green screen. And, it can be rather staid or stale at that. This has happened in both doctrine creation in an ecclesiastical context as well as scholarly study in an academic context. There is much "scholarly fiction" that masquerades as fact and abounds in the study of Paul, both in terms of Paul's ministry *and* his thought. Likewise, there is a lot of ecclesiastical and theological dogma that exists. As a hand-sewn banner that has always hung in the author's office states, "The Context is the Message." It was given to the author by students of the first Greek class he ever taught. It has hung in his office now for more than fifty years.

Regardless of all the ink that has been spilled regarding the "we" source employed by Luke in the book of Acts, a source of that nature could not be written by one who had never experienced sailing on the Mediterranean Sea to the places mentioned in ancient times. The "we" may or may not be a stylistic device, but underlying the account in Acts is an eyewitness who knew from the depth of personal experience that of which he wrote. It is a scholarly convenience to define Luke as a "sometimes companion of Paul." It is pure, improbable scholarly fiction to suggest one may imagine Luke on the voyage to Rome with Paul struggling to preserve his manuscripts and historical notes related to both the Gospel and Paul's ministry for benefit of future generations in the midst of a severe, life-threatening storm.

The narrative in Acts suggests a lengthy tempest in which cargo itself was thrown overboard in order to save the ship itself. Everything would have been thoroughly drenched. When it comes to life itself—when everything is on the line, possessions are of little concern. One may certainly imagine such scholarly assertion, but it is implausible. The biblical source description would suggest "Luke" would have been most concerned about preserving his very life through the unfortunate shipwreck—not to mention again the two-week long tempest which would have soaked everything not cast overboard. While fiction is not bound by plausibility, history is. And theology should be.

To debate to what extent the witness of Acts was a "companion of Paul" and whether or not Luke the author of Acts is the author of the "we" source are different issues entirely. Why is Luke, a gifted writer, never the co-sender of a Pauline letter? Why did he not ever serve as Paul's amanuensis? Why does "Luke, the writer of Acts," never even acknowledge that Paul wrote a single letter? In the present writer's judgment, the "we" source is marked by Lukan redaction just as the other portions of Acts. The present writer finds too many differences in the portrayal of Paul in Acts and the portrayal of Paul in the authentic letters to assume the traditional perspective of "Luke, the gentile physician, the companion of Paul" found in popular thought.

However, this does not mean that "Luke, the writer of Acts" did not use ancient sources of exceptional quality and veracity as he produced his own account of the ministry of Jesus and the development and spread of the early church through the ministry of Paul. We are greatly indebted to this "Luke," whoever he was, for his story of the Gospel and the early church. He wrote for *his* own audience, not for us. Still, the work of Luke and of Paul may yet speak *to us*. And together, they constitute virtually 50 percent of the New Testament.

Luke writes of the unhindered triumph of the Gospel of God, as it moved out into the larger Greco-Roman world through the ministry of folk like Paul (ἀκωλύτως, Acts 28:31). Paul would echo the freedom that Luke portrays. He affirms freedom from all slavery—even doctrinaire religious slaveries (ἐλευθεία, Gal 5:1). As Paul himself might express, he would offer a doxology: "*Glory be to God for all the things he has done 'in Christ.' To God be all glory forever, through Christ Jesus. Amen.*"

Conclusion

As set forth in the present work, Paul's ministry consisted of two major campaigns—the Foundation Campaign treated in the prior chapter and the Collection Campaign presented in this chapter. The years of Paul's Collection Campaign may be presented in the following table or chart. Again, for clarity's sake only a simplified and summary outline is presented here. A full chart of Paul's entire ministry, including Paul's Post-Collection years, replete with associated scriptural references, may be found in appendix A.

PAUL'S FINAL MINISTRY

COLLECTION CAMPAIGN—52–56 CE, from Antioch to Corinth

    Ministry in Galatia—52 CE

    Ministry in Ephesus—52–54 CE

        Imprisonment in Ephesus—54 CE

        Galatians—53–54 CE, from Ephesus

        Philippians—54 CE, from Ephesus

        1 Corinthians—54 CE, from Ephesus

            (*Painful Letter to Corinth*)

    Departure for Macedonia—55 CE

        2 Corinthians 1–13—55 CE, from Macedonia

    Move to Achaia

        Romans 1–15—56 CE, from Corinth

    Journey to Jerusalem for Pentecost—Late Spring 56 CE

        (Pentecost—June 11, 56 CE)

PAUL'S POST-COLLECTION YEARS—56–61 CE

    Fourth Visit to Jerusalem (J4)—"Collection" Visit, 56 CE

    Arrest in Jerusalem—Early Summer 56 CE

    Caesarean Imprisonment—Summer 56–Summer 58 CE

    Travel to Rome by Sea—Fall 58 CE

Winter on Malta—Fall 58–Winter 59 CE

Arrival in Rome—Early Spring 59 CE

Roman Imprisonment—Spring 59–61 CE

    Colossians   Early Summer 60 CE

        (Tychicus the bearer, Col 4:10; cf. Acts 20:4)

    Philemon   Early Summer 60 CE

        (Tychicus, with Onesimus, the bearer)

    Ephesians   Early Summer 60 CE

        (Tychicus sent to Ephesus, cf. Eph 6:21)

    Romans 16   Early Summer 60 CE

        (Timothy with Paul; letter carried by Tychicus to Ephesus, accompanied by Phoebe)

    Note: These four letters of Paul were carried by Tychicus and those who accompanied him to Ephesus and Colossae/Laodicea. Tychicus then returned to Rome.

First Trial before Nero—Midsummer 60 CE

    2 Timothy   Late Summer 60 CE

        (Timothy in Ephesus; Tychicus again sent to Ephesus, cf. 2 Tim 4:12)

    Note: Second Timothy is the last literary testament of Paul that we have.

Martyrdom—Late Spring or Summer 61 CE

SUMMARY CHRONOLOGICAL LISTING OF LETTERS

Letter	Place of Origin	Date
Foundation Campaign		
2 Thessalonians	Corinth	49 CE
Previous Letter to Corinth (see 2 Cor 6:14—7:1)	Illyricum	50 CE
1 Thessalonians	Corinth	51 CE
Collection Campaign		
Galatians	Ephesus	53–54 CE
Philippians	Ephesus	54 CE

1 Corinthians	Ephesus	54 CE
(Painful Letter to Corinth)		
2 Corinthians 1–13	Macedonia	56 CE
Romans 1–15	Corinth	56 CE

Post-Collection Letters

Colossians	Rome	60 CE
Philemon	Rome	60 CE
Ephesians	Rome	60 CE
Romans 16	Rome	60 CE
2 Timothy	Rome	60 CE

Letters Not by Paul

1 Timothy?	Pseudonymous, not Pauline on historical and stylistic grounds
Titus?	Pseudonymous, not Pauline on historical and stylistic grounds

6

Imagine the Gospel of Paul

IT IS SUGGESTED THAT there is a difference between the concept of the "gospel of Paul" and the "theology of Paul." Now that one has imagined the ministry of Paul, one may better imagine the gospel of Paul—the gospel, not his theology. The task of imagining Paul's *theology* must wait until the following chapter. From the author's perspective, there is often a problem in Pauline studies that manifests itself in the desire to formulate Pauline theology before one understands the nature of the Pauline gospel—or ministry, for that matter. By contrast, it is the nature of the Pauline gospel that is foundational for doing *Pauline* theology rather than engaging in some kind of imposition upon Paul of later theology found within Christendom.

The current chapter is focused upon imagining Paul's gospel, which is altogether appropriate before offering a treatment of the more common topic of the "theology of Paul." Most treatments of Pauline theology would be better informed if attention were first given to the ministry of Paul, followed by attention given to the nature of the gospel that he understood and proclaimed. The additional length and level of technicality of this chapter is necessary in order to adequately imagine the Gospel of God reflected in all of Paul's letters.

Paul's definition of the gospel is the foundation for appropriate appreciation of Paul's "theology." Perhaps the beginning salutation and thanksgiving of 2 Cor 1:1–14 may illustrate the points made. Paul affirms to the Corinthian church that had questioned his apostleship (1 Cor 9:1–27) that he was an apostle of Christ Jesus by the will of God. He defended his apostleship in a different manner from the autobiographical material of Galatians (Gal 1:11–17). Paul addressed the Corinthian Christians as "saints," and it should be noted that he actually addresses the saints in the whole of Achaia. That could include Athens and Beroea and others perhaps as far as Epirus.

Paul's letters include his usual commendation of "grace and peace to all of you from God our Father and the Lord Jesus Christ." While not often realized, Paul's salutation expresses basic elements of his *gospel* that could be further developed in explication of his *theology*. Paul clearly defines the nature of the God of the Gospel as one to be embraced rather than feared. He is not described as a celestial law-enforcer or Judge, but rather as a Father. Paul is the author of a gospel that is truly *good* news, for its content is grace and its result is peace.

God has acted in Jesus to bring grace and peace, exalting him as Lord and confirming him as his Anointed One or Christ. One could pursue terms and concepts theologically to develop their full meaning, but for the moment the focus is upon the applicational and definitional nature of the gospel. One may develop a full discussion of the concept of grace (theology), but as *gospel* it is significant to note that the gospel is first of all characterized by grace and not judgment, law, or condemnation. As gospel, it comes as both announcement and invitation, as *indicative* (what God has done) and *imperative* (our response, what we are to do).

The only way to imagine the gospel of Paul is to examine the letters of Paul on an individual basis with a single question in mind: How does this particular letter reflect or set forth the gospel that Paul preached, i.e., how Paul understood the Gospel of God (Rom 1:1)? This will be done by examining the letters in the number and order that the present writer has suggested they were dictated or written by Paul. There is much in Paul's letters of personal and relational nature that is not relevant to the present endeavor, even though such reference material is vitally important for understanding the *ministry* of Paul. Paul's ministry defined his gospel and his theology. While certainly important, at this juncture one may also largely pass over such material that deals with a gospel imperative of how we are to conduct our lives in Christ. The focal point here is upon what *God* has done in Christ, according to Paul's understanding and appropriation of the Gospel of God.

The chapter thus begins with the earliest letter of Paul (2 Thessalonians in the present writer's view), and concludes with the last letters of Paul, after which a summary conclusion will be presented. The length of treatment of each letter is only in part determined by the length of the letter itself. Some letters reflect the nature of the Pauline gospel to a greater degree than others, given the fact that Paul wrote occasional letters to deal with specific issues relevant to a given church situation. He exhibits no awareness that his occasional letters would one day be considered to be a part of Christian Scripture providing food for thought and faith for layperson and scholar alike.

Second Thessalonians (49 CE)

This letter of Paul was written approximately fifteen years after Paul's call experience. It is the earliest letter of Paul that we possess, although it is reasonable to assume that Paul had written even earlier letters that have been lost. Fifteen years is a long time within a single human lifespan, as the reader may reflect. Paul has not yet standardized his salutation (see 1 Thessalonians), compared to his later letters that we possess. He exhibits an awkward redundancy, yet he employs the same building blocks. Paul's gospel as proclaimed to the Thessalonians was focused on the kingdom of God (2 Thess 1:5) and the "parousia" (2 Thess 1:7–10). Paul's central content is focused upon the Lord Jesus (2 Thess 1:8).

If what Paul writes is any indication of what he preached while founding a predominately gentile church in Thessalonica, it is no wonder the Thessalonians sought clarification concerning eschatological speculation with regard to the return of Christ (see 2 Thess 2:1–12; 1 Thess 4:13–17). The problem groups (the weak, fainthearted, and the idlers) that developed in Thessalonica suggest some confusion arose with regard to Paul's traditional Jewish apocalyptic speculations in the light of their ongoing experience (see 2 Thess 3:6–12; 1 Thess 4:1–12; 5:14). The central issue was the timing of the parousia or return of Christ (see 2 Thess 2:1; 1 Thess 4:16–17), and this some nineteen years after Jesus's execution and resurrection.

Paul's description is couched in apocalyptic language of final judgment. The language is not unlike 1 Cor 15:20–28, although it has a different focal point there. As 2 Thess 2:1–12 suggests, Paul's gospel preached to the Thessalonians had been laced with apocalyptic thought and development along the lines of the Old Testament "day of the Lord," now understood as the advent of the risen Christ who would return in the name of God the Father.

Apparently, the apocalyptic thought triggered by Caligula's order to have his statue erected in the Temple had fueled lingering apocalyptic imagery and expectation that still remained in Jewish thought some years later. Who knew whether a future Roman emperor would attempt the same thing? Caligula ruled as emperor of Rome from 37 CE until he was assassinated in January 41 CE. Apocalyptic thought had been fueled by that event, harkening back to the memory of Antiochus's IV Epiphanes desecration of the Temple that had sparked the Maccabean revolt some two hundred years earlier (see 1 Maccabees).

Second Thessalonians appears to be a brief, early letter of Paul that seeks to encourage these early Christians to remain firm even in the face of persecution (2 Thess 2:15). Paul's gospel even here is implicitly focused on the resurrection, represented by reference to obtaining "the glory of our Lord Jesus Christ" (2 Thess 2:14), as well as by mention of "eternal comfort" and "good hope through grace" (2 Thess 2:16). Intertextually, Paul alludes here to what he later states directly in Phil 3:10–11—namely, the hope of resurrection. The general themes are still present in his subsequent letters that we possess.

Paul even introduces the thought of imitating his own conduct as an apostle in the face of the issue of idleness that has arisen because of a false expectation of the parousia that had developed (2 Thess 3:6–10). Similar thought of imitation of Paul is encouraged in Phil 3:17–21, where Paul is squarely focused on the resurrection in the light of the parousia. Paul's imperatival exhortation is focused on the problem group of the "idle," who have misunderstood Paul's gospel focused upon the parousia of Christ. As the first letter he actually wrote to the Thessalonians (see 2 Thess 2:15), Paul writes the final greeting in his own hand and appends his signature. He thereby establishes a mark of authenticity for any future correspondence he may have with the Thessalonians.

First Thessalonians (51 CE)

Paul writes a second letter within two years. Two other problem groups have developed, in addition to a lingering problem with the "idle." The parousia remains an issue (1 Thess 5:23), for it continues to be misunderstood and perhaps even more so with the additional passage of time. What the catalyst for this may have been, we do not know. Paul continues to employ apocalyptic imagery (1 Thess 4:6) in describing Jesus's return ("the day of the Lord," 1 Thess 5:2). Hope in the resurrection is still foremost (1 Thess 1:3), as the Thessalonian Christians continue to await the parousia (1 Thess 1:10). Paul recalls his initial time spent with them when he first preached to them the "Gospel of God" (1 Thess 2:2, 8; cf. 2:13), a phrase he uses several times (1 Thess 2:1–12). He obliquely addresses those living in idleness by recalling his own example of working while he was among them. The concept of the kingdom of God retains mention (1 Thess 2:12), as do basic elements of the kerygma understood apocalyptically (1 Thess 2:14–16).

There is a continuing focus on the parousia (1 Thess 3:13). As the time has lengthened, problems have arisen with regard to gentile morality (1 Thess 4:1–8) in relation to an ongoing process of sanctification (1 Thess 4:3). Mention is made of the gift of the Holy Spirit in this regard of ongoing Christian living (1 Thess 4:8). Apocalyptic imagery continues to be present, as seen in the extended description of the nature of the parousia (1 Thess 4:14–17). One is to continue to live in the hope of the coming resurrection, which will be occasioned by the welcoming of Christ at the parousia. Faithful obedience is called for, as the value of patient work and service in the Gospel is stressed.

Paul's language has been misunderstood in terms of a relatively new and artificially created doctrine known as the "rapture."[1] Paul does not describe the Thessalonians' "going" (or departure out of the world), but rather their "greeting" of Christ when he returns. The comprehension of the parousia continued to be a problem issue for the Thessalonians, compounded by the fact that one or more of their number had died. Had they missed out on the resurrection? Paul writes with what he hoped was clarifying language by way of a common analogy. The coming of the *Lord* Jesus Christ will figuratively be like the visit of Caesar or a commanding Roman general visiting any Roman city.

To understand what Paul says, one must understand that the "city of the dead" (a *necropolis*) lined the major roadways leading into the city of the living. Any visiting dignitary would thus pass through the necropolis in order to enter the city and reach the city of the living. He would be greeted with welcome and fanfare of the living along the way, before he settled into the city. If one searches "necropolis Pompeii" on the internet, one will be greeted with a number of visual images. One should read

---

1. One may have heard much about the "rapture." It is not a New Testament concept. One will not find the word anywhere in the New Testament. Check it out in a concordance. See the glossary.

what Paul writes in the light of an ancient city. One may clearly see arrangement of tombs lining the roadway leading into ancient Pompeii, for example.

Fig. 32. Tombs in the Necropolis of Pompeii. Watercolor by Luigi Bazzani prior to 1927, from the book *Pompeii*, by Amedeo Maiuri (Pompeii superintendent from 1924–61), published in 1929. Public domain, via Wikimedia Commons.

Paul does not describe our "going," but rather Christ's coming or parousia. He does so, not to craft some doctrine that was unknown to him and the remainder of the New Testament writers, but rather to comfort Thessalonian Christians who have lost loved ones to death (see 1 Thess 4:18). At Christ's coming, in the resurrection, we shall always be with the Lord. Paul offers comfort, expressed with typical apocalyptic language illustrated by common awareness and experience. Paul encourages all to live faithfully in the present according to the will of God (1 Thess 5:15–24), in the light of the coming parousia. This was the best he could do, in the light of the fact that no living person who speaks about the resurrection and the return of Christ to this very day has actually yet experienced such event. Paul lived in hope, firmly based upon the reality of the Gospel of God, and so must we. All three problem groups that Paul had to address in the Thessalonian church are mentioned together in 1 Thess 5:14.

By way of summary, Paul in the Thessalonian correspondence is focused upon the kingdom of God and the Gospel *of God* through the Lord Jesus Christ, who is the indirect agent of God's Gospel (see 1 Thess 5:9). He is focused both on the resurrection and the parousia, for it is the parousia that will lead directly to a general resurrection.

He employs apocalyptic description that was familiar to him through his Judaism, although it was not so familiar to the gentile Thessalonians who had difficulty understanding. In the interim, before Christ's return that was not far off in Paul's expectation, Paul calls upon the Thessalonians to live a life of faithfulness, even as Paul himself had been seeking to do. The Thessalonian correspondence was written from Achaia prior to Paul's return to Antioch at the conclusion of the Foundational Campaign and prior to Paul's Famine Visit and Conference Visit to Jerusalem (51–52 CE).

Galatians (53–54 CE)

Paul's letter to the Galatians emerges in the time frame after the Jerusalem Conference (52 CE), at the beginning of Paul's Collection Campaign. As Paul writes Galatians, he is angry because of the interloping Nomistic Evangelists who have invaded his mission field and whom he feels are threatening the faith of the Galatian Christians. It is a time that reflects the early stage of Paul's Collection Campaign. Paul gives much autobiographical testimony that we would not likely have if it had not been for the controversy in the Galatian churches that called both his apostleship and his gospel into question.

The controversy threatened the very faith of the Galatians. The interlopers were preaching an alternative gospel that Paul did not consider to be the gospel at all. Paul himself feels threatened, as is evident from the very first verse of the letter where he begins to defend himself. While the controversy may not have been good for Paul nor for the churches as a whole, it called forth an autobiographical response for which we should be most grateful. Because Paul is under attack or assault in the midst of a serious theological controversy, we see what is most basic to his understanding of the Gospel of God.

God raised Jesus from the dead, and in so doing he has delivered us from the powers of the present evil age, including Death itself. The Torah has fulfilled its role of guardian until Christ came. One may now live as full participants in a life of faith, freedom, and obedience to God in Christ, as one bears "fruit of the Spirit" now present.

Galatians 1:1–5 is as significant as Rom 1:1–6 in its summary of the Gospel of God. It is significant both for what it states and what it does not state or stress. First of all, Jesus is identified as the Messiah, "Christ" being his common identification or "cognomen," if you will. God is identified as "Father," as the one who raised Jesus from the dead. It should be noted that there is no mention here of the cross or stress on the manner of Jesus's death. Paul commands his usual "grace and peace from God the Father and the Lord Jesus Christ," which is now becoming stylized. Jesus could not be affirmed as either "Lord" or "Christ," apart from the resurrection and exaltation by God. At best, he would have simply been a dead founder of a social or religious movement or perhaps perceived as one more failed Jewish messiah.

Paul further describes Jesus as "the one who gave himself," for the purpose that he might deliver us from "the present evil age." Paul believed in the "Two Ages" conception present in his Pharisaic Judaism, even though he introduced the modification of the Age of Transformation. Such an eschatological perception of ultimate reality would have an affinity for apocalyptic description, which has already been seen to be prevalent in the Thessalonian correspondence. The descriptive phrase Paul uses here could be translated "the age of impending evil" (ἐνεστῶτος, perfect participle), describing that which has already drawn near in terms of a tumultuous transition of the ages. In other words, that which is indicative of final judgment and fulfillment had already begun. Paul knew himself and others to be living now in the Age of Transformation as a result of God's deliverance in Christ. Paul feels compelled to break out in a doxology of praise to God the Father, to whom "be glory unto the Ages of the Ages. Amen."

It should be noted there is no mention of sacrifice or atonement, other than Jesus's own giving of himself in behalf of our sins for the purpose of delivering us from the impending age of evil. There is a crucial point to be made that involves a degree of technicality, but which is significant for interpretation. How should Gal 1:4 be punctuated? The reader will recall that punctuation is not original to the text, but rather has been added in translation. Grammatically speaking, Gal 1:4 could be translated in two different ways. Verses 3–4 could read *"Grace to you all and peace from God our Father and the Lord Jesus Christ, the one who gave himself in behalf of our sins, for the purpose that he might deliver us from the impending age of evil according to the will of God and our Father . . . ."* In this rendering, the will of God is associated with our deliverance, for it occurs in a prepositional phrase within a purpose clause.

Verses 3–4 could also be rendered, *"Grace to you all and peace from God our Father and the Lord Jesus Christ who gave himself for our sins, for the purpose that he might deliver us from the impending age of evil, according to the will of God and our Father . . . ."* The difference rests in the placement of commas. In this rendering, the will of God is connected back to Jesus giving himself for our sins. If so translated, these verses could be suggestive of sacrificial and substitutionary atonement theory. The question is whether Paul's focus is upon deliverance or sacrificial atonement. Jesus gave himself in voluntary obedience as Paul stresses elsewhere (see Phil 2:5–13). Paul's metaphor would appear to revolve around obedience and deliverance rather than sacrifice.

In the present writer's judgment, and in the light of what Paul elsewhere writes (such as Phil 2:5–11), it is the former rendering that Paul would intend (see 2 Thess 1:7–10; 2:13–14; 1 Thess 1:10; 5:9–10; 1 Cor 15:20–28; Rom 1:1–5). In other words, Paul focuses upon the divine intention of God (Father of both Jews and gentiles) *to deliver* his people from an impending age of evil. Paul's focus is not upon the death of Jesus as a necessary and perfect atonement sacrifice. It is a misconception of Paul's thought to attribute Jesus's death to the intention of God as is done in much popular theology and hymnology. Paul's thought is in accord with the earliest kerygma (see 1 Cor 15:3–4; Acts 2:23–24; 10:39–40; 13:28–31).

The point made, while technical, is important, if we are seeking to imagine the Gospel of God as proclaimed by Paul. Jesus died on a *Roman* cross, according to the kerygma, at the instigation of Jewish authorities in Jerusalem. That was historical *fact*. Paul's call and gospel were born of the resurrection, according to what he proclaimed.

Paul can stress that Jesus's death had purpose, for it was a self-giving death out of love. For Paul, Jesus's death meant death to the Law as a means of being made right with God, such that he affirms that he himself "has been crucified together with Christ," as he seeks to live in faithfulness to God (Gal 2:19–21), according to the pattern of Jesus's own faithfulness. God, who has supplied his Spirit to the church, works miracles among the Galatians on the basis of faithfulness and not on the basis of Jewish Law (Gal 2:2–5). As Paul had come to realize on the basis of the Abraham story, rectification with God had always been on the basis of faithfulness (Gal 3:6–18) in response to the faithful promises of God (Rom 3:26).

Paul has to deal with the Law, for that is the point of contention with the Nomistic Evangelists who have now entered the Galatian theater with an alternative gospel. Which is it? Rectification on the basis of the Law or on the basis of faithfulness "in Christ"? Paul's position, *based on his own experience*, is that no one is made right with God on the basis of the Law (see Gal 2:15–16; 3:11). The Law simply cannot "make alive" (Gal 3:21). Given indirectly through the intermediary of angels (see Gal 3:19–20), the Law had a function before Christ came that was in keeping with the promises of God (Gal 3:21–24). In Christ, however, there is now equal access to God on the basis of faith—belief, trust, and commitment that leads to faithfulness before the God of all humankind regardless of ethnic, social, or gender status (Gal 3:26–29). Everyone is now potentially an heir of Abraham, having been set free in Christ.

One is now a child of the living God, whether Jew or gentile, slave or free, male or female, such that one can cry "Abba! Father!" (Gal 4:1–7). Jews have been freed from the curse and guardianship of the Law; gentiles have been freed from the challenge and slavery of the Law. All have been freed from the "elemental spirits of the cosmos" (the στοιχεῖα, Gal 4:3). One should not misunderstand. Paul the Christian saw the Law as "holy and just and good" (see Rom 7:12). However, Paul came to understand that the Law was weak and under the power of Sin. It simply had proven to be unable to effect final salvation (i.e., resurrection), such that it had been superseded in the Christ event. The Christ event highlighted the fact that since the time of Abraham long before Moses, proper relationship with God was based upon faithfulness and was independent of the Law.

In the light of the challenge posed by the Nomistic Evangelists, the threat of once again becoming slaves to the "Stoicheia" is real (Gal 4:9). Paul combats the sentiment that wishes to succumb to the Law by posing a query. "Do you not hear what the Law says?" (Gal 4:21). Paul affirms that Christ has set us free for freedom's sake and encourages the gentile Christians of Galatia not to become loaded down again with a yoke of slavery (Gal 5:1). If one chooses the "Law road" of circumcision as espoused by the Nomistic Evangelists, one is committing to the entire Law. If one would be justified on the basis of Law, one will have fallen away from God's grace in Christ. Paul affirms that we await the hope of righteousness through the Spirit on the basis of faithfulness (see Gal 5:4–5). This is but an alternative way of affirming that we await the resurrection, which indeed is the "hope of righteousness" and the glory of the Gospel.

While Paul has some blunt and unkind words for the alternative gospelers who were questioning his own apostleship and gospel ("I wish they would castrate themselves," Gal 5:12), he encourages the Galatians to let faith energize through love (Gal 5:6–15). He encourages them to walk according to the Spirit, not according to the Law (Gal 5:16–25). It is life in the Spirit that leads to resurrection and eternal life (Gal 6:8).

Paul writes with his own hand, such that we do not get any closer to Paul and his thought than we do here (see Gal 6:11–18). He charges his opponents with seeking to escape a cross imperative with persecution in favor of a gospel of circumcision based upon the Law. Paul only glories in the gospel of the cross, i.e., his own figurative crucifixion to the world rather than Jesus's cross. The thought is akin to Jesus's own emphasis that in order to be his disciple one must take up one's own cross and follow him (see Mark 8:34; Matt 10:37; Luke 9:23). This is an acknowledgment that opposition, persecution, suffering, tribulation, and even death may well await one who truly follows the Lord Jesus. However, those things are relativized and not seen as paramount. What matters is a new creation, of which the new Israel of God is but a part (see Gal 6:15–16). One becomes a member of the new Israel on the basis of faithfulness, not ethnicity nor legal ritual.

Philippians (54 CE)

Paul writes Galatians in roughly the same time frame as Philippians. He is engaged in his Collection Campaign, a campaign that has been interrupted by an unexpected severe imprisonment. The threat of the Nomistic Evangelists has begun to have a potentially disastrous effect upon the Galatian Christians. While they had not yet reached Philippi (Phil 3:2–3), the opposing Evangelists had already had an effect in Galatia. Geographical proximity of Galatia to Antioch and Jerusalem would suggest an overland movement that first affected the Galatian Christians prior to any effect in Macedonia and Achaia. At any rate, the situation was different in Galatia as compared to Philippi. Philippi was presently stable, provided the threat of disunity could be overcome—a threat that was the very antithesis of the purpose behind Paul's Collection Campaign.

Philippians is an intensely personal letter. Its content of personal encouragement is based firmly upon the Gospel of God in Christ. Paul stresses the effect of the Gospel of God upon his life. He encourages the Philippians to adopt an *imitatio*

Christi ("imitation of Christ") lifestyle that may be marked by suffering in the light of coming resurrection. As God's apostle, Paul could encourage the Philippians to follow his example. His appeal is not born of arrogance, but it arises on the basis of his called identity in Christ as an apostle.

Paul likely wrote Philippians in 54 CE as his Ephesian imprisonment was coming to an end. Paul is still focused upon the parousia and resurrection and faithfulness, and all the more so in the light of his serious imprisonment. He commends his usual greeting of grace and peace from God the Father and the Lord Jesus Christ to the saints in Philippi. Paul is now beginning to think of his collection campaign in Macedonia and Achaia, perhaps even especially in the light of the developing problems in Galatia.

Paul is very thankful for this church that has engaged in a continuing partnership with him in support of his proclamation of the gospel (Phil 1:3–11; 4:15–18). In a sense, the Philippian church had "mirrored" the very intent of Paul's Collection through their own actions. The church had even supported Paul during his imprisonment by sending gifts, service, and aid through one of their own, Epaphroditus, who in the course of service had become seriously ill (Phil 2:25–28). Paul himself has apparently turned the corner and is now expecting to be released from imprisonment. Christ means life to him, whether he lives or dies (Phil 1:19–26). Paul rejoices that the gospel continues to be proclaimed, even if it be by pretense out of envy and rivalry (Phil 1:12–18).

Paul has harsh words for what must be a reference to the partisan Nomistic Evangelists (or Judaizers) that had begun to create a significant undermining of the gospel among the Galatian Christians. Their influence could have potentially already been felt in Ephesus, although Paul simply seeks to give a warning to the Philippian Christians to be watchful against these false evangelists whom he calls "evil-workers" and "dogs" (Phil 3:2). Paul defends himself on the basis of what he considers to be his superior Jewish identity, in the face of those who have questioned even that (Phil 3:3–7).

In the light of his personal experience, Paul's thought is centered upon both a cross imperative of suffering and a resurrection victory of life in Christ (Phil 1:27–30; 3:12–16). Even in the midst of suffering and threat of death, Paul's faith in the gospel and joy in Christ is undaunted. Joy in the gospel becomes a primary theme in what Paul writes to the Philippians, even should they become involved in conflictual suffering. To live in selfless unity in Christ becomes the order of the day (Phil 2:1–4; cf. 4:2–3).

As it pertains to the living out of the gospel, Paul acknowledges that he has learned the secret of contentment in whatever state he might find life to take him (Phil 4:10–13). He had learned that he could overcome all things in Christ (Phil 4:13) and that one could live without anxiety and within the peace of God in Christ (Phil 4:19).

The present peace of God is transformative because the Lord is at hand (Phil 4:5). Paul's expectation is that Christ will return soon. In the interim time that remains, one should live a life focused upon the praise of God, i.e., focused upon excellence, grace, love, purity, justness, honor, and truth (see Phil 4:8–9).

Currently, the Age of Transformation affords opportunity for affection and sympathy even as the Philippians have expressed these concerns for Paul and Paul for them. It is the age of participation in the Spirit, incentivized by love, because of encouragement in Christ. It is in this context that Paul offers his summary of the Gospel of God and encourages the Philippians to continue working out their salvation with reverence and the trembling of awe, because God continues to work in them to accomplish his will according to his good pleasure (Phil 2:12–13).

The mind-set of Christ is to characterize the Philippians themselves—a mind-set that is theirs "in Christ Jesus." The Philippian hymn (Phil 2:5–11) affirms that Christ was of the nature of God but not equal with God. The Christological parabola describes Christ as taking on the nature of a servant in the form of a man. He became subject (obedient) to Death, even Death's cross. Jesus died by the most shameful of deaths on a Roman cross as a result of the collective sins of humankind that put him to death. It was not Death, however, that won out. The "wherefore" of Phil 2:9 affirms both resurrection and exaltation as Lord over all things in the perceived three-storied universe. Jesus's exaltation is signified by the confession "Jesus Christ (is) Lord," even as his subordination to God the Father is made plain (Phil 2:11; cf. 1 Cor 15:28).

Paul entertains a cross imperative that emerges from the historical reality of Jesus's own death. He envisions resurrection that emerges from a life of crucifixion (Phil 3:7–11). Paul's hope—even immediate hope—is to attain resurrection from the dead, although he clearly acknowledges that the power of resurrection only comes through sufferings even unto death. Paul has suffered almost unto death in the course of his imprisonment (Phil 1:19–26; 3:10–16). He encourages the Philippians to imitate his example (Phil 3:17; 4:9), even as he has sought as God's apostle to emulate the example of Christ to the Philippians (Phil 2:5).

Paul acknowledges that the Christian commonwealth is in heaven, from which the Savior, the Lord Jesus Christ, is awaited (Phil 3:20). The parousia looms (Phil 4:5). The prize of resurrection looms (Phil 3:14). It is an age of transformation based not upon Law but upon grace and continuing development of faithfulness as one embraces what God has done in Christ (Phil 3:21; 2:5; 2:12–13). Paul has now been at work in terms of active ministry post-call for twenty years.

First Corinthians (54 CE)

At a temporal marker some twenty years after his call experience, Paul identifies the Corinthians as "saints" enriched in Christ, who are lacking in no spiritual gift as they await the parousia of Christ (1 Cor 1:2–9). He affirms the faithfulness of God in the fellowship of Christ. He immediately turns attention to the problem of division that exists in the church, following which he rehearses the power of the gospel of the cross (1 Cor 1:10–17). Paul affirms the foolishness of a gospel of the cross when evaluated by the worldly standard of Corinthian wisdom. He affirms two things: the very foolishness of God is wiser than human wisdom; the very weakness of God is stronger than the strength any humans can muster (1 Cor 1:25). Humans have no boast before God, even though Jews demand signs and Greeks seek for wisdom. Paul preaches "Christ crucified," which on the surface of things is a stumbling block of utter foolishness for both Jews and gentiles (1 Cor 1:23–25). In the gospel, death is the prelude to resurrection.

Paul is focused on the wisdom of God in the Christ event, not upon his own words of wisdom in proclamation. First Corinthians 2:3 is often misrepresented. Paul knew not only Christ crucified, but also Christ raised (see 1 Cor 15:3–4). Paul can mention one or the other aspect as the occasion demands, but the other aspect is always nearby. As has already been seen in Galatians, Paul understood himself to have been crucified together with Christ (see Gal 2:20; Rom 6:6). The crucifixion itself was an historical event attributed by Paul to the "rulers of this age" (1 Cor 2:8). Although Paul is often seen to espouse a gospel of the cross, Paul's allusion to the cross more often refers to a cross imperative for Jesus's followers rather than the historical cross of Jesus. Paul champions the Spirit as the revealer of God and his wisdom—a force distinctly different from human wisdom and the spirit of the world (1 Cor 2:10–13).

Paul affirms that the Christian has the "mind of Christ," as those who enjoy the spiritual gifts of God. Those who are not spiritual persons in Christ cannot discern the things of God (1 Cor 2:14–16). Still, Paul acknowledges that he could not address the Corinthians as "spiritual men," but rather as only "babes in Christ" who yet remained as spiritual babes and "men of flesh" who were not yet ready for solid food (1 Cor 3:1–6). The petty jealousy and strife, their pride and self-centeredness, were characteristic of the world at large and the old age—not the new age in Christ.

Paul still speaks of "the Day" of coming judgment, although any apocalyptic sentiment is subdued (see 1 Cor 3:10–15). He has not finished addressing the topic of wisdom, a topic dear to the Greeks of Corinth. Paul, by contrast, affirms the wisdom of the "foolishness" of God that brings all things to those in Christ in the present and in the future, whether by life or death (1 Cor 3:18–23). As an apostle, he has become a fool for Christ's sake (one lacking wisdom), in order that the Corinthians might become truly wise in Christ. He is their spiritual father. He intends to visit them soon, either with a rod to discipline them or a spirit of gentleness to woo them in love (see 1 Cor 4:8–21).

Paul acknowledges the issue of severe immorality among the Corinthians, as well as lawsuits of Christian versus Christian before a pagan judge (1 Cor 5:1–5; 6:1–8). Paul apparently writes 1 Corinthians near the time of Passover (1 Cor 5:7), for he mentions that "Christ, our paschal lamb, has been slaughtered." He later mentions he intends to remain in Ephesus until Pentecost (1 Cor 16:8). The mention of Christ as a "Passover lamb" is certainly a metaphor used by Paul, in the light of the fact that Jesus was historically crucified at Passover according to the Gospel tradition. It should be noted that the focal point of Paul is not one of sacrifice for the forgiveness of sins, but rather celebration, a theme characteristic of general Passover observance. For Paul, the gospel is to be celebrated with the new unleavened bread of sincerity and truth (1 Cor 5:8).

First Corinthians 2:19 indicates that the wisdom of the world is foolishness with God. One has no boast based upon the wisdom of men—even if that of Paul, or Apollos or Cephas, even if that of the world that contemplates realities of life or death, present or future. Wisdom offered through human leaders and philosophical contemplation are secondary at best in the Present Evil Age. It is the mysteries of God that have been revealed and will be revealed in Christ (see 1 Cor 3:11–13, 16–17; 3:19—4:1). Paul and other human leaders are but stewards of the divine mysteries of God expressed in Christ, all of which are inherent to the Corinthians because they belong to Christ. Christ is the wisdom of God (1 Cor 3:22; 1:18–25).

Paul affirms that the Christians have already become wise in Christ (1 Cor 4:10), as he is called upon to defend his own apostleship in the face of Christian immaturity and factionalism, differentiating himself from others (such as Apollos) because he was their spiritual father in Christ (1 Cor 4:14–16). Paul has to address the spiritual immaturity of the Corinthians in the face of a misplaced spiritual arrogance. It is passages like those set forth in 1 Cor 4 that identify 1 Corinthians as the "painful letter" that Paul mentions in 2 Cor 2:4. Among other issues, Paul appears to single out a radical case of immorality in the Corinthian church that was providing a severe threat to the church as a whole. This was an issue he had been previously called upon to address in his second visit to Corinth upon his return from Illyricum.

One needs to remember that Paul was dealing with a comparatively small "house church," such that the actions of individuals would be magnified in terms of their overall influence upon the church as a whole. One could also imagine family centers of power within the overall church body. We don't know how many people made up the church in Corinth. Paul will deal with issues facing the church throughout the remainder of the letter, from which his gospel and theology may be abstracted. Paul had already written an earlier letter to Corinth (the "Previous Letter," likely from Illyricum) to warn of the threat of immorality (1 Cor 5:9).

Corinthian "wisdom" had apparently misunderstood or misrepresented Paul's instruction or correction, such that Paul now offers clarification to a continuing problem. It is tempting to identify the one guilty of immorality in 1 Cor 5:1–2 with the person who caused so much pain for Paul and the Corinthians, as mentioned in 2 Cor 2:1–11. From the later vantage point, it is time for redemption.

It is interesting that Paul alludes to Satan in both contexts (see 1 Cor 5:5; 2 Cor 2:11). Paul uses the word "Satan" but eight times in his letters—2 Thess 2:9; 1 Thess 2:18; 1 Cor 5:5, 7:5; 2 Cor 2:11, 12:7; Rom 16:20; see 1 Tim 1:20, 5:15. The word occurs but fourteen times in the Gospels, twenty times in the remainder of the New Testament.

of which eight times are in the book of Revelation. The word for "devil" (διάβολος) occurs thirty-seven times in the New Testament, twenty-three times outside the Gospels, eight times in letters ascribed to Paul (see Eph 4:27; 6:11; 2 Tim 2:26; 3:3; 1 Tim 3:6, 8, 11; Titus 2:3). Paul uses the concept of "Sin/sin" (ἁμαρτία) more frequently, sixty-four times in all ascribed letters, forty-eight times in Romans alone.

Paul's advice was strong—drive out the wicked person from the church (1 Cor 5:13), such that with a spirit of reconciliation he later has to encourage the church to reaffirm its love for him through comfort and forgiveness (2 Cor 2:6–8). Paul seeks to mend fences in the light of God's reconciling Gospel in Christ.

Paul still has a focus on the kingdom of God (1 Cor 6:9–11) as something that will be inherited. He mentions cleansing and sanctification and justification (all as aorist verbs, second person plurals) in the name of the Lord Jesus Christ and in the Spirit of God, the means of divine communication. While trifold language appears here (Jesus—Spirit—God), Paul is not addressing a view of the "Trinity." In the light of his gospel and theology, he simply alludes to Jesus as Lord and Christ, the one who was exalted by God. Paul sees the Spirit as the communicative and effective power of God given as a gift to the church. It is through the Spirit that the Corinthian Christians have been cleansed, made holy, and rectified by God.

Paul cannot treat all of the issues facing the Corinthian church at once—he must treat them one at a time (seriatim), as one must do in any written narrative. However, they all play in his head simultaneously as he writes, as is characteristic of thought. Thus, his treatment of a given issue is laced with the thought of other issues and the nature of the gospel that is brought to bear upon them all. Paul, for example, has not left the issue of false Corinthian "wisdom" and "slogans" (see 1 Cor 6:12, "all things are lawful"), as he proceeds further to address the issue of immorality (1 Cor 6:18). Before he turns his attention specifically toward the issues about which the Corinthians wrote to him, he employs his "body" analogy to affirm that the Corinthians collectively represent the Temple of the Spirit (or "Spirit of holiness"). He employs the word customarily used for "sanctuary" or most holy place (ναός), rather than the customary word for the larger temple complex (ἱερόν).

Paul affirms that it is God who is the source of the Spirit. The church as the body of Christ and as the dwelling place of God's Spirit is not of their own making. They are encouraged to glorify God in their body (singular), for they together were those redeemed as those who honor God (see 1 Cor 6:20, ἠγοράσθητε γὰρ τιμῆς, customarily translated "bought with a price"). Paul has a strong theological orientation here, much like his stress upon the church as a "praise of God's glory" later in Ephesians (Eph 1:6, 12, 14). The Corinthians were redeemed in Christ to live in honor of God, not in shame before God and man.

As Paul begins to address issues about which the Corinthians had written, he deals with the matter of marriage and sexual fulfillment. What Paul writes by way of advice is predicated upon the eschatological nature of the gospel. The present form of this world (a.k.a. the Present Evil Age) is passing away; the appointed time has grown very short (see 1 Cor 7:31, 29). In view of present realities in the light of the gospel, Paul feels it is good to remain in the state in which one was called to be in Christ (1 Cor 7:17–24, 26). Paul extends the basic principle to three examples—circumcision, slavery, and the issue of marriage. Paul claims the Spirit of God in his pronouncement (1 Cor 7:40).

As he turns his attention to the issue of eating food sacrificed to idols, Paul again confronts Corinthian sloganism associated with wisdom: "we have all knowledge" (1 Cor 8:1). An idol is nothing in the world, for in the light of his gospel in Christ, there is no god but one. There may be many so-called gods and lords, whether in heaven or upon earth, but in reality there is but one God the Father and but one Lord, Jesus Christ (1 Cor 8:6). Paul does not deal with "Trinity," but rather with gospel. God the Father has worked through Christ, such that all things have come about *through* him, including the Corinthian Christians themselves. In Greek, the suggestion is that God is the direct or principle author/agent of the Gospel that is expressed *through* Christ as the indirect agent of God. God is the author of the Gospel (see "Gospel of God," Rom 1:1), while Christ is the content and agent through whom God's Gospel is mediated or expressed. God's Gospel is personal. Paul's Christology is subordinationist.

Paul acknowledges that not all possess a clear knowledge of the gospel, that some with "weak conscience" hitherto accustomed to idols may continue to believe in the real existence of idol gods. It makes no difference whether one eats meat that has been offered as a sacrifice to an idol god if that meat is eaten as mere food. In Paul's day, a temple stood as a dwelling place of the deity, such that a statuary stood therein. Worshipers would offer sacrifices and participate in sacred meals together. A block away, one might find a butcher shop with meat for sale that had been previously sacrificed to a god at a temple.

The reader can imagine the connection. While it was one thing to participate in ceremonies within a temple dedicated to an idol god, buying meat in a butcher shop was another issue. In either case, however, Paul is concerned that the conscience of the more immature Christian not be damaged or misled. When one sins against a weaker brother or sister in Christ, one actually sins against Christ. All make up the "body of Christ." Paul is thereby willing to forego his rights in Christ, if they should lead to the behavioral and conceptional failing of a Christian brother or sister (see 1 Cor 8:9–13).

As opposed to pagan polytheism, Paul's gospel involves the singular God of Judaism who established his Gospel through his anointed one or messiah, whom he has now exalted as Lord and Christ (1 Cor 8:6; cf. Acts 2:36). The Gospel not only has an indicative foundation of the reality of what God has done, but it carries with it a foundational imperative of how one is to live in the light of God's Gospel. As he defends his own apostleship in 1 Cor 9, Paul returns to earlier thought that has been turning over in his mind. He affirms that the Corinthians are his workmanship in the Lord, that he is their "apostle" (see 1 Cor 3:10–15; 4:1–16; 9:1–27).

Much as he did with the topic of the questioning of his own apostleship, Paul returns to address further the matter of the worship of idol gods. Paul appears to be writing, perhaps dictating, seriatim, with a stream of consciousness that returns to prior thought. In 1 Cor 11 he affirms participation in the death and resurrection of Christ (1 Cor 10:15–16), as he mentions the cup and loaf of the Lord's Supper or Eucharist. He develops the theme further in the light of the problems in Corinth (see 1 Cor 11:17–34), but the terms of celebration (the cup and the loaf) are introduced here. He returns to the Corinthian slogan of "all things are lawful" (1 Cor 10:23; cf. 6:12). He elaborates further on conscience and scruples and food sacrificed to idols.

Paul will not finish with these swirling topics until he addresses the next issue of spiritual gifts (see 1 Cor 12–14), although he has essentially been dealing with issues of Christian living in the context of self-defense of his apostleship and Corinthian factionalism and fractionalism. For a second time, he encourages the Corinthians to become imitators of him (1 Cor 11:1; cf. 4:16). This is not out of arrogance, but rather it is a recognition that Paul is an apostle sent with the authority of God and Christ. Just as Paul seeks to imitate Christ as one sent with his authority, so also should the Corinthians recognize they are under Paul's authority but "in Christ."

Paul speaks of cultural issues pertaining to decorum and contentiousness in worship, but he does so in the context of authority. Theologically, God is the "head" of Christ and Christ is the head of every man, even as culturally, the husband is the "head" of his wife (see Eph 5:23–24). Paul then moves to generic issues of male and female decorum in worship in the light of his Jewish background and apparent issues that had arisen in Corinth. It should be noted that Paul assumes that women will both pray and prophesy in public worship, although they should model appropriate dress and behavior that did not mimic temple prostitutes of Corinth or the Pythia prophetess of nearby Delphi.

Paul undertakes discussion of spiritual gifts in the context of the unified gospel of Christ and in the light of those at Corinth who felt they were "spiritual persons" (πνευματικοῖ, 1 Cor 12:1). There are varieties of gifts, service, and words that are manifested in the church, but the same God and the same Lord manifested through the same Spirit for the common good—the building up of the body of Christ. All were baptized into the one body of Christ through the gift of the Spirit—whether Jew or Greek, slave or free (1 Cor 12:13). Unity in the Spirit is thus constitutive of the Gospel of God in Christ. Even as Paul spoke about faith energizing through love in Galatians (Gal 5:6, 13–15), the exercise of spiritual gifts should be on the basis of love (1 Cor 12:31b—14:1) and not on the basis of Corinthian egocentrism and pride.

Speaking in tongues was an issue in Corinth, which is perhaps not so surprising given its location across the Bay of Corinth from the oracle at Delphi. Paul does not address speaking in tongues in any other church setting than that of Corinth. Paul considered this phenomenon as one of the lesser gifts and saw it to be less than edifying for the church (1 Cor 14:1–40), apparently seeing its practice as an exercise in divisive Corinthian pride.

First Corinthians 15 is a decisive chapter, for it records some of the earliest Christian kerygma and addresses one of the two major centers of the Christian gospel ellipse, namely, the resurrection. In 1 Cor 15:3–4 Paul sets forth what he received, namely, "Christ died concerning our sins according to the scriptures, and that he was buried, and that he was raised on the third day according to the scriptures, and that he was caused to appear" to Cephas and to others, including last of all, Paul himself (see 1 Cor 15:3–8). Paul uses the Greek preposition ὑπέρ frequently, with the sense of "for the sake of," "in behalf of," "concerning."

In the light of their experience with the risen Christ, the earliest Christians searched their scriptures (some portion of what we term the "Old Testament") in order to explain what they had experienced. First Corinthians 15 is definitive for setting forth the Gospel of God as Paul understood it. Paul as a Jewish Christian Pharisee believed in the resurrection of the body as an element within theology. Paul as a Christian apostle believed in the resurrection as a direct result of God's direct revelation to him in Christ and his own experience of the resurrected Christ.

Paul's view stood in contrast to at least some of the Corinthians who questioned the nature of the resurrection. Gentile pagans might believe in the immortality of the soul, but not the resurrection of the *body*. Some at Corinth were apparently denying the *reality* of the resurrection altogether. Essentially, therefore, Paul deals with three issues in 1 Cor 15. First, the *reality* of the resurrection is addressed. Secondly, the *result* of the resurrection is addressed. Thirdly, Paul deals with the *nature* of the resurrection. As Paul affirms, apart from the resurrection there is no Christian faith and no Gospel (see 1 Cor 15:12–19).

With regard to the reality of the resurrection, if there is no such thing at all then Christ has not been raised. If Christ has not been raised, then Paul's preaching (*kerygma*) is empty, foolish, or senseless (κενός). If Christ has not been raised, then the faith of the Corinthians in the gospel is likewise empty, foolish, and senseless (1 Cor 15:14). Paul advances his argument through a series of what are known as "first class" conditional sentences in Greek that, for the sake of argument, assume the reality of the condition. What is set forth in the last part of each sentence naturally follows from the assumed "truth" of the first part of the sentence (the "if clause"). The condition need not be actually true; it may simply rhetorically be assumed as true for the sake of argument (see 1 Cor 15:12–19).

For clarity's sake, one might illustrate several of the sentences at this point. Standard English translations are not always clear in terms of Greek grammatical meaning. In 1 Cor 15:13, Paul asserts "If there is no resurrection from the dead [and let's assume there is none], then Christ has not been raised [he has not, for there is no such thing]." Or, in 1 Cor 15:17, "If Christ has not been raised [and let's assume he has not], then your faith is empty [and it is], for you all are still in your sins." Greek can express things rather precisely, while English may sometimes be vague and lack clarity. To illustrate the conclusion of Paul's argument by reversing the two halves of the sentence, "We are of all men most to be pitied, *if* in this life we are ones who have hoped in Christ only" (see 1 Cor 15:19). In other words, if we have hoped in a false resurrection that could never occur, then we are simply deluded and to be pitied. The conclusion will follow naturally from an assumed condition in a "first-class" conditional sentence in Greek. So much for the Greek grammar lesson!

As one thinks about what Paul has to say concerning the resurrection in the light of the Corinthians' question, it is interesting that Paul does not explicitly mention the cross. For example, Paul *could have written* 1 Cor 15:17 as follows: "If Christ had not died on the cross, your faith would be empty and you all would still be in your sins." That would accommodate much contemporary theology and presentation of the gospel centered on atonement. But, Paul did not take that position. Paul's gospel, like the early kerygma (1 Cor 15:3–4), included attention given to both Jesus's death and resurrection.

One could argue that Paul presents a graduated summary, with the historical reality of crucifixion and burial being superseded by the generative event of the resurrection. Paul's order (summary) may be more than a mere presentation of historical sequence. For Paul, the focal point of the gospel was the power of God exhibited in the resurrection, even though it is Paul who in New Testament theology is particularly associated with the cross. Nowhere else in the New Testament do we find as extensive and powerful attention devoted to the resurrection as here in Paul.

With regard to the result of the resurrection, neither Paul's preaching nor the Corinthians' faith is in vain or empty. Paul has faithfully proclaimed the truth of God's Gospel (see 1 Cor 15:15). The Corinthians are no longer living in their sins under the power of Sin (see Rom 6), provided they avail themselves of the gospel and grow up in their faith. Paul implies that those who may have died have not perished, but indeed live in Christ. Those in Christ have not placed their faith in the Present Evil Age, but rather now place their hope in the Age to Come now present in the Christ event. Lest there be any doubt or misunderstanding, Paul affirms that Christ has indeed been raised as the "first fruit" of all those who have died or "fallen asleep" (1 Cor 15:20). "First fruit" implies a later, full harvest.

Skipping for the moment 1 Cor 15:20–28, Paul employs the technique of *diatribe*, or debate with an imaginary debater, to treat the question of the *nature* of the resurrection body. It should be honestly noted that Paul had not yet literally experienced the resurrection personally, such that his argument is based upon analogy and support from scripture interpreted in the light of Christ. He employs a word that suggests foolishness of an ignorant or unlearned kind (ἄφρων) to address his debating opponent (1 Cor 15:36). This would not have been lost on those in Corinth who prided themselves in wisdom.

Paul employs the analogy of a seed that must "die" in order to produce growth for food or harvest. He differentiates among different kinds of bodies (human, animals, etc.), even as he acknowledges a difference in celestial bodies (sun, moon, stars). There is thus a difference between the physical body and the resurrection body—the one is physical, perishable, and "sown" in dishonor. The other is spiritual, imperishable, and "sown" in glory. In the resurrection, that which was physical, perishable, and sown in dishonor will be raised to the level of the spiritual, imperishable, and eternally glorious body.

Paul also employs scriptural imagery to build his case. In his comparison of Adam with Christ, he affirms the "first Adam" was a physical being, a man of the ground, who became a "living being" (see Gen 2:7). Christ, as the "last Adam" of God's new creation, makes one alive in the Spirit. The physical came first, only followed by the spiritual. We have borne the image of the first Adam, the man of dust—physical, weak, under the power of Sin. We shall bear the image of the last Adam if we are in Christ—spiritual, empowered, and freed from the domination of Sin.

One may consult Rom 5:12–21 to see how Paul further employs Adam imagery. In that context, Adam's sin and transgression (Gen 3) represented direct disobedience that led to the many being constituted sinners, whereas Christ's obedience opened the door of opportunity for rectification and righteousness. One sees the characteristic powers of the Two Ages at work here as they cluster together. Sin worked through the Law to bring about Death. In Christ, God's Grace has abounded unto Righteousness through Jesus Christ our Lord unto eternal Life.

Paul speaks of a mystery. That which is perishable does not inherit the imperishable, rather we shall be changed. Paul employs apocalyptic imagery of trumpet sound, even as he did in one of the earliest letters that he wrote (see 1 Thess 4:16). Paul brings his argument regarding the nature of the resurrection body to a close with citation of Old Testament scripture (see Isa 25:8; Hos 13:14). Again, the powers operative in the Present Evil Age cluster together. The Law is surprisingly the power of Sin. Death, the ultimate enemy of humanity, is the sting of Sin. But now, Death itself has been swallowed up in divine victory achieved by God's resurrection of Christ from the dead. That is the reason Jesus is now God's Son in power (see Rom 1:4).

This brings us back to 1 Cor 15:20–28, one of the most important and significant passages in all of Paul's letters in the definition that it gives to the Gospel of God. Christ has, in fact, been raised from the dead. Christ, as the "last Adam" in God's new creation, becomes the first fruit unto life. He becomes the one in whom all find life. At Christ's return or parousia, those in Christ will be raised, followed by the Telos or culmination of God's Gospel. Paul's attention to the kingdom of God is still present, even as it was in 2 Thess 1:5. Paul is still focused on the parousia (see 2 Thess 1:7–10; 2:1–12; 1 Thess 1:10; 2:19; 3:13; 4:15–18; 5:1–10; 5:23).

In the light of what Paul suggests, the *wrath to come* will involve the destruction of every rule, power, and authority that opposes God. Christ will continue to reign until *all* enemies are subjected and placed under his feet. The last enemy that will be *destroyed*, however, is Death itself. Indeed, God through Christ, has already conquered Death and, hence, Sin. With the destruction of Death, Christ himself as the Son will be subjected to God, that God might be "all things in all" [or "to all"] (1 Cor 15:28). Paul suggests the same or similar thought in Phil 2:9–11. God is the one who raised and exalted Jesus, that every "knee" in the entire universe should bow before him, including those in the realm of the dead, and every "tongue" should confess Jesus Christ is Lord. All confession and all victory will be to the "glory of God the Father" (Phil 2:11).

It should be noted in passing that these "victory" passages in 1 Cor 15:20–28 and Phil 2:5–11 and Eph 2:1–18 echo the content of Paul's salutations, which is where we first encounter Paul's expressed theology. Paul commends *grace* (the content of the gospel) and *peace* (the result of the gospel) from God the Father and the Lord, Jesus Christ.

Second Corinthians (56 CE)

Once again, we seek to glean insight into the Gospel of God as Paul understood it. When we imagine Paul's gospel, there is a sense in which we have to overlook the personal details in his letters that pertain to either Paul or the church to which he writes. While extremely important for understanding Paul, it is the incidental elements that define Paul's understanding of the gospel that must be ferreted from the overall text.

Paul is undoubtedly impacted by the severe affliction he suffered in Asia (2 Cor 1:8–11), but one should note how God is characterized *in the light of the gospel*. God is the one who not only raised Jesus but who raised Paul from deadly peril (2 Cor 1:10). Paul hopes in *that* God—the Jewish God who raises from the dead—with the confidence that he will again deliver (2 Cor 1:10). Personally, Paul is centered on God as one who comforts in affliction, in the light of his experience in Asia and his need to be reconciled to the Corinthians (2 Cor 1:3–7). God is the God of mercies who offers comfort of the gospel even in the context of deepest afflictions.

The gospel may lead to persecution and affliction, but it is that which brings comfort, help, and encouragement (παράκλησις). Paul uses this basic Greek word group an amazing ten times in five verses (2 Cor 1:3–7). One comes to understand the nature of the gospel as truly good news of help and encouragement and this from the God of comfort. This is definitional of the *gospel*, but one is not likely to encounter discussion of God as comforter in systematic treatments of *theology*. While Paul may be focused upon his own affliction and that of the Corinthians, through his presentation he says something indirectly about the nature of God and the gospel that, quite frankly, becomes an embarrassment of some theological characterizations of Paul's thought that are simply wrong or lacking in proper balance.

Paul still firmly acknowledges "the day of the Lord Jesus" (2 Cor 1:14). God's "Yes" is expressed in Christ, as he has established both Paul and the Corinthians "in Christ." God has offered his Spirit as a guarantee, as his seal upon us, such that Paul utters an "Amen" to the "glory of God" (2 Cor 1:20–22).

Paul's personal details of his relationship with the Corinthians (2 Cor 1:23—3:3) may be skipped, for it has little or no direct relation to the gospel topic at hand. In the context, however, Paul speaks of being a minister of a new covenant in the Spirit. The written code (Law) kills, but the written code in the Spirit (gospel) gives life (2 Cor 3:6).

Paul essentially speaks of the Two Ages concept in what follows, albeit in different terms (2 Cor 3:7–15). Paul affirms that the gospel removes veils of misperception (see 2 Cor 3:17). Paul does not advance Trinitarian doctrine with his mention of the Spirit. Rather, he affirms the Lord Jesus is the Spirit who brings freedom and change from one degree of glory to another. With veil removed, we reflect the glory of the Lord (resurrection?) as we are being changed into his likeness—and this comes from the Lord who is the Spirit (2 Cor 3:17–18). We know God and the risen Christ through a spiritual interface or relationship, much as we may know someone else personally and they us "spiritually."

Paul's overall thought in Second Corinthians continues to be laced with reflection upon his own afflictions and sufferings in the service of Christ—this permeates the letter (see 2 Cor 4; 6:3–10; 11), as does his reminiscence over his difficulties with the Corinthian church. It is a crucial time for Paul, who is engaged in his Collection Campaign (see 2 Cor 8; 9). He is less than assured that he has won the Corinthians back to himself; suspicions, selfishness, distrust, and dissension still appear to be the order of the day (see 2 Cor 12:14—13:10). If Paul fails in Corinth, his Collection ministry as well as his apostleship will collapse (see 2 Cor 8–9).

Paul points to a cross imperative and affirmation of the resurrection in 2 Cor 4:7—5:5. Paul bears in his body the death of Jesus (i.e., cross), so that the life of Jesus (i.e., resurrection) may be manifest in him. Paul has confidence that the God who raised Jesus will also raise him and other Christians (2 Cor 4:14). Paul appears to think in terms of an ongoing transformation from death unto life in the gospel as one faces afflictions, although there will be a culmination point in a literal resurrection. God is the author of the Gospel; his presence in the Spirit is the guarantee (2 Cor 5:5). Paul expresses belief in a final judgment in which Christ is judge (2 Cor 5:10) in thought that could echo Paul's portrayal of Christ as God's conquering general (see 1 Cor 15:24–26). Paul later speaks of God's final judgment through Christ (indirect agency) in his letter to the Romans written from Corinth (see Rom 2:1–16).

Christ died in behalf of all in a representative death, for Paul considers that all died at least in a figurative death with him (2 Cor 5:14). The figurative death to self results in a new lifestyle to be lived in Christ, the one who died and who was raised by God (2 Cor 5:15). Paul alludes to the basic kerygma he had earlier set forth for the Corinthians (see 1 Cor 15:3-4).

Paul acknowledges that already anyone in Christ is a new creation (2 Cor 5:17)—the "old" has passed away, the "new" had already come. God has reconciled us to himself through Christ. The Greek suggests God is the direct agent in redemption, as he works through Christ as his indirect agent (see 2 Cor 5:18-19). It should be noted that *it is humanity and not God who needed to be reconciled.* God himself was the inaugurator of a Gospel of reconciliation and redemption that did not "reckon" human trespasses against us. Those who are in Christ have not only died with him, but they now live a new life as a new creation—in expectation of a New Creation.

However, there is more, for one redeemed by the Gospel has now been entrusted with the gospel message of reconciliation. As representatives in behalf of Christ, i.e., those now defined by the Gospel, God presently makes his encouraging appeal through us (indirect agency). Paul uses the same word that he used multiple times as he began his letter (παρακαλέω, see 2 Cor 1:3-7). He will use the same verb again in 2 Cor 6:1 with the sense of strong encouragement ("beg" is not too strong). Paul strongly implores the Corinthian Christians to be reconciled to God (2 Cor 5:20) in "behalf of Christ." Paul then adds a final thought to what had begun as a continued defense of his apostleship (2 Cor 5:11): "The one who did not know sin he [God] made sin in our behalf, such that we might become the righteousness of God in him" (2 Cor 5:21).

The doctrine-makers seek to employ 2 Cor 5:21 in isolation as a proof-text for atonement theories, but that is to take the verse out of its context. The reader will pardon the technicality that must be introduced for the sake of clarity. The phrase translated "in our behalf" (ὑπὲρ ὑμῶν) cannot correctly be rendered "in our place," for a similar phrase "in behalf of Christ" (ὑπὲρ Χριστοῦ) occurs twice in 2 Cor 5:20. The preposition in both phrases should be translated in the same manner. If "in our place" in 2 Cor 5:21, then "in the place of Christ" in 2 Cor 5:20, which is not likely Paul's thought. As an apostle, Paul writes with God's authority in Christ but does not supplant Christ. What Paul means in 2 Cor 5:21 may be illumined by what he writes in Rom 8:1-11. It is also illumined in the same context in 2 Corinthians, for Paul has already affirmed that Christ died "in behalf of all" (ὑπὲρ πάντων), such that all have figuratively died in him. He died "in behalf of all," that those who live might live for the one who died and was raised "in their behalf" (2 Cor 5:14-15). Death is the prelude to resurrection, as Paul asserts that both Christ's death *and* resurrection are for our benefit.

Paul does not have in mind a substitutionary, sacrificial atonement theory of the doctrine-makers. What Paul has in mind is God's Gospel of reconciliation. Paul understood that sin kills. Personified, Paul knew that Sin brought Death (see Rom 6:23; 5:12-14). Paul upheld a Gospel indicative of what God had done in Christ (resurrection, new creation), but he also upheld a cruciform imperative (died with Christ, raised with Christ, live accordingly). Be reconciled *to* God, be reconciled *for* God, live out of the Gospel, become the righteousness of God. Incidentally, the "righteousness of God" or "rectification of God" is the theme of the letter to the Romans.

In 2 Cor 6:16 Paul affirms we are the temple of the living God, contained in what may be a fragment of the Previous Letter (see 1 Cor 5:9). Second Corinthians 6:13, as it stands, appears to connect directly with 2 Cor 7:2, such that 2 Cor 6:14—7:1 interrupts the context and apparently treats the subject of that earlier letter.

Paul returns to the theme of "comfort" in 2 Cor 7 in the light of his relational problems with the Corinthian church. He again offers explanation for his painful letter (2 Cor 7:8–13). Paul is building his case in support of his Collection ministry (2 Cor 8–9), which simply must not fail. Paul uses a metaphor of poverty and wealth to speak of the grace of the Lord Jesus Christ in the gospel. He appears to already have in mind a ministry farther to the west, as he later directly announces in Rom 15:23–24 (see 2 Cor 10:13–16). Paul is feeling the threat of those whom he characterizes (with a bit of sarcasm) as the "superlative apostles" (2 Cor 11:5; cf. 12:11), such that he again engages in personal apologetics to defend his own place before the Corinthians.

For Paul, the interlopers are only false apostles (see 2 Cor 11:13). For the remainder of the letter, Paul is engaged in personal defense (see 2 Cor 11–13). He does reiterate that Christ was crucified in weakness (i.e., in the domain of the flesh), but has been made alive (i.e., resurrection) by the power of God. Paul admits his human weakness, but he affirms the power of God in present and future living (2 Cor 13:4). The Corinthians are "in Christ" as a result of their acceptance of the gospel, but as they live out of the gospel, Christ lives "in them" (2 Cor 13:5). The thought is not unlike that expressed later in Col 1:27, "Christ in you all, the hope of glory."

Paul closes the letter by acknowledging God as a God of love and peace. He commends the grace of the Lord Jesus Christ and the love of God to the Corinthians as they share in the participation of the Holy Spirit (2 Cor 13:11–14). One may see the building blocks for what later became Trinitarian doctrine with a capital *T*, although Paul himself is neither troubled nor informed by later Christological debates in the history of Christianity. Paul lived long before the Council of Nicaea. For Paul, God is Father, Jesus is Lord, and the Spirit is the functional interface that conveys the ongoing truth of the Gospel to humanity. Paul had a functional understanding of the Gospel, theology, Christology, and pneumatology (study of the Spirit of God). He did not think in ontological or metaphysical terms, as did the later church fathers who debated from the standpoint of Greek philosophy and metaphysics, as well as Latin legal thought.

Romans 1–15 (56 CE)

Rightly or wrongly, Romans is the letter of Paul *sine qua non*, from which Pauline theology is understood and from which Christian theology is usually drawn. It should be noted that the present writer understands Rom 16 to actually be a letter written to

Ephesus that was appended to the Roman letter at some early point in time. It will be treated later. Thus, only the first fifteen chapters of Romans are examined here. The approach at this point, once again, is not to draw out theological themes in the light of systematic treatment, but rather to seek to discern how Paul understood and set forth the basic nature of the Gospel. There is a difference and an order to be observed between gospel and theology. One cannot correctly set forth Pauline theology without first of all setting forth Paul's description of the Gospel of God in a holistic sense. The elements of Pauline theology need to be understood in the light of the entire gospel of Paul. One must first of all actually read Paul's letters.

The Gospel of God

Simply put, Paul identifies the gospel as the Gospel *of God*, of which the content pertains to Jesus, God's "Son." According to his genealogy, Jesus was descended from David "according to the flesh," but he was designated "Son of God" in power on the basis of his resurrection from the dead and his exaltation by God. The dual description pertains to Jesus's earthly life and his present heavenly and eternal existence. God's action and interaction with humankind occurred through his spirit, as it always does. God exalted Jesus as Lord, affirming Jesus as the Anointed One or Christ (Rom 1:1–4). Scholars may debate whether Paul takes over earlier pre-existent Christian tradition or not, but if so, Paul is obviously in agreement.

It is *through* the Lord Jesus Christ (indirect agency, the direct agent being God) that Paul received the grace of the Gospel and his apostleship (see Gal 1). Paul's apostolic call or commission would mean the proclamation of the gospel to the gentiles in the name of Christ. The gentiles in Rome are now "called saints." The word "called" is an adjective and not a verb. The meaning is thus descriptive and not assertive. The Roman Christians are "called saints," not "called to be saints," as some English translations might suggest. They are "called saints" in Jesus Christ, beloved ones of God, to whom grace and peace are extended through God the Father and the Lord Jesus Christ (Rom 1:5–7). Paul serves God through his spirit in the Gospel, the content of which is what God has done in Christ.

Paul affirms the gospel is the power of God unto salvation for everyone who has faith, because the "righteousness" or rectification effected by God is revealed in it. It is a matter of faithfulness—God's faithfulness to his promises that calls forth the response of faithfulness on the part of both Jew and gentile, thus leading to life.

God's righteousness in Christ has been revealed in the gospel, as well as God's contemporary wrath or anger. In what is the longest treatment of the concept of the wrath of God in the New Testament, Paul speaks in terms of God turning humankind over to themselves for self-destruction (Rom 1:24, 26, 28). Humankind has no excuse. Humanity has been guilty of alienation, arrogance, and idolatry (Rom 1:19–23), such that God simply gave them up to their own undiscerning minds and their improper conduct that failed to acknowledge and honor God. Humankind's ensuing guilt was not a result of ignorance, but the result of deliberate refusal to honor God as well as approval of false conduct (Rom 1:32).

Whether Jew or gentile, humankind is without excuse before God; wickedness (literally, "unrighteousness") has been deliberate. No one is exempt from God's righteous judgment on the day of revelation of final judgment. Mere possession of the Law or expressed allegiance to it will have no saving value for anyone on that day. In other words, Jews may not depend upon Jewish heritage to escape the judgment of God, nor can gentiles plead ignorance through lack of possession of the Law. What matters is actual faithfulness and honoring of God through the demonstration that the expectations expressed in the Law are actually written on the heart (see Rom 2:1–29).

Paul wants to defend the blessed advantage of his own people, but at this juncture he is forced to conclude that Jews are no better off than gentiles. Scripture itself has led him to this conclusion, as he offers a collection of references (a *catena*) drawn basically from Psalms in support. Romans 3:15–17 is drawn from Isa 59:7–8. There is not so much as one who is righteous before God; there is no honoring of God. It is not enough to be "entrusted with the oracles of God" (Rom 3:2), for Paul has come to the conclusion that no human being (Jew or gentile) will be rectified before God on the basis of human boasting or works of the Law (Rom 3:20). Individual "sins" are not the ultimate problem for Paul. The ultimate problem as Paul understands the human predicament is the power of Sin, singular and personified.

Sin, as a power operative in the Present Evil Age, has enslaved God's good creation. It even works through the Law to bring about Death. Paul's theological understanding in this regard becomes more clear in Rom 5–8 as he develops his understanding of God and his actions in a thematic manner. The power of Sin is able to pervert even that which is holy and good, namely the Law, and to render the ultimate result of Death.

The Law is effectively powerless in the face of the specters of Sin and Death. Given the weakness of the Flesh (our domain of living in the current age), Sin is able to use the Law as an agent to prey upon the weakness of our Flesh, which becomes host to the power of Sin dwelling within. Sin pays wages, namely Death. It should be noted that Paul refers to the power of Sin singular in Rom 3:9 and to Sin singular in Rom 6:23. He does not say the wages of "sins" are death. It is Sin that manifests itself in symptomatic "sins," the greatest of which are perhaps idolatry and the arrogance of self-righteousness. By way of analogy, "fever" in one's physical body is not the problem, but rather it is symptomatic of a more serious condition, infection, or illness. When the *cause* of the fever is treated and conquered, the fever goes away. Paul thinks in similar terms with regard to "sins" and "Sin." Until the cause of sins is addressed, one will continue to commit "sins," small *s* and plural.

The gospel involves the rectification or operative righteousness of God apart from God's revelation in the Law and the Prophets. All "have sinned" and all "continue to fall short of the glory of God," whether Jew or gentile. Although Paul does not directly say so here, implied on the basis of what he says later (Rom 6), clarification would suggest all have committed "sins" because they remain under the lordship of Sin, and thus, continue to lack the glory of God. In other words, outside of Christ and the gospel, one bears the "glory of Sin," namely, Death. "In Christ," as a result of the Gospel of God, one bears the "glory of God," namely, Life in the name of the One who lives. God's rectification has come as a gift through God's own grace, through the redemption he put forth in Christ. Rectification includes revivification.

Romans 3:25 is a crucial and somewhat controversial verse in terms of its meaning. Few people readily know what the word "propitiation" or "expiation" mean as they appear in English translations. The underlying Greek word (ἱλαστήριον) is best understood in terms of a "*place* where sins are forgiven" or "provision made," rather than a "*means* of forgiveness." In fact, Paul really does not focus as much on "repentance" and "forgiveness" as we tend to do in Western Christianity. He employs the noun for "forgiveness" (ἄφεσις) but twice in letters attributed to him, letters that in fact many scholars deem not to be by Paul at all (see Col 1:14 and Eph 1:7). He likewise exhibits an absence of emphasis upon the word "repentance" (μετάνοια), which occurs but three times (see 2 Cor 7:9–10; 12:21; Rom 2:4). *Paul's gospel does not emphasize a "guilt-punishment" gospel, but rather one of deliverance and reconciliation.*

For Paul, the emphasis is upon "grace" and "joy" and "gladness." The words do not look alike in English, but all belong to the same word root (χαρ-) in Greek. Paul's gospel is more of a commitment to and *turning toward* the grace of the Gospel of God than it is of *turning away* from sins. Turning away from sins calls for freedom from the power of Sin, made possible only by the conquering grace of God. Even here, it is not a matter of human action or achievement concerning which one might boast; it is strictly about the victory of God in Christ, in which we may share and rejoice. It is not a boastful case of "I conquered Sin," but rather a case of doxology, "Thanks be to God for his victory in Christ Jesus our Lord. Amen." The one bespeaks narcissistic self-righteousness and arrogance, while the other bespeaks a praise of God's glory.

The phraseology, punctuation, and overall sense of Rom 3:25–26 are all subject to much debate. It is clear that God has chosen to pass over previously committed sins that were universal to all humankind, and he has done so on the basis of his own forbearance. God in his sovereignty could rightfully punish sin or he could choose to forbear. His purpose in forbearance, according to Paul, was to demonstrate his own righteousness or rectification in the present season apart from Jewish scripture. "Righteousness" is not first of all a "moral" concept, but rather a *character* concept of being right and doing right. Paul's major point is that God in all of his actions is just or right in his character, and that he is able to justify or rectify the one who expresses faithfulness (Rom 3:25–26). What is not clear is the subject and object or the basis and nature of "faith." Whose "faith" and "faith" in what or whom?

God's redemption of humankind *in Christ* represents the free action of God on the basis of his grace extended to all those who stand in need of rectification, namely, the entire human race that lacks the glory of God. It has failed to live up to what God created it to be (see Gen 1). Human beings were created to live as a "praise of God's glory" (see Eph 1:6, 12, 14). In Western Christianity the emphasis has fallen too often upon "all have sinned" to the neglect of attention given to the "glory of God," that which should define human beings (see Rom 3:23). One should understand Rom 3:25–26 on the basis of Paul's argument given before and afterward, for Paul sets forth "his gospel" (see Rom 2:16). Our lack of faithfulness does not nullify the faithfulness of God (Rom 3:3). Our lack of "rightness" does not nullify God's "rightness" (Rom 3:5). God is not unjust even when he brings wrath, for our falsehood and our wickedness does not establish God's righteousness either in fact or opportunity (Rom 3:5–8).

God is right and is able to make right (Rom 3:26). Paul understands the gospel to be a universal gospel addressed to both Jews and gentiles because he worshiped the living God, who was One. Consequently, he understood that God's glorification was not exclusive only to Jews on the basis of Law or Torah, but rather it was universal and predicated on faithfulness. Human boasting predicated on works, achievements, and privilege were excluded, such that the playing field was leveled universally for both Jew and gentile. Since God was One, he would justify both Jew and gentile on the basis of faithfulness (Rom 3:27–30).

Torah in Context

One must understand Paul in his context. He is in the final stages of his Collection Campaign, having reached Corinth to receive the Corinthian Christians' gifts. He has suffered a great deal of personal turmoil in the questioning of his gospel and his apostleship by the Nomistic Evangelists who have proclaimed an alternative gospel in at least several of Paul's congregations. Paul likely suffered a severe personal experience of imprisonment in Ephesus. He has been at severe odds for several years with those in Corinth. Paul's personal life has been anything but tranquil. Even as he writes Romans, Paul is torn between Rome and Jerusalem. He wants to go to Rome and gain support for a ministry to Spain (Rom 15:22–29). Who would know? Christ's parousia and God's Telos might be delayed until the entire known world (the Mediterranean as far as Spain) had had the Gospel proclaimed to it. At present, Paul has decided he must accompany the Collection to Jerusalem and there defend his gospel one more time (Rom 15:30–32).

Romans becomes a manifesto of his gospel to the Roman church/es, as well as a rehearsal of issues he will likely have to face in Jerusalem. His collective experiences in his immediate past now swirl in his consciousness and subconsciousness. Paul writes Romans for his own sake as much as for the sake of the Roman Christians. In part, it is also likely a reflection of his situation in Corinth, although there is no direct statement that the letter was written in Corinth.

It is in the light of the above that Paul affirms that he does not nullify the Law but rather affirms it (Rom 3:31). A part of our problem in understanding Paul is really a Greek and English problem. When we hear the word "law," which is a legitimate translation of the underlying Greek word νόμος, we think in terms of legal regulations. Paul would have thought in terms of *torah* or divine instruction given on the basis of God's grace and contained in the five "books of Moses."

While the Torah contained both moral and ritual prescriptions of both legal and righteous nature, it also contained much else, such as an historical accounting of covenants established through Abraham and Moses. The Torah is as much narrative description of Israel's formation based upon God's promise as it is "legal" prescription based upon God's expectations. It defines Israel as descendants or children of Abraham, as well as people of a covenant code through Moses. The basic credo of Israel found in Deuteronomy, for example (see Deut 6:1–25; 26:1–11), is one of faithfulness to the promise given to Abraham and the first commandment given in the Covenant Code through Moses. The point is that the "Law" is not just "legal prescription," but is primarily first of all covenant faithfulness and responsibility born of relationship and defined by the narrative of God's actions. The Torah was first about God, then about humankind. The Gospel was first of all about God, and then about humankind. In other words, Paul deals with a *theological* Torah and Gospel, both of which have *anthropological* ramifications.

As given by God, even through angels (see Gal 3:19–20) and even in terms of its legal prescription, Paul understood the Law as "holy and just and good" (Rom 7:12). He understood the Law as that which defined "sin" and "transgression," but that which in itself could not bring salvation. Against the position of the Nomistic Evangelists who argued for a gospel based upon legal prescription of Torah (circumcision and food laws, see Gen 17:9–14; Lev 11), Paul argued for a gospel of freedom and equality based upon the prior faith strands *present in Torah*. He quotes scripture: "Abraham expressed faith in God and it was accorded to him as righteousness" (Rom 4:3; cf. Gen 15:6). God's original covenant word given to Abraham contained no "rules," but only a call for faithful action of following God (Gen 12:1–3). Even after Abraham shows lapses of faith (see Gen 12:10–13; 15:1–4), God maintains his covenant promise to Abraham.

Abraham "believed" God, and it was reckoned as righteousness before God (Gen 15:6). It was only after the birth of Ishmael that God again renewed the covenant and at that point commanded Abraham and every male in his household to be circumcised for reasons not altogether plain (Gen 17:9–14). Those not circumcised, however, would not belong to the people of Israel (see Gen 17:14). With regard to gentile incorporation into the *eschatological* Israel, Paul argued on the basis of Gen 15:6 and the Nomistic Evangelists argued on the basis of Gen 17:9–14. While it may seem like an insignificant, misplaced argument, it is similar to some theological controversies of our own day. Interestingly, Ishmael was circumcised on the same day as Abraham (see Gen 17:22–27), while the biblical text never mentions the circumcision of Isaac through whom the Abrahamic covenant will be established (see Gen 17:15–21).

Paul found in Abraham a universal father of both Jew and gentile, circumcised and uncircumcised. It was ultimately the faithfulness of Abraham in all ways that gave glory to God (Rom 4:20). Abraham was convinced that God was able to do what he had promised (Rom 5:21), such that righteousness was reckoned to him (Rom 5:22), a word not only written about Abraham but written to us (Rom 5:23–24). Faith in the God who raised Jesus from the dead will result in the reckoning of righteousness (Rom 4:24). Paul acknowledges that Jesus was handed over because of trespasses against God that are endemic to the human race, as Paul has already established. It should be noted that Paul does not say explicitly (nor implicitly, in the present writer's judgment) that it was God who handed Jesus over. Jesus was betrayed not according to a divine need for a perfect sacrifice, but on account of universal human trespasses against the will of God and because humankind continues to lack the glory of God as intended in creation.

Rectification

Those who are about to be justified before God are those who express faithfulness before the God who raised Jesus from the dead. Romans 4:25a may well belong with Paul's assertion in verse 24. Paul is interpreting the text "it was reckoned to him unto righteousness" (Gen 15:6). His point is that those words were not written for the benefit of Abraham only, but also for our benefit, "to those to whom it is about to be reckoned, to those who come to faithfulness in the One who raised Jesus our Lord from the dead, who was handed over because of our trespasses. Indeed, he was raised because of our justification" (Rom 4:24–25). Romans 4:25a is descriptive in function, while Rom 4:24b is assertive. Paul's intended meaning is along the lines of "while he was handed over to death because of the sinful trespasses of men, God raised him from the dead with a view to rectify humankind." We are those who are justified on the basis of faithfulness, just like Abraham (Rom 5:1).

God is the one who brings life out of death, even when conceived metaphorically as was the case with Abraham and Sarah, who were too advanced in age to bear children (Rom 4:18–20). Abraham was convinced God was able to do what he had promised (Rom 4:20–21). By customary rabbinical interpretation, Paul applies the promise to Abraham more generally (Rom 4:23–24). God is the one who raised Jesus from the dead. "Indeed, he was raised on account of our justification" (Rom 4:25b). In Paul's understanding, justification ultimately means life out of death, or resurrection. To obtain resurrection, one must trust God and honor God through faithful living (see Phil 3:12–16). God's own intention to offer life from the dead is born out of both his freedom and his sovereignty.

Paul has made his argument *for* the gospel in Rom 1–4, such that in Rom 5–8 he will set forth his understanding *of* the gospel. The shift in emphasis is expressed by Paul's "therefore" which he announces in Rom 5:1. His next real change in topic in a macro sense will not come until Rom 9–11, when he is compelled to deal with the lack of faithfulness of his own people, Israel. In that context, before he breaks out in a doxology of praise before God (Rom 11:33–36), Paul concludes that God consigned all humankind to their disobedience, in order that he might show mercy to *all* (Rom 11:32). The word "all" is a rather inclusive word. An awareness of what Paul is doing in his overall letter helps us to understand the difficult and significant passage found in Rom 3:21–31.

In Rom 3:21–31 Paul contrasts the effective age of the gospel with the ineffective age of the Law. The Law could not justify (establish as "right") any human being before God (Rom 3:20), i.e., it could not bring righteousness leading to resurrection. It could only bring knowledge of Sin. In fact, the Torah has no connection with resurrection at all, which indeed is the hope of the Gospel of God for Paul.

God's righteousness and his right-wising activity, however, have been made known or revealed in the present time through his revelation in Christ. Apart from the gospel based upon faithfulness, humankind still sins and continues to exhibit a lack of the glory of God. Humankind fails to live up to the glory of God intended in creation (Gen 1:26–28) or the glory of God intended in the call of Abraham or the glory of God set forth in the Law of Moses.

God himself in the Gospel seeks to rectify human beings on the same basis that he rectified Abraham and the same basis by which Jesus himself was rectified before God—namely, on the basis of faithful, trustful living even unto death. Our redemption is thus in Jesus Christ, whom God himself sent forth as a merciful solution to humankind's need for rectification before God. Humankind's continuing sinfulness and continuing idolatry even in the present age calls forth God's wrath (Rom 1:18–32; 3:23).

God in Christ has sought to demonstrate his own rightness in the present age in Christ by passing over previously committed sins and rectifying those who exhibit the faithfulness of Christ in their own living. He did so on the basis of his own choice and sovereign freedom, not on the basis of some extrinsic compulsion. Those who are faithful like Abraham, and like Christ before them, will be justified before God through resurrection. As Paul will go on to demonstrate, those in Christ are freed from and are victorious over all present powers that would enslave and kill—Sin, the Law, even Death and all other entities that one might conceive (Rom 6–8). Nothing can sever one from the love of God in Christ (Rom 8:38–39). One is even delivered from "wrath" (Rom 5:9; cf. 1:18) both present and future. Paul does not say the wrath "of God" in Rom 5:9, it should be noted.

Since we are rectified on the basis of faithfulness, Paul encourages Christians at Rome to enjoy peace with God through our Lord Jesus Christ, because it is through him we have already come to have access (a perfect tense verb) or the right of entry by faith into the grace in which we have already been established ("come to stand," perfect tense, accomplished fact). Consequently, Paul encourages Christians to boast over the hope of the glory of God (Rom 5:2). The glory of God is assured in the resurrection, but one can even boast in the present in one's afflictions. Paul suggests that such sufferings produce endurance, endurance produces character, and character brings forth hope. Paul's words suggest an early Christian hymn.

The Christian hope is not an empty hope, because God's love has already been poured into our hearts through his holy Spirit that he has given us (Rom 5:5). Paul acknowledges that at the appointed time Christ died for us (he does not say "God put to death"), while we were in a weak and godless state. In other words, Christ died in our behalf (not "in our place") while we were still sinners subject to death (see Rom 3:23), God thereby demonstrating his own love through him (Rom 5:6–9). Therefore, having been justified by his death (lit., "his blood"), we shall be saved (future tense) from wrath through him (or, "blood" implied) (Rom 5:9).

Paul does not directly say the wrath "of God" in the Greek text, just "wrath." Paul then makes two significant points. Affirming reality, in Rom 5:10 Paul asserts that if we have been reconciled through the death of his Son (*and we have*), much more we shall be saved (future tense) by his life now that we are reconciled (*and we shall be*). Secondly, Paul identifies Christians as those who boast in God through our Lord Jesus Christ (indirect agency), through whom we have now received reconciliation (Rom 5:11). The word "reconciliation" was translated as "the atonement" in the King James Version (1611) as a synonym of "reconciliation," which it was at the time ("at-one-ment"). The same word group occurs twice more in Rom 5:10, both times being rendered with the concept of "reconciling."

Paul's whole point thus far in Romans has been a focus upon the alienation of humankind from God as a result of sin and idolatry. The need has been for reconciliation with God, of which the avenue has now been provided in Christ, Son of God in power through the resurrection. On the basis of Jesus's resurrection, even death itself can now be understood as only a temporary precedent. Jesus's faithfulness, even unto death by the powers (see 1 Cor 2:8–9), has provided both a model and a foundation for our own living and adoption by God as his adopted children.

Christ now lives as Lord of our own faithfulness unto resurrection as we glorify God and enjoy his peace. Although not our achievement, we have *received* reconciliation with God and have been rectified on the basis of faithfulness. So, let us enjoy peace with God through our Lord Jesus Christ, and let us boast even in our sufferings; let us boast in the sure hope of sharing in the resurrection glory of God (see Rom 5:1–11).

In the face of hope of future life on the basis of reconciliation with God, Paul begins to set forth his thought on the "powers" that enslave and kill and from which Christians have been set free, provided they continue in faithfulness. He treats the topic of the culprit of Sin (personified), which entered the world through Adam, and through Sin, Death (likewise personified). For Paul, it was not a case of the original guilt of all in Adam (as Augustine), but rather it was a case of a contagion that spread to all like a virus or an infection. The proof for Paul of Sin reigning universally was the fact that Death reigned universally. That all died and continued to die was the proof that Sin and Death reigned universally, even over those whose "sins" were different from the "transgression" of Adam, even over those who "sinned" before the Law was given through Moses (Rom 5:12–14).

One must have a known command to break in order to have a "transgression," but in the light of Paul's thought it is obvious one may "sin" apart from possession of the Law (see Rom 1–3). Every transgression is a "sin," but not every sin is a transgression. Once the Law was given, it actually served the function of defining and multiplying "sin" that now became even more grievous as direct "transgression" (see Rom 7). Sin became deliberate in transgression. Paul has already made his point that no one—not so much as one!—will be made right with God by works of the Law. Knowledge of sin as transgression comes as a result of the Law, but in itself the Law does not save. The reason in Paul's understanding is that the Law itself has fallen under the power of Sin.

Sin worked through the Law to enter humanity at our weakest point, the domain of our fleshly existence. The Law turned sin into transgression. The Law thereby became Sin's agent to effect death in our flesh, which became Sin's host. While the gnostics later understood "flesh" to be evil, Paul only understood it to be weak and highly subject to the contagion of Sin. Paul will use Adam as a type, or actually as an "anti-type" of Christ, who was to come as the "last Adam" of God's new creation (Rom 5:17–19). The imagery of Adam suggests a new creation, a new genesis, a new "beginning."

Dawn of a New Age

It is Rom 6–8 in particular that Paul's conception of the Two Ages concept becomes more readily apparent. He personified those "powers" or "realities" that characterize the Present Evil Age and the Age to Come that has now been inaugurated by God's Gospel in Christ. Adam let Sin loose through his trespass. The Law through Moses increased the trespass. Sin worked through the agency of the Law and through the weakness of Flesh to unleash Death. Adam-Sin-Flesh-Law-Trespass-Death become markers of the Present Evil Age. However, God's Gospel in Christ now inaugurates a new age, the Age to Come. Christ-Faithfulness-Grace-Spirit-Righteousness (Rectification)-Life now characterize the living of life unto resurrection in Jesus Christ our Lord (see Rom 5:15–21).

Paul thus recognized the Two Ages concept within Judaism in terms of a Present Evil Age dominated by Sin and characterized by human sins and transgressions and a glorious Age to Come that would be characterized by the "rightness" of God. Paul understood the shift of the Ages to have occurred when the power of Sin and Death were overcome by the resurrection of Christ as the "first fruit" of a greater harvest yet to come. Humanity was now freed to live under a different lordship, as Paul stressed the supremacy of Christ over all (see Rom 6:1–23; Col 1:15–29). In Paul's understanding, Jewish monotheism and present lordship now ushered in a third, interim age, namely, the Age of Transformation. The Age of Transformation marked the current period of overlap between the Age to Come now inaugurated and the Present Evil Age now being overcome.

As Paul continues to set forth his understanding of the gospel, one should note that to Paul it is not Sin that has died but those in Christ who have at least died a metaphorical death in him (Rom 6:1–4). By the metaphor of baptism, Paul asserts that we are baptized into Christ's death—that we have died and been buried with him, such that just as Christ was raised from the dead through the glory (indirect agency) of the Father, *we*, too, might live (lit., "walk") in a newness of life. For Paul, "resurrection" must be preceded by a death, whether metaphorical or literal. There is thus a cruciform imperative that stands before the Christian in any full Pauline gospel. While it likely has escaped the attention of the reader to this point because of popular Christian theology, Paul has nowhere mentioned the cross in the letter to the Romans. Nor will he do so in the remainder of the letter.

He has, of course, mentioned Jesus's death. By contrast, the theme of resurrection has been a dominant one. Only in Rom 6:6 does Paul use a compound verb based on the concept of "crucifixion." Paul affirms that our former self "has been crucified together" (συνεσταυρώθη) with Christ that the body of Sin might be destroyed, such that we might no longer serve Sin as a slave of Sin (see Rom 6:6). It takes a death to be freed from Sin ("to have been rectified," δεδικαίωται, perfect tense), such that if we have "died" together with Christ, we have faith that we shall live together with him, i.e., be resurrected with him (see Rom 6:8–11).

A note should be offered that there is a difference between resurrection and "resuscitation." A "resuscitation" implies a being brought back to the state of former life. When Jesus resuscitated Lazarus or the widow's son at Nain (see John 11:38; Luke 7:11–17), he brought them back to the normal life they had known. They lived to actually die again, just as many in our own day may report on their "after clinical death" experiences. The New Testament, Paul included, does not speak of Jesus's "resuscitation," but rather of Jesus's resurrection to heavenly existence. The difference is significant. Even when Paul speaks metaphorically of Christians already having been raised with Christ, he does not think of Christians being "resuscitated" to life in the old age of slavery to Sin and Death. He thinks of resurrection, of new life that even now begins to be lived unto God. The longed-for Age to Come has already broken in, such that the Age of Transformation has begun.

Christ, having been raised from the dead, no longer dies and Death no longer "lords" over him. His death represents a once-for-all death to Sin. The life he lives he lives to God. Emphatically, although the emphasis is often overlooked in English translation, Paul tells the Romans that *they* should consider themselves dead to Sin on the one hand, but now living unto God in Christ Jesus on the other hand.

Consequently, Paul can exhort them with a present tense imperative to stop letting Sin reign in their mortal body (sing.) to obey lustful desires. Nor should they render their members to Sin as instruments of wickedness (lit., unrighteousness). *Instead*, with a bit of emphasis, Paul encourages the Roman Christians to present themselves to God as those who live from the dead, and their members as instruments of righteousness to God. "Sin no longer lords over you all; for you all are not under Law but under Grace" (Rom 6:14).

Paul did not embrace a libertine gospel. Once one is freed from the power of Sin, one should not live a lifestyle of committing sins (i.e., disobedience) with the view that that will multiply available grace (Rom 6:15–23). The conclusion is often taken out of Paul's context and understood in the sense that personal sins (plural) lead to eternal damnation, whereas God's free gift is eternal life in Christ Jesus our Lord (Rom 6:23). Paul's argument involves the imagery of slavery to Sin or slavery to God. One has been set free *from* Sin, but one has now become a slave of Righteousness. One cannot be a slave to both simultaneously. The reward for being a slave of Sin is death; the return one receives as a slave of God is a life of sanctification that leads to life under God's eternal rule.

For Paul, literal slavery was a socioeconomic part of the Greco-Roman world. It was pervasive. Some estimates number 25,000,000 slaves in the Roman Empire. Paul and the other early Christians did not have political power to overturn the social reality of a literal slavery, even had they been so inclined. One must remember that the earliest Christians expected Christ to return very soon to institute the full reign of God (see 1 Cor 7:29, 17–24). Paul made metaphorical use of the imagery of slavery in the service of the gospel. He identified himself as a "slave" (δοῦλος) of Jesus Christ (Rom 1:1). To affirm "lordship" of Christ for Paul was to affirm a "saving slavery." He informs the Corinthians that if one were a literal slave, when one received the gospel, one became a "freedman of the Lord." The imagery is powerful, for a master at his will could free a slave. "For freedom, Christ has set us free," according to Paul in Gal 5:1.

At the same time, if one were a free person (non-slave) before becoming a Christian, one has now become a "slave" of Christ (1 Cor 7:20–24). Even Jesus suggested one cannot serve two masters (Matt 6:24; Luke 16:13). Paul affirms that one was once a slave of Sin, whose service leads to Death/death. One in Christ has now become a slave of God's righteousness that leads to life. Paul admits he speaks "in human terms," as he uses the metaphor of slavery in a most serious and transformative way—in Christ (see Rom 6). To become a slave in the gospel is to know life—and, paradoxically, freedom. Paul can also move beyond the metaphor of slavery to that of adoption as children of God (Gal 4:4–7). One should not overly literalize Paul's use of singular metaphors so as to lose sight of Paul's major emphasis.

In Rom 7, Paul will affirm both the holiness of the Law and the Law's subjection to Sin. Christians have died to the Law through the body of Christ and are freed from it, in order to belong to the lordship of the risen Christ. Discharged from the subjection to the Law, that had had the rousing effect of arousing sinful passions in the weakness of the domain of the Flesh, one is now free to bear fruit unto God. We are "dead" to the old written Law through which Sin killed; we are freed persons in the new life in the Spirit (Rom 7:1–6).

Paul clarifies his position. The Law is not sinful of itself. It defines sin and disobedience, such as covetousness. However, Sin finds opportunity in the Law and multiplies transgressions (such as covetousness). The Law ironically breathes life into Sin's effective power, such that the very commandment that promised life actually results in death (Rom 7:9–12). Sin worked through that which was good to bring about death. After further discussion of the fatal effects of Sin dwelling within, Paul cries out with a cry of futility, "Wretched man I am! Who will rescue me from the body of this death?" (Rom 7:24). Paul immediately breaks out in thanksgiving—"Grace be to God through Jesus Christ our Lord!" (Rom 7:25), even as he recognizes the continuing threat of Sin. Again, it is not Sin that has died but we who die to Sin, as we become subject to another Lord. It was not Sin nor the sins of man that "died" at the event of Jesus's crucifixion. Rather, it was Jesus who died. The sins of humanity were in full evidence in Jesus's death. Jesus, faithful to the Lord God, was raised to new life by him.

No Condemnation

In what is most certainly one of the favorite chapters in the entire New Testament, Paul affirms that there is no condemnation for those who are "in Christ Jesus" (Rom 8:1). The Law of the spirit of life in Christ Jesus has "freed" one from the Law of Sin and Death. God accomplished in Christ what the Law, weakened by the Flesh, could not do. God condemned Sin in the very lair in which it wielded its power (the domain of Flesh) to bring about death. Jesus entered the realm of the Flesh, and with his death, it appeared Sin and the powers had won out once again. But then, God broke the strangle-grip of Sin by raising Jesus from the dead—not just "un-doing," but rather *overcoming* the ultimate power and pay-off of Sin, namely, Death.

Those who live in Christ live in the spirit of grace and peace (Rom 8:6). One's body may be dead because of Sin (see Rom 8:6), but one's spirit is alive in Christ on the basis of God's rectification. God's Gospel comes with fullness of promise expressed with a first class condition that affirms reality: "Since the Spirit of the One who raised Christ from the dead lives in you all, the one who raised Christ from the dead will also make alive your mortal bodies through his indwelling Spirit in all of you" (Rom 8:11). In short, that is both the content and promise of the Gospel of God.

As a result, Paul acknowledges that we are debtors to God so as to put to death life lived according to Flesh in order to live according to the Spirit. Life in the Spirit means we have been adopted by God and are enabled to cry "Abba! Father!," as his children. Since we are God's children, we are heirs of God and fellow-heirs with Christ (Rom 8:16–17), which is absolutely an amazing assertion. There is but one qualification. We are fellow-heirs of God with Christ, *provided we likewise suffer with him*. Resurrection can only follow a faithful death (see Rom 8:17). Along with the whole of creation, we await final redemption with a fullness of hope. We were saved with a fullness of hope as the first fruit of the Spirit, as we wait with patience for the completion of full redemption. The Spirit intercedes for the saints according to God (Rom 8:22–23). Paul affirms that God works all things unto good for those who are called according to purpose (Rom 8:28). Called to what? A call according to divine purpose may well involve suffering evil that will be transformed by God into the ultimate divine victory, as was the case with Christ.

Paul may have drawn upon an early Christian hymn for what follows. "*Those whom he foreknew, indeed he set apart beforehand; Those whom he set apart beforehand, these indeed he called; Indeed those he called, these he also justified, those whom he justified, these indeed he glorified*" (Rom 8:29–30). This is seen even more clearly in Greek, for which translation has already been given, such that the following Greek is given for illustration purposes only.

> οὓς [δὲ] προέγνω, [τούτους] καὶ προώρισεν,
> οὓς δὲ προώρισεν, τούτους καὶ ἐκάλεσεν.
> καὶ οὓς ἐκάλεσεν, τούτους καὶ ἐδικαίωσεν,
> οὓς δὲ ἐδικαίωσεν, τούτους καὶ ἐδόξασεν

One may easily imagine Paul's words being chanted as a hymnic praise in the course of the worship of God, a capella style, in a context with wonderful acoustics.

Paul himself adds an additional comment that those whom God foreknew he marked out to become conformed to the image of his Son, such that he might be the first-born among many brothers (and sisters). Technically speaking, to be conformed to Christ involves a sharing in his suffering as well as his victory. Paul does not enunciate a theological doctrine of "predestination," but rather a perspective of divine adoption in Christ. What he offers is not offered in the vein of a systematic theological doctrine, but rather in the vein of worship.

One might have expected Paul to have offered a doxology of praise at this point, but in effect the praise has come through the hymn. Paul instead raises a rhetorical question, "What shall we say to these things?" Paul is not quite through. "Since God is for us [ὑπὲρ ἡμῶν], who is against us?" Romans 8:32 may be employed in atonement theology in support of doctrine, but Paul's purpose toward which he is building is quite different. With his series of rhetorical questions, Paul is not engaging in apologetics but in affirmation of the Gospel. The whole of Rom 8 is tied together in sequential rhetoric. There is no condemnation for those in Christ Jesus (Rom 8:1). The Spirit of God who raised Jesus from the dead dwells in them (Rom 8:11). Their mortal bodies will be made alive by that same Spirit.

A Sovereign Solution

In Rom 9–11 Paul deals with his own people who have not responded to the gospel. Paul's heart is laid bare as he expresses his great sorrow (Rom 9:1–3). Paul's Jewish kinsmen had been richly blessed with great privilege. Paul lists nine different things, including last of all sequentially, Christ (Rom 9:4). On the one hand, he is willing to give his own life to save his own people. On the other hand, as he thinks of the gospel, he must break out in worship of God (Rom 9:5). There has been a failure, as seen in Israel's overall lack of response. The question is where and why. How can a Jewish gospel be proclaimed to gentiles with acceptance and be rejected by Jews? How can an eschatological gospel be proclaimed that marked the very shift of the Ages and it not be universally inclusive? How can one have an ultimate gospel that lacks universal application?

It is not just the status of Israel that is at stake, but rather the very character of God that is on the line. Has God failed in his commitment and promises to Israel? Has he exchanged his covenant people for another? And, if God so easily casts aside one people for another, can God really be trusted? It is not a question of the reality of God's sovereignty, but one of how God chooses to exercise his sovereignty.

While Paul offers several comments that have become the subject of theological debate, his basic assertion is found in Rom 9:6—the word of God has not failed. That is not the cause of the problem. Not all who are physical descendants of Abraham and Isaac are children of God's covenant with Israel. The covenant passed through Jacob and not Esau. Paul denies that God is unjust, citing Moses's own words that God will have mercy upon whom he will have mercy and compassion upon whom he chooses (see Exod 33:19). Romans 9 is heavy with citation from the Jewish scriptures. Paul also employs the example of Pharaoh, who was raised up for the purpose that God might demonstrate his power and effect his will (Exod 9:16).

It is not a question of humankind's will or exertion, but rather a question of God's justice and sovereignty and mercy (Rom 9:14–18). Just as a potter might have power over the clay to make what he wished, so also God is sovereign in the working of his will. Paul finds a theological support for God's sovereignty in passages like Hos 1:10, 2:23, and Isa 1:9, 10:22–23, as well as in Exodus. While God's sovereignty is unlimited, Paul does not find Israel's problem to rest in that sovereignty. In fact, it is just the opposite. The problem rests with Israel. The solution is to be found in God's gracious sovereignty.

Paul essentially makes two points in Rom 9 aside from theological debates that swirl around this chapter. Paul affirms through Jewish scripture and examples that God is sovereign and can exercise his will, justice, power, wrath, mercy, and glory as he wishes (see Rom 9:9–29). That, in fact, is what "sovereignty" is about. Paul's second point is that Israel may be lost except for a remnant that God always has acted to preserve. So, how might the present situation of gentile acceptance and general Jewish rejection of the gospel be explained? Paul is confronted with an apparent contradiction and anomaly. Israel had all the blessed advantages, including the pursuit of righteousness on the basis of the Law, but Israel failed to attain righteousness based upon the Law. Gentiles, on the other hand, did not even pursue righteousness and did not possess the Law, yet they had attained righteousness through the gospel based upon grace available to faithfulness.

Paul's two basic points—God is sovereign and Israel may be lost—are bathed in Paul's sorrow for his own people, for he deeply wishes and cares for their salvation through the acceptance of the gospel (Rom 9:1–3; 10:1). One may debate theology, but until one can feel deeply with Paul his anguish for his own people, one has not yet understood him. Paul concludes in Rom 10 that Israel by and large is lost, but Israel is lost as a result of her own choice and not because of some arbitrary choice of God. Israel had sought to establish her own righteousness based upon works of the Law rather than embracing God's righteousness founded upon faith in the gospel (Rom 9:30—10:4). God's direct revelation through the risen Christ had convinced him of the truth of the gospel. It had convinced him that a right relationship with God had always been based upon response to God in faithfulness. This was all the more true in the eschatological age, such that confession of Jesus as Lord through faith in the resurrection will bring salvation (i.e., resurrection) to anyone who has faith. Paul cites Isa 28:16 in support of faith's confession.

There is no distinction to be drawn between Jew and gentile in this regard, for whoever calls upon the name of the Lord will be saved (Joel 2:32; Acts 2:31; Rom 10:13). Israel by and large is presently lost to the gospel, as Paul expresses his heart's sorrow (Rom 10:1). Faithfulness can come only on the basis of the proclamation of the gospel, by the preaching of Christ to all who will hear (Rom 10:14–17). Israel is lost, but where does the problem lie? Have they not heard? Indeed, Israel has heard (see Ps 19:4; Rom 10:18). Has Israel failed to understand; is it just a matter of comprehension? Paul replies by citing Deut 32:21 and Isa 65:1–2 (see Rom 10:19–20). The answers to the questions Paul posed were to be found in the Jewish scriptures themselves, for Isaiah reports God has been found by those who did not seek him (gentiles). On the other hand, Israel has proven to be a disobedient and obstinate people (Rom 10:20–21; cf. Isa 65:1–2), much to Paul's own anguish.

God is sovereign; Israel can be lost (Rom 9), Israel is lost, but it is lost by her own choice (Rom 10). Israel can be saved (Rom 11), because it is God's willful intention to show mercy to *all* (Rom 11:32). It is that final conclusion and realization that calls for worship and doxology on Paul's part (Rom 11:33–36; cf. Isa 40:13; Job 35:7; 41:11). Paul maintains that God has not given up on his covenant people, but Paul is mindful of Israel's scripture itself that testifies to Israel's recalcitrance (Rom 11:1–4). It is now as it has always been, there is a remnant characterized by grace. Grace, however, is unencumbered; it is not defined by human works (Rom 11:5–6), nor is it denied by human obstinacy. Nor is it bound by human theology or defined perspectives. As supported by Isaiah (Isa 29:10) and by "David" (Ps 69:22–23), Paul alludes to the current state of Israel, but he refuses to accept rejection of the gospel as the *permanent* state of Israel, his own people.

Paul can shift from second person ("you all, your") to first person ("we, our") or even third person ("as many as, these") and back again as appropriate. If, in the Spirit, you all put to death the practices of the body you will live. As many as are led by the Spirit prove they are children of God—children who cry "Abba!, Father!," adopted children who inherit with Christ, fellow-heirs who suffer together and who will be glorified together with him. We await our inheritance with expectant hope.

The Spirit intercedes with God's saints, as God works all things unto good for his children—known beforehand, marked out beforehand, called, justified, and glorified, conformed to the image of his Son. So, what shall we say? Who is against us? How will God not "grace" all things to us? Who will charge God's "called out" ones? It can't be God. Who will serve as a condemning, prosecuting attorney? Surely not Christ, the one who died, was raised, and intercedes in our behalf. Who will sever us from the love of Christ? Absolutely nothing, not Death nor anything else that may be imagined. Nothing, absolutely nothing, will sever *us* from the love of God in Christ Jesus our Lord.

Paul does not employ apologetic, for he does not have to defend the Gospel of God. Neither do we. While we may feel the need to protect our own dogma, we need not defend the Gospel of God. We only need to proclaim it. Overwhelmed by it, he can only proclaim it. Paul may again have offered a doxology of praise at the end of Rom 8 and may well have done so, if his heart had not been filled with so much sorrow for his own people (Rom 9:1–5). He cannot, however, express doxological praise until he has expressed his heart's deep sorrow (see Rom 9:5).

God's intention in the gospel, according to Paul, is to have mercy upon all (Rom 11:32). That is why Paul's heart can soar from depths of anguish to heights of ecstatic worship (Rom 11:25–26). While there may be divine mystery afoot (and there always is! See Rom 11:25–26), it is as Paul wrote in 1 Corinthians—the foolishness of God is wiser than the greatest wisdom of humankind, the weakness of God is more powerful than the greatest strength or ability of humankind (see 1 Cor 1:25). In Christ Jesus, all humankind finds its wisdom, rectification, sanctification, and redemption/deliverance (1 Cor 1:30). Paul alludes to Jer 9:23–24 LXX, which in itself is highly instructive. "Let the one who boasts understand and know that *I* am [ἐγώ εἰμι] the Lord who does mercy and renders judgment and righteousness/justice, upon the earth, because my will (is) found in these things, says the Lord." All the *more* reason to worship, in Christ.

Transformational Encouragement

It is on the basis of the mercies of God that Paul can make appeal for the Roman Christians (both Jew and gentile) to present themselves (lit., "bodies") to God in a sacrificial manner, as those living, holy, and pleasing to God, for that is their reasonable or logical service/worship (Rom 12:1). That is precisely the manner in which Christ offered himself to God (see Phil 2:5–11). Paul encourages the Roman Christians not to be conformed to this age, but rather to be transformed ("metamorphicized") by the renewal of the mind, such that they might discern the will of God. When this is accomplished, one finds that the will of God is good, pleasing/acceptable (same word as in Rom 12:1, εὐάρεστον) and complete (Rom 12:2).

It is generally recognized that Paul begins a new section of his letter in Rom 12, the "practical" section following the theological section. Paul rather builds precisely upon what he has just presented in Rom 9–11. In fact, if one excludes for a moment Paul's exclamation of worship (Rom 11:33–36). Paul's "therefore" connects directly with what he has just stated in Rom 11:32. The complete will of God is his mercy shown to all (Rom 12:2; 11:32). With themes similar to those in his Corinthian correspondence, Paul encourages a sober judgment of human wisdom and thought. He employs his "body" analogy not just to set forth varied functions in the church (Rom 12:4–8), but rather to stress unity in Christ and to stress the way the gospel should function in the living of Christians (Rom 12:9—13:10). "Thus, we the many are one body in Christ, the single body (being) a member of one another" (Rom 12:5).

In describing the encouraged behaviors of Christians, Paul offers encouragement in Christian living through the use of many adjectives and participles (verbal adjectives) rather than through the use of regular verbs. These are often translated into English as imperatives, such that we hear Paul saying "do this" or "do that." Paul's emphasis is more upon "*being those* who do this or that." There are only four regular imperative verbs in Rom 12:9–16—three in Rom 12:14 and one in Rom 12:16, for example. Paul's conception of the gospel informs the whole section, as illustrated by Rom 12:11–13—"in eagerness not (being) troublesome ones, (but being those) boiling over in the Spirit, serving in the Lord, rejoicing in hope, enduring in circumstances of affliction, being those devoted to prayer, contributing to the needs of the saints, rejoicing with the ones rejoicing, weeping with the ones weeping." Paul's use of participles rather than finite verbs gives a more unified and dynamic sense of Christian identity. The Gospel of God in Christ *is* dynamic and not static—something to be lived and not just "believed."

Even in this passage of encouragement, Paul acknowledges that the *lordship* of Christ, the present possession of the *Spirit*, the *hope* of final resurrection are what inform the way of living in the present season of time. Paul will return to those gospel themes (see Rom 15:13). Indeed, Paul concludes the entire section with the reminder of the eschatological hour or season, that salvation is nearer than the time when the Romans first came to faith. With metaphorical language, Paul asserts the night is far gone and the day has already drawn near. Thereby, he encourages Christians to conduct themselves in ways becoming of those who live in the light of day, as he encourages the Romans "to be clothed with" the Lord Jesus Christ (Rom 13:11–14).

Paul acknowledges that some may be weak in faith and he encourages those who are strong in faithfulness to bear with them. The Christian model is Christ, who did not act to please himself (Rom 15:3).

Gospel elements punctuate and inform Paul's behavioral injunctions. God is one of constancy or steadfastness—he does not go back on his promises (see Rom 3:26). Scripture offers encouragement of hope. We are with single voice to glorify the God and Father of our Lord Jesus Christ (Rom 15:4–6). Our behavior should *demonstrate welcome* in the light of the glory of God now manifested, for God has been true to his promises given to the patriarchs, such that both the Jews *and* the gentiles might glorify God for his mercy now shown in Christ. The gentiles now have hope (see Eph 2) in the God of hope. What God had promised in scripture—and Paul cites from all three divisions, the Torah (Deut 32:43), the Prophets (Isa 11:10), and the Writings (Ps 17:30; 117:1)—God has now brought to pass in Christ.

Paul is focused upon hope—the hope of resurrection, the final hope—from the God of hope who raised Jesus from the dead. Paul thus commends a benediction of joy and peace born of faithfulness (see Rom 1:16–17). Paul has come full circle. He even mentions again the "Gospel of God" directly (see Rom 1:1; 15:15). God's faithfulness should elicit our faithfulness, as one abounds in hope through the presence and power of the Spirit (Rom 15:13). Paul has worked for the God of his fathers "in Christ," such that the content of God's Gospel is the "gospel of Christ" (see Rom 15:17–19). As Paul cites from Isa 52:15, the referenced understanding on his part suggests the thought content of the theme of gentile inclusion and not just additional Pauline mission fields.

Romans is the last letter of Paul that we possess that was written prior to his final journey to Jerusalem. The letters that follow—Colossians, Philemon, Ephesians, Rom 16, and 2 Timothy—were written from a Roman imprisonment. Paul experienced incarceration in Jerusalem, Caesarea Maritima, and Rome that extended over a four- or five-year period, if Luke's presentation based on an underlying source is correct. We do not know what success, if any, Paul's Collection for the poor saints in Jerusalem enjoyed.

We do see, however, from Paul's final letters below that his spirit and faith in the gospel are undaunted. Paul remained a faithful proclaimer of the gospel, if Luke's account and final verse in Acts may be accepted (Acts 28:31). God had protected

Paul from death many times over (see 2 Cor 11:23–28); he would surely preserve him through death unto resurrection (2 Tim 4:6–8).

Colossians (60 CE)

There is a hope laid up in heaven (Col 1:5). The gospel represents the grace of God in truth (Col 1:6), for God has delivered us from the dominion of darkness to the kingdom of his beloved Son (Col 1:13). As a result of God's action in Christ, we have redemption, the forgiveness of sins (Col 1:14). In the face of a developing Colossian philosophical or theological heresy, Paul offers a Christ hymn (Col 1:15–20) that stresses the supremacy of Christ. All things were created through the Son (Col 1:16). Christ is pre-eminent, in whom the fullness of God dwells bodily (Col 1:19). Through him God has reconciled all things (Col 1:20). Christ is supreme, the hope of glory (resurrection), in whom one has full access to all wisdom and knowledge that leads to life.

Peace, in the sense of *shalom* or well-being, has been achieved through the blood of Jesus's cross (Col 1:20), surely a reference to the historical nature of Jesus's own death. One might go the next step to ask why. Paul's answer would be because the powers of death and enmity have been overcome and vanquished through the power of God in the resurrection. By Jesus's death, the prelude to eschatological victory, the Colossians have been reconciled (Col 1:22). Although the Gospel is a mystery that has been hidden for ages, it has now been made manifest (Col 1:26). As Paul writes to these gentile Christians, he exclaims that all the riches of divine mystery have been made known even to those who are gentile, namely, "Christ in all of you, the hope of glory" (Col 1:27).

One should savor the radical nature of Paul's affirmation, for it capsules his gospel. As even gentiles are to be found in Christ, Christ lives in them to bring to gentiles the hope of resurrection life. This mystery of God in Christ is that to which he has devoted his life since his call and commission to become an apostle to the gentiles (see Col 2:2). Because of the supremacy of Christ and the unfolding of hidden divine mystery, the Colossians are privy to all the treasures of wisdom and knowledge. Paul encourages them to live in Christ, such that they might become rooted, built up, and established in faith in Christ. Whatever the nature of the so-called Colossian heresy, they have no need for additional human philosophy that would amount to empty deceit and subjection again to the elemental spirits of the cosmos (the στοιχεῖα) once again.

The Colossians have already come to fullness of life in Christ (perfect tense, Col 2:10). The use of the Greek perfect tense (completed action, existing results) is certainly appropriate to describe the new status of *gentile* Christians. They have experienced a "circumcision" not made with hands (Col 2:11). Buried in baptism, they have been raised through faithfulness before the working of God, who raised Jesus from the dead (Col 2:12). Paul affirms that God has forgiven our trespasses and canceled whatever legal bond stood against us, nailing any such bond to the cross of Christ as a "paid in full" public notice to all the powers that placed Jesus there (Col 2:14).

There is no concern on the part of Paul to press his metaphor beyond the limit of his emphasis, such as to suggest divine payment to the devil or any such. Paul's metaphor simply stresses that the powers have no more claim. Even Death's claim has been nullified through the resurrection. It is simply public notice given of divine victory in the very place that appeared to be public defeat. In a reversal of images, a spectacle of shame has become a sign of divine triumph. God has disarmed the principalities and powers in Christ, making a public example or spectacle of them (Col 2:15).

One has died to the elemental spirits with Christ (Col 2:20), who, having been raised, is seated at the right hand of God (Col 3:1). Paul employs a customary metaphor of authority, that echoes the reality of lordship indicated elsewhere. It is sometimes suggested that the realized eschatology expressed in Colossians does not support Pauline authorship. For example, Col 3:3 asserts that the Colossians have died (aorist verb, single perspective summary) and their life has already "been hidden with Christ in God" (perfect verb, completed action, existing result). In reality, Paul simply expresses in different words what he asserts in Rom 6:1-11. The gospel is an accomplished fact. And again, the manner and content by which Paul expresses his thought is certainly appropriate to gentile Christians.

Paul continues to uphold the idea of the parousia, which in itself calls for right living (Col 3:4-6). There is a Christian imperative of living before Christ's return. The wrath of God is coming on account of the idolatrous desires and practices characteristic of the Present Evil Age, such that the Colossians are to put off the old nature and put on the new nature now being renewed in full knowledge in Christ (Col 3:5-11). They are to be reformed in the image of their Creator, who has now obliterated all customary human distinctions in Christ. Paul continues in an imperative and personal mode to define for the Colossians what Christ dwelling in them and they in Christ means (Col 3:12—4:6).

Ephesians (60 CE)

Following his usual greeting of grace and peace from God the Father and the Lord Jesus Christ, Paul writes of God's glorious grace freely bestowed in the Beloved One (Eph 1:1-8). Redemption and forgiveness of trespasses is accorded on the basis of the richness or wealth of God's grace. Paul acknowledges that God has made known the mystery of his will, namely, his plan for the fullness of time set forth in Christ to unite all things in him. As we know from elsewhere, there is not only a unification in salvation of Jew and gentile, there is also a unification in terms of judgment and subjection (Eph 1:19-23).

IMAGINE PAUL

In Praise of God's Glory

Paul knew the church in Ephesus quite well, for it had been his headquarters during his Collection Campaign. The church in Ephesus would have been a mixed church of Jews and gentiles. The benefits of God's Gospel are for both Jew and gentile, although Paul appears to be basically addressing gentile Christians (Eph 2:1–22). God is the Father of Glory, the God of our Lord Jesus Christ, who gives wisdom and revelation in knowledge of him (Eph 1:17). God's might is centered in his power to raise Jesus from the dead (Eph 1:19–20) and to exalt him. Christ is the fullness of God (Eph 1:23).

At a time when we were dead through our trespasses, God being rich in mercy and love made us alive together with Christ (Eph 2:5). The perfect tense verbs that Paul employs have prompted some to suggest alternative authorship, but surely Paul speaks metaphorically in the light of his own personal imprisonment in Rome and his warm regard for the Ephesian church. All humankind was under God's wrath, being given up for *self*-destruction. Paul apparently alludes to his own earlier visionary experience (see 2 Cor 12:1–5). Paul again is focused upon God's wealth of graciousness in Christ. Humanity has no boast before God, but rather has been saved by faithfulness to God on the basis of his graciousness (Eph 2:1–10).

Paul directly addresses gentile Christians, who at one time were strangers to the covenants of promise, alienated from Israel (God's covenant, servant people), and separated from Christ. They were those who lived without hope. God has now broken down the dividing wall of hostility between human beings (Jews and gentiles) and between human beings and God, such that all now have equal access to God the Father through the Spirit. Gentiles are now members of the household of God (Eph 2:19) in an echo of his thought in Galatians that identifies gentiles as children of God who inherit (see Gal 3:25—4:7). Paul also echoes his thought of Christians as the temple of God, as he suggested in Corinthians (see 1 Cor 3:16–17; 6:19–20).

The mystery of God's revelation in Christ has been made known through the Spirit (Eph 3:5), namely, that the gentiles are fellow heirs, members of the same body, and fellow partakers of the promise now realized in the gospel through Christ (Eph 3:6). That *is* the mystery of Paul's gospel in a nutshell. Paul proclaimed a reality lived out in the church at Ephesus, the headquarters of Paul during his Collection Campaign—a church with which he was very familiar.

Paul was called to be a proclaimer of this hidden mystery—the gospel now revealed by God's grace and worked by God's power to raise even the dead. The manifold wisdom of God has been demonstrated through the church to all rulers and authorities in the heavenly regions because God's own eternal purpose has now been realized in Christ Jesus our Lord, through whom both Jew and gentile have access to God and bold confidence through his faithfulness (Eph 3:8–12).

As Paul contemplates the mystery of God's glory revealed in the gospel, he is moved to worship (Eph 3:14–21). He wants the Ephesians to be thoroughly rooted in Christ, that they may fully comprehend the glorious Gospel of God in Christ. Empowered by the Spirit of God and grounded in the love of Christ, the Ephesians have knowledge beyond all human wisdom. Paul wants these gentile Christians in Christ to be filled with all the fullness of God. Just as Christ was the "fullness" of God (Eph 1:23, πλήρωμα), so now those in Christ are to be filled with the πλήρωμα of God (Eph 3:19). Paul is prompted to respond with a full doxology: "To the One who is able to do more abundantly above all things that we may ask or think according to (his) working power within us, to Him be glory in the church and in Christ Jesus unto all generations of the age of the ages, Amen" (Eph 3:20–21).

Paul's thought in Ephesians is sublime and focused on the glory of God in Christ, although one should not forget that he is imprisoned as he writes (Eph 4:1). Paul encourages the Ephesians to be faithful to their calling by exhibiting a single Spirit of unity. What he writes concerning the nature of the gospel is perhaps best comprehended by presenting the items and personages mentioned in reverse order (see Eph 4:3–6). There is *one God and Father* (above all, through all, in all; see 1 Cor 15:28) of us all (Jew and gentile), *one baptism* (unto Christ), *one faith* (like unto the faithfulness of Christ), *one Lord* (now risen and exalted), *one hope* (resurrection and divine rule), *one Spirit* (communicative power), *one body* (many members, but one in Christ). It may be significant or coincidental that Paul gives a series of seven persons or things, in view of the fact the number seven was considered the number of completeness.

With a Measure of Grace

To each one, grace was given according to the measure of Christ's gifts. Paul employs Ps 68:19 to support his thought. With beautiful, picturesque imagery, Paul suggests that Christ by his exaltation led captivity itself captive. God gained victory even over the captivity of Death when he raised Jesus from the dead and exalted him. Apparent defeat was transformed into divine victory. The one who died by the hand of the powers has now ascended to the realm of God, leading those same powers captive in his victory procession, that he might fulfill all things (Eph 4:8–10). Paul's second point is that he gave gifts to men. Christ himself established prophets, evangelists, pastors, and teachers for the purpose of equipping the saints for the work of ministry in building up the body of Christ (the church) until all should attain to the unity of faithfulness and full knowledge of the Son of God unto mature personhood, unto a measure of the stature of the fullness of Christ (Eph 4:11–13).

Speaking the truth with love, he encourages the Ephesians (hortatory subjunctive, "let us") to grow in all ways unto Christ, who is the head of the body (Eph 4:14–16). Paul encourages maturity in Christ, such that they may no longer be spiritual infants blown around by every doctrinal teaching or the crafty deceitfulness of men. The church must, however, build itself up in love.

IMAGINE PAUL

The Ephesians are no longer to live as gentiles with darkened minds, alienated from the life of God because of a hard-hearted ignorance. They are to put off the old nature and put on the new nature, the one that has been created by God in true righteousness and holiness (Eph 4:22–29). They have been sealed unto the day of redemption in/by the holy Spirit; they are to live as those who have been graced in Christ (Eph 4:30–31). They are beloved children of God who are to be imitators of God the Father. All are fellow heirs in Christ, members together in the same body of Christ, unified in service, and building up one another in love.

They are to conduct themselves in love, just as Christ loved us and gave himself in our behalf (ὑπὲρ ἡμῶν) as a fragrant offering and sacrifice to God (Eph 5:1–2). In other words, the Ephesians are to live in obedient conduct before God the Father after the manner of Christ, for the wrath of God is coming upon the children of disobedience (Eph 5:3–20). Paul encourages them to live in right and transformed relationships (Eph 5:21—6:9), as they are empowered by the Lord and the might of his strength (Eph 6:10).

Paul encourages the Ephesians to be clothed with the whole armor of God, for we do not contend with human foes but with rulers and authorities, with world power brokers of present darkness, with spiritual hosts of evil in the heavenly places. Because of these things or entities, the Ephesians are to be clothed with the "panoply" of God, such that they will be able to stand in the evil day after working against all of these forces (Eph 6:10–13). Paul once again mentions the "mystery of the Gospel," in behalf of which he is an ambassador or presbyter now in chains (Eph 6:19–20). Paul commends peace and faithful love from God the Father and the Lord Jesus Christ. He commends grace to all who love our Lord Jesus Christ with that which is imperishable (Eph 6:23–24). Paul has come full circle in terms of his emphasis upon the Gospel of God in Christ (see Eph 1:1–23).

Romans 16 (60 CE)

Most of Rom 16 consists of greetings to Christians and associates known to Paul in Ephesus, not in Rome, in the judgment of the present writer.[2] Paul does indicate that the God of peace will soon crush Satan under their feet (Rom 16:20). He mentions the mystery having been kept secret for long ages of time that has now been revealed in Paul's gospel and the preaching of Jesus Christ, having been made known to all the nations (gentiles) unto an obedience of faith according to the command of the eternal God. Satan is defeated, as all people are included within the eschatological people of God. The Gospel of God has had full effect, as the parousia and Telos is awaited. In the interim, as Paul has encouraged the Ephesians, Christians are to be clothed with the whole panoply or armor of God. And, Paul must break out in a final doxology

---

2. Full supportive argumentation is given in the author's earlier work, *The Ministry of Paul the Apostle: History and Redaction*.

(Rom 16:25–27). Some consider this final doxology is not original to Paul, while others think that Rom 16 as a whole is integral to Rom 1–15.

Second Timothy (60 CE)

The "promise of life in Christ Jesus" surely refers to the resurrection (2 Tim 1:1). God's purpose and grace has been given in Christ Jesus, who has been manifested in the present time through the appearance of our Savior Christ Jesus, who on the one hand abolished death and on the other hand brought to light life and incorruption through the gospel. Paul was appointed a preacher and teacher, such that he is undergoing suffering. Paul, however, is not ashamed, for he remains faithful and stands persuaded that God is able to guard what had been entrusted to him unto "that day" (2 Tim 1:11–12).

While much of 2 Timothy is personal, Paul encourages Timothy to remember Jesus Christ, the one risen from the dead, of the seed of David, according to Paul's gospel. Paul is bound like a common criminal, but the word of God remains unfettered (2 Tim 2:8–10). The word is sure and faithful—if we have died with him, indeed we shall live with him; if we endure, we shall reign with him (2 Tim 2:11–13, a possible hymn). Paul still lives with an eschatological viewpoint (2 Tim 3:1; 4:1). Christ will judge the living and the dead. He and his kingdom will come. Timothy is to remain faithful and fulfill his ministry (2 Tim 4:2–5).

Paul himself is near the point of martyrdom (2 Tim 4:6–8). He looks for a *victor's* crown of righteousness and not a diadem (στέφανος, not διάδημα, a "royal" crown); his race is nearly finished (2 Tim 4:8). In words reminiscent of the Model Prayer (2 Tim 4:18; cf. Matt 6:13), he has all confidence that the Lord will rescue him from every evil and will save him for his heavenly kingdom. Even in the midst of his final suffering, he must break out in doxology—"To whom (be) glory unto the ages of the ages, Amen" (2 Tim 4:18). He ends his letter with a grace wish extended to the entire church (2 Tim 4:22).

Given its personal nature and brevity, there is nothing in the letter to Philemon that contributes to the definition of the gospel, although perhaps one point can be made. What Christ has done for us, Paul offers to do for Onesimus. He provides an example of sacrifice and love for fellow believers. First Timothy and Titus are deemed to be non-Pauline by the present writer.

Conclusion

The presentation in this chapter has been descriptive, drawn from Paul's own letters written over about a twelve-year period of time to his several church communities. Explanatory comment has also been included where needed or appropriate. What Paul has to say in the course of his occasional correspondence sets forth the nature and definition of the gospel as Paul understood it. The concern in the chapter has not been to develop Paul's "theology" or to offer any doctrinal apologetic in defense or advancement of any particular theological viewpoint, even though some comment has been made as deemed appropriate.

Theological definition of doctrines may appropriately belong to subsequent chapters in terms of their relevant development. The present question is, in the light of what Paul actually wrote, how *did* he understand the nature and content of the Gospel of God in the light of its foundational parameters? The topic of the present chapter may thus be addressed in terms of persons, entities, and issues.

Experiencing Gospel

If one is to re-imagine the Gospel of God in Paul's thought, then one must lay aside at least for the time being the issues that plagued later Christian history and even the critiques of modern scholarship. One must do one's best to hear Paul on his own terms. One must imagine Paul's gospel in the light of what Paul actually wrote within the context of his lengthy ministry. One must view Paul's gospel in terms of its whole, before one begins to dissect and explain the parts.

The mystery of God's Gospel and the fulfillment of God's promises have been manifested in Christ. That which has been hidden now stands revealed. That which had been long promised now stands fulfilled. Old distinctions have passed away and are obsolete. Dividing walls have been broken down. Powers that have enslaved have themselves been conquered, led in subjection as unwilling participants in God's victory procession in Christ. The darkness of the Present Evil Age has been penetrated by the rays of light of the Age to Come that have now dawned in the event of Christ's resurrection and exaltation, totally overcoming the darkness of the cross.

The entire Christ event becomes a mini-narrative of the Gospel of God that is part of a larger story understood both foundationally and eschatologically. First Corinthians 15:20–28 and Phil 2:5–11 are very instructive here. God's drama in the Gospel involves incarnation, the faithfulness of Jesus, the resurrection of Jesus from the dead, and the exaltation of the risen Jesus as both Lord and Christ. Contrary to common theology, the cross of Jesus is not the culmination of the divine Gospel but rather an interruption of God's Gospel event. God quickly overcame the action of Sin and evil that perpetrated the worst that Sin can do, namely, to give one over to Death. God raised Jesus from Death and exalted him as Lord and Christ. It was not a "rescue" from Death, but rather a demonstrated victory *over* Death and all evil powers that had put Jesus to death. It resulted in a victory procession that is portrayed as leading vanquished powers captive.

God was not a co-conspirator in Jesus's death because he needed a "perfect sacrifice," but rather he was the one who acted by his very Gospel to overcome the worst that evil has ever done. He effected victory over Death, the worst enemy of humankind and creation since the time of the first Adam. God's victory over Death in Christ, the last Adam, represented the beginning of God's new creation in the Gospel. It is the vanguard of God's redemption of his entire creation. It is the redemption of humankind in reconciliation.

To come to understand this is to *experience* grace. No longer a topic for theological discussion among the doctrine-makers, it becomes rather the living experience of God's Gospel that establishes Life itself. And, having experienced God's grace as opposed to man's "doctrines of grace," one lives with a sense of well-being or peace under the continuing lordship of Jesus Christ. Even though there be a "cross" for the believer, as there was for Jesus, as there was for Paul, it is that which leads to life and life eternal, as suggested by both the teaching of Jesus himself and that of Paul. The gift of the presence of God (Spirit) heralds both the "first fruit" of a bountiful harvest of those who love God, as well as the "guarantee" of the fulfillment of faith. God is both right and the one who is able to make right or rectify those who have the reality of the faithfulness of Jesus manifest in their living. The narrative of God's Gospel is profound yet simple; it is profound yet sure. Christ living in us is the hope of glory, i.e., life lived eternally unto the glory of God.

One begins to "imagine" the gospel of Paul by setting aside one's preconceived notions about Paul (e.g., Paul was arrogant, Paul didn't like women) and "knowledge" of Paul based upon theological hearsay distilled from historical accretions (e.g., original guilt, predestination). On the one hand, it is a very simple task to sit down and read what Paul actually said. Through actually reading Paul, even in English translation, one may not only see what he said, but one may begin to develop an awareness of some things he did not say. On the other hand, it is difficult to hear Paul's gospel because of the clutter of our own cultural setting and the theological static of developed theological doctrines that surround us on every hand at every level. We often fear the loss of giving up "what we already know," in the face of experiencing what is new. Personal enrichment, however, only comes through new experiences and the exercise of imagination.

When one discovers Paul, instead of what one has heard about Paul, the beauty of the Pauline gospel radiates the glory of God in Christ afresh. Perhaps the needed task is not just to "imagine," for we already "imagine" Paul in one way or another. Perhaps the task is to "re-imagine" the gospel that Paul proclaimed in the light of alternative gospels that are partial or incomplete, inaccurate or misleading, even mischaracterized or false. Paul's own faith in what God had done in Christ is found in the gospel he proclaimed. To "imagine" Paul's gospel by actually reading what he wrote may be to "re-imagine" Paul and his theology, as well. The latter task involves a more detailed exegetical or analytical approach, while the present endeavor of imagining Paul's gospel has involved a more descriptive task.

From his very earliest letters sent to the Thessalonians, Paul is focused upon the resurrection in the light of the parousia. He is focused upon the nature of God as loving Father and the person of Christ as living Lord exalted by God. The prior two sentences deserve to be read again before one proceeds. The gospel comes as a result of the grace of God and brings a sense of well-being, peace or *shalom*. The rule or kingdom of God surely comes and it will come with both judgment (self-exclusion) and gentile inclusion. Paul portrays Jesus's parousia and the coming of God's rule with a brevity of apocalyptic description or imagery which he does not develop. Such imagery does, however, betray his Jewish orientation and awareness of the Old Testament conception of the "Day of the Lord" interpreted "in Christ." This is something Paul himself awaits and thus must "imagine."

Paul focuses upon the Gospel of God in terms of the basic kerygma, which had been in development for twenty years or more since the time of the execution and resurrection of Jesus. Paul acknowledges that his own people, the Jews, killed the Lord Jesus even as they had the prophets before him. He acknowledges Jewish opposition to the inclusion of gentiles as a part of Israel—opposition that incurs a final wrath because it is opposed to God's Gospel (see 1 Thess 2:14–16). There are now multiple *churches*, even in Judea.

Paul identifies God as Father, the one who raised Jesus from the dead, and Jesus as Lord. Jesus's resurrection, of course, even by definition, had to be preceded by Jesus's death. It should be noted, however, that Paul makes no direct mention of the cross in his earliest letters (2 Thessalonians, 1 Thessalonians, Galatians) or even in Romans. He does speak of being "crucified with Christ" (Gal 2:20; Rom 6:6). He describes Jesus as the one who gave himself. The emphasis is upon faithfulness and obedience born of reconciled relationship wrought by the grace of God's deliverance from a pervasive age of evil. Paul does speak of the cross of Christ in Gal 6:14 as the rubric under which Paul himself has been crucified to the world. The usage is that of a deliverance metaphor of freedom from the Present Evil Age.

In Galatians, Paul is forced to deal with the issue of Jewish Law in the light of severe opposition from the Nomistic Evangelists. For those conservative Jewish Christians, gentile inclusion in Israel and rectification with God had to be on the basis of embracement of Torah, for that defined the covenant of God's graciousness that defined Israel. For Paul, rectification and inclusion was simply on the basis of faithfulness, even as had been the case with Abraham. Paul had discovered that while the Law was holy and just and good (Rom 7:12), it was obsolete and ineffective at the point of establishing righteousness or effecting rectification with God (see Gal 3; Rom 7). *We may not have yet learned how obsolete and ineffective our own dogmatic theology is in establishing righteousness or effecting rectification with God.*

It is not the Law that defines inclusion or exclusion, but rather faithfulness in Christ that defines who are Abraham's offspring (Gal 3:23–29). If God is true to his promises in the eschatological age, rectification and reconciliation come as a result of deliverance from slavery to elemental spirits/forces/powers (τὰ στοιχεῖα) and our adoption as children of God (Gal 4:1–7). Through the Spirit, all are able to cry, "Abba!

Father!" The hope of such adoption and righteousness based upon faithfulness is the resurrection, our inheritance in Christ.

Christians lack in no necessary spiritual gift as they await the parousia and consequent resurrection, which is the hope of righteousness (Gal 5:4, 25; 1 Cor 1:7–9). God is faithful in the fellowship of Christ through the Spirit. Paul speaks of "heaven" in Eph 2:5–7, although much like John in Revelation, he must describe visions of heaven that are currently unrealized.

Paul, along with the early Christian kerygma, proclaimed "Christ crucified" (1 Cor 1:23–25), which was the *historical* fact but also a stumbling block of utter foolishness. It should never be forgotten, however, that Paul knew Christ crucified *and* Christ raised. For Paul, the gospel was a cause for celebration (1 Cor 5:8), as God's revelation of divine mystery in Christ, in the light of the resurrection.

It is Tertullian (d. 220 CE) who provides the impetus toward the development of "the Trinity." Paul does not have a metaphysical doctrine of the Trinity with a capital *T* as later introduced into Christian thought in subsequent centuries. His theology was monotheistic in keeping with his Judaism ("Hear, O Israel, the Lord our God is One"), while his descriptive language is functional. He never offers a "Trinitarian" salutation in any of his letters and clearly presents Jesus as Lord and Christ who is exalted by God and who is subservient to the Father (see 1 Cor 15:28). He has a subordinationist Christology. God the Father works through Christ and communicates through his Spirit. For Paul, it is not "God in Three Persons, Blessed Trinity." It is Tertullian in the third century that provides impetus toward that formulation. Rather for Paul, it is "God the Father and two personal agencies, Blessed Unity." While the word "agency" sounds somewhat impersonal, in reality it is quite personal. The characterization simply reflects the functionality of the underlying Greek text (see John 1:1–4, as well).

The "agent" in any sentence is the entity that performs the action of the verb. Sometimes the "agent" is also the grammatical subject of the verb, sometimes not. Sometimes the grammatical subject works through another agent, perceived as "direct," "indirect," or "impersonal." Greek has a particular manner of expressing each kind of agency, which is often theologically significant. In John 1:3, for example, it is implied that God created "through" the Logos [indirect agency]. In Rom 1:21, the righteousness of God has already been manifested "by" [direct agency] the Law and the prophets. Without becoming more technical, it simply should be said that English translation does not always make the distinction clear. However, the concept of agency does become important in understanding Paul.

The limitations of our human language to describe the ultimate reality of God, as well as our accumulated dogma originally addressed to problems of earlier ages occurring after the time of Paul, are what create our present problems of understanding. Paul was a Second Temple Jew schooled in the Old Testament scriptures, not a metaphysical and ontological thinker attuned to a later day of third- and fourth-century church debates in a Hellenistic environment. Paul sought to celebrate the deliverance of the Gospel of God in Christ. That Gospel was an announcement of God's faithfulness that called for faithful response through the power of God's indwelling Spirit. Christ is the "first fruit" of the Gospel of God for Paul, while the gift of the Spirit is the guarantee of the fulfilling of that same Gospel of God for all.

The Gospel revealed the powers of evil for what they are. Their evil has been undone by God's resurrection of Christ. The power of Death itself has been swallowed up in divine victory. God is the God of mercies who has made the mystery of his good news announcement (Gospel) known in the Christ event. He has brought deliverance, redemption, reconciliation, comfort, help, encouragement, and peace through his gracious action in Christ.

The *content* and *promise* of the Gospel of God is found in Rom 8:11—"the Spirit of the One who raised Christ from the dead will also make alive your mortal bodies through his indwelling Spirit in all of you." The *hope* of the Gospel is seen in Col 1:27, "Christ in you, the hope of glory." The *means* of the Gospel is to be seen in Gal 5:25, "Since we are alive by the Spirit, let us walk in step with the Spirit." The *challenge* of the Gospel is seen in Phil 2:12, as we are to continually work out our salvation with fear and trembling, "for God is the one working in you all both to will and to work according to his good pleasure." The *result* of the Gospel is the experience of grace and peace from the God of peace, such that "the peace of God, which passes all understanding will guard your hearts and your minds in Christ Jesus" (Phil 4:7; cf. 4:9).

Re-Imagining Gratitude

As one is called upon to imagine or re-imagine the Gospel of God in Paul's thought, we have a tendency to speak of the "gospel of Christ." In Paul's thought it is God's Gospel that is wrought in Christ, the one who is the content of the Gospel. If, indeed, Paul introduces us to the Gospel of God, then everything depends upon the nature of the God of the Gospel. For Paul the emphasis is not upon sin and guilt and punishment, but rather, the emphasis is upon grace, love, joy, and gladness inherent in deliverance.

In the foregoing presentation, one may have noticed a comparative absence or a greatly diminished frequency of usual theological terminology that most often accompanies attention given to Paul. It is not that theology itself has been absent, for Paul's own theology underpins his gospel. At the same time, however, his gospel informs his theology. It is "gospel" that has been the focus of this chapter. In summarizing Paul's gospel, the concern is more broad. Finer points, which are subject to debate, are what address Paul's theology. Some of these finer points will be addressed in the following chapter.

Paul understood *God* as the Father of grace, mercy, and love, who is faithful and right. God is the one who acts to redeem his fallen creation and to create a new people of Israel in Christ. The *Gospel* itself is thus about grace and reconciliation, enacted through God's power and sovereignty. While rejection of "good news" brings its own self-judgment and ultimately self-destructive idolatry, Paul acknowledges but does not focus upon the conception of judgment. He is too overcome with doxology in the worship of God for his action in Christ to give undue attention to "bad news."

Without minimizing other Christological identity, *Christ* is God's faithful agent, obedient and faithful even to the point of death, whom God raised from the dead and exalted as both Lord and Christ. Death had come through a man, and now through a man has come resurrection from the dead (see 1 Cor 15:21). Christ shall rule as God's regent until the Telos (time of fulfillment), subduing all enemies, until he returns the kingdom to God the Father (see 1 Cor 15:24–28). *Salvation* itself represents the operative righteousness of God. There is freedom and deliverance from all alien powers. There is the hope of future resurrection.

What matters now is the actual faithfulness and honoring of God. There is peace *with* God, as one enjoys the peace *of* God. Christ in one now is the hope of glory later. God communicates and guides through the *Spirit*. The Spirit of God aids us in our weakness and intercedes in our behalf, even when we do not know how to pray. The Spirit is the intercessor because God knows the "mind of the Spirit" (it is his Spirit) and he searches the "hearts of men," who are his creation (see Rom 8:26–27). There is no place in the kingdom of God for the "works of the flesh." Now in the present, one is to keep pace with the Spirit in one's living, as one bears fruit unto God (see Gal 5:16–25).

Everything associated with the Gospel is dependent upon the nature of the God of the Gospel. The human *problem*, wrought by both weakness and by deliberate will, was that of alienation, idolatry, and enslavement. The *problem* was that of a creation that had become corrupt and subservient to powers such as Sin and Death. It was not God who had a problem that had to be overcome, but rather it was creation itself and humankind that stood in need of rectification. The *need* was thus reconciliation to the Creator and a renewed commitment to the single God of Israel. God's *solution* was the Gospel of God in Christ, a Gospel of grace and peace.

And, that Gospel yet involves *promise*. Paul metaphorically reminds the Romans that in view of the "hour," it is time to awake from sleep. The day is at hand. The works of darkness need to be cast off in favor of the armor of light. One needs to "put on" the Lord Jesus Christ (see Rom 13:11–14). God is "for us" (ὑπὲρ ἡμῶν). He relinquished his Son, who died and was raised, for us (ὑπὲρ ἡμῶν). Nothing can sever us from the love of Christ (see Rom 8:31–37). But even more than that, Paul is persuaded that "neither Death nor Life nor angels nor rulers nor things present nor coming things nor powers nor height nor depth nor any other 'creation thing' will be able to sever us from the *love of God* in Christ Jesus our Lord" (Rom 8:38–39, emphasis added). We are now children of God in Christ, God's own adopted children who inherit all that God has to give.

Ephesians 2:1–10 points to human plight and divine solution. *Philippians 2:5–11* offers a narrative of gospel realities in verse. *Colossians 1:26–27* celebrates the hope of glory through a now-revealed mystery. *First Corinthians 15:20–28* celebrates final divine victory and God's rule through Christ. *Romans 5:1–5* encourages the enjoyment of the peace we now have with God that transforms sufferings and infuses the hope of sharing the glory of God. *Romans 5:6–11* affirms kerygmatically God's Gospel of reconciliation in Christ. One might try reading these passages from Paul in the order given and meditating upon Paul's thought, for in one way or another they offer significant building blocks for the re-imagination of the actual nature of Paul's gospel in Christ. They offer at least a week's worth of scriptural reading and enough meditation food for life.

And all of this prompts Paul to worship. "*O the depth of wealth and wisdom and knowledge of God; his judgments are far beyond human scrutiny understanding and his ways are far beyond human understanding. 'For who has known the mind of the Lord? Or who has become his advisor?' 'Or who has given a gift to him, or who will repay him?' For all things are from him and through him and unto him; to him be glory unto the ages, Amen*" (Rom 11:33–36).

Paul's gospel began with a new revelation of the risen Christ given to him directly by God (Gal 1:11–17). Paul had to re-imagine everything, including his own life and the nature of his own religion. Paul's gospel concludes with worship (2 Tim 4:18), even though he is imprisoned and facing death. We should take note, for the Gospel of God is truly good news by which life is sustained. First and foremost, the only proper response to the Gospel of God is the gratitude of worship, not the dogma of humanly formulated theology of the doctrine-makers.

Having now examined the Gospel of God in the light of what Paul actually wrote in his letters, one may now be in position to consider Paul's theology, but to consider it from a mode of worship. Now, re-imagine Paul's theology—not just as rationalized doctrines, but as relational worship.

7

Now, Re-Imagine the Theology of Paul

MOST TREATMENTS OF PAUL'S theology offer systematic definitions and developments, replete with points and sub-points. Some may offer a rather shallow and arbitrary summary of a few elements in defense of dogmatics. By contrast, others may offer a rather detailed, historically developmental and exegetical treatment of manifold elements. However, the author has done that elsewhere, largely either as a prelude or follow-up for the current work.[1] While the author has developed a more thorough exegetical treatment of Paul's theology elsewhere, the present work offers a more expositional approach based upon Paul's gospel structures and themes. Paul has been appreciated, abused, misunderstood, and in our day ignored. One joins either an ongoing conversation or a silence when one writes or reads about Paul.

It is time, however, to re-imagine Paul's theology on the basis of his letters in the light of the gospel he proclaimed. It is time to cut the theological "Gordian Knot" of tangled theological opinions and pay attention to Paul's theological gospel evidenced in his letters. It is time to recover the dynamism inherent in Paul's theology. The topic, again, calls for an extended treatment.

The title of the present chapter is "Now, Re-Imagine the Theology of Paul." The former chapter treated the gospel of Paul. The distinction should not be lost. Theologians often spend time dicing and dissecting Paul's theology, organizing it into a systematic outline of topics, while at the same time missing Paul's gospel. The order of gospel—theology is thus important. Paul was an evangelist who had a theology, but who proclaimed a gospel. The distinction is significant. Consequently, Paul often expressed his theology in doxological worship. Thus, it seems better to imagine Paul's theology in the light of his gospel, rather than lose Paul's gospel in a sea of theological terminology systematically defined and delineated. The former may become a dynamic enterprise teeming with life, while the latter may become static and lifeless.

It is not possible to develop the whole of Paul's theology in an exhaustive sense in a book such as the current work. The author has sought to do that elsewhere. It is possible to imagine and present the basic structures and salient themes that appear to constitute the gospel that Paul proclaimed and was called upon to defend. While Paul manifests foundational convictions imported from Judaism, Paul entertained other

1. The author's other works are listed in the bibliography.

convictions born of his encounter with the risen Christ. Paul's Christian theology matured as he came to appreciate more fully the import of the death of Jesus in terms of the resurrection and resultant lordship of the risen Christ. Faith in the resurrection is certainly an essential part of his gospel, even as it was for other early Christians.

Introductory Considerations

Paul's identity as a Pharisaic Jew before he encountered the risen Christ is one of the most significant factors that determined the manner in which he lived, what he believed, and how he understood the world in which he lived. His religion, theology, and worldview were all altered by his encounter of the Gospel of God in the risen Christ. He did not forsake his Judaism with its set of core convictions, but rather he came to understand that the time for the fulfillment of Israel's covenant promises had dawned. All of the covenant promises that God had made to Israel—to Abraham, Moses, David, and others—had now been fulfilled in Christ.

Paul's gospel came as an announcement made to him by God through a direct revelation of the risen Christ. Paul's gospel, and hence, his theology was "evangelical" in the most true and biblical sense of the word. He was not a systematic theologian seeking to propose a rational system defined by high-sounding theological words and debated in the halls of apologetics and polemics. His was a theology of "good news" to be lived, born of God's revelation in Christ.

An "Epistolic" Theology

The word "epistolic" belongs to the author. One might find "epistle" and "epistolary" in the dictionary, but not the word "epistolic." By creating the word, the author simply means that which is based upon or drawn from Paul's own letters. Paul's personal background matrix and cultural context certainly become important. However, the later theological barnacles that became attached to the Pauline wood are largely irrelevant to the present task.

Paul was not privy to the later debates and affirmations of church history, even though much so-called "Christian" theology lays claim to a theological basis supposedly found in Paul. How Paul has been understood may be important for us to comprehend how we got to where we are, theologically speaking. Very often, however, the historical foreground only reveals the attached barnacles for what they are. On the other hand, Paul's own background matrix and that of the earliest Christians in his churches largely determine both what he wrote and why he wrote what he did.

Paul's gospel as he proclaimed it has already been treated in the prior chapter on a letter by letter or church by church basis. There is a sense in which Paul's theology available to us can only be the sum of what he wrote in his letters. We can never be privy to Paul's entire theology any more than we are privy to the entire thought of any other *living* person. We are only privy to what Paul writes in his extant letters as that may be ordered and reconstructed. Paul's theology is "epistolic," that is, what he wrote in his extant letters, but even then, there are assumptions. Issues such as the order and unity of the letters, as well as which letters attributed to Paul were actually written by him, are frequently raised. Beyond what he actually wrote, which always requires interpretation, we can only discern his non-epistolic (to create another word) theology on the basis of projected trajectories one may imagine from his epistles.

There is a *foundational core* inherent to Paul's gospel, even as there was for other first-century Christians. It marks the basic gospel that was preached, the "exceedingly good news announcement" (εὐαγγέλιον) to which the term *kerygma* might be applied. Paul's salutations in both Romans and Galatians, for example, contain elements of foundational theology that Paul proclaimed in terms of gospel. In addition to a core theology that is universally foundational, Paul responds to particular church needs with theological applications and clarifications that are *situationally contingent*.

Whether *core* or *contingent* theology, the only theology of Paul to which we are privy to is Paul's *literary* theology expressed in his letters. Paul's personal theology, as is true for anyone, was more extensive than his expressed theology. In fact, much of Paul's contingent theology would have remained unexpressed had it not been for the conflicts or particular church needs that called it forth. This highlights once again the importance and integral relation of the contours of his ministry and his theology.

Paul had a theology, but he proclaimed gospel. Paul's theology does not first of all consist of theological theory systematized (all of the big *-tion* and *-logy* words). While one may hear a lot about things like *justification* and *sanctification*, *eschatology* and *ecclesiology*, Paul himself was a pastoral evangelist and not a systematic theologian. Paul had a gospel to proclaim, not a theology to define and itemize. While Paul announced God's good news in Christ, he also had to address problems of theological understanding or moral behavior that arose in specific church contexts. Paul's letters represent occasional correspondence written to specific churches at specific points in time to address specific problems or issues. Paul announced the gospel; response to that gospel called for faith. In a word, simplified, Paul's theology is an announcement of "this is what God has done" (which scholars term "the indicative") and "this is how one should live in response to that Gospel" (which scholars term "the imperative").

Paul did not leave a legacy of a singular, grand, comprehensive statement of the gospel he proclaimed. We are not privy to his entire teaching nor to his entire theology. Paul carried out an oral ministry extending over a quarter of a century. Paul does not give us a comparative chart of his theology as a Pharisee as that might be compared with his theology as an apostle of Christ. He did leave a legacy of isolated letters that, taken together, may offer a framework of essential elements of his gospel. Paul's "gospel" is more than conceptual ideas or abstract beliefs or systematic doctrines. Essentially, we see Paul's own lived experience in vignetted snapshots, as well as the spirituality he sought to nurture and inculcate in the churches he founded or with which he had contact. We have no "videos" or "DVDs" to watch. The Christ event brought to Paul a change of life marked by deep spirituality and worship of the living God who had acted in Christ.

While scholars debate the authorship of Paul's supposed letters, the present writer entertains a broad Pauline canon for reasons argued elsewhere. As has been seen, the author accepts both Colossians and Ephesians as Pauline. Colossians and Ephesians were written from Rome in 60 CE within a year of Paul's martyrdom. They exhibit some overlapping themes, although Colossians must deal with the "Colossian heresy" that had been brought to Paul's attention. Remarkably, following four long years of imprisonment after the delivery of Paul's Jerusalem Collection, Paul's spirit soars high in his theological characterization of the gospel. After a quarter of a century of the proclamation of the Gospel of God in Roman provincial cities around the *Mare Nostrum*, Paul can celebrate the Gospel he has served that now carries him, as it always had since the beginning of his call. The challenges of his calling now become crystallized in both affirmation and final hope.

Ephesians represents the distillation of the Gospel toward which Pauline themes lead. Working backward, what is stated in Ephesians suggests the conclusional point toward which Pauline trajectories lead. In the writer's judgment, Ephesians represents the maturity of Paul's thought near the end of his life. It stands as one of a pair of theological bookends surrounding Paul's final years—Romans written in 56 CE, Ephesians in 60 CE. Of all of Paul's letters, these two epistles reveal the heart and soul of the Pauline gospel, comparatively devoid of personal polemic and apologetic. It is within Ephesians that Paul encourages his beloved Ephesian brothers and sisters in Christ to become *imitators of God*, as beloved children (Eph 5:1). It is also in Ephesians, whether Pauline or a trajectory based upon Paul's gospel, that Paul stresses unity or oneness: one God and Father of us all, one baptism, one faith, one Lord, one hope, one Spirit, one body (see Eph 4:4–5).

The overall approach taken in this book is to re-imagine the theology of Paul that centers upon Paul's gospel conception of "oneness" in God and "unity" in Christ. That theme governed Paul's theological thought from the time of his call, through the time of his Collection Campaign ministry, even to the end of his life. This "oneness" is reflected in the theological outline of the present chapter.

A Jewish Apostle

Paul was an apocalyptic Jewish Pharisee. The Pharisees had a broad canon of scripture and a deep love for scripture. Paul's Christian theology developed out of interpretations of Israel's sacred texts, notably expressed in the Greek of the Septuagint (LXX). As a Pharisee, Paul would have been immersed in the scriptures of Israel, as evidenced by his quotations, allusions, and appropriations of biblical themes and examples. He was steeped in the Old Testament stories and language of scripture.

What we term the "Old Testament" was the "Bible" of the earliest church; the "New Testament" had not yet been written. Altogether, Paul quotes from some sixteen Old Testament books. Biblical imagery and echoes of scriptural themes permeate his letters. He experienced a direct revelation of God that brought a sense of the beginning of the time of apocalyptic realization and revitalization of the whole creation.

Paul's encounter demanded a total reorientation of his life and gave him a distinct sense of mission. The content of Paul's commission, as he understood it, was to continue the mission that God had begun in Jesus. The reality of the resurrection had confirmed the messianic identity of Jesus. The reality of the Messiah confirmed the time of eschatological fulfillment. The new Age to Come had been set in motion, with the resurrection of Jesus and the advent of the Spirit as the "first fruit" of future harvest. Again, Paul demonstrates an apocalyptic perspective. Could the parousia of Christ, the resurrection of Christians, and the finality of God's ultimate rule in the Telos be far behind? The Lord Jesus would conquer all powers and forces of evil, including Death itself, that last enemy, before turning all kingdom rule over to God the Father.

As one begins to think about this Jewish apostle's theology, one certainly thinks of the foundational belief expressed in Jewish worship, the Shema. "Hear, O Israel: YHWH is our God, YHWH alone; and you shall love YHWH your God with all your heart, and with all your soul, and with all your might" (Deut 6:4–5). In the midst of a polytheistic environment, Israel proclaimed allegiance to the single God of the covenant (see Exod 20:1–3). Paul believed in the singularity of the Jewish God, before whom there was no other.

Paul's theology is, as is his gospel, profoundly and thoroughly Jewish. Paul's theology concerns the God of Abraham, Isaac, and Jacob. It is this God who spoke through Moses and the prophets. It is this same God who has now acted to fulfil his long-standing promises. And, in terms of Paul's gospel, it is this God who has now enabled his people to inherit their covenant blessings through the coming of Jesus, the Messiah. Paul was a Jew throughout his life, although we might characterize him as a Christian, a Jewish Christian, or a Christian Jew. The word "Christian" is anachronistic for Paul's life time. Paul was called to a movement known as the "Way" in the book of Acts. Paul certainly found his way "in Christ."

While Paul's theology is marked by foundational convictions represented in Paul's underlying Judaism, his theology as a Christian evangelist and pastor is also conditioned by the contingent situations in which he found himself with reference to each of his very different churches and his conflicts with opponents, notably the Nomistic Evangelists who dogged his steps during his crucial Collection Campaign that followed the Jerusalem Conference in the spring of 52 CE. Many of Paul's most significant letters were written in the course of this campaign, such that the Collection runs like a "red thread" through the "Pillar Epistles" of Galatians, 1 Corinthians, 2 Corinthians, and Romans that enables their firm ordering in the period 54–56 CE.

By the categories and standards of his day, Paul lived and died a Jew. His foundational identity determined how he understood the world (worldview), how he lived (religion), and what he believed (theology). The convictions he inherited and the convictions he sharpened through his Jewish Pharisaism even marked his expression of the gospel he proclaimed. Paul experienced a radical, transforming call by God (Gal 1; cf. Acts 9) that marked a confirmation, transformation, and even denial of earlier convictions. Yet Paul remained a Jew, now a Jew "in Christ."

A History of Interpretation

The theologians of the Christian church have for virtually all the centuries of Christian history looked to Paul in order to formulate a system of Christian theology. That is not to say that the remainder of Christian Scriptures (both the Old Testament and the New Testament) do not contribute greatly to theological understanding. It is to affirm that Paul's thought expressed in his letters is central, that, historically speaking, his understanding of God and the gospel stands at the very heart of Christian belief. That is very remarkable for a first-century Jewish Pharisee called by God to proclaim the Gospel of God to the gentile world, who left behind but a handful of occasional letters addressed to small house churches he founded or established. Paul did not leave behind an extended and systematic treatise of carefully developed theological topics according to some logical ordering. In short, not even the influential letter to the Romans offers a systematic theology of Paul.

Some have suggested Paul created a theological system from the simple religion of Jesus. The legitimacy of such an enterprise may be questioned, in view of the fact that Paul's letters are occasional and situationally specific. To reiterate, there is no "systematic theology" found in any of Paul's writings, not even in his letter to the Romans. While the division in this book between "the theology of Paul" and "the gospel of Paul" may seem to be somewhat artificial to some, it affords a viable rubric to treat a complex subject of Paul's rather strong Jewish theology expressed in God's Gospel "in Christ." This chapter combined with the former chapter offers understanding of how Paul's basic religious viewpoint becomes interpreted in the light of his call and his interpretation of events regarding Jesus of Nazareth.

Paul believed that in the Christ event involving the life-death-resurrection-exaltation of Jesus, the Jewish God had taken steps to put the world right again. God had re-established life, by overcoming the forces of evil (including the power of Sin); God had inaugurated a new age in Christ. This became Paul's "gospel," his announcement of good news, his proclamation of what God had done. There is a sense in which this chapter treats underlying structural realities of Paul's theological mind-set, whereas the previous chapter sets forth the specific nature of Paul's gospel in living address to churches, constructed on the underlying foundation of Paul's structural theological realities.

For example, Paul certainly emphasizes gospel in the Galatian epistle. Our knowledge of both Paul and his theology would be impoverished if we did not have the Galatian letter. Situationally speaking, for Paul, things were serious in Galatia at a very delicate time. The very gospel of Christ was being called into question through the insistence upon an alternative "gospel," not that such an alternation actually existed (see Gal 1:6–7). For Paul, the only gospel that existed depended upon what God has done in Christ and upon one's faith in that action that operates by love (Gal 5:6).

God's Gospel brought freedom, whereas that of the Nomistic Evangelists brought renewed slavery based upon ritual commitment to Torah. In Paul's view, one has been severed from Christ and has fallen away from grace, should one look to justification based upon ritual requirement of Torah (see Gal 5:4). To fall away from Grace is to fall again under Law, the agent of Sin, the harbinger of Death in Paul's view. The Nomistic Evangelists threatened Paul's gospel and person, the very faith of the Galatian Christians, and the Collection plans of Paul to seek to unify a church divided over the Jew-gentile controversy of what was necessary to be "really" Christian.

Not all that Paul believed or thought is to be found in his occasional letters, even though one may detect and even assume principles and guidelines pertaining to his theological mind-set. That mind-set was formed by his matrix within Judaism, although it was altered by his experience "in Christ." His theology is foundational within Judaism; that theology becomes interpreted in the light of the gospel "in Christ." Hence, this chapter is devoted to Paul's theology—the underlying, major theological conceptions that inform his understanding of the gospel "in Christ."

While Paul would not have used the label "theologian" to describe himself, Paul left a more extensive record of his theological understanding in the form of the letters that he wrote than any of his early Christian contemporaries. While we may treat them as a repository of his theological perspectives, it needs to be remembered that Paul's letters are occasional correspondence written to different specific church or personal situations at specific points in time to address particular issues pertaining to a specific situation. Thereby, none of Paul's letters are totally "neutral" theological treatises meant to record Paul's "last theological will and testament" in any neat, comprehensive manner. Each one of the letters has a distinct underlying purpose. Again, Paul himself offered no systematic summary of his own beliefs for theology's sake.

Consequently, *any* contemporary treatment of theological topics offered represents an abstracting of Paul's theology by a modern interpreter drawn from the existing evidence of the letters of Paul. This fact gives rise to the many and varied interpretations of Paul, as scholars discuss major and important areas of Paul's thought. As an old Jewish proverb suggests, we do not see the world as it is but we see it as we are. This is true for the study of Paul, not only for the average student of Paul in the modern world, but for the most accomplished scholar as well. We do not see Paul as he was, but as we are. What Paul wrote continues to call forth ongoing debate as to what is central and what is tertiary, what is culture-bound and what has continuing relevance. To one degree or another, everyone must imagine Paul.

Some interpreters abstract a systematic theology from Paul, while others question whether an overall Pauline theology can be written. Was Paul always consistent or not? Did his theology change over the ten- to twelve-year period (48–60 CE) that his existent letters represent or did it not? In this regard, the letters do not even cover the entire period of Paul's ministry from his call to his death (34–61 CE)—a period of ministry that approximated twenty-seven years. Did Paul's theology develop and change over that time from that of a Jewish Pharisee to that of a Jesus-follower (or Christian)? If so, how so? What kind of Jew was Paul before his call? What kind of Christian did Paul become? Why did this former Pharisee, now believer in Christ, have such conflicts with fellow Jews and even fellow Christians? Paul was complex and so were his letters. So was his overall and underlying theology. So might be the reader's own theology.

One Story

Judaism in Paul's day was not a religion of legalistic works-righteousness as often supposed; it was rather a covenantal religion called into being by the one true God. The keeping of Torah was the Jewish response to God's gift of covenant initiative. Covenant was basic to Judaism as well as to Paul's beliefs. Election naturally leads to covenant. The covenant between God and Israel was an act of divine grace. God was faithful; Israel was called to faithfulness.

A Theological Narrative

According to Scripture (LXX), the one God elected a people through whom to extend his blessings to all the peoples of the earth. The family of Abraham was destined to be God's representative to the world. In the call of Abraham, himself a "gentile" at the time, God promised Abraham that if he would leave his home and family and follow him, God would give him a land and many descendants, and that through Abraham's family all the peoples of the world would be blessed (Gen 12:1–3). Abraham followed and YHWH was with him (Gen 12:4a). While modern politics have created various crises in what is now termed the "Middle East," the biblical account speaks of Abraham's descendants as God's servant people occupying a strategic body of land as a light to the nations.

Election of Abraham and his descendants was an act of God's grace. The covenant established through Moses in the event of the exodus and the giving of the Torah was an act of God's grace. Prior to the Christ-event, people became members of the elect community through birth (i.e., through a Jewish mother). Those not born a Jew could embrace Judaism through conversion (including circumcision, if male). One remained in Judaism by following the Torah given through Moses, which provided the supreme and complete guide for covenant living.

Paul the Pharisee followed the Torah, shall we say, "religiously." He belonged to the Pharisaic party that sought to extend religious purity according to Torah to every area of life. The Pharisees not only followed the written Torah, but they also developed the "oral torah" in seeking application to every contingent situation of living. Long after Paul's day, this "oral torah" was later incorporated into a work known as the Mishnah that, along with further interpretation, became the Talmud.

There is perhaps overlap between the conception of election and covenant, but there are also distinguishing difference. The word "election" involves choice—God chose the family of Abraham to be a servant people. The family line of Abraham-Isaac-Jacob is established solely on the basis of God's grace and not upon any usual human action or standards. The lines of Abraham-Ishmael or Isaac-Esau were not established, for example. Election involved divine choice beyond any customary human standard or achievement and consequently the omission of customary cultural standards, such as the succession of the first-born son.

Covenant, on the other hand, involves stipulated relationship. In the case of God's covenant with Israel, it is again an act of God's grace. It is not something "negotiated" between God and his servant people. The covenant that God set before Abraham was "unconditional," in the sense that God called Abraham to faithfulness without defined stipulations or termination clauses. The covenant that God established through Moses was a covenant that came with "conditions." If the people were faithful, God would bless them. If they became unfaithful, God would discipline or seek to correct them even through severe measures. Israel's theological narrative involves both election and covenant-making.

Paul was not interested in a timeless, abstract, a-historical system of salvation. For Paul, the Gospel of God was not a set of propositions to be understood in systematic fashion and predicated toward individual salvation adopted by affirmation. Rather, the Gospel was an announcement of divine activity. It was the announcement of God's definitive but benevolent intervention into human history and the entire cosmos to set things right. It was the announcement of God's action of intervention into the history of Israel to bring the promises made to Abraham to full fruition. For Paul, Abraham becomes the model of the kind of faith that leads to righteousness (see Rom 4:1–25; Gal 3:6–9). Although Paul will develop a "First Adam-Last Adam" typology comparison (see Rom 5:12–21), Abraham in his own way through his faithfulness becomes the very antithesis of Adam's disobedience in Israel's story.

The Gospel of God marked the action of God toward transformation in Christ; it was the good news of redemption, not the announcement of final judgment. It was re-creation and not destruction. It was a call to faith and not to fear. The gospel is a corporate narrative about God on many levels, beginning with a world gone wrong and cosmic powers, extending to community redemption within the body of Christ.

The death of Christ is an inclusive event—it embraces all in its inclusive, universal significance. Sin and Death came to all through Adam; now Grace and Righteousness and Life come to all through Christ.

Paul's gospel was not first of all about an individual invitation to eternal life at the point of individual death based upon a personal and confessional "I do." Rather, Paul's gospel was a call to new life in this world under the lordship of a new Lord and in the company of many companions of faith. Many presentations of the gospel today are at best misunderstandings and at worst perversions of what Paul proclaimed. Paul did not preach an individual "health and wealth" gospel of something for nothing. Rather, his gospel proclaimed a cross on both sides of the resurrection—Jesus's cross and ours.

Corruption and Subjection

However, in spite of God's graciousness, Israel had become sinful, had broken covenant, and had become deeply compromised. The cardinal points of Jewish theology in Paul's day were monotheism, election, covenant, and eschatology. These were nourished by both Torah and the prophets. The latter, in particular, emphasized in one way or another the future fulfillment of election and covenant by the one true God of Israel, such that eschatology became increasingly significant in its various forms, including an apocalyptic emphasis. Zeal and observance of Torah could hasten the time of fulfillment.

Paul the Pharisee, like many other Jews of his day, wanted God to act and to redeem Israel. Paul was zealous for both Israel's God and for Torah; he had a zeal for the realization of the kingdom of God, for it was the keeping of Torah that would vindicate Israel. It was Israel's faithfulness to covenant that would vindicate the people in the time of God's greatest lawsuit. In the "Day of the LORD," God would find favor in his people and thus rescue them, while pagan nations that held Israel hostage would be condemned. Evil doers—gentiles and renegade Jews—would be judged and punished appropriately.

The hope of Israel was sustained through the Jewish scriptures. The latter half of Isaiah (Isa 40–66), often referred to as "Second" or "Deutero" Isaiah, celebrates the creative and redemptive activity of Israel's singular God, Yahweh. The latter half of Isaiah is focused upon God's redemption of his people from foreign bondage. Multiple copies of the prophet Isaiah were found among the Dead Sea Scrolls at Qumran, indicating its significance for at least one apocalyptic Jewish community located at the northern end of the Dead Sea during the time of Jesus and Paul.

While Deutero-Isaiah looked to the fulfillment of freedom from a Babylonian exile, in Paul's day it was not apparent that the predictions of prophets had been permanently fulfilled. The Jews found themselves under a Roman overlord, the Roman Empire, in which Caesar was proclaimed as divine lord. The prosperity, national forgiveness, comfort, and peace envisioned earlier by Isaiah (Isa 40–55) as promised in "scripture" had never come to full realization.

In the day Jesus was born, Jews were looking for the "consolation of Israel," variously described (see Luke 2:25, 38; 23:51; 24:19–21). The years of the first century marked a rising period of tension between the Jews and the Romans, especially in the light of client Herodian rulers and the presence of Roman prefects and procurators. These tensions culminated in the Jewish-Roman War (66–70 CE) and the destruction of Jerusalem and its great temple (70 CE). Jewish hopes were high in Paul's day and were pinned to an apocalyptic view that God was suddenly going to act and to redeem his covenant people from both foreign and celestial powers that held them captive.

Jesus earlier had seized upon the political tensions of the day by proclaiming the nearness of the kingdom of God and the need for a different mind-set (repentance; see Mark 1:15). Luke portrays Jesus not as a political revolutionary of violence but as an apocalyptic prophet of healing (see Luke 4:17–22a). Luke omits Isa 61:2b that speaks of God's vengeance. According to Luke, Jesus's words are gracious and mark the fulfillment of scripture, although overall Jesus and his message were not well-received. Over-familiarity with his person coupled with the implied inclusion of impure gentiles doomed his message in his own hometown (Luke 4:22–30). The inclusion of gentiles and the basis of inclusion became a central if not *the* central issue in the early church, as reflected in both Acts (Acts 10:1—11:18; 15:1–21) and Paul's letters (e.g., Galatians). Paul, of course, emphasized faith as the key in the eschatological age, such that in Christ old boundary markers were no more (see Gal 3:27–29): there was no difference between Jew and gentile, slave and free, male and female in Christ.

Principalities and Powers

Worldviews are to be found at a foundational level, such that some scholars suggest that the center of Paul's thought is the underlying narrative story of Israel. Paul's arguments, discourses, and exhortations emerge from God's saving actions in the world. The accounting of Israel's religion is to be found in the Pentateuch, in stories associated with the exodus and establishment of the covenant, as well as in the exile, recognition of which is found in the prophets and the Psalms. The concept of "revelation" is basic to both the Old Testament religion of Israel and the fulfillment of Israel's promise in Christ.

As Paul came to understand eschatological fulfillment of Israel's story, he believed that God had inaugurated the New Age in the life-death-resurrection of Jesus that promised victory over Sin and all forces of evil. The Gospel of God in Christ is essentially a retelling of a very Jewish story, one that is now reconstructed around Jesus. It marks the climax of Israel's unfinished story. The grand story may involve many subplots and elements that Paul understood to merge together in Christ, according to those who embrace this view as central. Paul's gospel also looked beyond the story of Israel to the entire cosmos.

Paul's "theology" is very much attuned to the story of Israel in terms of divine creation and relationship, reflected in the archetypal stories in the Pentateuch (Genesis–Deuteronomy). One should not presume that those stories were not revised in the light of Israel's later history and eschatological fulfillment. The one creator God (Gen 1–2) fashioned all that is, as Israel's later prophets (Isa 45–46) or the psalmist insisted (Ps 104). The psalmist celebrated the many great deeds God had also done on behalf of his covenant people whom he had called into being (Ps 105). However, coupled with God's great deeds is the confession of sin and call for help (Ps 106), as well as hope for deliverance.

Paul's hope as a Pharisee was one with that of his own people, namely, that the one God of Israel would fulfil all of his promises made to his covenant people. That hope for fulfillment could be described with a modern theological term *eschatology*, based upon the Greek word ἔσχατος, which suggests a meaning of "last" or "final." It is often misunderstood as "last things" in terms of the end of the world. Paul did not think in terms of the "end of the world," but in terms of final fulfillment, i.e., a final age in which all evils would be overcome and God would rule over all. The eschatological age would not be the end of all things, but rather an everlasting age of all things good under the rule of God. This is reflected in later Christian apocalyptic, such as the book of Revelation, where a "new heaven" and a "new earth" are depicted. A "new Jerusalem" *comes down* from heaven (see Rev 21).

A particular type of eschatology is known as *apocalyptic*, a word which suggests a "revealing" or an "unveiling" (Greek, ἀποκαλύπτω). All apocalyptic is eschatological, although not all eschatology has to be of the apocalyptic type. Apocalyptic literature as a genre is marked by the use of great symbolism, of which the most familiar may be the book of Revelation. It tends to be persecution literature or at the least to reflect a time of deprivation and frustration. A movement known as "apocalypticism" entered into Jewish thought through prophetic voices that announced the ultimate victory of God and his people over all forms of evil. There were many Jewish apocalyptic works abounding in Paul's day.

Apocalyptic tends to focus on the radical and sudden in-break of God into history to enact his victory and "make things right." Apocalyptic writers within Judaism believed in a historical scheme of what is termed "the Two Ages,"—a conception that has previously been introduced. It is now appropriate to discuss this further. The Present Evil Age was a fallen age under various powers, while the Age to Come was a more glorious age when God would restore or make all things right. From an apocalyptic perspective, help must come from God above, for the forces of evil and the demonic are too great an adversary for human beings themselves to conquer alone.

Within apocalyptic Judaism, the Age to Come would succeed the current Present Evil Age. The Present Evil Age would be destroyed and the new creation of the Age to Come would dawn and come to fruition. The Age to Come would be characterized by Righteousness, Grace, Life, and Spirit. That it would come "some day" was the belief within Judaism. Paul *the Pharisee* had an apocalyptic worldview that expected God to act—some day.

Jesus's proclamation of the kingdom of God was an apocalyptic message (see Mark 1:15; 15:3–37). Jesus himself apparently embraced this Two Ages concept as he proclaimed the kingdom of God as his dominant theme. He came proclaiming the Gospel of God in terms of present fulfillment: "The appointed time stands fulfilled [perfect tense verb], indeed the rule of God has drawn near [perfect tense verb]," such that one should come to a different mind-set and express faith in the Gospel (see Mark 1:14–15). Again, perfect tense verbs in Greek express action that has already occurred, but the effect of which continues with existing result or impact. The appointed time has at last *already* dawned and will have its impact. The rule of God—long expected with hope at some point in the future—has indeed *already* become reality, such that one must respond with a new mind-set and with faithfulness. The hope of time has become now. Paul and other early Christians came to realize that the Gospel of God who rules included the story of Jesus himself, including his execution on a Roman cross and especially including his resurrection and exaltation by God (see Phil 2:9–11; 1 Cor 15:3–4; Rom 1:1–4).

Paul, like apocalypticists within Judaism, believed in such a two-age schema. The current age was subject to powers of evil, such that it was seen as the "Present Evil Age." It was an age characterized by things like Sin, Law, Death, and Flesh—powers and domains personified. Sin was a power that worked through the agency of the Law to bring about death. Death itself, like Sin, was a tyrant that held humanity in its unflinching grasp. The weakness of our humanity "in flesh" led to "Flesh" being Sin's host. Paul describes Death itself as the last enemy to be destroyed (1 Cor 15:54–56), as he offers thanksgiving unto God for the victory over the powers and weaknesses of human existence that he has provided through our Lord Jesus Christ (1 Cor 15:57).

For Paul, "sin" was an inborn tendency of humankind learned from living in a fallen world as descendants of Adam—a tendency that ultimately led to idolatry of creation and self-idolatry (Rom 1:20–23). Sin marked an inward weakness, by which predisposition toward evil could be exploited. However, as has been suggested, it also marked a power over human beings—a force that could invade and take control of human life. Paul personifies "sin" (especially in Romans), such that it could be spelled with a capital S, thus Sin, as evidenced in this work. For Paul, Sin was a power that held sway in what could be termed "the Present Evil Age." Sin was the culprit. It was Sin that brought about sins (Rom 7:7–25). In Rom 6:23, for example, Paul does not say the "wages of *sins*" is death (as is customarily assumed), but rather the "wages of *Sin*" is death.

Although Paul embraces and expresses an apocalyptic worldview, he was not an "apocalypticist" as was John, the author of the book of Revelation. To understand Paul's theology, however, one must comprehend the "Two Ages" that Paul held in common with apocalyptic Judaism. Once one becomes sensitive to the concept and its characterizations, it becomes readily apparent. Each of the Two Ages has particular characteristics, such that in the present writer's judgment Paul cannot be understood apart from his conception of the Two Ages. One begins to notice how the conceptions that characterize each age are juxtaposed or cluster together (see Rom 6; 1 Cor 15:56). In Paul's letters, the Present Evil Age is characterized by Sin, Law, Death, and Flesh, all of which may be personified. Cruel powers of the Present Evil Age exercised a stronghold dominion over humankind (see Gal 1:4; Eph 5:16; 6:12).

The Age to Come is characterized by Righteousness, Grace, Life, and Spirit, all of which may be personified. The power of Sin, Death, Flesh, and the Law represented one dominion of the Old Age opposed to the dominion of the New Age inherent in the power of God, his Grace, Christ, and the Holy Spirit. As one may see, the Age to Come is a polar opposite to the Present Evil Age. For the rabbis, the Two Ages were held in separation, for the Age to Come had not yet dawned. The two sets of powers stand in separate polar opposition, as they influence the entire cosmos and the human race. For Paul the Pharisee, now called by God in Christ, the Age to Come had been inaugurated and now overlapped the Present Evil Age, an Age that would soon disappear because its powers had been defeated.

Paul the Christian understood that God had already acted in Christ to usher in the new age, the Age to Come. No longer was it in the distance; it had already broken in, as evidenced by the resurrection and the gift of the Spirit. By overcoming the very worst that Sin (personified) could do, namely, bring about Jesus's death on a Roman cross, such that Death won again, Paul understood the resurrection to be the harbinger of the in-break of the New Age. The spiritual forces of the Present Evil Age had lost what seemed to be an ageless war and were on the run, even though the last battle had not yet been fought. God had won a tremendous victory in Christ. Because the remnant of the Present Evil Age had not totally disappeared, there was overlap between the Two Ages that called for those in Christ to continue to battle, but now equipped with the full armor of God (Eph 6:10–20).

The still present, but defeated, Present Evil Age was understood to be ruled by powerful forces that were contrary to the will of God. Paul can give attention to elemental spirits and powers of evil that threaten humanity and the entire creation. He even personifies the power of Sin and Death, as has been seen. Sin is not just a list of transgressions; rather it is a power and a domain. People live unto Death in the domain of Sin. In Christ there is freedom for new life.

In Paul's perspective, if the turning point had already occurred with Christ's resurrection, the fulfillment in the parousia and "Telos" could not be far behind. Paul expected the completion of the turning point of the ages to occur suddenly at some point with a great reversal, at which point all evil would be totally overcome by the victory

God had already wrought. Righteousness, life, and peace would follow. Paul visioned a change in power structure and thought, both in the world and in the cosmos.

For Paul the "Two Ages" concept experienced a rebirth of imagery in the most unexpected ways. No longer was the Age to Come a future event, but it had already dawned. Not only was it now proleptically present, but it explicitly had come about through the Christ event. Many Jews, including the Pharisaic Paul, would not have viewed Jesus as the Messiah. By all appearances according to Paul's pre-Christian Pharisaic theology, Jesus's death on a cross involved the curse of God (see Gal 3:13; Deut 21:23). His death on a Roman cross also suggested that he was a false messiah. How could the true Messiah of Israel be killed by the Romans, Israel's enemy? Jesus died in subordinate public shame on a human cross; he was not killed by a Roman arrow in a battle for freedom against the Romans. How could the real Messiah even be cursed by the Torah? By contrast, the resurrection of Jesus by God in a sense represented the public shaming of Sin and Death. Resurrection of Jesus by God and Paul's experience with the resurrected Christ convinced Paul of God's new reality, God's Gospel, God's New Age, now present through the restoration of God's Spirit (see Gal 1:12, 15–16; 1 Cor 15:8).

Paul's understanding of the Two Ages in his *pre-Christian* perspective could be understood in terms of two successive but separate circles. Within Judaism, the advent of the Age to Come belonged to an unknown future time. But now, proleptically, in Christ, the "Age to Come" had been inaugurated and could be experienced in the present. Thus, in Paul's *Christian* perspective, the Two Ages could be understood in terms of two overlapping circles that actually created a third age. This third age is termed the "Age of Transformation" by the present writer (see Fig. 33 and Fig. 34).

The Present Evil Age (1) had been eclipsed but it had not yet totally passed away; the Age to Come (2) had already dawned. There is thus an overlapping of the Two Ages (1 and 2), such that the new, intervening, overlapping age is the Age of Transformation (3). The early sermons presented in Acts make clear who is responsible for Jesus's death and who is responsible for Jesus's resurrection (see Acts 2:23–24; 4:10–11; 10:39–40). Jesus's death on the cross was effected by evil powers, domestic and celestial, and is representative of the Present Evil Age (1). Jesus's resurrection by God is representative of God's New Age that has dawned and is now present in an interim Age of Transformation (3). The proof for Paul rested in the appearances of the *risen Christ* and in the *gift of the Spirit* to those in Christ. Christians now lived in the overlap of the Age of Transformation (3) that was steadily eclipsing the old, Present Evil Age (1). The interim age itself would soon be eclipsed by the Telos, the fulfillment of the Age to Come (2). This may be illustrated in the following two figures below.

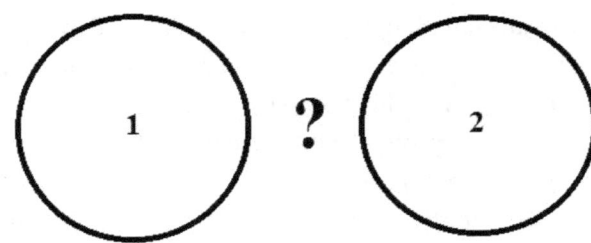

Fig. 33. Jewish Concept of the Two Ages.

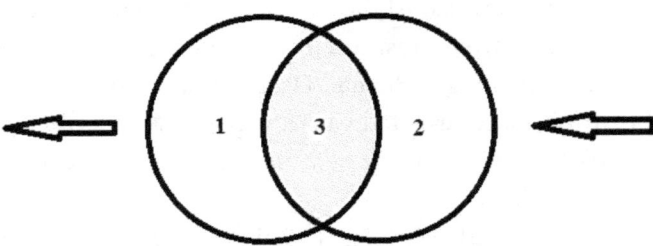

Fig. 34. Paul's Concept of the Three Ages. Conception by G. Roger Greene.

Thus, for Paul the Christian, one should imagine a dynamic overlap, with present life being lived in the Age of Transformation (3). The overlapping of the ages created a tension between the "already" and the "not yet." Those in Christ, sealed with the Spirit, live out of the Gospel of God in the present Age of Transformation as more than conquers, as "super-conquerors" (see Rom 8:37). Already united with Christ in both suffering and in victory, already sealed by the Spirit as the guarantee of future inheritance, already forgiven of sins and delivered from Sin, Christians must yet do battle in the power of the Spirit with Sin and Death which nevertheless remain active as wounded adversaries. Those "in Christ" now do so, however, equipped with the full power of God's Spirit present, with the full armor of God (see Eph 6:10–20). Believers continue to live in the time between the resurrection and the expected return (the parousia) of Lord Christ, who at the Telos will achieve total victory and will rightfully return all rule to God the Father (1 Cor 15:28).

The Present Evil Age is passing away and will be totally eclipsed. The Age to Come has already dawned—God's victory has been won in resurrection—and it comes on apace. The Age to Come will continue to eclipse the Present Evil Age until the time when the advent of the Age to Come will stand as the sole reality at God's Telos.

Paul proclaimed the Gospel of God as that which delivered one from the slavery of powers that killed. Paul came to understand that the striving after works could not save. The Law itself was ineffective in this regard—it could define, but under the power of Sin it could not save. By extension, one could say that Paul came to understand that religion itself could not save, a lesson the Nomistic Evangelists had not yet learned. Religion will always be negatively or positively defined in terms of law or rules, as works of conformity, as a call to orthodoxy or orthopraxy. Paul came to understand that we had been set free in Christ for freedom's sake (Gal 5:1), that one might live in faithfulness before God even as was true of Abraham. As one seeks to live in faithfulness, one will always remain on a road or way characterized by God's grace.

Problems are still to be faced in the New Age, for the forces of evil even in retreat are still active and aggressive in the remnant of the Old Age. In the present writer's judgment, to underscore a point, one cannot really understand Paul without an appreciation of the Two Ages conceptualization, however one chooses to understand that in modern terms. According to Paul's schema, we now continue to live in a third age, the Age of Transformation.

Paul's proclamation of the Gospel of God was an apocalyptic message. God had done something quite unexpected in the Christ event. The great event of the fulfillment of the ages that Paul along with many others had expected to come some day had now already come in Christ. The good news was here—God had raised Jesus from the dead as his Son and Messiah and had installed him as Lord over all forces of evil, both terrestrial and celestial. The eschatological age had begun in ways Paul had never expected. And, if one believed in that Gospel, the earliest Christians (Paul included) had to come to grips with and explain the event of the cross.

The word "cross" came to be used metaphorically. It does not, however, mean that Jesus's death on the cross was willed by God as is commonly touted. If Jesus indeed were the Messiah of God, Jesus's cross needed to be explained. How could one who was truly the Messiah be killed by Israel's enemies? That only happened to "false messiahs." Perhaps the best analogy for understanding Jesus's death on the cross is Jesus's own parable or allegory of the Wicked Tenants (see Mark 12:1–12 par.). The vineyard owner and father in Jesus's parable sent neither his servants nor his son to be killed, but rather to claim what was rightfully his. Certainly, the father and vineyard owner would have understood the risk of sending his son after he servants had been shamefully treated and killed, a point Jesus himself would certainly have understood. In terms of the Gospel of God, apparent defeat was to be seen in a *Roman* cross but the victory of God was to be seen in the resurrection. For Paul, the "cross" was far more or other than just a perfect sacrifice for sin required by God. It is far more than that. One should meditate on Jesus's own parabolic words.

Paul perceives the cross metaphorically beyond the literal event. It becomes primarily a cross imperative for him and for those who are in Christ. It stands as an all-inclusive cosmic event in the context of a cosmos that is understood to have a dualistic structure of evil over against God's good. The dominion of powers hostile to God has been conquered, their reign overcome and their dominion stripped. The dominion of the risen Christ is now in effect. Paul's patterns of thought include the thought of Christ as the Last Adam, and that of dying and rising with Christ.

As Paul imagined the Gospel, he developed a vision not only of the salvation of the individual, but more particularly a vision of the renewal and restoration of the entire cosmos. The concept of "life" is central to Paul's understanding of the gospel in terms of the new age that had dawned with Christ's resurrection.

The Jewish scriptures and apocalypticism left indelible marks upon Paul's theological structures and themes. Although not a Pauline word in terms of frequency, Paul in essence was called upon to "repent" from a more parochial mind-set to a more universal mind-set in Christ. The basic idea in "repentance" is the concept of coming to a different mind-set that leads to a change of lifestyle in terms of behavior or application. Paul "repented" of his rather strict Pharisaism based firmly upon Torah, in order to embrace an inclusive stance of faithfulness to God akin to that represented in the call and covenant that God established with Abraham long centuries before the Law (Torah) was given through Moses. God had initiated fulfillment in Christ that marked the demise of the Present Evil Age and that ushered in the advent of the rule of God in the Age to Come. The new state of affairs marked the redemption of creation and the inclusion of the gentiles into the people of God and Israel on the basis of faithfulness, just like Abraham who was himself a gentile and forefather of both Jews and gentiles. The new "life" offered by God was available to all, both Jew and gentile. It involved the total creation. It was all inclusive.

One God of Israel

Paul's chosen form of greeting in all of his letters is "grace to you all and peace from God our Father and the Lord Jesus Christ," of which Gal 1:3 is but an example. Paul's salutations are actually our first introduction to Paul's overall theology. The gospel itself is constituted by the extended "grace" of God as its originating reality, whereas "peace" is the intentional result. Grace is that which is freely given and peace is holistic well-being, akin to the Hebrew *shalom*. Neither is compelled; both are profoundly refreshing. God is identified further with the familial term "Father," rather than a designation of "King" or "Judge" or the like. Jesus is affirmed in his identity as "Lord" and "Christ" (the Greek equivalent of the Hebrew "Messiah"). Neither identity could be affirmed apart from the reality of Jesus's resurrection by God. One who remained dead by Roman crucifixion would not be proclaimed as "Lord" and would appear to be only a false Jewish Messiah. Crucifixion was not a divine action, it was a Roman action. Resurrection could *only* be a divine action.

It is thus important to hear what Paul really affirms as he begins each of his letters, for the gospel "in a nutshell" is expressed in each of his greetings. It bears repeating. *Paul's salutations are our first introduction to Paul's theology.* Ultimate authority belongs to God, who as Father is far more than a Roman *paterfamilias*. His authority accrues for the entire human family in terms of his extended graciousness, which results in well-being and wholeness. As a result of God raising Jesus from the dead, God has made him to be Lord over all things as God's Anointed One. Paul does far more in his salutations than simply say "Hello!," even though these are generally verses we skip over to get to the "real stuff" of Paul's "theology."

As a Jew, Paul inherited the concept of the worship of a singular God (monotheism). The Shema (see Deut 6:4–6) stood at the center of Israel's faith confession. Paul did not abandon monotheism once he came to believe in what God had done in Christ. The one God was the Creator, Judge, Redeemer, and ultimate Power in the universe (cosmos). As a Christian, Paul did not become a "tri-theist" or believer in three gods. He was not Trinitarian with a capital *T*, as much later Christian theology became.

A Jewish synagogue service in Paul's day might begin with confessional recital of the Shema: "Hear, O Israel: YHWH is our God, YHWH alone; and you shall love YHWH your God with all your heart, and with all your soul, and with all your might" (Deut 6:4–5). Reminder would be given that, according to Moses, these words should be upon one's heart, should be taught to one's children, should be spoken of everywhere at every time, should be bound upon one's hand and on frontlets before one's eyes, and should be written upon the doorposts of one's house. In a first-century world of belief in many gods and goddesses—Greek, Roman, Oriental, Egyptian, and even Caesar—Jews believed in uncompromising monotheism. The word "theology" in its simplest definition suggests thinking or expressed thought about God.

Paul, as any Jew of his day, was a Jewish monotheist. Paul began, where any Jew would begin, with uncompromising monotheism. This singularity of the divine provides support for the power of God. God has revealed his eternal power and deity in and through his *creation* activity (Rom 1:19–20; cf. 1 Cor 11:12; Rom 11:36). As Paul writes to the church at Corinth, he affirms that idol gods have no existence, that there is no God but one (1 Cor 8:4). He describes God as "Father," not as "Judge," here, as in all of his salutations in his letters. While he acknowledges that many "gods" and "lords" are worshiped by others, he affirms that for the Christians at Corinth there is only "one God the Father," from whom all things come to be and unto him we have our being (1 Cor 8:6).

In all of his salutations, Paul describes Jesus as "Lord" and as "Christ," two identities that come as a result of Jesus's obedience unto death and his resurrection by God. Jesus is God's instrument and indirect agent in creation (see John 1:3), the image of the unseen God, the firstborn of all creation, in whom all things were created (Col 1:15–16). He identifies Jesus Christ as the "one Lord" through whom (indirect agency) all things come to be, including we ourselves through him. Paul describes Jesus as "Lord," through whom God worked. Faith in the singular God of Judaism provides the foundation stone of Paul's theological thought. What God accomplished in Christ becomes the foundation for Paul's gospel thought found in chapter 6 of the current work. Paul's gospel is the foundation of the larger context of Paul's theology.

It is often assumed that Paul's gospel is focused upon Christ—especially his death and resurrection. In reality Paul's theology is *theocentric*. Paul had a firm *theol*ogy before he ever had a *Christ*ology rooted in Jesus of Nazareth. Paul's conviction was that the one Jewish God had acted in Christ in a decisive and final manner through the resurrection (Rom 1:4). His action, however, was preparatory for the return of Christ (the parousia) and the advent of the Telos, the time of God's final victory and final rule (1 Cor 15:20–28). This, indeed, was the "Gospel of God" (Rom 1:1) that Paul proclaimed in his gospel.

To ask the question in modern dress, "Do you believe in God?," is non-specific, as it might have been in Paul's day. A gentile pagan would believe in all the "gods," such that the question would sound silly. Monotheistic belief would be the hurdle for gentiles. Paul as a Jewish Christian would have worshiped only the single God of Israel, whose acts were manifest in the larger structures of creation, election, covenant, and redemption. The Jewish scriptures told the story of this God, who had made covenant promises to Abraham, who had given the Torah through Moses, and who had redeemed a sinful Israel through many trials as he spoke through his servants, the prophets. Paul understood that this one true God had now acted in Christ. The general question is sharpened, then, if phrased "Do you have faith in the one God of Israel?" Faith in the future under the rule of the one God (monotheism) of Israel lay at the bedrock of Judaism. "Hear, O Israel, the LORD our God is one. And you shall love him with all of your being . . . ." God is the Creator, Redeemer, Provider, and ultimate Judge.

Belief in the one true God of Israel provides the foundation stone for Paul's theological thought (1 Cor 8:4, 6). Paul refers to God as "Father" in all of his letters, as seen in all his salutations at the very least. The affirmation of one God, in keeping with Judaism, suggests power, might, and majesty—and one who is just. Consideration of this one God, especially in the light of the Christ event, causes Paul to break out in worship and doxology (Rom 11:36). Coupled with Paul's affirmation of God as "Father," Paul invokes the nature of God in terms of God's authority, expressed in kindness, grace, love, and mercy. The one God is the Creator and the Redeemer, while the Son is his agent or instrument (1 Cor 8:6; Col 1:16; Eph 3:9). God's creative activity marked self-revelation of his nature and deity (Rom 1:19–23). Paul thought of himself as being set apart even before he was born to a called apostleship in order to proclaim the Gospel of God in Christ (Gal 1:15–16; Rom 1:1–6).

God had acted to reconcile and restore the human race to himself. God's action was for the benefit of humankind. Paul was called by God. He had an encounter with the risen Christ. Belief in Christ's resurrection both corrected and motivated him. As he affirms, "God was *in Christ* reconciling the world to himself, while not reckoning to them their trespasses, indeed establishing in us the word of reconciliation. Therefore, we are ambassadors in behalf of Christ since God makes his appeal through us; we beseech in behalf of Christ, you all be reconciled to God" (2 Cor 5:19–20). Reconciliation and the overcoming of human alienation are the themes that Paul emphasizes, not the need for some type of divine satisfaction or transaction. These themes in turn call for human responsibility before God in community with God and humankind, as one lives *in* proper relationships *out of* restored relations.

Paul's theology begins where the Jewish scriptures begin, with God's act of creation. The disobedience of Adam marked the time and person through whom Sin/sin entered into the world (Rom 5:12–14). Sin becomes that which corrupts and enslaves; it becomes at its root the problem of idolatry, from which humanity stands in need of deliverance (Rom 1:18—3:20). The foundational basis of idolatry ultimately moves beyond mere ignorance to arrogance and human narcissism.

In Paul's understanding, God is a heavenly Father who adopts us as his children in Christ. He is one characterized by "love, joy, peace, patience, kindness, goodness, faithfulness, gentleness, self-control." He is One who is right and who is able to make right one who is in Christ (see Gal 5:22–23; Rom 3:26). To see God as primarily a God of wrath who condemns is not Paul, but the product of later theological systems with dogma and doctrine to protect.

Paul's gospel is one of rescue and deliverance, grace and peace, wholeness and provision, love and acceptance, unity and mercy and love. It is the refusal of those things that in reality bring divine wrath and self-destruction. The most extensive treatment of God's wrath in Paul and in the entire New Testament is found in Rom 1:18–32, where Paul describes God's wrath in a threefold emphasis of God turning humankind over to themselves for *self*-destruction (Rom 1:24, 26, 28). The righteousness or rectification of God and the wrath of God are both revealed as two sides of the same gospel coin (Rom 1:16–18).

One Gospel

The gospel is, indeed, the proclamation of exceedingly good news (εὐαγγέλιον), for there is not a single negative element expressed in Paul's salutations. If one were to read no further, Paul's theology expressed in his salutations offers a freedom from so many different yokes of slavery and religiously induced guilt that have become ingrained as a result of guilt-inducing dogmatic sermons—echoed in hymnology—and ill-based, ineffectual theological dogmas born of both ignorance and arrogance.

Paul's gospel was about God's Gospel—about God's benevolent, dramatic, and cosmic intervention in the resurrection. It was an announcement of good news from God, concerning victory in the voluntary death of his Son in our behalf that culminated in the resurrection defeat of Sin and Death (see Rom 1:1–17; 3:21–26). It is a word from God that heralds salvation and deliverance. It is a word from God that heralds transformation and redemption of the entire cosmos (Rom 8). As a gospel of fulfillment, Paul found it only natural to express that gospel in the theological thought of Jewish apocalyptic—thought or language that expressed the end of the Present Evil Age and the in-break of God's Age of justice and righteousness.

"Christ" for Paul is not a name, but a title. It does not mean first of all a "divine" being in Paul's thought. Christ for Paul meant "Messiah" or "Anointed One." Jesus Christ, and specifically his death and resurrection, are held to be at the heart of Paul's Christian message. Christ's death and resurrection are of equal importance for Paul, although they carry different significance for him. Both are central to early Christian tradition and confession of faith (see 1 Cor 15:3–5). Christians had to reconcile the nature of Jesus's death with his proclaimed identity.

The resurrection spawned the gospel. Paul, along with other early Christians, came to believe that the one Jewish God had raised Jesus from the dead and had exalted him as Lord. Paul's language about Christ is essentially Jewish. The Greek word *Christos* (Χριστός) is the equivalent of the Hebrew *Mashiah*, Messiah. The affirmation of Jesus as Lord is the most fundamental Christian expression (κύριος Ἰησοῦς, see Rom 10:9; 1 Cor 12:3). Paul can identify Jesus as "son of God" (Gal 2:20; 2 Cor 1:19; Rom 1:4), although the Hebrew scriptures can identify Israel (Exod 4:22) and Israel's king (Ps 2:7) as God's "son." Although the LXX may use "Lord" (κύριος) as an equivalent of YHWH, the covenant name for God in Hebrew, the term "lord" itself was used widely as a general term indicative of authority in Paul's world (e.g., husbands, masters, even the emperor). Paul does not use the term "son" in the sense of later Trinitarian creedal confession.

Salvation has everything to do with God; we are but the recipients, such that we have no boast but only doxology. Such a gospel—the Gospel of God—becomes lyrical as the grace of the Gospel resonates with God's peace.

Jesus, crucified by the powers, was vindicated as God's Messiah when God raised him from the dead. Paul was called to proclaim the Gospel of God as the fulfillment of the true story of Israel's God in his redemption of the entire cosmos. Paul did not understand "gospel" as an *ordo salutis*—an order or description of how individual people become "saved." If we wish to "imagine Paul," however, we have to pursue the meaning of the word "gospel" as it was understood in Paul's world and by Paul. Paul understood the Gospel of God as far more than an objective and individualistic salvation plan that saved one from hell.

Jewish usage of the root word is found in passages such as Isa 40:9, 52:7, 60:6, and 61:1. It is the announcement of YHWH's coming reign. On the other hand, Roman usage is found in the proclamation in so many words that "Caesar is Lord," as represented by the Priene inscription (Asia Minor, 9 BCE). The gospel message is about both *enthronement* and *dethronement*. To affirm Caesar as Lord for the Roman world meant victory and peace through war. Caesar was enthroned and someone or something else had been dethroned. To affirm Christ as Lord meant that God had established the one who apparently had been defeated in death and had enthroned him as Lord. That meant the dethronement of all other entities and powers.

Fig. 35. Augustus of Prima Porto. Wikimedia commons, CC BY-SA 4.0.
Image has been cropped. http://commons.wikimedia.org/wiki/Image:Statue-Augustus.jpg.

That meant that the apparent victors in Jesus's death, including Caesar and Sin, had been dethroned. It meant that victory belonged to God; the demise of the "powers" that opposed, wherever they might be found, had been accomplished. To announce that God (YHWH) rules is to announce Caesar and celestial powers are no longer in charge. Paul's announcement was that the crucified Jesus of Nazareth had been raised from the dead, and that as YHWH's Viceroy, he had been installed as Lord of the world. While certainly not the Roman gospel, that was the Christian gospel. Paul's gospel bore the announcement that Israel's God had reversed the world's values and had overcome the principalities and powers (see Col 2:14–15). The gospel addressed the entire cosmos with the full weight of Jewish tradition behind it.

The Gospel of God involved his activity in the incarnation. God sent his Son into the very lair of Sin and Death. God sent his Son in the likeness of sinful flesh in the fullness of time for the purpose of redemption (Gal 4:4; Rom 8:3). It involved his activity in the resurrection of Jesus—Jesus did not raise himself (see Gal 1:1; Rom 4:24–25). The cross for Paul did not involve the action or condemnation of God, but rather the redemption of God. The crucifixion *as gospel* requires the resurrection, for there is no Pauline gospel apart from resurrection (see 1 Cor 15). The rule of Death had continued in the action of the cross, suggesting the continuing rule of all of the powers. The powers of the Present Evil Age, Death included, were broken only by the resurrection of Jesus, as God raised him to new life and exalted him as Lord (Phil 2:9–11).

Rulers, powers, authorities, and sinful humankind perpetrated the worst of evils in putting Jesus to death, but God raised him from the dead. Paul's understanding of the Christ event echoes the thought of the kerygma presented in Acts (see Acts 2:22–24; 3:13–15; 10:37–41; 13:27–30)—thought that has been sublimated and ignored by contemporary dogmas of Christendom. The full kerygma in Acts takes on a greater narrative character that includes a focus upon Jesus's life and mighty works. As a result of Paul's encounter with the *risen* Christ, Paul does not so much focus on the earlier life and ministry of Jesus.

In terms of Paul's epistolary purposes, he need not stress or recite a presumedly known full kerygma. The context of 1 Cor 15:3–4, for example, is the specific issue of resurrection. Jesus's death must be the prelude, but Jesus's very real death and resurrection would not be the sole elements of the kerygma for Paul. He would know the story and meaning of Jesus's entire life and ministry. Paul would have known a gospel. Jesus did not live or die to change the attitude of God from wrath to love. For Paul, who focuses upon the risen Christ, Jesus was the proclaimer of a redeemer God of love and life and not the pacifier of a God of wrath and death.

It may be surprising to learn that Paul does not emphasize *forgiveness* of sins. Paul only uses the word for "forgiveness" five times (ἀφίημι, 1 Cor 7:11, 12, 13; Rom 1:27; 4:7). While humankind is *guilty* of sin and as a consequence will experience the wrath of God's judgment that turns humanity over to self-destruction (Rom 1:24, 26, 28), humankind is also the *victim* of Sin and other powers. What Paul realizes and emphasizes is that humankind needs to be delivered from slavery to Sin that will unavoidably lead to death (Rom 6:23). Humankind needs to be transformed through peace with God wrought by God's grace.

It is God's grace in Christ that has overcome the power of Sin and Death and opened the door for the possibility of *transformation*. Humankind is helpless before the powers and, hence, lives unto destruction under the wrath *of* the powers *and* the operative wrath of God. One is sold under Sin as its slave and is free only unto death (Rom 6:23). One becomes free, perhaps paradoxically, as one becomes a slave of God in Christ. Paul maintains the metaphor of slavery, which would have spoken strongly to a first-century audience, and perhaps Paul's general audience.

Redemption is thus a more central concept in Paul's thought than is "forgiveness of sins." The symptomatic problem of "sins" remains as long as one is a slave of Sin. The remedy of transformation and redemption rests in what God has done in Christ to break the power of Sin. Sin has not yet "died," but its power has been broken if one is no longer enslaved to it. The worst Sin could effect was to bring about death or eternal destruction. The resurrection broke Sin's power, even shattered it, as Sin became shamed by Life rather than honored by Death. Christ has now been exalted by God and is powerful over all adversaries, to the glory of God the Father (see Phil 2:9–11).

Consequently, one is to continue to work out one's salvation with fear and trembling (Phil 2:12–13), as one commits to the operative grace of God in Christ. It is no longer the destructive fear and trembling of terror before a power of Sin to which one is enslaved or to the Specter of Death or to a judgmental God of condemnation. Rather, it is the fear and trembling in the light of one's salvation as Paul states, that is, the "fear and trembling" of *reverential astonishment* and *amazed awe* of God's Gospel in Christ.

One Lord

Following his call, Paul did not abandon but rather embraced Jewish monotheism. His understanding of God in the present, however, was revolutionized by his personal experience with the risen Christ. Paul experienced a "Christophany," or appearance of Christ that compelled him to embrace new theological realities. Paul remained a monotheist—he did not become a di-theist (belief in two gods) nor a tri-theist (belief in three gods). The risen Jesus, whom Paul came to understand as Lord and Christ, remains subordinate to the Father even in Paul's mature theology (1 Cor 15:20–28) and is seen to be "Son of God in power" only on the basis of the resurrection (Rom 1:4). In fact, according to Paul's thought, Jesus could only become "Lord" and "Christ" on the basis of the resurrection, as a result of God's action and exaltation (Phil 2:9–11; Eph 2:20–23; Col 1:11–20).

Jesus's death had deep significance and meaning for Paul that was significantly deeper than much contemporary theology that merely emphasizes a substitutional transactionalism. Many theologians and preachers have emphasized substitution of required satisfaction of some sort in terms of some theory of "atonement." In contemporary circles, one may most often hear a phrase like "penal substitutionary atonement," a characterization that comes not from Paul but that comes to us as a Reformation legacy.

Paul recognizes that "Christ died in behalf of the ungodly" (see Rom 5:6) or that he was "obedient unto death, even death of a cross" (see Phil 2:8), but he himself did not emphasize what became later theories of substitution or satisfaction. Paul recognized the importance of the resurrection, although he was not fixated upon the historical event of the cross. The cross was an historical reality that had to be explained, if indeed Jesus were the expected Messiah. The resurrection was a powerful, revolutionary, and generative event that altered the course of history itself.

The present writer does not imagine that Jesus's death on the cross was a direct act of God, as much supposed Christian theology affirms. The death of Jesus Christ in Paul's understanding did not represent a better or more perfect cultic sacrifice required by God. For Paul, it was not God who had the problem that required the satisfaction of his honor or his sense of justice or his "feelings." For Paul, it was God who had the solution.

The problem for Paul was a twofold one of subjection and alienation that required reconciliation. Jesus's death did not represent the absorption of the wrath of God as payment for human sins for all time. Jesus's death represented the very worst that the power of Sin and other elements could effect in an age pervasively evil. Death was always the final enemy that had reigned from Adam to the present, as a result of conspiratorial cooperation with Sin and slavish submission to it. With Jesus's death, it appeared that Sin and Death had won again. But God had a trump card. As a result of Jesus's obedience, God raised him from the dead and exalted him as Lord and Christ (see Phil 2:8–11). In the resurrection and exaltation of Christ Jesus, God triumphed over the worst that all the powers detrimental to humankind and opposed to God could effect.

The purpose of the universal lordship of the risen Christ is to "annihilate death and its allies" through his current activity. Both Sin and Death have lost their dominion "in Christ." The risen and exalted Christ stands as a life-giving power. Salvation involves far more than the "forgiveness of sins," a point Paul does not emphasize. Salvation means resurrection, personal transformation, and life in union with the risen Christ. Resurrection serves as the basis of hope in the manifestation of the love, power, and faithfulness of God. God raised Jesus as the "first fruit," so will he raise those who are faithful in him.

Shared titles and functions have blurred the lines between God and Jesus in Christian history and theology. Historical debates (such as the Council of Nicaea, 325 CE) have wrought doctrines that remain confusing and that move well beyond the understanding of Paul, who is rather clear. Paul did not confuse Christ with God the Father. Christ is the risen one who, as exalted Son and Lord, will at the Telos ("time of fulfillment") vanquish all enemies—rulers, authorities, powers, and even Death. He will then deliver the kingdom and himself in subjection to God (1 Cor 15:20–28). Paul plainly states that Christ the Son has always been and always will be subject or subordinate to God the Father. It is God who gives victory through our Lord Jesus Christ (1 Cor 15:57).

Paul, of course, moves beyond his salutations to develop his thought, but his thematic foundation is exhibited in his greetings. Paul writes his most extended introduction to the "saints" in Rome, a church or multiple churches that he has never visited (see Rom 1:1–6). There, he speaks of the "Gospel of God," the content of which is defined in terms of Jesus. Of royal blood, Jesus was of the seed of David according to fleshly descent. Most significantly, Paul affirms Jesus was marked out as Son of God in power by means of his resurrection from the dead. Paul affirms Jesus as Christ and as Lord. He affirms that he himself received grace and the commission of apostleship with a view toward proclaiming obedience to all the gentiles based upon faith.

In Galatians Paul affirms that his apostleship has come through Jesus Christ and from God the Father, who is identified as the one who raised Jesus from the dead (Gal 1:1). One of the things that is interesting in both Romans and Galatians is that

Paul stresses the resurrection, but he never mentions the cross in either salutation. In fact, the noun for "cross" and the verb "crucify" never occur in Romans at all, other than in a compound form where Paul affirms in a singular occurrence that he has been crucified together with Christ (see Rom 6:6). The noun only occurs ten times in all letters attributed to Paul, while the simple verb occurs eight times and in its compound twice. On the other hand, Galatians manifests the highest concentration of "cross" language in all of Paul's letters—the noun is used in Gal 5:11, 6:12, 6:14 and the verb in Gal 3:1, 5:24, and 6:14 (see Gal 2:19). Thirty-eight percent of Paul's usage of the noun (σταυρός) is found in Galatians, along with 30 percent of his usage of the verb (σταυρόω).

Paul does two other things in his salutation in Galatians. He affirms that Jesus, who is identified as both Lord and Christ only as a result of the resurrection, gave himself for the purpose that he might bring us out from "the Present Evil Age" according to God's will (Gal 1:4). As has been seen, the conception of the "Two Ages" in Paul is a very significant one, apart from which one will not comprehend Paul's gospel. The second thing that Paul does is to break out in a doxology of praise to God, as he frequently does in his letters (Gal 1:5).

In the verses that follow in Galatians, Paul uses some of his strongest language found anywhere in his letters. Paul is defending his own ministry and apostleship, his own person and his integrity, his very gospel and (as the present author would say) his Collection before the Galatian churches. The situation is that interlopers in the person of Judaizers or Nomistic Evangelists have entered into Paul's Galatian churches and are preaching a different gospel that requires commitment to the Mosaic Torah, particularly it seems with regard to circumcision. Paul's whole Galatian letter becomes a polemic against the misunderstanding and mis-emphasis upon Torah. With harsh words, Paul essentially condemns his opponents to hell not once but twice (see Gal 1:6–8) and suggests they should mutilate themselves to the fullest extent (Gal 5:12).

Paul's framework for his proclamation of end-time realities is that of Jewish apocalyptic. Paul entertains a view of the world and history nearing its culmination and end, modified by association and union with Christ. The parousia, final resurrection, and life with Christ after death become unique features within a more general apocalyptic framework.

Paul announced to the world that the crucified Jesus was the world's rightful Lord, thus calling into question Jewish pride and rebellion, Roman arrogance and rule, pagan confusion and idolatry. This was a Christian message that emerged from an underlying Jewish narrative. Although Paul the Pharisee had entertained different expectations, Jesus's resurrection meant that the eschaton of Jewish expectation had arrived and the Age to Come had dawned.

Paul came to recognize Jesus's true identity as Messiah (confirmed by God's resurrection) and Lord (confirmed by God's exaltation). He came to understand that the gentiles were a welcome part of God's people apart from the Law, that both Jews and gentiles had been adopted by God on the basis of faithfulness. Through his call and commission, Paul came to understand that he had a distinct role in bringing about acceptance in Christ on the basis of faith.

While Paul was greatly influenced by what has become known as his "Damascus road experience," Paul received traditions from those who were in Christ before him in the four to five years prior to his call (34 CE). Paul records hymns to Christ (Phil 2:6–11; Col 1:15–20; cf. 1 Tim 3:16), addresses God as "Abba" (Gal 4:6; Rom 8:15), proclaims basic kerygma (1 Thess 1:9–10; 1 Cor 15:3–7; Rom 1:3–4), affirms the Lord's Supper (1 Cor 11:23–25), and offers traditional prayer with "Maranatha" ("Our Lord, come," 1 Cor 16:22) and "Amen" (Gal 6:18; cf. 1 Tim 1:17). In these, Paul is one with the preaching and practices of the early church.

For Paul, Jesus was not God. Jesus was Christ and Lord. Paul always carefully distinguishes between God the Father and Jesus the Son. Jesus was God's Son in a unique way (see Rom 1:1–4), but Paul always saw Jesus as subordinate to God the Father. While one might find and extract from Paul's letters the raw materials that later defined the development of Trinitarian thought and speculation, neither Paul nor the New Testament develops a formal doctrine of the Trinity with a capital *T*. Historically speaking, that development rests with a post-Tertullian (d. 220 CE) and post-Nicaean (325 CE) world. Paul could speak of God the Father as a true Jewish monotheist and of God's Gospel in Christ. He could speak of God's revelation and redemption in Christ, marked out as Son of God in power by means of the resurrection (Rom 1:4).

Paul had a monotheistic theology and a functional rather than metaphysical Christology. The Spirit was the interface of communication between God and his people, the down-payment and guarantee of what was to come. One should take note of all of Paul's salutations, none of which are "Trinitarian" in statement: "Grace to all of you and peace from God the Father and the Lord Jesus Christ." It would not appear to be helpful for understanding Paul to try to accommodate his thought to later Christian theology of subsequent centuries, as some scholars seek to do by affirming Jesus as the image of God or revision of monotheism to include Jesus within the divine identity within Judaism. Judaism did not understand the Messiah to be "divine."

Paul never confused Christ with God the Father. They remained distinct "persons" for Paul, even though titles and functions might at points overlap and blur their difference. Clarity may be seen in various considerations. God raised Jesus from the dead and exalted him; Jesus did not raise himself. Clear distinction is maintained in all of Paul's salutations. In Paul's brief summary statement to the Roman church, he speaks of the Gospel *of God*, the gospel concerning the son of David who was designated Son of God in power through the resurrection, who is now Jesus Christ (Messiah) our Lord (Rom 1:1–4). That is Paul's view.

As Paul writes to the Corinthians concerning the resurrection, he speaks of the Telos (End) when Christ will return all rule to God the Father after subduing every enemy, including Death. With total victory over all powers antithetical to God's purposes, the Son who now rules will be subject to God the Father who placed all things under Christ (see 1 Cor 15:20–28). Other references could be adduced, but it is evident Paul was a Jewish monotheist who had a functional Christology under the umbrella of the "Gospel of God."

Paul was forced to reflect on the meaning of the cross. Following his encounter with the risen Christ, he had to rethink the place of the Torah or the Jewish Law in terms of salvation and God's covenant with Israel. Notably, what Paul says in Galatians and Romans called forth the time-honored Reformation view of "justification by faith" as a central avenue for comprehension of Paul's overall theology (see Gal 3:6–14; Rom 4:1–24).

The Christ event brought a change in the power structure existing since Adam. The Old Age had come to an end in terms of its domination; the New Age had come with opportunity in Christ. End-time reality had begun. The notion of the two dominions underlies Paul's thinking—two spheres of reigning powers, as has been seen. The powers of subjugation have been rendered impotent, specifically through Christ's death *and* resurrection. Their strength has been nullified, although their presence has not been annihilated. Those in Christ have the Spirit and are being transferred to the dominion of Christ.

Deuteronomy 21:23 for the pre-Christian Saul (see Gal 3:13) suggested that Jesus was not the Messiah and that he was condemned by God. When God revealed his Son to Paul, Jesus was both confirmed and affirmed as risen Lord by God himself. Jesus's death and resurrection meant the inauguration of the New Age. The kerygma of the church at Antioch (see 1 Cor 15:3–4) may well have suggested Paul's own radical confession that questioned the continuing validity of the Law. Galatians 4:4 and Rom 8:3–4 suggest that the Son sent by God shared both our human nature and our human domain.

God sent his Son to condemn Sin in its own lair (the flesh), such that the just requirements of the Law might be fulfilled by those in Christ who walk by the Spirit. It should be noted Paul says "just requirements." Does that exclude other things, such as ritual requirements and definitional boundary markers? When Sin was condemned in the flesh—and when the gentiles were included on the basis of faith—the Law was superfluous and no longer needed for the reasons that it was important in an earlier time. God's people were now defined by faithfulness in Christ and not by Torah. Abraham, himself a gentile, became the father of faithfulness for both gentile and Jew alike.

In a rebirth of images, Paul took the cross, itself a symbol of ultimate shame and ignominy and transformed it into a symbol of divine victory as seen in the resurrection. Even as was the case with the Jesus tradition (see Mark 8:34 par.), the challenge of a "cross" marks the identity of those in Christ. Faithfulness may lead to suffering, even death, but suffering produces hope, and there is no resurrection apart from death. The present life of believers under the sign of the cross is a gift of God; future life of believers in terms of the resurrection is likewise a gift of God, given to those who are his people. The cross becomes a window on faithfulness and the symbol of resurrection to come.

Christ crucified becomes a mode of salvation, although not because God needed a "perfect sacrifice." Salvation comes through faithfulness. Christ remains the "crucified one," but he also lives as the "resurrected one," exalted as Lord. Christ crucified becomes the model for Christian living in terms of a participatory pilgrimage of faithfulness. The way of the world is boasting, power, and inflicted death. The way of God is humility, apparent weakness as seen in the cross, and life granted by God on principles other than the world's way.

One Spirit

The objective character and universal significance of the Christ event are essential to Paul's thought. His thought is rooted in Jewish apocalyptic and in the Christian kerygma. One might think in terms of the "Christ event," which would combine Paul's thought of both death on the cross and resurrection, two halves of a whole. However, the overall Christ event will continue to unfold through the present gift of the Spirit and the coming parousia and Telos.

Paul's theology is focused upon the one God of Israel, who is Creator and Redeemer and now Father, who has acted through Jesus Christ the Son, who is present in power through his Spirit. The "Spirit" is God's presence and power in the world, present even from the time of creation (Gen 1:2). The Spirit is thus God's empowering presence, his mode of communication with his creation and people. Paul was not a Trinitarian who worshiped three gods, although the language of "Father, Son, and Spirit" is found in Paul and provided building blocks for the formal *ontological* doctrine of the Trinity developed in the fourth century.

For Paul, the one God of Israel had acted in Jesus of Nazareth, had raised him from the dead following his crucifixion by forces of evil, had exalted him as his Son in power as a result, and now continued to manifest himself through his Spirit as he had always done, the presence of the Spirit of God being understood as an eschatological gift to the church.

Paul's core convictions remained, although now there was necessary modification. It was a new day. Paul believed in the singular God of Judaism, although that God was now best understood through his actions in Christ, whom Paul identifies as the Son of God in power on the basis of the resurrection, an action of God (Rom 1:1–4). God raised Jesus and then exalted him (see Phil 2:9–11). The future had become now, for God had decisively acted to inaugurate the long-hoped for Age to Come. This was signified not only by God's resurrection of Jesus, but also by the gift of the Spirit present and given to the church. The dominant view within Judaism was that the Spirit of God had been taken from Israel with the last of the Old Testament prophets, but that he would restore his Spirit in "the last days." The outpouring of the Spirit certainly provided foundation for Peter's Pentecost sermon (see Acts 2:16–21; Joel 2:28–32).

The early Christians envisioned themselves as those for whom the words of the prophet Joel had come to pass, as the Spirit was poured out upon all as eschatological event (see Joel 2:28–29; Acts 2:17–18). For Paul, the mark of a true Christian was the Spirit (1 Cor 12:3; Rom 8:9), who affirms one's identity as God's child (Gal 3:26; 4:4–7; Rom 8:14–29) and imbues persons with diverse gifts for the building up of the community in Christ (1 Cor 12:4–11). The Spirit of God produces fruit for living a new life in Christ (see Gal 5:22–26) that stands in clear dichotomous contrast with life "according to the flesh" (see Gal 5:16–21). Life "according to the flesh" follows in the train of the disobedience of Adam, whereas life "according to the Spirit" follows in the train of the obedience of Christ imbued by the presence of God (see Rom 5:12–21).

Paul could speak of the Spirit of God or of Christ as a gift given to the church as a guarantee and down-payment of the fulfillment of the Gospel. The Spirit was, as it were, an empowering and energizing and encouraging force between God and his adopted children. The Spirit becomes the mode of interface or communication between either God or the risen Christ and his people. The Spirit empowers, energizes, and directs the lives of God's people in Christ until the parousia, until the Telos. Paul was not privy to nor troubled by later Christological and Trinitarian controversies of later centuries, some of which were even constructed from underlying Pauline wood.

One Faith

Paul's doctrine of "justification by faith" has been at the heart of much theological thinking since the time of the Reformation. In fact, for the last five hundred years it has often been viewed as the central theme or the foundation stone of Paul's thought in Protestant circles. Traditional interpretation of this doctrine has suggested that humanity stands in the docket before the court of God as a guilty sinner who is only deserving of death. God has been satisfied by the perfect sacrifice of Jesus on the cross, such that God the Judge can acquit the sinner with a verdict of "not guilty." The obedient and innocent Son dies, such that the guilty can go free. While it may be true that God has overcome the sinfulness and guilt of humanity, it is difficult to find in Paul any concept that God has rendered a verdict of "not guilty" to a guilty humankind. God's integrity and his righteousness become issues at question.

There is a sense in which Paul's encounter with the risen Christ caused him to rethink and recover the foundational purpose of Israel's story—it went back to Abraham, beyond Moses. By an act of divine grace, God chose a gentile by the name of Abraham through whom to establish his covenant. Through his election, his descendants would constitute a blessing to all peoples of the earth. The Law, given later through Moses, defined how this covenant people were to live in faithfulness before God, both morally in their living and ritually in their worship.

It was not an ethnic story, but a human story that even extended back beyond Abraham to creation and transgression in Adam. Paul reread his scripture in the light of the Christ-event. It had always been God's plan to include gentiles within the singular people of God. And, in the light of the Christ event, gentiles did not have to become Jews any more than did father Abraham. Righteousness before God and inclusion within his people had always been predicated upon faithfulness and not upon law or ethnicity (see Gen 15:6; Rom 4:1–25).

The one covenant people of God had now been fulfilled in terms of God's original covenant with Abraham, the promise that he would be a blessing to all peoples of the earth (Gen 12:1–3). The new Israel of eschatological fulfillment now incorporated gentiles in the time of God's new future. While Paul understood the Gospel of God in terms of Israel's scriptures (the Old Testament) and Israel's worship (one temple), his appreciation of both the place of the Torah (Law) and temple had to undergo revision. Paul came to understand the church as the body of Christ, as a living temple unbound by place and particularity that had no dividing walls. Paul recognized the value of the Law, but largely saw its function to have been superseded in Christ in the New Age of the Spirit. Neither the Torah nor the Jerusalem Temple were any longer defined by Jewish particularity, but that does not mean that either one was unimportant to Paul.

Relationship is heralded in the matter of "faith," which should be comprehended in the Old Testament sense of faithfulness or trusting commitment. Like an Abraham, one exhibits a basic trust in the essential righteousness of God. It is only because God *is* right and does right that he is able to make right the one who is in Christ (Rom 3:26). It is the fact that God *is* right that calls forth Gospel. It is God alone who determines what is righteous, because he alone is right. God's righteousness formed the basis of his relationship with Abraham, with Israel, and with the world. His own righteousness is that which insures he will always act in accordance with his own character.

God is faithful to his covenants and relationships even when humanity is not. One can imagine the opposite—a god who is capricious and arbitrary, a god who plays "favorites," a god who can be "bought," a god who is neither just nor righteous. One can imagine such a god, but one can then be thankful for the God of Jesus and Paul who is quite the opposite, who takes steps to reconcile humanity to himself in Christ. The singular God is faithful and seeks to reconcile humanity and his creation to himself. The God of Jesus and Paul can be trusted.

The phrase "in Christ" is perhaps the most dominant note that sounds forth in Paul's letters. Paul had a theology before he had a Christology, but what God accomplished in the Gospel he accomplished "in Christ." The phrase has a somewhat mystical association with it, although that should not cause one to shy away from it. It is not a case of absorption that results in one becoming lost in a "sea of deity." There is not a loss of conscious individuality, but there is rather a new sense of belonging and relationship. To be "in Christ" is to be a part of his people and to gain a new identity through the relational reconciliation as a participant in the Gospel of God. It is to find life and new individuality in its deepest sense, but only in corporate solidarity with Christ and those who express faithfulness in him.

Technically speaking, one may understand being "in Christ" as a "locative of sphere." The preposition "in" may indicate a physical place where one is located, such as one is "in a room." One may also, however, be "in love," which is a locative of sphere. Being "in Christ" is more like being "in love" than being "in a room," which is not a bad comparison with Christian experience based upon what God has done "in Christ." It is metaphysical relationship characterized by incorporation into the family of God. The meaning is corporate, as well as individual. In fact, according to Paul, one belongs to the *body* of Christ (see 1 Cor 12:12–21; Rom 12:4–8). As the church lives as the body of Christ, it witnesses to the world that God's New Age has already dawned.

As a result of the dispersion or spread of the Jews that began at the time of the exile, Jews were scattered throughout the Greco-Roman world in a movement known as the diaspora. While Delphi was the "center of the world" for Greeks, the Jerusalem Temple was the very center of the world and religious worship for Jews. The temple marked God's earthly dwelling place, the locus of God's presence, the holiest place in the world.

Paul retained the concept of sacred space, but now it was not the physical location of the temple in Jerusalem but the living body of Christ, the church, that represented the true temple of God in the New Age. It is Christ-believers gathered in his name that creates a living sacred space—a sacred living sphere—in honor of God. Paul could retain the language and symbols, while bringing a new birth of meaning. There was no longer a "dividing wall of hostility" that separated the Court of Israel from the Court of the Gentiles as found in the Jerusalem Temple (Eph 2:14–15). Paul saw the collective body of the church to be the Temple of the Holy Spirit (1 Cor 3:16–17; 6:19; cf. 2 Cor 6:16–18), the Temple of the Lord (Eph 2:21).

Attainment of the promise involves faith, love, and hope. Paul did not address the matter of interim existence between one's personal death and the general resurrection, nor did he posit anything like a millennial reign between the parousia of Christ and the end-time kingdom of God. "Transformation" marks the mode of the resurrection (1 Cor 15:35–55). Transformation marks the mode of living by faith now (Rom 12:1–2). Faith finds its direction and definition "in Christ." Faith energizes through love—love of God, love of humankind (see Gal 5:6). Faith gains its own energy through wholeness and hope, through divine "grace and peace."

Romans 6:1–11 is a basic text. Resurrection life begins now. Paul's understanding is that God sent his Son into the world to share fleshly existence under the dominion of the powers of the Present Evil Age (Phil 2:6–11; Gal 4:4–5; Rom 8:3–7). Christ's death on the cross was ultimately death to Sin, which appeared to have won once again. In God's act of resurrection, Sin was condemned in the very domain of its power, the flesh, for death wrought by Sin was overcome and its universal power was broken. Through Christ, Sin's hold on humanity has been broken. Just as the risen Christ lives unto God, so also in Christ the believer must die to Sin in order to become free to live unto God. It is the resurrection, not the death, that broke the stranglehold of the old dominion.

One might think of a parabola. One side of the parabola leads to death, the usual end of the dominion of Sin. At the nadir of the parabola rests the divine mystery of death and burial followed by resurrection and new life. The other side of the parabola now heralds the dominion of God in the Age to Come operative through grace, righteousness, and Spirit now found in new life in Christ. The resurrection broke the hold of the old dominion of Sin by ushering in the dominion of the risen Lord. Dying with Christ becomes a participation in God's past event, but not as a repetition of that event. As one embraces a cross imperative, one embraces a hope of resurrection. The two parallel perspectives may be illustrated in the form of two parabolas as given below—the first parabola depicting the Christ event, the second depicting the comparative nature of the Christian life.

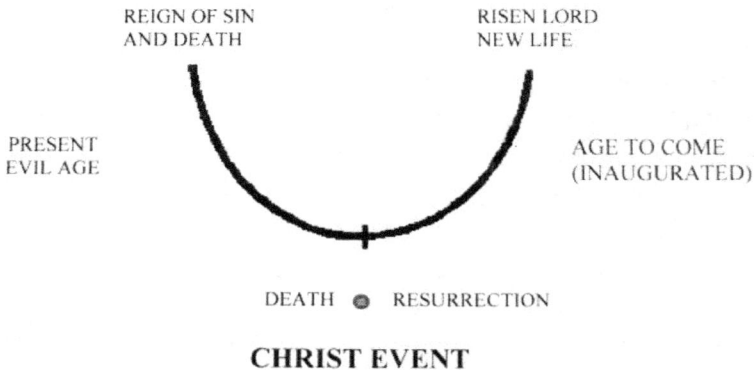

Fig. 36. The Christ Event. Conception by G. Roger Greene.

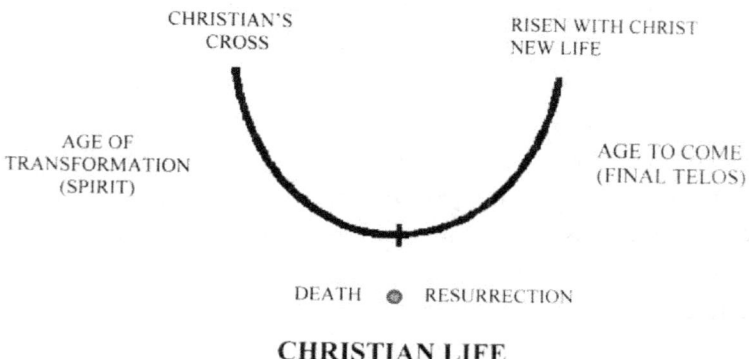

Fig. 37. The Christian Life. Conception by G. Roger Greene.

The cross is certainly a part of Paul's gospel, but it is not the whole cloth of *the* Gospel. The cross cannot be correctly understood apart from the resurrection and exaltation of Christ. It should be understood in the light of the believer's dying and rising with Christ, both metaphorically and literally, in hope of bodily resurrection. Paul's gospel would not be the Gospel apart from the cross, for the life of the Christian must be conformed to the Gospel of the cross.

However, it is the resurrection of Jesus that became the generative event that marked the in-break of the Age to Come that was now inaugurated. The presence of the Spirit as the first fruit and guarantee of future inheritance becomes the identity marker and enabler of those who have embraced the Gospel of God in Christ. As both Jesus and Paul maintained, the Christian life in the present age is cruciform (see Mark 8:34; Gal 6:14; Rom 6:1–6).

Paul's theology was influenced by his own sufferings as an apostle (notably seen in 2 Corinthians, see 2 Cor 1:3–11; 6:4–10; 11:23–33; cf. Phil 1:21–23). Paul learned to rely upon God. Reliance upon God is what it means to be faithful. One abandons the ways of the world and trusts in God. It is a summons to selflessness. It is on the basis of the spirit of the cross that the Christian community achieves unity on the basis of its resurrection faith in God. The cross apart from the resurrection only heralds death. With a rebirth of images, the cross in the light of the resurrection heralds life and becomes the visible symbol of Christian living and resurrection.

The matter of *faith* has been prominent in discussion of Paul's theology and enters into any search for the "center" of Paul's thought. To ask what the "center" of Paul's *faith* was may be different from the question of the "center" of Paul's *theology*. Faithfulness is a mode of living, guided by a constellation of theological comprehension. Martin Luther, during the Protestant Reformation, suggested "justification by faith" as the center of Paul's thought, and that theme continues to be seen as central by many some five hundred or more years later. Others have argued that justification by faith was inherent to Paul's doctrine of redemption and, hence, cannot be the center of Paul's gospel. It has also been noted that justification by faith tends to be prominent only in Galatians and Romans, where Paul engages in polemical thought with the Nomistic Evangelists (or Judaizers) who were advancing the Law and circumcision as a requirement for salvation and entry into Israel.

By contrast, the rather mystical doctrine of "being-in-Christ" was advanced as the true center of Paul's thought. Ultimately, however, being "in Christ" appears to be derivative of something else, namely, the comprehensive saving acts *of God* expressed through Jesus the Messiah. Reconciliation has been suggested as the center—reconciliation of humanity to God, reconciliation of Jew to gentile and vice versa (see 2 Cor 5:18–21; Col 1:15–20). Enmity between humanity and God, as well as hostility between Jew and gentile, has been overcome in Christ. The "center" of Paul's *faith* was the Gospel of God, characterized by grace and peace in Christ, lived out unto transformation and new creation (see the concluding section below).

One Hope

In the light of the Gospel of God in Christ, there are now pockets of the kingship of God already present. It is its completeness that is longed for in terms of future hope. God's rule has been inaugurated with a clarity of love and life, characterized by his righteousness and grace. The death of Jesus on the cross marked the crowning event of the Present Evil Age. The resurrection of Jesus marked the inaugural event of the Age to Come, the "first fruit" and the guarantee of things to come in the restoration, reconciliation, and renewal of the whole of God's good creation, including those created and now recreated in God's image. Paul not only preached an "inaugurated" eschatology, but he proclaimed a "participatory" and "anticipatory" eschatology. He encouraged the Philippians to live up to what they had already attained, even though the goal stood yet before them (Phil 3:12–16). He encouraged the Galatians to keep step with the Spirit, for it was by the Spirit of God that they had been made alive (Gal 5:25).

What happened in Christ must necessarily happen to those in Christ, i.e., Christ's death and resurrection corresponds to dying and rising with Christ. The universal possibility of salvation life only becomes effective through incorporation into Christ. Incorporation into his death will mean incorporation/assimilation unto his life. There is a sharing in the cross of Christ before there is a sharing in his resurrection, even though this may be seldom "preached" or highlighted in theological "doctrines." The cross is Paul's interpretation of Christ's death and resurrection. The language of the cross, of the death of Christ, of dying with Christ never occurs, however, without affirmation of life. The "already" but "not yet" structure of present Christian living manifests a dynamic orientation toward both the present and the future predicated upon a past event. The present life of faith is a way of suffering and thus not yet risen life (Phil 3:20–21; 1 Cor 15:51–55; 2 Cor 4:14).

The Torah defined the election privileges of Israel, but now the new Israel was defined as was the original Israel, i.e., on the basis of faithfulness, as was the case of the original promise given to Abraham (Gen 12:1–3). The one in Christ, made alive by the Spirit, is characterized by a single faithfulness energizing through love (Gal 5:6). One acting through love spontaneously does what is deemed to be right. Even Hillel, long before Jesus, had suggested the whole Torah was summarized in the two great commandments of loving God and loving one's neighbor, that all the rest of the Torah was commentary.

The "oracles of God" (Rom 3:2) were entrusted to the Jews, along with many other privileges (Rom 9:3–5). But now, the playing field is leveled "in Christ," as God's Gospel calls for equal faithfulness on the part of both Jew and gentile. For Paul, anyone who loves fulfills the Law (Rom 13:10). Love provides the energy for faithfulness. Love enables a unified body of Christ to function appropriately. Faithfulness expressed through love leads to unity of the people of God in Christ. God's new Israel, even according to his intention in Abraham, is based upon faithfulness in Christ, not upon the ritual boundary markers of the Torah or particularistic privilege.

The kingdom of God or the rule of God is the ultimate object of hope (Gal 5:21; 1 Cor 6:10; 15;50), i.e., the ultimate transformation to the New Age (Phil 3:20-21; 1 Cor 15:50-56; Rom 8:23). Paul's hope has redemptive and salvific significance. For Paul, Christ is God's agent in both creation and redemption. Hope is informed by the knowledge of the mystery of God's salvation wrought by God in Christ Jesus (1 Cor 2:8-10; Col 1:26-27), "Christ in you all, the hope of glory." "Glorification" (which ought to be given at least equal attention with "justification") is both a promise and a hope, for those whose love for God and their brothers and sisters faithfully energizes through love.

God's redemptive love is poured into those who identify with Christ through the gift and guiding of the Spirit. It is the will of God expressed through his love in the commandment of Christ, given through the presence of the Spirit. God is the Father of comfort and mercy (2 Cor 1:3-6), the one who raises the dead (2 Cor 1:9), who demonstrates his redemptive love (2 Cor 4:7-12) and abeyance of judgment (Rom 3:25) in Christ. One can express hope in a God like that, even and especially beyond and through a cross, both Jesus's and ours. The entire cosmos shares in the hope of the glory of God (Rom 8:18-25).

The ultimate goal and ground of hope is God himself. The Christian hope is not groundless nor nebulous. The Christian hope is based upon what God has already done in the Christ event—the resurrection of Christ and the inauguration of a New Age. Yet it is a hope based upon future events—the parousia and the rule of Christ until all enemies are totally vanquished and the kingdom is given over to God the Father at the Telos. The Christian hope thus remains a hope, sustained by the presence of the Spirit until the parousia and the Telos (1 Cor 15:20-28). The individual participates in Christ with a view toward the resurrection and living life now as a "praise of the glory of God" (Eph 1:6, 12, 14). Paul's hope is eschatological. Paul never abandoned hope, although there was a dawning awareness that he might personally die before the Lord returned (2 Tim 4:6-8). And such proved to be the case.

What Paul teaches about the resurrection of Christians is a projection of what Paul knows about the resurrection of Christ. The death of Christ becomes a pattern for those in Christ. Death itself is seen as the ultimate enemy power (1 Cor 15:26), the last of many forces hostile to God and those in Christ. Christ's present reign is not one of peaceful possession of power and glory in a heavenly realm, but rather one of "a present and active enforcement" of God's rule in the entire cosmos as his reign works to establish the rule of God over all. The resurrection marks a continuing warfare against all evil that will reach its ultimate completion and purpose in the victory of the kingdom of God (1 Cor 15:28). The parousia marks the completion or culmination of the lordship of the risen Christ.

The pre-Christian Paul was a Pharisee who entertained apocalyptic expectations of the coming end of the age. When the Present Evil Age came to an end and the Age to Come dawned, the righteous dead would be given new life in a world to come. As has been seen, the word *apocalyptic* suggests an "unveiling" or a "revealing," a "disclosure" of the fulfillment of God's purpose that would come with signs and wonders. The term can be applied to a particular way of viewing coming reality in terms of a radical and sudden in-break of God to make things right. It can be applied to works belonging to a particular literary genre that expresses an apocalyptic viewpoint. As a noun, apocalypticism appears to be a development for later prophetic voices that announced the ultimate victory of God over evil. It tended to arise out of an uncertain social context of upheaval, deprivation, and persecution. It provided a genre of hope during the uncertain times between the Old Testament and the New Testament (see for example Dan 8:1–14; Zech 5:1—6:8; Joel 2:28–32; 1 Enoch 90:1–42; 4 Ezra 3:1—5:13).

There are many characteristics of apocalyptic, including the use of much symbolism, such as may be seen also in the New Testament book of Revelation (no *s*!). The present apocalyptic conception of the world was extremely pessimistic, with a seeming dominance of evil. It was hoped that God would decisively and suddenly act to overcome all evil threats. Apocalyptic thus expresses a dualistic, yet linear view of unfolding history. History is moving toward fulfillment in a new age; it is not a series of repetitive, endless cycles. The current age, which is seen to be pervasively evil, cries out for resolution. But, there is hope.

For Paul the man in Christ, the one God of Israel offers hope through one Lord and one Spirit and though his singular Gospel, as one lives faithfully before him. The Christ event fosters hope. To live "in Christ" is to live in hope.

One New Creation

While the nature of Pauline eschatology may be debated, Paul's gospel was an eschatological gospel. The Age to Come had arrived in the risen and exalted Christ, affirmed by the gift of the Spirit to the church. Paul inherited the basic kerygma of the early church that included the expectation of Christ's imminent return. In the early part of his foundational ministry, Paul set forth a rather literalistic apocalyptic interpretation (see 2 Thess 2:1–12; 1 Cor 7:26). As time went on with the delay of the parousia, Paul appears to have shifted his thinking. In the Thessalonian correspondence (which actually marks about a fifteenth-year anniversary of Paul's call), Paul apparently understood persecution in itself as a sign of the coming parousia.

However, Paul's experience in Ephesus during his Collection Campaign underscored for him the distinct possibility that he himself could die before Christ returned (see Phil 1:20–21). While he did not give up his belief in Christ's parousia, he appears to begin to at least balance the apocalyptic interpretation with a more internal, individualistic, and spiritual kind of thought. Paul can speak of his own desire to go and be with Christ (Phil 1:19–20), rather than Christ's universal appearance. He appears to focus upon the believer's fate at the time of death while maintaining an uninterrupted relationship with God that is not broken by death.

In his later letters written from a Roman imprisonment after the earlier completion of his Collection ministry, he appears to express a realized eschatology that begins to focus more upon a continuing Christian imperative (see Col 2:6—4:6; Eph 4:1—6:20). Some scholars interpret the change of eschatological emphasis in Colossians and Ephesians in particular as evidence that these letters were written by someone other than Paul. It would seem to the present writer that the more natural assumption would be that Paul simply adjusted his own thought in the light of the continuing delay of the parousia as his own death drew nearer. Paul's own theology would have likely also experienced a cross-fertilization with that of the Roman Christians.

The reader will pardon a bit of explanatory technicality. Paul makes use of what are called "aorist" verbs in Greek in Col 3:1, 3 to acknowledge that Christians have died and been raised with Christ. In its basic usage, an *aorist* verb suggests a single perspective, non-descriptive, summary of an action. Verb "tense" in English primarily expresses time of action—either "past," "present," or "future." Verb "tense" in Greek has more to do with *kind* of action than with *time* of action. The aorist ("without a horizon") verb in Greek simply affirms an action, often without any reference to time or particular description. It is the default tense in Greek, unless one wishes to affirm the continuation or the perfection/completion of an action. In Col 3:3 Paul shifts from an aorist ("you all died") to a perfect tense ("your life has been hidden and remains hidden"), suggesting the Colossians' collective life remains hidden together with Christ in God. He emphatically emphasizes that whenever Christ should appear (φανερωθῇ, an aorist subjunctive), the Colossians themselves will be manifest together with Christ in glory (ὑμεῖς φανερωθήσεσθε, future passive with emphatic subject). The fact that the Colossians died (aorist ἀπεθάνετε) to the elemental spirits of the world/cosmos is what makes possible the Christian imperative (see Col 2:20).

Paul also uses aorist verbs in Eph 2:5–7 to affirm that we have died, been made alive, and been raised, and established "in the heavenlies" in Christ (see Eph 2:5–6). These things have "happened." With what is termed a perfect tense periphrastic construction, Paul twice affirms to the Ephesians that they are those who already stand saved by God's grace in Christ (Eph 2:5, 8). One should remember that Paul is addressing gentiles, who were once excluded from Israel and who were without access to God. They are now no longer strangers and aliens, but they are fellow members of the household of God (see Eph 2:11–19). They, too, are part of the living Temple of God in Christ (Eph 2:20–22). They "have been saved by grace." Paul's affirmation addresses what God has already done, i.e., the indicative of God's Gospel. One should not, however, overlook the imperative of living "in Christ."

The word "eschatology" has to do with fulfillment of the "end goal" of God. It does not mean the "end-of-the-world" or the space-time universe. Jews and early

Christians did not mean "end-of-the-world" language literally. For a Jew, according to scripture, everything that God created was good (see Gen 1). Although the creation itself had been polluted by human sin and evil powers, the time of fulfillment would be a time of renewed creation. That which God deemed to be "good" would be redeemed, not destroyed. The word "apocalyptic" suggests a revealing or an unveiling. It describes a particular kind of eschatology that suggests a radical and sudden in-break of God to overcome all evil powers of opposition, as he conquers the powers and restores his creation according to his will.

One is not automatically transformed by mere entrance into the new life or mere assenting commitment to it. One is not magically transported to a different realm of existence, but one is offered the opportunity for a different quality of living, even and in spite of suffering. Present Christian life may become a difficult struggle—there is a Christian imperative, although now one has been equipped with power beyond oneself for that struggle. Paul himself experienced suffering in Christ, although he did not seek it. As illustrated by Philippians, his joy in Christ over-mastered his personal sufferings. Although many commentators read Rom 5:1 in terms of an indicative verb—"we *have* peace with God through our Lord Jesus Christ," the better textual support in ancient manuscripts is expressed in the subjunctive mode: "*Let us have* peace with God through our Lord Jesus Christ." Theologically, both points may be underscored. Because we have peace with God (Rom 8:1–2, "there is no condemnation for those in Christ Jesus"), let us rejoice with hope even in afflictions.

The reference in Rom 5:1 is a difficult textual problem, for the difference rests in but a change of a single vowel in Greek that would have been pronounced like the other vowel (both with an "o" sound). To illustrate, and the reader will pardon the technicality, it is the difference between ἔχομεν ("we have peace") and ἔχωμεν ("let us have peace") in Greek. The latter not only has the better textual support in ancient manuscripts, but it is also consonant with what Paul goes on to say: "Since we have been justified out of faithfulness, *let us continue to have peace* with God through our Lord Jesus Christ . . . *let us continue to rejoice* over the hope of the glory of God, . . . *let us continue to rejoice* in afflictions . . ." (see Rom 5:1–3).

The idea of "new life" that is available to all persons regardless of status stands out in all of Paul's letters. This is the most important concept, religiously speaking, in Paul's letters. God has done something to extricate humanity from Sin/sin that it could not do for itself. Sin could be understood in multiple ways. It was an inherent weakness that manifested itself in an active predisposition toward evil. It was an outside force that could take control, as it invaded human life and actually incited one to sinning.

For Paul, it is this power of Sin that is most serious—a power manifested in various acts of committing "sins." Transgressions and "sins" are but the symptom, while the real culprit is Sin. For Paul, the deadly grasp of Sin that has held sway over humanity has been broken by God's action in Christ. Although the results of the Christ event are clear to Paul (particularly, the resurrection), Paul does not fully explain exactly what happened. It remains a revealed mystery. Paul himself had experienced God's transforming power—*that* he knew, even in the face of divine mystery.

Paul became aware of Jesus's resurrection as a result of his encounter in his call experience (see Acts 9; Gal 1). The event is of paramount importance in understanding Paul's eschatology. Paul the Pharisee had looked forward to what God was going to do at the end of the age, when he would vindicate Israel from her suffering at the hands of pagans. This would herald a great reversal, with the fulfillment of all Old Testament expectations. With a flourish of trumpets and other events, the defeat of evil would be once and for all, as the Age to Come was ushered in—at some point in the future.

With surprise to Paul, and without the flourish of trumpets, the resurrection of Jesus of Nazareth signaled for him the advent of reversal of the ages. The resurrection affirmed Jesus as the true Messiah, which in turn meant that the Age to Come had begun. Paul had to radically rethink his perspective of how YHWH was to effect his plan of salvation. Paul came to realize that Jesus's death and resurrection marked the inauguration of God's great eschatological event of new life.

Paul understood that the Age to Come now overlapped the continuing Present Evil Age that would soon pass away. The Age to Come had been inaugurated specifically in Jesus's resurrection (see Rom 1:4); Paul himself had been called to be God's agent to the gentiles (see Gal 1). Paul saw himself as privileged to live in the Age of Transformation. He understood the time span of the Age of Transformation to be short—a comparatively brief period before the parousia and Telos. He did not envision, nor could he have foreseen, a time frame of two thousand years. Still, Paul presents a divine imperative suitable for any interim period and singular life-span.

Paul calls for the renewing of the *mind* (Rom 12:2). That is repentance. Repentance is renewal, sometimes from sin, sometimes from inadequate perspectives. It is not momentary; rather, it is a reorientation followed by a new lifestyle. And, if the mind is to be renewed with a different mind-set, that will involve imagination—the ability to envision a new reality that has not existed but that may come into existence. For Paul, the stimulus was the love of God expressed in Christ, i.e., the Gospel of God. Neither faith nor hope nor love in the gospel may be realized apart from imagination, the ability to imagine and then to realize a new creation in Christ.

Grace restores and heals; love recreates because it imagines what can be and what one can become. Faith becomes the exercise of grace and love that marks the creation of hope. By contrast, a systematic theological perspective known as substitutionary atonement offers a trauma-filled and trauma-informed model of divine violence, as God the Father requires the death of his innocent Son, so that the guilty may go free. Such a view offers a different perspective of God, the Christ event, and the new community of God in Christ than that which is found in Paul.

Far too often, a religion promises freedom but delivers a slavish control of the worst kind. Instead of building people up, it breaks people down. It instills shame, fear, guilt. Or, perhaps, it offers magical thinking that evades real life and responsibility. Paul embraced real life with the responsibility inherent to his calling to proclaim the Gospel of God. Paul preached a gospel that involved salvation here and now. The future surely belonged to God, but it had begun now in Christ. For Paul, there was no division between the secular and the sacred, as though life could be so compartmentalized. Life "in Christ" was not superstitious magical thinking, nor did it mark the installation of fear and guilt. It was good news of life before God as his adopted child.

Conclusion

Many forces and factors came together to influence Paul's theology. His Jewish background and inheritance, enhanced and revised by his Christophany experience in his call, were coupled with the kerygmatic traditions of the earliest church and his own missionary experiences to form a unique perspective of the Gospel of God.

Paul's expressed epistolary theology is a result of (1) his foundational experience within the umbrella of first-century Judaism and (2) his experience of the risen Christ. Those two experiences determine Paul's expressed theological viewpoints. It is significant and important to note that his theology is based upon the experience of covenant-making and not upon doctrinal theory. The focus of this chapter is not so much upon understanding "theology," a rather general and abstract concept in and of itself. Rather, the focus is upon imagining Paul's theology in the light of the Gospel of God. Theological issues, of course, enter into giving definition to Paul's conception of the Gospel of God in Christ. These can become quite complicated as scholars debate the finer points and alternatives of theological issues of note and relevance. For Paul, however, the issues were more pragmatic. Why has humankind been alienated from God? What has God done in Christ to overcome that alienation? What is the result?

If one is at all familiar with traditional approaches to Paul's theology, one can discern a distinctive difference in the foregoing presentation that has, for the most part, ignored a systematic theology treatment and evaded the more usual theological discussion and argument. One reason for this is the consistent structural and thematic focus on Paul's "epistolic" theology itself, rather than a focus upon pietistic apologetic or scholarly polemics. Another reason is the theme of this chapter and this book—now, re-imagine Paul.

One may move beyond the treatment of this book to more customary definitional and apologetic approaches as one wishes. There are many different interpretations of Paul's theology available, including other publications by the present author. There are certainly many resources to be found in the religious and theological marketplace. It is hoped, however, that one will carry forward one's developed imagination of Paul and his theology, as one augments one's present comprehension of this original apostle of God in Christ. For Paul, the rubric of "Gospel" determined his theology.

Scholars have long sought a "center" or "central theme" that provided the backbone for Paul's theology. Such a center would be defined as the "starting point" or "conceptual foundation" or "cornerstone" of Paul's dynamic theologizing. It would represent that which was presuppositional for Paul, that which underlies Paul's arguments expressed in his letters. And many thoughts have been offered in the attempt to identify a center, from general themes like "salvation" to very specific ones such as "justification by faith." Is there a coherent theme that permeates Paul's contingent interactions with his various churches? Various and multiple criteria have been suggested as a tool for discovering such an underlying or consistent theme.

Perhaps the "central theme" may be understood in general terms and supported by specific elements. One criterion is to seek for a center that is generational, in that it provides support or meaning for everything else. Another criterion is Paul's experience itself and any central theme that might arise from that experience base. And, finally, Paul was focused upon God first of all and not man. Paul's center was first of all *theo*logical, compared to much contemporary theology that is first of all *anthropo*logical. Paul had a theology, before he ever entertained a *Christ*ology or an *anthropo*logy. In a word, Paul's theology as well as his gospel was God-centered.

Most proposed "centers" of Paul's thought that focus on theological conceptions have in common a focus upon the person and work of Christ—they tend to be "Christological." Paul finds the story of Jesus to be prefigured in the Old Testament scriptures, such that Christ becomes the central key that unlocks the mysteries of God. Such a perspective is said to recognize that a word about Christology is a word about God. Monotheism is affirmed in principle in many proposed theologies, although description hints at a defense of the doctrine of the Trinity with a capital *T*. Paul clearly never lost a sense of functional distinction between God and Christ and never compromised his monotheism. But, then, he did not have to defend doctrines that arose in a post-Nicaean environment (325 CE and later) or doctrines that arose in the light of the Reformation.

Paul's "center" does not reside in a theological concept, the realm of myth and legend, nor in the locus of tradition. Paul's gospel is firmly centered in the Gospel of God, effected in the resurrection, the generative event of God's new creation in Christ. It marks the fulfillment of God's covenant for the world, both Jew, gentile, and the whole of creation.

The present writer would suggest that *Paul's foundational domain is his understanding of the now revealed Gospel of God in Christ established on the generational reality of the resurrection*. Some would say that is too broad, while others would suggest such a characterization represents a multiple theme. However, if one unpacks the characterization, Paul staked his life not on theology, but on the God of the Gospel now revealed to him in Christ. God had acted decisively to usher in the New Age. "In Christ" defines the nature of God's intervening and continuing action and Christian living. And, specifically, it is the reality of the resurrection that is generational for everything else, including Paul's hope for the future.

The resurrection is solely a divine event effected by God and the only aspect of the Christ event that cannot be manipulated by humankind. The reality of the resurrection was the event that convinced Paul that Jesus was blessed and not cursed by God, that Jesus was alive and exalted as Messiah and Lord. This writer understands the broad concept of the Gospel of God to be that which Paul announced throughout his ministry.

To be "in Christ" was his dominant expressed theme, occurring in one way or another some 164 times in his letters, but he was "in Christ" in the light of the Gospel of God. And, it was the reality of the resurrection that defined both Paul's proclamation of Christian faith and Paul's hope. There are, of course, many significant themes that emerge in Paul's letters—grace, peace, unity, justification, sanctification, etc. All of these find their meaning in the Gospel of God in Christ crucified *and* resurrected.

Although the "righteousness of God" has often been seen to be the theme of the letter to the Romans, for example (and the present writer has taught Romans in that manner for many years), what Paul actually announces and unpacks is the Gospel of God that now not only reveals the wrath of God (Rom 1:18), but the righteousness of God in his action of redemption and reconciliation. Paul's letter is an invitation to rectification—to freedom and faithfulness.

While Galatians (53–54 CE) and Romans (56 CE) were written several years apart, the fact that they exhibit common or related themes is indicative of abiding elements within Paul's theology. It appears much less likely that Paul used Galatians as an existing model for crafting Romans. The two letters address different contexts, even though they share common themes. Paul's letter to the Romans is an encouragement of transformation in the light of the eschatological "Gospel of God." That is why the letter to the Romans is filled with invitations to worship and why Paul most often breaks out in doxology.

Paul's theology is best seen in his two contextual bookends of the letter to the Romans written in 56 CE prior to his Jerusalem Collection visit and the letter to the Ephesians written from a later Roman imprisonment (60 CE). Paul's gospel unfolds in real time in his other letters, as one sees the application of his epistolic theology. Romans is *invitation*, in the light of expected continued proclamation of the gospel. Ephesians is *celebration* in the light of closing windows of opportunity for Paul near the end of his life—a fact that makes the epistle all the more remarkable. Both letters are an acknowledgment of God's Gospel in Christ.

It is perhaps appropriate to close this chapter with a catena (a connected series) of Pauline scripture, following the example of Paul himself as he employed Jewish scripture (see 1 Cor 3:19–20; 15:54–55; 2 Cor 6:16–18; Rom 3:10–18; 11:8–10; 11:34–35; 15:9–12). It is through Paul's own words that his gospel and his theology emerge with clarity. It should be noted that the "you" pronouns and imperatives are plural and not singular in the Greek. One needs to remember that Paul basically writes to churches composed of men and women seeking to live their lives in Christ, not to individuals. Also, in these examples, the personal pronouns that refer specifically to God are capitalized for clarity's sake. The translations are original to the author of the current work.

> *Rejoice in the Lord always; again I will say, 'Rejoice.' Let your graciousness be made known to all men. The Lord is near. Do not worry about anything, but in every prayer and petition let your requests be made known to God. Indeed, the peace of God, that (peace) that surpasses all understanding, will guard your hearts and your thoughts in Christ Jesus.* (Phil 4:4–7)

> *For from Him and through Him and unto Him are all things. To Him be glory unto the ages. Amen.* (Rom 11:36)

> *May the God of hope fulfil you with all joy and peace in faithfulness, so that you may abound in hope by the power of the holy Spirit.* (Rom 15:13)

> *Indeed, if you should do anything in word or in deed, (you all do) everything in the name of the Lord Jesus, while giving thanks to God the Father through him* [indirect agency]. (Col 3:17)

> *Since therefore you all were raised in Christ, continue to seek the things that are above, where Christ is seated at the right hand of God. Be mindful of the things above, not (mindful) of things upon earth. For indeed you all have died, and your life has already been hidden together with Christ in God. Whenever Christ should appear, your life, then also you all will appear together with him in glory.* (Col 3:1–4)

> *To the One who is able above all things to do far more exceedingly than whatever we may ask or think according to the power of the One working in us, to Him (be) glory in the church and in Christ Jesus unto all the generations of the Age of the ages. Amen.* (Eph 3:20–21)

> *Blessed (be) the God and Father of our Lord Jesus Christ, the One who has blessed us with every spiritual blessing in the heavenly places in Christ, just as He chose us in him before the foundation of the world, so that we should be holy and blameless ones before Him in love, because He set us apart beforehand unto adoption through Jesus Christ* [indirect agency] *unto Himself, according to the good pleasure of His will, unto a praise of the glory of His grace of which He graced us in the beloved one, in whom we have the redemption through his blood, the forgiveness of transgressions, according to the wealth of His grace which He lavished upon us, with every (element of) wisdom and insight, because He made known to us the mystery of His will, according to*

IMAGINE PAUL

His good pleasure which He set forth in him unto a plan of the fullness of the appointed Ages, that all things be headed up in Christ, things in the heavens and things upon earth in him, in whom we indeed were called, having been marked out beforehand according to the purpose of the One who worked all things according to the intention of His will, for the purpose that we the ones who have hoped beforehand in Christ might live unto a praise of His glory, in whom indeed you all having heard the word of truth, the gospel of your [pl.] salvation, in which indeed having become faithful you were sealed by the Spirit of promise, by the holy one, which is the guarantee of our inheritance, unto a deliverance of possession, unto a praise of His glory. (Eph 1:3–14)

[Note: In Greek, Eph 1:3–14 is one long sentence in which the primary verb "be" must be supplied. Paul's pleonasm is remarkably occasioned by his celebration in and of the Gospel.]

Now to the One who is able to strengthen you according to my gospel and the kerygma of Jesus Christ, according to the revelation of a mystery that was kept in silence for long ages but that is now made known through prophetic writings according to the command of the eternal God, unto an obedience of faith having been made known to all the gentiles—to the only wise God, through Jesus Christ [indirect agency], *to Him be glory unto the ages. Amen.* (Rom 16:25–27)

Meditate upon Paul's own words. They herald God's Gospel.

Now, re-imagine the theology of Paul in terms of the Gospel—and worship, free of all encumbering shackles that enslave.

8

Re-Imagine the Legacy of Paul

PAUL DID NOT LEAVE a legacy of a singular, grand, and comprehensive statement of the gospel he proclaimed. We are not privy to his entire teaching nor to his entire theology. Paul does not give us a comparative chart of his earlier theology as a "Pharisee" which might be compared with his later theology as an "apostle of Christ." He *did* leave a legacy of random letters that, taken together, may offer a framework of essential elements of his gospel. And that is more than we have from anyone else in the earliest period of Christianity. Paul's "gospel" is more than conceptual ideas or abstract beliefs or systematic doctrines. Paul's gospel is relational.

Essentially, we see in Paul's letters his own lived experience, as well as the spirituality he sought to nurture and inculcate in the churches he either founded or with which he had contact. The Christ event brought to Paul a change of life that was marked by deep spirituality and worship of the living God who had acted in Christ.

We know very little about Paul's contemporaries, such that the canonical influence of Paul's letters after his death may be disproportionate to the actual significance of Paul during his lifetime. On the basis of the surviving literature, Paul was the most significant person in early Christianity. Jesus himself, of course, was not a Christian (he was the Christ!) and left nothing in writing. We know only "Jesus remembered," through the Gospels. Paul's letters antedate the actual Gospels themselves and represent the earliest New Testament literature that we possess. However, many different Pauls live today in the memory and "museums" of modern Western culture and Christendom. We are not the first to "imagine" Paul, nor shall we be the last, although it is not the purpose of this book to chronicle the ways in which Paul has been understood or misunderstood. There are many works which do that, several of which may be found in the bibliography.

Paul's Person

When Paul's life came to an end, he was still supported by a few friends and associates like Timothy (see 2 Timothy) and the legacy of a few struggling house churches primarily located in the area of western Turkey and in Greece, i.e., the provinces of Galatia, Asia Minor, Macedonia, and Achaia. Paul's plan of fulfilling his commission and call to carry the Gospel of God to the gentiles by working counter-clockwise through the eastern provinces of the Roman Empire came to an unexpected end with his extended imprisonment and death in Rome. We do not know whether Paul's Collection for the poor saints in Jerusalem was successful or not. By all appearances, supported by a lack of any further reference to it, the safe assumption is that it failed to achieve what Paul had hoped it would (see Rom 15:22–32; Acts 21:15–26:32). And, of course, Paul himself was apparently arrested in Jerusalem, imprisoned in Caesarea Maritima, carried to Rome as a prisoner, and martyred there.

In the present writer's judgment, Paul's life came to an end around 61 CE, although other scholars suggest dates as late as 68 CE. It appears to this writer that Paul had passed from this life prior to the beginning of the Jewish-Roman war of 66–73 CE in Judea, for there is no mention or allusion to the war in any of Paul's letters. It would seem that even the outbreak of the struggle would have revived apocalyptic images for Paul, such as that seen in the Thessalonian correspondence (2 Thess 2:1–12; 1 Thess 4:13—5:2) or even the Corinthian correspondence (see 1 Cor 15:26–28). Paul's life had most certainly ended before the destruction of the temple and the city of Jerusalem in 70 CE. We do not know when Paul was born (6 BCE–6 CE?), but he was likely in his sixties when he died as a rather spent man.

There are no unambiguous citations of Paul before the time of 1 Clement 47:13 (ca. 95 CE) and Irenaeus (ca. 130–202 CE), such that Paul's immediate impact appears to have waned very quickly. Luke's book of Acts has been variously dated from ca. 85–120 CE. One might muse over how Paul's various churches would have remembered him. How might one imagine the church at Ephesus have remembered Paul or the church at Philippi, and for how long? On the other hand, how might one imagine the church at Corinth to have remembered Paul? All of Paul's churches had to face growing pains and changing times after Paul's successive imprisonments and subsequent death. Times were changing, even within the mind-set of a cultural continuum.

Multiple theologies of the gospel were developing in the time after the fall of Jerusalem. Multiple "false teachers" arose perhaps particularly on Pauline mission fields, as the gospel continued to be adapted to a Greco-Roman world and to a church written large that had become predominately gentile, perhaps especially as a direct result of the Pauline mission. Jesus had not returned and the church had to settle down for extended life in the world. Regardless of what appears to be a complicated origin, multiple expressions of what is collectively known as Gnosticism began to threaten the developing Christian church. It may have been among the gnostics that Paul's letters began to find a universal significance, as they found the language and emphases of his letters to be congenial with the dualism of good and evil, flesh and spirit, and celestial powers.

Paul is the most influential thinker in church history other than Jesus. Paul was loved by friend and foe of the mainstream church of the second century. He had "fought the good fight," or, more literally, he had "agonized the good agony" (2 Tim

4:7). And, yet were it not for the pages of fragile papyrus that recorded his letters, Paul may well have passed from the pages of history altogether, aside from Luke's story recorded in Acts. And Luke never acknowledges that Paul wrote letters.

It is Irenaeus (d. 202 CE) who first offers unambiguous citation of Paul's letters, although church fathers from Clement of Rome to Justin Martyr (period, ca. 95–152 CE) appear to have known the various letters. There are comparatively few references to Paul for the first one hundred years after his death. The writer of 2 Peter (2 Pet 3:15–16, ca. 125 CE?) mentions Paul and his letters (pl.), acknowledging that they are difficult to understand and that they were apparently in use by unorthodox elements within early Christianity. The earliest surviving list of Paul's letters comes from Marcion (ca. 140 CE), who is known only secondhand through Tertullian (d. 220 CE).

Paul, of course, has been influential upon Christian theology down the centuries through folk like Augustine (doctrine of original sin), Thomas Aquinas (the father of natural theology), Martin Luther (justification by faith), and John Calvin (predestination, atonement). Some have understood Paul as the "second founder" of Christianity, who transformed the very practical agenda of Jesus by offering instead a spiritualized gospel with Christ as the object of faith. According to some, in keeping with Hellenistic mystery religions, Paul turned the prophet Jesus into a cosmic Lord. According to others, Paul offered up a "being-in-Christ mysticism" on the basis of his own spiritual experiences.

Paul was both loved and hated—even during his own lifetime. He has been a major center of controversy ever since. Reaction to Paul during his lifetime may suggest something about the temperament and character of Paul himself, of which we see only glimpses in his letters. We should be careful not to over-characterize Paul. That Paul could express moods of great elation and great despondency only acknowledges his humanness. It is remarkable, however, that he could express elation and joy even in a context of imprisonment in which at one point he despaired of life itself (see Phil 1:12–26). He was but a "ceramic" vessel, a pottery vessel of clay (2 Cor 4:7).

We do not have enough material to complete a full "biography" of Paul. The limited number of letters ascribed to him, along with Luke's account in Acts, cannot even come close to fully charting his more than a quarter of a century ministry. By comparison, according to the Synoptic Gospels, Jesus's own public ministry likely lasted only a maximum of about two years. Still, we can know quite a lot about Paul, even though it may be fragmented. We should not, however, "know" more or less than there is to know. If history is an encounter with what is known, then each generation must do its own work of recovery and understanding in turn in the light of latest knowledge and application.

Paul's world does not change; it is what it was. However, our comprehension of that world most certainly does change. While there may be no final knowledge of evolving reality, there will always be a new quest for the historical Jesus and the historical Paul as long as people seek to understand the New Testament. History involves not only knowledge of Paul and his writings from the first century, but also the impression Paul makes upon us through the reading of his letters. History always involves events that happen, facts that are remembered about those events, *and* interpretations that are given.

Paul has always been controversial. He was so in his day. He has been so in the history of interpretation. He remains so today, whether viewed antagonistically, favorably, or indifferently. Paul dominates the pages of the New Testament, appearing on perhaps half of its pages, with approximately a third of the New Testament itself being ascribed to him. Still, in view of the many portraits of Paul and his thought offered in the scholarly and pietistic marketplace of Christendom, the question for the average person who seeks to understand Paul and his letters may be "Will the real Paul please stand up?"

There are even different Pauls reflected in the New Testament itself. There is the Paul of the authentic letters, the deutero-Paul(s) of the letters ascribed to him the authenticity of which is questioned, the Paul of Acts, the implied Paul opposed by the Nomistic Evangelists, the "hard to understand, twisted" Paul entertained by the ignorant and unstable (2 Pet 3:15–16). While we may be most interested in what Paul wrote, Paul the man insofar as he may be recovered may be more important than we realize. How can we rightly interpret his thought without an appropriate understanding of the man? This work has invited one to imagine Paul—the man, his message, and the myths that have come to surround this first-century apostle of Christ.

Paul transposed Jesus's theological vision to a new key. He understood the power of God as that which reversed the Law's condemnation (as even it had of Jesus, Gal 3:13) and affirmed the Law's inclusion of all of Abraham's descendants on the principle of faithfulness (see Gen 15:6). Some scholars have written an obituary for Paul, in which he is seen as the "Founder of Christianity." Paul did not institute a new religion, because he never left his old, ancestral religion. Paul remained a Jew, who understood God's promises to Israel to be fulfilled in Christ. The emergence of Christianity as distinct from Judaism was a long process, which Paul did not initiate, but to which he made a distinctive contribution.

Paul should not be termed the "founder of Christianity," for he was not. It may be appropriate to term Paul the inadvertent "founder of Christendom," in view of the way his writings came to be interpreted within the official church of Christian history. On the other hand, Paul's Jewish identity determined his religion, his theology, and his worldview. The Gospel determined the way he lived. It needs to be frankly admitted that Paul did not recast his monotheism into Christendom's later third-fourth century doctrine of the "Trinity." Paul maintains a strong note of subordination of the Son even in the midst of the most exalted eschatological passages (see Phil 2:11c; 1 Cor 15:28c). God the Father is responsible for Jesus's resurrection (1 Thess 1:9–10; Gal 1:1; 1 Cor 6:14; 15:15; 2 Cor 4:14; Rom 1:4; 6:4; Col 2:12; Eph 1:20).

Paul never confused Jesus the Son with God the Father, even though he could baptize in the name of Jesus/Christ, celebrate a meal in the name of Christ, employ hymns of praise in honor of Christ, confess Christ as Lord, and even dedicate doxologies to Christ. Paul did not confuse monotheism with agency, exaltation, functional nature, and subordination, as many interpreters of Paul's letters have done. Jesus's view of God is inherent in his address to God as "Abba," an address that carried over to Paul's gentile churches (Gal 4:6; Rom 8:15). Not a single one of Paul's salutations is couched in Trinitarian language, although they all commend "grace and peace from God the Father and the Lord Jesus Christ." The term "Christ" represents Jesus's identity as Jewish "Messiah," God's anointed one, although the term likely became a name upon gentile soil. The term "Lord" represents Jesus's identity as the all-powerful one, God's exalted one, risen from the dead.

Paul's Pharisaic zeal led to fanatic opposition to those earlier Jerusalem Christians who announced what appeared to be a ridiculous and offensive assertion of a crucified Messiah. Paul's vision of Christ changed his life. He came to a new understanding of the place of the gentiles, the Jewish Torah, and faithfulness. Paul went so far as seeing some elements within the Torah to be obsolete (as did Jesus, as did Stephen). In the context of his ministry, he was deemed to be an apostate by Jews, a heretic by more conservative Jesus-followers. He faced opposition from both the synagogue and some factions of the early church. Expressed in modern terms, it is doubtful the church at Corinth would have called Paul as their pastor.

Conservative Jewish-Christians came to view Paul's Jewish heritage as ambiguous. Paul himself experienced strong tensions between his inherited values and his new convictions in Christ. He became selective in observance of Torah. His proclamation of the gospel and his apostleship were not deemed legitimate in some quarters. Paul redefined those who were descendants of Abraham in contrast to the customary views of his day. As he came to understand, God always intended to include gentiles; there had never been an exclusive covenant for Israel as an ethnic people. That is not to deny that a particularistic view of Israel developed in the period of post-exilic and Second Temple Judaism as one strand of interpretation, as in Ezra, for example. That was balanced, however, by an alternative universal viewpoint, present in Second-Isaiah (Isa 40–66), for example. Paul was a Hellenistic Jew living in a Roman-dominated world.

Fig. 38. Icon of Saint Paul. Photograph by G. Roger Greene.

While no one knows what Paul looked like physically, portraits of both Paul and Peter began to decorate church walls in the early Christian centuries. Paul was given the traditional appearance of slender-faced philosopher who emphasized his role as a theologian, teacher, and letter writer. Iconography began to emphasize the Roman church's claim to a dual apostolic foundation. It is "Saint Paul" that is depicted along with "Saint Peter." Artistic representations of Paul since the time of the Reformation, such as portraits by Rembrandt, tend to depict Paul as a letter writer. Other depictions are drawn from the narrative portrayal by Luke in Acts. A different work, the *Acts of Paul and Thecla*, provides an imaginative presentation of Paul in the late second century as a small, bald man with crooked legs, although it is not accorded much historical credence.

Both the church and Christian faith existed before and alongside Paul. We know something of its experiences, rites, beliefs, and ethics through the various source materials available to us from the New Testament and church history. Even gentile Christianity also existed before and alongside of Paul. Someone other than Paul, for example, founded the church at Rome or in Alexandria, Egypt, or in Antioch, for that matter. Paul was a debtor to his predecessors in Christ, perhaps even more so than is admitted in his letters. His story is a part of the story of the rise of Christianity. Our ignorance of Paul is at the same time an ignorance of primitive Christianity. Paul's letters become a sole witness. Paul's letters reflect much of the same kind of perspectives, addressed to groups of people, with much the same range of subject matter. Paul's personality is stamped on everything he wrote. Paul was a product of a particular age and set of circumstances. He was a man "in Christ" within five years of Jesus's own death and resurrection. As his letters became important in the mainstream church, he became "Saint Paul."

Paul's Gospel

Neither Jesus nor Paul offered a new religious system, yet both offered gospel (see Mark 1:14–15). The perceived identity of Jesus and his sacrificial death are not the key to a new religious system supposedly proposed by Paul. As an example, "justification by faith" (discussed below) is too abstract to be the key to Paul's theology or his gospel. It is a phrase even misunderstood in connection with Paul's gospel. It may be manipulated by humankind in ways the Gospel of God cannot be manipulated.

Lest we forget, the word "gospel" (εὐαγγέλιον) suggests "*good* news." Paul's gospel is the *announcement* of what the God of Israel has done to fulfil his covenant promises made long ago in Abraham. In Christ, God had acted to fulfil the basic promise to bless all nations through Abraham (Gen 12:3). That basic promise, handed down by tradition and found in Torah, was given long before the provision of the Torah itself through Moses. Paul's Jewish gospel, for many of his contemporary Jews and Christians, was regarded as dangerous—even false and heretical. It created a basic tension between continuity and discontinuity, for it focused not upon the history of the past but upon the discontinuity wrought by an eschatological present and future.

Torah and Israel

The "new Israel" now consisted of Jews *and* gentiles. While God's plan from the time of his covenant with Abraham was to incorporate gentiles into the one people of God, which Paul can term the new "Israel of God" (Gal 6:16), that did not mean that gentiles had to embrace the Mosaic Torah (to live like Jews) in order to receive God's blessing. In fact, Paul affirms that neither circumcision nor uncircumcision makes any difference (Gal 6:15). What does make a difference is embracing Jesus's cross as our own, as well as in faithfulness that is distinctively different from worldly ways, even if it involves persecution and suffering. Paul writes with his own hand in Gal 6:11–18, such that we don't get closer to Paul than what he writes there.

Paul understood admission to the "new" Israel of God apart from the Torah (see Gal 6:15–16) to be on the basis of faithfulness, in the light of the foundation of faith expressed in the Abraham stories. God had ratified the covenant made with Abraham some 430 years before the Torah was given through Moses (see Gal 3:15–20). The order of references in Genesis determined Paul's understanding of the gospel. God established his covenant with Abraham in Gen 12:1–3. Abraham trusted God and his faith was reckoned to him as righteousness (Gen 15:6).

Both actions were prior to a later-presented tradition whereby the establishment of the covenant was ratified by the rite of circumcision (see Gen 17:1–14). Paul had opposition from his own people, as well as Christian "Nomistic Evangelists" who called for the necessity of circumcision for completion of admission into Israel or the "new Israel" in Christ. This resulted in rejection from his own people or repeated punishment in synagogues or the undermining of his authority and his own person in churches that he had established (see 1 Thess 2:14–16; 2 Cor 11:23–27).

Theologically, as Christians, we too often live where *Paul the Pharisee* lived, with a religion based upon ritual and a rational code, a safe haven laced with a "sound and a feeling" that soothes our minds and hearts and circumscribes the Gospel according to our comfort. When Paul received his call and commission to become an apostle to the gentiles, the *inclusive* aspects of Torah became central over the *exclusive* aspects of Torah or "Law." Abraham became his foundational model of faithfulness to God. For Paul the Christian, who followed the "Christ Way," he did not forsake his Judaism. Rather, he came to celebrate his Judaism in terms of God's original covenant with Abraham based upon relational faithfulness that antedated God's *conditional* covenant expressed through Moses.

The Mosaic covenant was given hundreds of years later than the *unconditional* covenant through Abraham. The latter was inclusive; the one through Moses was exclusive. One should not approach the two covenants moralistically, but rather historically. One should realize the difference (see Gen 12:1–5; Deut 30:15–20). The Mosaic Torah defined the people of Israel as a people in distinction from neighboring peoples, even beginning with the first commandment (see Exod 20:2–3). Distinctive exclusivity is characteristic of the Mosaic religion in the formative period of Israel's national history, inherent also in the prosecution of "holy war" under Joshua during the conquest of the land. An exclusive people were defined by an exclusive God, with exclusivism defined in terms of "holiness" and "righteousness."

The earlier traditions associated with Abraham are recounted in the light of the exodus event and Mosaic covenant-making; Abraham, Isaac, and Jacob are understood as the ancestors of Israel. Yet there is an ambivalence. Abraham is the forefather of what became historical Israel, yet at the same time of an Israel that was meant to be inclusive of all peoples of the earth. In fact, Abraham was a "gentile" when called by God. Paul the Christian came to understand the temporal distance of Moses from Abraham, but in the light of his own call by God to be an apostle to the gentiles or nations (see Gal 1:15–16). Paul had experienced a dramatic divine intervention in terms of the resurrected Christ. Within a universal gospel, a Jew might continue to live under Torah as always. A Jew need not discard the Torah, foundational as it was to covenant. However, to require a believing gentile to embrace the Torah as necessary for salvation marked a denial of the efficacy of resurrection and the value of faithfulness. The value of faithfulness was evidenced by Torah itself (Gen 15:6) in the period of Abraham, long before Moses.

Paul understood God's victory in Christ in terms of the two critical moments of the resurrection and the parousia. Full redemption awaits the future *of* God and *with* God, in a time when Sin and Death are no more. For the present, while defeated in Christ's resurrection, they are still active. Christ-believers are united with Christ, sealed with the Spirit, forgiven of sins by Grace, no longer under the lordship of Sin.

Whether our apprehension and imagination of Paul is accurate or not—and hopefully it is in at least some respects—the theology of Paul remains the theology of Paul. All interpretations of Paul and his theology are not equal. It is faulty thinking on the part of theologians to assume they stand at the end of a long line of faithful trustees of the Pauline tradition, safely guarded so as to guarantee the delivery of the precious original deposit unchanged down to their own generation.

The more we can view Paul *as he was* rather than *as we are*, the better we shall comprehend and the better we shall be able legitimately to appropriate Paul's understanding of the Gospel of God. Such a Paul may appear as a stranger in our midst, rather different from the many anachronistic portraits of Paul that have been offered us. So, what *is* the test to insure one is seeing Paul as *Paul*? To be frank, the real Paul will only be found through the careful study of Paul's letters in context. Like anything else, the context is largely the message.

Personal religion does not necessarily value the historical Paul as a theologian. It looks instead for food for the soul. Theologically speaking, however, one should avail oneself of the best "soul food" available. Paul's thought is not life itself for us but rather food for us. Paul himself would direct us to the gospel as that which gives life. It can still nourish. It can still inspire. The "doctrine" of Paul is not obligatory for every age who would call themselves Christian. The "doctrine" of Paul is actually post-Paul, having been developed in later ages. The "doctrine" of Paul has been thrust upon us to the exclusion of the gospel of Paul.

With the proclamation of the gospel, Paul offered life "in Christ." His personal theology supported his understanding of the gospel. The "gospel" would echo Paul's core convictions, while his expressed "theology" offers theoretical answers to contingent situations in which he was called upon to do something or to address a problem. Paul declares the kerygma, the mighty acts of God in Christ. He declares the Gospel of God.

The foundations of Paul's doctrines are Jewish. Freed from rules and rituals, some see Paul as one who shackled believers with dogmas of grace, atonement, and salvation based upon a belief in Jesus the Messiah and the bodily risen Son of God. Paul substituted faith for deeds and transformed the kingdom of God into a mythical and mystical conception in contrast to the prophetic message of the restitution of a nationalistic society. Paul's conception of Christianity was considerably similar to that of the mystery religions and had great appeal to gentile pagans who were already attuned to such. And, Paul held great appeal for developing Gnosticism.

For Paul, favored as he was (see Phil 3:4–6; Rom 9:4–5), favoritism did not invalidate God's impartiality. The Law did not establish God's partiality, even though it may have been so interpreted. For Paul, nothing less than God's own trustworthiness was at stake (Rom 3:26).

The crux of the difference between Paul and others within Judaism was the conception of the age in which Christians now lived post-resurrection. The fact that Paul came to believe the New Age had dawned meant eschatology became imperative in practical terms. Paul's acquired conviction gave him a distinctive understanding of Jesus's crucifixion, the Torah, the resurrection, and the inclusion of the gentiles within the Israel of God. Paul had a distinctive understanding of the gospel compared with that of the Jerusalem apostles.

Jerusalem apostles awaited the coming of the New Age, the restoration of the kingdom to Israel (see Acts 1:6). With the parousia, the Torah would have fulfilled its God-given function, although presently it remained as valid as ever. In the mind of the conservative element of the Jerusalem church, Torah remained obligatory for all those who joined the company of the saints awaiting the parousia. The delay of the parousia spoke against Paul's view, although the growth of the gentile church and especially the destruction of Jerusalem (70 CE) contributed greatly to the growth of Paul's esteem at a time after his death. This esteem grew over time with the collection and usefulness of the Pauline correspondence for the developing church.

Paul creatively transformed the Old Testament concept of the "Day of Yahweh" into that of the "Day of the Lord Jesus Christ," such that Paul becomes the major source for the use of the term "parousia" for the future coming of Christ (2 Thess 2:2; 1 Thess 5:2; Phil 1:6, 10; 2:16; 1 Cor 1:8; 5:5; 2 Cor 1:14). Paul draws apocalyptic language and imagery from the Old Testament (see 1 Thess 1:9–10; 4:13—5:11). There is a close association between the parousia and final judgment (1 Thess 3:13; 1 Cor 3:12–15; Rom 2:1–11). Paul's own calling and the gentile mission are related to the fulfillment of God's promises to include all nations under his blessing and rule in the fullness of time. Paul saw his own ministry to which he had been called by God to be a part of God's eschatological activity.

When the parousia did not occur, it was over time postponed to the "end of the world." Continued use of old phraseology became conventional and Paul's theological spontaneity was lost. His terminology remained, but the meaning of Christ, his death and resurrection, salvation, sacraments, and sanctions all changed. Over time, the plants that grew in Paul's garden were those of Augustine, Luther, Calvin, and others. Largely, these later thoughts were their own theology read back into Paul and not a continuation or revival of Paul's thought.

To begin with the theology of Paul and imagine a context later than Paul's day is to run the risk of losing contact with the reality of Paul. This is commonly the fault of historical critical studies of Paul. To do so is to run the risk of losing both Paul and the gospel he proclaimed.

Paul's gospel destroys the danger of elitism within the church from both a sociological and theological perspective. Such election suggests that election is actually based upon justification by works—"I am better than you because of who I am or what I do." It is diametrically the opposite of justification by grace. Grace leaves no one with a boast, but calls for gratitude and worship. Paul neither judges nor addresses those outside the community of faith. The church remains the servant of the new creation. God has acted for his *world*—for *his* world, with the church as his servant. We can celebrate the new creation wherever it exists. Salvation is restoration to authentic creatureliness. According to Genesis, humankind was created in the image of God for relationship with him and given the responsibility of stewardship over the remainder of creation as God's representative.

Paul's theology proved not to be *directly* "transferable" beyond his own generation, although Paul's name and words became hallowed in the church of the empire. Over time, a catholic theology sublimated that of the early church in such a way as to promote creeds and ecclesiastical organization as required for a post-Pauline new age. However, the theology of Paul cannot be simply lifted out of the first century and deposited into the fourth, sixteenth, or twenty-first century without the occurrence of some change. One should not expect Paul's theology "as is" to be an exact fit when transported into an alternative social, cultural, and religious context existing in the environment of a different worldview. There has been a Copernican revolution in more ways than one since the time of Paul.

Much of what is heard in Christian preaching is not to be found in Paul, even though it is often attributed to him. Much of what is found in Paul, it also need be said, is never heard in Christian preaching. As any serious concordance and examination of references will show, the use of the word "cross" in Paul's letters refers more to Christian living than it does to Jesus's death. Paul lived in a world of literal religious sacrifice, but interestingly he does not affirm that God needed a "perfect sacrifice" in order to be able to forgive sins. In fact, as has been pointed out, Paul only *very* seldom speaks of forgiveness of sins. One can, again, easily follow Paul's emphases through the use of a concordance index.

In fact, as has been seen, Paul does not emphasize forgiveness in his letters. Paul does not develop atonement theory in single, isolated verses. Neither does Paul affirm that "Jesus died for our sins so we could go to heaven." Paul does not affirm that "Jesus died in our place" in a substitutional, transactional atonement that required the shedding of blood. He simply does not. Where is the evidence? The Greek phrasing of ὑπέρ ὑμῶν ("in our behalf," "for our benefit") does not accommodate "in our place" in Paul's general usage, as some advocates of "Pauline theology" would maintain. Paul, whether one agrees with him or not, has been misunderstood, misapplied, and even abused in much post-Reformational theology and preaching. It is important to note what Paul himself said by actually reading his letters with a degree of understanding and appreciation. And, it makes a difference whether one reads them in a gospel mode of worship versus a laboratory mode of theological dissection versus a propaganda mode of alternative agendas.

In Search of Gospel

Many people today may see Paul's thought as mythological, locked into an ancient worldview no longer entertained by contemporary people. Many people today may see Paul's thought as perhaps having only an historical interest for a diminishing number of people with interest in such. One may imagine Paul, but one should not see either Paul or his gospel that he proclaimed as imaginary. "God was in Christ reconciling the world to himself, not reckoning their trespasses to them, and entrusting to us the word of reconciliation" (2 Cor 5:19). Can one still imagine that? Paul could and did, and it changed his life.

We need to appreciate Paul's gospel in terms of Paul's presuppositions, his suppositions, and his hope—God's action in Christ, Christ's sufficiency for our need, *and* Christ's resurrection as a harbinger of hope—rather than substituting our doctrines as paramount to the Gospel. We live in a different age, such that we may have different presuppositions and suppositions, even some based upon Paul's thought. Paul can cause one to think through a lot of things that one holds dear and cause one to evaluate them in the light of his understanding of what, indeed, is "gospel" and what is not. He provides the earliest "yardstick" for measuring our "gospels" and a plumb line or standard of soundness like none other available to us.

Paul's gospel provides not only food for much thought, but it also provides food for one's soul—"soul food," to borrow a metaphor from the southern part of the United States. While we may not be able to embrace his culturally locked presuppositions or his suppositions contingent upon specific situations, there is still the matter of gospel and that of hope. What hope shall we substitute? Or, shall we live without either good news or hope? One may even choose not to embrace Christianity as a personal choice, but if not, one must and will choose an alternative. One may choose to believe in God or not, but one must define an alternative, even if it be an atheistic nihilism.

If one does not choose to embrace Christianity, then one needs to posit the absence of hope or to find hope elsewhere. *Christendom* may only need a doctrinal Paul, but *Christianity* needs a gospel Paul. Such a "gospel Paul" still has much to offer. Perhaps it is we who need to develop ears to hear and eyes to see. There's a word for that—the word "imagine." Imagine Paul's gospel. Paul's "theological reflections" provide a center where being and doing become a single unity. Imagine it is "true," just as he proclaimed it and lived it. The Gospel of God can still change our lives, even as it changed Paul's, in ways that doctrine, ever how correct, never can. Paul discovered that very thing with reference to Torah (the Law) no less.

There are many beliefs that belong to a bygone age that are no longer seriously entertained by contemporary persons. It becomes all the more incumbent to understand not only what Paul had to say, but why he said it. Not everything needed by modern persons may be distilled from first-century documents. It needs to be admitted that not everything Paul had to say remains relevant to twenty-first-century Christians. Frankly, this needs to be acknowledged for the Bible itself overall. Blind dogma no longer satisfies, nor is it sufficient to meet human need in a contemporary, postmodern world.

One needs to exercise discernment. There are some doctrines used to describe the Bible that have outworn their perceived usefulness. They are outmoded, inadequate, or simply wrong. These have caused depreciation of biblical truth, even as similar doctrines have wrought depreciation of Paul. What is needed is a more adequate hermeneutic that offers appropriate discernment. Paul understood himself to be living in a New Age, which, for us, is no longer new. His words are most applicable to those who shared his world and his view of eschatological fulfillment, but that does not automatically mean they are irrelevant to us who live in a different age.

Paul's gospel was a paradoxical call to freedom. For too long, we have sought to live on doctrines—codified and impersonal "truths," when in reality they can never bring life. Within Christendom, we have created a new "oral torah." Paul, if a Pharisee, must have spent a good portion of his life defending and debating and refining the "oral torah." Jesus himself criticized the oral torah (see Mark 7:5–13 par.). In Christ, Paul came to understand that all the theological debate in the world and no "doctrine" created by humankind could save, redeem, and restore.

In fact, "doctrines" tend to fracture and separate, rather than to reconcile. They tend to mark off "us" and "them." Paradoxically, perhaps, to live according to doctrines is akin to setting one's mind on the "flesh," which according to Paul, is the way of death (Rom 8:6). As Paul said of the Law, if a law had been given that would make alive, there would have been no need for Christ to die. To paraphrase, if a doctrine had been given that could make alive, there would be no point to Christ's death. Indeed, there would be no need for the Gospel of God. There would be no relevance for a "cross imperative."

Paul and his letters came to be used for a "confessedly and dogmatic purpose" to support and circumscribe the church at the beginning of Christendom. One may overly tout the pre-Pauline tradition or the post-Pauline tradition and simply make Paul to be a mouthpiece for alternative gospels of later ages. Given the chance, Paul himself would criticize today's alternative "gospels" just as strongly as he criticized the alternative gospel of the Nomistic Evangelists presented to the Galatian Christians (see Gal 1:6–9).

Theology

As we come to consider "theology" in this section, all the remaining elements in this chapter could be subsumed under this broad rubric. However, because the remaining topics are primary elements inherent to Paul's gospel, they are treated separately and individually. Here, among other themes, the post-Reformational and time-honored theme of "justification" is treated. Paul's own life represented two alternative ways to become "right with God." The theology of Paul the Pharisee called for one to become or remain "right with God" on the basis of Mosaic Torah, as augmented by the developing oral torah. Paul the follower of Christ discovered in that same Torah a prior and foundational strand of "faithfulness" associated with Abraham, who had lived long before Moses.

In fact, the story of Abraham actually began *Israel's* ancestral history (Gen 12–50) following the Torah's introduction of primeval history. The primeval history (Gen 1–11) established the fact of the sinfulness of humankind and a fallen creation in need of reconciliation and redemption. The covenant God made with Abraham becomes the first step toward reconciliation and redemption, i.e., the first step toward God's salvation of humankind as a whole (Gen 12:1–5).

"Pauline theology" is always a construct. It is always "culturized" at both ends. It belongs to Paul's culture. It belongs to our cultural inheritance. It is likely better to speak of Pauline "themes" rather than Pauline "doctrines." We can examine "themes" more generally, while "doctrines" carry vested interests and evoke either our own apologetic or polemic. This is not to deny the reality of interpretation, but it is to speak more neutrally and to imagine Paul, rather than later theological accretions. With that in mind, there are two themes that emerge that have some significance for understanding Paul: "justification" by law and "justification" by faith. Actually, those two themes give evidence for three items for discussion—"justification," "law," and "faith." A fourth theme, that of "grace," may also enter into understanding the theological themes inherent to and at issue with Paul's gospel.

There are actually three thematic triads that are examined in the remainder of this chapter, although topically they may call for different treatment. In the current section, the time-honored theme of justification by faith merits consideration, although that necessarily introduces the third element of the Law. The first thematic triad thus involves "justification, faith, and the Law." The theme of "justification by faith" that emerged in the Reformation was proposed in contrast to a characterization of Judaism as a religion of "Law." God, Christ, and salvation provide a second triad, even though the topics warrant separate treatment. And, finally, the separate topics of church, eschatology, and a gospel imperative bear a degree of inter-relatedness.

Justification by Law

One needs, first of all, to be clear about terminology. English words such as "just," "justice," "righteous," and "righteousness" connote very different concepts in English. In Greek these words are all based on the same root (δικ-). There is confusion in English because of the perceived difference between "justice" and "righteousness," although the Greek word δικαιοσύνη (root δικ-, "to show" or "point out") may be translated in either manner, depending upon context. Paul's usage stems from a confluence of themes in biblical thought. Because God is right, his judgments are just. God's current wrath is just, as he turns humankind over to themselves (Rom 1:24, 26, 28). God's final judgments are just (Rom 2:3–11). Paul's assumptions are based upon the convictions that the God of Israel's covenant is just or righteous. God expects his covenant people to be just and righteous. Creation has been "fallen" since the time of Adam, and Sin has worked its way through the entire human race, such that "not so much as one" is righteous or lives with kindness (see Rom 3:10–12).

The theme of the book of Romans could be expressed in terms of the "righteousness of God" (δικαιοσύνη τοῦ θεοῦ), although that should be understood in the context of the Gospel of God (εὐαγγέλιον τοῦ θεοῦ, Rom 1:1, 16–17). In the biblical language of Paul, God is said to be right in himself and in his actions (Rom 3:26). Only one who is right can judge rightly or take steps to rectify one who is not right. From an Old Testament perspective, one is said to be "righteous" when one is living in accordance with covenant. That would actually mean that one was living in a right relationship with the covenant God, who indeed established the covenant. Righteousness was accorded to Abraham by God on the basis of his faithfulness (Gen 12:6). While we may focus on Abraham, Paul first of all focused upon God. No matter how "good" Abraham may have been, it is the character and action of God that makes all the difference then and now.

The term "righteousness" may carry a lot of theological baggage subject to misunderstanding. It is seen to be "religious" language. In common perspective, "righteousness" can be understood as that which accrues when one "lives by the rules." Paul's language of "righteousness" can also be understood in terms of a divine declaration of substitute righteousness, i.e., one is considered righteous (even though not) because of the saving death of Christ. One "believes" in God's salvation in Christ on the basis of his death. One is seen to be either declared righteous (imputed) or made righteous (actual) according to some requirement. The term "righteousness" simply carries a lot of opportunity for religious mischaracterization.

The term is subject to manipulation by humankind, such that it becomes a status accorded to some and denied to others on the basis of some established and extended standard. To give a simple example of the point, one who attends church regularly could be deemed "righteous," while one who does not attend could be deemed "unrighteous." While this example may seem simple, the Nomistic Evangelists of Paul's day who opposed the gospel of Paul would deem those male gentiles who became circumcised as "righteous," while gentiles who remained uncircumcised could be judged to be "unrighteous," irrespective of any other considerations.

It seems better to understand the concept of δικαιοσύνη ("righteousness," "justice," "right relationship") in dynamic rather than static terms. One might assume with Paul that δικαιοσύνη is inherent with God. With human beings, "righteousness" is always a moving target. A better translation of the concept might be "rectification," the idea of being "made right," or, to make use a contemporary legal metaphor, "made whole." Theologically speaking, to see δικαιοσύνη as reference to "being made whole" is actually a healthy conception. God is "right" and he is able to "make right" or "make whole" those who exhibit the faithfulness of Jesus (Rom 3:26).

God is right and rectifies through his redemptive activity. One in Christ becomes rectified on the basis of faithfulness in God's grace expressed through Christ. God's rectification is revealed apart from the Law and the Prophets (i.e., the scripture). It occurs freely through his grace. God himself establishes a place of mercy and provision. God passes over previously committed sins. God "forbears," that he might demonstrate his δικαιοσύνη in the present season (see Rom 3:21–26).

"Justification" is something we feel we can do. We "justify" or defend our actions or inactions all the time. We rationalize our behaviors and beliefs. That we "justify" ourselves, however, does not mean that we *are* right. Δικαιοσύνη is more than self-rationalization. It is that which comes as actualization. "Imputed justification" is an invention of the doctrine-makers and belies factuality. It is a human standard that belies divine reality at the point of both the indicative of what God has done and the imperative of what we are to do. It is altogether too easy to miss the point that there can be no δικαιοσύνη apart from a right relationship with either God or fellow human beings. Actual "rectification" makes possible right relationships, those characterized by "justice" and "rightness."

We need to be reminded that in biblical thought, Paul included, human beings are created in the image of God to have relationship with God, to be representative of God in the midst of creation, and to be responsible before God. Sin and idolatry are representative of the attempt to become "gods" unto ourselves. All that we are to be and all that we may actually become is simply to realize our God-given identity in creation, i.e., to be a "praise of God's glory" (see Eph 1:6, 12, 14). To be faithful before God, as Abraham was, is to be reckoned as "righteous." Abraham was not "justified," although he was accorded as right before God. "Justification" is human language of "vindication" and is really inappropriate to describe Paul's understanding of the gospel in terms of human vindication. *Rectification* describes the action of God in the Gospel.

Discussion of Paul's ambivalent view of the Law is well known in the context of scholarly discussion as a major issue within Pauline theology. Paul appears to embrace the Law (Torah)—it is "holy and just and good" (see Rom 7:12). Actually, literally, Paul writes that the *Law* is "holy," and the *commandment* is both just and good. The Torah prescribes celebration, for example, in terms of Sabbath or Passover (1 Cor 5:7-8; 16:2; Col 2:16). It also defined at least a basis of final judgment (see Rom 2:6-16). Paul the Pharisee could see himself to be "blameless" in relation to the Law (Phil 3:6), but on the other hand he had come to realize that no law could make one alive (Gal 3:11).

In Greek, Gal 3:10-14 is instructive. Paul quotes from Deut 27:26 in v. 10 to support his affirmation that "as many as are 'out of works of law' are under a curse." He cites Hab 2:4 (see Rom 1:17) to affirm that it is evident that no one is justified/rectified before God by law, because the one who is right will live by means/reason of faithfulness (ἐκ πίστεως). The Law is not "ἐκ πίστεως," but the one who does these things shall live by them (see Lev 18:5; Rom 10:5). Paul had experienced a freedom in Christ (see Gal 5:1-6) that had delivered a Pharisee schooled in the finer points of the Torah from the curse of the Torah. In fact he cites Deut 21:23 to support his affirmation that Christ has redeemed us from the curse of the Law ("purchased from the marketplace," ἐξαγοράζω, a slave market metaphor).

We have focused so much upon substitutionary atonement theory that we have missed Paul's point, which is found in Gal 3:14 and not Gal 3:13. Paul's point is seen in Gal 3:10 and 14, namely, that the Law is burdensome (its curse) and that the original blessing in Abraham (that antedated Mosaic Law) has come to the gentiles through faithfulness. This was the identical action represented in Abraham. That God had rectified the gentiles was evidenced by the reception of the promise of the Spirit on the same basis as Jews.

There is a sense in which what Paul asserts here is no different than the discovery that Peter made according to Luke, i.e., God shows no partiality. The gift of the Spirit was extended on the same basis to gentiles as to Jews (see Acts 10:34-35; 11:15-17). It should be remembered that Paul (on being pressed by the Nomistic Evangelists) writes to gentile Christians in Galatia in the context of legal prescription of circumcision on the basis of the Torah.

One other point might be made. It is instructive to read Deut 21:23 in its larger context. It is found in the context of Moses's second address to the people of Israel (Deut 5-26; 28) recounted in the light of a cultic and liturgical ceremony that dramatizes Israel's covenant responsibilities (Deut 27:1-26). The entire chapter may be a later insertion into the book of Deuteronomy, for it interrupts Moses's address (see Deut 26 and 28) and speaks of Moses in the third person. Deuteronomy 27 apparently records an ancient ceremony carried out by the presiding Levitical priests at

Shechem that preserves a list of twelve curses observed in a liturgical ceremony and setting, in which the people were to make response by solemnly affirming covenant responsibilities.

Deuteronomy 21:23 belongs to a collection of miscellaneous laws that Israel was to observe so as not to defile the covenant community or the land that God was about to give them for possession. It has to do with capital punishment (impalement on a tree) for capital crimes and, applicationally, with defilement of God's gift of the land. One might criticize Paul for his hermeneutical approach to scripture, for what at times appears to be a proof-texting, "post it note" citation of Old Testament scripture. However, one should not criticize Paul and then replicate the same action or approach in the utilization of Pauline texts themselves.

Living under Law

As a gift of God to Israel, Paul could appreciate the Law as "holy and just and good" (Rom 7:12). Paul also understood that the Law had fallen under the power of Sin and actually increased its severity by moving "sins" into the direction of transgression (Rom 7:7–25). The wages of Sin is death (Rom 6:23). The effect of the Law, that has become Sin's agent under the power of Sin, is not righteousness but wretchedness (cf. Rom 3:9–19; 7:24).

We need to realize that our dependence upon doctrines is the equivalent of Paul the Pharisee's life of dedication to the Torah. To live on the basis of or by doctrines and liturgy is to live in "Christendom," but not necessarily "in Christ" on the basis of the Gospel of God.

Did Paul have a theology? Yes, of course he did. Humans are rational beings who like organization and classification in thought and practice. Should we have a theology; should we have organized doctrines? Should we have organized worship, shall we say a "doctrine of worship"? Of course, we should. We will. On the other hand, we should not confuse theology with gospel. If we apply Paul the Christian's standard, there is no doctrine that has ever been given that, when embraced by one's thought, can save and make alive. None—not so much as one.

Every doctrine has been crafted by human thought at some point in time to address a particular issue or to seek to establish a particular point of view. Doctrines are human-centered. The gospel is first of all God-centered. How often, for example, has even evangelism been carried out in a human-centered way rather than in a God-centered manner? How often has it been carried out with a view toward *indoctrination* coupled with rote mental assent, rather than salvation toward relationship and personal or interpersonal rectification?

Galatians and Romans are the two Pauline epistles where the concept of righteousness occurs. Romans is not polemical, as is Galatians; it represents Paul's main exposition of "justification by faith" (see Rom 1:17; 3:21–26; 9:30–33; 10:1–13). In

Galatians Paul defends his gospel against the Nomistic Evangelists who sought to make the Torah rather than faith to be the means of inclusion into the people of Israel. According to Paul, it was faith and not the Torah that resulted in adoption as children of God, as participants in the promise to Abraham, and as receivers of the Spirit.

Paul gives his argument for rectification in Gal 2:19-21. Faith, as opposed to Law, is stressed in Gal 3-4. One is Abraham's offspring and an heir to God's promise on the basis of faith and not Law, even as in Abraham. One is an heir of Abraham and a child of God who is able to cry, "Abba! Father!" (Gal 4:6-7). It is highly significant that Paul, schooled in the Torah, chose Abraham and not Moses as his example of appropriate response to God.

Justification by Faith

Justification by faith is commonly thought to be the center or hallmark of Paul's theology. The phraseology comes as a residual legacy of the Reformation. Justification by faith is considered to be the central doctrine in Paul within Protestantism. Justification by faith has often been juxtaposed over against a salvation by works. For Protestants, generally, justification is a judicial act of God on the basis of Christ's saving death based on pure grace and not works. For Lutherans, justification by faith is *the* doctrine for understanding Christianity.

Within Catholicism, justification by faith is but *one* of Paul's theological themes—one of many metaphors describing new Christian existence. Opposition between justification by faith and works has not been stressed within Catholicism, as within Protestantism. Essentially, justification by faith suggests that God grants the undeserved gift of imputed righteousness to guilty sinners—a gift of pure grace received through faith. As some expressions would suggest, our sins are transferred to Christ and his righteousness is imputed to us.

Christ is God's offer of salvation that, when accepted, establishes one as right with God—either declared or made so. Is one only "declared" righteous, while remaining guilty? Is one judged "guilty" and offered redemption and rehabilitation? A pure judicial interpretation is seen to be inadequate by the present writer, if only imputed righteousness is envisioned. Alternatively, the justified actually become righteous, holy, transformed in the inner self. Humanity may cooperate with God's grace and, indeed, must do so.

In biblical thought, God in himself is righteous and acts in righteousness in accordance with his sovereign will. In Paul, righteousness concerns man as a sinner in need of *actual* rectification. The question may be asked as to whether the phrase "righteousness of God" is subjective or objective, whether it refers to God's own righteousness (subjective) or righteousness extended from God (objective).

Extended discussion of the topic of "justification by faith" in Paul occurs only in Galatians and Romans, such that other centers of Paul's theology have been proposed as alternatives, such as "participation in Christ." All of these terms—justification, faith, participation, "in Christ"—may lend themselves to misinterpretation. The word "justification" suggests legal terminology, "faith" as opposed to works may connote "religion lite" focused only on belief, "participation" in search of definition may be nebulous, and "in Christ" may be seen as "mystical."

The central statement on justification by faith in Romans is found in Rom 3:21–26, as Paul resumes the theme of the righteousness of God. Romans 4 repeats the argument of Gal 3. The same emphasis upon faith is found, although Paul intensifies insight into human sinfulness, the power of Sin, the role of the Law, and the action of God in justification. Even so, justification by faith is not the main theme of Romans. That honor belongs to the concept of the righteousness or rectification of God (δικαιοσύνη τοῦ θεοῦ) expressed in the Gospel (Rom 1:16–17), with which Paul contrasts the wrath of God (ὀργὴ θεοῦ, Rom 1:18) revealed against the "unrighteousness of men" (ἀδικία ἀνθρώπων, Rom 1:18). Both the righteousness of God and the wrath of God are now *revealed*. God's wrath results in the self-condemnation of humankind as God turns humankind over to itself for self-destruction (Rom 1:24, 26, 28). The lack of righteousness on the part of human beings is exhibited in a lack of godliness and a suppression of the truth.

To say that gentiles become a part of the covenant people of God "by faith in God's crucified and resurrected Messiah" suggests an objectification of faith and even Christ himself, when Paul treated Christ as personal and faith as subjective. Paul called for full personal participation in Christ and in the Gospel of God.

Paul discovered the Mosaic Torah was not able to explain fully the ways of God. His paradoxical experience of the risen Christ caused him to broaden his conception of God. Paul found a biblical precursor in Abraham. Paul interpreted Jesus's death and resurrection in the light of biblical promises, the image of barrenness and new-life conception in Abraham. Typologically, Paul found humankind's plight in Adam and he found God's solution in Abraham and in Jesus, Abraham's true offspring (Gal 3:16). The true offspring (pl.) of God are those like Abraham and like Jesus, who live in total faithfulness, who live from death unto life.

Historical interpreters of Paul have suggested an understanding of justification laced with law court imagery that is often set forth as legal fiction. Does Paul speak of *imputed* righteousness (Protestant) to those who are not right with God, based upon the atoning merits of Christ's death? The doctrine of substitutionary atonement accompanies such a view. Does Paul speak of *imparted* righteousness (Catholic) actually given to those who trust in Christ? Or, the present writer would ask, does Paul believe in neither? A divine judge who accords people as righteous even though they are not bespeaks an unjust God who traffics in cheap grace and cheap justification.

Some contemporary interpretations of justification understand it in terms of covenant membership apart from works of the Law, i.e., gentile inclusion yet without observation of the ritual aspects of the Law. To leave "justification" in the realm of legal language with the primary metaphor of God as Judge does not get to Paul's level of characterization. Paul acknowledges that God is right, and that he is able to rectify those who exhibit the faithfulness of Jesus (subj. gen.) in themselves. God judges faithlessness, but at his own initiative God acts with grace and makes provision for redemption. What God does is not to "justify" but to "rectify" (see Rom 3:26).

When one thinks in terms of rectification, one thinks in terms of a Redeemer and that which has real and lasting effect. One is not focused upon legal transaction whether real or imputed. One lives in the realm of covenant reconciliation, familial redemption, community inclusion, and new life. Romans 5:1–11 becomes constructive and provides a window of understanding. The action of rectification means provision means reconciliation means actual rectification.

Views of justification that privilege only a judicial metaphor miss the deeper aspects of Paul's covenantal thought based upon the reality of reconciliation and relational identity. One begins to have to nuance the language of legal justice in phrases like "restorative justice" or "restrictive justice" or "retributive justice." A term that has to be carefully nuanced may not be appropriate to begin with, nor does it necessarily get to the heart of the matter. Would Paul's audience have heard a point of "divine justice" in a world where Caesar's "justice" called for destruction of the enemies of Rome and subjection of those who might be potential enemies? God's "justice" was a matter of the manifest faithfulness and grace of God. What sense would the "absorption" of violence by God on behalf of the enemy make?

Normal forms of justice accepted in Paul's world were alien to the gospel. Grace-filled "justice" is alien to "violence-filled" justice. Paul's gospel calls for actual transformation of people in the light of the actual grace of reconciliation and restoration.

A wrong understanding of "faith" may distort the meaning of the phrase as well. Faith for Paul is conviction, trust, and confidence in God. However, faith is a bi-directional term. It is also more than trust—it is loyalty or faithfulness. God is faithful to his creation, to his promises. Jesus was faithful to God's purposes in the Gospel. Christians are called upon to express loyalty or fidelity to God. One of the high water marks in the Old Testament is the question posed by Micah and the answer that he gives. "What does the LORD require? But to do justice, to love covenant loyalty, and to walk humbly with your God" (Mic 6:8).

That statement made by Micah capsules the two great commandments and, hence, faithfulness to God. Faith is covenant knowledge and allegiance expressed toward God and the distribution of the qualities of God's kind of life unto others. Faithfulness is life lived in acceptance of God and expression of God in a manner representative of a praise of his glory. Ultimately, this may mean fidelity in life even to the point of death, and then continued fidelity even unto death.

Paul sees faith as sharing in the faithful death of Jesus. One is co-crucified with Jesus, becoming completely identified with his mode of obedience. It is a response to grace. The new covenant community formed in Christ re-enacts Jesus's own covenant loyalty on a daily basis. One experiences liberation from violent powers that can only kill. As one shares in the faithful death of Jesus, one will also share in his life.

"Rectification" comes as a result of God's grace, his faithfulness coupled with our reconciliation. Faith is incarnational and incorporational. Faith is learning to live unto God in a "we" culture rather than living unto ourselves in a private "me" culture. Galatians 2:20 marks the heart of cruciform spirituality for Paul.

Scholars have long searched for the "center" of Paul's theology, the conceptual starting point from which Paul's "theologizing" emerges. Paul's theology consists of interaction between coherence and contingency. To say that the essentially Jewish story of Jesus constitutes the true center of Paul's theology is to stop short. It is Jesus who is the key to unlocking the mysteries of God. Fundamentally, Christology is a word about God. A phrase like "Christological monotheism" is not really Pauline. Paul does not think theology in an abstract, impersonal way. "Christological monotheism" is high-sounding theologizing, but it is not Paul. Paul spoke simply of the Gospel of God, i.e., being interpreted, the good news announcement of the action of Israel's God expressed in Christ. (See further below.)

The Christ event marks the gracious invasion of God's astounding grace. The key to Paul's theology is the Gospel of God, that culminates in the resurrection and exaltation of Christ. It is living out of the Gospel, living in Christ, that makes sense of all of Paul's theology. It is not a principle, however, but a person. Paul's theology includes things transient and things lasting, things temporal and things eternal. Paul himself not only provided doctrine; he provided an example of what it meant to live in Christ. Paul has a lifestyle theology, whether one is speaking of "redemption" or "justification" or "salvation" or "faith" or "Spirit."

Is the Law still necessary? It did not provide the necessary discipline to ward off or restrain the power of Sin. It was not itself based upon trust. At the same time, trust did not invalidate the Law. It was effective in calling attention to sin (Rom 3:20; Gal 3:19). It was not effective in preserving one from Sin/sin. In fact, it could lead one away from grace (Gal 5:2–6).

The mind of Paul is not an encyclopedia of first-century theology. There is a difference between understanding the mind or intent of the author and using what is written by an author for one's personal need. The use of Paul's letters to meet individual needs may vary in different times and for different people. Paul was not a systematic theologian. Paul's interest was not in theology, nor even in a static religion that established a status quo. Paul was claimed by the dynamic Gospel of God to an experience-based faith of the risen Lord that led unto dynamic living rather than a faith in static belief.

Paul gives a theology rooted in the biblical witness. It is not an abstract mythology, but rather a construct deeply rooted in the transformation of persons by God's act in Christ. Paul's theology addresses Christian identity. Paul's theology is representative of event-become metaphor-become event, as God's indicative becomes transformative in terms of a corporate cruciform existence, paradoxically the embodiment of God's triumph expressed in communal health and hope.

God

While a dangerous and inaccurate caricature, many people have the idea of an angry, punitive, and warlike God of the Old Testament contrasted with a loving God of the New Testament, shall we say a God of John 3:16 or Rom 8 contrasted with the "holy war" God of Joshua. In the early church, one like Marcion discarded the Old Testament because he could not reconcile the different portrayal of God.

The Nature of God

One may set forth identity and character traits entertained by Paul and his fellow Jews. As the eternal one, God was the single one, the creator and the redeemer, such that Judaism was staunchly monotheistic.

God was holy, distinctive in character and action from human beings. He was relational and good, establishing relationship through covenant and choice of an elective servant people. God was a faithful keeper of promises, who was fair and just. He was gracious, loving and kind. He was merciful and forgiving, yet he was holy and demanding. He was a God worthy of obedience, praise, and honor. Human beings were created and Israel was chosen to be a praise of his glory.

Both Jesus and Paul offered a new view of God that caused each of them to be considered social and religious radicals in their time and context. Paul's root understanding of God was fundamentally akin to that of Jesus. They each perceived God as a sovereign Father who extended his grace and mercy of inclusion to those formerly excluded from God's covenant family. Paul's summary of the *human* (not Jewish or gentile) condition is that everyone has sinned (Rom 3:23) and continues to fall short of God's glory as intended in creation. No one is exempt. Paul's argument for God's impartiality and universality meant parity that is not nullified by privilege (see Rom 3:1–19).

Paul's gospel is first of all about God—his identity, his initiative, his story, his intention. The point of this section is not to develop a "doctrine" of God, but rather to come to an understanding of Paul's perception of God in the light of the Christ event. The cross of Christ is the definitive theophany of redemption, revelation, and reconciliation. The first introduction to Paul's theology and his understanding of God is found in all of Paul's salutations, as Paul commends "grace and peace to all of you from God the Father and the Lord Jesus Christ."

"Grace and peace" become the hallmark of Paul's experience with God. He begins all of his letters with "grace and peace," and ends them with benedictions that echo these words. Paul commends his own experience to his churches. One should take seriously Paul's conceptualization of the God of the Gospel, whom Paul describes as "Father," as compared to later portrayals of God colored by alternative cultural and theological realities in Christian history.

In the judgment of some scholars and others, Paul's religious claims about God and his Gospel belong in a museum of theology. According to their views, the sophistication of the modern world makes it rather difficult to believe as Paul did that Jesus rose bodily from the dead as a result of God's action. Such a view certainly marks a denial of the Gospel of God itself, as well as Paul's perception of God himself. It marks a disbelief in God or a view of gnostic theodicy that bespeaks the weakness of many religious people who claim to know what in reality they do not know and in fact cannot know.

From Paul's perspective and that of Christianity, one might call Paul's religious claims "gospel" and belief in them "faith." Paul's claims were based upon his personal and subjective experience. But as Paul himself honestly acknowledged, if Jesus has not been raised, i.e., if the gospel is not true, then Christians of all people are most miserable and to be pitied and may even be found to be misrepresenting God (see 1 Cor 15:12–19). We would not have Paul's thought regarding the resurrection, had the troublesome gentile Christians at Corinth not asked him to clarify the matter. Paul himself clearly believed in God and in the Gospel of God. He did not worship an antiquated "God of the gaps" in human knowledge. He worshiped the God of Abraham, now revealed in Christ.

The folly of covenantal disobedience is more than matched by God's apocalyptic grace extended to a dysfunctional human family that had infected the entire cosmos. God's power is demonstrated in self-giving service displayed in seeming weaknesses marked by serendipitous triumph. Far too often, rather than bending the knee to the will of God, we seek to bend the will of God to our own self-righteousness and self-satisfaction, even our own violence. We often worship an inverted God bound to anthropology, rather than understanding anthropology in terms of bended knee before God.

A Universal Monotheism

For Paul, the whole world was in need and was to be held accountable to an impartial God. There was only one God, who would redeem or judge everyone (Jew and non-Jew) on the same basis of faithfulness. Jewish monotheism is found in the creedal assertion of Deut 6:4, a central affirmation of Jewish faith and expectation. Echoes of the Shema are found in Rom 3:30, Gal 3:20, and 1 Cor 8:4. "Deeds" do matter, with or without the Mosaic Law (see Rom 2:6; 2 Cor 5:10). God is reliable and his integrity exists apart from the Law (Rom 3:21). After all, it was *his* Law freely given. God's integrity—justice, righteousness, loyalty to covenant—may be trusted, *before* Mosaic

Law, *during* the realm of Mosaic Law, and *post*-Mosaic Law. God is right, and he is able to make right, now and always.

As a result of God's revelation to Paul and his encounter with the resurrected Christ, Paul's monotheism was enhanced with new character. While Israel was prohibited from making images of Yahweh (Exod 20:4), the writer of Hebrews affirms that Jesus the Son is of the very "character" (χαρακτήρ) of God's nature (Heb 1:3). God's primary identity is no longer defined in terms of lawgiver and judge, but in terms of power and creation. In contrast to a prevailing view of God as a Lawgiver and Judge who looked for sacrifice and offerings as atonement for human sin, Paul contrasted a God who was Father and Creator of that which was new (see 1 Cor 3–4; 6:15–20; 12:12–31). The church was a spiritually and divinely generated family (1 Cor 3:1–4; 4:1–6).

Paul calls for health and well-being that begins with a healthy conception of a healthy God. Paul's new understanding of God caused him to trespass Jewish taboos and definitions as well as Greco-Roman conventions. The idea of God as "Father" who effects spiritual re-creation pervades Paul's letters. The resurrected Jesus had and has priority as God's "first-born" Son, now born twice unto a new creation as risen Lord. Jesus's exaltation may be singular, but his resurrection would not be singular according to Paul (see 1 Cor 15:20). His resurrection was the first fruit of a coming multitude.

Paul emphasizes God's generative power that is also beneficent and personal—ever greater than that of Caesar and all other powers and principalities. Paul combines the universal with the particular. Paul personalizes the creative power of God with the metaphor of a father's procreative, nurturing power that is able to bring new life even out of death. The power of the same God who created the universe is now exhibited in Christ and Abraham. This same God is undoing the pattern established in Adam, in whom things went so terribly wrong. Paul personalizes by choosing family imagery as metaphors of understanding. God is "Father," Christ is the exalted Son—and why not, for *Messiah* or *Christ* means "anointed one." The larger family of those in Christ provides the symbol of the church.

While many today may reject a "too small God," it may not be God who is rejected, but rather the limited conceptions of God that people have been presented. For example, to characterize God as one who had to have a "perfect sacrifice" in order to be able to "forgive sins" not only flies in the face of Paul's conception of God, but it also denies the entire biblical conception of God who has always sought to deal with human sinfulness on the basis of redemption. Not only do some worship their own conception of a "too small God" (otherwise known as idolatry), they also read a "too small Paul" in support of their viewpoints.

Paul did not create Hellenistic Christianity, nor is it accurate to draw a straight line from Paul to fourth-century creeds that confess Jesus's divinity in metaphysical terms. Paul did advocate a view of God marked by social egalitarianism. *The*ology was more important to Paul than *Christ*ology; he did not confuse the two. Greco-Roman class status and definition of the family of Abraham and of God were revised by Paul in the light of the Gospel of God in Christ.

Christ

Paul maintained a functional difference between God and Jesus the Son, but he could transfer Old Testament texts and divine attributes to the risen Christ, who was now the viceroy of God. The language of "Sonship" implies a shared identity, but it also suggests a sharing of divine purpose and power. Paul was a Jewish monotheist (see 1 Cor 8:4; Deut 6:4–5). Christian scholars have popularized the characterization of "Christological monotheism," a phrase that in the present writer's judgment Paul would not have embraced. The phrase marks an attempted accommodation of Jewish monotheism to Christian trinitarianism. The phrase suggests an incorporation of Jesus Christ as Son and Lord into the identity of God. Paul's answer to the contemporary question "Well, Jesus was God, wasn't he?" would be "no." Paul's Christology was not guided by philosophical concerns, informed by Greek ontological expression or later Latin description, as likely called forth by later theological controversies. Paul's orientation was Jewish. Paul identifies Jesus as Son, as Lord, as Christ. He does not confuse Jesus with God. We should stop trying to accommodate Paul to later Christian theology that arose in Christological controversies and simply let Paul remain a first-century Jewish Christian.

Jesus as Lord

To express "Jesus is Lord" in Paul's world was a pledge of ultimate allegiance in a world where Caesar *was* Lord. It was a subversive confession. The Gospel of God in Christ was a counter-imperial theology that in an eschatological time had refuted all of Caesar's claims. Yet the Jewish God who now fulfilled his promises was not a vindictive God but a reconciling God of grace and well-being (peace) toward the entire cosmos. As the people of a gracious and benevolent God, the church as church was to live as a transformed community engaged in transformation of society rather than conformation to it (see Rom 12:1–2). God's Gospel was personal, but not private. Paul's gospel was not first of all a private message of personal salvation. Jesus was not crucified for telling popular moral stories that we call "parables," or for offering self-help advice regarding an inward search for God in satisfaction of personal appetite.

Abraham and Christ mark two movements by God to right the wrong in the archetypal figure of Adam. Christ, of course, is identified as the Last Adam by Paul. Abraham, however, becomes the first antitype to Adam's *faithlessness*, as Abraham becomes the archetype of *faithfulness*, providing a foundation for the birth of Israel. Christ becomes the antitype of Adam in a much more complex manner in the eschatological age, as Paul sees Abraham to be a prototype of Christ. Christ is seen as the "seed" of Abraham (Gal 3:15–16). God's revelation in Christ marks the promised fulfillment of Israel. Christ undoes the faithlessness in Adam through his own faithfulness, even but not only his death on a cross (Phil 2:8). God through Christ is undoing the pattern established in Adam, in whom things went terribly wrong. Paul transposes the fundamental Jewish story to an eschatological key that involves all powers and principalities, primary of which may be Sin and Death.

The story of Abraham already alluded to is important to Paul in another sense. Abraham and Sarah were as "good as dead" when new life came to them in their old age. In effect, God brought life out of "death." God can do that which he has promised (Rom 4:19, 21). Of course, the ultimate act of God in the gospel was the raising of Jesus from the dead (Rom 4:24; 8:11; Gal 1:1). Scripture provided for Paul the motto that "the justified will live by faithfulness or trust" (Hab 2:4). Mosaic Law itself was not based upon trust, but upon obligation and practices.

For Paul, the "scandal of the cross" (Gal 5:11; cf. 3:13) became transformed into a symbol and sacrament of redemption—a blessing that could only be received through faithfulness. Cruciform identity is found throughout Paul and in fact is his predominant use of references to the "cross." His language, arguments, and concepts all seek to foster and inculcate a cruciform ethos and practice within his communities.

History between the time of Adam and Christ came to an end with the resurrection of Christ, that in itself introduced a new age. In effect, the crucifixion of Jesus marked the end of the old age, while the resurrection marked the beginning of the new age. Not the "end" of the world, but a new creation. There is not a linear salvation-history process in Galatians. The two nodes of Abraham and Christ are not two ends of an elongated historical continuum of God's dealing with ethnic Israel. They are dual representations, although representative of different import.

It was not the death of Jesus, a fellow Jewish countryman, on a Roman cross that was significant for Paul. Rather, it was the identity of Jesus as the Christ that was paramount. That awareness marked Paul's Christian life. Paul's conception of the resurrected Christ only deepened as time went on, as the key to God's eschatological future. Jesus was now Christ and Lord. Three men were crucified the day Jesus died (see Mark 15:27), but only one was confessed as raised, as Lord and Christ.

Being in Christ

There is no evidence Paul was ever challenged on the central issue of Christology. Paul was not fixated on Christ, although Christ was certainly important as the mediator of God's salvation. Paul consistently spoke of being "in Christ." To live "in Christ" for Paul was to live a cruciform life of obedience in hope of resurrection. Paul was not overly concerned with the unique or unrepeatable concerning Christ's death and resurrection.

Paul had a functional Christology that ultimately is subsumed under his *theo*logy. For us, we speak of the "gospel of Christ," as though he were the "author."

Paul spoke of the "Gospel of God" (see Rom 1:1). How could we have missed that? It occurs in the first verse of the most significant letter of Paul over the course of Christian history, as well as elsewhere. The answer most likely is that we have been in too much of a hurry to get to Paul's "theology"—the "real stuff" that we can manipulate, with the result that we lost sight of the foundation of Paul's gospel. Paul spoke of the "Gospel of God," of which Christ is the personal content and expression.

The word "cross" may be used metaphorically by Paul. Although it is commonly assumed, Paul did not view the literal death of Jesus on the cross as willed by God. Those who killed Jesus are not deemed "righteous" by God, nor by Paul, nor by the early sermons in the book of Acts. The "blood of Christ" refers to his life poured out upon the cross. It becomes a concentrated expression for the whole cross event understood as the mediating cause of redemption, rectification, and reconciliation. However, the "efficient cause" of forgiveness/rectification is not the death of Christ, but rather the love of God that changes one, the love of God that brings life out of death.

On the other hand, faithful commitment even to the point of death on a Roman cross becomes the way of salvation to be appropriated by those who follow Christ. Paul moves beyond this fundamental point to understand Jesus's death as an all-inclusive cosmic event in the context of a cosmos understood to have a dualistic structure. The dominion of powers hostile to God has been conquered, their reign overcome and their dominion stripped. The dominion of the risen Christ is now in effect. Paul's patterns of thought include that of Christ as the Last Adam, and that of dying and rising with Christ, who is now Lord.

By way of summary, Adam was disobedient, in that he sinned, transgressed, and let Sin and Death loose in the world. Abraham, as good as dead, was obedient before God and becomes an illustration of God's re-creative power at work in the faithfulness of Abraham to overcome "death" and fulfil his promises. Christ, of the seed of Abraham and David (see Gal 3:16; Rom 1:3; cf. Matt 1:1), was faithful and obedient even to the point of death on a cross. The result of Jesus's faithfulness in the face of lawless men and the powers of Sin and Death was his resurrection and exaltation by God, thus marking him out as Christ and Lord, as God gained victory over the powers of evil through Jesus's faithful obedience.

A Cruciform Life

Paul, along with other early Jesus followers by necessity, had a special interest in Jesus's death. He did not, however, view it primarily as a sacrificial atonement for other people's sins. Other metaphors predominate in Paul over sacrificial metaphors. Paul first encountered the risen Christ, who had been resurrected by God. As he sought to "learn Christ," he moved back beyond the resurrection and was immediately arrested by the fact of Jesus's death that called out for explanation and understanding. How could such a shameful death by Roman crucifixion be explained, such that it came to represent an honorable death in a first-century world where the cultural values of "honor-shame" held sway?

The change in Paul's thought came about through God's direct revelation and call (see Gal 1:11–17). The early kerygma also became formative for Paul. He and the other earliest Christians first thought retrospectively, not prospectively. Paul did not seek to write a "gospel" that narrated the life and ministry of Jesus. He was called to proclaim a gospel that had a clear focus on the present living and resurrected Christ. His contribution came by way of announcement, not by way of recollection, however interpreted.

Paul refers to only one event between Jesus's birth and death, namely, the Lord's Supper (or Eucharist; see 1 Cor 11:23–25). Paul knew Christ as risen, such that he does not emphasize the life and ministry of the historical Jesus. Jesus is not unimportant to Paul, for his obedience must be predicated upon his historical life and ministry, even as his death on a cross (see Phil 2:5–11). The Lord's Supper as Paul presents it is commemoration not only of the Lord's death but also of his return (see 1 Cor 11:26). The death of Christ marks a significant orbit of the Christ event for Paul in terms of his understanding or thought regarding salvation. However, Paul did not hold it in isolation. It always stands in concert with both incarnation and resurrection.

To give a human example, military missions may be charted. It is not the will of a commander that anyone should be killed or even injured. The will of the commander is that the mission be accomplished. Some of the most dangerous of missions call for volunteers. Jesus's own death is perhaps best understood in terms of his own words as ascribed to him in the Gospels (see Mark 12:1–12 par.). The father in Jesus's parable of the Wicked Tenants did not send his son nor his servants to be injured or killed, but rather to claim what was rightfully his, to accomplish a mission. The divine mission was that of redemption and reconciliation. The death of Jesus was a supreme act of surrender, commitment, and submission to the mission of God. The mission to which Jesus made commitment resulted in a voluntary commitment to pain and shame.

The death of Jesus is directly connected with sacrifice in but three passages in Paul—1 Cor 5:7, Rom 3:25, and Eph 5:2. First Corinthians 5:7 is a celebratory Passover metaphor. Romans 3:25 is a divine provision metaphor that demonstrates God's reconciling rectification. This is but one of several metaphors Paul employs in the same context, the others being related legal justification, the exodus, and slavery. Ephesians 5:2 affirms that Jesus freely gave himself "in our behalf" as an offering to God, but it occurs in a thoroughgoing *imperative* context of Christians presenting themselves as beloved children of God who walk in love.

Comparative clauses affirm that God has "graced" us in Christ, that Christ has loved us with an unparalleled demonstration of love. If anything, a cross imperative is implied as Christians are to live as points of light following the example of Christ.

To live a cruciform life even metaphorically is to follow the example of the crucified Christ (historical fact) and to experience divine grace and peace from a rectifying and reconciling Father. The "cruciform image *of God*" is an inaccurate theology that is not Pauline.

Salvation

Salvation, in a word, is coming to life again. In Paul's letters salvation means deliverance and rescue. However, it is a truncated misunderstanding to assume that Paul is focused upon the salvation of the individual from one's misdeeds that we term "sins." Paul does not proclaim such a restrictive gospel. Paul's gospel is that of communal life that overcomes the isolated individualism stressed in much Christianity. There is no personal salvation that is not characterized by mutuality and consummated within a believing community.

The "old" and "customary perspective" on Paul promoted a wrong view of justification as conversion, the moment of coming to faith in a personal salvation. Such a view tended toward a "one size fits all" perspective. Justification by faith for Paul was never about how people get saved or converted. "Justification" by works of the Law (circumcision, food laws) or by faith was one of the fiercest controversies in the early church. It marked a severe threat to church unity in Christ.

Comprehension

At least statistically, Paul exhibits a greater usage of the word "salvation" than any other New Testament writer. For Paul, salvation is what God has done in his great saving act in Christ that we term "gospel." It is not too much to affirm that salvation in a broad sense is the very purpose of the incarnation and entire Christ event. Salvation is a comprehensive word that extends far beyond an individual getting "into heaven." It involves other theological conceptions—redemption, reconciliation, sanctification, rectification, as those realities are even extended to the entire cosmos. "Salvation" is eschatological. The act of salvation involves the death and resurrection of Jesus. As Christ, it also involves Jesus's exaltation, his current rule, his parousia, and the final re-creation of the cosmos at the Telos.

Paul nowhere speaks of salvation wrought by human effort, not even in Phil 2:12. The initiative belongs with God (2 Thess 2:13). Salvation comes as a gift of God. It is not a matter of human effort of achievement over which one may boast. Rather, it is about faithfulness, about living in a manner that trusts in God as did Abraham and as did Jesus. It is God in Christ who saves. Salvation is the negation of boasting in human achievement.

Philippians 2:12 ("*work out* your own salvation . . .") is phrased in the plural; it is addressed to the church. The imperative is not a command directed toward good works supportive of human boasting. It is rather a view toward the past and toward the future in the light of the present. The imperative verb is present tense and plural: "you all keep on working out your salvation . . . ." In Paul's view, salvation is a past-present-future process, contrary to some theological perspectives of today that focus upon the past or the future. In Paul's understanding, "salvation" is a process very different from a momentary inoculation of a medicinal vaccine. Paul's own life of ministry serves as a clear example.

Salvation thus has, even especially has, a present component in Paul, basically because *the faithfulness upon which salvation is based must always be present tense.* Faithfulness in the past or in the future, coupled with *unfaithfulness* in the present, is not salvation. This is the basic logic underlying Phil 2:12, as the Philippians are encouraged to continuing faithfulness, moving forward with reverence and awe over what God has done, is doing, and will do in Christ.

The Philippians are encouraged to "work out" their own salvation, which is not just an invitation to moral good works. Rather, it is encouragement to live by the salvation offered in Christ, rather than some other. Paul's world offered "salvation" on a number of fronts. A different "lord" offers a very different or distinctive salvation. "Peace and security," for example, was imperial rhetoric, the virtual definition of Roman "salvation." However, Paul saw Caesar's salvation to be a hollow sham of real salvation provided by the alternative Gospel of God in Christ. Christ marked the royal presence of the true Lord. Caesar's empire was but a temporal parody.

Incarnational Identity

The gospel is the power of God unto salvation now for those who are "being saved" (1 Cor 1:18). For those who "are perishing," again a present tense participle, the cross and Christ event as a whole is "foolishness" (1 Cor 1:18). As a present colony of heaven, we currently await a Savior, the parousia of the Lord Jesus Christ (Phil 3:20). Paul's words should not be misunderstood. One is to live out a Christian life, even to the point of a cruciform imperative, as is made plain in many sections of Paul's letters.

It should also be noted that just as salvation is a present, ongoing experience, so also is judgment. Over against those who are being saved are those who are perishing (2 Thess 2:10; 1 Cor 1:18; 2 Cor 2:15). Although 2 Thess 2:10 is sometimes poorly translated, what Paul says is instructive: "with every deception of unrighteousness to those who are perishing [pres.], because they have not received [aor.] the love of truth with the result that they may be saved." There will also be a final judgment, just as there will be final salvation (1 Cor 15:20–28). Those who are perishing are deceived by their own lack of righteousness, they do not have a love of the truth, and consequently they are not being saved.

Paul looks forward to the day when the Lord would save him into his heavenly kingdom (2 Tim 4:18). Romans 5:9–11, the only place where the word "atonement" occurred in the New Testament of the King James Version, is likewise instructive. Those who have been rectified by Jesus's faithfulness unto death will be saved through him (indirect agency) from wrath (see Rom 5:9). "For since being enemies we were reconciled [aor. pass.] to God through the death [indirect agency] of his Son, much more since we are reconciled we shall be saved by his life; but not only so, but indeed we are those who boast in God through our Lord Jesus Christ [indirect agency], through whom we have received [or "we receive," aor.] reconciliation." Salvation is dependent upon reconciliation and faithfulness unto rectification.

Salvation is a broad term for Paul. It is collective and cosmic. We have been delivered from Death and will be delivered—that is faithful hope (2 Cor 1:10). Rectification is in play through the power of the active Spirit of God. One has been delivered from the fear of Death; one is offered triumph over all forces of evil.

Salvation, however, is not just deliverance "from" something, but it is deliverance "for" something. That something is wholeness, wellness, goodness, and health, i.e., *shalom* or "peace." In essence, Paul commends God's salvation to his churches in all of his salutations—salvation is "grace and peace from God the Father and the Lord Jesus Christ." The indicative of unredeemed humankind in sin, living under the power of Sin unto Death, calls forth an imperative of divine judgment. The indicative of God, living under grace and peace unto Life, calls forth an imperative of human gratitude and faithfulness in Christ unto God though his singular Gospel.

For Paul the decisive moment in God's universal salvation plan was begun in Abraham's total trust in God's promise (Rom 4:3; Gal 3:6) and culminated in the Christ event. Abraham's trust in God becomes the paradigm for everyone who exhibits the same kind of trust (Rom 4:24) now in Christ—whether Jew or non-Jew. Abraham, himself a gentile, becomes the ancestor of the gentiles (Gen 17:5; cf. Rom 4:12).

Salvation for Paul is the fulfillment of Israel's story, the formation of a new people composed of Jews and gentiles, the creation of a new humanity, reconciliation, liberation from and victory over evil powers. "Salvation" ultimately includes the acclamation of Jesus as Lord (Phil 2:9–11), an acclamation that delivers one from all other lordships. It is far, far more than just a focus upon individual life after death. Salvation also involves mission. Where there is no mission, there is no church. Where there is no church, there is no evident divine mission. The gospel is incarnational and corporate. "Christendom" may exist without mission, but not Christianity. Christianity thrives on incarnation inherent in mission.

A particular understanding of the message of Paul rather than that of Jesus is the primary basis upon which Christendom has been constructed. This is illustrated by the older rubric of the "theology of Paul" and the "ethics of Jesus." Christendom is really built upon the idea of accrued righteousness through ritual and preservation of the institutional church now with promise of heaven later. The real emphasis is upon social activity in the name of God that preserves a certain personal identity within a coveted power structure, coupled with a self-preservation characterized as religion.

Church

It is sometimes said that we need to go back and become like the early church, a view advanced as a panacea to solve or cure the problems that exist in the contemporary church. Generally, when one makes that statement, it is the earliest church in Jerusalem that one has in mind. Based upon Luke's summary description given in Acts (see Acts 4:31–37), we imagine a picture of total unity and sweetness without any problems. Everyone is nice and seeking to meet one another's needs. It is like viewing a photograph where everyone is smiling at the moment of the picture, when the underlying reality may be far different.

We neglect to read further in Acts (Acts 6; 15), and we do not take note of the dissension and divisive differences that also arose and affected the unity of the church. We neglect to take into account the trouble that Paul had with the Nomistic Evangelists over the course of his ministry that prompted him to consign some conservative fellow Christians to "hell" and to write some other unkind things regarding them (see Gal 1:8, 9; 5:12; Phil 3:2). We neglect to consider the immorality, immaturity, and self-centeredness of the church at Corinth (see 1 Cor 1–6).

New Testament Church?

When we make such a general statement ("we need to be like the New Testament church") without pursuing knowledgeable understanding, we are not imagining but rather engaging in the imaginary. The early church was not a utopia such as we may sometimes think. We succumb to Luke's *summary* description, without pursuing his full story—and that even apart from any consideration of the distinct differences of the modern world with the social culture of the Greco-Roman world.

"We need to go back and become like the New Testament church." To which church do we refer? The Jerusalem church, which appears to be more fundamental and authoritative, or the church at Antioch, which appears to have had a more liberal, universal outreach to the gentile world? To which church of Paul do we refer or imagine? To the naivete and gullibility of the Galatian churches that were so willing and eager to swallow an alternative gospel that was a "no gospel" at all, a "gospel" of law that was focused upon externals and not internals? To a "gospel" of law that has departed from grace and faithfulness?

Which church? The Corinthian church with all of its "I" problems of excessive pride that called forth self-centered immoralities, exploitations of spiritual gifts, exclusive groups within the church, derisive neglect of the needs of fellow church members, and even abuse of the Lord's Supper? Although the Corinthian church should have become mature in Christ, they remained immature "babies in Christ" whom Paul had to continue to feed with baby food (see 1 Cor 3:1–4). Which church? The Thessalonian church, which, for all its faithfulness in the face of religious and social persecution, continued to be characterized by moral weakness, lack of a confident faith in a full gospel, and a false preoccupation with the end time?

Which church? The Philippian church that, for all its expressed care and concern for Paul, still suffered from the threat of disunity within? Or the church at Colossae, which was facing and was in danger of adopting an alternative and false philosophy or "theosophy" (i.e., an alternative gospel), that marked a departure from faith in the centrality and superiority of Christ? Which church? In the present work, we consider the churches associated with Paul, but one may also recall John's description of the seven churches in Asia given in Rev 2–3. The list could be extended, but we know very little about other churches in Paul's day, including the church at Rome. *There was no single model of a "New Testament" church that did not face problems and growing pains.*

We should, however, be thankful for those New Testament churches reflected in Paul's letters, for apart from Paul's address of their problems and challenges we would lose a significant portion of Paul's description and prescription of what it means to live out of the Gospel of God in Christ. It is those fledgling, imperfect churches that called forth the necessity of Paul's letters, as he sought to instruct them as to the basic nature of the gospel and one's conduct in the light of it.

Among Paul's churches, the church at Ephesus was perhaps the church that Paul knew best, for he had headquartered among them during the course of his Collection Campaign. This is likely the reason why, in his final years while imprisoned in Rome, Paul felt compelled to write a brief letter of thanksgiving greetings to all the "little saints" of God who had been so instrumentally faithful to living out of the Gospel of God in Ephesus. It is, in fact, hard for us to imagine the sacrifices and the change of social lifestyle that they had to effect when they embraced the singular Gospel of God in Christ in the context of a Greco-Roman culture of polytheism.

It may well have been Paul's experience in that church that called forth his magnificent praise to God (Eph 1:3–14) for the gospel that was working itself out in their midst (Eph 1:3–23). Paul set forth the nature and impact of the Gospel (Eph 2:1—3:32), as he encourages the Ephesians to become mature in the Gospel, even encouraging them to become imitators of God (Eph 4:1—6:20; cf. 5:1). He is encouraging, but not at all critical. Reading between the lines of his encouragement, one gains an awareness of potential cultural, social, and religious issues that were having to be faced by Christian congregations in that first-century Greco-Roman world.

A People of God

The basic nature and definition of the Gospel of God was being hammered out in Paul's day. What it meant to be a Jesus-follower—one who embraced the Gospel of God—was cause for the creation of differing interpretation. How the previous promises of God to Israel and how one was to be incorporated into the new people of God was cause for serious conflict, not only religiously speaking, but culturally and socially.

What constituted appropriate belief? What constituted appropriate behavior? Then? And now? There was no single "New Testament" church and there is yet no single "modern" church, in the face of more than 30,000 different Christian groups/denominations in the contemporary world. Even within each denomination, every church is different because people are different both in nature and levels of maturity. Paul helps us understand that. Paul can help us give up romantic notions that are imaginary and to imagine what indeed it actually does mean to live in accord with the singular Gospel of God in Christ. Paul's encouragement can help us to become mature in Christ.

Paul can understand the church as a colony of heaven that awaits its Lord (Phil 3:20–21). It is an outpost awaiting consummation and incorporation. Paul does not say that Jesus's parousia will be the time when his people will be taken away to live in heaven, but rather Paul speaks of Jesus's return from heaven to transform a weary world and us. Paul doesn't think in terms of a "raptured" dualism, where some will be taken and others left behind, but he thinks rather of a re-creative unity of heaven and earth.

Κοινωνία or community describes the church for Paul, a.k.a. the people of God. The church is to be a community of life in God, constituted by grace, defined by love, characterized by peace and hope and faithfulness in Christ. For the church, the gospel story defines what it means to be Christian. It is the church that narrates the gospel story to the world. How can the world at large believe in a credible gospel that features a man hanging on an ancient Roman cross, if the congregation of people who claim to believe such a gospel do not live by it? Evangelism is not a mere program nor a mere proclamation; it is rather the church living out the gospel. The church becomes the gospel. One must become the gospel in order to advance the gospel. The church is God's redeemed humanity, the new model of what it means to be human.

People in Paul's world sought a sense of belonging to something beyond themselves. Clubs, associations, and guilds within the gentile world offered that sense of belonging. The early Christians went a step beyond this sense of belonging, for no other group lived as though they were a new version of the human race. Still, church disunity was present almost from the beginning. Paul's Collection ministry was a unity exercise, that by all appearances was not the success for which he had hoped. It was a model of community—community with God, with creation, with one another.

The church as the body of Christ was a community that lived under a new Lord, through whom Sin and Death and all the powers had been conquered. It was a community that lived by grace, celebrating and extending that grace through love. The church today is not a community that boasts in power on the basis of Flesh, but rather that which boasts in God on the basis of the empowering Spirit of God. It becomes hypocritical when it exchanges a gospel of man for the Gospel of God.

Renewed Identity

As he writes to a strongly gentile church, Paul can encourage the Ephesians to become imitators of God himself and conduct themselves in love, as beloved children (Eph 5:1). That is a tall order—and invitation. Faith(fullness) energizes through love because it is not a private possession. It is a shared-in reality. Reconciliation is not a private experience; it always involves another party with whom relationship is restored. Love is the gift of the Spirit itself that becomes the living presence of God in the midst of his people. Love is not lived out singularly.

For Paul "the life of Christ" meant the lordship of the crucified and risen one, present now in the Christian community that lives by faithfulness. Faith(fullness) is not mere acceptance of intellectual or abstract truth. Faith is living out reconciliation in love as God's new community in the world. The gift of love is the presence of the Spirit of God. Grace is the gift of God's love. Faith is the manner in which we receive and grow into the gift of God. Peace and hope are the consequence of love's reception through grace.

The church is God's redeemed humanity—both in identity and in practice. Insofar as the church does not practice its identity, it loses that identity and slips back into a self-chosen identity that this writer has termed "Christendom." "Christendom," among other things, adopts the ways of the world to accomplish its own self-centered goals, to protect its own institutional existence, to enhance its own status, to build its own new temple of Babel.

The church is called to live and work characterized by (1) a firm and fixed foundation of what God has done and (2) a command to improvise—to stay in tune and in time with what God is doing. The questions become "What was the foundation then and the foundation now?," and, musically speaking, "Do we know the tune and the time?" Have we redefined or exchanged the foundational score? Do we know the "tune" of God's Gospel or do we sing a new tune of our own making? And, even if we have memory of the "tune," are we trying to perform it in "four-four" time when in reality it is "three-four"? Are we missing "the beat"?

The two questions together may appear to be paradoxical or oxymoronic. Answer to each of them must be found in different ways. Recovery of the Pauline foundation must be based upon a hermeneutic of value that is willing to read, study, and investigate both the *what* and the *why* of the Pauline correspondence. Having done our homework, it involves a commitment to imagine, even following the direction of the Spirit, that which for Paul was more than a metaphor. To "sing God's song" is to become immersed in the Gospel, such that life in Christ grows lyrical.

The command to improvise involves a commitment to follow the leading of God, even to learn a new "tune" that is his tune, to experience the gifts of the Spirit that empower the life of the church, and to employ those gifts by allowing the love of God in Christ to energize in ministries of repentance, redemption, and reconciliation. Repentance involves a change of mind-set, redemption an alteration of identity, and reconciliation a restoration of relationships on a multi-relational front. Foundational improvisation involves the church in a process of living out of the gospel and learning to live the Gospel of God. Paul's imperatives become a focal point of how to do this in ways that are still relevant within the context of a new, rapidly moving postmodern world.

Christian living is not "living in the Flesh" according to the standards of the Old Age and its temporary Torah. It is not living in accordance with a new law governed by formulated doctrines. The life of love is not born of duty, so much as it is born of identity, will, and destiny. The Spirit of God that raised Jesus from the dead now works in the church to give it life. The Spirit marks the guarantee and down-payment of future inheritance, but it is also the power that creates new life now. It enables God's people to live above the level of illusion, to imagine new life that transcends a mundane world of repetition or even despair.

For the church as the people of God, Paul talked about broken down walls and destruction of barriers (see Gal 3:26–28; Eph 2:14–21). Paul can speak in different ways of broken barriers and reconciliation effected between Jew and gentile, men and women, slave and free, humanity and God. People in the modern and postmodern world live in a context of over population and twenty-four/seven sensory overload. We have erected walls of culture and race, economics and politics, doctrines and religion—walls that seemingly grow ever taller. Paul spoke of an egalitarian gospel that proclaimed no difference between Jew and Greek, slave and free, male and female (Gal 3:26–29). He spoke of an egalitarian community that was defined as the singular body of Christ.

Although it does not describe all churches, many churches in "Christendom" erect, tend, and maintain doctrinal, racial, economic, social, and sexual segregation on both a formal and informal basis. Factions, schisms, judgments against false teachings, cults of personality all scream out "They are not like us!" In a post-denominational age in which threat is perceived even from the church down the street, the wagons are circled, the barriers are up, and the defenders are ever more rigid in their doctrines and practice. The church does not appear to have a center about which it has confidence. "How do I feel?" has replaced "What is the responsible thing to do?," i.e., "How do I/we live?" The church which tends its own existence and allows the world to set the church's agenda has no right to think that God will continue its existence no matter what.

Paul has a corporate and not individual vision that was first of all *theo*logical. Paul expressed a corporate hope in the power of God that could transform both individual and corporate identity. Identity is defined in terms of the triangle of God-others-self. Personhood is fundamentally relational, rather than being defined in terms of rampant individualism or power brokerage. The sphere of the Spirit and being "in Christ" defines the church as a collective fellowship. Christian existence is cruciform, empowered by the Spirit and informed by the Gospel. The church lives in residence under a living Lord, the crucified and resurrected Jesus, now the exalted Christ. No one could accuse Paul of apathy or a lack of action. Paul knew that those who lived by full participation in Christ would suffer for the sake of the gospel but also reap the rewards of the Gospel.

Eschatology

Paul, like Jesus, entertained an apocalyptic perspective of fulfillment. Almost every Pauline letter is conditioned by an eschatological perspective involving Jesus's death and resurrection as the inauguration of the long-awaited Age to Come. Virtually every letter of Paul either expresses eschatological presuppositions or explicit eschatological references. Paul's eschatology provides the substrata and backdrop for other significant topics within Pauline theology. Ultimately, this involves other areas of Pauline expression such as pneumatology, soteriology, and even Paul's basic *theo*logy. While eschatology and apocalyptic are in themselves "big words," other large theological words find their foundation here: anthropology; Christology; pneumatology, rectification, justification, sanctification, reconciliation, ecclesiology; soteriology; even ethics.

Apocalyptic Vision

Paul experienced an apocalyptic vision that heralded a new covenant and a new creation. The intersection of the ages had occurred in Jesus's resurrection. The time was at hand. It was time for the Gospel. For Paul, the Christ event marked the transition from the Present Evil Age to the long-awaited Age to Come. The New Age had invaded the Old Age in a manner that marked an inaugurative transition, such that the overlap of the Two Ages marked the intervening third Age of Transformation. As Paul affirms in 2 Cor 5:17, if anyone is in Christ such a one is a "new creation" (see Gal 6:15).

As has been indicated, this apocalyptic framework of the Two Ages is fundamental to understanding Paul. God inaugurated the Age to Come in the Christ event to herald the new Age of Transformation, with the demarcation line being the new creation in the resurrection. In one sense, the cross event was actually the culminating event of the Present Evil Age. The death and burial of Jesus becomes the point at which the Age to Come intersects with the Present Evil Age in its inaugural event of the new Age of Transformation—God's resurrection of Jesus from the dead and his exaltation as Lord.

Israel's story was a long story in search of an ending. And it was a *story*, couched in *narrative*, whether it be psalmic word or prophetic hopes and apocalyptic expectations. Israel believed God would act again in a re-creation, in order to right what had gone wrong in Adam. The creator and covenant God would not only come to judge the world, according to prophetic voices, in the Day of Yahweh, but he would also come to vindicate his people Israel and incorporate the gentiles. He would act to fulfill his covenant established in Abraham that would incorporate all people on the basis of faithfulness and not ethnic origins. In fact, "ethnic origins" is a humanly created category, not a divine one.

Apocalypticism tended to arise out of a social context of exclusion, subjection, deprivation, and persecution. In times of great social and religious stress, prophetic voices announced the ultimate victory of God over all forces of evil (see Dan 8:1–14; Zech 5:1—6:8; 1 Enoch 90:1–42; 91:11–17; 93:1–10; 4 Ezra 3:1—5:13). Powerful spiritual and cosmic forces contrary to God were seen to rule the Present Evil Age. In Paul, there is a certain fluidity in his reference to the "powers"—the Tempter (1 Thess 3:5), the Devil (Eph 6:11), Satan (2 Cor 4:4; Rom 16:20), angels good and bad, rulers of this age (1 Cor 2:6–9), principalities and powers (1 Cor 15:24; Rom 8:38; Col 2:15; Eph 6:12), elemental spirits (Gal 4:3; Col 2:8, 20). Salvation in Christ's resurrection meant freedom from the powers.

Paul inherited an apocalyptic worldview from Judaism that led him to believe the turn of the ages had occurred with the resurrection of Jesus. This heralded an age of transition and transformation. For Paul, the resurrection of Jesus was an eschatological act of God that heralded the New Age had arrived, closely associated as it was with Christ's exaltation to a position of power (Rom 8:34), which in itself marked a change of power structure. Jesus's credentials as Son of God are intimately linked to his resurrection (Rom 1:4).

God's apocalyptic intervention in the resurrection marked the advent of the Age to Come and the inauguration of a time of dynamic Age of Transformation overlap between the Two Ages. Whereas the earlier Jewish schema understood the Two Ages as separate and successive, Paul now understood the Age to Come to be advancing in triumph while the Present Evil Age was retreating in defeat. The present time was thus the Age of Transformation, a period of overlap. According to the Pauline model, we are still living in a time of overlap of the Age of Transformation. Transformation is what remains central until the Telos.

Both the Present Evil Age and the Age to Come still affect the present, although victory belongs to God and to his Christ. Sin and Death have been conquered and, wounded, are on the run. Final and total victory is yet in the future and will occur with Christ's parousia and the Telos (1 Cor 15:20–28). God has acted, is acting, and will act. The overlap of the ages for Paul was thus a dramatic story in three acts. Paul and his churches were participants in the second act, the Age of Transformation, as are we. Perhaps put theologically, the cross was past (indicative) and present (imperative). The resurrection of Christians was present and future. It is inaugurated eschatology in process of full realization. That is Paul's bi-directional view, as the present continues to be affected by the past and shaped by the future

Pauline eschatology is not monolithic nor uniform in expression through his various letters, nor should we expect it to be in a group of occasional letters that were written over a twelve-year period against the backdrop of a twenty-five-year-plus ministry. Scholars may debate the "dimensions" of Paul's eschatology, whether it be "vertical/spatial" (earthly/heavenly) or "horizontal/temporal" (present/future), but the language of debate is non-Pauline. Paul himself was convinced that with the resurrection the new order had begun, the inauguration of events leading to the Telos had already occurred. Paul used a variety of expressions drawn from his Jewish heritage in accordance with the varied needs of his churches at a given point in time. The Thessalonian Christians had questions about the parousia. The Corinthians had questions about marriage in current time and about the resurrection. The Philippians needed encouragement. The Colossians needed Christological correction. The Ephesians and Paul needed affirmation. Situational needs varied over time. What does the church "need" today? What does your church need?

Righteousness, life, and peace would rule in the Age to Come and replace the darkness and stress of the Present Evil Age. For Paul, the resurrection heralded the vanguard of God's renewal. The light was already shining; the darkness was already receding. The dawn marked the Age of Transformation. In the period of Second Temple Judaism, themes of both judgment and redemption developed in various ways. Eschatological expectation varied from one group to another.

An Eschatological Corollary

Paul was proud of his Jewish heritage that in the first century included not an "end" but a "conclusion" to Israel's story, i.e., an eschatological expectation of fulfillment—victory over evil, subjection of pagan rulers, the coming of the Messiah, the creation of a new Israel, the resurrection of the dead (figurative and literal dead), the dawn of God's new future. Fundamentally, eschatology was a corollary of monotheism and covenant. Paul the Pharisee shared Israel's comprehensive hopes.

Paul found nothing wrong with Judaism and in fact as a persecutor of the church defended Judaism against what he perceived to be an aberrant form represented by the Jesus-followers. However, once Paul had his experiential encounter with the risen Christ, he realized that God *had* acted to fulfill Israel's hopes in a totally unexpected way. Paul found nothing wrong with Judaism—it was not an inferior religion based upon Law. However, once Paul encountered the risen Christ, he embraced a Judaism of fulfillment that we term early Christianity.

We might say that Paul found nothing wrong with Judaism, except that it was not Christianity. What might that mean? The Judaism Paul had previously known was not *eschatology inaugurated*. God had now vindicated Jesus in the resurrection, but at the same time God had vindicated his own promise through the inauguration of the long-expected and hoped-for Age to Come. The present inspiration of the

Spirit in an Age of Transformation provided the "down-payment" or "guarantee" of long-awaited fulfillment.

This meant that Paul had to re-imagine what he held dear. To "re-imagine," however, is simply to imagine anew. He had to update his understanding of God, covenant, the Law, the people of God, eschatology, the Messiah, God's kingdom. Paul did not undergo a religious conversion, but he did have to undergo a *theological revision*. He had to think through the Christ event in the light of his own experience with the risen Christ. He had to imagine what the resurrection meant. He had to re-imagine how the cross should be properly understood. He had to imagine what it meant to proclaim the gospel to the gentiles. He had to imagine what gentile inclusion into the people of God meant and would entail. This process would have certainly begun in the time immediately following his call experience (the three years past Damascus), but it continued throughout his ministry.

Non-Eschatological Truncation

Paul re-imagined the traditional themes of Jewish eschatology. Contemporary fundamentalism of evangelical Christianity at the popular level has collapsed Paul's Jewish eschatology into a very un-Jewish dualism of the saints of God snatched up to heaven in a "rapture" (a non-Pauline, non New Testament doctrine), while the rest of the world is left to divine judgment. The key passage of supposed "rapture" theology is 1 Thess 4:16–18, whereby Paul utilizes typical apocalyptic imagery to describe Christ's return and not the Christian's departure. Meeting the Lord in the air is but the prelude to the implied triumphant return to earth where the Messiah will reign. It is not travel to a safe haven somewhere else, from which to view destruction of a wicked earth. His purpose in crafting the passage is to comfort the Thessalonian Christians who have experienced the death of loved ones before the parousia occurred, as he plainly states. Paul's eschatology yet involved the return of Christ (parousia) and the final victory (Telos) of God, the point at which the Lord Christ returns all rule to God the Father (see 1 Cor 15:20–28).

Christendom truncates Paul's eschatology to the event of Jesus's cross. "Jesus came to die for my sins so I could go to heaven." There is not even any need for the eschatological event of the resurrection, or the parousia, or the Telos. There is no awareness of the eschatological conception of the Two Ages or of the Age of Transformation, which is evident throughout Paul's letters, nor of the respective powers that characterize each age. There is no emphasis or lived awareness of cruciform existence involving the Christian's cross as proclaimed by both Jesus and Paul. Laypersons have not been encouraged to read Paul, much less to imagine the meaning of what he writes. And many of those who preach to them have no interest nor necessarily adequate knowledge to imagine beyond a status quo. Christendom acts to preserve itself.

A New Creation

Paul's gospel is filled with eschatological understanding, beginning with the resurrection. The crucified Jesus is the resurrected Christ, exalted by God as Lord over all. The cross did not "serve notice" on the powers, Sin, Death, and others; rather, it lulled them into complacency prior to their defeat. The "powers" did to Jesus what they always did—they put to death. But this time, it would be different.

The Christian life itself is eschatological living, in that it is being lived "in Christ" in the interim time between the resurrection and the parousia. Paul served a present and living Lord, not an absentee substitute for divine judgment. Jesus's ministry was and would be eschatological from the time he began to proclaim the kingdom of God (Mark 1:14–15) to the resurrection to his exaltation to the time of final eschatological fulfillment in Christ's parousia and the Telos (see 1 Cor 15:20–28).

Heaven and earth in the cosmology of apocalyptic Judaism are not separated at some great distance. Paul's cosmology of heaven and earth has been redrawn around the Christ event and the active presence of the Spirit. Creation is good. It stands in need of redemption. God has begun just that in Christ. The word "parousia" suggests presence, and not just expected coming, as is made plain by Paul's contrasting reference to "presence" (παρουσία) and "absence" (ἀπουσία) in Phil 2:12.

God's coming New Age has begun with the Age of Transformation. The Age to Come will be consummated in the future with Jesus's parousia and the Telos, the time of God's full and final rectification. The good news has to do with the nature of God's "restorative justice," i.e., God's rectification. God's new creation in Christ will reverse the storied corruption of Gen 3–11. The resurrection is the advance announcement that God has dealt with Sin and Death. It is also a summons to the obedience born of reconciliation and faithfulness. The present time must be lived in proper anticipation of eventual fulfillment. It is yet an Age of Transformation that calls for a patient and expectant imperative of transformation on the part of those "in Christ" (see Phil 2:2–13; Rom 12:1–2).

In Paul's re-imagined Jewish eschatology, there is a single future for a single world recreated and loved by a single God who has expressed his single Gospel through the resurrection and exaltation of his Son. That which Paul re-imagined, Paul actually lived out with a spirit of eschatological freedom in Christ (Gal 5:1). The defensive armor of Eph 6, for example, suggests inaugurated eschatology, initiated by the victory of Jesus's resurrection.

Part of Paul's task was to educate the imagination of those in Christ, to enable those earliest Christians to lift their eyes beyond limited horizons of narrow, assumed worldviews. Salvation and justice, along with words like gospel and lord and savior, were all *imperial* buzzwords before they were given Christian meaning. Christians reinterpreted them and applied them to Christ in the service of the Gospel of God. Jesus, the Davidic Messiah, raised from the dead (Rom 1:4), was the world's true Lord, constituted as such by his resurrection. The Gospel of God trumped the gospel of Caesar. Jesus was proclaimed as the world's true Lord and Christ.

God had revealed his saving justice in Abraham (Rom 1–4). He had acted to create a worldwide family of faith promised to Abraham. Paul's pneumatology understood the Spirit to be the first fruit (Rom 8:23; cf 1 Cor 15:20) and down-payment or guarantee of things to come (2 Cor 1:22; 5:5; Eph 1:14). The gift of the Spirit thus marks both our adoption (Gal 4:5; Rom 8:15; 9:4; Eph 1:5) and our inheritance (1 Cor 6:9–10; 15:50; Gal 5:21).

The eschatology of Rom 12–15 sustains the community of the church across traditional boundaries. Paul's exhortations, as in Rom 12–13, are totally conditioned by Paul's eschatological perspectives. Sociological approaches which seek to understand the function of eschatology within the eschatological community enable the application of Paul's teachings in contemporary contexts, in areas such as human sexuality, cosmic ecology, and definition of community in terms of identity (Gal 3:28) and responsibility (Gal 5:16—6:10).

How we view the nature of history will have a great effect upon our appreciation of the historical aspects of the Christian faith. At least some of Paul's visions were no longer tenable after Paul and the first generation in his churches died out. The parousia had not materialized; the post-apostolic age could not adopt Paul's own characteristic convictions in a post-70 CE world, even while they collected and tended Paul's letters and felt obliged to make use of Pauline phraseology. The book of Acts may be seen as a prime example of a re-interpretation of the time of Paul in a post-70 CE world. First Timothy and Titus mark the perpetuation of the figure of Paul and his perceived authority in a later age of a new generation of Christians.

"What time is it?" is a significant question after some two thousand years. Have we outgrown an outmoded eschatological view of history that sees God moving toward some type of fulfillment in Christ? If so, we leave Paul's gospel behind. It is a significant question, but it is not a new question. Paul essentially faced the same issue in the question concerning the resurrection posed to him by the Corinthians (see 1 Cor 15). If one surrenders eschatology, one surrenders Paul's gospel and perhaps a lot more, perhaps even the Gospel of God.

The Cross and Resurrection

Paul's apocalyptic theology is rooted within actual historical events. The Age to Come had arrived with Jesus's resurrection that intersected the Present Evil Age event of the cross. The cross-resurrection event thus marks the intersection of the Two Ages, the point at which the two come together. What looked like defeat marked the beginning of divine victory.

In the world in which Paul lived, the cross was a sign of Roman power and control. Those are the facts of the matter, but imagine the scene of the event. Imagine the original scene of Jesus's crucifixion between two insurrectionists against Roman rule, Jesus himself being crucified as the "King of the Jews" according to the placard above his head on the cross as reported in all four Gospels (see Mark 15:26 par.; John 19:19). No one that day, no one, not even the disciples, looked upon that event and confessed the love of God or breathed a sigh of relief because now all sins had been forgiven by the Jewish God. Not a single person. According to the Gospels, the disciples stood far off except for "the disciple Jesus loved" (John 19:26–27). Rome was in control—and at Passover, yet. And Jesus died—on a *Roman* cross.

The first-century Greco-Roman world was a world in which values of limited goods and honor-shame held sway. In the social context of an honor-shame society and culture where honor and shame were paramount values, it was Sin acting through human perpetrators that was honored in the crucifixion of Jesus, as Jesus was publicly executed with full public shame. One might affirm that God was *quietly* honored by Jesus's willing obedience unto even death on a cross. God is always honored by faithful obedience to his will and ways, and that is what is good for God's human creatures (see Rom 12:1–2). Personified, Sin accomplished its usual action in concert with Death, such that in this instance Sin and the gods of Rome were "honored" through Jesus's death. The powers of evil had won out.

God overcame the worst that Sin working through sinful human beings could do, namely, put to death—yea, even the most shameful of deaths. God wrought new life through the resurrection. It is God's honor that is proclaimed in the Gospel. God's honor is exhibited through both the resurrection and the exaltation of Jesus, who now reigns as Lord at God's behest over all powers that would corrupt, enslave, and seek to kill and destroy.

To understand the crucifixion in terms of a limited goods and honor-shame scenario provides for a radically different understanding of the Christ event than the customary one of penal substitutionary atonement—the need for a "perfect sacrifice" in order to forgive sin and to placate the satisfaction of a rather transactional and impotent god according to an ancient human ritual. The creation and development of such a limited conception of sacrificial imagery belongs to the doctrine-makers and not to the God of Israel whom Paul knew and who is to be praised (see Eph 1:3–14). There is so much in Paul that has been misconstrued. There is so much in Paul that has been neglected or overlooked. Many "theological barnacles" have firmly attached themselves to the beautiful Pauline wood of the gospel.

While Paul may stress Christ's death as God's act of love (Rom 5:8), he can *only* do so in the light of the resurrection. The cross for everyone that Passover eve was seen as a symbol of imperial violence and deterrence, an emblem of personal suffering and shame. Actually, Rom 5:8 affirms the original event: while we were yet enemies of God, Christ died at the hands of humankind. The cross was an "enemy" action, not a divine action.

Although it is commonly stated that the focal point of the Gospel of God was the crucified Messiah, or, differently, the cross of Christ stands at the center of Paul's understanding of Israel's one true God, this is not so if one carefully pays attention to what Paul actually wrote. Such viewpoints betray echoes of Christendom. Paul can speak of the "word of the cross" (1 Cor 1:18) and of preaching only "Christ crucified" (1 Cor 2:2). The cross *is* significant because it is not just an act of Jesus, but rather it becomes *through the resurrection* a definitive act of the self-revelation of God. In essence, Christians are to become a "self-revelation of God" as they live as a "praise of God's glory." Christianity is an incarnational religion, not a substitutionary transaction.

For Paul, it is God's action in the resurrection that is his focal point or center (see Rom 1:4). For *Paul*, it is the resurrection that is the generative event. For *Paul*, there is a cross on both sides of the resurrection: Jesus's cross—Jesus's resurrection—the Christian's cross. In actuality, Paul's cross language is directed more toward Christian living or the Christian imperative. Paul personally suffered for the cause of Christ and spoke of being "crucified with Christ" (Gal 6:14; Rom 6:6). Paul lived the cross and sought the resurrection—a cross imperative combined with a resurrection hope (see Phil 3:12–16; Gal 6:14–15; Rom 6:5–11).

The reason Paul understands the cross in terms of a cruciform imperative for Christians is that the promised resurrection would once again follow a cross. *Paul knew no cross apart from resurrection.* The cross of Jesus seen from the perspective of the resurrection represents God's own self-giving nature and his saving, rectifying action. It reveals God's power and glory, his "honor." It also reveals he had a plan. What appeared to be weakness and foolishness actually proved to be God's power and wisdom, in retrospect (1 Cor 1:30).

There is no question that the cross is the distinctive symbol of the Christian faith, but then how could one symbol the resurrection? While it is commonly acknowledged today that "Christ died for us [ὑπὲρ ὑμῶν]" (and Paul supports that, Rom 5:8), it is seldom acknowledged today that "Christ was raised for us," even though that is the "good news" part of Paul's gospel. Atonement doctrine in one form or another seems ever present in sermons and especially the music of Christendom; whether it be old-time hymnology or contemporary Christian choruses. Those who wrote the songs generally do not have the depth of theological foundation nor imaginative reflection to write more than what is generally heard or commonly confessed. The song-writers write what they have heard or what they have been taught. The song-writers generally enforce the doctrine-makers within Christendom.

Sermonic dogma dare not imagine alternative theological models within the guilt and sin culture of Western Christendom. Dogma maintains the power of the clergy. Christians "cling to" and "cherish" the "old rugged cross," because that is where they are told that Jesus died "for their sins." Christians seldom think of their own cross in any significant way. As one pastor said some years ago in the presence of the present writer, "I don't preach on sin anymore because it doesn't motivate 'baby-boomers.'"

This may be the opposite approach to a guilt-laden "sin" sermon, but we don't preach on "our" cross anymore either, because it does not motivate comfortable and casual Christians within Christendom. Jesus's death and cross as a substitute "for me" is fine; "my death and cross" is not so appealing.

We live with an apathetic ignorance of Paul and a truncated gospel that Paul would not embrace. So what? Why should we embrace Paul's gospel? Many theological claims are made for Christ and for God in the light of the cross—e.g., the cross tells us something about God's character or the cross reveals God's traditional attributes. Or, the cross is a theophany that reveals the face of God in terms of sacrificial love, wise folly, or power in weakness. Paradox and mystery prevail in the cross as the heart of the gospel. If, however, the cross is primarily an imperative, then the supposed things revealed *about God* are also revealed *about Christians* who are called to live according to the Gospel. They, too, should exhibit wisdom in apparent folly, power in apparent weakness, and love though sacrifice.

Apart from the resurrection, the cross was meaningless, even as noted by John Calvin. It is the resurrection that turned the cross of Jesus from defeat to victory, from denial to validation, from desertion to vindication. It is the resurrection that makes possible exaltation. It is the resurrection that establishes the identity of Jesus as Son of God, Messiah, Savior and Lord. It is the resurrection that offers hope for the future. In response to the Corinthians' question pertaining to the resurrection, Paul clearly sets forth why the resurrection matters, going so far as to say that faith is vain or empty apart from the resurrection (1 Cor 15:12–19). He does not say the same thing anywhere about the cross. Preaching, hymnology, and rhetoric ought to take note and to reflect better that reality.

Paul almost always speaks in the passive—"God raised him" or "he was raised." Jesus did not raise himself, but was raised *by God*, the only one who could raise the dead. Encounter with the risen Christ transformed Paul from persecutor to proclaimer of the gospel. It changed Paul's theology. It changed his life. Paul had to revise his understanding of Jesus's death on a Roman cross. It was Jesus's cross born of faithfulness. And, God's resurrection action, likewise born of faithfulness, marked the victory of God and the shaming of Sin and Death themselves.

Resurrection of the dead was thought to be a sign of the age of fulfillment. The resurrection of but *one man now* signaled for Paul and others the *beginning* of the eschatological age and a coming general resurrection and re-creation anticipated in earlier Pharisaic thought. Paul's references to the resurrection, as a direct result of Christ's appearance to him, heralded a literal experience and not mere metaphorical description.

The resurrection marked a central concept that appears in Paul, namely, the concept of being "in Christ." It is the reality of the living presence of Christ through the Spirit that claims allegiance and marks identity. Paul could term the church itself the "body of Christ" (1 Cor 12:12–31). Those defined as the "body of Christ" are defined by the confession "Jesus is Lord" and "Lord Jesus." Lordship transcends sentimentality. The language of lordship was the language of power in the Roman world. The emperor was "lord." The Christian gospel is thus counter-imperial and counter-cultural, both then and now.

The resurrection is participatory and definitional. Apart from the resurrection, Christianity collapses. Apart from the resurrection, Christianity is never born. Apart from the resurrection, there is no Paul. For Christians in the present, resurrection power takes the form of a cross exhibited in Paul's cruciform imperative. The cross becomes the mark of the presence of God in the truly Christian community.

Confession of Jesus/Christ as Lord marks the rejection of other power claims and paradoxically means freedom. Our minds become transformed and renewed, as we become conformed to the mind of Christ. The church lives as the body of Christ in a world of hurt that seeks redemption and longs for meaning. It seeks to help by reconciling and offering hope. It stares the face of Death down in all of its manifestations and embraces life. It proclaims a gospel of resurrection.

A Gospel Imperative

Paul was a man of his time who understood history itself in terms of two ages—now three, in Christ. It is not necessary to take every part of Paul's accounting as factually true. We do not, for example, still believe in a biblically oriented "three storied universe" with a flat Earth at the center, even though we have retained some spatial language with regard to "heaven" and "hell" that doesn't really work given our understanding of a much larger cosmic order. While many Christians may still talk about "Satan" in rather literal terms, few think about "Sin" as an actual or metaphorical power over humanity that causes people to commit sins, as did Paul. One may no longer think in terms of a "lordship of evil" as did Paul, but if not, how does one envision the "lordship of Christ"? Can we imagine that? If we can't imagine the one, how can we imagine the other?

While a Christian may commit acts of sin (see 1 John 1:7—2:2), one does not engage in a lifestyle of sin because one has been delivered from the power and bondage of Sin, according to Paul (Rom 6:5–14). One formerly had no option as a slave of Sin, for one was guilty of the kind of unrighteousness that killed. One in Christ has now been set free from Sin but has become a slave unto God, such that one lives unto a process of sanctification of which the end is eternal life (see Rom 6:20–22). "The wages of Sin is death, but the gracious gift of God in Christ Jesus our Lord is life eternal" (Rom 6:23). Paul speaks of "Sin," not "sins."

The Christian ethic is based upon a building up and not a tearing down, just as God's Gospel is based upon redemption and not judgment, life and not death. As Paul writes to each of his churches, it is always "grace and peace to you all from God the Father and the Lord Jesus Christ." Paul characterizes the new Christian life as walking in the Spirit, as one bears the fruit of the Spirit—"love, joy, peace, patience, kindness, goodness, faithfulness, gentleness, self-control" (Gal 5:22–23). It should be noted that Paul characterizes these expressions as the "fruit of the Spirit"; and he employs a different set of characteristics as the "works of the flesh" (see Gal 5:19–21). One should recall that "flesh" is associated with weakness under the power of Sin, whereas the Spirit is the communicative link as the gift of God in the New Age unto redemption and transformation. By extension, while Paul gives the "fruit of the Spirit" as human expression in Christian living, God is not absent.

Life "in Christ" has both vertical and horizontal dimensions. The invitation to accept Christ is also a summons to serve Christ. Twenty-first-century Christianity is not merely a "walk in Galilee" or a "visit to Bethlehem," literally or metaphorically. Existence in Christ is cross-shaped; it is cruciform. It involves both participation in and embodiment of the cross. It is self-giving faithfulness energized through receiving and extending love. Love, like grace, mercy, and forgiveness, is a flow-through reality. It flows freely or it spoils into self-centered narcissism and self-righteousness.

A Gospel imperative offers a number of challenges in our day that differ from those Paul faced, as well as others that echo Paul's own challenges. Paul expresses the very depths of God's liberating and redeeming/reconciling act of love in the Gospel that found him. Dare we come to faith in that Gospel that is still able to find us and help us find ourselves? Do we dare?

Imagine Paul. Imagine the Gospel. Imagine life. Re-imagine theology, such that we find liberation from the imaginary theology that only enslaves as it dissolves the Gospel into something more manageable, palatable, more doctrinalized, and more manipulatable. By contrast, the Christian lifestyle is to embody eschatological existence in the present through the power of the Spirit. There is a pattern of conformity—conformity to the pattern of faithfulness expressed in Christ in terms of loving, self-giving service. Paul does not offer a recipe for theology, but he does call for an incarnational pattern of cruciform living through his theology. Not transaction or truncation, but transformation. That is Paul's legacy. Even more so, that is the legacy of the Gospel of God, according to Paul.

9

Imagine Incarnation

PAUL IS OFTEN TERMED "Saint Paul," and not just "Paul." "Saint Paul" emerges as a somewhat unreal figure from the hidden folds of human piety and religious devotion, himself clothed in the ecclesiastical dress of long-standing doctrines and formulated belief of Christendom. Much of what the church has become over time may be attributed to the influences of *Saint* Paul, with whom the theologians and pietists have flourished as they have read their theology into sacred texts and fashioned icons of devotion to stimulate support of official religion. After all, better for theology and religion to stay away from history, lest history undermine and challenge and even correct our pretensions (see 2 Tim 3:16–17). The church has interested itself in the theology of Paul almost exclusively as an explication of a divine plan for individual human salvation, as well as institutional preservation. The concept of Paul the theologian characterized as "Saint Paul" has eclipsed the figure of Paul the man.

The historical Paul, of course, could describe all those in Christ as "called saints," as children of the holy God of a new Israel, composed of both Jews and gentiles (see 1 Cor 1:2; Rom 1:7). Paul himself was a "saint" of God with a small s, although he knew himself to be an "apostle" sent out to proclaim the Gospel of God under the authority of God. It is ironic that Paul became a source for two different streams of Christian tradition—dogmatic orthodoxy on the one hand, and "heretical" opposition to conventional Christianity on the other. Paul could be read as much to refute orthodoxy as much as he could to enshrine it. Contemporary Christendom has no more interest in a historical Paul, however, than it has in a historical Jesus. Conception of either one may be too threatening, should they be different from our usual theological construct. Still, behind the plastic figure found in the holy book, liturgies, and creeds of Christendom, stands one who was a real man in Christ.

Images

Imagine if we should again see Paul's theology as Gospel instead of only doctrine. Just imagine. Romans 12:1–2 would truly become incarnational. "History" is only generally welcomed if it be deemed to lend support to theological doctrines already established, even though they themselves were established for particular purpose at some point in history. It is certainly true that every generation can view the world only from its own vantage point, imagining the present, as well as the past and the future. Still, there is no "magical mountain" from which to view the full and final sum of history. "History" is not so simple as gathering the facts, only to arrange all of them in a proper order according to the "right" interpretation found in our doctrinal gallery. Such action is akin to "arranging flowers" to our liking.

Still, historical study of Paul, so as to imagine Paul (or Jesus, for that matter) in his first-century setting, can offer a liberating function for a twenty-first-century audience. It can free from iconic and dogmatic images of "Saint Paul" that have emerged over time and that are reinforced through denominational dogma and formal worship. Latent images of "Saint Paul" even lodge in the minds of scholars and remain to haunt like ghosts or demons that lurk in dark corners. Paul was a real person and the gospel he proclaimed was for real people. Appropriate study coupled with contextual historical reconstruction can actually allow Paul (and Jesus) to remain in the first century, even as we learn how better to imagine the world in which Paul first proclaimed the Gospel of God. We do not need to venerate Paul or make him over in our image.

We need to *hear* Paul. We need to hear *Paul*. The real Paul would not ultimately point us to himself, but rather to the Gospel and God whom he proclaimed as a "man in Christ." The operative word is thus not "icon" or "idolization," but rather "incarnation." Through ancient words of Paul we can re-imagine an incarnational vision of Paul's gospel for the context of our own culture. That is not unimportant, but it is not easy.

It is not easy in part because we no longer live in Paul's world. It is not easy also because we have chosen to leave Paul's world behind, seeing much of it to belong to ancestral ignorance. We live in our own world with an overwhelming mass of greater knowledge available in less than a second on a worldwide web. We live with higher levels of education termed literacy, and we have developed psychological techniques that serve to dispel ignorance and guilt complexes that today trouble the inner psyche. Over the past nineteen centuries since the time of Paul, we have become "wise" in our own progress. At the same time, it need be said that humanity today can exhibit a "tower of Babel" mentality that embraces the concept of no limitations, that there is nothing we cannot do or achieve.

Ours is an age of self-referentiality (either ego- or ethno-centrism) that results in disregard for others not like us or that even sees others like us as a vehicle of self-advancement. The breakdown of values and patterns that normally promote the health and well-being of society is evidenced in increased anxieties and isolation. It is evidenced by increased "name calling" on every hand. Current "social media," for example, is an oxymoron and misnomer that may describe avenues of interaction that are more convenient and *addictional*, but in the end, less social and less personal, even hurtful. They become substitutionary for those real things for which we truly yearn, yet representative of a façade that may actually disappoint, conceal, and lead to despair. We so easily succumb to propaganda, and in the technological AI (artificial intelligence) world in which we live, we can literally no longer believe or trust what our eyes and ears tell us. How does one recognize what is true anymore? It becomes a case of "no one is true but me and thee and I'm not sure of thee."

Change, even rapid change, becomes a god worshiped with various human currencies of secularism, while in other quarters the god "Status Quo" sits protected in theological temples erected in yesteryear under a banner called "religion." The god of secularism rules in idolatry. The god of secularism is a very demanding god that highlights the demonic in human living. The god of Status Quo becomes a more and more irrelevant god in the eyes of modern, secular humanism that prides itself in being righteous in its own eyes. In an age of such social advancement, as a new tower of Babel is raised, theology for many becomes a relic of a bygone age.

However, theology still lives, and it is not an unimportant concern. According to biblical thought, the divine concern is human wholeness. While theology may be foundational to both faith and living, theology itself often stands in need of transformation. Without a theological transformation, there can often be no life of transformation, completely apart from God's or Jesus's power to heal or make whole.

By way of analogy, the gospel story speaks of a paralyzed man who was let down through a roof into the presence of Jesus (see Mark 2:1–12 par.). Jesus first of all said to the man, "My son, your sins are forgiven," before he ever healed him of his paralysis. Why did Jesus do that? Because in the *theological* understanding of the day, sin was the direct cause of illness or infirmity (see John 9:1–5). There was reason in the order of events. Without Jesus's correction of a mistaken theology, there could be no healing. An appropriate faith is required for life transformation. Otherwise, we may only limp along with an inadequate and ossified theology that fails to confront adequately the real issues of living in a new age. It makes a difference as to what one believes and incarnates. Paul himself discovered that his Pharisaic theology in the end neither saved nor satisfied. In Christ, he repented of his Pharisaic theology.

One sometimes needs to repent of theology (again, see 2 Tim 3:16–17). Paul did—and it transformed him from persecutor to proclaimer of the gospel. We may need to repent of theology, such that we may again grasp and be grasped by the Gospel in a postmodern age. We need to imagine again the gospel of Paul and the God of the Gospel whom Paul proclaimed. As we turn attention again to Paul and his letters and actually study them for ourselves, the Gospel of *God* may again become free of the structures of Christendom that shackle, so as to both challenge and console, to imagine and make whole. There may yet be life in theological valleys of dry bones.

As the writer of 1 John understood, one cannot love God fully until one can love God without fear (see 1 John 4:16–19). As the lyrics of a country music song suggested, God's gonna "get cha" for every little thing that one does.[1] How far removed is that from Paul's or Jesus's conception of God? And the tragedy is that we don't even

---

1. Collins, "God's Gonna Get 'Cha (For That)."

recognize it from our theological wells or canyons. How close that is, however, to many contemporary portrayals of God in supposed underlying theological expression based upon Paul. In how many Christians does that fearful view of God live incarnate today? How many people are saddled with the heavy burden of a "git cha, got cha" god that actually imprisons rather than frees?

Paul's greeting is *always* "grace and peace from God the Father and the Lord Jesus Christ," a greeting that affirms the primary nature of God as gracious and the exalted yet subordinate nature of the risen Jesus as both Lord and Christ. God is not a celestial traffic policeman handing out tickets nor a condemnatory "hanging" judge—at least in Paul's presentation, as some theology might suggest. While we may define the word *gospel* as "good news" in a "Sunday School" setting, we need to learn in our actual living that the gospel is, indeed, the good news of a God who *is* good and who wills good for all his creation.

In a first-century world of the Roman Empire, Jesus and Paul could be viewed as parallel preachers of a doctrine of salvation. Jesus addressed a Jewish audience with the theme of the reign of God. Jesus was not an end-time sage, but one who taught God was making himself known in the everyday experiences of life. The earliest stage of the Jesus tradition consisted of parables, of which the most authentic parables nowhere announce a cataclysmic end of history. One must balance the Sermon on the Mount with the Cross on the Hill. They may not be as far apart as they may first appear to be. Paul's thought expressed how to do the kingdom of God in fresh ways. Still, the questions that were so pressing for Paul are not the ones on our contemporary agendas.

Judgment and the wrath of God are not popular ideas in a postmodern world "come of age," but neither is "salvation" in an age in which we "save" ourselves. We live by self-created illusions of peace and security in an individual world populated by gates and locks and security systems and bank accounts and a countless parade of passwords. And, there are "pills" for our every ill. A cell phone becomes our "gospel" and even god of choice.

The real tragedy in many so-called Christian quarters today is that laypersons in Christendom have never even been exposed to the terminology and encouraged to imagine a full Christ event or a full Gospel of God by those supposedly called to lead them. They have never been challenged nor required to grow toward spiritual maturity in Christ. They remain infants, as Paul said of the Corinthian Christians (see 1 Cor 3:1–4). The current writer once heard a story about a layman who asked a serious theological question of his pastor. The seminary-trained pastor's response was "We've known about that for fifty years," to which the layman retorted, "Then, why in the hell haven't you told us about it!"

Must laypersons be shielded from biblical truth? In reality, it is not a case of the need to shield laypersons. Laypersons can think for themselves, given permission and opportunity. Laypersons likewise have the ability to imagine—even to imagine theologically when given permission. It is too often a case of keeping laypersons enslaved to ecclesiastical institutionalism. One is reminded of Paul's own words to the Galatian Christians that if anyone comes preaching a different or heterodox gospel (ἕτερον εὐαγγέλιον), then let them "go to hell" (see Gal 1:6–9). Paul's understanding of the Gospel of God was one of sequential eschatology that had already been inaugurated by a gracious God who offered the fullness of peace to those who incarnated the gospel and grew toward maturity in the light of a final goal (see Phil 3:12–16).

To imagine Paul is not easy. We prefer to remain on the familiar surface of things with fifteen-second sound bites or brief text messages. If it's what we have always heard, we *dismiss* it, sometimes even by voicing "Amen!"—it is ever so familiar and may be affirmed. Familiarity breeds contempt. If it's not what we've always heard, we *dismiss* it as strange, irrelevant, or simply wrong. If we disagree, we dismiss it as "misinformation" and mal-characterize the messenger. We still *dismiss* it—either way. We only hear what we want to hear, or, to express the thought negatively, we refuse to hear what we choose not to hear. How many times in the Gospels did Jesus use the expression "The one who has ears to hear, let that one hear"?

The majority of the people in Christendom past or present may have found Paul and his message to be strange or alien, to be irrelevant or unreal. The majority of laypersons are convinced that Paul always belongs to the domain of preachers, priests, and theologians. In turn, the clergy and theologians have neither encouraged nor entrusted Paul to laypersons. Average church members have been convinced that Paul is too difficult for them to interpret. What does this say about discipleship, a kindred word to discipline? What does this say about a vibrant Christianity?

Laypersons have not been given permission to "imagine Paul" on their own. The fact remains that Paul's gospel has been the greatest source of revival and renewal within the Christian church itself over many centuries. The true antithesis may be between those truly committed to God in Christ and those who have no need for God, whether one be ironically *in* the church or *outside* the church. No one is so far from God as those who are dying in their own self-righteousness. Paul's old-fashioned terminology has lost its force with a sophisticated humanity-come-of-age or with those who leave it to others to do their theological thinking for them.

Paradoxically, that which Paul wrote about may *not* sound strange to us, because Christendom has adopted Paul's language without adopting or at least understanding Paul's conception of reality. To be sure, our world is not Paul's world. One needs to discern between Paul's abiding gospel and his cultural expression of that gospel, especially in view of the fact that Paul's legacy comes to us in the form of letters written to first-century Christian congregations. One cannot treat what Paul said as a post-it note. Many people rightly object to or even reject a theology that has become ossified in static doctrines that have long lost their meaning. Theology is only static if it becomes a "downloaded" repetition of words from a past era. In present-day computer terms, it becomes a "save as" to be filed away in another folder of whatever name, for reference if or as needed. It becomes hidden away in cyber-space. By contrast, Paul's theology was a dynamic theology for actual living. It provided an open "window" for real living on a day-by-day basis.

In contrast to shallow stream beds that may run dry, Paul thought deeply about the gospel. It controlled his life. By contrast, contemporary religious expression is often very shallow and often dry. For example, religious moralism's conception of sin as a rather insignificant moral wrong choice or "personal peccadillo" (as some have defined) if even taken seriously, may be easily dispatched by "confession" or liturgical assertion—"My brothers and sisters, your sins are forgiven." If it is as easy as liturgical confession, sin must not be much of a real problem.

Paul did not engage in such facile forgiveness. In fact, he seldom spoke or wrote of "forgiveness," as consultation of any concordance will demonstrate. He addressed a larger and deeper problem. Dietrich Bonhoeffer wrote of "cheap grace," as contrasted with "costly grace."[2] We are offered not only "cheap grace" in the religious marketplace of today, but also "cheap forgiveness" that excuses a "cheap" conception of sin. Is "sin" only a religious conception? Or, is it a theological reality? Do we no longer recognize its seriousness because we no longer feel the need for God at all, because we have fashioned self-solutions to recognized needs or even dismissed deeper human needs as irrelevant or unreal? Or, because we are actually living under the power of Sin?

If the language of "Sin/sin" is irrelevant, then the language of "grace" is likewise passé. If we no longer believe in a God who can deliver, pardon, and set us right, then conceptions of life—"redemption," "justification," "rectification," and "reconciliation"—carry no import. All become simply antiquated catchwords of a now ancient soteriology suitable for display in an ever less popular museum of theology that fewer and fewer people visit on any regular basis.

Paul spoke of the symptoms of a deeper malady of indwelling Sin and the corruption of one's heart that defies all our self-medications and proffered self-helps. Paul recognized a problem within humankind that was greater than confusions borne of ignorance, psychological maladjustments, and institutional corruption. Paul spoke of "powers" ever greater than the ability of human "cures." Paul recognized a level of evil that could infect and affect the entire cosmos, a level of evil even more insidious than a pandemic virus. And, Paul sought to deal forthrightly with the last enemy of humankind that rules over all of our self-remedies, namely, Death. The mortality rate down the centuries remains 100 percent, even for "faith-healers" and those who patronize them.

So, does Paul *really* have *anything* to say to our world? One should not come to a premature judgment before one has conducted personal investigation. Rediscovering Paul is not easy. Is the journey even worth undertaking? A question that faces us is whether we accord any authority to Paul. If we do, is Paul authoritative merely because his letters are in the New Testament? Or, is it because we believe that what he says is

---

2. Bonhoeffer, *Cost of Discipleship*, 43–56.

true, because he gives us a vision that can introduce us to the transforming power of God in Christ. Is it because we have experienced Paul's vision?

In the context of postmodernity, the questions are all the more pragmatic—"What difference does it all make?" "What was it like to live in Paul's day?" "Why should Paul and his letters even matter today?" Paul may be dismissed as passé and irrelevant in the light of all our technological advances and sociological and psychological understandings. How is *Paul's* word the "word of God"? With the pride of mind and with longing, empty hearts, the real question may even extend beyond Paul. "What difference does *any* of this 'word of God' stuff make anymore?"

Paul did not write to non-Christians, to people who were outside the church. Perhaps the surprising question for our day is whether people *within* the church find Paul to be relevant. And, the prior question may be whether the Bible itself—a book today more praised than read, much less Paul, is really authoritative for the contemporary church, much less humanity in general at all. The question of "Scripture" looms large in our day, *even for the church*, if we are honest.

The Reformation answer of *sola scriptura* ("Scripture alone") in general proposed as an alternative to "church alone" may no longer suffice in a world come of age and caught in the tension and turmoil of rapid change. The Reformation's answer in the sixteenth century was proffered in response to what Christendom had become in that day. Human arrogance would still qualify as "sin" for Paul (see Rom 1:18–31). Paul's answer to the human predicament was given before his letters themselves were deemed scriptural. It may be there is need for a new reformation of Christian faith—not "church alone" or "Scripture alone" but "grace alone" that redirects our vision to theological issues that really matter.

The church itself is always caught up in the sociological change of the general society. However, sociological change within the church itself may become problematic. An illustration may be given that typifies the issue. One problem today within the church is perhaps surprising, namely, Christian music. Older hymnody reflects an ossified doctrinal theology of yesteryear with lyrics that have lost their fizz. While there is a generational divide within the church pertaining to music media—hymns and pipe organs of yesteryear versus choruses and Christian rock—the underlying theology remains either ossified or shallow. "Praise" comes not only with a beat, but with feigned and rote expression of meaning.

The central problem with contemporary Christian music is not the medium, but the shallow nature of underlying theology that is reflective of an easy "gospel" that entertains but has no cost and, thus, has little substance according to the standards of Jesus or Paul. The secular beat and the rhythm may be fine and moving, but the message only parrots the ossified theology of a Christendom substituted for Christianity. As a result, the church has become a marketplace, even as the temple of Jesus's day had become a marketplace (see Mark 11:15–19; John 2:16, where the word "emporium" or market is used). And, people today "shop" churches.

For Paul, neither God nor Christ belonged to the past. Neither was either absent or only an idea. Neither was praised with canned praise. They were present and personal, and hence, important. To them belonged the future. Paul thought in terms of the lordship of Christ and a God who was Father. Paul's presuppositions, Paul's gospel, and Paul's theology may not only appear old-fashioned but even irrelevant to people today both within and outside the church. Those outside the church may have no need for "religion," much less Paul's brand of Christianity. On the other hand, those who have been brought up in traditional "Christian" homes, familiar with customary teaching and practice of "Christendom," may find Paul's theology to be irrelevant, inconvenient, or even irritating.

Paul not only lived in a now "never, never land" far away, but he thought deeply about the Gospel of God that had changed his whole life in such a radical fashion. Paul found meaning. We search for meaning in an increasingly impersonal world. Paul's voice has been silenced through granting iconic "sainthood" and through long centuries of the growth of theological barnacles that have overlaid the underlying Pauline wood with layers of doctrinal incrustations. For these reasons and others, Paul needs to be re-imagined such that the voice of Paul and the Gospel he proclaimed speaks afresh once again. We have the capacity and resources today to imagine Paul's world more clearly than ever before, but are we free enough and brave enough to imagine and embrace Paul's gospel?

One can never get away from interpretation (*hermeneutics*). There is no uninterpreted scriptural text. Perhaps what is needed is a hermeneutic of courage, a hermeneutic of discovery, a hermeneutic of imagination, an historical and metaphorical hermeneutic without the overly literal or the overly critical, i.e., factual without the fantasy. Perhaps we need a hermeneutic without the arrogance of the Enlightenment, the self-idolatry of modernity, or the homeless critique of postmodernity that is yet in search of an identity.

Perhaps we need a hermeneutic willing to pioneer through postmodernity that pursues the question "How does a human become truly human?" Can Paul's understanding of the gospel help with that? Rather than dismissing Paul, to imagine Paul and his gospel may mean that we get to know ourselves better, as we learn Paul again for the first time. Perhaps we can learn from Paul what it means to live together as a "praise of God's glory."

The Essence of What Paul Believed

To imagine Paul and his gospel is to get to know him better, to recognize his strengths as well as his weaknesses. To recognize his gospel and his theology is to wrestle with its depth and its relevance. Paul was not personally nor religiously perfect, he was "saint Paul" but not "Saint Paul." He may have been more right than wrong. What if Paul were right? What does one substitute for the Gospel of God? What other platform offers grace and peace, love and hope, as one finds a faithfulness beyond one's own current slavery and the emptiness of narcissistic self-idolatry?

Paul retains his vibrancy because he calls upon the church in every age, even the church in a postmodern period, to hear, comprehend, and to become living representatives of the Gospel of God. That takes the courage to imagine the application of the gospel of Paul, as it is transposed from a cultural world strange to us into a cultural world that would be strange to Paul. We may challenge and question Paul, but if we read him with any degree of comprehension, he still challenges and questions us. While we may challenge the apocalyptic husk of Paul's imagery, the larger question is whether we shall embrace Paul's eschatological foundation of the Gospel of God.

Is there a "word of God" to be found in the words of Paul? A "death of God" theology emerged in the mid-twentieth century, born from the smoldering optimism of the nineteenth century that had been called to account by two world wars. Serious questions emerged. Did God still exist? As scientific "progress" advanced in a world come of age, humanity seemingly had less need for a perceptively inactive God. Christendom circled its wagons to defend an impotent God who seemed to be increasingly less powerful and authoritative before the corrosive acid of modern science and human "progress." Indeed, does God have a future?

That question, however, is not a new one. It was asked by the psalmist following the destruction of the temple and Jerusalem by Babylon in 586 BCE, "How can we sing Yahweh's song in a foreign land?" (Ps 137:4). And, in a personal way, two of Jesus's disciples on a road to Emmaus lamented Jesus's crucifixion, "We had hoped he himself was the one destined to redeem Israel" (Luke 24:21). Their reaction at the end of Luke's Gospel stands in stark contrast to Simeon's confession in the temple at the beginning of Luke's Gospel that he had seen God's salvation for all peoples (Luke 2:27–32). Where was God the day Jesus died, in April of the year 30 CE? Where was God through the years of the Black Death (1348–53 CE)? Where was God when 50,000,000 people died in the Second World War (1939–45 CE), including 6,000,000 Jews? Where was God during the COVID-19 global pandemic of 2020 CE? Where is God in the sufferings and conflicts of today? The questions asked by theodicy are not new, nor were they necessarily asked by Paul. His testimony is that God is not absent but present. Paul proclaimed those elements that heralded God's presence in the context of the Gospel. It was the Gospel that helped Paul to re-imagine his theology.

Did God indeed act in final, re-creative ways in the Christ event or did he not? Is Christ Lord now or is he not? Do we still believe (i.e., have faith in the gospel) now or not? Or, have we discarded an ancient apocalyptic mythology, while at the same time we cling to an ecclesiastical husk of a ritualistic gospel of a Christendom with no eschatological meaning and only a promised, postponed future? How do *we* imagine Paul? How do *we* imagine the Gospel of God?

How do we imagine awareness of Paul's gospel of God? There are a handful of passages in Paul's letters that one should "live with" until their truth shines clear and before one makes any kind of final decision regarding Paul. The first is Paul's greeting to each of his churches, in which he commends *"grace and peace to all of you from God the Father and the Lord Jesus Christ."* Live with that—every word is significant—live with that until the truth of every word sinks into one's being. *Live* with that, as life itself becomes re-imagined through incarnation of its truth. Paul's salutations are, in fact, our very first introduction to Paul's theology. The heart of the Gospel resides in them. Imagine God as Father and Jesus as Lord and begin to discover what that means. Imagine life filled with God's grace, experienced with the wholeness of God's peace. Imagine—and live!

Paul should be allowed to speak for himself. So, other passages are given below in an order in which the author believes them to have been written, with proposed dating. The passages given below were written over a period of time from fifteen to twenty-six years after Paul's original call experience by God, an event that likely occurred in 34 CE. By the time his letters are written, Paul had had ample opportunity to incarnate the gospel in his own ministry. He was a "man in Christ."

Deliberately, the material has been selected because it has significance for understanding both Paul's gospel and his theology. Both realities are always a construct. Even the assemblage here and the translation from the Greek belong to the present author and is thus a construct. However, the material is representative of what Paul wrote to his churches. In this instance, italics are employed for clarity's sake to distinguish the present author's original translation of what Paul actually wrote. Italics are used in lieu of quotation marks to carefully set off Paul's thought from the present author's commentary. It is thus the present author's intention to let Paul "speak" for himself, as he proclaims the Gospel of God (Rom 1:1). Paul lives "in Christ." Christianity yet lives by the word of the Gospel of God found in Paul's own testimony.

During his Foundational Campaign, Paul wrote the following.

Corinth, 49 CE

⁴We stand persuaded [pf.] *in the Lord concerning you all, that what things we announced/instructed (you), indeed you all are doing and you all will do. ⁵May the Lord guide your hearts unto the love of God, indeed.* (2 Thess 3:4–5)

Corinth, 51 CE

⁸. . . let us be sober because we are those clothed with a breastplate of faithfulness and love and a helmet (that is) hope of salvation; ⁹because God has not appointed us unto wrath but unto a gaining of salvation through our Lord Jesus Christ [indirect agency], *¹⁰the one who died for us* [ὑπὲρ ἡμῶν] *for the purpose that whether we may be awake and alert or whether we may be asleep* [euphemism for death] *together at the same time we might live with him. ¹¹Therefore you all comfort one another and encourage one another, just as you are doing.* (1 Thess 5:8–11)

During his Collection Campaign, Paul wrote the following.

Ephesus, 54 CE

4. *³¹Wherefore, brethren, we are not children of the maid woman but of the free woman. 5. ¹Christ freed us for freedom; therefore you all stand firm and do not again become subject to a yoke of slavery. ²Behold I Paul say to you all that if you should be circumcised, Christ will benefit you nothing. ³For I bear witness again to every man being circumcised that he is obligated to do the entire Law. ⁴You all have been cut off from Christ, whichever ones would be rectified by law, you all have forfeited grace. ⁵For we out of faithfulness expectantly await (the) hope of rectification. ⁶For in Christ Jesus neither circumcision avails for anything nor lack of circumcision, but faithfulness energizing through love (is what avails).* (Gal 4:31—5:6)

Ephesus, 54 CE

⁵Have this way of thinking among yourselves that was also in Christ Jesus, ⁶who while being in the nature of God did not consider to be equal with God something to grasp after ⁷but/rather he emptied himself taking on the nature of a servant/slave and while being found in outward likeness as a man, ⁸he humbled himself because he became one obedient unto death [Death?], even Death's cross. ⁹For this very reason, God exalted him and graciously granted to him the name, the name above every name, ¹⁰such that at the name of Jesus every knee should bow—of things in heaven and of things upon earth and of things under the earth, and ¹¹every tongue should confess that Jesus Christ is Lord, unto the glory of God the Father. ¹²Therefore, my beloved ones, just as you all have always been obedient, not only in my coming [παρουσία] but now much more in my absence [ἀπουσία], with fear and trembling you all continue working out your salvation, ¹³for God is the One working in you both to will and to work for the sake of (his) good pleasure. (Phil 2:5–13)

Ephesus, 54 CE

²⁰But now Christ has been raised from the dead, the first fruit of the ones who have fallen asleep. ²¹For since through a man Death (came), also through a man (came) resurrection from the dead; ²²for just as in Adam all die, thus indeed in Christ all will be made alive. ²³But each one in one's own time: Christ the first fruit, then those of Christ at his parousia. ²⁴Then (comes) the Telos, whenever he should hand over the kingdom to (our) God and Father, whenever he may abolish every rule and every authority and power. ²⁵For it is necessary for him to rule until which time he may put all enemies under his feet. ²⁶Death is destroyed (as) the last enemy; ²⁷For "all things will be subjected under his feet." But whenever it should be said (that) "all things have been subjected, it is evident that the One who subjects all things (is) an exception. ²⁸But whenever he should subject all things to himself, then indeed the Son himself will be subjected to the One who subjected all things to himself, in order that God may be all things in all. (1 Cor 15:20–28)

Macedonia, 55 CE

[11]Therefore, while knowing the fear of the Lord, we persuade men, but we have been manifest to God and I hope also to have been made manifest to your collective consciences. [12]We are not again commending ourselves to all of you but giving to you all an opportunity for boasting in our behalf, in order that you may have [an answer] for those who boast in outward appearance and not in interior intention. [13]For if we appear to be out of our mind, (it is) for God; if we appear to be right-minded, (it is) for all of you. [14]For the love of Christ surrounds us, because we have concluded this, that he died in behalf of all, consequently all died; [15]indeed, he died in behalf of all, in order that those who live may live no longer for themselves but for the one who died and was raised in their behalf.

[16]So that from now on, we regard no one according to human nature. We concede we have regarded Christ according to human nature, but now we do not regard (him so) any longer. [Christ has been raised and exalted.] [17]The result is that if any one (is) in Christ, (such a one is) a new creation; old things have passed away, behold new things have already come to be. [18]But all things are from God, who reconciled us to himself through Christ [indirect agency] and who gave to us the ministry of reconciliation, since God was reconciling the world to himself in Christ, not reckoning to them their trespasses and placing in us the message of reconciliation. [20]Therefore, in behalf of Christ we are representatives as God speaks words of encouragement through us [indirect agency]. We beg (you all) in behalf of Christ, become reconciled to God. [21]He made the one who did not know sin (to be) sin in our behalf, in order that we might become [an example of] rectification of God in him. (2 Cor 5:11–20)

Corinth, 56 CE

[21]But now the rectification of God has already been manifested apart from law, being directly witnessed by the Law and the prophets [direct agency], [22]the rectification of God through the faithfulness of Jesus Christ [indirect agency, subj. gen.] unto all those living faithfully; for there is no distinction. [23]For all have sinned [aor.] and continue to be in need of the glory of God, [24]being rectified freely by his grace [impersonal agency] through redemption/release/setting free, that is in Christ Jesus, [25]whom God put forth as a place to receive mercy through faithfulness [indirect agency] by his life-blood [impersonal agency], unto a demonstration of his [God's] rectification through the passing over of previously committed sins [indirect agency] [26]by the forbearance of God [impersonal agency], pertaining to the demonstration/evidence of his rectification in the present season, that He might (prove to be) right and (be) One who rectifies the one (who is) of the faithfulness of Jesus.

²⁷*So where is boasting? It is excluded. Through the basis of what principle? Through works? No, but through the principle of faithfulness.* ²⁸*For we consider a man to be rectified by faithfulness apart from works of the Law.* ²⁹*(Is) God (the God of) the Jews only? Is he not also (God of the) gentiles? Yes, indeed, of the gentiles,* ³⁰*since God is One, who will rectify the one circumcised on the basis of faithfulness and the one uncircumcised through faithfulness* [indirect agency]. ³¹*Do we therefore nullify (the) Law through faithfulness? Not at all. Rather, we establish (the) Law.* (Rom 3:21–31)

Corinth, 56 CE

¹*Wherefore there is now no condemning judgment against the ones in Christ Jesus;* ²*for the law of the Spirit of life in Christ Jesus has freed you* [sing.] *from the law of Sin and Death.* ³*For the inability of the Law, in which inability it is weakened by the flesh (Flesh)* [indirect agency]*, God having sent his own Son in the likeness of sinful Flesh and concerning Sin, he condemned Sin in the Flesh,* ⁴*in order that the righteous judgment of the Law might be fulfilled in all of you who do not walk according to (the) Flesh but according to (the) Spirit.* ⁵*For the ones who live according to the Flesh set their minds on the things of the Flesh, but the ones (who live) according to the Spirit (set their minds on) the things of the Spirit.* ⁶*For the mind-set of the Flesh (is) Death, but the mind-set of the Spirit (is) life and peace;* ⁷*because the mind-set of the Flesh (is) an enemy unto God, for it is not subjected to the Law of God, nor is it able (to be).* ⁸*For the ones living (in the realm of the) Flesh are not able (to be) pleasing to God.* ⁹*But you all are not in (the domain of) the Flesh but in (the domain of) the Spirit, if indeed the Spirit of God dwells in all of you. But if anyone does not have the spirit of Christ, this one is not of him.* ¹⁰*If Christ (is) in all of you, on the one hand the body (is) dead because of Sin, but the Spirit/spirit (is) life because of rectification.* ¹¹*But since the Spirit of the One who raised Christ from the dead dwells in all of you, the One who raised Christ from the dead will make alive also the mortal bodies of all of you through his indwelling Spirit* [indirect agency] *in all of you.*

¹²*So therefore, brethren, we are debtors, not to (the realm of) the Flesh to live according to the Flesh;* ¹³*for if you all live according to Flesh you are about to die, but if by the Spirit you put to death the practices of the body you all will live.* ¹⁴*For as many (as are) led by the Spirit of God, these are children of God.* ¹⁵*For you all did not receive the spirit of slavery again unto fear, but you all received a spirit of adoption, whereby we cry, "Abba, Father!"* ¹⁶*The Spirit itself bears witness together with our spirit because we are children of God.* ¹⁷*But if (we are) children, (we are) indeed heirs: on the one hand, heirs of God; but on the other hand fellow heirs of Christ, since we suffer together (with him) in order that we may be indeed glorified together (with him).*

¹⁸*For I consider that the sufferings of the present Age* [time] *(are not) worthy (to be compared) to the coming glory to be revealed to us.* ¹⁹*For the eager longing of creation waits expectantly the revelation of the children* [sons] *of God;* ²⁰*for the*

creation was subjected to futility, not willingly but because of the One subjecting (it), because of hope, ²¹because indeed the creation itself will be freed from the slavery of decay unto the freedom of the glory of the children of God. ²²For we know that the whole creation groans together and experiences pains of birth until the present time. ²³But not only so, but indeed we ourselves who have the first fruit of the Spirit, we indeed ourselves groan in ourselves, while eagerly we expectantly await adoption, the redemption of our body. ²⁴For we were saved by hope. But hope being seen is not hope; who hopes for what he sees? ²⁵But if we hope for what we do not see, we wait expectantly through steadfast endurance.

²⁶But likewise indeed the Spirit helps with our weakness. For we do not know the thing whatever we should pray as is necessary, but the Spirit itself intercedes with unspoken groanings; ²⁷But the One who searches hearts knows what is the mind of the Spirit, because it intercedes in behalf of the saints. ²⁸We know that for those who love God it works all things unto good, to the ones called according to steadfast purpose. ²⁹Because ones whom he foreknew, indeed he worked out beforehand the same likeness of the image of his Son, with the result that he is the first born among many brothers and sisters: ³⁰"Whom he marked out beforehand, these indeed he called. And whom he called, these indeed he rectified. And whom he rectified, these indeed he glorified" [Paul here quotes an early Christian hymn].

³¹Therefore, what shall we say to these things? Since God is for us, who is against us? ³²Who did not spare his own Son but gave him over in behalf of all of us [ὑπὲρ ἡμῶν], how will he not also grant/grace all things to us together with him? ³³Who will call out against the elect ones of God? God (is) the One who rectifies. ³⁴Who shall level charges? Christ Jesus (is) the one who died, rather the one who was raised, who indeed is at the right hand of God, who indeed intercedes in our behalf [ὑπὲρ ἡμῶν]. ³⁵Who will sever us from the love of Christ? Affliction or trouble or persecution or hunger or poverty or peril or violent death? ³⁶Just as it stands written, "For your sake we are put to death all day long, we are reckoned as sheep for slaughter." ³⁷But in all these things we are super conquerors through the One who loved us. ³⁸For I stand persuaded [pf.] that neither death/ Death nor life nor angels nor rulers nor things present nor things about to come nor powers ³⁹nor height nor depth nor any other thing in creation will be able to sever us from the love of God, the love in Christ Jesus our Lord. (Rom 8:1–39)

And, during his Post-Collection period, Paul wrote the following from Rome toward the end of his life.

Rome, 60 CE

³We continually give thanks to God the Father of our Lord Jesus Christ, praying always concerning you all ⁴because we have heard of your faith in Christ Jesus and the love that you have for all the saints ⁵because of the hope that has been stored away for all of you in the heavens, the (hope) that you heard in the word of the truth of the gospel ⁶that has come to you all, just as indeed in all the world it is bearing fruit and growing . . . ⁹Because of this, indeed, from which day we heard, we do not cease praying and offering petitions in your behalf [ὑπέρ ὑμῶν], *in order that you all may be filled with full knowledge of his will in all wisdom and spiritual understanding, ¹⁰that you might conduct yourselves worthily of the Lord in every way pleasing, in every good work (being those) bearing fruit and growing in full knowledge of God, ¹¹being those empowered with all power according to the might of his glory unto every endurance and patience, with joy ¹²giving thanks to the Father who makes you fit for a share of the inheritance of the saints in light, ¹³who rescued us from the authority of darkness and brought (us) unto the kingdom of his beloved son, ¹⁴in whom we have redemption, the forgiveness of sins . . .* (Col 1:3–6, 9–14)

Rome, 60 CE

¹And you all being dead in your trespasses and sins, ²in which then you conducted yourselves according to the age of this world, according to the ruler of the authority of the air, the spirit now working in the children of disobedience. ³Indeed, among these we all lived then by the strong desires of our flesh while carrying out the wills of the flesh and reasonings, indeed we were by nature children of wrath as indeed all the rest; ⁴ but God being rich in mercy, because of his abundant love with which he loved us, ⁵even when we were dead through trespasses, he made alive in Christ—by grace you are those who have been saved [pf.]*—⁶indeed he raised us and established us in the heavens in Christ Jesus, ⁷in order that he might demonstrate in the coming ages the surpassing wealth of his grace in kindness over us in Christ Jesus. ⁸For by grace you all are those who have been saved* [pf.] *through faithfulness; indeed this is not of yourselves, (but it is) the gift of God; ⁹not of works, lest anyone should have a boast. ¹⁰For we are his workmanship, because we have been created in Christ Jesus for good works which God prepared beforehand, in order that we might conduct ourselves in them.* (Eph 2:1–10)

That which Paul writes is gospel informed by his theology. Paul speaks for himself in the above passages. One can only illustrate a difference in interpretation here. Several of the above passages are often viewed as significant theological or "doctrinal" passages in Paul—passages that theologians and scholars dice, dissect, and debate, with various positions recited by pietists. Romans 3:21–31 is usually treated as a significant "theological" passage in Paul. It is vigorously and assiduously debated and parsed by scholars. In this work, why not imagine reading this passage as "gospel" instead of "theology." Does that make a difference?

On the other hand, Rom 8:1–39, and especially vv. 28–39, are usually treated as a "gospel" passage especially employed by laypersons in times when comfort is needed. To be sure, Calvin found support for his theological doctrines of "predestination" here (see Rom 8:28–30). Why not imagine reading this entire passage as "theology" rather than as "gospel comfort"? And, why not allow a theology of practical application emerge rather than doctrinal abstraction that only becomes a substitute for living? Imagine it as a theological passage that informs one of the nature of God and his Gospel, rather than as a recipe for human comfort in terms of our doctrinal gospel. Does that make a difference? Indeed, might not the resultant theology lead to grateful worship of God, if we allow it to do so? Other passages could be examined in the light of the same rubric. There is Bible reading, study, and spiritual insight for living for more than "a month of Sundays" contained in Paul's words.

When one begins to think of God and to imagine him in the terms that Paul uses, "grace and peace," "love, joy, peace, etc.," one begins a transformational theological journey of coming to imagine God as a loving and gracious Father instead of a celestial Judge who requites and condemns. How do the other passages read? Does it make a difference to imagine them as "gospel," rather than just a collection of theological doctrines, perhaps represented at times only in singular verses (e.g., 2 Cor 5:21)? What do they have to say about God? About the Gospel? About Christ? About us? Their order of writing is not insignificant for appropriate perspective.

The legacy of Paul is not just a category of thought that we call "theology." Paul's legacy also involves gospel. "Gospel" is always something that once heard is meant to be embraced and lived, for it is truly good news. "Gospel" is always announcement that comes with invitation. While we may interpret some of the themes Paul treats in a different manner in the light of different religious and socio-cultural settings, Paul still challenges us to re-think or re-imagine the Gospel of God, even in the light of an historical continuum. He still introduces us to the God of the Gospel and invites us to worship in the name of Christ. He leaves the decision to us. It is we who must decide to incarnate the Gospel of God or not.

For Paul, life is "cruciform." The fabric of life itself becomes defined by the self-giving love of the cross. Faith, love, and hope are grounded in the integrity of God. The cruciform principle of "power in weakness" signals love's transformation. Faith is a death experience that leads to the new life of resurrection. Faith is not just a "belief" system. Rather, faith lived out becomes a living organism, a covenant community, not a calcified fossil remain or an artifact displayed in a theological museum. Love is not an emotion, but an action of the will. Love is the freedom of liberating identity unto liberating service. The love that serves is a correlate of the faith that saves.

While love is faith's expression, hope is faith's fulfillment. Hope is the future tense of faith and love. Hope is the antidote to despair. Laced with hope, even suffering may launch a chain of endurance and hope. Christ without eschatological hope is a Christianity that has no future. It is the resurrection that offers the triumph of hope (1 Cor 15:19, 30–32). Paul's conviction that love is preferable to faith and hope is noteworthy, because love is open-ended. Faith and hope may be fulfilled; love remains, always fulfilling (see 1 Cor 13:13).

Images for the church are abundant in Paul—body, temple, assembly, unity, diversity, adoption, "fictive family," alternative polis, incorporation. The church as church meets to worship, to encourage. It meets to recite narratives. It also meets to enact and incarnate narratives. It meets to proclaim the Gospel of God. It meets to live life together. The Gospel of God for Paul was good news of a new age of fulfillment and a living Lord. It was not an industry or a marketplace geared for profit, self-preservation, or religious illusion.

Paul celebrates salvational realities within the church as a community of faith—the emotional and intellectual life of authentic persons for whom joy, peace, freedom, mutual love, and hope are all qualities of the reality of a church living under justification by grace, as faith energizes through love (Gal 5:6). In the Old Testament, Israel was a people set apart by a holy God to be a distinctive people in identity and behavior, not in isolation but in influential inclusion.

For Paul, Christian existence is charismatic existence. The Spirit gives life in covenantal relationship. The church is multi-cultural and counter-cultural in every age, if it holds Christ above culture. It lives as the church only as the people of God unto a "praise of his glory" (Eph 1:6, 12, 14). The scriptural concept of the "word of God" for Paul was not a doctrinal abstraction, but rather it was a living Word in Christ. It was not a Word to be praised, but rather a Word to be incarnated and lived.

A Concluding Postscript

This book was begun as I sat for a week in a darkened hospital room with my beloved eldest son who had survived a totally unexpected heart attack and who was recovering from open heart surgery. I simply began to write to occupy my time and mind while he rested and slept. I had no resources to draw upon other than pen and paper and my years of living with the New Testament, Jesus, and Paul through courses taught to undergraduate students and occasional adult church groups, as well as my own faith's pilgrimage and pastorates.

This book, with some degree of irony, was essentially brought to its conclusion during weeks of self-quarantine at home as a result of the COVID-19 virus pandemic that swept the United States and the world and that continues to be a threat. Never in all my life had I ever experienced anything like that, which virtually shut down the entire world. This was not, however, the first pandemic the world has ever experienced. (The author has often mused over the religious impact of the pandemic of the Black Death or Plague in the fourteenth century that killed an estimated 75–200,000,000 people and the effect that it must have had on Christian life and thought.) Both of these events, one personal and the other truly global, had the effect of jarring the author out of a spirit of modern complacency and a spirit that can only be characterized as an illusion of peace and security established on a purely secular plane. And, even and especially today, we live in an increasingly uncertain and postmodern world in which time-honored landmarks are disappearing and even being deliberately destroyed in a search of soul.

"Christendom" becomes institutionalized self-protection and does not realize how secularized it has become, employing methods and entertaining values that are sub-Christian. One may find difficulty personifying the "principalities and powers" of Paul's day, yet such personification is not unknown in our day. "Powers" still do business under different names. People speak of "the market," "the media," "the economy," "the government," "the party," "drugs," as though these had an identity and power of their own. There are still "powers that be" in the postmodern world that rival Paul's powers in his world, *some empowered by people but all with power over people*. And, superstitions still seek for magical solutions.

Ancient minds likewise grappled with the human predicament in ways both like and unlike our modern minds, such that the norms of antiquity may seem strange in a postmodern age. The vocabulary of Paul's religion comes to us in words like sin, Sin, atonement, grace, righteousness, justification, etc. The Christian movement began with a small group of Jesus's disciples in Jerusalem, the center of Judaism, but it developed into a self-sufficient gentile church that moved beyond Jewish markers of dietary laws, festival calendars, and religious rites. Uniquely Christian markers came into being, such as baptism and the Eucharist. Sunday, the Lord's Day substituted for the Sabbath, was observed, while other holy days such as Pentecost took on a Christian meaning. And now, there is a liturgical "Christian year," punctuated by special seasons and populated by "ordinary" time.

God's faithfulness and grace are rooted in God's promises (Rom 4:11–17). God's grace is reconciling and transforming. Grace is not just cheap forgiveness although many of our religious "justifications" are just that—cheap. The peace and grace of God are not merely private. The *shalom* of God is peace with real-world consequences. God's grace and peace comes to fullest expression in Christ (1 Cor 1:4; Rom 5:15).

The divine goal for the entire creation according to Paul is reconciliation, rectification, liberation from suffering and death, participation in the life and glory of God as a praise of his glory. The Gospel of God offers solution to dysfunctional humanity, still unfortunately in search of itself, that increasingly blames others for one's own dysfunction.

Unless contemporary theology is rooted in the proclamation of the gospel found in the basic perspectives of the historic earliest church, and especially Paul, then the danger exists of succumbing to a modern Gnosticism or a secular relativism. When Christianity becomes only one way of helping people realize their supposed human potential, it has become only an anthropological humanism on the way to becoming "Christendom." It is then called upon to protect and defend and appropriate its own structures erected and employed by humankind, whether those be physical plants or theological doctrines. And, at some point, who can say when or how, the human structures we have erected and have imagined to be sufficient for our peace and security will fail, as their inadequacy becomes demonstrated in the crucible of life.

By contrast, Christianity is first of all centered upon the actions of God in the historical Christ event in which Paul found himself to be a participant. It was the action of God that shook Paul out of his Pharisaic complacency, as he now came to imagine a new reality, a new world, and a new life. On the one hand, it is easy to deceive ourselves and speak about a Paul of our own making who never existed (and a made-over Jesus as well, for that matter). There was, however, a real Paul, even as there was a real Jesus. And, maybe, each was very different from what we have previously imagined.

The Christ event challenged Paul, even as it embraced and enveloped him. That is what the Christ event needs to do for us. We need to become enthralled. We need to allow its embrace and envelopment, as well as its challenge. It is a creative mind open to faith that welcomes new experiences, that questions and debates, and that makes profitable use of such opportunities, even opportunities of challenge. Paul had a creative mind that embraced the Gospel of God, even as that Gospel enveloped him with a call to faith. It was not a singular transaction that animated Paul, but rather an ongoing experience. In the power of the Spirit, Paul incarnated that Gospel that had claimed him in his living witness. Paul imagined, but he did not engage in the imaginary.

By contrast, and perhaps for a number of different reasons, we have become far too comfortable with the *imaginary* and see no real need to imagine positively anything other than what we have always been taught and have come to believe. And "belief" has become mere assent without cost, or to use Dietrich Bonhoeffer's phrase, "cheap grace" sold as works in the religious marketplace of today. Imaginary gospels carefully crafted with theological barnacles called doctrines offer only an imaginary salvation—perhaps a comfortable one, without personal cost, but one that will not deliver in reality what it promises.

Paul wrote to the Galatian Christians who were being duped by a substitute gospel based upon the law—one that he did not consider to be the gospel at all. "*Is the Law against the promises of God? For if a law had been given—one able to make alive* [and none ever has], *then rectification would be on the basis of law* [but it is not]. *On the contrary, the scripture made all things a prisoner under Sin, that the promise of faithfulness in Christ Jesus might be given to those who respond in faithfulness*" (Gal 3:21–22). Paul employed a second class, contrary to fact conditional sentence in verse 21, as the current author's interpretive comment makes plain. One could also substitute the word "doctrine" for the word "Law" in contemporary application. All "doctrines" are human creations fashioned in time; the Gospel is God's timeless action "in Christ." *No doctrine* has been given that is able to make alive. One is not saved by formulations no matter how timely they may be or how elaborately they may be expressed. Rather, one is saved by the operative grace of God expressed and experienced in faithfulness. One is both saved and enabled by the Gospel of God through which one receives new identity and orientation to life.

In contrast to many false gospels that lack truth and balance, the God of the Gospel that arrested Paul in the midst of his Pharisaism still seeks to claim us with *his* Gospel. Paul learned to live out that Gospel, one characterized by the *"scandal of the cross"* (Gal 5:11) that revealed new life unto resurrection (Phil 3:7–11). It was a Gospel through which faithfulness energized through love (Gal 5:6). In Christ, one is called to the freedom of indebted service to one another through actions of loving service (Gal 5:13). The tenor of Paul's practical emphasis upon faithfulness may be seen in Rom 12:9–21 and 13:8–10. Even one's doctrine should serve one's neighbor, as Paul affirms that the whole Law is fulfilled in a single imperative, *"You shall love (your) neighbor as yourself"* (Gal 3:14; cf. Lev 19:18).

In Rom 12:1–2, Paul calls for living service to others as that which is sacrificially holy and acceptable to God as one's logical worship. In contrast to being "schematized" to the current age, Paul calls for transformation or renewal of one's mind-set, in order to discern what is truly the will of God. When one experiences that new mind-set, then one discovers the will of God to be good and pleasing and characterized by wholeness. It is "Grace and Peace from God the Father and the Lord Jesus Christ," as Paul himself experienced and testified. As we imagine living out that Gospel in actual, incarnational situations, then reconciliation with God and incarnational living in the power of the Spirit becomes expression of the Gospel in terms of gratitude, praise, worship, and service that is truly life-giving. We learn to live on a daily basis in manifold ways as a *"praise of God's glory"* (Eph 1:6, 12, 14).

When one imagines the Gospel of God, one (like Paul) is drawn to worship God with gratitude and with praise. One is freed and empowered to live as a "praise of God's glory," thus fulfilling one's own God-intended identity (see Rom 12:1–2; Eph 1:3–15). So, to borrow from Paul's personal example, this work may be closed with a doxology: *"Glory be to God for all the things he has done 'in Christ.' To God be all glory forever, through Christ Jesus. Amen."*

Imagine that.

APPENDIX A

A Chronology of the Ministry of Paul

Revelation and Initial Ministry

Initial Call and Ministry

    Revelation and Calling—34 CE (Gal 1:11–17; cf. Acts 9:1–9)

    Ministry in Damascus and Arabia—34–37 CE (Gal 1:15–17; cf. Acts 9:19–22)

    First Visit to Jerusalem (J1)—"Acquaintance" Visit, 37 CE (Gal 1:18–24; cf. Acts 9:26–29)

    Ministry in Syria and Cilicia—37 CE (See Acts 9:30; 11:25–26)

Foundation Campaign around to Illyricum—38–51 CE

    Phase I of Foundation Campaign, Anatolia (likely 3–5 years), 38–42/43 CE (See Acts 13:1—14:28)

    Phase II of Foundation Campaign, Anatolia to Illyricum (likely 5–8 years), 43–51 CE (See Rom 15:19; Acts 16:1—19:41)

        2 Thessalonians—Early 49 CE, from Achaia? (1 Thess 3:1)

        Previous Letter to Corinth (see 2 Cor 6:14—7:1 Fragment)—Early 50 CE, from Illyricum (See 1 Cor 5:9; Rom 15:19)

    Stay in Corinth—Summer 51 CE, appearance before Gallio (July 51?) (See Acts 18:12–17)

        1 Thessalonians—Early 51 CE, from Corinth

    Second Visit to Jerusalem (J2)—"Famine" Visit, Fall 51 CE (+17 years) (Gal 2:1–10; see Acts 11:27–30)

    Conflict with Nomistic Evangelists (Judaizers) in Antioch—Early Spring 52 CE (Gal 2:11–14)

APPENDIX A: A CHRONOLOGY OF THE MINISTRY OF PAUL

Third Visit to Jerusalem (J3)—"Conference" Visit, Spring 52 CE (See Acts 15:1–35)

Collection Campaign—52–56 CE, from Antioch to Corinth

Conflict with Nomistic Evangelists (Judaizers) in Antioch—Summer 52 CE (Gal 2:11–21)

Ministry in Galatia—52 CE (See 1 Cor 16:1)

Ministry in Ephesus—52–54 CE (See Acts 19:1)

Imprisonment in Ephesus—54 CE (See 1 Cor 15:30–32; 2 Cor 1:8; 11:23)

Galatians—54 CE, from Ephesus (Gal 6:7–10; cf. 2 Cor 9:6–15)

Philippians—54 CE, from Ephesus (Phil 1:27–30; 3:2–3; 3:17–20; 4:1–3)

1 Corinthians—54 CE, from Ephesus (1 Cor 16:1–12; 2 Cor 2:3)

(*Painful Letter to Corinth*)

Departure for Macedonia—55 CE

2 Corinthians 1–13—55 CE, from Macedonia (2 Cor 7:6; 8; 9)

Move to Achaia

Romans 1–15—56 CE, from Corinth (Rom 15:26)

Journey to Jerusalem for Pentecost—Late Spring 56 CE (Pentecost—June 11, 56 CE) (See Acts 20:3–16)

Paul's Post-Collection Years

Fourth Visit to Jerusalem (J4)—"Collection" Visit, 56 CE (Rom 15:25–29; cf. Acts 24:17)

Arrest in Jerusalem—Early Summer 56 CE (Acts 21:27–34)

Caesarean Imprisonment—Summer 56–Summer 58 CE (Acts 24:27)

Travel to Rome by Sea—Fall 58 CE (Acts 27:1—28:10)

Winter on Malta—Fall 58–Winter 59 CE (Acts 28:1, 11)

Arrival in Rome—Early Spring 59 CE (Acts 28:11–14)

APPENDIX A: A CHRONOLOGY OF THE MINISTRY OF PAUL

Roman Imprisonment—Spring 59–61 CE   (Acts 28:16, 30)

   Colossians   Early Summer 60 CE

      (Tychicus the bearer, Col 4:10; cf. Acts 20:4)

   Philemon   Early Summer 60 CE

      (Tychicus, with Onesimus, the bearer)

   Ephesians   Early Summer 60 CE

      (Tychicus sent to Ephesus, cf. Eph 6:21)

   Romans 16   Early Summer 60 CE

      (Timothy with Paul; letter carried by Tychicus to Ephesus, accompanied by Phoebe)

Note: These four letters of Paul were carried by Tychicus and those who accompanied him to Ephesus and Colossae/Laodicea. Tychicus then returned to Rome.

First Trial before Nero—Midsummer 60 CE

   2 Timothy   Late Summer 60 CE

      (Timothy in Ephesus; Tychicus again sent to Ephesus, cf. 2 Tim 4:12)

Note: Second Timothy is the last literary testament of Paul that we have.

Martyrdom—Late Spring or Summer 61 CE

Summary Chronological Listing of Letters

Letter	Place of Origin	Date
Foundation Campaign Letters		
2 Thessalonians	Corinth	49 CE
Previous Letter to Corinth (see 2 Cor 6:14—7:1)	Illyricum	50 CE
1 Thessalonians	Corinth	51 CE
Collection Campaign Letters		
Galatians	Ephesus	54 CE
Philippians	Ephesus	54 CE
1 Corinthians	Ephesus	54 CE
(Painful Letter to Corinth)		

2 Corinthians 1–13	Macedonia	56 CE
Romans 1–15	Corinth	56 CE

Post-Collection Letters

Colossians	Rome	60 CE
Philemon	Rome	60 CE
Ephesians	Rome	60 CE
Romans 16	Rome	60 CE
2 Timothy	Rome	60 CE

Letters Not by Paul

1 Timothy?	Pseudonymous, not Pauline on historical and stylistic grounds
Titus?	Pseudonymous, not Pauline on historical and stylistic grounds

This chronology was first developed in the author's earlier work, *The Ministry of Paul the Apostle: History and Redaction*, published by Lexington Books/Fortress Academic (2019). It is used in this application with permission.

APPENDIX B
God's Table Spread

OTHER THAN THE HISTORICAL narration of Jesus's last meal with his disciples as found in the Gospels, it is only Paul in the New Testament who offers insight on the practice of the "Lord's Supper," or the sacrament of the Eucharist as found in Christendom (1 Cor 11:23–27). It sometimes referred to as "Communion." Paul treats the Supper in the context of addressing Corinthian self-righteousness in wisdom, worship, and spiritual gifts (1 Cor 10–14). We may easily forget that Paul wrote what he wrote in the context of a factious and idolatrous worship by an immature church at Corinth that had to be fed with infant milk rather than solid food (see 1 Cor 11:17–34; 3:1–3).

Within Christendom today, some churches practice "open communion," while others practice "closed communion." Some churches practice "inclusion," while others practice "exclusion," while each claims support of a doctrinal "scripture." Contemporary social issues and differences in theological doctrines threaten to tear churches and denominations apart. It appears that the contemporary church has not grown much beyond the legalism and antinomianism—and consequent self-righteousness—of Paul's church at Corinth. Again, it may be time to imagine Paul's Gospel, even at the time of most sacred celebration within Christianity. With that in mind, the present author offers a hymn for the celebration of unity in Christ unto a praise of God's glory.

APPENDIX B: GOD'S TABLE SPREAD

God's Table Spread

Children of light who come now from a darkened night,
Abundance full, God's mercy, grace, and light.
Dividing walls now broken down, no power enslaves.
A meal prepared for all who seek his grace.

> We do receive far more than what we asked of Thee,
> For we have found far more than what we sought.
> So let us take our place before your table spread,
> And celebrate the love of God with all around.

Around this table, now, we share both cup and bread.
One table spread for all who live in Christ.
A table spread, by grace alone, where love abounds,
Where there's a place for us and everyone.

> One Lord, one Spirit, and one Father of us all.
> One faith, one call, our invitation plain.
> Renewal of soul, our hearts and minds are filled with joy,
> We celebrate the love of God with table spread.

Go forth in joy, be led in peace, let God be praised,
For we are freed from powers that enslave.
Melodious song, with hymns of praise, our psalms we sing.
Incarnate now a loving heart around.

> One Lord, one Spirit, and one Father of us all.
> One faith, one call, our invitation plain.
> Renewal of soul, our hearts and minds are filled with joy,
> We celebrate the love of God, his love unbound.
> One Lord, one Spirit, and one Father of us all.
> One faith, one call, our invitation plain.
> Renewal of soul, our hearts and minds are filled with joy,
> We celebrate the love of God, his love unbound.

G. Roger Greene. "God's Table Spread." Provine Chapel, November 2023
(May be sung prayerfully to the tune of "Londonderry Air" or "Danny Boy.")
Copyright © 2023 by G. Roger Greene. All rights reserved.

Glossary

Agency—An "agent" is a person or thing that creates the action of a verb expressed in a sentence. In the "active" voice, the agent and the grammatical subject are one and the same. In the "passive" voice, the grammatical subject is acted upon and receives the action. One may have a "direct" agent expressed or implied or an "indirect" agent through which the direct agent accomplishes the action. "Agency" in Paul is theologically important and significant.

Agora—The marketplace in a Greco-Roman city, usually consisting of shops and perhaps some temples and public buildings.

Aorist Tense Verbs—The so-called aorist tense in Greek is the default verb tense. It offers a "single perspective summary" of action that has occurred or occurs without describing the *kind* of action that took place. It is "without a horizon." It is first of all "kind" of action that is set forth in Greek, rather than "time" as in English.

Apocalyptic—A particular type of perspective and literature within Judaism and early Christianity that looked for the radical and sudden in-break of God to make things right and establish his rule. It expressed future destiny by the use of much symbolism.

Apostle—One who is sent out on a mission with the authority of the sender. Paul characterized himself as an apostle of God in Christ.

Canon—An accepted or authoritative listing of books accepted as Holy Scripture. The New Testament canon of twenty-seven books developed over time and was acknowledged by Athanasius in 367 CE. Paul's letters are the earliest writings contained in the New Testament.

Christendom—The official expression of Christianity that has come to be and that developed through the centuries of Christian history. Conformity to the accepted practices of Christian faith.

Christian—One who is a follower of Christ who expresses faith in the gospel of Christ. While common today, the word only occurs three times in the New Testament and never once in Paul.

Christianity—Religious expression based upon faith in Christ. It developed out of first-century Judaism and expressed faith in Jesus as the Messiah and Son of God.

Christology—The theological expression and interpretation of the meaning of the person and events pertaining to Jesus as the Christ of God.

Cruciform—That which takes on or has the shape of a cross. For Paul, the Christian life was cruciform, whether literally or metaphorically. As in the case of Jesus, one may face suffering and even death. "Cruciformity" would precede resurrection.

Diaspora—The movement or migration of people away from an ancestral homeland. In Paul's day, the Jewish Diaspora represented Jews living throughout the Mediterranean world outside of Palestine.

Diatribe—Most often, a debate or interchange with an imaginary opponent in speech or writing. It is a technique used in rhetoric that Paul frequently employed.

Doctrine—Teaching or principles that are accepted and taught as a system of belief. Hence, it becomes an official statement of religious belief. Doctrine arises at particular points in time to address specific issues.

Dogma—Something held as an authoritative statement or tenet, often held without adequate evidence or warrants. A body of accepted beliefs formally stated and authoritatively proclaimed by the church.

Ecclesiology—The study of things pertaining to the church in terms of expressed faith and practices. Drawn from a Greek word, *ekklesia* (ἐκκλησία), most often translated "church."

Eisegesis—The interpretation or presentation of the meaning of one's own ideas read into a scriptural text. The opposite of exegesis, it is technically an invalid approach to a scriptural text.

Epistolic—A word coined by the author. An adjective based upon the noun "epistle" to refer to that drawn from or based upon Paul's epistles, as in "epistolic theology."

Eschatology—A word drawn from the Greek word for that which is "last" or "final." It refers to that which is ultimate in terms of final things, although not necessarily to that which is "last in a temporal sequence." The Gospel of God in Christ was eschatological, i.e., it marked the ultimate response of God to redeem a broken creation.

Exegesis—An interpretation or explanation of a scriptural text, based upon a thorough examination of the text in its overall context. The opposite of eisegesis, it technically represents a valid approach to the meaning of scripture.

Gentiles—A term that refers to people or nations at large who are not of Jewish origin. In Paul's day, one might be a believer of Jewish origin or non-Jewish origin, a Jewish Christian or a gentile Christian.

Gnosticism—A term that describes a religious movement in the early centuries of Christianity distinguished by the dualistic conviction that matter is evil and that spiritual emancipation comes through *gnosis* or knowledge.

God-fearers—A term used to describe gentiles who were attracted to Judaism and participated in Jewish worship, but who did not wish to fully convert to Judaism. Cornelius, in Acts 10, was a God-fearer. The issue of circumcision as a religious rite would often separate a "God-fearer" from a full-fledged convert to Judaism.

Hermeneutics—The methods and principles employed in biblical interpretation of scripture.

Imagination—In a positive sense, the act or power of forming mental images of something not present or directly experienced. It represents the creative ability to perceive alternatives beyond one's immediate frame of reference.

Judaizers—A term used in the study of the New Testament writings to describe those very conservative Jewish Christians within early Christianity who insisted that a gentile must first become a Jew in order to become a Christian. See "Nomistic Evangelists" below.

Manuscript—Something produced by hand. Every writing had to be produced by hand prior to the invention of the printing press in the fifteenth century. Inevitably, as copies were written by scribal activity, errors, additions, and variants were created.

Nomistic Evangelists—A phrase coined by the present author to describe the conservative Jewish Christian opponents of Paul who were insisting upon following the Jewish Law, including circumcision and food laws. They proclaimed an alternative gospel (hence, *evangelistic*) to that of Paul, insisting upon keeping the Law in all its requirements (*nomos*, in Greek).

Parables—A form of Jesus's teachings that drew a *comparison* between everyday experience and the reality of God and his rule for earthly life. A parable need not be a "story," although a number of Jesus's parables were just that. And, the meaning to be understood is "earthly" and not "heavenly." About 35 percent of Jesus's teachings in the Synoptic Gospels were in parable form. Interestingly, there are no parables in the Gospel of John.

Parousia—The early expectation of Christians, Paul included, was that Jesus would return soon. The term comes from Greek (παρουσία) and is used to mean "coming" or "presence." It is thereby associated with the "second coming" of Christ. *Parousia* is found in the New Testament, while the phrase "second coming" is not.

Patronage—A strong social system of exchange in the ancient world, whereby a wealthy or influential person would grant favors to those of lower social standing in order to curry favorable support or high honor. The first-century world was a world of "patrons" and "clients" from Caesar on down through various social classes.

Perfect Tense Verbs—In Greek, perfect tense verbs express action that was occurring but which has now come to a state of completion. The focus is upon the kind of action expressed (completed), rather than ongoing action or mere time. The general focus is upon an existing state that comes about as a result of the earlier, now complete past action or activity.

Pseudonymity—A practice in the ancient world that involved writing under another's name in order to gain a hearing or to honor another person. The term is descriptive and involves more than just the idea of a fictitious pen name meant to hide or deceive.

Rapture—A term used in Christian theology to describe a doctrine of the taking-up of Christians into heaven during or before perceived end-time events. The term was coined in the nineteenth century and is generally held by very conservative Christians. The word itself occurs nowhere in the New Testament, although it is often based upon a misunderstanding of what Paul writes in 1 Thess 4:15–18.

Redaction—A word that describes deliberate change made by an author or writer to an underlying literary work. Redaction analysis, for example, may be used to demonstrate how Luke has employed deliberate changes to his underlying sources utilized in the Gospel of Luke or the book of Acts. An author may express his or her own viewpoint through changes made in source materials in the final use or organization of those materials.

Scripture—A term used to describe a body of writings considered to be sacred or divinely authoritative, for example, the Bible. In order to be considered to be scripture, a work must be written, carry with it the idea of divine authority, and be accepted as such by a given religious community.

Septuagint—The translation of the Hebrew Old Testament into Greek, likely in the third century BCE. Jews living in the Diaspora needed the scripture available in the common Greek that was used on a daily basis. The Septuagint, abbreviated with the Roman symbol "LXX," was the "bible" of the earliest church. Paul's Old Testament quotations most often come from the Septuagint.

GLOSSARY

Soteriology—That aspect of theology that treats matters pertaining to salvation. In Christian theology, matters pertaining to the action of God in Jesus Christ.

STA—An abbreviation that represents the "Source Tradition of Acts" as coined by the present author in a former work. Luke used source materials in the production of the book of Acts and redacted them in the telling of his story or the giving of his account of the development of the early church.

Stoicheia—An English translation or transliteration of the underlying Greek word στοιχεῖα. The word may refer to elemental entities or supernatural powers. Paul uses the term to refer to supernatural powers believed to exist in the ancient world that had control over the fate of humans.

Telos—A term drawn from Greek (τέλος) which suggests the accomplishment of an ultimate end. Paul can use the term in a technical sense to refer to ultimate or final events following the return of Christ. It thereby refers to God's final fulfillment, which may in reality represent new beginning. See 1 Cor 15:24–28.

Textual Analysis—A methodology employed whereby scholars evaluate all of the available ancient manuscripts of biblical books in order to discern what appears to be the most original reading of a given passage. Changes known as variants unavoidably occurred, as scribes copied and handed down biblical writings.

"We Source"—A source employed by Luke in the writing of Acts. It is first apparent in Acts 16:10, as the shift is made from third person presentation to first person ("we," "us"). It continues to Acts 16:17, but then the presentation reverts to third person. The source appears again in Acts 20–21. It is likely a source used by Luke and need not suggest that the author of Acts was an eyewitness and companion of Paul.

Zugoth—A term that refers to "paired" Jewish scholars in ancient times—one more conservative in viewpoint, one more liberal. Hillel and Shammai were "zugoth" before the New Testament period.

Bibliography

Achtemeier, Paul J. "The Continuing Quest for Coherence in St. Paul: An Experiment in Thought." In *Theology and Ethics in Paul and His Interpreters: Essays in Honor of Victor Paul Furnish*, edited by Eugene H. Lovering Jr. and Jerry L. Sumney, 132-45. Nashville: Abingdon, 1996.

Aland, Kurt, et al., eds. *The Greek New Testament*. 3rd ed. (corrected). Stuttgart: Biblia-Druck GmbH, 1983.

Aquinas, Thomas. *The Summa Theologica of St. Thomas Aquinas*. 2 vols. Edited by Paul A. Böer Sr. Translated by Fathers of the English Dominican Province. Repr., Houston, TX: Veratatis Splendor, 2012.

Arnold, Clinton E. "Colossae." In *The Anchor Bible Dictionary*, edited by David Noel Freedman, 1:1089-90. 6 vols. New York: Doubleday, 1992.

Aulen, Gustaf. *Christus Victor: An Historical Study of the Three Main Types of the Idea of the Atonement*. Translated by A. G. Hebert. Reprint ed., Eugene, OR: Wipf & Stock, 1931.

Aune, D. E. "Eschatology (Early Christian)." In *The Anchor Bible Dictionary*, edited by David Noel Freedman, 2:594-609. 6 vols. New York: Doubleday, 1992.

Bainton, Roland. *Christendom: A Short History of Christianity and Its Impact on Western Civilization*. 2 vols. The Cloister Library. New York: Harper Torchbooks, 1964.

———. *Christianity*. The American Heritage Library. Boston: Houghton Mifflin, 1964.

———. *Here I Stand: A Life of Martin Luther*. New York: Abingdon, 1950.

Baker, Mark D., and Joel B. Green. *Recovering the Scandal of the Cross: Atonement in New Testament and Contemporary Contexts*. 2nd ed. Downers Grove, IL: IVP Academic, 2011.

Barrett, C. K. *A Commentary on the Epistle to the Romans*. Harper's New Testament Commentaries. New York: Harper & Row, 1957.

———. *The First Epistle to the Corinthians*. New York: Harper & Row, 1968.

———. *Luke the Historian in Recent Study*. Reprint ed., Eugene, OR: Wipf & Stock, 1961.

———. "Pauline Controversies in the Post-Pauline Period." *NTS* 20 (1973-74) 229-45.

Bassler, Jouette M., ed. *Pauline Theology*. Vol. 1, *Thessalonians, Philippians, Galatians and Philemon*. Minneapolis: Fortress, 1991.

———. "Paul's Theology: Whence and Whither?" In *Pauline Theology*, edited by David M. Hay, 2:3-17. Minneapolis: Fortress, 1993.

Bauer, Walter. *A Greek English Lexicon of the New Testament and Other Early Christian Literature*. Translated and adapted by William F. Arndt and F. Wilbur Gingrich. 2nd ed. revised and augmented by F. Wilbur Gingrich and Frederick W. Danker. Chicago: The University of Chicago Press, 1979.

Beilby, James, and Paul R. Eddy, eds. *The Nature of the Atonement: Four Views*. Downers Grove, IL: IVP Academic, 2006.

Beker, J. Christiaan. *Heirs of Paul: Their Legacy in the New Testament and the Church Today.* Grand Rapids: Eerdmans, 1996.

———. *Paul's Apocalyptic Gospel: The Coming Triumph of God.* Philadelphia: Fortress, 1982.

———. *Paul the Apostle: The Triumph of God in Life and Thought.* Philadelphia: Fortress, 1980.

Betz, Hans Dieter. *Galatians: A Commentary on Paul's Letters to the Churches in Galatia.* Hermeneia. Philadelphia: Fortress, 1979.

Bonhoeffer, Dietrich. *The Cost of Discipleship.* Translated by R. H. Fuller, edited by Irmgard Booth. New York: Simon & Schuster, 1995.

Bonner, Gerald. "Augustine as Biblical Scholar." In *The Cambridge History of the Bible 1: From the Beginnings to Jerome*, edited by P. R. Ackroyd and C. F. Evans, 541–63. 3 vols. London: Cambridge University Press, 1970.

Bonsirven, Joseph. *Palestinian Judaism in the Time of Christ.* Translated by William Wolf. New York: McGraw-Hill, 1964.

Borg, Marcus. *The Gospel of Mark.* Conversations with Scripture. Harrisburg, NY: Morehouse Publishing, 2009.

Borg, Marcus, and John Dominic Crossan. *The First Paul: Reclaiming the Radical Visionary behind the Church's Conservative Icon.* New York: HarperCollins, 2009.

Boring, Eugene. *An Introduction to the New Testament: History, Literature, Theology.* Louisville: Westminster John Knox, 2012.

Bornkamm, Günther. *Paul.* Translated by D. M. G. Stalker. New York: Harper & Row, 1971.

Bowman, John W. "Eschatology in the New Testament." In *Interpreter's Dictionary of the Bible*, edited by George A. Buttrick, 2:135–40. 4 Vols. Nashville: Abingdon, 1962.

Brondos, David A. *Jesus' Death in New Testament Thought.* 2 vols. Mexico City: Theological Community of Mexico, 2018.

———. *Paul on the Cross: Reconstructing the Apostle's Story of Redemption.* Minneapolis: Fortress, 2006.

Brown, Raymond E. *An Introduction to the New Testament.* Abridged ed. Edited by Marion L. Soards. New Haven, CT: Yale University Press, 2016.

Bruce, F. F. *Paul: Apostle of the Heart Set Free.* Grand Rapids: Eerdmans, 1977.

Buck, Charles H., and Greer Taylor. *Saint Paul: A Study of the Development of His Thought.* New York: Scribner, 1969.

Bultmann, Rudolf. *Faith and Understanding.* Vol. 1. Edited by Robert W. Funk, translated by Louise Pettibone Smith. New York: Harper & Row, 1969.

———. "New Testament and Mythology." In *Kerygma and Myth: A Theological Debate*, edited by H. W. Bartsch, translated by R. H. Fuller, 1–16. London: SPCK, 1957.

———. *Theology of the New Testament.* 2 vols. Translated by Kendrick Grobel. New York: Scribner, 1951, 1955.

Buttrick, George A., ed. *The Interpreter's Dictionary of the Bible.* 4 vols. Nashville: Abingdon, 1962.

Cadbury, H. J. *The Making of Luke-Acts.* London: SPCK, 1958 [1927].

———. *The Style and Literary Method of Luke: The Diction of Luke and Acts.* Harvard Theological Studies 6. Cambridge, MA: Harvard University Press, 1919.

Calvin, John. *Institutes of the Christian Religion.* 2 vols. Translated by Henry Beveridge. Grand Rapids: Eerdmans, 1989.

Campbell, Douglas A. *Framing Paul: An Epistolary Biography.* Grand Rapids: Eerdmans, 2014.

Campbell, T. H. "Paul's Missionary Journeys as Reflected in His Letters." *Journal of Biblical Literature* 74:2 (June 1955) 80-87.

Carroll, John T., et al. *The Death of Jesus in Early Christianity*. Peabody, MA: Hendrickson, 1995.

Chamblin, J. K. "Psychology." In *Dictionary of Paul and His Letters*, edited by Gerald F. Hawthorne and Ralph P. Martin, 765-75. Downers Grove, IL: InterVarsity, 1993.

Childs, Brevard S. "Adam." In *Interpreter's Dictionary of the Bible*, edited by George A. Buttrick, 1:42-44. 4 vols. Nashville: Abingdon, 1962.

Collins, E. E. "God's Gonna Get 'Cha' (For That)." Recorded by George Jones and Tammy Wynette. Epic Records, 1975.

Corley, Bruce, ed. *Colloquy on New Testament Studies*. Macon, GA: Mercer University Press, 1983.

Cousar, Charles S. *A Theology of the Cross: The Death of Jesus in the Pauline Letters*. Overtures to Biblical Theology. Edited by Walter Bruggemann. Minneapolis: Fortress, 1990.

Crossan, John Dominic, and Jonathan L. Reed. *In Search of Paul: How Jesus's Apostle Opposed Rome's Empire with God's Kingdom*. New York: HarperSanFrancisco, 2004.

Cullmann, Oscar. *Christ and Time: The Primitive Christian Conception of Time and History*. Rev. ed. Translated by Floyd V. Filson. Philadelphia: Westminster, 1964.

———. *Salvation in History*. London: SCM, 1967.

Culpepper, Robert H. *Interpreting the Atonement*. Grand Rapids: Eerdmans, 1966.

Culy, Martin M., and Mikeal C. Parsons. *Acts: A Handbook on the Greek Text*. Waco, TX: Baylor University Press, 2003.

Dahl, Nils Alstrup. *Jesus the Christ: The Historical Origins of Christological Doctrine*. Edited by Donald H. Juel. Minneapolis: Fortress, 1991.

Davies, Brian, and G. R. Evans, eds. *Anselm of Canterbury: The Major Works*. Oxford World's Classics. New York: Oxford University Press, 1998.

Davies, G. Henton. "Glory." In *Interpreter's Dictionary of the Bible*, edited by George A. Buttrick, 2:401-3. 4 vols. Nashville: Abingdon, 1962.

———. "Presence of God." In *Interpreter's Dictionary of the Bible*, edited by George A. Buttrick, 3:874-75. 4 vols. Nashville: Abingdon, 1962.

Davies, W. D. "Conscience." In *Interpreter's Dictionary of the Bible*, edited by George A. Buttrick, 1:671-76. 4 vols. Nashville: Abingdon, 1962.

———. *Paul and Rabbinic Judaism: Some Rabbinic Elements in Pauline Theology*. Rev. ed. New York: Harper & Row, 1948.

Deissmann, Adolf. *Paul: A Study in Social and Religious History*. 2nd ed. Translated by William E. Wilson. New York: Harper & Row, 1927 [1912].

Dibelius, Martin. *The Book of Acts: Form, Style, and Theology*. Edited by K. C. Hanson. Minneapolis: Fortress, 2004.

Dodd, C. H. *The Apostolic Preaching and Its Development*. New York: Harper & Row, 1964 [1936].

Donaldson, Terence L. *Paul and the Gentiles: Remapping the Apostle's Convictional World*. Minneapolis: Fortress, 2006.

Donfried, Karl P., ed. *The Romans Debate*. Rev. and exp. Peabody, MA: Hendrickson, 1991.

Downey, G. "Antioch (Syrian)." In *Interpreter's Dictionary of the Bible*, edited by George A. Buttrick, 1:145-48. 4 vols. Nashville: Abingdon, 1962.

Dunn, James D. G. "In Quest of Paul's Theology: Retrospect and Prospect." In *Pauline Theology 4: Looking Back, Pressing On*, edited by E. Elizabeth Johnson and David M. Hay, 95–115. Atlanta: Scholars Press, 1997.

———. *Jesus, Paul, and the Law: Studies in Mark and Galatians*. Louisville: Westminster/John Knox, 1990.

———. *Jesus Remembered*. Christianity in the Making 1. Grand Rapids: Eerdmans, 2003.

———. *Romans 1–8*. Word Biblical Commentary 38. Edited by Bruce M. Metzger et al. Nashville: Thomas Nelson, 1988.

———. *The Theology of Paul the Apostle*. Grand Rapids: Eerdmans, 1998.

Dupont, J. *The Sources of Acts*. Translated by Kathleen Pond. New York: Herder and Herder, 1964.

Elliott, Neil, and Mark Reasoner, eds. *Documents and Images for the Study of Paul*. Minneapolis: Fortress, 2011.

Ellis, E. Earle. *The Gospel of Luke*. Rev. ed. Greenwood, SC: The Attic Press, 1974.

———. *Paul and His Recent Interpreters*. Grand Rapids: Eerdmans, 1961.

———. *Paul's Use of the Old Testament*. Eugene, OR: Wipf & Stock, 1981.

Evans, C. F. "The Kerygma." *Journal of Theological Studies* New Series 7.1 (Apr. 1956) 25–41.

Fee, Gordon D. "Toward a Theology of 1 Corinthians." In *Pauline Theology 2: 1 and 2 Corinthians*, edited by David M. Hay, 37–58. Minneapolis: Fortress, 1993.

Ferguson, Everett. *Backgrounds of Early Christianity*. 3rd ed. Grand Rapids: Eerdmans, 2003.

Finegan, Jack. *Handbook of Biblical Chronology*. Rev. ed. Peabody, MA: Hendrickson, 1998.

Finlan, Stephen. *Options on Atonement in Christian Thought*. Collegeville, MN: Liturgical, 2007.

———. *Problems with Atonement: The Origins of, and Controversy about, the Atonement Doctrine*. Collegeville, MN: Liturgical, 2005.

Finlan, Stephen, and Vladimir Kharlamov, eds. *Theōsis: Deification in Christian Theology*. Princeton Theological Monograph Series, edited by K. C. Hanson. Eugene, OR: Pickwick, 2006.

Fitzmyer, Joseph A. "The Letter to the Romans." *The Jerome Biblical Commentary*, edited by Raymond E. Brown et al., 2:291–331. 2 vols. Englewood Cliffs, NJ: Prentice Hall, 1968.

———. "The Letter to the Romans." *The New Jerome Biblical Commentary*, edited by Raymond E. Brown et al., 830–68. Upper Saddle River, NJ: Prentice Hall, 1990.

———. "Paul." *The New Jerome Biblical Commentary*, edited by Raymond E. Brown et al., 1329–37. Upper Saddle River, NJ: Prentice Hall, 1990.

———. *Paul and His Theology: A Brief Sketch*. 2nd ed. Englewood Cliffs, NJ: Prentice Hall, 1989.

———. *Romans*. Anchor Bible Commentary. Edited by William Foxwell Albright and David Noel Freedman. New York: Doubleday, 1993.

Flood, Derek. "Substitutionary Atonement and the Church Fathers: A Reply to the Authors of *Pierced for Our Transgressions*." *Evangelical Quarterly* 82:2 (2010) 142–59.

Freedman, David Noel, ed. *The Anchor Bible Dictionary*. 6 vols. New York: Doubleday, 1992.

Funk, Robert W. "The Enigma of the Famine Visit." *Journal of Biblical Literature* 75 (1956) 130–36.

Furnish, Victor Paul. "The Letter of Paul to the Galatians." *The Interpreter's One-Volume Commentary on the Bible*, edited by Charles M. Laymon, 824–33. Nashville: Abingdon, 1971.

———. *The Moral Teaching of Paul: Selected Issues*. 3rd ed. Nashville: Abingdon, 2009.

———. *Theology and Ethics in Paul*. Nashville: Abingdon, 1968.
González, Justo L. *Church History: An Essential Guide*. Nashville: Abingdon, 1996.
———. *A History of Christian Thought*. Rev. ed. 3 vols. Nashville: Abingdon, 1987.
———. *The Story of Christianity*. Rev. and updated. 2 vols. New York: HarperCollins, 2010.
Good, Edwin M. "The Meaning of Demytholization." In *The Theology of Rudolf Bultmann*, edited by Charles W. Kegley, 21–40. New York: Harper & Row, 1966.
Gorman, Michael J. *Apostle of the Crucified Lord: A Theological Introduction to Paul and His Letters*. Grand Rapids: Eerdmans, 2004.
———. *Cruciformity: Paul's Narrative Spirituality of the Cross*. Grand Rapids: Eerdmans, 2003.
———. *Reading Paul*. Eugene, OR: Cascade, 2008.
Grant, Robert M., and David Tracy. *A Short History of the Interpretation of the Bible*. 2nd ed., revised and enlarged. Minneapolis: Fortress, 2005.
Green, Joel B. "Death of Christ." In *Dictionary of Paul and His Letters*, edited by Gerald F. Hawthorne and Ralph P. Martin, 201–9. Downers Grove, IL: InterVarsity, 1993.
———. "Kaleidoscopic View." In *The Nature of the Atonement: Four Views*, edited by James Beilby and Paul R. Eddy, 157–85. Downers Grove, IL: IVP Academic, 2006.
Greene, G. Roger. "God's Lamb: Divine Provision for Sin." *Perspectives in Religious Studies* 37:2 (Summer 2010) 147–64.
———. *The Ministry of Paul the Apostle: History and Redaction*. Lanham, MD: Lexington, 2019.
———. "The Portrayal of Jesus as Prophet in Luke-Acts." Unpublished Ph.D. diss., Louisville, The Southern Baptist Theological Seminary, 1975.
———. *A Theology of Paul the Apostle, Part One: Paul's Eschatological Gospel*. Eugene, OR: Pickwick, 2023.
———. *A Theology of Paul the Apostle, Part Two: Cross and Atonement*. Eugene, OR: Pickwick, 2023.
Grensted, L. W. *A Short History of the Doctrine of the Atonement*. London: Longmans, Green, 1920.
Gundry-Volf, J. M. "Expiation, Propitiation, Mercy Seat." In *Dictionary of Paul and His Letters*, edited by Gerald F. Hawthorne and Ralph P. Martin, 279–84. Downers Grove, IL: InterVarsity, 1993.
Guthrie, Donald. *New Testament Introduction*. 3rd ed. Downers Grove, IL: InterVarsity, 1970.
———. *New Testament Theology*. London: InterVarsity, 1981.
Haenchen, Ernst. *The Acts of the Apostles: A Commentary*. Translated by Bernard Noble et al. Philadelphia: Westminster, 1971.
Hafemann, S. J. "Paul and His Interpreters." In *Dictionary of Paul and His Letters*, edited by Gerald F. Hawthorne and Ralph P. Martin, 666–71. Downers Grove, IL: InterVarsity, 1993.
Hague, Dyson. "At-one-ment by Propitiation." In *The Fundamentals: A Testimony to the Truth*, edited by R. A. Torrey et al., 3:78–97. 4 vols. Los Angeles: The Bible Institute of Los Angeles, 1917. Reprint ed., in 2 vols. Grand Rapids: Baker Books, 2003.
Hanson, R. P. C. "Biblical Exegesis in the Early Church." In *The Cambridge History of the Bible 1: From the Beginnings to Jerome*, edited by P. R. Ackroyd and C. F. Evans, 412–53. 3 vols. London: Cambridge University Press, 1970.
Harris, Murray J. *Raised Immortal: Resurrection and Immortality in the New Testament*. Grand Rapids: Eerdmans, 1985.

BIBLIOGRAPHY

Hawthorne, Gerald F., and Ralph P. Martin, eds. *Dictionary of Paul and His Letters*. Downers Grove, IL: InterVarsity, 1993.

Hay, David M., ed. *Pauline Theology*. Vol. 2, *1 and 2 Corinthians*. Minneapolis: Fortress, 1993.

Hay, David M., and E. Elizabeth Johnson, eds. *Pauline Theology*. Vol. 3, *Romans*. Society of Biblical Literature Symposium Series, edited by Christopher R. Matthews. Minneapolis: Fortress, 2002.

Hays, Richard B. *Echoes of Scripture in the Letters of Paul*. New Haven, CT: Yale University Press, 1989.

———. *The Faith of Jesus Christ: The Narrative Substructure of Galatians 3:1—4:11*. 2nd ed. Grand Rapids: Eerdmans, 2002.

———. *The Moral Vision of the New Testament: Community, Cross, New Creation: A Contemporary Introduction to New Testament Ethics*. San Francisco: HarperSanFrancisco, 1996.

Heim, S. Mark. *Saved from Sacrifice: A Theology of the Cross*. Grand Rapids: Eerdmans, 2006.

Hendin, David. *Guide to Biblical Coins*. New York: Amphora Books, 1987.

Hendrix, Holland L. "Philippi." In *Anchor Bible Dictionary*, edited by David Noel Freedman, 5:313–17. 6 vols. New York: Doubleday, 1992.

Hengel, Martin. *The Atonement: The Origins of the Doctrine in the New Testament*. Philadelphia: Fortress, 1981.

Hennecke, Edgar. *New Testament Apocrypha*. Edited by W. Schneemelcher. 2 vols. Translated and edited by R. M. Wilson. Philadelphia: Westminster, 1964.

Hill, Charles E., and Frank A. James III, eds. *The Glory of the Atonement: Biblical, Historical, and Practical Perspectives*. Downers Grove, IL: IVP Academic, 2004.

Hodge, Charles. *Systematic Theology*. 3 vols. Peabody, MA: Hendrickson, 2016.

Holmes, Michael W., ed. *The Apostolic Fathers: Greek Texts and English Translations*. Grand Rapids: Baker Books, 1999.

Horrell, David G. *An Introduction to the Study of Paul*. 3rd ed. London: T&T Clark, 2015.

Howard, George. "Faith, Faith of Christ." In *The Anchor Bible Dictionary*, edited by David Noel Freedman, 2:758–60. 6 vols. New York: Doubleday, 1992.

Humphreys, Fisher. *The Death of Christ*. Nashville: Broadman, 1978.

Hunter, A. M. *Interpreting the New Testament 1900–1950*. London: SCM, 1951.

Jackson, F. J. Foakes, and Kirsopp Lake. *The Beginnings of Christianity*. 5 vols. Grand Rapids: Baker, 1979 [1920–32].

Jeffery, Steve, et al. *Pierced for Our Transgressions: Rediscovering the Glory of Penal Substitution*. Wheaton: Crossway, 2007.

Jewett, Robert. *A Chronology of Paul's Life*. Philadelphia: Fortress, 1979.

Johnson, E. Elizabeth, and David M. Hay, eds. *Pauline Theology 4: Looking Back, Pressing On*. Society of Biblical Literature Symposium Series, edited by Gail R. O'Day. Atlanta: Scholars Press, 1997.

Johnson, Franklin. "The Atonement." In *The Fundamentals: A Testimony to the Truth*, edited by R. A. Torrey et al., 3:64–77. 4 vols. Los Angeles: The Bible Institute of Los Angeles, 1917. Reprint ed., in 2 vols. Grand Rapids: Baker Books, 2003.

Johnson, Luke Timothy. *Scripture and Discernment: Decision-Making in the Church*. Rev. ed. Nashville: Abingdon, 1996.

———. *The Writings of the New Testament*. 3rd ed. Minneapolis: Fortress, 2010.

Josephus. *Josephus*. 9 vols. Translated by H. G. Thackeray et al. Loeb Classical Library. Cambridge, MA: Harvard University Press, 1926–63.

Kähler, M. *The So-Called Historical Jesus and the Historic Biblical Christ.* Philadelphia: Fortress, 1956 [1896].

Käsemann, E. *Essays on New Testament Themes.* Studies in Biblical Theology 41. Translated by W. J. Montague. London: SCM, 1964.

———. *New Testament Questions of Today.* Translated by W. J. Montague. Philadelphia: Fortress, 1969.

———. *Perspectives on Paul.* Translated by Margaret Kohl. Philadelphia: Fortress, 1971.

Keck, Leander. "Jesus' Entrance upon His Mission: Luke 3:4—4:30." *Review and Expositor* 64 (1967) 465–88.

———. "Paul and Apocalyptic Theology." *Interpretation* 38 (1984) 229–41.

Keck, Leander, and J. Louis Martyn. *Studies in Luke-Acts.* Nashville: Abingdon, 1966.

Kelly, J. N. D. *Early Christian Doctrines.* Rev. ed. New York: HarperOne, 1978.

Knox, John. *Chapters in a Life of Paul.* Rev. ed. Macon, GA: Mercer University, 1987.

Koester, Helmut. *Introduction to the New Testament: History and Literature of Early Christianity.* 2nd ed. New York: de Gruyter, 2000.

Kraftchick, Steven J. "Seeking a More Fluid Model: A Response to Jouette M. Bassler." In *Pauline Theology 2: 1 and 2 Corinthians*, edited by David M. May, 18–34. Society of Biblical Literature Symposium Series, edited by Christopher R. Matthews. Atlanta: SBL, 1993.

Kreitzer, L. J. "Adam and Christ." In *Dictionary of Paul and the His Letters*, edited by Gerald F. Hawthorne and Ralph P. Martin, 9–15. Downers Grove, IL: InterVarsity, 1993.

———. "Eschatology." In *Dictionary of Paul and His Letters*, edited by Gerald F. Hawthorne and Ralph P. Martin, 253–69. Downers Grove, IL: InterVarsity, 1993.

Kümmel, W. G. *Introduction to the New Testament.* Rev. ed. Translated by Howard Clark Kee. Nashville: Abingdon, 1975.

Ladd, George Eldon. *A Theology of the New Testament.* Rev. ed., edited by Donald A. Hagner. Grand Rapids: Eerdmans, 1993.

Lake, Kirsopp, trans. *The Apostolic Fathers.* 2 vols. Loeb Classical Library. Cambridge, MA: Harvard University Press, 1912–13.

Lampe, Peter. *From Paul to Valentinus: Christians at Rome in the First Two Centuries.* Translated by Michael Steinhauser, edited by Marshal D. Johnson. Minneapolis: Fortress, 2003.

———. "The Roman Christians of Romans 16." In *The Romans Debate*, edited by Karl P. Donfried, 216–30. Rev. and exp. ed. Peabody, MA: Hendrickson, 1991.

Liddell, Henry George, and Robert Scott. *A Greek-English Lexicon: With a Supplement 1968.* Revised by Henry Stuart Jones and Roderick McKenzie. New York: Oxford University Press, 1994.

Lincoln, A. T. "Ephesians 2:8–10: A Summary of Paul's Gospel." *Catholic Biblical Quarterly* 45 (1983) 617–30.

———. *Ephesians.* Word Biblical Commentary 42. Edited by Bruce M. Metzger et al. Nashville: Thomas Nelson, 1990.

Louw, Johannes P., and Eugene A. Nida. *Greek-English Lexicon of the New Testament Based on Semantic Domains.* 2 vols. 2nd ed. New York: United Bible Societies, 1988–89.

Lüdemann, Gerd. *Early Christianity according to the Traditions in Acts: A Commentary.* Translated by John Bowden. Minneapolis: Fortress, 1989.

———. *Paul the Apostle to the Gentiles: Studies in Chronology.* Translated by F. Stanley Jones. Philadelphia: Fortress, 1984.

———. *Paul: The Founder of Christianity*. Amherst, NY: Prometheus Books, 2002.

Lührmann, Dieter. "Faith, New Testament." *The Anchor Bible Dictionary*, edited by David Noel Freedman, 2:749–58. 6 vols. New York: Doubleday, 1992.

Luther, Martin. *Commentary on Galatians*. Translated by Erasmus Middleton, edited by John Prince Fallowes. Grand Rapids: Kregel, 1979 [1850].

MacDonald, Margaret Y. *The Pauline Churches*. Society for New Testament Studies Monograph Series 60. Cambridge: Cambridge University Press, 1988.

Macquarrie, John. "Philosophy and Theology in Bultmann's Thought." In *The Theology of Rudolf Bultmann*, edited by Charles W. Kegley, 127–43. New York: Harper & Row, 1966.

Malina, Bruce J. *The New Testament World: Insights from Cultural Anthropology*. 3rd ed., rev. and exp. Louisville: Westminster John Knox, 2001.

Manschreck, Clyde L. *Melanchthon: The Quiet Reformer*. Eugene, OR: Wipf & Stock, 2008 [1958].

Manson, T. W. *The Teaching of Jesus: Studies in Its Form and Content*. Cambridge: Cambridge University Press, 1967.

Marshall, I. Howard. *Luke: Historian and Theologian*. Grand Rapids: Zondervan, 1971.

Martin, Ralph P. *Reconciliation: A Study of Paul's Theology*. Grand Rapids: Academie Books, 1989.

Marty, Martin E. *A Short History of Christianity*. 2nd ed., rev. and exp. Philadelphia: Fortresss, 1987.

Martyn, J. Louis. *Galatians*. The Anchor Bible. Edited by William Foxwell Albright and David Noel Freedman. New York: Doubleday, 1997.

May, Herbert G., and Bruce M. Metzger, eds. *The New Oxford Annotated Bible with the Apocrypha*. Revised Standard Version. New York: Oxford University Press, 1977.

McGrath, Alister E. *Christian Theology: An Introduction*. 5th ed. West Sussex: Wiley-Blackwell, 2011.

———. "Theology of the Cross." In *Dictionary of Paul and His Letters*, edited by Gerald F. Hawthorne and Ralph P. Martin, 192–97. Downers Grove, IL: InterVarsity, 1993.

Meeks, Wayne A. *The First Urban Christians: The Social World of the Apostle Paul*. 2nd ed. New Haven, CT: Yale University Press, 2003.

———, ed. *The Writings of St. Paul*. New York: Norton, 1972.

Mela, Pomponius. *Pomponius Mela's Description of the World [de Chorographia]*. Translated by F. E. Romer. Ann Arbor: University of Michigan Press, 1998.

Mellink, M. J. "Cilicia." In *The Interpreter's Dictionary of the Bible*, edited by George A. Buttrick, 1:626–28. 4 vols. Nashville: Abingdon, 1962.

———. "Tarsus." In *The Interpreter's Dictionary of the Bible*, edited by George A. Buttrick, 4:518–19. 4 vols. Nashville: Abingdon, 1962.

Mertens, Herman-Emiel. *Not the Cross, But the Crucified: An Essay in Soteriology*. Leuven Theological and Pastoral Monographs. Leuven: Peeters, 1992.

Metzger, Bruce M. *A Textual Commentary on the Greek New Testament*. London: United Bible Societies, 1971.

Meyer, Paul W. "Pauline Theology: A Proposal for a Pause in Its Pursuit." In *Pauline Theology 4: Looking Back, Pressing On*, edited by E. Elizabeth Johnson and David M. Hay, 140–60. Atlanta: Scholars Press, 1997.

Mish, Frederick C., ed. *Merriam-Webster's Collegiate Dictionary*. 11th ed. Springfield, MA: Merriam-Webster, 2014.

Mitten, C. L. "Atonement." In *The Interpreter's Dictionary of the Bible*, edited by George A. Buttrick, 1:309–13. 4 vols. Nashville: Abingdon, 1962.

Moo, Douglas J. *The Epistle to the Romans*. Grand Rapids: Eerdmans, 1996.

———. *Theology of Paul and His Letters: The Gift of the New Realm in Christ*. Biblical Theology of the New Testament Series, edited by Andreas J. Kostenberger. Grand Rapids: Zondervan Academic, 2021.

Moore, George Foot. *Judaism in the First Centuries of the Christian Era: The Age of the Tannaim*. 3 vols. Peabody, MA: Hendrickson, 1997 [1927, 1930].

Morgenthaler, Robert. *Statistik des neutestamentlichen Wortschatzes*. Zurich: Gotthelf-Verlag, 1958.

Morris, Leon. *The Atonement: Its Meaning and Significance*. Downers Grove, IL: InterVarsity, 1983.

———. *The Cross in the New Testament*. Grand Rapids: Eerdmans, 1968.

———. "The Meaning of *hilastērion* in Romans iii.25." *New Testament Studies* 2 (1955–56) 33–43.

Mowinckel, Sigmund. *He That Cometh*. Translated by G. W. Anderson. New York: Abingdon, 1954.

Munck, Johannes. *Paul and the Salvation of Mankind*. Translated by by Frank Clarke. Richmond, VA: John Knox, 1959.

Murphy-O'Connor, Jerome. *Paul: A Critical Life*. New York: Oxford University Press, 1996.

———. *Paul: His Story*. Oxford: Oxford University Press, 2004.

Neill, Stephen, and Tom Wright. *The Interpretation of the New Testament 1861–1986*. Oxford: Oxford University Press, 1988.

Norris, Frederick W. "Antioch of Syria." In *The Anchor Bible Dictionary*, edited by David Noel Freedman, 1:265–69. 6 vols. New York: Doubleday, 1992.

Oakes, Peter. *Reading Romans in Pompeii: Paul's Letter at Ground Level*. Minneapolis: Fortress, 2009.

Ogden, Thomas C., gen. ed. *Ancient Christian Commentary on Scripture*. Multiple volumes. Downers Grove, IL: InterVarsity, 2000–.

Ogg, George. *The Chronology of the Life of Paul*. Eugene, OR: Wipf & Stock, 1968.

Packer, J. I. "What Did the Cross Achieve? The Logic of Penal Substitution." The Tyndale Biblical Theology Lecture 1973, delivered at Tyndale House, Cambridge, July 17, 1973. https://www.the-highway.com/cross_Packer.html. Accessed June 2021.

Parsons, Mikeal C. *Acts*. Paideia Commentaries on the New Testament. Grand Rapids: Baker Academic, 2008.

Perrin, Norman. *The Kingdom of God in the Teaching of Jesus*. The New Testament Library. Philadelphia: Westminster, 1963.

Pervo, Richard I. *Dating Acts: Between the Evangelists and the Apologists*. Santa Rosa, CA: Polebridge, 2006.

———. *The Making of Paul: Constructions of the Apostle in Early Christianity*. Minneapolis: Fortress, 2010.

———. *The Mystery of Acts: Unraveling Its Story*. Santa Rosa, CA: Polebridge, 2008.

Polhill, John B. *Paul and His Letters*. Nashville: Broadman & Holman, 1999.

Purdy, A. C. "Paul the Apostle." In *Interpreter's Dictionary of the Bible*, edited by George A. Buttrick, 3:681–704. 4 vols. Nashville: Abingdon, 1962.

Ramsey, William M. *St. Paul the Traveller and Roman Citizen*. 3rd ed. Grand Rapids: Baker, 1979 [1897].

Richardson, Alan. *Introduction to the Theology of the New Testament*. New York: Harper & Row, 1958.

Ridderbos, Herman. *Paul: An Outline of His Theology*. Translated by John Richard DeWitt. Grand Rapids: Eerdmans, 1975.

Riesner, Rainer. *Paul's Early Period: Chronology, Mission Strategy, Theology*. Translated by Doug Scott. Grand Rapids: Eerdmans, 1998.

Robinson, John A. T. *Redating the New Testament*. Philadelphia: Westminster, 1976.

Russell, D. S. *The Method and Message of Jewish Apocalyptic: 200 BC–AD 100*. The Old Testament Library. Philadelphia: Westminster, 1964.

Sanders, E. P. *Paul: The Apostle's Life, Letters, and Thought*. Minneapolis: Fortress, 2015.

———. *Paul, the Law, and the Jewish People*. Minneapolis: Fortress, 1983.

———. *Paul and Palestinian Judaism: A Comparison of Patterns of Religion*. Philadelphia: Fortress, 1977.

———. *Paul: Past Master*. Oxford: Oxford University Press, 1991.

Sandmel, Samuel. *The Genius of Paul: A Study in History*. Philadelphia: Fortress, 1979.

Schnelle, Udo. *Apostle Paul: His Life and Theology*. Translated by M. Eugene Boring. Grand Rapids: Baker Academic, 2005.

Schoeps, H. J. *Paul: The Theology of the Apostle in the Light of Jewish Religious History*. Translated by Harold Knight. Philadelphia: Westminster, 1959.

Schweitzer, Albert. *The Mysticism of Paul the Apostle*. Translated by William Montgomery. New York: Seabury Press, 1931.

———. *Paul and His Interpreters: A Critical History*. Translated by William Montgomery. New York: Schocken Books, 1964 [1912].

Scroggs, Robin. *Paul for a New Day*. Philadelphia: Fortress, 1977.

Shelley, Bruce L. *Church History in Plain Language*. Updated 3rd ed. Nashville: Thomas Nelson, 2008.

Sherwin-White, A. N. *Roman Society and Roman Law in the New Testament*. The Sarum Lectures, 1960–1961. Oxford: Oxford University Press, 1963.

Simonetti, Manlio. *Biblical Interpretation in the Early Church: An Historical Introduction to Patristic Exegesis*. Translated by John. A. Hughes, edited by Anders Bergquist and Markus Bockmuehl. Consultant editor William Horburg. Edinburgh: T&T Clark, 1994.

Smallwood, E. Mary. *The Jews under Roman Rule from Pompey to Diocletian: A Study in Political Relations*. Atlanta: SBL, 1976.

Snodgrass, Klyne. *Ephesians*. The NIV Application Commentary. Edited by Terry Muck. Grand Rapids: Zondervan, 1996.

Stacey, W. David. *The Pauline View of Man in Relation to Its Judaic and Hellenistic Background*. London: Macmillan, 1956.

Stagg, Frank. *The Book of Acts: The Early Struggle for an Unhindered Gospel*. Nashville: Broadman, 1955.

Stegner, W. R. "Paul the Jew." In *Dictionary of Paul and His Letters*, edited by Gerald F. Hawthorne and Ralph P. Martin, 503–11. Downers Grove, IL: InterVarsity, 1993.

Stendahl, Krister. *Paul among Jews and Gentiles and Other Essays*. Philadelphia: Fortress, 1976.

Stewart, James S. *A Man in Christ: The Vital Elements of St. Paul's Religion*. Grand Rapids: Baker, 1975.

Suetonius. *Suetonius*. 2 vols. Translated by J. C. Rolfe. Loeb Classical Library. Cambridge, MA: Harvard University Press, 1913–14.

Tacitus. *Tacitus.* 5 vols. Translated by John Jackson et al. Loeb Classical Library. Cambridge, MA: Harvard University Press, 1914–37.
Talbert, Charles H. *Reading Acts: A Literary and Theological Commentary on the Acts of the Apostles.* Rev. ed. Macon, GA: Smyth & Helwys, 2005.
Tambasco, A. J. *A Theology of Atonement and Paul's Vision of Christianity.* Zacchaeus Studies, edited by Mary Ann Getty. Collegeville, MN: Liturgical, 1991.
Tannehill, Robert C. *Dying and Rising with Christ: A Study in Pauline Theology.* Berlin: Alfred Töpelmann, 1967.
Taylor, Vincent. *The Atonement in New Testament Teaching.* 3rd ed. London: Epworth, 1958.
———. *The Cross of Christ: Eight Public Lectures.* London: Macmillan, 1957.
Theissen, Gerd. *The Social Setting of Pauline Christianity: Essays on Corinth.* Edited and translated by John H. Schütz. Eugene, OR: Wipf & Stock, 2004 [1981].
Thielman, F. "Law." In *Dictionary of Paul and His Letters*, edited by Gerald F. Hawthorne and Ralph P. Martin, 529–42. Downers Grove, IL: InterVarsity, 1993.
Throckmorton, Burton H. Jr., ed. *Gospel Parallels.* 4th rev. ed. Nashville: Thomas Nelson, 1979.
Townsend, John T. "Missionary Journeys in Acts and European Missionary Societies." In *Society of Biblical Literature 1985 Seminar Papers*, edited by Kent Harold Richards, 433–37. Atlanta: Scholars Press, 1985.
Vielhauer, Philipp. "On the Paulinism in Acts." In *Studies in Luke-Acts*, by Leander E. Keck and J. Louis Martyn, 33–50. Nashville: Abingdon, 1966.
Walker, Peter. *In the Steps of Paul: An Illustrated Guide to the Apostle's Life and Journeys.* Grand Rapids: Zondervan, 2008.
Westerholm, Stephen. *Perspectives Old and New: The "Lutheran" Paul and His Critics.* Grand Rapids: Eerdmans, 2004.
Whiteley, D. E. H. *The Theology of St. Paul.* Philadelphia: Fortress, 1966.
Wiles, M. F. *The Divine Apostle: The Interpretation of St. Paul's Epistles in the Early Church.* Cambridge: Cambridge University Press, 1967.
Williams, David J. *Paul's Metaphors: Their Context and Character.* Peabody, MA: Hendrickson, 1999.
Wink, Walter. *Naming the Powers; Engaging the Powers: Discernment and Resistance in a World of Domination.* Minneapolis: Fortress, 1992.
———. *Naming the Powers: The Language of Power in the New Testament.* Philadelphia: Fortress, 1984.
Witherington, Ben. *The Acts of the Apostles: A Socio-Rhetorical Commentary.* Grand Rapids: Eerdmans, 1998.
———. *The Paul Quest: The Renewed Search for the Jew of Tarsus.* Downers Grove, IL: InterVarsity, 1998.
Wright, N. T. *Jesus and the Victory of God.* Christian Origins and the Question of God 2. Minneapolis: Fortress, 1996.
———. "The Letter to the Romans." In *The New Interpreter's Bible*, edited by Leander E. Keck et al., 10:393–770. 12 vols. Nashville: Abingdon, 2002.
———. *Paul and the Faithfulness of God.* Christian Origins and the Question of God 4. Minneapolis: Fortress, 2013.
———. *Paul and His Recent Interpreters: Some Contemporary Debates.* Minneapolis: Fortress, 2015.

———. *What Saint Paul Really Said: Was Paul of Tarsus the Real Founder of Christianity?* Grand Rapids: Eerdmans, 1997.

Zetterholm, Magnus. *Approaches to Paul: A Student's Guide to Recent Scholarship.* Minneapolis: Fortress, 2009.

About the Author

G. Roger Greene is a professor of Christian studies. He served as an associate professor of religion at Palm Beach Atlantic College, before serving for forty-six years at Mississippi College. He has taught general courses of introduction in both the Old and New Testaments. He has taught New Testament Greek, using his own Greek grammar, *A Structural Grammar of New Testament Greek*. He has taught a full complement of upper-level New Testament courses in the Gospels, Acts, and the letters of Paul. He has taught courses pertaining to the context of the New Testament, including the intertestamental period, the text and canon of the New Testament, and distinctive ideas of biblical thought. In addition to teaching responsibilities, he has participated in archaeological work in Israel and has led travel groups to the lands of the Bible, including Israel, Jordan, Greece, and Turkey. He is an ordained Baptist minister and a graduate of The Southern Baptist Theological Seminary, with an undergraduate degree from Louisiana Tech University. *The Ministry of Paul the Apostle: History and Redaction* (Lexington/Fortress Academic), *A Theology of Paul, Part One: Paul's Eschatological Gospel* (Pickwick Publications), and *A Theology of Paul, Part Two: Cross and Atonement* (Pickwick Publications) are among his published works.

Scripture Index

Old Testament

Genesis

1–11	328
1–2	280
1	240, 308
1:2	298
1:26–27	1
1:26–28	244
2:7	233
3–11	356
3	233
12–50	328
12:1–3	242, 276, 300, 304, 322, 328
12:3	321
12:1–5	322, 328
12:4a	276
12:6	329
12:10–13	242
15:1–4	242
15:6	171, 242, 243, 300, 318, 322, 323
17:1–14	322,
17:5	346
17:9–14	171, 242
17:14	242
17:15–21	243
17:22–27	243

Exodus

4:22	290
9:16	251
20:1–3	273, 322
33:19	251

Leviticus

11	xvii, 242
18:5	331
19:18	382

Deuteronomy

5–26	331
6:1–25	242
6:1–11	242
6:4–5	273, 287
21:23	383, 297, 331, 331, 332
27	331
27:1–26	331
27:26	331
28	331
30:15–20	322
32:21	252
32:43	255

Ezra

3:1—5:13	306

Job

35:7	253
41:11	253

Psalms

2:7	290
17:30	255
19:4	252
68:19	259
69:22–23	253
104	280
105	280
106	280
117:1	255
137:4	371

Isaiah

1:9	251
2:1–3	123
2:3	165, 172, 175, 188
2:2–4	92

409

SCRIPTURE INDEX

Isaiah (continued)

10:22–23	251
11:10	255
25:8	233
29:10	253
40:9	290
40:13	253
42–53	44
45–46	280
52:7	290
52:15	255
59:7–8	239
60:1–5	188
60:2	165, 172, 175
60:3	175
60:6	290
61	45
61:1	290
61:1–2	7, 44, 47, 127
61:2b	279
65:1–2	252

Jeremiah

9:23–24 [3:1–5 LXX]	253

Ezekiel

37	xiii

Daniel

8:1–14	306, 353

Hosea

1:10	251
2:23	251
13:14	233

Joel

2:28–32	53, 56, 299, 306
2:28–32 [3:1–5 LXX]	61
2:28–29	299
2:32	252

Micah

4:1–4	92
4:1–2	123
4:1	165, 175, 188
4:3	172

6:8	335

Habakkuk

2:4	331, 341

Zechariah

5:1—6:8	306, 353

NEW TESTAMENT

Matthew

1–2	40
1:1	342
1:16	40
1:18—2:12	38
1:18–25	40
2:1	40
2:2	40
2:11	40
2:23	54
3:13–17	41
4:12–17	41
5:1—7:28	38
5:17–48	49
5:22	49
5:28	49
5:29–30	47
5:32	49
5:34	49
5:39	49
6:4	248
6:13	261
7:4–5	47
10:37	223
11:2–6	45
13:1–9	48
13:36–43	47
13:53–58	7
13:55	41
16:13–20	67
21:12–17	38
21:33–46	50
23	88
26:32	51
27:22	86
27:37–43	86
27:62–66	52
28	66
28:1–8	51
28:9–10	51, 53
28:16–20	51, 53

28:18–20	63
28:19–20	51, 53

Mark

1:1	41
1:4	42, 42
1:9–11	41
1:14–15	281, 321, 356
1:14	41
1:15	41, 42, 46, 58, 62, 86, 90, 279, 281
2:1–12	365
2:17	46
2:22	46
3:6	46, 50
4:1–9	48
4:11	49
4:14	49
4:15–20	46, 47
4:21–34	49
4:26	49
4:30	49
5:1–20	46
5:21–24	47
5:35–43	47
6:1–6	7, 41, 104
6:3	41
6:12	43
6:30–44	47
7:5–13	327
8:31	51, 53
8:34	223, 297, 303
8:35	60
9:30–32	53
9:31	51
10:32–34	53
10:33–34	51
11–16	50
11:15–19	38, 369
11:27–33	50
12:1–12	50, 285, 343
12:18–27	59
14:28	51, 51, 53, 62
15:3–37	281
15:9	86
15:26	358
15:27	341
16:1–8	51, 201
16:7	51
16:8	51, 53
16:9–20	51, 201

Luke

1–2	40, 61
1	194
1:1–4	39, 72, 111
1:5–25	39
1:26–35	40
1:46–55	65
1:57–79	65
	2 56, 65
2:1–11	65
2:1	65
2:1–2	40
2:4–7	40
2:3–14	40
2:11	65
2:14	65
2:16	65
2:25–38	42
2:25	279
2:27–32	65
2:30–32	65
2:38	279
3:3	42
3:21–22	41
3:23	38, 40, 42
4:16–30	7, 41, 104, 127
4:16–21	15
4:17–19	44
4:17–22a	279
4:18–21	47
4:18	44
4:21	7, 44
4:22–30	279
7:11–17	45, 47, 247
7:18–23	45
7:21–23	47
7:23	45
7:24–35	45
7:36–50	88
8:4–8	48
9:23	223
9:51—19:28	39, 61
9:51—18:14	52
15:1	48
16:13	248
19:45–48	38
20:9–19	50
23:2	86
23:38	86
23:51	279
24	56
24:1–11	51
24:13–53	53

Luke (continued)

24:13–49	51
24:13–27	51
24:19–21	279
24:21	60, 371
24:27	51
24:44–47	51
24:47–49	63
24:50–53	61
24:51	52
24:52–53	39, 52

John

1:1–4	265
1:1	41
1:3	265
1;40	45
1:41	45
1:42	181
1:45	40, 45
1:46	40, 45
1:49	45
2:1–12	47
2:13–22	38
2:13	38
2:16	369
3:16	16, 337
4:16–19	365
6:1–15	47
6:4	38
9:1–5	382
11:1–44	47
11:38	247
11:46–50	50
11:55	38
19:19–22	86
19:19	358
19:26–27	358
19:19	358
20	53
20:1–10	51
20:11—21:23	51
20:13	52
20:19–29	52
21	52, 53
21:14	52

Acts

1–12	62
1–2	61
1	66, 194
1:1–18	67
1:1–11	53, 61, 62
1:1–3	72
1:1	39
1:3–9	52, 52
1:6	324
1:8	63
1:11	39
1:15–26	62
1:15	61
1:21–26	
1:21	130
1:35	66
2	53, 56, 62, 163, 164, 170
2:5	xviii
2:7	54
2:9–11	131
2:10	xviii
2:14–36	71
2:16–36	63
2:16–21	299
2:17–18	299
2:22–24	54, 292
2:23–24	222, 283
2:31	252
2:36	50, 63, 65, 229
2:41–47	128
2:44	54
3–6	61
3:13–15	292
3:14–15	54
3:22–23	44
4:1–31	128
4:10–11	283
4:10	54
4:17–18	54
4:31–37	347
4:32—5:11	128
4:32–37	67, 128, 347
4:36	131
5:12–16	128
5:17–40	128
5:26–28	54
5:30–32	54
5:33–39	100
5:34–39	99
5:35–37	54
5:41–42	128
6	347
6:1–6	128
6:7	128
7–28	121
7:54–60	67

7:58	94	13:31	54
7:60	109	13:46	103
8:1–3	37, 100, 101	14:8–11 (STA)	199
8:1	99, 127	14:19 (STA)	132
8:3	94	14:25 (STA)	132
8:4–13	67	14:26 (STA)	132
8:26–40	67, 84	15	xvii, 39, 67, 104, 115, 118, 123, 156, 168, 169, 170, 171, 347
9	169, 274, 309		
9:1–22	67	15–21	168
9:1–9	xvi, 383	15:1–35	123, 384
9:1–8	63	15:1–21	279
9:1–2	37, 94, 100, 101	15:1–12	104
9:2	37, 37, 54, 61	15:2 (STA)	171
9:3–19	101	15:1–3	104
9:4	94	15:3 (STA)	172
9:17	94	15:1–2	114, 115, 171 (STA)
9:19–22	383	15:1	169
9:20–23	117	15:2 (STA)	171
9:21	129	15:40—16:1	105
9:26–30	123	15:7–11	169, 171, 181
9:26–29	114, 383	15:6–7 (STA)	181
9:26–27	123	15:7 (STA)	171
9:30	383	15:13–29	104
10	169	15:13:21	172
10:1—12:18	279	15:22–29	171
10:1—11:18	137, 169, 181	15:22	40
10:1–48	67, 84	15:35 (STA)	172
10:34–35	331	15:36	132, 132 (STA)
10:34–43	71	15:37–40	132
10:37–41	292	15:39	169
10:39–40	222, 283	15:40 (STA)	155, 173
11	171	16:1—19:41	383
11:1–11	67	16:1–3	105
11:15–17	331	16:6–7	105
11:25–26	383	16:7–10 (STA)	160
11:26	xvi, 37, 54, 61	16:7–9	105
11:27–30	123, 162 (STA), 168, 191, 383	16:10	105, 136 (STA), 393
11:28	160 (STA)	16:13–15 (STA)	136
11:29–30	114, 115	16:14–15	105
12:25	114, 115, 123	16:15 (STA)	136
13–18	122	16:16–24 (STA)	136
13–14	115, 170, 170 (STA)	16:17	393
13:1—14:28	383	16:19–21	105
13:1 (STA)	131	16:22–30	105
13:3—14:28	102	16:25–34 (STA)	136
13:3 (STA)	131, 173	16:35–39	106
13:9	94	16:35 (STA)	137
13:13—14:25	102	16:37	95
13:13	131 (STA), 132,	17:2	106, 136, 137
13:14—14:21 (STA)	132	17:3	106
13:26–41	71	17:5–15	137
13:27–30	292	17:6–9 (STA)	139
13:28–31	222	17:7	106

413

John (continued)

17:9 (STA)	137
17:10	106, 137 (STA), 139 (STA), 153 (STA)
17:11 (STA)	139
17:12 (STA)	139
17:14 (STA)	139
17:15–16 (STA)	139
17:15	106, 139 (STA)
17:16–34	80
17:17 (STA)	142
17:18–33 (STA)	142
17:18	106, 147 (STA)
17:22–30	106
17:34 (STA)	142, 149
18:1–18 (STA)	150
18:1–17	106
18:1–11 (STA)	150
18:1 (STA)	140
18:2	31, 106
18:3	10, 149 (STA)
18:4 (STA)	149
18:5	106, 140 (STA), 140 (STA), 149 (STA)
18:6–7 (STA)	149
18:7–8 (STA)	149
18:7	117n1, 149, 149 (STA)
18:6	103, 149
18:11	140 (STA), 149 (STA), 150 (STA)
18:11–16	106
18:12–18 (STA)	150
18:12–17	383
18:12 (STA)	149, 150, 152
18:18	106, 153 (STA)
18:18–21	31
18:18–21c (STA)	158
18:19 (STA)	155, 178
18:22	106, 107n3, 114, 158, 158 (STA)
18:24–28 (STA)	181
18:25–26	61
19:1	174 (STA), 179 (STA), 384
19:8–12 (STA)	179
19:8–10	31
19:8–9 (STA)	178
19:8	176, 176 (STA), 176 (STA)
19:9	61
19:9 (STA)	178
19:10	107, 176, 176 (STA), 177n2
19:11–12	176, 176 (STA)
19:17	176, 176 (STA), 179 (STA)
19:19 (STA)	176
19:21–22	108, 183 (STA), 186 (STA), 187 (STA)
19:21 (STA)	198
19:22 (STA)	176, 155
19:23—20:1	107
19:23–41	176
19:23	61
19:23–24 (STA)	182, 183
19:23–25 (STA)	179
19:27–34 (STA)	179
19:29–34 (STA)	176
19:33–34 (STA)	186
19:34	177n2
20–21	393
20:1–6	108, 119
20:1–6 (STA)	186, 187
20:1–4 (STA)	186
20:2–3 (STA),	185
20:3–5	107
20:4	385, 139 (STA), 198 (STA), 205 (STA)
20:3–16	384
20:3	150, 186 (STA)
20:6	107
20:31	107, 176
21–28	108, 187
21:10–11 (STA)	191
21:10	107
21:15—26:32	316
21:15–17	114, 123
21:15	107
21:16 (STA)	191
21:17	123, 191(STA)
21:18–26 (STA)	193
21:19 (STA)	191
21:21 (STA)	192, 193
21:27–34	384
21:27–31a (STA)	194
21:27 (STA)	192, 193
21:29	194
21:38	54
22	169
22:3	80, 95, 97, 112, 118
22:3–8	193
22:4–5	37
22:6–16	101
22:6–11	63
22:13	94
22:25–29	95
22:25	118
22:7	94
23	109
23:16	95, 191 (STA)
23:27	95

Reference	Page(s)
23:29 (STA)	195
24–26	25
24:5–6	195
24:5	54
24:17	187, 384
24:22	37, 61
24:23	207
24:27	384
25:11	109
26	169
26:4–11	193
26:9–11	37
26:12–18	63, 101
26:14	94
26:28	xvi, 54, 61
27	198, 198 (STA)
27:1—28:10	384
27:2 (STA)	198
27:4 (STA)	198
27:12 (STA)	198
28	170, 194
28:1–3 (STA)	199
28:1	384
28:7–10 (STA)	199
28:5–6 (STA)	199
28:11–14	384
28:11–12 (STA)	199
28:11	384
28:14 (STA)	200
28:15 (STA)	200
28:16–31	25
28:16	201 (STA), 207, 385
28:17–28	109, 207
28:23–31	61
28:23–25 (STA)	201
28:23 (STA)	201
28:24–29	103
28:28	149
28:30–31	207
28:30	109, 385
28:31	40, 52, 255

Romans

Reference	Page(s)
1–15	27, 36, 209, 261,
1–11	28
1–4	244, 357
1:1–17	289
1:1	xviii, 229, 248, 255, 288, 329, 342, 272
1:1–4	62, 148, 238, 281, 296, 298
1:1–6	220, 288, 294
1:1–5	116, 221
1:3–5	57
1:3	342
1:3–4	296
1:4	233, 238, 290, 293, 296, 309, 318, 353, 356, 359
1:4–7	63
1:5–7	238
1:7	363
1:8–15	27
1:8–13	200
1:16–18	289
1:18—3:20	289
1:16–17	255, 329, 334
1:17	331, 332
1:18–31	369
1:18–32	79, 244, 289
1:18–31	369
1:18	244, 312, 334
1:19–23	238, 288
1:19–20	287
1:20–23	281
1:21	265
1:24	238, 289, 292, 329, 334
1:26–32	91
1:26	238, 289, 292, 329, 334
1:27	292
1:28	238, 289, 292, 329, 334
1:32	239
2:1–29	239
2:1–20	83
2:1–16	235
2:1–11	324
2:3–11	329
2:4	240
2:6–16	331
2:6	338
2:16	241
2:17–29	99
3:1–19	337
3:2	304
3:3	241
3:5–8	241
3:6–9	277
3:9–19	332
3:9	239
3:10–18	312
3:10–1	329
3:15–17	239
3:20	239, 336
3:21–31	244, 375, 377
3:21–26	289, 330, 332, 334
3:21	338
3:23	241, 244, 245, 337
3:25–26	240, 241
3:25	240, 305, 343

SCRIPTURE INDEX

Romans (continued)

3:26	222, 241, 255, 289, 300, 330, 329, 335
3:27–30	241
3:30	91, 338
3:31	242
4	334
4:1–25	99, 277, 300
4:1–24	297
4:3	242, 346
4:7	292
4:9–11	28
4:11–17	380
4:12	346
4:18–20	243
4:19	341
4:20–21	243
4:20	243
4:21	341
4:23–24	243
4:24	59, 243, 341, 346
4:24–25	243, 291
4:25a	243
4:25b	243
5–8	239, 244
5:1–11	245, 335
5:1–3	308
5:1–5	268
5:1	243, 244, 308
5:2	245
5:5	245
5:6–11	268
5:6–9	245
5:6	293
5:8	358, 359
5:9–11	345
5:10	245, 245
5:9	244, 245, 346
5:11	245
5:12–23	299
5:12–21	246, 277
5:12–14	236, 246, 289, 380
5:15	246
5:17–19	246
5:21	243
5:22	243
5:23–24	243
6	282
6:1–23	247
6:1–11	257, 301
6:1–6	303
6:1–4	247
6:4	59, 318
6:5–11	359
6:5–14	361
6:6	226, 247, 264, 359
6:8–11	247
6:6–8	244, 246
6:14	248
6:15–23	96, 248
6:17	96
6:20–22	361
6:23	236, 239, 248, 281, 292, 361
7	246, 249
7:1–25	100
7:1–6	249
7:7–25	281, 332
7:9–12	249
7:12	100, 222, 242, 264, 332
7:14	83
7:24	249, 332
7:25	249
8	251, 289, 337
8:1–39	376, 377
8:1–11	236
8:1–2	308
8:1	249, 251
8:3–4	297
8:3	291
8:3–7	301
8:6	249, 327
8:9	299
8:11	59, 266, 341
8:12	250
8:14–29	299
8:15–17	250
8:15	319, 357
8:17	250
8:18–25	305
8:22–23	250
8:23	305, 357
8:25	296
8:26–27	267
8:28–39	377
8:28–30	58, 250, 377
8:28	250
8:31–37	267
8:34	353
8:37	284
8:38–39	244, 267
8:38	353
9–11	244, 251, 254
9	252
9:1–5	253
9:1–3	251, 252
9:3	112

9:3–5	304	15:19	107n3, 117, 123, 150, 383
9:4–5	xviii, 324	15:22–29	109, 113, 184, 241
9:4	251, 357	15:22–24	27, 200
9:5	251, 253	15:23–24	237
9:6	251	15:24	109
9:9–29	252	15:25–33	119
9:14–18	251	15:25–32	123
9:30—10:14	252	15:25–29	27, 108, 123, 175, 184, 187, 384,
9:30–33	332	15:25–27	25, 27, 122
10:1–13	332	15:25	114, 115, 162
10:1	252	15:26	186, 384
10:4	182	15:27	188
10:5	331	15:28–29	27
10:9	59, 290	15:28	109
10:13	252	15:30–32	187, 241
10:14–17	252	15:30–31	185
10:19–20	252	15:31	162
10:20–21	252	15:32	27, 200
11	252	16	27, 30, 31, 32, 36, 121, 186, 202, 208, 209, 237
11:1–4	253	16:1–2	32
11:1	95, 99, 112	16:3–4	31
11:5–6	253	16:3	148
11:25–26	253	16:7	182, 182
11:32	244, 252, 253, 254	16:20	227, 260, 353
11:33–36	244, 253, 254, 268	16:22–23	32
11:34–35	312	16:22	110
11:36	287, 288, 313	16:25–27	30, 210, 261, 314
11:8–10	312	16:27	32
12–15	28		
12–13	357	*1 Corinthians*	
12	254		
12:1	16, 254	1–6	347
12:1–2	301, 356, 358, 363, 382	1:2–9	225
12:2	254, 309	1:2	363
12:4–8	254	1:4	380
12:9—13:10	254	1:7–9	265
12:9–21	382	1:8	324
12:9–16	254	1:10–17	226
12:4–8	301	1:10–13	27
12:5	254	1:11–17	181
12:11–13	254	1:11–16	31
12:14	254	1:11	27, 181
12:16	254	1:12	181
13:8–10	382	1:14–16	147
13:10	304	1:14	149, 181
13:11–14	255, 267	1:17—2:5	147
15	32, 118	1:18–25	227
15:3	255	1:18	345, 359
15:4–6	255	1:23–25	226, 265
15:9–12	312	1:23	93
15:12–32	316	1:25	226, 253
15:13	255, 313	1:26–29	209
15;15	255		
15:17–19	255		

1 Corinthians (continued)

1:26	147, 148
1:30	253
2:2	359
2:3	147, 226
2:6–9	353
2:8–10	305
2:8–9	245
2:8	226
2:10–13	226
2:14–16	226
2:19	227
3–4	339
3:1–6	226
3:1–4	14, 339, 347, 366
3:1–3	387
3:1	147
3:10–15	226, 229
3:11–13	227
3:11	148
3:12–15	324
3:16–17	227, 258, 301
3:18–23	226
3:18–20	147
3:19—4:1	227
3:19–20	312
4	227
4:1–16	229
4:10	227
4:12	148
4:14–16	227
4:15	147
4:16	230
4:1–6	339
4:8–21	226
5:1–5	181, 226
5:1–2	227
5:1	27
5:5	227, 324
5:7–8	331
5:7	226, 343
5:8	227, 265
5:9	22, 24, 148, 151, 180, 227, 237, 383
6:1–8	226
6:9–11	79, 148
6:9–10	357
6:10	305
6:11	209
6:12	228, 230
6:14	318
6:15–20	339
6:18	228
6:19–20	96, 258
6:19	301
6:20	228
7–15	26
7:1	26, 27, 181
7:2	36
7:5	227
7:8	99
7:11	292
7:12	292
7:13	292
7:17–24	229, 248
7:18–19	148
7:20–24	248
7:21–23	148
7:22	83
7:26	229, 306
7:29	229, 248
7:31	229
7:40	229
8:1–6	148
8:1	229
8:4	287, 288, 338
8:6	229, 287, 288
8:9–13	229
9	83, 229
9:1–27	215, 229
9:1–7	181
9:1	101
9:1–2	67n1
9:19–21	192
9:20	148
9:21	148
9:24–27	83
10–14	387
10:5–16	230
10:14–21	148
10:14	91
10:21	91
10:23	192, 230
11	230
11:1	230
11:12	287
11:17–34	230, 387
11:17–22	26
11:18	27
11:23–27	387
11:23–25	296, 343
11:26	343
12–14	26, 230
12:1	230
12:2	148
12:3	290, 299
12:4–11	299

SCRIPTURE INDEX

12:12–31	360
12:12–21	301, 339
12:13	230
12:31b—14:1	230
13:13	378
14:1–40	230, 231
15	62, 63, 231, 291, 357
15:1–8	62
15:1–4	148
15:3–8	53, 63, 231
15:3–7	92, 296
15:3–5	57, 290
15:3–4	51, 222, 226, 231, 232, 236, 281, 292, 297
15:8–10	xvi, xvi, 62, 99
15:8–9	101
15:8	52, 283
15:10	357
15:12–28	63
15:12–19	231, 338, 360
15:13	231
15:14	231
15:15	232, 318
15:17	231, 232
15:19	232, 378
15:20–28	56, 56, 217, 221, 232, 233, 234, 262, 268, 293, 294, 297, 305, 345, 353, 355, 356, 374
15:20	232, 239
15:21	267
15:23–28	28
15:24–28	267, 393
15:24–26	235
15:24	353
15:26–28	316
15:26	305
15:28	225, 234, 259, 265, 284, 305
15:28c	318
15:30–32	378, 384
15:32	107, 182
15:35–55	301
15:36	232
15:50–56	305
15:50	305, 357
15:51–55	304
15:54–55	312
15:54–56	281
15:57	281, 282, 294
16:1–12	384
16:1–9	108
16:1–4	119, 175, 187
16:1–3	175
16:1	118, 119, 384
16:2	331
16:5–9	182
16:8–9	176
16:8	179, 181, 226
16:9	182
16:15	147, 148
16:17	181
16:19	148
16:22	296

2 Corinthians

1–9	26
1:10–13	26
1:1–14	215
1:3–11	303
1:3–6	305
1:3–7	234, 236
1:3–11	303
1:8	384
1:8–9	107, 182
1:8–23	182
1:8–11	184, 234
1:9	305
1:10	234, 346
1:14	324, 235
1:16	184
1:19	147, 290
1:20–22	235
1:22	357
1:23—3:3	235
2:1–11	227
2:1–2	153, 180
2:1–4	26, 152
2:1	150, 184
2:3	184, 384
2:3–4	22, 180
2:4	227
2:5–11	181
2:6–8	228
2:11	227
2:12–13	184
2:13	150, 184
2:15	345
3:6	235
3:7–15	235
3:17–18	235
3:17	235
4	235
4:4	353
4:7—5:5	235
4:7–12	305

419

2 Corinthians (continued)

4:7	17, 317
4:14	59, 304, 318, 235
5:2	236
5:5	235, 357
5:7	236
5:9	26
5:10	235, 338
5:11	236
5:11–20	374
5:14–15	236
5:14	235
5:16	100
5:17	352
5:18–21	303
5:19–20	288
5:18–19	236
5:19	326
5:20	236
5:21	236, 377
6:3–10	235
6:4–10	94, 303
6:13	36, 235, 237
6:14—7:1	24, 26, 36, 151, 164, 237, 385
6:16–18	301, 312
6:16	237
7	237
7:2	237
7:5–16	184
7:5	184
7:6	184, 384
7:8–13	237
7:9–10	240
7:13	184
7:14	184
8–9	26, 108, 118, 119, 184, 185, 187, 235, 237
8	150, 175, 235, 384
8:1–15	186
8:4	162, 187
8:6	117
8:14–15	188
8:16–17	149
8:16	117
8:19	187
8:23	117
9	150, 235, 384
9:1–5	186
9:1	162
9–10	184
9:6–15	384
9:12	162
9:13	162
10:10–12	97
10:10	94
10:13–16	237
11–13	185, 237
11:1—12:13	97
11:5	237
11:8–9	148
11:12–23	184
11:21–22	95
11:21b–29	94
11:22	68, 95, 99, 11
11:23–33	303
11:23–29	94
11:23–28	256
11:23–27	322
11:23–25	25
11:23	183, 384
11:24–27	107
11:25	132, 136, 140n1
11:32–33	128
12:1–5	287
12:7	227
12:11	237
12:13	237
12:14—13:10	235
12:21	148, 240
13:11–14	237
13:4	237
15	236
15:5	237

Galatians

1–2	67n1, 115, 116
1	238, 274, 309
1:1	59, 291, 294, 318, 341
1:1–5	220
1:3–5	101
1:3–4	221
1:3	286
1:4	221, 282, 295
1:5	295
1:6–9	25, 180, 367, 328
1:6–8	295
1:6–7	275
1:8	347
1:9	347
1:11–17	67, 114, 215, 268, 343, 383
1:12–17	99
1:12–16	128
1:12	101, 116, 283
1:13–17	99

1:13–16	92, 101	3:15–20	322
1:13–14	98	3:15–16	341
1:13	37, 101, 116, 128	3:15	83
1:14	112, 116	3:16	334, 342
1:15–17	62, 383	3:19–20	222, 242
1:15–16	52, 101, 116, 121, 283, 288, 323	3:19	336
		3:20	338
1:16–24	117	3:21–24	222
1:17–18	117	3:21–22	381
1:17	114, 128	3:21	222
1:18–24	159, 383	3:23–29	99, 264
1:18	114, 115, 117, 123, 129	3:25—4:7	258
1:21	102, 117	3:25–29	93
1:22–23	127	3:26–28	351
1:23	37, 101, 102, 128, 131	3:26	299
2	169, 171	3:26–29	222, 351
2:1–10	123	3:27–29	279
2:1	102, 114, 115, 117, 134, 149, 159	3:28	357
		4:1–7	222, 264
2:10	164, 165, 172, 187	4:1–2	83
2:11	169, 172	4:3	222, 353
2:1–10	150, 156, 162, 168, 181, 184, 383	4:31—5:6	373
		4:4–7	249, 299
2:1–3	150, 155	4:4–5	301
2:2–5	222	4:4	291, 297
2:2	102	4:5	357
2:3	149, 164, 171	4:6–7	333
2:4–5	165	4:6	296, 319
2:6–10	171	4:9	96, 222
2:6–9	164	4:13	132
2:9	172	4:21	222
2:11–21	123, 384	5:1–12	180
2:11–16	181	5:1	96, 212, 223, 248, 285, 356
2:11–13	163	5:1–6	331
2:11–14	169, 383	5:2–6	336
2:14	169	5:4	265, 275
2:14–21	171	5:6—6:10	357
2:15–21	171	5:6–25	223
2:15–16	222	5:6–15	223
2:19–21	222, 333	5:6	230, 275, 301, 379, 382
2:19	295	5:11	295, 341, 382
2:20	91, 226, 264, 290	5:12	223, 295, 347
3–4	333	5:13–15	230
3	264, 334	5:13	382
3:1–5	180	5:16–21	79, 299
3:1	295	5:16–25	267
3:6–14	297	5:19–21	362
3:6–18	222	5:21	305, 357
3:6	346	5:22–26	299
3:10–14	331	5:22–23	289, 362
3:10	331	5:24	295
3:11	222, 331	5:25	265, 266, 304
3:13	283, 297, 318, 331, 341	6:7–10	108, 119, 384
3:14	331, 382	6:8	223

421

Galatians (continued)

6:11–18	223, 322
6:11–16	171
6:12	295
6:14–15	359
6:14	264, 295, 303, 359
6:15–16	223
6:15	99, 321, 352
6:16	321
6:18	296

Ephesians

1:1–23	260
1:1	30, 32
1:1–8	257
1:3–23	348
1:3–14	30, 30, 314, 348, 358
1:3–15	382
1:5	357
1:6	228, 241, 305, 330, 379, 382
1:7	240
1:12	228, 241, 305, 330, 379, 382
1:14	228, 241, 305, 330, 357, 379, 382
1:15–23	203
1:17–23	30
1:17	258
1:19–23	257
1:19–20	258
1:20–23	30
1:20	59, 318
1:23	258, 259
2	255
2:1—3:32	348
2:1–22	258
2:1–18	234
2:1–10	258, 377
2:5–8	307
2:5–7	265, 307
2:56	307
2:5	258
2:6	30
2:11–22	30, 203
2:11–19	307
2:14–21	351
2:14–15	194
2:19	258
2:20–23	293
2:20–22	307
2:21	301
3:6	258
3:8–12	258
3:9	288
3:14–21	30, 258
3:19	359
3:20–21	259, 313
4:1—6:20	307, 348
4:1—5:20	30
4:1	259
4:3–6	259
4:4–5	272
4:8–10	259
4:11–13	259
4:14–16	259
4:22–29	260
4:27	228
4:30–31	260
5:1–2	260
5:1	272, 348, 350
5:2	343
5:3–20	260
5:16	282
5:21—6:9	29, 30, 260
5:23–24	230
6	356
6:10–20	204, 282, 284
6:10–13	260
6:10	260
6:11	228, 353
6:19–20	260
6:21	205, 385
6:21–22	208
6:23–24	260

Philippians

1:3–11	224
1:4	135
1:5	135
1:6	324
1:10	324
1:12–26	317
1:12–18	224
1:12–14	24
1:17	83
1:18	135
1:19–26	25, 224
1:19–26	25
1:19–24	182
1:19–20	182, 225, 307
1:20–26	107
1:21–23	303
1:21	63
1:25	135

1:27–30	224, 384	4:8–9	225
2:1–4	224	4:9	225, 266
2:2–3	223	4:10–16	135
2:2–13	356	4:10–13	224
2:2	135	4:10	135,
2:5–13	221, 373	4:13	224
2:5–11	28, 221, 225, 234, 254, 262, 267, 343	4:15–18	224
		4:15–16	137
2:5	225	4:15	135, 142
2:8	293, 341	4:16	135
2:6–11	58, 296, 301	4:19	224
2:9–11	234, 281, 292, 293, 294, 298, 346		

Colossians

2:11	225, 234	1:3–6	377
2:11c	318	1:5	256
2:12–13	225, 293	1:6	256
2:12	266, 344, 345, 356	1:7–8	202
2:16	83, 324	1:7	179
2:17–18	135	1:9–14	377
2:25–30	25, 176,	1:11–20	293
2:25–28	224	1:14	240, 256
2:25	182	1:15–29	247
3:1	135	1:15–20	29, 256, 296, 303
3:5–6	112	1:15–16	29, 287
3:7–11	225	1:16	256, 288
3:2–11	25, 180, 224, 347	1:19	256
3:3–7	224	1:20	256
3:3–7	224	1:22	256
3:4–6	68, 99, 324	1:26–27	267, 305
3:4–5	95	1:26	256
3:4–11	63	1:27	237, 256, 266
3:5–11	115	2:2	256
3:5–6	98	2:6—4:6	307
3:5	95, 98	2:8–23	29
3:6	112, 116, 331	2:8–9	29
3:7–9	99	2:8	91, 353
3:8–16	63	2:10	256, 353
3:10–16	225	2:11	29
3:10–11	217	2:12	59, 256, 318
3:12–16	93, 24, 244, 304, 359, 367	2:14–15	291
3:14	225	2:14	257
3:17–21	217	2:15	257, 353
3:17–20	384	2:16–23	29
3:20–21	304, 305, 349	2:16	29, 331
3:20	83, 225, 345	2:20–21	29
3:21	225	2:20	257, 307
4:1–3	384	3:1–4	313
4:1	135	3:1	28, 257, 307
4:2–3	25, 224	3:3	257, 307
4:4–8	xxi	3:4–6	257
4:4–7	313	3:5–11	257
4:4–6	25	3:12—4:6	257
4:5	224, 225	3:18—4:1	29
4:7	266		

Colossians (continued)

4:7–17	29, 208
4:7–14	202
4:7–9	202
4:7	205
4:9	205
4:10	198, 202, 205, 385
4:11	110, 205
4:12	202, 205
4:14	110, 206

1 Thessalonians

1:1	140
1:7–8	138
1:9–10	59, 296, 318, 324
1:9	138
1:10	218, 221, 233
2:1–20	137
2:1–12	138, 218
2:1	106, 138
2:2	138, 218
2:8	218
2:12	218
2:13	218
2:14–16	137, 218, 264, 322
2:16	151
2:17	138
2:18	227
2:19	83, 138, 233
3:1–10	138
3:1–5	140, 141
3:1	138, 383
3:5	353
3:6	142
3:13	218, 233, 324
4:1–12	217
4:1–8	218
4:1	138
4:6	218, 233
4:8	218
4:9—5:22	23
4:9–10	138
4:13—5:11	324
4:13—5:2	316
4:13–17	217
4:14–17	218
4:15–18	233, 292
4:16–18	355
4:16–17	217
4:16	83
4:18	138, 219
5:1–10	233
5:2	218, 324
5:8–11	372
5:9–10	221
5:9	219
5:14–22	138
5:14	138, 217, 219
5:15–24	219
5:23	218, 233

2 Thessalonians

1:1	140
1:3	138
1:4–12	137
1:5	216
1:7–10	216, 221, 233
1:8	216
2:1–12	23, 63, 138, 217, 233, 306, 316
2:1	62, 217
2:2	324
2:9	227
2:10	345
2:13—3:5	138
2:13–14	221
2:14	217
2:15	217
2:16–17	138
2:16	217
3:4–5	372
3:6–13	138
3:7–9	138
3:6–12	217
3:6–10	217
3:30–35	138
4:14	62

1 Timothy

1:17	296
1:20	227
3:6	228
3:8	228
3:11	228
3:16	296
5:15	227

2 Timothy

1:1	261
1:10	206
1:11–12	261
1:15	186
1:16–18	186

1:17	109
2:8–10	261
2:11–13	261
2:26	228
3:1	261
3:11	132
3:15–17	5
3:15–16	363, 365
3:16	xv
3:3	228
4:1	261
4:2–5	261
4:6–18	34
4:6–8	208, 256, 261 305
4:7	317
4:8	261
4:9–17	208
4:9–16	208
4:10	117, 150
4:11	205'
4:12	205, 213, 385
4:13	31, 109
4:14–15	186
4:14	202
4:16	186
4:17	208
4:18	63, 261, 268, 345
4:19–21	208
4:19	148, 186
4:20	206
4:22	34, 210, 261

Titus

2:3	228
3:12–13	208
3:12	151

Philemon

2	29
9	94
18	83
23–24	29, 95
23	202
24	202, 205
25	29

Hebrews

1:3	339

1 Peter

4:16	xvi, 54, 61
5:12	110

2 Peter

3:15–17	15
3:15–16	317, 318

1 John

1:7—2:2	361

Jude

14–15	33

Revelation

2–3	19, 348
18:11–13	96
21	280

"Imagine owning one volume to which you could turn for the life and work, travels and letters, history and geography of Paul, along with timelines and maps which help it all come clear—all offered in the thoughtful voice of a pastoral scholar who has given much of his life to learning Paul and teaching Paul in and for the university and the church. Imagine that, and you will have imagined a bit of G. Roger Greene's *Imagine Paul*."

—**Charles Eugene Poole**, retired Baptist pastor

"A devoted Christian disciple and lifelong student of Paul invites readers on a pilgrimage through the landscape of Pauline letters to encounter Paul unshackled from millennia of interpretation. Meet the first-century Pharisaic Jewish apostle and evangelist to the Greco-Roman world who became a new man in Christ and proclaimed the Gospel of God. Paul's resurrection faith as presented by the author yet calls for faithful response. *Imagine Paul* is good tonic for the modern soul!"

—**Susan Hooks Meadors**, associate pastor, Northside Baptist Church

"Developed through decades of extensive research and experience, *Imagine Paul* seeks to allow the apostle Paul to live again. G. Roger Greene invites the reader to imagine, or to reimagine, Paul and his message within Paul's own historical, cultural, and spiritual matrices as presented in the New Testament record. Scholar, student, and seeker alike will profit from Greene's informed, insightful, and innovative treatment."

—**Edward L. Mahaffey**, professor of Christian studies, Mississippi College

"Consciously tying himself to the mast of Paul's epistles, G. Roger Greene rigorously constructs an understanding of the apostle from what he said, rather than what was said about him—even in Acts. His original concept of Paul's 'epistolic' theology is worth the price of the book. I found myself alternately enlightened, encouraged, challenged, convicted, even irritated here and there, but most of all, stretched. Greene's gift is to move his readers beyond illumination to doxology and worship."

—**Cary Stockett**, senior pastor emeritus, Galloway United Methodist Church

"In *Imagine Paul*, G. Roger Greene has provided a comprehensive treatment of the apostle Paul's historical context, biography, letter writing method and purposes, and theology. Unique is Greene's well-reasoned argument that understanding Paul must go through every interpreter's imagination within the constraints of actual historical, geographical, lexical, and archaeological evidence. One foundational aspect of such evidence is that Paul's biography should start from his letters with Acts serving in a supportive role. Highly recommended!"

—**Bennie R. Crockett Jr.**, professor of religion and philosophy, William Carey University

www.ingramcontent.com/pod-product-compliance
Lightning Source LLC
Chambersburg PA
CBHW081755300426
44116CB00014B/2122